Facility Planning and Design

for Health, Physical Activity, Recreation, and Sport

13th ed.

SAGAMORE VENTURE

©2013 Sagamore Publishing LLC
All rights reserved.

Publishers: Joseph J. Bannon and Peter L. Bannon
Director of Sales and Marketing: William A. Anderson
Marketing Coordinator: Emily Wakefield
Director of Development and Production: Susan M. Davis
Technology Manager: Christopher Thompson
Production Coordinator: Amy S. Dagit

ISBN print edition: 978-1-57167-720-4
ISBN ebook: 978-1-57167- 721-1
LCCN: 2013943127

SAGAMORE ◆◆ VENTURE

1807 N. Federal Dr.
Urbana, IL 61801
www.sagamorepub.com

This book is dedicated to my grandson, Grayson James Rosselli.

He is a builder at heart and always makes his grandfather proud.

Contents

   Todd L. Seidler, University of New Mexico
   Bernie Goldfine, Kennesaw State University

Section I
Common Facility Components

Section II
Field and Court Specifications

Section III
Recreational Spaces

Section IV
Specialty Areas

Section V
Trends, History, and Standards

31 Equipment and Facility Design Standards
Thomas H. Sawyer, *Indiana State University*
Tonya L. Gimbert, *Indiana State University*

Appendices

Foreword

As the cost of construction for sports- and health-related facilities skyrockets, it becomes ever more paramount for those who plan, design, construct, and use these facilities to have access to a comprehensive facilities guide. The 13th edition of *Facility Planning and Design for Health, Physical Activity, Recreation, and Sport* is a tool for all professionals involved in facility planning and construction use.

The 21st century is a time of increased interest in health, fitness, recreation, physical activity, and sport. A synopsis of the historical development of this text is important. In 1945, at the board of directors meeting of the American Alliance for Health, Physical Education, Recreation, and Dance (AAHPERD) in Washington, D.C., support was given to a proposal submitted by Caswell M. Miles, AAHPERD vice president for recreation, to prepare a grant to finance a national workshop on facilities. Subsequently, a request for $10,000 was submitted to and approved by Theodore P. Bank, president of the Athletic Institute, to finance the first workshop. The December 1946 workshop at Jackson's Mill, West Virginia, resulted in the publication of the premiere edition of the *Guide for Planning Facilities for Athletics, Recreation, Physical and Health Education.*

The 1956 edition of the guide was a product of the second facilities workshop, held May 5-12, 1956, at the Kellogg Institute, and was held again January 15-24, 1965, at the Biddle Continuing Education Center, Indiana University in Bloomington. Two years later, April 29-May 8, 1967, another workshop was held at Indiana University. Among those invited were a number of outstanding college and technical personnel engaged in planning and administering programs of athletics, recreation, outdoor education, physical education, and health education. Other planning authorities and specialists receiving invitations included city planners, architects, landscape architects, engineers, and schoolhouse construction consultants.

The 1974 guide was reconstructed in such a way that it would serve as a more practical tool for school administrators, physical education heads, architects, planning consultants, and all others interested in planning new areas and facilities or checking the adequacy of those already in use.

The Athletic Institute and AAHPERD Council on Facilities, Equipment, and Supplies initiated the 1979 revision of the guide. A blue-ribbon steering committee was appointed by the Council. Edward Coates from Ohio State University and Richard B. Flynn from the University of Nebraska at Omaha, were appointed as coeditors and contributing authors.

Professionals well known for their expertise in facility planning, design, and construction were invited to assist in a complete rewrite, which resulted in Planning Facilities for Athletics, Physical Education, and Recreation.

The 1985 edition of *Planning Facilities for Athletics, Physical Education, and Recreation* represented a continuing effort on the part of The Athletic Institute and AAHPERD to keep the text current and relevant. Richard B. Flynn was selected to be editor and contributing author. Many of the contributors to the previous edition updated their chapters, and some new material was added.

The American Alliance for Health, Physical Education, Recreation, and Dance published the 1993 edition, entitled *Facility Planning for Physical Education, Recreation, and Athletics*, and Richard B. Flynn again was asked to serve as editor and contributing author. Again, many of the contributors to the previous edition updated their chapters, and some new material was added.

The AAHPERD Council on Facilities and Equipment selected Thomas H. Sawyer of Indiana State University to serve as chair of the editorial committee and editor-in-chief of the 1999 and 2002 editions of *Facilities Planning for Physical Activity and Sport*. Many new contributors were selected to complete a major revision of the text, which resulted in a great deal of new material and many fresh ideas and concepts. The editorial team for both the 1999 and

2002 editions was Thomas H. Sawyer, Ed.D. (Indiana State University); Michael G. Hypes, DA (Indiana State University); Richard L. LaRue, DPE (University of New England); and Todd Seidler, Ph.D. (University of New Mexico). There were 21 authors involved in writing 29 chapters in the 1999 edition, and 21 authors involved in writing 37 chapters in the 2002 edition.

The revised 2013, 13th edition, with Thomas H. Sawyer again serving as editor-in-chief, fulfills the intent of the Council on Facilities and Equipment to update and revise the text on a regular basis. Regularly revising and updating a text of this magnitude is no easy task. Basically, at the completion of one edition, the planning for a new edition begins—therefore never-ending work for the editor, editorial board, and authors. I would like to commend these selfless individuals. With rapid changes in both technology and construction methods, the regular updating of this text is a necessity. This new edition now adds one new chapter.

It should be noted that much of the material in this text reflects the composite knowledge of many professionals who have contributed to past AAHPERD text editions, as well as of those individuals who were solicited to serve as authors, editors, and reviewers for the current text. The American Alliance for Health, Physical Education, Recreation, and Dance, the American Association for Active Lifestyles and Fitness (AAALF), and the Council on Facilities and Equipment (CFE) have endorsed this book as one of the best on the topic of planning facilities for sport, physical activity, and recreation.

Having had the pleasure to work closely with Thomas H. Sawyer and the editorial board and the Facilities and Equipment Council and having been an author in four editions of the text, I would at this time give my sincere thanks and appreciation to all of those involved in this 13th edition of this text—a job well done! I recommend this edition of *Facility Planning and Design for Health, Physical Activity, Recreation, and Sport* as the most comprehensive source guide for planning, designing, and constructing facilities related to health, physical activity, and sport.

From its inception, this text has been a milestone resource for sports and physical activity facility designers, users and managers. Each edition builds on and adds to the field of knowledge in sport and physical activity facility design, planning, and construction. I give my highest endorsement to this 13th edition of the "bible" for facility designers and planners.

With gratitude,

Edward (Ed) Turner, PhD
Professor Emeritus
Department of Health, Leisure and Exercise Science
Appalachian State University

Acknowledgments

Appreciation is expressed to the editorial committee members of the Council for Facilities and Equipment (CFE) for assuming initial responsibility for outlining the content and chapters for the text and selection of the chapter authors. While some served as authors/editors for specific chapters in the text, all served as reviewers for assigned chapter drafts. The editorial committee members for the 13th edition consisted of:

- Dr. Thomas H. Sawyer, NAS Fellow, Chair and Editor-in-Chief, Contributor, 1999-2014 (9th, 10th, 11th, 12th, and 13th editions), Indiana State University, Chair CFE, 1995-97
- Dr. Julia Ann Hypes, Morehead State University, Chair CFE, 2007-08
- Dr. Michael G Hypes, Morehead State University, Chair CFE, 2008-2009
- Dr. Jeffrey C. Peterson, Baylor University, Chair CFE, 2005-07

We are indebted to a number of authoritative sources for permission to reproduce material used in this text:

— The National Collegiate Athletic Association (NCAA) for permission to reproduce drawings from selected 1997 NCAA rulebooks. It should be noted that these specifications, like others, are subject to annual review and change.
— Athletic Business for permission to reprint selected drawings.
— Selected architectural firms for supplying photographs, line drawings, artists renderings, and other materials.

Special recognition is due to those professionals who served as chapter authors or assistant editors, including Kimberly Bodey, Mark Cryan, Steven Dalcher, Tonya Gimbert, Bernie Goldfine, Susan Hudson, Julia Ann Hypes, Michael G. Hypes (Contributor and Assistant Editor), Lawrence W. Judge, Richard LaRue, David LaRue, John Miller, Jeffrey Peterson, Donald Rogers, Gary Rushing, Todd Seidler, Donna Thompson, LeLand Yarger, Hal Walker, Todd Weaver, and Jason Winkle. These individuals worked diligently to present chapter material in an informative and useful manner.

Without great assistance from a number of very special and important folks, this book would not have been possible: Julia Ann Hypes, who was responsible for the glossary and author information; Meghan "Muffin" Sawyer Rosselli for her graphic and photography expertise; and Susan Davis and Amy Dagit of Sagamore Publishing for invaluable advice, counsel, patience, and encouragement during the final edit and design of the manuscript.

Prologue

Todd Seidler, *University of New Mexico*
Bernie Goldfine, *Kennesaw State University*

Have you ever seen a facility with so many design problems that it left you shaking your head in disbelief? Each facility presents its own unique design challenges; if these challenges are not addressed and overcome, the result is a facility with design problems. Typically, the larger a building project, the greater the likelihood that mistakes will be made in the planning and design process. Often, details are overlooked, and sometimes even major mistakes are made in the planning process and not discovered until after the facility is built and opened for use. For example, most of us have seen buildings with poor lighting, ventilation, or access control that could have been prevented with appropriate planning. In particular, one of the most common design flaws in recreational, physical education, and sports facilities is a lack of proper storage space. Surely, we have all visited buildings where hallways, classrooms, and even activity spaces were used for temporary or permanent storage of equipment.

Inadequate planning has resulted in countless design flaws in sports and recreation facilities. Can you imagine a high school football team playing on an 80-yard football field? What about a recreation center with access to the locker rooms available only by crossing the gym floor? Do you believe a facility designer would locate a locker room toilet one foot lower than the septic field it was supposed to drain into? How about a gymnasium with large picture windows directly behind the basketball backboards? And how safe is an indoor track constructed as part of a pool deck that has water puddles present in every running lane? Impossible? Unfortunately, it is not.

These "building bloopers" are real and not as uncommon as we would like to believe. Such mistakes can be embarrassing, expensive, amazing, and sometimes humorous (if it is not your facility). These and many other design errors can usually be traced to insufficient planning. An example of an outrageous building blooper is Olympic Stadium in Montreal. Constructed as the track and field site for the 1976 Montreal Olympics, it has yet to be completed satisfactorily. Originally estimated to cost about $60 million, the price thus far is in excess of $1 billion.

Building bloopers are often caused by devoting insufficient time, effort, and/or expertise to the planning process. The earlier in the process that mistakes are discovered and corrected, the less they will cost to rectify. It is inexpensive to change some words on a paper, somewhat more expensive to change lines on a blueprint, and outrageously expensive or even impossible to make changes once the concrete has been poured. Furthermore, the impact of a poorly designed building is staggering when compared with other management problems. Problematic staff can be relieved of their responsibilities. Funds can be raised for underfinanced programs. However, the consequences of a poorly designed building will have to be endured for decades. Therefore, it is essential to devote all available resources early in the planning process.

All too often, facilities are planned without in-depth consideration of the programs that they will support. Basically, a facility is a tool. The better it is planned, designed, and constructed, the better it will support the objectives of the programs it will house. Strange as it may seem, sport facilities often are designed without a great deal of consideration given to programming and user desires. Aesthetics, the interests of one popular sport or program at the time, or the personal desires of decision-makers may, in fact, dictate the design of the facility. Implementing a new program in an existing or poorly planned facility often requires designing the programs based on the limitations of the facility. Poorly designed venues may limit or even prevent some activities from taking place. Conversely, a well-designed facility will support and enhance the desired programs. Planning and building a new facility is a great opportunity to ensure that it will optimally support these programs. Furthermore, well-planned venues allow for flexibility when the popularity of activities and user demand fluctuate. Planned with an eye toward future trends, these facilities are designed to be easily altered so that new activities can be added as needs change.

This book is intended to provide a basic understanding of the planning and design process as well as the unique features of many different areas and types of facilities. Although there is no such thing as a perfect building, with significant time, effort, and expertise devoted to the planning and design process, future building bloopers can be kept to a minimum. It is hoped that those of you involved with the planning of sports facilities will find this book to be a significant resource.

Section I

Common Facility Components

Section 1

Planning Facilities

Master Plan, Site Selection, and Development Phases

Thomas H. Sawyer, *Indiana State University*

Michael G. Hypes, *Morehead State University*

Tonya L. Gimbert, *Indiana State University*

Anyone who has been involved in facility planning and development understands that errors are common during the planning and development process. The challenge is to complete a facility project with the fewest number of errors. Before becoming too deeply involved in the planning and development process, it is important to review some of the common errors that have been made in the past (Conklin, 1999). Conklin (1999), Farmer, Mulrooney, and Ammon (1996), Frost, Lockhart, and Marshall (1988), and Horine and Stotlar (2002) suggested these errors include, but are not limited to (see photos on p. 5), (1) failure to provide adequate and appropriate accommodations for

---

25 Years of Indoor Innovations

According to Dennis Read (2013), it is extremely hard not to be amazed by all the new features facilities offer spectators and players. This is a list of the top 25 innovations in indoor facilities since 1989:

1. Video scoreboards
2. Unbreakable basketball goals
3. Bleacher seats with full backs, comfortable cushions, armrests, cup holders, and seats that fold
4. Portable basketball goals
5. Wood lockers
6. Synthetic gymnasium floors
7. Green floor finishes
8. Enhanced sound systems
9. Volleyball posts
10. Game clocks that stop and start on the official's whistle and shot clocks
11. Automated delivery of pool chemicals
12. Scoring tables with high-definition messages through LED lighting
13. Wall mats
14. Energy efficient lights
15. Practice structures
16. Gymnasium dividers
17. Customized sideline chairs
18. Indoor track surfaces
19. Antimicrobial locker rooms
20. Bleacher safety
21. Antimicrobial indoor surfaces
22. Wireless scoreboard controls
23. Floor and wall graphics
24. Faster pools with larger gutter systems and improved lane lines to reduce turbulence
25. Floor cover storage

(*Source:* Summarization of "Indoor Innovations," by D. Read, 2013, *Athletic Management, 25*(2), 55–61)

persons with disabilities throughout the facility; (2) failure to provide adequate storage spaces; (3) failure to provide adequate janitorial spaces; (4) failure to observe desirable current professional standards; (5) failure to build the facility large enough to accommodate future uses; (6) failure to provide adequate locker and dressing areas for both male and female users; (7) failure to construct shower, toilet, and dressing rooms with sufficient floor slope and properly located drains; (8) failure to provide doorways, hallways, or ramps so that equipment may be moved easily; (9) failure to provide for multiple uses of facilities; (10) failure to plan for adequate parking for the facility; (11) failure to plan for adequate space for concessions and merchandising; (12) failure to provide for adequate lobby space for spectators; (13) failure to provide for an adequate space for the media to observe activities as well as to interview performers; (14) failure to provide for adequate ticket sales areas; (15) failure to provide adequate space for a loading dock and parking for tractor trailers and buses; (16) failure to provide adequate numbers of restroom facilities for female spectators; (17) failure to provide adequate security and access control into the facility and within the facility; (18) failure to provide adequate separation between activities (buffer or safety zones) in a multipurpose space; (19) failure to provide padding on walls close to activity area, as well as padding and/or covers for short fences, on goal posts, and around trees; (20) failure to plan for the next 50 years; (21) failure to plan for maintenance of the facility; (22) failure to plan for adequate supervision of the various activity spaces within the facility; and (23) failure to plan to plan.

Planning Facilities for Health, Fitness, Physical Activity, Recreation, and Sports

The planning process defined in this chapter should be used for planning any of the following facilities/venues:

- stadiums for baseball, football, soccer, softball, or track and field;
- arenas for basketball, football, or ice hockey;
- gymnasiums for public and private schools, colleges and universities, YMCAs, YWCAs, or Boys and Girls Clubs;
- natatoriums (indoor aquatic centers);
- outdoor aquatic centers;
- municipal parks and recreation areas;
- skateboard parks; and
- adventure areas, including rope courses, challenge courses and climbing walls, and combative areas.

Furthermore, the process should include a planning committee, a master plan, a predevelopment review, a facility checklist, and site selection and development phases.

Development of a Master Plan

Master planning is a decision-making process that promotes changes that will accommodate new and revised needs and will search for ways to improve existing conditions. The master plan is critical during periods of excess and limited resources. The planning process can and does change attitudes about the needs and utilization of current assets, as well as provides a way for communicating with the stakeholders.

The master planning process requires coordination, organization, and integration of program, financial, and physical planning. Such planning is cyclical in nature and requires the architectural, strategic, and master planning staff to develop and implement procedures and schedules to ensure that the various activities occur in the proper sequence (see Figure 1.1).

Another important characteristic of the master planning process is its ability to respond to changing needs. It must be a flexible and dynamic plan so that it is easy to amend, taking into consideration future projections as reflected by the realities of the present and the absolutes of the past. This means the process will be more important than the eventual product.

Master planning is a process structured to promote cost-effective development decisions that best serve the goals and objectives of the organization. The process operates on the premise that the development of facilities and their ongoing management can best serve specific program needs if the organization's standards of space planning, facilities programming, design, and construction management are closely linked.

Typical Phases of a Master Plan

The master plan can be used to answer three common questions: Where are we? Where do we want to go? How do we get there? This approach is flexible to allow the individual organization to reflect local conditions, priorities, and emphases.

Establishment of an Ad Hoc Program Committee and a Plan for Planning

The organization's ad hoc planning advisory committee (sometimes called the program committee) should be composed of

- program specialists,
- end users,
- financial consultants,
- maintenance personnel,
- community representatives,

Dos

This is an example of proper use of safety fencing for a baseball or softball shelter. Notice the 4-ft fence has a protective cover.

This is an example of proper use of a protective covering for a short fence that provides a greater measure of safety for the players.

This is a good example of proper design with a warning track, 8-ft fence with protective covering, and a wind screen.

Don'ts

This is an example of an unsafe fence without a protective covering for a short fence.

This is an example of a proper 10-ft safety buffer zone, but with an unprotected wall. This wall should be covered with mats under the basket.

This is an example of poor planning with the exit doors located directly behind the basketball backboard.

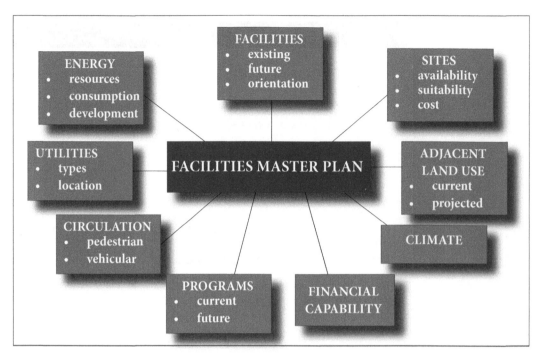

Figure 1.1. **Facilities Master Plan** (*Source:* White & Karabetsos, 1999; Sawyer, 2002, 2005, 2009)

- management representatives,
- facility consultants, and
- risk management and safety consultants.

The role of the planning advisory committee includes representing all of the organization's constituencies; overseeing and reviewing the ongoing work; communicating with the various stakeholders about the work in progress, findings, and results; validating the process; resolving unsettled issues; and endorsing the results and forwarding the master plan for approval.

The committee should be assisted by the office staff within the organization, who should keep the senior administration advised of the ongoing work, coordinate and schedule the planning efforts, serve as committee recorder, assist in communicating the ongoing work to the stakeholders, and represent the committee at planning work sessions and related meetings.

Organization Briefings and Initiation of Organization Master Plan Studies

The committee should organize and schedule information meetings to (a) notify the organization and the community of the organization's planning activity, purpose, method, and schedule; (b) solicit immediate concerns, comments, and suggestions; (c) encourage participation in the planning process and identify organization or community issues; and (d) identify the planning staff who will be available for further discussions of these and related matters.

Identification and Confirmation of the Organization's Goals and Objectives

Now detailed planning can begin with three concurrent studies: development of an organization profile, identification of capital improvements, and analysis of existing conditions. The development of the organization's program statement is intended to generally describe the organization's niche (see Figure 1.2). The statement should include, but not be limited to, a brief history of the organization; the organization's mission; the organization's programs, products, and services; the administrative structure; critical issues and strategic responses; goals and objectives for the organization; details about clientele; an outline of short-range planning, mid-range planning, and long-range planning; and other programmatic features that describe the organization as a distinctive operational entity (see Table 1.1). The statement should conclude with a descriptive overview of how the existing situation is expected to change strategically during the period covered by the proposed organization master plan and the implications and consequences such changes may have on the physical development of the organization.

It is important to compile a 10-year listing of projected capital improvements for the organization. Capital improvement items should include buildings, landscape, circulation (i.e., pedestrian and vehicular traffic), infrastructure (i.e., chilled air, electricity, roadways, sewage, sidewalks, steam, telecommunications, water, etc.), land acquisition, and actions that will change and modify the existing physical plant (e.g., new state highway right-of-way).

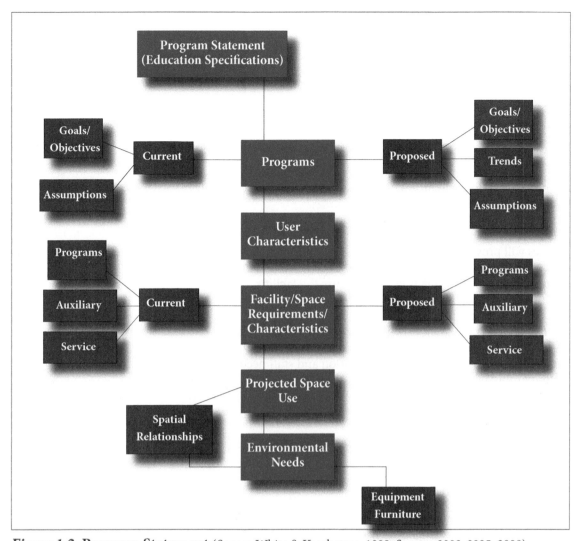

Figure 1.2. **Program Statement** (*Source:* White & Karabetsos, 1999; Sawyer, 2002, 2005, 2009)

The objective of the survey of existing conditions is to discover and describe elements that, in combination, typically create, inform, and/or express the organization as a physical place designed and operated for a specific purpose and located in a setting that has tangible physical characteristics. Certain items should be identified and defined in graphic and narrative formats so as to describe location, function, and physical character of elements. Such items include land ownership, land forms and topography; microclimate, soils and related subsurface conditions; recreational, social, and cultural patterns; land use; building use; buildings rated by physical condition; building entrances, exits, and service points; pedestrian and vehicular circulation systems; public transportation; parking; landscapes; ecological and natural settings, views, vistas, and related design features; major utilities by location, type, and condition; site history and heritage; site and building accessibility; and site and building problems.

Synthesis and Evaluation of Findings

After an ad hoc planning advisory committee is established, briefings are completed and plan studies are initiat-

ed, and master plan goals and objectives are identified and confirmed, it is time to synthesize and evaluate those findings. This effort should begin to clarify issues and opportunities that the organization should address and should establish and confirm the direction of the master plan. The issues and opportunities that should surface during the synthesis and evaluation effort relate to

- the organization's image;
- a sense of place for the improvements;
- existing and new initiatives that may require new building(s) and infrastructure, improvements and revitalization of existing physical resources, and potential demolition;
- the expansion of present facilities, which should occur only after careful and thorough evaluation of projected needs and capabilities of existing facilities; and
- the following approaches, which are listed in priority order, and which are generally considered the most appropriate way to proceed with the program requirements: (1) higher usage of existing space, (2) renovation of existing structures, (3) infill (i.e., adding ver-

Table 1.1

Sample Building Program Statement Outline

Part I. Objectives of the Programs
    a. Instructional (professional service)
    b. Recreational sports
    c. Adapted activities
    d. Athletics (interscholastic and intercollegiate)
    e. Club sports
    f. Community/school programs
    g. Others

Part II. Basic Assumptions to be Addressed
    a. Facilities will provide for a broad program of instruction, adapted activities, intramural and other sports
    b. Demographics of the population who will use the facility
    c. Existing facilities will be programmed for use
    d. Basic design considerations. What is most important?
    e. Facility expansion possibilities will be provided for in the planning
    f. Outdoor facilities should be located adjacent to indoor facilities
    g. Consideration will be given to administration and staff needs
    h. Existing problems
    i. Others

Part III. Comparable Facility Analysis
    a. Visit comparable facilities that have been recently constructed
    b. Compare cost, design features, etc.

Part IV. Factors Affecting Planning
    a. Federal and state legislation
    b. Club sports movement
    c. The community education or "Lighted School" program
    d. Surge of new noncompetitive activities being added to the curriculum
    e. Expansion of intramural sports and athletic programs
    f. Sharing certain facilities by boys and men and girls and women (athletic training rooms and equipment rooms)
    g. Coeducational programming
    h. Emphasis on individual exercise programs
    i. Physical fitness movement
    j. Systems approach in design and construction
    k. New products
    l. Others

Part V. Explanation of Current and Proposed Programming
    a. Instructional
    b. Intramural sports
    c. Club sports
    d. Adaptive programs
    e. Community/school
    f. Recreational programs
    g. Priority listing of programs
    h. Others

Part VI. Preliminary Data Relative to the Proposed New Facilities

---

(*Source:* White & Karabetsos, 1999; Sawyer, 2002, 2005, 2009)

tically or horizontally to existing structures), and (4) expansion of facilities into new areas on the organization's site.

The master plan, during this phase, needs to consider generally accepted land use guidelines such as (1) the highest and best use should be made of all land, (2) land use conflicts should be avoided (i.e., neighboring residential and commercial areas), (3) areas should complement each other and promote a visual interest and functionally fit the remainder of the organization's site, (4) facilities should be constructed only on sites that best meet programmatic and environmental objectives of the organization, and (5) the organization should develop a no-build policy relating to the preservation of historic sites or open spaces.

Furthermore, the master plan should contain goals and objectives for circulation and transportation on the organization's site. These goals and objectives should include, but not be limited to, (1) general access to the organization, (2) vehicular circulation, (3) parking, (4) pedestrian and bicycle circulation, and (5) transit.

Another extremely important aspect of the master plan is the utilities and service elements. A consolidated utility system consistent with the projected needs of the organization should be developed. This system should be designed for simplicity of maintenance and future needs for extension or expansion of the utility network.

The master plan should consider the landscape design. The primary landscape goal for the campus should be to present an image with a high degree of continuity and quality. The landscape design should consider the organization's buildings and grounds, accessibility issues, fire, security, energy conservation, and desired development beyond the organization's property line.

The following steps assume an organization planning a new facility from the ground up.

Regional Analysis

Sufficient data must be gathered about the off-site surroundings to ensure that the project will be compatible with surrounding environments, both man-made and natural. This part of the design process is referred to as the regional analysis. It should include the following:

- service area of the facility under construction (i.e., major facilities such as parks, large commercial areas facilities, and minor facilities such as children's playgrounds, senior citizen centers, local library, etc.),
- user demand (i.e., determine the kind of use clients desire, activity interests, demographic makeup of residents, and local leadership and calculate the number of users),
- access routes (i.e., major and secondary routes),
- governmental functions and boundaries (i.e., contact the local planning agency and local government offices),

- existing and proposed land uses (i.e., gather information about abutting land ownership, adjacent land uses, land use along probable access routes, off-site flooding and erosion problems, off-site pollution sources, views [especially of aesthetic and historic interest], and significant local architectural or land use characteristics), and
- regional influences (i.e., check for anything unusual or unique that could either enhance or cause problems to the project).

Site Analysis

The planning committee will need to consider various pieces of information prior to selecting the building site. The considerations for site selection (Flynn, 1985; Sawyer, 1999, 2002, 2005, 2009) include

- access to the site (i.e., ingress and egress, surrounding traffic generators, accessibility via public transportation);
- circulation within the site (e.g., roads—paved and unpaved—bicycle trails, walking and hiking trails);
- parking;
- water supply;
- sewage disposal;
- electrical service;
- telecommunication service;
- other utilities, including oil/natural gas transmission lines or cable TV;
- structures to be constructed or renovated;
- environmental concerns and conditions on and off property (e.g., noise, air, water, and visual pollution);
- easements and other legal issues (e.g., deed restrictions, rights-of-way, and less than fee simple ownership);
- zoning requirements (i.e., changing the zoning is usually time consuming and expensive and frequently not possible);
- historical significance;
- any existing uses (activities) on the site;
- climactic conditions prevalent in the area by season (e.g., temperature; humidity; air movement velocity, duration, and direction; amount of sunshine; precipitation—rain, sleet, snow; sun angles and subsequent shadows; special conditions—ice storms, hurricanes, tornadoes, heavy fog, heavy rainstorm, floods, and persistent cloud cover);
- nuisance potentials (children nearby, noise, etc.);
- natural features (e.g., topography, slope analysis, soil conditions, geology, hydrology, flora and fauna);
- economic impact of a site (e.g., labor costs, growth trends, population shifts, buying power index, available workforce, property taxes, tax incentives, surrounding competition, utility costs, incentives, area of dominant influence, designated market area, and established enterprise zones);

- natural barriers and visibility;
- supporting demographics (age, gender, occupation, marital status, number of children, expenditures, education, income, number of earners in the family, ethnic background, etc.) and psychographics (e.g., lifestyle data or lifestyle marketing); and
- security concerns (e.g., proximity of police, fire, emergency medical personnel, hospitals).

The most important aspects of site selection are location, location, and location. If the site is not in the most accessible location with a high profile for people to recognize, the success of the venture will be negatively affected.

The following seven steps apply to both new ventures and established organizations planning major overhauls (Flynn, 1985; Fogg, 1986; Miller, 1997; Sawyer, 1999, 2002, 2005, 2009):

1. **Master plan agenda**. The master plan agenda is a specific list of issues, opportunities, and projected physical improvements. The plan will include the number and type of structures to be constructed or renovated, the estimated capital costs over a set period of time, approximate locations of new structures, and probable priority to be considered in the preparation of the master plan (see Figure 1.3).

2. **Review and discussion**. This step offers the organization and its stakeholders the opportunity to review and comment on the work completed on the master plan to date. The planning committee should be present at these open forums to answer questions and understand the issues and concerns raised. The presentations for these open forum meetings should include

- a description of the process,
- a summary of the organization's profile,
- a review of the projected capital improvements,
- a summary of the surveys and analysis of existing conditions,
- an accounting of issues and opportunities,
- a list of items on the master plan agenda, and
- a description of the next steps in the planning process.

The committee should review and evaluate all reactions and concerns raised at the meeting(s).

Then the committee should determine appropriate modifications to the master plan.

3. **Preparation of the draft master plan**. The preliminary master plan should be expressed in both general and specific terms. The former is intended to communicate the major features of the campus plan. The latter view enriches the vision by showing in greater detail the character, justification, feasibility, and phasing of selected significant improvements. The following components typically appear in a master plan: (1) new construction; (2) building and site reconstruction, renewal, and demolition; (3) revisions to and extension of the circulation systems; (4) new and improved landscape projects; (5) parking patterns; (6) transportation proposals; (7) infrastructure projects; (8) joint organization and community development; (9) drawings and illustrations; (10) block models; (11) organization design guidelines for buildings and building materials; and (12) landscape guidelines including views, boundary identification, major entrances and exits, service entrances and exits, building sites, vehicular and pedestrian circulation systems, parking, water features, rock formations, gardens, open spaces, and passive or recreational spaces.

4. **Review of preliminary plan**. The planning committee will present the preliminary plan to the organization's constituencies, administration, board, and community at large. These groups will review the preliminary plan. After careful review, a combined report will be generated with suggested modifications and justifications for the modifications.

5. **Revision of the master plan to obtain consensus and approval**. After the preliminary plan review has been completed, the master plan should be revised to include recommended changes from the stakeholders. The revised plan should be published and distributed as a draft master plan for use in the plan approval process. The master plan remains a dynamic and flexible document even after approval.

6. **Documentation and dissemination of the master plan**. The ad hoc planning advisory committee is transformed into a standing planning advisory committee with the following responsibilities: (1) serve as a conduit for the organization's community to present issues and suggestions regarding the master plan; (2) review all capital expenditure projects; (3) confirm conformance to the campus plan; (4) expedite the resolution of nonconformance; (5) review, resolve, and recommend plan amendments; and (6) participate in an annual review of the master plan and cyclical master plan revisions.

7. **Master plan amendment process**. The master plan will need to be amended periodically to stay current with new trends and developments. The standing planning advisory committee should plan to revise the master plan every 5 years. The process is the same as the original process that established the master plan. The standing planning advisory committee will annually review the master plan. If the administration plans a major new initiative that requires modifying the master plan or a structure or utility fails, the committee can request that the master plan be modified. This recommendation would be forwarded to the administration and board for approval.

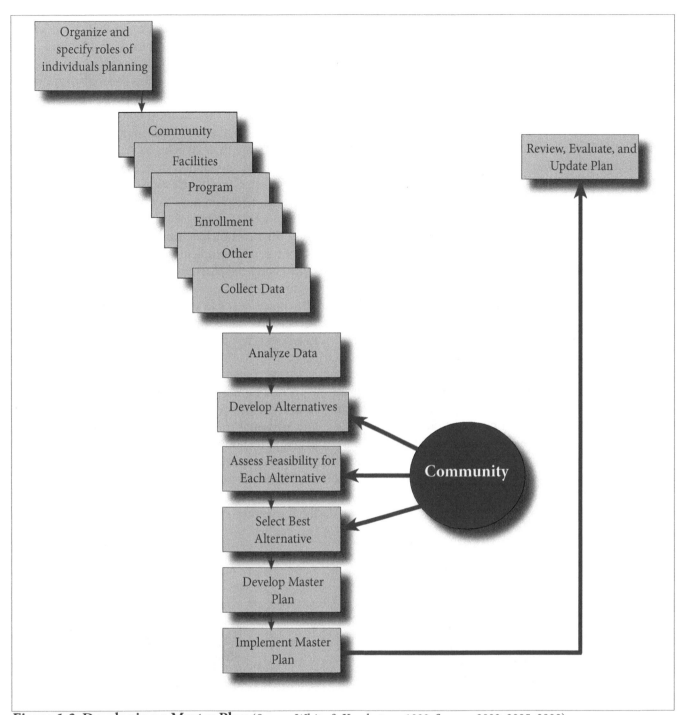

Figure 1.3. **Developing a Master Plan** (*Source:* White & Karabetsos, 1999; Sawyer, 2002, 2005, 2009)

Implementation of Plan

After the master plan has been approved as a guideline for the organization's future planning, it is important to remember that the master plan is a guide for the entire organization. It is not a specific plan for a particular structure. Once approval and funding have been gained for a specific structure, then the developmental process begins for that structure. The common components of a development process for a single structure or complex include re-

search; regional analysis; site analysis; program; functional analysis; combined site, function, land use; refinement and site plan/overall design; construction documents; bidding; construction; and review.

Design Team

The design team (see Figure 1.4) is composed of the project planning committee, architect(s), engineers, facility consultant(s), interior designer(s), construction manager, acoustical consultant(s), and turf management specialist(s). Generally, the architectural firm the organization selects employs engineers (e.g., civil, electrical, mechanical, and structural), interior designers, acoustical consultants, and turf management specialists. The organization often hires a facility consultant to work with the program committee and architect. However, in some cases, the architectural firm as part of the design team may employ the facility consultant.

A facility consultant can provide numerous services. If the consultant is part of the owner's team rather than the architectural team, this individual should serve as a liaison between the project planning committee and the architect. It is important to understand that the majority of architects an organization employs have little or no experience in designing these types of facilities. It would be preferable to select an architectural firm familiar with these types of facilities. If this is not possible, then the facility consultant becomes very important to the process.

Selecting an Architectural Firm

The selection of an architectural team should be based solely on the reputation and experience of the company and a formal review process. Once a project is approved, an advertisement (a request for qualifications [RFQ]) should be placed in the news media seeking qualifications of interested architectural firms for the specific project. Later, a letter should be sent to specific firms who qualify inviting them to submit proposals.

Tips for Drafting the Request for Proposal

The request for proposal, or RFP, is composed of the following components: (1) Prepare an RFP and communicate to a broad list of applicants to ascertain their qualifications and experience for this particular type of project (Noyes & Skolnicki, 2001; Sawyer, 2009). (2) Draft an evaluation sheet for the selection committee to use to determine who is qualified. (3) Based on responses to the RFQ, select no more than 20 firms to which to send the RFP. (4) Draft a second evaluation sheet to narrow the pool to three to five finalists for the selection committee. (5) Provide the applicants adequate time to prepare a proposal—between 3 and 4 weeks, or longer if holidays are involved. (6) Request the firms include in their proposals the following: a list of recently completed projects (last 10 years), the estimated budgeted costs and actual costs for each project, and in-house professionals available to work on the project. (7) The owner needs to provide the applicants with adequate background for the project. (8) The finalists will participate in an interview process.

Prior to the Interview

Prior to interviewing the finalists, the program committee, facility consultant, and administration representatives should travel to at least two facilities built by each firm and review the final result of their efforts. The travelers need to speak with the facility manager and users and ask about the best features and the worst features of the facility. What would they do differently? After completing the tours, they should draft a number of questions to ask the architect during the interview.

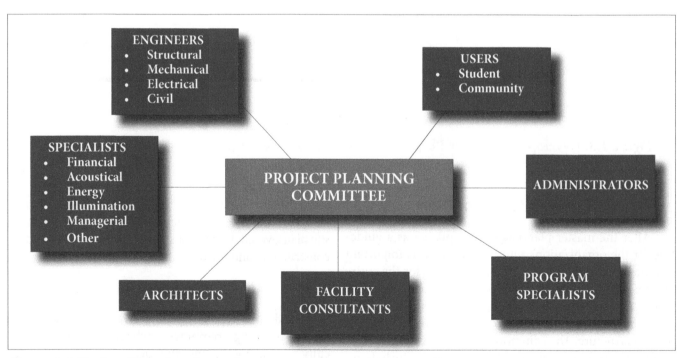

Figure 1.4. **Project Planning Committee** (*Source:* White & Karabetsos, 1999; Sawyer, 2002, 2005, 2009)

The Interview

After the field of applicants is narrowed to three to five, the firms should be interviewed. Each firm should demonstrate its competence and philosophy in the following areas (modified from the American Institute of Architects suggestions):

- client's role in the design process,
- number and type of consultants required,
- design or build versus conventional design versus fast-track process,
- extent of engineering services,
- construction supervision,
- number of sets of plans or specifications to be provided,
- construction cost,
- factors that may influence construction,
- time schedule and target dates for completion,
- architectural fee and payment schedule, and
- development of a budget.

Criteria for Selection

The successful firm should be open and flexible with the program committee and facility consultant experienced with this type of project and able to demonstrate that they have completed facilities within the budget developed (Noyes & Skolnicki, 2001; Sawyer, 2009). The firm should be able to demonstrate awareness, a user-friendly process, past success with other similar projects, and past fees as related to similar projects. Finally, the firm should be willing to provide accessibility to the architects and engineers during the planning and building phases.

Research for Facility Development

In its research, the planning committee should be concerned with (1) knowing and understanding the current and future needs and desires of the people who are involved in and/or affected by the proposed project and (2) knowing everything reasonably possible about the project function and/or activity and the space requirements.

Designers Design for People

At least four groups of people may need to be involved in the research and eventually be satisfied, including clients (e.g., board of directors), users, affected neighbors and/or public, managers and operators, and possibly others. Each of the relevant groups must be identified and its needs, concerns, and desires understood. Conflicts will almost certainly exist between the various groups. Understanding these problems in advance may make resolving them during the design phase possible.

Maintenance and Operations

Maintenance and operational needs, small but significant, must be clearly understood. They can make a project successful or doom it to future failure. The following are specific items to consider:

1. Maintenance

- Will maintenance be conducted by in-house labor or by contract?
- Is special equipment used or needed (e.g., riding lawn mowers)?
- Does maintenance staff require or prefer certain standard equipment (e.g., motors, lights, showerheads, pumps, etc.)?
- How capable is staff to maintain sophisticated equipment?
- What are maintenance space requirements, such as equipment clearance around motors and pumps, so routine maintenance can be performed?
- Are there any special fire protection requirements?
- What special storage requirements are needed for flammables and chemicals?

2. Operations

- Security—Is it needed? If so, what type (patrol, electronic, entrance only, dogs, by whom)? If patrolled, how—by foot, car, motorcycle, horse, bike, or boat?
- Hours of operation—Is night lighting required?
- Trash pickup—In-house? Contract? Kind of equipment used?
- Deliveries—Food, supplies, etc. When are separate entrances and exits needed?
- Communications system—Speakers, phone, radio, bell system, public address system?
- Safety/first aid—Are special facilities needed? Where? Extent? Emergency vehicle access?
- Peak use—How is it handled? Restrict use or provide overflow capacity?

3. Special Programs

- Will there be any? If so, what kind (e.g., concerts at noon, employee training, visitor information and/or education, arts and crafts shows, special exhibits)?
- Any special space requirements for programs? Lighting? Service areas? Other utilities?

Facilities and Their Requirements

Most facilities have specific site requirements. Technical data must be gathered on all the proposed facilities. At a minimum, the following must be known:

- size (actual dimensions plus any buffer spaces or required accessory space);

- grade requirements (i.e., maximum and minimum heights);
- special construction requirements (e.g., aquatic centers, tennis courts, or ice hockey rinks); and
- utility needs (i.e., type and amount).

Predevelopment Review

Along with the master planning process, a thorough review of facility needs should be completed for a proposed new or renovated facility. This review should be completed before an architect or consultant is brought on board. This can save time and money, as well as ensures that the structure will fit the proposed program. It is important to develop a checklist at the beginning, not the end, of the planning process. This will help focus and guide the dream and planning process. See Appendices A through D for examples of specific checklists to guide you in developing your own checklist for the proposed project.

Program

Program, as used here, is the organization of the information needed for planning a project to provide an appropriate facility to meet the needs of the affected people (client, users, neighbors, and staff). Program needs should include a list of activities, facility needs for each activity listed, number of participants in each activity during peak periods, size of each facility ranging from minimum to ideal, and a description of the relationship between activities and facilities (i.e., Can certain activities coexist with other activities at the same time in one facility?).

Functional Analysis

Functional analysis is the process of analyzing and organizing the information provided in programming and relationships by translating that analysis into graphic symbols. It establishes the preferred or ideal physical relationships of all the components of a project. The process commonly consists of four parts: space diagrams, relationship charts and/or diagrams, bubble diagrams, and land use concepts. All of the elements contained in the activity/program must be considered and their desired functional and physical relationships accommodated.

Combined Site, Function, and Land Use

Two issues are key to land use: people's needs and site constraints. At this point, the various constraints and opportunities the site presents must become integrated with people's needs. It is also the time when the reality of the site constraints may require changes in the program. This step combines the site analysis with the functional analysis. If changes are made in the program, the changes must be in-corporated throughout the functional analysis phase. This step in the site design process is where analysis of the site data is most completely utilized.

If the site selected is too small, the following options should be considered:

- Physical modification of the site. This may be the least desirable option because it is almost always undesirable from an environmental standpoint. It frequently is not aesthetically pleasing, and it is usually expensive.
- Expand the site if adjacent land is available. This is frequently not possible and can be expensive.
- Change to another site. This can be expensive, and alternate sites may not be available.
- Cancel the project. This is not usually desirable or possible.
- Creatively look at new ways of solving the problem.

The location is the most difficult choice. It is always difficult to abandon the proven acceptable way of designing and operating facilities. When successful, however, it often leads to outstanding, innovative solutions.

Refinement and Site Plan/ Overall Design

After the land use step has been completed, the planning committee needs to refine the focus of the building project before it moves to the site plan/overall design step. After the refinement is complete, then, and only then, should the planners consider site planning and overall design. A site plan shows the entire existing and proposed site features superimposed on a topographic base map at an appropriate scale. It functions as the coordinating plan that ensures that all the project parts fit together. This is the point in the site design process where imagination and creativity are really important. In addition, this plan is almost always the feature part of any presentation to the client and other interested parties. Finally, accompanying the site plan will be a number of drawings, including utilities (e.g., water sources, sewer lines, and electricity/communication lines), grading and drainage, circulation, scale drawings, relationships, and three-dimensional aspects.

Construction Documents

Construction documents control the actual constructed results and consist of two separate parts: working drawings and specifications, the written companion to the working drawings. Upon completion of the working drawings and specifications, the project is bid and, if the bids are satisfactory, the contract is awarded.

Working Drawings

All working drawings must be clear, concise, and understandable to the people who are going to construct the building. Only as much detail as is necessary to build the project should be included. More detail might give the client more control but will definitely cost more money for design and will result in higher bids. All pieces must be clearly presented in a manner that will allow accurate building.

All construction drawings must be accurate, clearly labeled, and dimensioned. If in doubt as to the need for a label or a dimension, include it! Normally, written numbers on the plan take precedence over field-scaled distances.

A useful tool in outlining the numbers and kinds of construction drawings is a plan control list. Each drawing expected to be needed is listed by description. This enables the designer(s) to coordinate work and ensures that all aspects of the project are included.

With the completed list of plans, an estimate of time required to complete the working drawing and the necessary scheduling of work assignments can be carried out. This plan control document will probably be revised during the preparation of drawings. In its final form, it will become the drawing index listing for Sheet 2 of the working drawings package.

The more detailed and elaborate the working drawings are, the higher the cost of preparing them and, very frequently, the higher the cost of building the project. A rule of thumb: The smaller the job, the fewer the construction documents. Small contractors do not like excessive control and paperwork. They frequently will not bid on projects with elaborate specifications, and if they do, they bid high. Frequently, too much control will cause bids to be higher but does not result in an increase in quality.

The construction drawings must be reviewed by the maintenance staff to (1) ensure compatibility of parts with existing facilities, (2) see whether the project can be effectively maintained at reasonable cost, and (3) determine whether alternative materials or design modifications would reduce the costs and/or simplify maintenance. A detailed cost estimate is almost always necessary at this point in the design process. If costs estimated for the time of construction are too high, then the project may have to be reduced in scope and/or redesigned. Be certain that lifetime operations and maintenance costs are also considered in the estimate.

The construction drawings should include the following: demolition and site preparation, utilities, landscape and site improvements, structural, architectural, mechanical/HVAC, mechanical/plumbing, mechanical/fire protection, and electrical/telecommunications.

Specifications

The written portion of the construction documents comes in three parts: bidding and contract requirements (including the bid documents)—Division 0; general requirements—Division 1; and construction specifications—Divisions 2–16.

This part of the design process is often most disliked by designers because of the massive detail required. It is, however, of the utmost importance in ensuring that the design is actually built according to the way it was envisioned.

Specifications should be organized in the 16-division format developed by the Construction Specifications Institute as follows (AIA, 2009):

Division 0:	Bidding requirements, contract forms, and conditions of the contract
Division 1:	General requirements/special conditions
Division 2:	Site work
Division 3:	Concrete
Division 4:	Masonry
Division 5:	Metals
Division 6:	Wood and plastic
Division 7:	Thermal and moisture protection
Division 8:	Doors and windows
Division 9:	Finishes
Division 10:	Specialties
Division 11:	Equipment
Division 12:	Furnishings
Division 13:	Special construction
Division 14:	Conveying systems
Division 15A:	Mechanical (HVAC)
Division 15B:	Mechanical (plumbing)
Division 16:	Electrical

General Notes

- Include everything in the specifications that you want to see in the final constructed product.
- Make sure that Division 1 includes the contractor providing "as-built" drawings, catalogue cuts, and, where appropriate, an operation manual and training of operating and maintenance staff.
- Include only information necessary to the specific project—especially if it is a small one. As with plans, small contractors do not like and frequently do not understand long, involved specifications; therefore, they will not bid or may increase their bids accordingly. The heavier, thicker, and more complicated the specifications are, the higher the bid.
- Conversely, the less detail you have in the specifications, the greater the opportunity for misunderstandings between the owner and the contractor.
- All phases of specifications are readily adaptable to computerization and/or word processing. Much time

can be saved if "canned" specifications are used, thus speeding up this tedious but crucial task. Computerization will probably lead to standardization of details and format.

Schematic Design Phase

In the schematic design phase, the architect prepares schematic design documents that consist of drawings and other documents illustrating the scale and relationship of project components. These are based on the mutually agreed-upon program with the owner, the schedule, and the construction budget requirements, and they are submitted to the owner for approval.

The products from this first phase of the project consist of the following: renderings (architect's conception of the building) and models, floor plans and elevations, narrative (a description of the project with sufficient detail to allow an initial review by the organization), outline specifications (e.g., exterior materials, interior finishes, mechanical and electrical systems, identification of significant discrepancies between the project requirements and the budget), and cost estimates.

The project management issues for this phase consist of cost and budget, program expansion, schedule slippage, design review, quality assurance, use of design and estimating contingencies, code compliance, and building committee(s).

Design Development Phase

Based on schematic design documents and any adjustments the owner authorizes in the program, schedule, or construction budget, the architect prepares further design development documents for approval by the owner. These consist of drawings and other documents to fix and describe the size and character of the project as to architectural, structural, mechanical, and electrical systems, materials, and other appropriate elements.

The products for this phase include drawings (site and landscape, utilities, structural, architectural, mechanical, electrical, and special equipment), narrative, specifications, and cost estimates.

The project management issues for this phase consist of cost and budget, scope creep (common elements previously eliminated from the project that reappear in design development), design review, technical review (specific reviews initiated by the owner to ensure the organization's guidelines for design and construction are being complied with), and use of design contingencies.

Construction Approaches

Lump-Sum Contract

The traditional approach is commonly known as the lump-sum contract. In this method, a general contractor is selected based on the lowest bid. The general contractor is responsible for selecting all subcontractors and all construction materials. It is not advisable to enter into this type of contractual relationship because the general contractor has too much control of the profit and loss for a job.

Pros. This is a simple, traditional approach with a defined project scope, suitable for small or straightforward projects, and fiduciary architect/engineer (A/E) and nonfiduciary general contractor roles are clear.

Cons. The builder has no input in design; the price is uncertain until bids are received; it is the slowest project delivery; there is no control over subcontractor selection; an adversarial relationship could exist among the A/E, owner, and contractor. It is prone to cost growth through changes and claims; there is a high incidence of litigation.

Construction Manager

Many public projects employ a construction manager to oversee the progress of the construction through all phases. This method allows for multiple bids, such as one for mechanical, another for electrical, and another for general construction of the structure.

Pros. There is builder selection flexibility, pre-construction services, a faster delivery schedule, early budget input and control, and change flexibility. Money is saved with controlled purchasing, optimal trade contractor selection through competitive bidding, and effective minority- and women-owned business enterprises procurement.

Cons. The owner assumes contractual cost and schedule risk, and there is no single point of contract accountability. The owner must manage more contracts, and the price is not guaranteed. Potential additional design costs and potential claims exist.

Design and Build

The next approach is design and build. This method places the responsibility for completing the project on the architect and builder who work for the same company. This option sets a fixed price, encourages interaction, and eliminates additional costs arising from design changes. A variation of design and build is called fast tracking. It is used in large projects in which contracts are let incrementally or sequentially so that the construction time may be reduced. This variation may be not be allowed in public projects due to federal or state mandates.

Pros. There is a single point of responsibility for design and construction; it offers the fastest schedule for delivery and allows for early identification of guaranteed costs.

Cons. There can be loss of owner control, quality, or both and loss of checks and balances. Contractors' profits may be excessive, and competitive bid design and build selection with guaranteed maximum price is problematic.

Design/Build/Finance/Leaseback

Another approach is design/build/finance/leaseback. This approach encompasses all the design associated with the construction project as well as obtaining funding and securing a location for the project. Furthermore, this approach also includes operations and maintenance support after the building is occupied for a specific time frame. The financially challenged owner will find this approach more acceptable. The owner will lease the facility for a specific number of years and will own the facility at the end of the term.

Pros. This approach offers a lease commitment versus a capital expense and an early lease cost determination. There is single-source management of the entire program and risk assumption, lease, financing, and ownership flexibility, and it avoids long-term capital ownership commitment.

Cons. Potential interest rates are a risk. There is diminished owner control and potential for higher operating costs. Future facility control is limited, and residual value is reduced or eliminated.

Building Project Budget Components

It is important to understand what a building project will cost. The following are the common cost components suggested by the AIA (2009, see http//:www.aia.org):

- land acquisition costs;
- land development costs;
- permitting procurement costs;
- utility tie-in, connection, or impact fees;
- attorney's fees for zoning and permitting;
- regulatory costs;
- consultant fees;
- costs of relocation, staff, and new building simulation drills;
- costs of building commissioning and activation;
- furniture, fixtures, and equipment costs;
- data, security, and telephone infrastructure costs;
- costs of testing and inspection services;
- costs of A/E;
- costs of a construction manager; and
- construction costs.

Construction Document Phase

Based on the approved design development documents and further adjustments in the scope or quality of the project or in the construction budget authorized by the owner, the architect prepares construction documents for the owner's approval. These consist of drawings and specifications that set forth in detail the requirements for the construction of the project.

Construction documents (developed by the AIA and the Associated General Contractors of America) consist of the following: invitation to bid, instructions to bidders, in-

formation available to bidders, bid forms and attachments, bid security forms, construction agreement, performance bond, payment bond, certificates, contract conditions (i.e., general conditions and supplementary conditions), specifications (Divisions 1–16), drawings, addendum(s), and contract modifications.

The program management issues for the phase consist of code compliance, scope creep, schedule slippage, design review, technical review, quality assurance, use of design and estimating contingencies, design contract interpretation and enforcement, bidding and construction strategy (i.e., a lump-sum bid for all components or multiple bids for general contractor, mechanical, electrical, and add-ons or reductions), cost overruns or underruns, design-bid-build (i.e., project designed by an architectural firm and bid out to construction firms to build), design and build, and a variation of design and build called fast tracking.

All designers must keep current on the latest product information available in their field of expertise. When the plans and specifications are completed, the project is ready for bid.

Bidding

Bids are opened in front of witnesses, usually the contractors or their representative(s), and an attorney (normally required by a government agency). The bidding process includes (a) bidding and advertising, (b) opening and reviewing bids, and (c) awarding the contract. The bid documents include invitation to bid, instructions to bidders, the bid form, other sample bidding and contract forms, and the proposed documents (e.g., drawings and specifications).

Bidding and Advertising

Bidding is the process of receiving competitive prices for the construction of the project. A bid form should be provided to ensure that all bids are prepared in the same manner for easy comparison. The bids can be received in many ways. The most common are

- lump sum (one overall price),
- lump sum with alternatives (either add-ons or deletions), and
- unit prices.

All bids on large projects should be accompanied by some type of performance bond, ensuring that the contractor will perform the work as designed at the price bid in the time specified. This ensures that bidders are sincere in their prices.

The time and place of the receipt of the sealed bids must be clearly shown on all bid packages. No late bids can be received without compromising the entire bidding process.

Small Projects (Up to $25,000)

A bid of this size can normally be handled informally. The process of calling a selected list of local contractors will usually be sufficient and will probably result in obtaining the best price.

Larger Projects (Over $25,000)

A formal bid process is usually necessary to ensure fairness, accuracy, and a competitive result. The process starts with advertising for bids. Advertising frequently is initiated prior to completing the plans with an effective date for picking up the completed plans and specifications. The larger, more complex the project is, the wider the range of advertising necessary. Governmental agencies usually have minimum advertising standards. They advertise in the legal advertisement section of the local paper and papers in larger nearby cities and in professional construction journal(s). In addition, designers or clients frequently have a list of contractors who have successfully built past projects and/or who have indicated an interest in bidding on future projects.

As a minimum, the advertisement should consist of
- a description of the project and kind of work required,
- the date and place plans can be picked up,
- the cost of plans and specifications (usually only sufficient to cover printing costs),
- the bid date and time, and
- client identification.

The approximate value of the project is sometimes included; however, some designers and clients do not wish to give out this information. With complex projects, it is desirable to schedule a pre-bid conference to explain the design and bidding process to prospective bidders. During the bidding period, one or more prospective bidders frequently raise questions. If the questions require design modifications or clarifications, they must be answered in writing in the form of an addendum to all holders of plans.

Opening and Reviewing of Bids

The designers or their representatives are usually present at the bid opening. After the bids are opened and read, it is necessary to analyze them and decide to whom the contract is to be awarded. The technical analysis is usually by the designers who consider whether the bid is complete, the prices are reasonable, and the contractor is able to do the work. A recommendation is then made. The legal analysis by the attorney is conducted concurrently with examining whether bonds are attached, all necessary signatures are included, and all required information is provided.

Award of Contract

Assuming favorable analysis by all involved and that the bids are acceptable to the client, the contract will be awarded. Most contracts are awarded to the lowest qualified bidder. Sometimes, however, the low bidder is not large enough or does not have the expertise to do the work required. Occasionally some bids are improperly prepared. In these situations, they may be rejected and the next lowest qualified bidder will be awarded the contract, or the project is rebid. This can lead to problems with the disqualified bids or bidders and is why an attorney should be present.

Payments

Drawdown. Who pays what and when? The key to a successful construction project is timely payments. Normally there is an agreed-upon payment schedule based on the submission of proper invoices for work completed and materials used from the contractor to the owner. This is generally done on a weekly basis.

Progress payments. The owner agrees to make progress payments to the contractor percentage of work completed. The payment requests are submitted based upon the amount of work completed on a line item from a pre-approved schedule of values.

Retainage. This is the portion of the construction contract amount that the owner typically holds back until all elements of the work are satisfactorily completed. This amount is established in the beginning of a project and is normally specified in the contract as a percentage.

Construction Phases

The architect should visit the site at least twice monthly at appropriate intervals during the construction stage and make the owner generally familiar with the progress and quality of the work in writing. The architect has other responsibilities, including certifying the payments presented to the owner.

The construction step of a project goes through several phases. The number of phases depends upon the scope of the project and the contracting agency. Two general guidelines govern the construction step: (1) the larger the project, the more steps required and (2) governmental projects usually have more contractual controls. At least some, and perhaps all, of the following steps will be required during construction.

Pre-Construction Conference

A meeting should be held between the contracting agency and the contractor(s) prior to the commencement of construction to review the contract items and make sure there is an understanding of how the job is to be undertaken.

Construction

The actual construction begins this phase, which could take as long as 5 years, depending on the scope of the project. However, construction can generally be completed in 18 to 24 months on an average project.

Change Orders

Change orders are defined as official documents requested by either the contractor or the contracting agency that change the approved contract documents. These changes usually include an adjustment of the bid price and a benefit to the contractor. It is better to avoid all change orders. Where this is not possible, be prepared to pay a premium price and to accept delays in contract completion.

The owner (or construction manager) needs to do the following to manage change orders:

- evaluate the proposed change for impact on the construction budget and schedule,
- determine whether the proposed change is cost effective,
- secure independent estimates of verified change order requests and recommend approval levels,
- challenge the validity of change order pricing by the contractor,
- prepare a proper change order agreement,
- make changes to the project budget and schedule, and
- maintain a log of all change orders approved.

Pre-Final Inspection and Preparation of Punch List

The initial review of a completed construction project is called a pre-final inspection. This inspection should have the affected parties' decision makers present including the owner or his or her representative, the architect, the contractor(s), and any subcontractors. At this time, it is also desirable to have the facility operation supervisor present. During this review, a "punch list" is prepared of any work the contractor needs to complete prior to a final inspection. All items that are not completed or are not completed according to specifications should be included on the list. The punch list is then agreed upon and signed by all affected parties. The contractor must then correct and/or finish all the items on the list. When the punch list is completed, it is time to call for a final inspection.

As-Built Drawings and Catalogue Cuts

As-built drawings and catalogue cuts are the drawings prepared by the contractor showing how the project was actually built. These drawings will be of great value to the operations and maintenance staff. They must know exactly what facilities were actually built and their locations to be able to maintain the project effectively.

Catalogue cuts are printed information that the manufacturers supply on materials and equipment used in the project construction. This material is necessary so that the operating staff will be able to learn about the material and equipment. In addition, it is needed for locating necessary replacement parts. It must also be included in working drawings and specifications of future renovations and/or expansion of the project.

Preparation of an Operations Manual

An operations manual contains written instructions on how to operate and maintain special equipment. The minimum data should include how to start up, how to shut down, inspection(s) time intervals and what should be inspected, schedule of required maintenance, safety precautions, and whom to contact for specialized repair assistance.

Training on How to Operate the Project

This contract item is usually included only for larger projects that are unfamiliar to the people who will operate them.

Final Inspection

The final inspection should concentrate on items not found acceptable during previous inspections. The same review team that made the pre-final inspection should be assembled for the final inspection.

Acceptance of Completed Project

Assuming all the work has been completed as shown on the plans and described in the specifications, the project should be accepted and turned over to the owner or operator. Furthermore, if the contractor has posted a performance bond guaranteeing the work, it should be released by the contracting agency.

If at all possible, avoid partial acceptances. Sometimes it is necessary to take over a part or parts of a project prior to completing the entire project. If this becomes necessary, the contractor will have the opportunity to blame future problems and/or delays on having to work around the people using the project.

Maintenance Period

When living plants are involved, many contractors have a maintenance period included after the acceptance of the project. This can last anywhere from 30 days or more for lawns to 90 days for flowers and, frequently, one full growing season for ground cover, vines, shrubs, and trees.

Bond Period

Most government projects and some larger projects require the contractor to post not only a performance bond but also a 1-year (or some other specified period) warranty on the quality of the work. Usually the bond requires the contractor to replace or repair any defective or damaged items during the time covered by the bond. Typical items are leaking roofs, infiltration of groundwater into sewer lines, puddling of water in parking lots or tennis courts, and so forth.

Bond Inspection and Final Acceptance

At the end of the bond period, the original final inspection team holds another inspection. Prior to release of the bond, any problems that have been uncovered during this inspection must be rectified at no cost to the contracting agency. It is important to note that when the bond is released, the contractor no longer has any responsibility to the project.

Review

The project has been completed and turned over to the client. Does the project do what it was designed to from the standpoint of the (a) client, (b) user, (c) affected neighbors and/or public, (d) manager and operator, and (e) design team? There are two basic kinds of information to be gathered: information on people and information on physical conditions.

Planning Facilities for Safety and Risk Management

Todd L. Seidler, *University of New Mexico*

Sports and recreation facilities that are poorly planned, designed, or constructed often increase participants' exposure to hazardous conditions and not only render the facility harder to maintain, operate, and staff, but also significantly increase the organization's exposure to liability. A poorly designed facility can usually be traced to a lack of effort or expertise of the planning and design team. It is not uncommon for a sport, physical education, or recreation facility to be designed by an architect who has little or no experience designing that type of building. For those without the proper background and understanding of the unique properties of sport and recreation facilities, many opportunities for mistakes exist that may lead to increased problems related to safety, operations, and staffing.

Design problems commonly seen in activity facilities include inadequate safety zones around courts and fields, poorly planned pedestrian traffic flow through activity areas, poor security and access control, lack of proper storage space, and the use of improper building materials. Often, safety problems related to design are difficult, expensive, or impossible to fix once the facility has been built. It is essential that professionals with activity-related knowledge and experience plan and design these facilities.

To protect themselves from claims of negligence, managers of sport and recreation programs and facilities have a number of legal responsibilities they are expected to perform. In this case, negligence is the failure to act as a reasonably prudent and careful sport or facility manager would act in the same or similar circumstances. In general, facility managers are required to run their programs so as not to create an unreasonable risk of harm to participants, staff, and spectators. One of their specific legal duties is to ensure that the environment provided is free from foreseeable risks or hazards. Unsafe facilities are one of the lead-

ing claims made in negligence lawsuits related to sports and physical activity. Facility liability has been called one of the largest subcategories within the broad spectrum of tort law. More specifically, managers of sports facilities are expected to provide a reasonably safe environment and at least to carry out the following five duties:

- keep the premises in safe repair,
- inspect the premises to discover obvious and hidden hazards,
- remove the hazards or warn of their presence,
- anticipate foreseeable uses and activities by invitees and take reasonable precautions to protect the invitee from foreseeable dangers, and
- conduct operations on the premises with reasonable care for the safety of the invitee.

According to van der Smissen (1990), "The design, layout, and construction of areas and facilities can provide either safe or hazardous conditions, enhancing or detracting from the activity in which one is engaged" (p. 235). A properly planned, designed, and constructed facility will greatly enhance the facility manager's ability to effectively carry out these legal duties. Common safety problems in sports facilities can usually be traced to two primary causes: (1) poor facility planning and design and (2) poor management.

When discussing safe facilities, Maloy (2001) stated, "Most liability problems dealing with safe environment, however, stem from maintenance and operation of the premises, not their design and construction" (p. 105). Even though this may be true, it is important to understand that sport managers can take many actions during the planning process that will enhance the their ability to safely and properly maintain and operate the premises. A well-designed facility makes the management process more effective and efficient. It follows that the easier it is to maintain a facility, the more likely it is that it will be done well. Jewell (1992), in his book *Public Assembly Facilities*, stated, "Public safety begins with good architectural design..." (p. 111). Therefore, the majority of this chapter will focus on the planning and design of safe facilities.

Planning Safe Facilities

To plan and build a facility that is safe, efficient, and optimally supports the activities likely to occur in each area, a thorough understanding of those activities is required. During the planning process, each individual space within the facility must be studied to identify every activity that will, or might, take place in that space. After this has been done, the requirements of the space necessary for each of the activities must be determined. For example, if a multipurpose room is to house classes in aerobic dance, martial arts, yoga, and gymnastics and to also act occasionally as a small lecture setup with portable chairs, the needs of each of these activities must be met even though some may conflict with others. After the design requirements have been identified for each activity, a master list for each area should be developed. This master list is then used to plan that area to reduce the number of design errors as much as possible. The following are areas where errors in planning often create hazardous situations within facilities.

Security and Access Control

When a facility is designed, access should be controlled (1) to the facility and (2) within the facility. Controlling access to sport, recreation, and fitness facilities is an important function of facility managers. Legal liability, deterrence of vandalism and theft, member safety and satisfaction, and exclusivity and value for those who pay for the privilege of using the facility are a few of the reasons it is necessary to deny access to those who do not belong. A properly designed and equipped facility, along with the use of computerized controls and a well-trained staff, can make access control relatively easy to deal with.

Many facilities, especially older spectator facilities, can be a nightmare to control. Fire regulations require many outside doors for quick evacuation. When limited access is desired, how can these doors be secured, monitored, and controlled without violating fire codes?

Having one control point through which everyone entering or leaving the building must pass is often an advantage. This control point is usually staffed during open hours, so the appropriate fee is paid, ID cards are checked, or permission is given to those who are eligible to enter. If a higher degree of control is desired, a door, gate, or turnstile can also be used.

Many computer software programs are now available to help with access control. If patrons and staff are issued ID cards, such as in a club, school, or corporate setting, systems with magnetic strip or bar code readers can be used to quickly check a person's status. Swiping the ID card through an electronic card reader can determine whether the user is eligible to enter. In systems designed for high traffic flow, the computer can be connected directly to a turnstile. If, after scanning the ID, the computer determines that the person should be permitted to enter, it sends a signal to release the turnstile and allow the individual to come in. However, this does not prevent an unauthorized person from using someone else's ID. For increased security, picture IDs are desirable to ensure that the person using the card is the legal owner. Other new systems of access control include software programs that upon scanning an ID card, display a picture of the patron on a computer monitor. If a higher level of security is desired, some systems use biometric identification. These systems may scan a patron's fingerprint, palm print, or even retina and compare it to records in the computer's memory. Facial recognition systems are now being used in high-security situations to identify individuals that may pose a threat to a facility or event. These security/access control systems are used to not only admit members but also track attendance and adherence to fitness programs, determine patrons' attendance habits, help set staffing levels to provide services at the proper times of the day, and provide information for marketing efforts.

Another aspect of access control that is improving with advances in technology is the replacement of standard door locks and keys. Systems now exist that place an electronic card reader at each door. Instead of a key, each authorized person is issued a card that can be passed through, or near, the card readers. A central computer receives the information from the card and compares it with the information stored in memory. The computer determines whether the person who was issued that card is authorized to open that particular door and either unlocks it or refuses access.

This type of system has many advantages. The computer can be programmed to allow access only to certain areas for each individual cardholder. A part-time employee may have a card that works only on certain doors, and the facility manager's card can be programmed to open them all, like a master key. Also, the computer may be programmed so that certain cards only work during specified hours.

In the case of regular locks, if someone loses a key, it is often necessary to rekey many of the locks in the building. New keys must then be issued to everyone, often at great expense. With the card system, if someone loses an access card, that card can simply be turned off on the computer and a new card issued to the owner. The old card then becomes useless.

Another feature of the card access system is that each time someone uses a card to open a door, it can be recorded on the computer. For example, computer records may show not only which door was opened on Tuesday night at 11:05, but also whose card was used and whether the person went in or out through the door. This information can be extremely valuable for facility security. The system can also be connected to the fire alarm and programmed to automatically unlock any or all of the doors when the alarm is triggered. Though installing the card reader system initially may be more expensive than installing standard locks, the system usually pays for itself in increased efficiency, convenience, and long-term cost.

Access control to certain areas within a facility is often desirable. Most buildings limit access to areas such as equipment rooms, office areas, mechanical rooms, or storage, but when a multiuse facility has more than one event or activity taking place at the same time, it may also be desirable to separate different parts of the building. For example, in a college activity center, it is not uncommon to have a varsity basketball game in the main arena while the rest of the facility is kept open for recreation. With good planning, this can be accomplished by physically separating the spaces through the use of different entrances and exits and different floors and by locking doors, gates, and fences to restrict passage from one area to another.

There are two basic concepts with which to be familiar for controlling access within a facility: (1) horizontal circulation control and (2) vertical circulation control.

Horizontal circulation control is a common method of managing access to different parts of a facility when a need exists to separate areas on the same floor. In the above example, when the entire facility is open for recreation, an open access plan is utilized. However, when a varsity basketball game is scheduled, certain doors, gates, and fences can be opened or closed to restrict spectator access to the arena without having to close down the rest of the building.

Sometimes the most efficient plan for managing access is through vertical circulation control. For example, it may be desirable in a large arena to limit access to the lower level. This level may include the playing floor, locker rooms, business offices, coaches' offices, training rooms, and storage areas. Limiting public access to the entire floor makes securing each individual area much easier. In some arenas and stadiums, the luxury suites are located on one floor, and access to that floor can be gained only by certain elevators, stairways, or gates. Patrons in general seating areas cannot gain access to the suite level, thereby enhancing security and also providing a feel of exclusivity for suite holders. If vertical circulation is needed for a large number of people, providing nonskid ramps with good handrails or escalators may provide a safer method than stairs.

Buffer Zones

Some activities require a certain amount of space surrounding the court, field, or equipment to enhance the safety of the participants. An inadequate amount of space for a buffer zone or safety zone can present foreseeable risks of injury. A number of lawsuits have been based on claims that an injury occurred as a result of an inadequate buffer or safety zone. Whether they are to separate two adjacent courts or to provide room between the court and a wall or another object, buffer zones must be considered.

Indoor

It is recommended that basketball courts be designed to have at least 10 ft of clear space beyond the end lines that is free from walls, obstructions, or other courts. This should be possible when designing a new facility, but if it is not, a minimum of 6 ft is needed, and anything less than 10 ft should be fully padded to soften the impact where players are likely to hit if they lose control while going out of bounds. As for the sidelines of the court, it is recommended that at least a 6-ft buffer space be provided between adjacent courts or to obstructions including bleachers, walls, tables, benches, or stored equipment. It is important to remember that if cross-courts are used, then adequate buffer zones and padding must be provided beyond the end lines of those courts. However, the collegiate (NCAA) and high school (NFHS) rule books specify that a minimum of 3 ft of space is required around the perimeter of the court, but a 10-ft clearance is preferable. All too often, facility planners see the 3-ft minimum specified in the rule book and design to that. It is the author's belief that a 3-ft buffer zone is inadequate for safety, and anything less than 6 ft presents a foreseeable risk of collision. There is no reason for continuing to build brand new gymnasiums that contain dangerous conditions from the day they open. The smaller the buffer zone is, the greater the risk of injuries occurring from collisions with walls, benches, bleachers, or tables. A full 10-ft buffer zone is recommended beyond the end line of basketball courts.

Because gyms are often used for activities other than basketball, it is recommended that all walls and obstructions be fully padded. It is suggested that wall padding cover from no more than 4 in. off the floor to a height of at least 6 ft 4 in. and extend at least the entire width of the court. On many existing courts, it is not uncommon to have padding begin 6 in. to 12 in. above the floor, rise only to 5 ft or 6 ft, and extend only the width of the lane. In these facilities, players diving for a ball and sliding into the wall, those over 6 ft tall, or others outside the lane receive no protection.

Another common problem in basketball is with the scorer's table and team benches. These are commonly placed within 3 ft of the sideline and are often unpadded. Padded scorer's tables are available, but too few are in use, especially at the high school level.

The American Society for Testing and Materials (ASTM, 2009) established standard specification F2440-04 to identify a minimum level of protection for impact and shock absorption properties for wall padding. The ASTM standard is an important step in the safety of sport and recreation facilities, and it is recommended that any padding that is purchased meet or exceed the ASTM standard.

Activity spaces and surrounding areas should also be designed to be free of obstructions such as doors, poles, columns, and supports. If any obstruction cannot be moved or eliminated from the activity area or safety zone, it must be padded. All other protrusions that may cause a safety hazard in the gymnasium should be avoided if possible. Common examples of such protrusions include drinking fountains and fire extinguishers, which can easily be moved or recessed into a wall during the planning process. Standard doorknobs located in an activity area can also present a hazard, and alternative types of knobs that are recessed in the door are available. Such handles are commonly used on racquetball courts.

It should be recognized that an activity area such as a gymnasium might be used occasionally for activities other than those for which it was designed. It is not uncommon for outdoor activities such as softball, ultimate frisbee, or track practice to be moved indoors during inclement weather. These activities must be considered when planning a safe gym. The main point is that not all activities will use the traditional court markings for their activity area. This means that the distance from the out-of-bounds line to the wall is not always a safety factor for those activities that ignore the floor markings. If these activities can be identified and planned for before construction, there is an opportunity to provide a safe environment for them also. Otherwise, it becomes a management concern and a potentially hazardous aspect of the facility that must be compensated for.

Allowing more than one activity to take place in one area can be dangerous. Playing more than one basketball game on two or more courts that overlap, such as using a side basket for one game and an end basket for another, produces a situation in which an injury is foreseeable.

Another area where buffer or safety zones are important and often overlooked is in the weight room. Placing weight equipment too close together can present a serious safety hazard. Most weight equipment should be spaced a minimum of 3 ft apart. This should be measured with the movement of the machine or exercise in mind. Some exercises require a horizontal movement, and the buffer zone should be measured from the extremes of this movement. An example occurs with many leg extension machines. As the movement is executed, the legs straighten and extend another 2 ft or so out from the machine. The buffer zone should be measured from the point of full extension. Some exercises require more than a 3-ft buffer zone. Certain free weight exercises such as squats and power cleans require

more room because of the amount of weight and relative lack of control typically encountered during such exercises.

Outdoor

Outdoor fields and courts have many of the same problems. Overlapping fields are a common occurrence and can cause a significant safety hazard if activities are allowed to occur simultaneously. A common example is two softball fields that share a part of the outfields. If games are being played at the same time on each field, the outfielders are at risk of collision. Overlapping courts and fields should be avoided if possible. An alternative might be to turn the fields around.

Two activity areas adjacent to each other can be just as dangerous as those that overlap. It is not uncommon to see a baseball field located next to a track. Sometimes this can lead to joggers on the track having to dodge errant baseballs. All adjacent activity areas must be planned with the idea that activities may occur simultaneously so that foreseeable dangerous situations can be avoided.

Another common design that can produce several hazardous conditions is the typical football field that is surrounded by a track. Often, facilities for field events are constructed inside the track and include asphalt runways and pit areas in addition to the track and pit areas constructed with concrete curbs. In this situation, there is often little distance between the football sidelines and the inner perimeter of the track, much less the runways, pits, and the commonly used concrete pole vault box.

Ideally, two activity areas, such as a football field and a track, should not be combined in one space. Realistically, though, sufficient space is often not available to construct the two separately, and they must be combined. If this type of mixed-use field is necessary, it is recommended that no obstructions be within a minimum of 15 ft of the sidelines or end zone of the football field. At the very least, the jumping and vaulting runways can be placed outside the track. If bleachers on the opposite side of the field are not adequate to accommodate crowds, removable bleachers can be temporarily installed over those runways and pit areas. The high jump approach as well as the shot put and discus pads can be located more than 15 ft from the end zone without encroaching on the track.

Other common obstructions that can create hazardous conditions are telephone, water, and/or electrical boxes used during football games that are often placed adjacent to the inner perimeter of the track. These are typically metal boxes mounted on poles several inches above the ground. A runner (either track or football) who is bumped, stumbles, or is tackled can fall and strike the sharp metal receptacle and be severely injured. If such boxes are essential, they should be placed underground with the top flush with the field surface. Obstructions that are within 15 ft of the field should be padded for safety. The primary problem with padding obstructions is that, even when padded, they are still a hazard. Also, the padding deteriorates over time, or disappears, or people become lax about installing it prior to usage of the field. It is better to plan and construct the area without such hazards in the first place.

Many fields have been built with steel manhole covers or storm drain grates in, or next to, the playing area. Also, fences are constructed or trees are planted just outside the boundary lines, typically with no thought for the safety of the people using the field. It is important to understand that not all activities occur within the playing field. Whether chasing a fly ball into foul territory or getting tackled on the sideline, obstructions that are just out of bounds can be significant hazards. With proper planning, these can often be easily avoided.

Another common safety hazard often seen in high school baseball and softball facilities is open dugouts. All dugouts should be screened in front to protect those within from line drive foul balls and errant throws. Providing protected access to and from the dugout is also important. Water fountains and bat racks should be placed inside or behind the dugout, with players being able to gain access to them from the dugout without being directly exposed to the field.

Portable soccer goals that are left out on fields also can create a hazardous situation. Several children are killed or severely injured each year by climbing on goals that are not anchored to the ground. These goals are often heavy, are poorly balanced, and tend to tip over when someone hangs on them. Injuries typically occur when a child hangs from the crossbar and is then crushed as it tips over. Permanently anchoring soccer goals or using a chain or cable to lock them in place can prevent these incidents.

Pedestrian Traffic Flow

A common flaw in planning a facility that can cause safety problems is failure to properly plan for pedestrian traffic flow from one area to another. Requiring people to walk through an activity area to get to their desired destination can result in a needlessly high-risk situation. A common example is when the main entrance to the locker room can only be reached by walking across the gym floor. The result is people entering and leaving the locker room while an activity is taking place in the same space.

Another example of poor traffic flow planning often occurs when pedestrians are forced to walk across a court or between two adjacent courts to get to another part of the facility. This also puts pedestrians in a situation where a collision with a participant is likely.

Planning pedestrian traffic flow within some activity areas is important to consider. A weight room can be more hazardous if people do not have good, clear, open pathways to move around to different parts of the room.

The design and layout of the weight room should account for the movement of the users, especially during times of peak occupancy. Laying out the optimal pathways within the weight room that provide users with easy access to the more popular areas or machines will help prevent excess traffic between machines.

Storage

One of the most common complaints that facility managers report when asked about their facility is a lack of adequate storage space. The following is a typical example of how this often occurs. A new facility is planned with plenty of storage space in the early stages of planning. Sometimes as the design is developed and the estimated cost of construction becomes clearer, it is determined that the project is over budget and cuts must be made. Storage areas are often the first spaces to go.

Without proper storage space, equipment will usually be stored in a corner of the gym, in one of the hallways, or on the side of the pool deck. Besides that improperly stored equipment is more likely to be vandalized or stolen, it may also attract children (see attractive nuisance below) or others to use or play with it, usually unsupervised and not in the manner for which it was designed. Equipment such as mats and port-a-pits, gymnastic apparatus, standards, nets, goals, chairs, hurdles, tables, ladders, maintenance equipment, and so forth are often stacked in the corners of gyms. No longer a common sight, trampolines were often pushed into a corner and left unattended. This improper storage and poor supervision has led to many catastrophic injuries and deaths and has resulted in trampolines being eliminated from most programs today. It is essential to plan and construct adequate storage space that is readily accessible and easily secured to prevent unauthorized use of the contents.

Lack of sufficient storage space for outdoor equipment is also often a problem. Providing a fenced, lockable storage area for items that are too large to be moved indoors, such as blocking sleds, is recommended. A fully enclosed storage area for pole vault and high jump pits, hurdles, judges stands, and other moveable equipment will provide protection from the weather and vandals and will prevent creating an attractive nuisance.

Proper Materials

Many factors must be considered when selecting materials to be used in the construction of a sport or recreation facility. Among these are initial cost, functionality, durability and expected life span, ease, and cost of maintenance and aesthetics. Another factor that is often overlooked is safety. Without proper consideration, building and finishing materials can play a large role in the inherent safety of the facility. The activities that may occur in every space must be studied thoroughly to ensure that the facility will optimally support each.

Flooring materials must be chosen with great care. Poor selection of the floor surface can contribute to significant safety hazards. One of the most dangerous examples commonly occurs in wet areas, such as locker rooms, shower areas, training rooms, and pool decks. The material selected for the floors in these areas should be a long-lasting, easily maintained, nonslip surface. All too often, these wet areas are constructed with a smooth finish, such as smooth or polished concrete, linoleum, or terrazzo. These are excellent surfaces in the proper situation and are usually selected for cost, durability, and ease of maintenance. But they all can become extremely slippery when wet. Many excellent nonslip surfaces are available for areas where they may get wet. One of the best surfaces for wet areas is rough-finish ceramic or quarry tile. All wet areas should be designed to slope toward a floor drain to avoid standing water.

Wall surfaces also offer opportunities for hazards to be designed into a facility. A major hazard often introduced into a facility is the use of glass in or near activity areas. Glass in doors or windows or covering fire extinguishers is a common cause of injury. Even the use of glass embedded with wire mesh should be questioned in activity areas. This type of glass is often mistaken for safety glass, which it is not. It is designed for fire protection and can be easily broken. If someone were to put their hand or head through such a window, the wire mesh would likely make the injury much worse than the same incident with regular glass.

Another relatively common problem is using glass in what most people think of as a non-activity area. The trophy case in the lobbies of most high school gyms is a good example. Planners often overlook that lobby space is frequently used for activities, whether it is the wrestling team running in the halls during inclement weather, cheerleaders practicing, or just the everyday horseplay that occurs with teenagers. Safety glass of some sort should be used in this area. Mirrors used in weight rooms and dance studios must be selected and located with care. They should be made of high-strength, shatterproof glass designed for activity areas. Weight room mirrors should be mounted about 18 in. above the floor to avoid contact with a barbell that may roll against the wall.

It is also important to select proper ceiling materials. Acoustic ceiling panels can be excellent for classrooms and offices but can become a maintenance headache and safety hazard when used in activity areas such as gyms. Acoustic panels are not meant to withstand abuse from balls and often break or shatter when hit.

The materials selected must be chosen with care to withstand the abuse likely to occur in each particular area. Lighting fixtures in activity areas must be appropriate to withstand the activities that will take place. In gyms where balls or other objects may hit the lights, each fixture must be designed to withstand potential punishment. The proper light typically has a plastic cover and a wire screen for protection. If the fixture is struck hard enough to shatter the bulb, the broken glass will be contained by the plastic cover and prevented from falling to the floor. Fixtures without this feature may shower broken glass on the participants below when struck.

Supervision

Designing a facility so that it can be supervised efficiently is a great advantage for two major reasons. First, a lack of proper supervision is one of the most common allegations made in lawsuits regarding negligence in sport and physical activity programs. The design and layout of the facility are often overlooked as a primary reason for poor supervision. Some facilities are inherently easy to supervise and some are not.

Second, a poorly designed facility may require five staff members to properly supervise activities, whereas a well-designed building of similar size and offerings may require only three. The cost of paying even one extra supervisor, calculated using the number of hours the facility is open each year over the life of the facility, can result in a dramatic increase in operating cost.

A well-designed facility can be adequately supervised by a minimum number of staff members. Design features that enhance efficiency of supervision include activity areas that are close together and easily monitored. Instead of activity areas being spread around the perimeter of the facility, one efficient method is to design a long central hallway or mall off of which the activity areas are placed. With proper windows or other means of observing, a supervisor can view many different areas in a short period of time.

Locker rooms are another area that is often poorly designed for adequate supervision. Concrete floors and walls, steel lockers with sharp corners, and standing water all make locker rooms perhaps the single most dangerous facility in sport and recreation. In school settings, a lot of time is unstructured with classes coming and going, showering, and changing clothes. It all adds up to a need for close, active supervision. Most locker rooms are laid out in rows of high lockers, which make it difficult to supervise the activities and easy for someone to hide. All too often, the teacher/coaches' office is located in a position that does not allow an adequate view of the entire room. Providing the ability to easily and adequately supervise must be considered when planning and designing a locker room.

Another innovation that is seeing increased usage is closed-circuit television (CCTV) systems. A well-designed system can allow a supervisor in one location to visually monitor many diverse locations, both within and outside of the facility. Often the supervisor is equipped with a two-way radio to stay in constant communication with attendants on duty inside and outside the building. If a problem is observed on the CCTV monitor, the supervisor can direct an attendant to respond immediately. A properly planned system may allow for a smaller staff than might otherwise be required and may actually increase supervisory coverage of the facility.

Miscellaneous Considerations

All facilities must comply with all applicable codes. This includes all Occupational Safety and Health Administration, Americans With Disabilities Act, fire, safety, and health codes that are appropriate for a given situation.

Humidity must be controlled throughout the facility. Excessive humidity not only reduces the comfort level but also can corrode and deteriorate building materials. Under the right conditions, high humidity also can condense onto activity floors, steps, walkways, and so forth and can create a dangerous condition. Lighting levels must be sufficient for the activity. Improper lighting can cause a hazardous situation, especially in areas where participants must visually track fast-moving objects such as in racquetball.

Signage can be an important part of a facility risk management program. Rules, procedures, instructional signs, and warning signs must be developed and posted in proper locations.

3 Sustainable Design, Construction, and Building Operations

Rick Gonzales, *University of Wisconsin–Eau Claire*
Jeffrey C. Petersen, *Baylor University*

The need to become more sensitive to global warming, rising energy prices, increased contamination, the increase in environmental related diseases and ailments, material shortages, overflowing landfills, and other related issues has caused significant concern not only in the scientific community but also with the general public. Increased news coverage, Academy Award-winning documentaries, and Nobel Peace Prizes, along with increased awareness, have brought this issue to the forefront of human concern.

Background

People and organizations can have many different reasons why they adopt or promote sustainable design methods. Some reasons why such practices should be considered include, but are not limited to, the following:

- **Altruistic objectives**—such as demonstrating commitment to environmental stewardship and social responsibility by showing leadership in transforming the built environment.
- **Carbon reduction**—is an essential ingredient of all fossil fuels (coal, oil, gasoline). When these fuels are burned to provide energy, carbon dioxide (CO_2), a greenhouse gas, is released into the earth's atmosphere.
- **Greenhouse gases (GHG)**—any gas that absorbs infrared radiation in the atmosphere. Greenhouse gases include, but are not limited to, water vapor, carbon dioxide (CO_2), methane (CH_4), nitrous oxide (N_2O), chlorofluorocarbons (CFCs), hydrochlorofluorocarbons (HCFCs), ozone (O_3), hydro fluorocarbons (HFCs), perfluorocarbons (PFCs), and sulfur hexafluoride (SF_6; U.S. Environmental Protection Agency [EPA], 2008).

- **Reduce energy consumption**—any program that promotes the implementation of energy efficiency improvements in buildings to reduce energy consumption and create energy savings.
- **Reduce nonbiodegradable waste generation**—encouraging consumers to avoid using disposable products and designing products that use less material to achieve the same purpose. In construction, the challenge is to produce high-quality projects with minimal generation.
- **Conserve water**—to reduce the withdrawal of freshwater from an ecosystem to stay within its natural replacement rate.
- **Reduce harmful greenhouse gas emissions (GHG)**—primary sources of GHG include home heating and cooling, electricity consumption, agriculture, and transportation.
- **Protecting the rights of future generations**—development that meets the needs of society without compromising the ability of future generations to meet their own needs. Implicit in this definition is the recognition of rights of future generations—the right to achieve a sustainable level of development and the right to be able to utilize natural resources.
- **Improve air quality**—eliminating sick building syndrome, improving occupant health and psyche, reducing lost work time, and improving productivity.
- **Reducing the production of toxic chemicals**—moving away from chemicals that can harm human health or unnaturally enhance food production.
- **Moving America away from oil dependency**—developing better fuel sources that are good for national security, the economy, and the environment.
- **Global warming**—rising earth temperature's effects on species survival, food production, and weather.

- **Saving the wildlands**—defending the wild places of the world, including forests, parks, wetlands, and wilderness areas.
- **Reviving the oceans**—overfishing, pollution, and habitat destruction.
- **Financial incentives**—local communities, state agencies, and some federal agencies may give developers some type of financial incentive for building sustainable buildings. If the protection of a historic structure is involved, then financial incentives may be available for the restoration of such a structure.

Whatever the reasoning is for proceeding with sustainable objectives does not matter; it is the right thing to do. No reason is better than another.

There is no common definition of what sustainability means. Green design, socially responsible design, high performance buildings, ecologically efficient, environmentally friendly, healthy buildings, ecodesign, natural resource efficient, whole building design, and other terms are widely used synonymously.

To practice sustainable methods requires a complete "cradle-to-grave" approach. The cradle-to-grave approach is an analysis of the impact of a product from the beginning of its source-gathering processes, through the end of its useful life, to disposal of all waste products. *Cradle-to-cradle* is a related term signifying the recycling or reuse of materials at the end of their first useful life.

Sustainability is most often considered to be the condition of being able to meet the needs of present generations without compromising those needs for future generations. It is achieving a balance among extraction and renewal and environmental inputs and outputs as to cause no overall net environmental burden or deficit. To be truly sustainable, a human community must not decrease biodiversity, must not consume resources faster than they are renewed, must recycle and reuse virtually all materials, and must rely primarily on resources of its own region.

Many organizations promote sustainable design practices. These organizations may stress a particular aspect of sustainability, such as site design, products and materials, recycling, or other key aspects in the cradle-to-grave approach.

Sustainable Design for Facilities/Venues for Health, Fitness, Physical Activity, Recreation, and Sports

Health, fitness, physical activity, recreational, and sports facilities fall behind other types of facilities with sustainable features in mind. There is no apparent reason why this industry has lagged behind others. Locating green facilities is not as easy as one might think. Facilities can be green but not be certified. Multiple certification programs are available, each with certification criteria.

It is important to note that of the many LEED-certified (Leadership in Energy and Environmental Design) buildings, only a small percentage qualify as facilities or venues for health, fitness, physical activity, recreation, and sports. The number of LEED-certified sport and recreational facilities is as follows:
- recreation—42,
- park—eight, and
- stadium/arena—three.

Known sustainable sport facilities that have been completed to date include the following:
- Los Angeles Community College Fieldhouse,
- Harbor College PE/Wellness Center,
- Montclair State,
- Haverford College,
- Grinnell College,
- Dow Diamond,
- Coors Field,
- Great American Ball Park,
- Detroit Lions HQ and Training Center,
- University of South Carolina Baseball Stadium,
- University of Connecticut Football Training Facility, and
- Murray State University.

The University of Connecticut facility was the first collegiate athletic facility to achieve LEED silver certification. This facility was completed in 2006. This supports the concern that green industry is still in its infancy, especially when it comes to sport and recreation facilities.

Other sport facilities are planned but have yet to be completed. The details of what will make them sustainable are unknown. In 2008, or shortly thereafter, other green sport facilities expected to be fully operational include, but are not limited to, the following:
- University of Connecticut Football Complex,
- Minnesota Twins Ballpark,
- Washington Nationals Ballpark,
- University of Michigan Gymnastics Facility,
- Orlando Magic Arena,
- Citi Field,
- Thunder Bay Community Center, and
- Aquinas College Rec Center.

There has been significant movement to build sustainable schools and universities. These facilities may include gymnasiums that utilize sustainable design as well. These types of facilities are not broken down to a point that will allow for an easy analysis of the various green components that each educational facility may have.

The movement toward sustainable buildings is not just an American effort. Many countries have embraced the need for more environmentally friendly structures in sport. The United Kingdom, Australia, Canada, and others are aggressively pursuing the benefits of sustainable buildings.

Key Concepts of Sustainability
Need for Integrated Design

Ensuring design success on any project, not just sustainable building projects, requires an integrated approach to the process. This approach requires that all design team members, including the designers, stakeholders, and construction workers, work together to set project objectives and select appropriate building materials, systems, and project delivery methods. In the United States, most construction projects are structured on an adversarial level where designers, owners, and constructors have different agendas and there is little mutual trust. This is the "low-bid" mentality. Everyone is looking for a bargain, but sometimes those bargains hurt everyone. No one wants the contractor who had a large mistake in tabulating his bid constructing his project. No one should want an unqualified design team to design a project just because they were willing to do the project for the lowest price or because they knew the right person.

Building Certification Programs

There are multiple certification programs of various types in the marketplace, but there are two primary programs that focus on advancing responsible building practices and one that focuses on responsible product design and fabrication.

The U.S. Green Building Council (USGBC) has also compiled an extensive library of available resources that many industry professionals use, even if their goal is not to achieve LEED certification. For this reason, many USGBC publications, periodicals, and data will be cited extensively in this chapter.

To date, LEED has the strong brand name recognition and appears to be the front-runner among multiple certification methods. The LEED process has been adopted for use by the federal government and many state and local governments.

Another excellent certification program is the Green Globes program developed by the Green Building Initiative. This program has similarities to the LEED format. The Green Globes process assesses potential points in seven areas, including
• project management;
• site;

• energy;
• water;
• resources;
• emissions, effluents, and other impacts; and
• indoor environment.

The primary reason for these similarities is that both share a common beginning. Both systems were based on the Building Research Establishment's Environmental Assessment Method from the United Kingdom.

The Green Globes method is less rigid, easier to use, and costs much less to certify a building. It is important to remember that a building does not have to be certified to be sustainable. The decision to certify is the choice of the building owner.

The Energy Star certification program developed by the EPA and the Department of Energy is a program that promotes energy-efficient products and practices for the benefit of American consumers.

The intent of this chapter is not to promote any one sustainable design organization, but it is important to note that the USGBC's LEED system is rapidly becoming the national norm. Many organizations in many fields promote sustainability methods, but few give guidelines as to how that goal can be achieved. The USGBC provides more of a "how to" to sustainability, and that has significantly helped in the adoption of the program. This organization has experienced incredible growth in the last 11 years. In 1996, the USGBC membership was 61 members. By July 2008, the membership had risen to 16,727. By July 2012, the membership had risen to 31,286 with 77 chapters nationwide (USGBC, 2012).

LEED Rating System Product Portfolio

According to the USGBC (2012), green design is the design and construction practices that significantly reduce or eliminate the negative impact of buildings on the environment and occupants. The LEED process varies by project type. USGBC has developed multiple processes with subcategories that include the following:
• new construction and major renovations (LEED-NC, Version 2.2),
• existing buildings (LEED-EB, Version 2.0),
• commercial interiors (Version 2.0),
• core and shell (Version 2.0),
• homes (Pilot Version 1.11a), and
• neighborhood development (Pilot Version).

Most projects that professionals in the sport and recreations industry may face should fall along the LEED-NC or LEED-EB process; for that reason, greater emphasis will be given to detailing those processes. LEED building certification is a voluntary consensus-based national standard for developing high-performance, sustainable buildings.

LEED-NC and LEED-EB

These two processes for distinctively different types of projects have great similarities in what is measured. In both processes, the same six broad areas of concern are measured:
- sustainable site planning;
- safeguarding water and water efficiency;
- energy efficiency and renewable energy;
- conservation of materials and resources;
- indoor environmental quality; and
- innovation in upgrades, operations, and maintenance.

The six broad areas of concern may not vary by either measuring process, but how an area is measured and what is measured vary by process. The specific differences are as follows:

- LEED-NC Process
  Total points possible are 69.
  For certification, a project must earn the following point levels:
  -Platinum—52 to 69 points
  -Gold—39 to 51 points
  -Silver—33 to 38 points
  -Certified—26 to 32 points

- LEED-EB Process
  Total points possible are 85.
  For certification, a project must earn the following point levels:
  -Platinum—64 to 85 points
  -Gold—48 to 63 points
  -Silver—40 to 47 points
  -Certified—32 to 39 points

The higher number of available points for existing buildings diminishes the value of each point. An existing structure may be able to do little about its site configuration, thus making it hard to achieve points in that area. Existing buildings are prime candidates for improvement in the areas of energy and atmosphere, materials and resources, and environmental air quality.

Of all of the LEED-certified buildings, only a small number of buildings in any of the LEED processes are platinum certified. In 2012, the number of buildings per certification level for all of the LEED rating systems, regardless of project type (i.e., NC, EB, or any other LEED category), were as follows:
- Platinum—91, or about 5% of the total
- Gold—407, or about 22% of the total
- Silver—454, or about 25% of the total
- Bronze—3 (no longer offered), or less than 1% of the total
- Certified—387, or about 34% of the total
- Total number of LEED-certified buildings—1,838 as of May 2012 (USGBC, 2012)

Benefits of Green Buildings

Sustainable practices can substantially reduce the impact on natural resource consumption. Green buildings can also reduce energy consumption. According to the USGBC (2012), sustainable buildings on average consume
- 30% less energy,
- 30% less carbon,
- 30% to 50% less water usage, and
- 50% to 90% less cost due to waste generation.

In addition to the potential financial benefits, green buildings can also
- promote building occupant health and decreased risk management,
- reduce the impact on local infrastructures,
- increase building valuation,
- decrease vacancy in commercial buildings,
- be excellent for public relations,
- increase morale, and
- reduce the growth of mold.

The general public has a positive perception of brands and products that are aligned with social causes. According to the USGBC (2008),
- 89% choose brands aligned with social causes,
- 74% listen to brands aligned with social causes,
- 69% shop for brands aligned with social causes, and
- 66% recommend brands aligned with social causes.

It is still unknown whether green buildings live up to expectations. Only time will tell whether these buildings actually deliver the intended benefits. Despite this fact, there are still perceived benefits to green buildings (USGBC, 2008):
- 8% to 9% decrease in operating expenses,
- 7.5% increase in building values,
- 6.6% improvement in return on investment (ROI),
- 3.5% increase in occupancy, and
- 3% rent increase.

If the Benefits Are So Great, Why Isn't Everyone Building Sustainable Buildings?

The sustainable products, materials, and equipment industry is still in its infancy. New items are becoming available every week. Only time will tell which of these will catch on and survive in the long term. At this point in time, sustainable structures cost more to construct than conventional construction, but the cost is decreasing at a reasonable rate (Kibert, 2005).

Kibert (2005) also found that compared to standard construction methods, the cost to construct sustainable facilities at LEED standards can cost above and beyond that of conventional construction as follows:

- Platinum—6.5% higher
- Gold—1.8% higher
- Silver—2.1% higher
- Certified—0.7% higher

Since the LEED certification process is relatively new, there is little hard data to examine that confirms or refutes whether sustainable facilities reduce operating costs over time. If costs are found to be reduced, then recouping the high first-costs investment that these types of facilities require is possible.

In 2007, Compass Resource Management issued the report *Towards a Green Building and Infrastructure Investment Fund* in conjunction with the Vancouver 2010 Olympic and Paralympics Winter Games effort. In this report, the researchers conducted multiple surveys and studied multiple models to determine the increased cost of LEED-certified construction as well as the potential benefits. This report confirmed that LEED certification increases cost above and beyond that of conventional construction as follows:

- Platinum—4.7% to as high as 10.3% more
- Gold—0.4% to as high as 8.1% more
- Silver—0% to as high as 4.3% more
- Certified—0% to as high as 2.4% more

It is important to note that this same study (Compass Resource Management, 2007) also found that LEED-certified buildings have a significant impact on reducing the overall building consumption. The observed reductions were as follows:

- Platinum—60%
- Gold—47%
- Silver—33%
- Certified—24%

Rapidly rising energy costs will continue to rise, and reducing long-term operating costs could be an attractive alternative to relatively low first costs required for construction. Not all of a project's incurred costs will provide a return on investment. The soft costs of a project, such as specialized design work, LEED certification process, and so forth, are actual costs but will not provide financial return directly. Reducing water runoff or recycling resources equates to benefits to society but does not equate to actual measurable savings (The American Chemistry Council, 2003).

Avoided costs are also hard to measure. For example, it may be harder than one would think to quantify productivity improvement or reduced maintenance costs. Sustainable buildings can contribute to savings in both of these; but will people actually work harder if they are more comfortable and less likely to become ill? In factory settings, this case can easily be made, but in office environments or classrooms, or even sport and recreation facilities, the effects will be undetectable. People will do what they have to do and seldom will they exceed that accepted limit. Reducing costs can also imply to some that staff may be reduced, as fewer people will be required to do the same amount of work. The concept that people could lose their jobs because productivity is up and costs are down could make sustainable facilities a hard sell (The American Chemistry Council, 2003).

Building owners and developers must also be sold on making investments in sustainable buildings. Higher first costs could mean higher rents or higher costs to be passed on to the consumer. Could doing the right thing price someone out of the marketplace? Renters of commercial or residential properties generally do not care about increased investment costs, as they know that those costs will be passed on to them (Brown, Southworth, & Stovall, 2005).

According to the *Whole Building Design Guide* (2007), the first cost of construction will only amount to about 2% of the total cost of building ownership in the first 30 years. If building owners and developers fully understood the negligible impact of the first cost of construction, would they be more likely to embrace sustainable design at a higher initial cost? The CSBTF (2003) study also found that going green would result in a 20% savings in the total life cycle cost of the structure.

Other costs that cannot be easily quantified are the human and community benefits. How does one measure moral, decreased turnover, absenteeism, and other human factors? How does one begin to measure community factors such as reduced land erosion, controlled stormwater runoff, and watershed pollution? For that matter, what is the moral responsibility of building owners?

It is important to note that as the sustainable products, materials, and services industry matures, the costs will continue to go down, thus reducing the first-cost premium. Government regulation of some type may also mandate the movement toward more sustainable buildings, thus making it more mainstream.

As many contractors are not savvy on the intricacies of sustainable development, there may be some wariness in bidding or pricing such structures. Cost can be impacted when a contractor perceives the sustainable requirements as onerous or risky. When faced with uncertainty, the contractor will add a contingency to his or her pricing or refuse to participate if he or she believes that the contingencies will price them out of the project. If the bidding pool diminishes, then there is less competition, and the bid prices will most likely rise (Matthiessen, 2004). Proceeding with projects using the integrated design approach will help to prevent these types of problems.

Quantifying the Benefits

Understanding the life costs of a facility is a part of the design, construction, and operational stages that is essential for making good decisions. To fully understand the concepts of life cycle costing, it is necessary to understand the concepts of compounding, discounting, present value, and equivalent annual value.

It is not the purpose of this chapter to delve into all of these concepts in detail, but a number of sources are readily available to assist one's understanding of life cycle costing concepts. Life cycle costing could easily be a chapter in itself. Available resources include, but are not limited to, those discussed below.

Building for Environmental Economic Sustainability (BEES)

This free software was developed by the National Institute of Standards and Technology (NIST) to assist users in measuring the environmental and economic performance of various building products.

Cost Effectiveness for Capital Asset Protection Version 3.0

This is another NIST-developed product that allows the user to create models to compare risk mitigation strategies based on established economic evaluation practices.

The National Renewable Energy Laboratory (NREL) Life Cycle Inventory (LCI) Database

This is a publicly available database for commonly used materials and products in the construction industry.

Green Building Initiative Life Cycle Assessment (LCA)

This tool allows designers to compare alternative design scenarios to assist in the decision-making process.

American Society for Testing and Materials (ASTM) Life Cycle Costing Standards

The ASTM has published 143 different standards that relate to building sustainability. These standards include, but are not limited to, the following:

- ASTM E833-06 Standard Terminology of Building Economics,
- ASTM E964-06e1 Standard Practice for Measuring Benefit-to-Cost and Savings-to-Investment Ratios for Buildings and Building Systems, and

- ASTM E917-05 Standard Practice for Measuring Life Cycle Costs of Buildings and Building Systems.

Asset Lifecycle Model for Total Cost of Ownership Management

A core group of facility management members have published this free product that can be useful for existing facilities that need to make good decisions on day-to-day operations. Core participants include the Association of Higher Education Facilities Officers, Federal Council, International Management Association, and the National Association of State Facilities Administrators.

The Athena Institute's EcoCalculator for Assemblies

This is a good tool for comparing the environmental impact of different assemblies (exterior and interior walls, roofs, floors, windows, etc.).

Federal Energy Management Program's (FEMP) Building Life Cost Cycle (BLCC) Program

This is a free program; there are multiple life cycle costing models and software packages available for sale, but the free packages serve most needs just fine.

One of the biggest obstacles to analyzing the potential benefits of LEED certification effectiveness is the inability to establish a baseline for measurement. Government regulation, building code requirements, or even the availability of resources may cause a move toward sustainability that might happen anyway (The American Chemistry Council, 2003).

Financial Incentives

The U.S. Department of Housing and Urban Development, through its Brownfields Economic Development Initiative (BEDI), offers loan guarantees to finance projects that redevelop abandoned, idle, or underutilized industrial or commercial facilities that may be burdened by real or potential environmental contamination. Detailed and up-to-date listings of financial incentives are available at the USGBC website (https://www.usgbc.org) or at the Database of State Incentives for Renewables and Efficiency (DSIRE) website (http://www.dsireusa.org). Financial incentives may include

- tax incentives,
- grants,
- bonds,
- lease purchase programs,
- loan programs,
- personal income tax incentives,
- property tax incentives,
- rebate programs, and
- sales tax incentives.

There are other types of incentives that are not financial in nature but are beneficial to a developer nonetheless. This other type of potential incentive is favorable zoning permissions. Some municipalities may grant preferable zoning or rezoning approvals to projects that meet municipal sustainability objectives. These incentives can also be found on the previous two websites.

A number of large, well-funded real estate portfolios heavily invest in green projects worldwide. The interest in these properties is because of the higher rents that can be commanded, lower tenant turnover, quicker space absorption, and substantially reduced annual operating costs. Sustainable buildings may also receive high valuations from real estate appraisers, thus improving the value of the investment.

Sustainability and Government Regulation

There is little federal government support or requirement for sustainable facilities funded by state, municipal, or private sectors. It is a mandate for most federal agencies, but that is the limit of federal involvement. A complete listing of requirements by state and municipalities can be found in the Database of State Incentives for Renewables and Efficiency (DSIRE, http://www.dsireusa.org).

Large societal paradigm shifts as to what society values will be required before substantial changes will occur. In the near term, simply bringing current building practices up to the level of best practices will yield tremendous energy and cost savings. Past studies have shown that many climate-friendly and cost-effective measures in the building sector are not fully utilized in the absence of policy intervention (Brown et al., 2005). Studies have suggested that significant improvements in the energy efficiency of buildings appear to be cost effective, but they are not likely to occur without extensive policy changes.

Sustainable Operations

In the day-to-day operations the operating personnel can do a variety of tasks to promote sustainability. These operations can reduce operating costs, promote air quality, reduce pollutants, and conserve resources. Areas where sustainable practices can make a difference include, but are not limited to, those discussed below:
- Green cleaning—use biodegradable and environmentally friendly chemicals.
- HVAC maintenance—use HEPA filters, keeping ductwork free of dust and water collection.
- Energy conservation—turn off lighting and equipment when not in use.
- Water conservation—understand current water usage and how that impacts operating costs. Develop a

plan that works to reduce water usage. Identify in the plan areas where water consumption can be reduced, for example, the use of low-flow fixtures and low water use landscaping. Examine the operations for leaks and drips to reduce waste. Use automatic timers where possible on faucets, sprinklers, and so forth. Work with building occupants to change behavior through education.
- Green vehicles—use hybrid or all electric vehicles when possible.
- Recycling programs—make recycling a routine process.
- Food service operations—limit food waste, buy local products, use environmentally friendly chemicals, reduce water usage, recycle frying grease.
- Green groundskeeping—use environmentally friendly or natural pesticides, use local plants, recycle clippings, reduce water usage, and xeriscape when possible.

The above is not a complete listing of what could be accomplished to make day-to-day operation sustainable. It is just a short list to help the reader understand that much is possible with a little forethought.

Tips for a Successful Sustainability Program

Predesign
- Select your design and construction team members carefully. Use the integrated design approach on the project.
- Develop a sustainability checklist of features that are desired for the project. Prioritize these features accordingly, as not all may be necessary to make the project a success.
- Determine whether financial incentives are available for the project before moving the plan forward.
- Facilities can be designed and constructed that meet all sustainable criteria. Is it necessary to certify the building?
- Stop the practice of building disposable buildings. This concept runs contrary to the practice of building new stadiums and arenas with the latest and greatest technology and amenities as part of the facilities "arms race" mentality. There is great truth to the old adage, we don't build them like we used to. Save and reuse old structures rather than demolishing them.
- Consider alternative energy options such as wind, photovoltaic, geothermal, anaerobic digestion, fuel cells, or solar power.
- Use native vegetation; drought-resistant or low-maintenance vegetation is also preferable.
- Orient facilities properly. Always take advantage of south-facing windows, use trees to cool outside walls,

use wind to provide ventilation or water to reduce the heat island effect.

- Do not overbuild. Design facilities that can be easily added onto when needed rather than building for a future that may never be required.
- Set your preliminary budgets accordingly. If you launch into a green project with a budget for a conventional project, there will be problems. Understand what your green project will entail, so that it accurately reflects your first budget. Project funding will probably be based on this first budget, so work hard to get it right.

Design

Keep it simple; you can go green with a tight budget. Do not limit yourself, explore all possibilities, and do not sacrifice performance for the sake of first-cost savings.

Set your project objectives early and stick to the plan. Do not allow "scope creep" unless it is absolutely necessary.

- Design in flexibility. Try to predict potential future uses as best as possible.
- Do not rely on technology. You can do many things that are reasonable in cost, have good paybacks, and rely on simple and straightforward concepts.
  Tried and true products and materials are available for use without taking undue risks. Again, do your research!
- Use low-flow water fixtures. Not all low-flow fixtures are made equal. Some low-water-use toilets can end up being more trouble than they are worth if these units fail to properly remove solid waste material. Low-flow toilets that require multiple flushes or fail to remove all waste are not solutions but rather additional problems. Do your research before buying or specifying products.
- Use natural lighting whenever possible, but use it wisely. Too much lighting or glare can prove detrimental to any kind of sport, fitness, and recreation or for spectators.
- Properly select the products, finishes, and materials to be used.
- Use recycled or reclaimed water when possible. Check with local health and building code officials before proceeding.
- Properly size the HVAC equipment for the intended use. Remember that building codes are minimums and not ideals. It is just as important to not undersize airflow and changes as it is to oversize a system. Make sure that all systems, new or existing, are properly balanced and operational.

Water Harvesting

- Capture rainwater to offset the need for additional potable water for landscaping needs.

- Remember that life safety codes are minimums and not ideals. So do not underinsulate buildings, do not undersize ventilation systems, and so forth.
- Specify low-VOC products and materials. Low-VOC items will not contribute to poor indoor air quality.

Construction

- Minimize construction waste. Make recycling easy by identifying where materials of different types can be stored and work to educate the construction staff.
- Reduce the tendency to clear the site. Save as many trees as possible and protect the site's topsoil.
- Use quality local products when possible.

Startup and Occupancy

Consider the use of a qualified building commissioning firm. Commissioning provides documented confirmation that building systems function according to criteria set forth in the project documents to satisfy the owner's operational needs. Commissioning existing systems may require developing new functional criteria to address the owner's current requirements for system performance. According to the BCA, building commissioning can be useful in existing buildings as well. Retrocommissioning is the systematic process for investigating, analyzing, and optimizing the performance of building systems to improve their operation and maintenance and ensure their continued performance over time. Retrocommissioning makes the building systems perform interactively to meet the owner's current facility requirements.

Operations

- Institute a comprehensive recycling program.
- Maintain all mechanical and electrical systems to ensure optimal performance and to prolong useful life.

Use HEPA Filters

- Regularly change out filters to ensure optimal performance.
- Use green cleaning products and equipment.
- Use environmentally friendly pesticides and herbicides.
- Use recycled water.

Renovation

No design project can accurately predict the future. All facilities will need some type of strategic renovation for any of a multitude of reasons. Keeping up with technological changes such as computerization, lighting, and so forth may require renovation to keep facilities fit for duty.

Demolition

- Adapt and reuse existing facilities when possible. When you knock something down, the debris has to go somewhere.

- Remember that nothing will last forever and plan replacement facilities before it is too late.
- Do not let all of the possibilities overwhelm you and prevent you from doing the right thing. Use well-trained and experienced professionals to help you through the maze of this dynamic and ever-changing industry.

Potential Downsides to Green Buildings

The industry is still in its infancy, and only time will tell whether facilities live up to the green hype. Already there is a growing industry in lawsuits related to facilities that failed to live up to expectations. Potential legal questions and issues that could someday impact green buildings being designed and constructed today include the following:

- Does a green building add another layer of risk?
- Fraud, negligence, or breach of contract might happen if facilities fail to perform as expected.
- What are the legal implications if someone intends to build to a green certification level such as LEED, but does not seek certification?
- Will there be insurance implications?
- Can there be trademark implications if the name of certifying organizations is used but no payments are made to that organization?

- Are there issues on the design professional's standard of care?
- How will standard contracts need to be modified?

Pitfalls to Avoid

Reliance on Technology

Going green does not require high technology. The federal government launched full speed into the construction of sustainable buildings and relied heavily on technology. The high cost of technology when the green marketplace was so young resulted in many high-profile design failures.

Use of Untrained and Experienced Support Professionals

Select professionals for their unique and related experience. This should not be an on-the-job training opportunity. Not all professionals have the same credentials.

Avoid the Low-Bid Mentality

Even with public money, there are ways to select the most qualified design and construction firms without having to settle for the lowest offer.

4 Universal and Accessible Design: Creating Facilities That Work for All People

Richard J. LaRue, *University of New England*
Donald Rogers, *Indiana State University*

This chapter presents historical, conceptual, and regulatory information as well as planning resources related to universal and accessible design. Primary to the regulatory development of accessibility planning today are the key statutes from the 1990 Americans With Disabilities Act (ADA) and information regarding the most recent accessibility guidelines as published by the Architectural and Transportation Barriers Compliance Board (Access Board). Given the nonspecific nature of the regulations, the interpretations of many ADA statutes have been tested in court. The results of this litigation have created a body of case law under each ADA title. Case law is useful when planning facilities where accessibility issues are not clearly defined. Generally, the government was unresponsive to early accessibility legislation such as the 1968 Architectural Barriers Act (ABA). Today, accessibility is not the overlooked factor that it once was in the design of public and private facilities. However, many questions still exist about compliance and how to best meet the access needs of people with disabilities.

Even with published standards and guidelines, plus regular updates, it is possible for planners and designers to make misinterpretations and oversights. This chapter attempts to provide facility planners and designers with accessibility standards and guidelines associated with typical design features such as parking, restrooms, entryways, ramps, and information areas. Additional resources will be provided in the form of websites and other references to assist in locating timely information. It is important to realize that beyond the supporting features associated with facilities addressed in this book, there are often specific activity space, program, and equipment accessibility features to consider.

In this chapter and in resources located on the Internet and other places, differences between the terms *final rule, guidelines,* and *standards* may be difficult to understand. For example, in many of the documents found on the Access Board's website, the term *final rule* is used. This would seem to indicate that this is now an enforceable mandate, but, in fact, it may not be. The sequence begins with the law, and then guidelines are developed, and finally, they become standards or regulations after the necessary agency or agencies review and approve them. This means that when the Access Board publishes final rules, these are only guidelines until the Office of Management and Budget (OMB) reviews them, and then the entities responsible for enforcement must approve them, and only then do they become enforceable standards or regulations. Enforcement responsibilities are also explained in this chapter. A unique situation exists with the ABA that allows final rules by the Access Board to become standards as soon as the OMB approves them. This happens because the Access Board is responsible for enforcing the ABA, whereas other entities are responsible for the ADA and its subsequent titles.

Although the final rules are not enforceable, they represent the latest thinking on accessibility for that particular facility or situation and should be viewed as guidelines for new construction and proposed remodeling. In situations where guidelines have not been established, or standards and regulations are not in effect, the ADA is clear that all covered entities must still comply with the law, which prohibits discrimination against people with disabilities. In these situations, enforcement entities expect planners to use current best practices when designing and building for accessibility. Guidelines that have been published, but have not become standards, then would likely constitute best practices or minimum requirements. When no guidelines exist, then the planners and designers are responsible for researching what is being done with regard to accessibility in the types of facilities they are creating. It is useful to involve people with disabilities in this type of information-gathering process to get a sense of what the real needs are and whether new design ideas or adaptations will be functional.

Terminology is important to consider when discussing, writing about, and reporting on matters that involve people with disabilities. A number of trendy terms are used in these situations; however, most violate basic principles of acceptable terminology. A deliberate effort was made in this chapter to follow what is known as *person-first* terminology. The federal government uses this approach, and scholars writing in the field prefer it. Perhaps most important, it is widely endorsed by the professional community of people with disabilities. Its usage is prominently seen in the ADA and the Individuals With Disabilities Education Act. This approach acknowledges the person ahead of the disability, emphasizing that the disability is a fraction of the whole person. Although a person can undeniably have a disability, he or she should not be considered disabled. The term *handicapped* is often used with regard to accessibility as with handicapped parking or a handicapped restroom or toilet stall. In fact, when these facilities meet code, they are actually accessible features. When they do not meet code, they present a barrier to a person with a disability, which creates a handicapping situation. Helping designers create accessible and universal facilities instead of "handicapped" facilities is the primary purpose of this chapter.

The two final topics of foundation knowledge and awareness are the concepts of accessible and universal design. Frequently, these two terms are used interchangeably when considering the access needs of people with disabilities. Although they are related in some ways, each has a unique meaning. *Accessible* has a popular or nontechnical meaning that suggests something is made usable or available through some type of adaptation for individuals who have disabilities. It also has a well-developed legal meaning in the context of the ADA and ABA. Consider the situation where a ramp does not comply with the Americans With Disabilities Act Accessibility Guidelines (ADAAG). Some would say that the ramp provides access, even in cases where it is steep. Others who have knowledge of the ADA might reference the ADAAG, which requires an "accessible" ramp to be no steeper than 1:12. In either case, the term *accessible* refers specifically to meeting the needs of people with disabilities.

The second term, *universal design*, moves beyond the narrow concept of accessible. Accessible design juxtaposes accessible components with typical construction to eliminate or minimize environmental barriers for people with disabilities. Universal design creates a broadly inclusive environment that effectively blends a variety of design concepts, including accessible, into a range of meaningful options for all users. In a universally designed facility, modifications that have been made for a specific person or group are not evident. This approach facilitates inclusion by focusing on people's abilities and emphasizing socially meaningful roles.

Exploring the complexities of universal and accessible design can be an overwhelming prospect. Designers and planners are expected to follow so many codes and regulations, in addition to accessibility issues, that the process may seem restrictive to the point of stifling creativity.

Although codes and regulations present boundaries of a sort, they also provide concrete beginning points that can stimulate creative design ideas. A helpful suggestion is to envision a comprehensive plan of accessibility that goes beyond minimum standards and considers the many potential uses of the space by people with a wide range of needs and abilities.

Civil Rights Legislation for Persons With Disabilities

Public Law 90-480 (known as the Archictual Barrier Act) authorized four primary agencies to issue accessibility standards in accordance with its respective statutory authority. Those agencies are the General Services Administration (GSA), the Department of Defense (DOD), the Department of Housing and Urban Development (HUD), and the U.S. Postal Service (USPS). The problem that surfaced with this approach is that guidelines were inconsistent between the agencies, resulting in much confusion. To address the issue of compliance with the ABA, Congress established the Access Board in Section 502 of the Rehabilitation Act of 1973.

The Access Board is composed of representatives from the four initial agencies, seven other governmental agencies (Defense, Health and Human Services, Interior, Justice, Labor, Transportation, and the Veterans Administration), and 12 members appointed from the general public by the President of the United States. A 1978 amendment to Section 502 of the Rehabilitation Act of 1973 added to the Access Board's functions. This amendment required the Access Board to issue minimum guidelines and requirements for the standards then established by the four standard-setting agencies (GSA, DOD, HUD, and USPS).

The four standard-setting agencies determined that the adopted uniform standards would, as much as possible, conform to the Guidelines of the Access Board and be consistent with standards published by the American National Standards Institute (ANSI). ANSI is a nongovernmental organization in the United States that oversees standard setting procedures and applications. It accredits standards developing organizations that must adhere to the ANSI

Essential Requirements, which emphasize an "open" process to standard creation. A similar open process is used in creating accessibility standards and revisions by the Access Board, allowing public input and feedback to influence the final standards. It is important to note that ANSI's standards, (specifications for making buildings and facilities accessible to, and usable by, the physically handicapped). formed the technical basis for the first accessibility standards adopted by the federal government and most state governments. The development of ANSI's revised standards was based upon research funded by HUD. The ANSI standards were generally accepted by the private sector including the Council of American Building Officials. Updated versions of *ICC/ANSI A117.1: Accessible and Usable Buildings and Facilities*, were published in 1998 and 2009. The 2015 ICC/ASC A117.1 standards are currently being developed.

In 1984, the Access Board updated the MGRAD and published the *Uniform Federal Accessibility Standards* (UFAS), which became the standard used by the four agencies responsible for accessibility to enforce the ABA. The UFAS followed the ANSI 1980 standards in format and, with regard to scope provisions and technical requirements, met or exceeded the comparable provisions of MGRAD.

The ADA of 1990 significantly expanded the role of the Access Board. Under the ADA, the Access Board became responsible for developing accessibility guidelines for entities covered by the ADA and for providing technical assistance to individuals and organizations on the removal of architectural, transportation, and communication barriers.

In 1991, the Access Board published the *Americans With Disabilities Act Accessibility Guidelines for Buildings and Facilities* (ADAAG), which is considered more stringent than the UFAS guidelines. The Access Board maintains responsibility for revisions of the ADAAG as well as the UFAS. In November 2000, the Access Board published a comprehensive proposal to update and merge both its ADA and ABA/UFAS accessibility guidelines into the *ADA/ABA Accessibility Guidelines*. This was intended to provide more consistency between the ADA and ABA, simplify and clarify the language, and broaden the scope of what is covered. After extensive review and public comment, the Access Board approved the guidelines in final form on January 14, 2004, and published them as revised guidelines on July 23, 2004 (available at http://www.access-board.gov/ada-aba/final.cfm). On June 17, 2008, these proposed regulations were published in the *Federal Register*. At the time of this writing, these proposed guidelines were in the "notice of proposed rulemaking" stage and will become enforceable once issued as rules/standards by the DOJ.

The Access Board's recent efforts to update the ADA and ABA/UFAS guidelines and provide ANSI with guidance with A117.1 will produce standards that are highly consistent with each other. The new ADA–ABA version will read much like model building codes and industry standards. This should be more helpful for designers, planners, and architects as they integrate accessibility requirements into the vast array of building codes they must consider. The goals of the new standards include greater consistency across standards, added scope to meet the needs of people with disabilities, and updated formatting for improved usability and a "building code-like" presentation. It is projected that these changes will result in improved compliance with accessibility requirements.

On September 25, 2008, the president signed the Americans With Disabilities Act Amendments Act of 2008 ("ADA Amendments Act" or "Act"). The Act made important changes to the definition of the term *disability* by rejecting the holdings in several Supreme Court decisions and portions of U.S. Equal Employment Opportunity Commission's (EEOC) ADA regulations. The Act retained the ADA's basic definition of disability as an impairment that substantially limits one or more major life activities, a record of such an impairment, or being regarded as having such an impairment must be documented. However, it changes the way that these statutory terms should be interpreted in several ways. Most significantly, the Act

- directed the EEOC to revise that portion of its regulations defining the term *substantially limits*;
- expanded the definition of *major life activities* by including two nonexhaustive lists:
  — the first list includes many activities that the EEOC has recognized (e.g., walking) as well as activities that the EEOC has not specifically recognized (e.g., reading, bending, and communicating);
  — the second list includes major bodily functions (e.g., functions of the immune system, normal cell growth, digestive, bowel, bladder, neurological, brain, respiratory, circulatory, endocrine, and reproductive functions);
- stated that mitigating measures other than ordinary eyeglasses or contact lenses shall not be considered in assessing whether an individual has a disability;
- clarified that an impairment that is episodic or in remission is a disability if it would substantially limit a major life activity when active;
- provided that an individual subjected to an action prohibited by the ADA (e.g., failure to hire) because of an actual or perceived impairment will meet the "regarded as" definition of disability, unless the impairment is transitory and minor;
- provided that individuals covered only under the "regarded as" prong are not entitled to reasonable accommodation; and

- emphasized that the definition of *disability* should be interpreted broadly.

The EEOC began evaluating the impact of these changes on its enforcement guidance's and other publications addressing the ADA. The effective date of the ADA Amendments Act was January 1, 2009 (EEOC, n.d.). Subsequent to publication of these changes on its enforcement, the EEOC published the performance and accountability report (EEOC, 2008).

Guidelines for play areas were issued as a supplement to ADAAG on November 17, 2000. The information that follows outlines the guidelines contents.

The guidelines covered the number of play components required to be accessible, accessible surfacing in play areas, ramp access and transfer system access to elevated structures, and access to soft contained play structures. They also addressed play areas provided at schools, parks, child care facilities (except those based in the operator's home, which were exempt), and other facilities subject to the ADA. (available at http://www.access-board. gov/play/finalrule.pdf)

These play area guidelines were issued as part of the 2004 final rule ADA–ABA guidelines and awaited adoption as law by the DOJ and other agencies.

In addition, a final rule (guidelines) covering recreation facilities was published in September 2002 as a supplement to ADAAG. These guidelines covered newly constructed and altered recreation facilities in the areas of amusement rides, boating facilities, fishing piers and platforms, miniature golf courses, golf courses, exercise equipment, bowling lanes, shooting facilities, swimming pools, wading pools, and spas (available at http://www.access-board.gov/recreation/final.htm). The guidelines also followed the same timetable as the above-mentioned changes to ADA–ABA and were part of the proposed rulemaking process. Most recently the ADA standards for both play areas and recreation facilities are covered in the DOJ's *2010 ADA Standards for Accessible Design* (available at http://www.access-board.gov/ada-aba/ada-standards-doj.cfm).

In 2009, the Access Board generated a report that contained the draft guidelines for outdoor developed areas, which includes trails, beaches, picnic areas, and campgrounds. Although these regulations will be enforceable only with regard to state and federal lands, they offer invaluable information regarding the construction of like facilities on private land (Access Board, available online: http://www.access-board.gov/outdoor/draft-final.htm)

Proactively, the U.S. Forest Service developed accessibility guidelines to provide guidance for its own agency "to maximize accessibility while at the same time recogniz-ing and protecting the unique characteristics of the natural setting of outdoor recreation areas and hiker/pedestrian trails. These guidelines apply to new or reconstructed areas within the National Forest System" (U.S. Forest Service, 2008; available at http://www.fs.fed.us/recreation/programs/accessibility).

The publication (September 15, 2010) and implementation (March 15, 2012) by the DOJ, of the *2010 ADA Standards for Accessible Design* came after significant work by the Access Board and through public comment.

The 2010 Standards set minimum requirements—both scoping and technical—for newly designed and constructed or altered state, local governmental facilities, public accommodations, and commercial facilities to be readily accessible to and usable by individuals with disabilities.

Adoption of the 2010 Standards also establishes a revised reference point for Title II entities that choose to make structural changes to existing facilities to meet their program accessibility requirements; and it establishes a similar reference for Title III entities undertaking readily achievable barrier removal. DOJ; 2010 ADA Standards for Accessible Design, p. 1 (available at http://www.ada.gov/2010ADAstandards_index.htm)

The DOJ revised parts of both Title II and Title of the 2010 Standards on May 24, 2012. This revision was directly related to "Accessible Pools: Means of Entry and Access" (DOJ: ADA 2010 Revised Requirements, available at http://www.ada.gov/pools_2010.htm).

Presently, the only areas not covered by accessibility legislation in the United States are churches and private clubs. Exceptions include those churches that rent or lease facilities to the public; these facilities are covered. Private clubs must also demonstrate sufficient cause for existing as such. They cannot just charge a fee, generate a list of "members," and then expect to be exempt from accessibility law.

An area that is considered exempt by some is historically significant facilities protected by the 1966 Historic Preservation Act. However, historic preservation law does not supersede accessibility law, and the reverse is also true. In such situations, it is expected that accessibility law will be applied sensitively to these types of facilities with thoughtful designs that do not compromise important historical features and create the greatest degree of access possible. A more detailed discussion with illustrations to assist in making historically significant facilities accessible can be found in *Preservation Briefs 32: Making Historic Properties Accessible* (National Park Service [NPS], available at http://www.nps.gov/history/hps/tps/briefs/brief32.htm)

from the U.S. NPS Heritage Preservation Services Office in Washington, D.C. See also DOJ Advisory 202.5 Alterations to Qualified Historic Buildings and Facilities, p. 52, 2010 ADA Standards for Accessible Design.

The Telecommunications Act of 1996 (most recently published December 21, 2000) requires the Access Board to develop and maintain accessibility guidelines for telecommunications and customer premises equipment (e.g., mandated closed-captioning options on the newest models of televisions). Access standards for electronic and information technology in the federal sector were issued under Section 508 of the Rehabilitation Act Amendments of 1998 "which requires that such technology be accessible when developed, procured, maintained, or used by a Federal agency" (Access Board, p. 1; available at http://www.access-board.gov/sec508/standards.htm).

The roots of the ADA are in well-intentioned charity and rehabilitation efforts to include people with disabilities in society. As more is learned about having and living with a disability, the complexities of disability are better understood. The approach to accessibility is now a matter of how people with disabilities interact with and within a particular environment. This ecological approach to accessibility is the future of accessibility laws and codes.

The Five Titles of the 1990 Americans With Disabilities Act as Amended by the DOJ 2010 ADA Standards for Accessible Design

The ADA recognizes and protects the civil rights of people with disabilities and is modeled after earlier landmark laws prohibiting discrimination on the basis of race and gender. The ADA covers a wide range of disability, from physical conditions affecting mobility, stamina, sight, hearing, and speech to conditions such as emotional illness and learning disorders. The ADA addresses access to the workplace (title I), State and local government services (title II), and places of public accommodation and commercial facilities (title III). It also requires phone companies to provide telecommunications relay services for people who have hearing or speech impairments (title IV) and miscellaneous instructions to Federal agencies that enforce the law (title V). Regulations issued under the different titles by various Federal agencies set requirements and establish enforcement procedures. To understand and comply with the ADA, it is important to follow the appropriate regulations. Under titles II and III of the ADA, the Board develops and maintains accessibility guidelines for buildings, facilities, and transit vehicles and pro-

vides technical assistance and training on these guidelines. The ADA Accessibility Guidelines (ADAAG) serve as the basis of standards issued by the departments of Justice (DOJ) and Transportation (DOT) to enforce the law. The building guidelines cover places of public accommodation, commercial facilities, and State and local government facilities. The vehicle guidelines address buses, vans, a variety of rail vehicles, trams, and other modes of public transportation. Regulations issued by DOJ and DOT contain standards based on ADAAG and also provide important information on which buildings and facilities are subject to the standards. It is important that the regulations be used along with the design standards they contain or reference. (Access Board; p. 1, available at http://www.access-board.gov/about/laws/ada.htm#Overview)

Responsibility for enforcement of the ADA is shared by multiple government agencies based on each title of the law. While individuals can complain directly to federal agencies, it is preferred that they try to work through the dispute at the source of the problem. The DOJ (2010) stated:

Through lawsuits and settlement agreements, the Department of Justice has achieved greater access for individuals with disabilities in hundreds of cases. Under general rules governing lawsuits brought by the Federal government, the Department of Justice may not sue a party unless negotiations to settle the dispute have failed.

The Department of Justice may file lawsuits in federal court to enforce the ADA, and courts may order compensatory damages and back pay to remedy discrimination if the Department prevails. Under title III, the Department of Justice may also obtain civil penalties of up to $55,000 for the first violation and $110,000 for any subsequent violation. (DOJ, p. 1. available online: http://www.ada.gov/enforce.htm)

To research and/or stay current with enforcement activities, the DOJ publishes quarterly reports that include ADA litigation, formal settlement agreements, other settlements, and mediation activities (available at http://www.ada.gov/enforce.htm#anchor201570). Additionally, the DOJ provides technical assistance manuals and publications for state and local governments (available at http://www.ada.gov/publicat.htm).

It was never the intent of the U.S. government to establish accessibility legislation that would create an atmosphere of conflict around the needs of people with disabilities. A thoughtful, rational, and cooperative process that involves all parties will more effectively educate an entity on the needs of people with disabilities. Improved awareness, sensitivity, and knowledge will provide a basis for understanding the guidelines and valuing accessibility. This approach has greater potential to result in accessible facility designs that are optimally functional and relationships that will promote inclusion.

Striving for Inclusion: Accessible and Universal Design

It is important not to get drawn into the "standards game" when designing facilities that are accessible to people with disabilities. The ADA (including the DOJ's *2010 ADA Standards for Accessible Design*) is not meant to be seen simply as a set of building codes. The ADA legislation's primary purpose is as civil rights legislation that makes it illegal to discriminate against people with disabilities, because of their disabilities. To assist in implementing these efforts, there are additional regulations to follow, including the ADAAG (2004) and applicable state and municipal accessibility codes/guidelines. Designers then have a choice to either apply the existing minimum standards in an effort to comply with accessibility law or incorporate the guidelines into a universal design approach.

Although the design of sports and recreation facilities strives to meet aesthetic goals, the primary purpose is usually based on some desired experience for the users. Whether the facility is designed for specific or multipurpose use, there will typically be a variety of human interactions for which to plan. Such interactions will likely occur during staff meetings, at the information desk, in activity/event spaces, in support areas (e.g., restrooms, water fountains, locker rooms, and concessions), and so forth. Universal design provides opportunities for these interactions to happen in dignified and meaningful ways, creating a foundation for full inclusion for all participants and staff.

Universal design has its roots in accessible design beginning with the ABA. As a result of early accessible design efforts, before the ADA, it became apparent that creating accessible facilities helped more than just people with disabilities. It helped everyone at different times and in different ways.

In addition to accessibility, universal design embodies other important concepts that benefit all people. These concepts include

- providing a range of choices in how a space can be utilized or an activity can be experienced. People with and without disabilities can select from the same choices.
- offering a range of challenge levels for everyone within those choices. Do not assume that similar individuals want similar challenge levels.

- using a minimal amount of signage to indicate special services or access features. By nature, universal design reduces the need for this type of signage because functional options are more apparent.
- providing access and services in and through the same space for everyone. Do not use a design that sends different people to separate features.
- going well beyond the minimum standards when providing accessible spaces and features such as more accessible restroom stalls, easier ramp grades, and wider doors and passageways.

Most people, at some time in their lives, will experience either temporary or permanent sensory impairment and/or physical disability. These range from broken bones to age-related changes in functioning. Approximately 57 million Americans live with a disability, representing approximately 19% of the population (U.S. Census Bureau, 2012, available at http://www.census.gov/people/disability/, see Report), with countless others affected indirectly by them. Although there are legal mandates to create accessible facilities for all people, those of us in the leisure, recreation, and sport fields have a moral imperative to apply universal design strategies. It is during leisure-time experiences that our diverse society finds merge points between different classes, races, beliefs, and abilities. All people are capable of leisure, just as we are capable of creating universal facilities that serve the leisure needs of all people.

Accessibility and Public Accommodations

Like no other previous legislation, Title III of the ADA (including the DOJ's 2010 *ADA Standards for Accessible Design*), Public Accommodation, covers private, for-profit businesses, and not-for-profit agencies. This casts a huge legal net covering most sport and recreation facilities, programs, and services. Some situations by law permit alternative and partial methods of compliance, and those will be discussed in this section.

Place of public accommodation means a facility operated by a private entity whose operations affect commerce and fall within at least one of the following categories:

- place of lodging (see also the Fair Housing Amendments Act. In instances where such housing is "rented" to the public [e.g., student dormitories], specific accessibility requirements must be met.);
- a restaurant, bar, or other establishment serving food or drink;
- a motion picture house, theater, concert hall, stadium, or other place of exhibition or entertainment;
- an auditorium, convention center, lecture hall, or other place of public gathering;

- a bakery, grocery store, clothing store, hardware store, shopping center, or other sales or rental establishment;
- a laundromat, dry cleaner, bank, barbershop, beauty shop, travel service, shoe repair service, funeral parlor, gas station, office of an accountant or lawyer, pharmacy, insurance office, professional office of a health care provider, hospital, or other service establishment;
- a terminal, depot, or other station used for specified public transportation;
- a museum, library, gallery, or other place of public display or collection;
- a park, zoo, amusement park, or other place of recreation;
- a nursery; elementary, secondary, undergraduate, or postgraduate private school; or other place of education;
- a day care center, senior citizen center, homeless shelter, food bank, adoption agency, or other social service center establishment; or
- a gymnasium, health spa, bowling alley, golf course, or other place of exercise or recreation. (ADA, 2010)

Public accommodation means a private entity that owns, leases (or leases to), or operates a place of public accommodation (ADA, 2010).

A public accommodation shall remove architectural barriers in existing facilities, including communication barriers that are structural in nature, where such removal is readily achievable (i.e., easily accomplishable and able to be carried out without much difficulty or expense).

Examples of steps to remove barriers include, but are not limited to,
- installing ramps;
- making curb cuts in sidewalks and entrances;
- repositioning shelves;
- rearranging tables, chairs, vending machines, display racks, and other furniture;
- repositioning telephones;
- adding raised markings on elevator control buttons;
- installing flashing alarm lights;
- widening doors;
- installing offset hinges to widen doorways;
- eliminating a turnstile or providing an alternative accessible path;
- installing accessible door hardware;
- installing grab bars in toilet stalls;
- rearranging toilet partitions to increase maneuvering space;
- insulating lavatory pipes under sinks to prevent burns;
- installing a raised toilet seat;
- installing a full-length bathroom mirror;
- repositioning the paper towel dispenser in a bathroom;
- creating designated accessible parking spaces;

- installing an accessible paper cup dispenser at an existing inaccessible water fountain;
- removing high pile, low density carpeting; and
- installing vehicle hand controls. (ADA, 2010)

A public accommodation is urged to take measures to comply with the barrier removal requirements of this section in accordance with the following order of priorities:

1. A public accommodation should take measures to provide access to a place of public accommodation from public sidewalks, parking, or public transportation. These measures include installing an entrance ramp, widening entrances, and providing accessible parking spaces.
2. A public accommodation should take measures to provide access to those areas of a place of public accommodation where goods and services are made available to the public. These measures include adjusting the layout of display racks, rearranging tables, providing Braille and raised character signage, widening doors, providing visual alarms, and installing ramps.
3. A public accommodation should take measures to provide access to restroom facilities. These measures include removing obstructive furniture or vending machines, widening doors, installing ramps, providing accessible signage, widening toilet stalls, and installing grab bars.
4. A public accommodation should take any other measures necessary to provide access to the goods, services, facilities, privileges, advantages, or accommodations of a place of public accommodation. (ADA, 2010)

The ADA is designed to allow an otherwise-covered public accommodation to limit or "customize" its compliance using auxiliary aids and services or alternative means of providing equal goods, services, facilities, privileges, advantage, or accommodations. This is only required if those methods are readily achievable (ADA, 1990). In rare cases, due to concerns with an undue burden or a fundamental alteration in the nature of the service, program, or activity, a covered entity may not be required to provide accessible facilities and/or access to equal services. Language within the ADA that guides these decisions is explained in the following.

Undue burden means significant difficulty or expense. To determine whether an action will result in an undue burden, one should consider the following factors:
- the nature and cost of the action needed under this part;
- the overall financial resources of the site or sites involved in the action; the number of persons employed at the site; the effect on expenses and resources; legitimate safety requirements that are necessary for safe operation, including crime prevention measures; or

the impact otherwise of the action upon the operation of the site;

- the geographic separateness, and the administrative or fiscal relationship of the site or sites in question to any parent corporation or entity;
- if applicable, the overall financial resources of any parent corporation or entity; the overall size of the parent corporation or entity with respect to the number of its employees; the number, type, and location of its facilities; and
- if applicable, the type of operation or operations of any parent corporation or entity, including the composition, structure, and functions of the workforce of the parent corporation or entity. (ADA, 2010)

In the process of meeting the needs of individuals with disabilities, public entities are required to make reasonable accommodations. Should it be determined that the accommodation will drastically change (i.e., fundamentally alter) the service, program, or activity, the accommodation may not be required. A formal legal procedure is required to evaluate and substantiate this defense.

Similar to the standard of undue burden is the consideration of whether an accommodation is readily achievable. To be readily achievable means easily accomplishable and able to be carried out without much difficulty or expense. To determine whether an action is readily achievable, factors to be considered include

- the nature and cost of the action needed under this part;
- the overall financial resources of the site or sites involved in the action; the number of persons employed at the site; the effect on expenses and resources; legitimate safety requirements that are necessary for safe operation, including crime prevention measures; or the impact otherwise of the action upon the operation of the site;
- the geographic separateness, and the administrative or fiscal relationship of the site or sites in question to any parent corporation or entity;
- if applicable, the overall financial resources of any parent corporation or entity; the overall size of the parent corporation or entity with respect to the number of its employees; the number, type, and location of its facilities; and
- if applicable, the type of operation or operations of any parent corporation or entity, including the composition, structure, and functions of the workforce of the parent corporation or entity. (ADA, 2010)

An important provision in the ADA is the concept of Equivalent Facilitation. This provides an entity with an option to identify alternative methods of accommodating for the needs of patrons with disabilities. The Access Board (2010) defined equivalent facilitation as the following:

Departures from particular technical and scoping requirements of this guideline by the use of other designs and technologies are permitted where the alternative designs and technologies used will provide substantially equivalent or greater access to and usability of the facility. (retrieved from Access Board at http://www.access-board.gov/adaag/about/AIAcourse/ADAAG/Adaag.htm#2.2)

The intention of the Access Board is to encourage ongoing creative solutions to accessibility needs as long as they meet the minimum expectations of existing standards.

Short- and long-range strategic planning is an integral part of an organization's stated intention to comply with federal accessibility regulations. These plans should include specific actions and timelines for compliance. If an organization claims undue burden to avoid financial strife, they will only get short-term relief. Planning to permanently discriminate against people with disabilities is not an option. It is important to note that the ADA itself is not static legislation. It will continue to evolve, as it has numerous times since its passage in 1990, increasing in scope and degrees of accessibility. Waiting to comply when it is convenient for the organization is an ill-advised strategy. It is imperative that organizations plan ahead, take advantage of federal tax incentives, and strive to at least meet, and where possible, exceed current accessibility legislation.

Compliance with public accommodation accessibility regulations is required with all new construction, with most remodeling projects, and when offering programs and services to the public. All elements of new recreation and sports buildings, parking facilities, and site development must be accessible. Where specific guidelines are not available for new facilities, then the best information available should be used. All remodeling of facilities and developed areas must meet applicable standards and guidelines with consideration being given to concerns of undue burden and impact on the essential nature of the service or experience.

To assist with ADA compliance, it is suggested that state and local building oversight agencies pursue certification of their codes. Under Title III of the ADA (2010) the DOJ remains authorized to certify state and local accessibility building standards/requirements, ensuring that these codes meet or exceed ADA requirements. Certification promotes voluntary compliance and provides oversight through plan approval and building inspection. This approach can also save substantial costs by identifying design or compliance problems during the planning stages.

Making programs and services accessible will range from relatively simple to complicated. Modifying seating, installing a wheelchair lift on a van, widening a racquetball court door, and providing large print literature are examples of accommodations that allow participants with disabilities access to the same program or service available to other participants. In some cases, however, it will be necessary to create equitable alternatives to provide program access. Usually, a variety of ways to provide accessible options are available. In these situations, it is suggested that people with disabilities and technical experts be consulted to identify the best and most cost-effective option.

Additional Accessibility Resources and Notations

American Acoustical Society of America (ASA)

The ASA, in partnership with the Access Board, has revised *ANSI/ASA S12.60-2010/Part 1 American National Standard Acoustical Performance Criteria, Design Requirements, and Guidelines for Schools, Part 1: Permanent Schools*, which applies to facilities that include a classroom space. Specific acoustical requirements are detailed in these standards; the document is available online through the ASA store (as a downloadable PDF file at no cost; http://asastore.aip.org).

American Society of Mechanical Engineers (ASME)

The EEOC's new regulations (March 25, 2011) stipulate that impairments need not prevent or severely or significantly restrict performance of major life activity to be considered a "disability" and that mitigating measures, include assistive devices, auxiliary aids, accommodations, and medical therapies and supplies do not impact coverage. The regulations also clarify coverage of impairments that are episodic or in remission that substantially limit a major life activity when active (e.g., epilepsy or post-traumatic stress disorder). These regulations are available online (http://www1.eeoc.gov//laws/regulations/adaaa_fact_sheet.cfm?renderforprint=1).

Federal Communication Commission (FCC): Broadband Plan

The National Broadband Plan was introduced in 2010. It targets universal access to broadband Internet services. There is specific content benefiting access for persons with disabilities in Chapter 9 of the plan. For more information, visit http://www.broadband.gov/.

Federal Emergency Management Administration (FEMA)

Guidance on Planning for Integration of Functional Needs Support Services in General Population Shelters provides planning guidance to emergency managers and shelter planners to ensure equal access for people with disabilities to sheltering services and facilities; the document is available at http://www.fema.gov/pdf/about/odic/fnss_guidance.pdf.

Fair Housing Administration Act (FHA Act)

Fair Housing Accessibility First offers guidance on the Fair Housing Act. Under this law, new multifamily housing in the public and private sectors must conform to guidelines for accessibility and adaptability. Student housing falls under the FHA Act. See http://fairhousingfirst.org for more information.

International Code Council (ICC)

The ICC publishes the Updated A117.1 Accessibility Standard ICC A117.1-2009: Accessible and Usable Buildings and Facilities. The latest version includes changes and additions, including a new chapter on recreation facilities, for greater consistency with the Access Board's ADA and ABA Accessibility Guidelines; the document is available (for purchase) at http://www.iccsafe.org/Store/Pages/Product.aspx?id=9033S09.

ICT Section 508 Homepage: Information and Communication Technology (2011 Draft)

Section 508 standards and its Section 255 guidelines address access to computer hardware and software, websites, media players, electronic documents, telephones and cell phones, PDAs, and other information and communications technology products at http://www.access-board.gov/508.htm.

Inclusion Design and Environmental Awareness (IDEA) Center

A major study was completed by IDEA (2010), Anthropometry of Wheeled Mobility Project, regarding people who use wheeled mobility aids (e.g., manual chairs, power chairs and scooters). Key findings included the need for "clear floor space" to accommodate users of wheeled mobility aid; the need for greater clearances for maneuvering and turning required by some mobility aids (particularly scooters); and the variability of "reach ranges" for individuals using wheeled mobility aids; see http://www.ude-world.com/anthropometrics for more details.

National Center on Accessibility (NCA)

The NCA has published *A Longitudinal Study of Playground Surfaces to Evaluate Accessibility: Year One Findings: Executive Summary* (March 11, 2011), which is available at http://www.ncaonline.org/news/news playground surface year1findings 05-2011.shtml

New England ADA Center

ADA Checklist for Readily Achievable Barrier Removal is available at http://www.adachecklist.org as part of the updated ADA 2010 Standards.

Revised Title III Regulations

Part 36 Nondiscrimination on the Basis of Disability in Public Accommodations and Commercial Facilities (as amended by the final rule published on September 15, 2010) is available at http://www.ada.gov/regs2010/title-III_2010/titleIII_2010_withbold.htm.

To find the accessibility-related building codes of specific states, visit http://www.access-board.gov/links/state-codes.htm.

5 Electrical, Mechanical, and Energy Management

Richard J. LaRue, *University of New England*
Thomas H. Sawyer, *Indiana State University*

At its best, technology should conform to the way we work, the way we play, and the way we live. Through electrical and mechanical engineering we have an opportunity to create extraordinary environments through the manipulation of basic components: lighting, sound, and other electronic technologies; heating, ventilation, air-conditioning, and refrigeration (HVAC-R); and humidity and air quality control. Advancements in engineering these technologies, in both indoor and outdoor spaces, require planners to understand the basics and expect unlimited potential for new technologies. Planners must avoid setting limits on how far ahead they look. Only a few years ago, the computer was a luxury. Now computers are a necessity of everyday life, operating everything from membership systems to the building automation and HVAC systems of intelligent buildings. Today's engineering must be about providing for the way we will work, the way we will play, and the way we will live.

Lighting is an important factor when selecting facility surfaces. With increased efforts to manage aesthetics, as well as participant and spectator satisfaction, lighting should be addressed in the planning phase of building construction. Indirect lighting is largely viewed as ideal for most competitive sports and recreation settings. Indirect lighting, however, is heavily influenced by its surroundings. Paint type (flat vs. gloss), paint color, shadows, HVAC-R systems, sprinkler pipes, and acoustical features can impact lighting efforts (Cohen, 2002a). As mentioned throughout this text, the knowledge and related efforts of the architect can significantly impact a variety of design elements within a facility.

Furthermore, energy-efficient lighting retrofits can offer an extraordinary chance to cut operating costs and improve lighting quality. However, along with the opportunity for improvement comes the opportunity for costly mistakes. Table 5.1 outlines common lighting mistakes that should be avoided.

Table 5.1

Common Lighting Mistakes

- Selecting the wrong project team
- Conflicting change of command
- Neglecting frontline people
- Engaging experts too late
- Underestimating the importance of an audit
- Buying based on price
- No "what-if" planning
- Not testing thoroughly
- Botching up installation
- Falling for "bargain" products
- Failing to thoroughly scrutinize proposals
- Using average electricity rates to calculate savings
- Falling in love with hardware
- Overlooking opportunities

Electrical Engineering

A theoretical basis of electrical engineering includes an understanding of circuits, electronics, electromagnetics, energy conversion, and controls. Conceptually, when planners consider lighting and sound, they are also considering the broader areas of illumination and acoustics. Therefore, the planning basics of lighting, sound, and other electronic technologies, in this text, include information relevant to the design of electrical systems, which goes beyond electrical engineering in its strictest sense. The chapter also considers the growing body of knowledge regarding nontraditional and renewable energy sources.

Basic Considerations in Lighting

Lighting is simply a means to illuminate or further brighten an object, individual(s), area, or space. The two primary lighting options are energy-produced lighting and natural lighting. The product of lighting in combination with other variables, such as the level of darkness, the amount of reflective light (from surfaces), distortion, and the color of the lighting, results in illumination (good or bad).

Illumination is measured by the foot-candle. Brightness is the luminous intensity of any surface and is measured by the foot-lambert. Glare, which is an important consideration in physical education and sports facilities, is nothing more than excessively high or accentuated brightness.

The amount of light in any given area and the quality of light are equally important. Providing efficient illumination is complicated and challenging, and the services of an illumination engineer are recommended to obtain maximum lighting efficiency. Gymnasiums, classrooms, corridors, and other areas have specific and different lighting requirements. Planning for illumination requires that each area be considered relative to its specific use.

The foot-candle is a measurement of light intensity at a given point (e.g., the water or floor surface). Light intensity, measured in foot-candles, is one vital factor in eye comfort and viewing efficiency, and intensity must be considered in relation to the brightness balance of all light sources and reflective surfaces within the visual field.

The reflection factor is the percentage of light falling on a surface that is reflected by that surface. To maintain a brightness balance with a quantity and quality of light for good visibility, all surfaces within a room should be relatively light, with a matte rather than a glossy finish.

The foot-lambert is the product of the illumination in foot-candles and the reflection factor of the surface. For example, 40 foot-candles striking a surface with a reflection factor of 50% would produce a brightness of 20 foot-lamberts (40 x .50 = 20). These values are necessary when computing brightness differences in order to achieve a balanced visual field. Table 5.2 gives a relative indication as to a comparison of illuminations for specific indoor spaces.

Table 5.2

Levels of Illumination Recommended for Specific Indoor Spaces

Area	Foot-Candles on Tasks
Adapted physical education gymnasium	50
Auditorium	
Assembly only	15
Exhibitions	30 to 50
Social activities	5 to 15
Classrooms	
Laboratories	100
Lecture rooms	
Audience area	70
Demonstration area	150
Study halls	70
Corridors and stairways	20
Dance studio	5 to 50[2]
Field houses	80
First aid rooms	
General	50
Examining table	125
Gymnasiums	
Exhibitions	502
General exercise and recreation	35
Dances	5 to 50[2]
Locker and shower rooms	30
Gymnastics	50
Archery	
Shooting tee	50
Target area	70
Badminton	50[1]
Basketball	80[1]
Deck tennis	50
Fencing	70[1]
Handball	70[1]

Table 5.2 (cont.)

Area	Foot-Candles on Tasks
Paddle tennis	70[1]
Rifle range	
Point area	50
Target area	70
Rowing practice area	50
Squash	70[1]
Tennis	70[1]
Volleyball	50
Weight-exercise room	50
Wrestling and personal defense room	50
Games room	70
Ice rink	100[2]
Library	
Study and notes	70
Ordinary reading	50 to 70
Lounges	
General	50
Reading books, magazines, and newspapers	50 to 70
Offices	
Accounting, auditing, tabulating, bookkeeping, and business-machine operation	150
Regular office work, active filing, index references, and mail sorting	100
Reading and transcribing handwriting in ink or medium pencil on good quality paper, and intermittent filing	70
Reading high-contrast or well-printed material not involving critical or prolonged seeing, and conferring and interviewing	50
Parking areas[1]	
Storerooms	
Inactive	10
Active	
Rough bulky	15
Medium	30
Fine	60
Swimming pools	
General and overhead	50[3]
Underwater[3]	
Toilets and washrooms	30

Note. These standards have been developed by a panel of experts on facilities for health, physical education, and recreation after careful consideration of the activities involved. In all instances, the standards in this table are equal to, or exceed, the standards that have been recommended by the Illumination Engineering Society, American Institute of Architects, and National Council on Schoolhouse Construction. Courtesy of Illuminating Engineering Society of North America (IESNA). The IESNA also provides educational publications, including *Sports and Recreational Area Lighting* (available from the IESNA at http://www.ies.org/store/product/sports-and-recreational-area-lighting-1033.cfm).

[1]Care must be taken to achieve a brightness balance to eliminate extremes of brightness and glare. [2]Should be equipped with rheostats. [3]Must be balanced with overhead lighting and should provide 100 lamp lumens per square foot of pool surface.

Installation

Lights in arenas, gymnasiums, and other high-ceiling activity spaces need to be a minimum clearance of 24 ft above the playing surface so they will not interfere with official (sport-regulated) heights for indoor competition.

Indoor lighting systems are generally of two types: direct lighting and indirect lighting. Direct lighting systems face directly down at the floor. Indirect lighting systems face in some direction other than the floor, such as sidewalls or ceiling, to reflect the beaming light in an effort to reduce glare. Indirect lighting is more expensive to operate because with each reflection the light is diminished. Therefore, more energy is consumed with indirect lighting as compared to direct lighting, to obtain the same final illumination of an area.

Both lighting systems should meet the required level of foot-candles without causing glare or shadows on the playing surface. The type of lighting—incandescent, fluorescent, light-emitting diodes (LED), mercury-vapor, metal halide, quartz, or sodium-vapor—will likely depend upon the type of space and the way the space will be used (see Figure 5.1), as well as the projected cost of installation, operation, and maintenance. The style of fixture may have more to do with aesthetics than functionality, but the advantages and disadvantages of aesthetics versus functionality should always be considered.

Designed for Impact

In spaces where the play may involve hitting, kicking, or throwing balls, lighting fixtures should be designed to deflect or absorb impact. Lighting systems are available that include shock-absorbing characteristics. Perhaps more important is the additional protection these lights require in the event that they are struck and a bulb(s) is (are) broken. Falling shards of glass from broken lights should be avoided at all costs.

Lights need to be covered with a transparent polycarbonate sheeting (a screen may not be enough) that will catch broken glass bulbs and also protect the bulbs from direct impact. The sheeting or cover should also keep softer, potentially flammable sports implements (e.g., tennis balls, shuttlecocks, and Nerf or Wiffle balls) from lodging within the fixture against a high-temperature bulb.

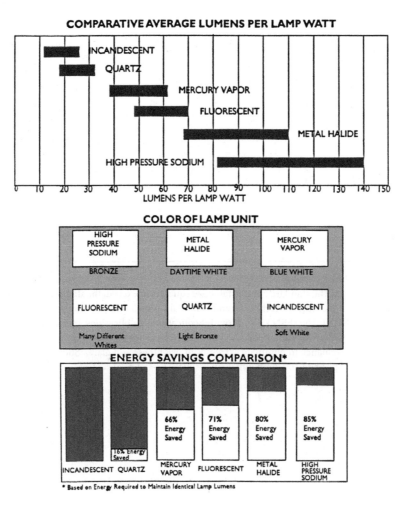

Figure 5.1. Comparison of Various Lamps

Lighting Types

Incandescent light. The incandescent light is instantaneous, burns without sound, and is not affected by the number of times the light is turned on or off. Incandescent lights and fixtures are considerably cheaper in initial cost; are easier to change; and the lamp, within limits, may vary in size within a given fixture. Incandescent fixtures, however, have excessively high spot brightness and give off considerable heat, a problem when high levels of illumination are necessary.

In December 2007, H.R. 6, the Energy Independence and Security Act of 2007 was signed into law, and the incandescent lightbulb, as we know it, will be phased out in favor of more energy-efficient lamps. "The new devices include current products such as compact fluorescents and halogens, as well as emerging products such as light-emitting diodes and energy-saving incandescent bulbs" (Davidson, 2007, p. 1). Compact fluorescent bulbs, costing approximately 4 times as much as incandescent, last about 6 times longer, therefore meeting the new standard established by the law. "Under the measure, all light bulbs must use 25% to 30% less energy than today's products by 2014" (p. 1). The phase-in began with 100-W bulbs in January 2012 and will end with 40-W bulbs in January 2014. "By 2020, bulbs must be 70% more efficient" (Davidson, 2007, p. 1).

Fluorescent lamps. Fluorescent lamps also have the advantage of long life and give at least 2 and a half times the amount of light that incandescent lamps give for the same amount of electrical current used. They frequently are used in old buildings to raise the illumination level without installing new wiring.

Mercury-vapor lighting. Mercury-vapor lighting is expensive in terms of initial installation. The overall cost of mercury-vapor lighting, however, is cheaper than incandescent lighting. The primary objection to mercury-vapor lighting is its bluish color. However, when incandescent lighting is used in addition to mercury-vapor, a highly satisfactory lighting system results. Mercury-vapor lights are being phased out in favor of metal halide lights.

Metal halide lights. Metal halide lights do not last as long as mercury vapor lights but give a better light output and operate more efficiently. Metal halide lights do not have the bluish tint of mercury-vapor lights. Quartz lights and high-pressure sodium lights are outdoor lights. Only over the past few years have these lights been used indoors. Quartz lights are not much different than incandescent lights, except they have a slight bronze color and are slightly more efficient. High-pressure sodium lights might be the indoor activity light of the future. They have long life expectancy, are highly efficient, and give the best light output of all the lights mentioned. The only problem with high-pressure sodium lights is the yellow-bronze hue associated with them.

Lighting Levels

A number of systems exist that allow different levels of lighting so that special events or lighting requirements can be met. As early as 1989, the Jack Breslin Student Events Center at Michigan State University afforded such variety using an intricate Holophane lighting system. The lighting levels are turned up or down through a computerized control system, which is preprogrammed for different lighting and uniformity levels. On another control panel, a single button designated for one of eight different preprogrammed scenes can adjust the lights. For example, facility personnel can press one button to set the lighting for televised basketball games, another for nontelevised games, another for pregame setup, and so forth.

When the Dan and Kathleen Hogan Sports Center at Colby-Sawyer College opened in 1991, the NCAA lighting standard for swimming was 60 foot-candles at the water's surface. Today 100 foot-candles of illumination are required for U.S. swimming and collegiate championship events. Because the planners decided upon a higher-than-minimum level for lighting the natatorium at the center, the facility continues to meet required lighting standards without any modification. However, now every light must be in working order to meet the newer NCAA standard.

Using Natural Lighting

Windows and other translucent materials allow natural light into a facility. Natural lighting can reduce operational costs and enhance the aesthetics of an indoor space. The major problem with windows is that it is difficult to control the glare that they allow to enter. Avoid windows in any activity area where visual acuity is an important commodity for both learning activity skills and safety. However, other translucent building materials are available that do several things windows cannot and have several advantages over windows:

- provide higher values for insulation, reducing both heat loss (during colder seasons) and/or heat gain (during warmer seasons);
- diffuse the light that comes through, reducing glare; and
- provide greater resistance to breaking, so they are safer to use in spaces where broken glass is a serious problem, and they are harder to break into from a security standpoint.

Translucent materials are not perfect. Translucent panels or blocks in a high-moisture area will still allow moisture to condense on the inside surface if it is colder outside, and they do not allow clear images to transfer. Windows can also have movable shades, shutters, curtains, or blinds that assist with controlling glare and can improve insulating levels. Skylights are acceptable in "slow movement areas," and vertical skylights are recommended to keep glare and leakage to a minimum. Regardless of the materials used, natural light seems a worthy goal when the facility is designed and used appropriately.

Maintenance

Planning must also account for the need to change bulbs or replace fixtures. Unless there is a catwalk or crawl space in the ceiling, the lights will need to be changed from the floor using poles, ladders, scaffolding, or hydraulic hoists. Experience informs us that changing all the lights in a space at the same time is the most cost-effective approach to maintenance. However, if lighting fails to meet required levels whenever a single fixture is out, the bulbs will need changed more frequently. Consider adding a couple of fixtures more than are required in each space (e.g., if the space/activity standard calls for 50 foot-candles on task, you may wish to exceed this standard by four fixtures so that you can have up to four lamps fail and still meet the minimum). When four bulbs are gone, it is probably time to replace all the bulbs in the space. As you plan for the need to change bulbs and replace fixtures, remember the characteristics of the space. Even telescoping poles need minimum clearance to get inside a space. Racquetball courts with standard-sized doors can allow the use of a small hydraulic hoist rather than a giant stepladder. Finally, direct-lighting bulbs can sometimes be changed using only a pole (standing on the floor), and indirect lighting can only be changed using a catwalk, crawl space, or other more time-consuming approach. Therefore, when planning your lighting system maintenance, consider designs that will serve the facility without being labor intensive (which also influences cost).

Unique Lighting Settings and Issues

Unique settings in sports and recreation facilities often require special lighting systems, special fixtures, or carefully planned designs. In spaces with a higher level of moisture (pool areas, shower and toilet areas, locker rooms, etc.), vapor-proof lighting units are recommended. Remember that broken glass in any such area is a mini-disaster. If a bulb breaks in a space where participants might be barefoot, extensive cleanup will be required. Locker rooms and athletic training rooms are two examples of spaces where light placement will directly affect the quality of the environment. Fixtures should be placed to enhance the areas between lockers in locker rooms, to afford clear reflections at mirrors, and to brighten places where visibility is critical to the operational goals in athletic training rooms.

Aquatic facilities. Lighting indoor swimming spaces has never been the easiest part of natatorium design; although frequently, and with regrettable results, it has been treated that way. With today's multipurpose aquatic centers frequently accommodating diverse programming activities in a shared environment, it has become an even greater creative challenge to get the lighting right. Natural light is an increasingly attractive option for indoor aquatic facilities. Large windows or open fenestration can be energy-efficient ways to supplement artificial heat and lighting, and they add interest for users and a much-appreciated connection to the outside for employees who work all day in an enclosed environment. With all its advantages, however, natural light can also be accompanied by glare.

If windows are used in aquatic areas, the glare trade-off must be addressed during the planning stages. Glare is not an exclusive problem of natural lighting. Glare can result from improperly located artificial lighting, when the lights reflect off either the water surface or the sidewalls. With safety a major consideration in aquatic facilities, every effort must be made to control for glare and/or the blind spots caused by glare. Underwater lighting can reduce some of the glare problem and can further enhance visibility in deeper water (underwater lighting is required in some jurisdictions), and in aquatic facilities, there are maintenance issues related to the location of light fixtures over the pool (the preferred location for competitive facilities). The YMCA's Walter Schroeder Aquatic Center in Milwaukee, Wisconsin, was able to locate light fixtures directly over their 50-m indoor pool after determining that by using the two movable bulkheads, a hoist could be positioned anywhere a fixture required relamping. This avoided the added construction expense of a catwalk or crawl space and the labor intensiveness of using a scaffolding setup in an empty pool to replace bulbs. Finally, artificial lighting in pool areas must consider the variability of water depth.

Outdoor lighting. Outdoor lighting for sports fields can have specific requirements. Lighting levels used for night sports are the highest commonly encountered in the nighttime environment. Recommended levels for social or recreational sports, including most municipal sports activities, range from 200 to 500 lux (20 to 50 foot-candles); levels for professional sports, with large spectator attendance and television coverage, can reach 3,000 lux (300 foot-candles).

The lighting fixtures commonly used for sports lighting can be huge sources of direct glare to spectators and players actually using the fields and at considerable distances from the sports fields. The brightest single sources of light visible in city nighttime landscape views are often these facilities. It is no surprise that such lighting is probably the single greatest source of complaint and neighborhood tension.

In the past, available fixtures and lighting designs often left little choice for communities and designers seeking to minimize spill and glare in sports lighting. Fortunately, several manufacturers have recently begun producing fully shielded luminaires suitable for sports lighting, particularly for the most commonly encountered levels of lighting. These designs provide major reductions in off-field spill and can eliminate direct uplight in all but the brightest lighting levels required for professional level sports. Furthermore, many feel that these designs deliver substantially improved lighting quality on the field for the players.

Although specific considerations apply when planning illumination of a specific-use field, for the purpose of this chapter, the discussion of outdoor lighting will focus on multipurpose installations.

Multipurpose sports fields are more complicated to light than single-purpose fields, but you will save money by combining activities on one field. Several issues need to be addressed when lighting a multipurpose field. Light levels and pole placement become big factors, and design decisions become critical. However, controlling spill and glare is perhaps one of the most important issues to be addressed in recent years!

Today, thanks to advances in design of reflectors and components that aim light, as much as 70% of the light generated can be directed onto the playing service, resulting in fewer fixtures to purchase, install, and operate. Longer lamp life, pole materials, and lamp design also contribute to reduction in operating and maintenance costs over the life of the system... (Rogers, 2008, p. 2)

This can also make lighting a multipurpose field extremely cost-effective. The Illuminating Engineering Society of North America (IESNA) publishes light level guidelines for outdoor sports (see IESNA's website for further information: http://www.iesna.org).
Planning steps include the following:
- Use a professional lighting design service to develop a scheme, taking into account the need to restrict obtrusive light;
- select floodlights that do not give upward light when they are mounted in their normal configuration;
- ensure that the lighting design "cuts off" near the boundary so that spillage (trespass) is minimal;

- if possible, select playing surfaces of lower reflectance to minimize upward reflected light;
- light only to the required level, and no more;
- ensure the floodlights are installed and aimed as planned; and
- when the job is finished, maintain the system. (Thorn, 2013, p. 4)

Regarding the selection of poles, the American Society of Civil Engineers (ASCE) is planning to examine these structures and create a new design standard for the industry. Specifically, the ASCE Athletic Field Lighting Structures Standard Committee was created in the fall of 2011 and is working to create a national consensus standard for the proper specification, design, and system support of these structures. Until the new committee comes up with a new formal standard, the committee recommends the following interim measures:

1. Design professionals should use the *AASHTO Standard Specifications for Structural Supports for Highway Signs, Luminaries and Traffic Signals*, 5th edition, with 2010 and 2011 interim revisions.
2. Designs should be made for a minimum life of 50 years and Fatigue Category I as it applies to the *AASHTO Standard Specifications*.
3. Owners should be encouraged to develop routine scheduled inspection and maintenance programs and contact qualified inspection professionals if cracks or corrosion is observed (further information is available online: http://www.asce.org/Press-Releases/2012/Civil-Engineers-Creating-Design-Standard-for-Athletic-Field-Light-Structures/).

Supplementary and special lighting requirements. It is advisable to provide supplementary lighting on areas such as those containing goals or targets. Supplementary light sources should be shielded from the eyes of participants and spectators to provide the proper brightness balance. Other special lighting requirements include
- night lighting—lights that remain on 24 hr per day (can be the same circuit as the emergency lighting), lighting large spaces, lobbies, corridors, stairwells, and classrooms;
- exit lighting—located at all exits (including exit-only locations), should be mounted according to local and state codes. Because these lights are often required to remain on 24 hr per day, cost savings can be realized if fluorescent or LED bulbs are used instead of incandescent bulbs. All exit lighting should be on special circuits that will remain on even if the power is lost; and
- emergency (white) lighting—should be provided for exits (including exterior open spaces to which exits lead). This lighting should be on a special emergency

circuit (battery powered) that will power up whenever normal power is lost.

Lighting Controls

When planning for lighting, the methods of control are also important to consider. The central light switch box should be located at a major entrance area, and all teaching [or activity] spaces should have individual light switches. A relatively unusual approach to controlling illumination in spaces where lighting is only on as needed (e.g., individual racquetball or squash courts, restrooms) is motion sensor or "occupancy sensors" switching. If the sensor detects no movement over a period of 10 to 15 min, the lights automatically switch off. The lights come back on as soon as someone enters the room. Light level sensors are also available for use indoors as well as outdoors. These sensors can adjust the lighting level in response to the amount of natural lighting. Replacing the all-or-nothing on/off switch in parking areas or skylit rooms can give just the right amount of artificial light needed as the natural light fades.

Basic Considerations in Sound and Acoustics

Sound and Related Electronic Media

Sound is an important part of everyday life, and subsequently it is an important part of sports and recreation. From the public address system to the wireless microphone and headsets, the ability to hear what is going on is almost as critical as seeing what is happening. The reality is that both hearing and seeing support each other in completing the act of communication. From the sound quality expected in aerobic dance and fitness facilities to the audio system required for a halftime show in the Super Bowl, technology is advancing the availability of high-resolution sound.

For the sports or recreation facility, sound design starts with creating a suitable sound environment. Beginning in the lobby, where users first enter, several approaches can be used:

- Install a high-performance audio system throughout the facility that can be used to communicate with patrons; serve as an integrated part of the facility warning system; and assimilate and distribute other kinds of electronic media through information monitors and system-integrated computer stations.
- When integrating the sound and media technologies, ensure that such integration includes the ability for expansion/upgrading as needed, that it can be used together with live-streaming media from on-site programming/events, and that the technology is secure and relatively easy to operate.

In strength training spaces, the major sound considerations are even distribution, the ability to overcome background noise, and low-fatigue factors. Correct selection and placement of appropriate speakers will provide even distribution, reduce the impact of background interference, and satisfy low-fatigue requirements. Wall-mounted speakers usually work best, although clubs that have a lot of tall equipment in rooms with low ceilings should use ceiling speakers. Whenever possible, include in your design a dedicated sound system for free weight areas to increase your flexibility in sound sources and level control.

In cardiovascular areas, the most satisfactory approach for most clubs is to supply each exercise station with a headphone and flexibility in source selection, along with one or more video monitors visible to several stations at once.

The aerobics room is the one area where facility users most expect to hear sophisticated, high-quality sound. Achieving this in a room full of hard surfaces and highly active people is difficult. A well-designed and properly operated sound system will add precision and impact to classes, establishing a sense of timing and inspiration without fatigue, stress, or hearing damage created by distortion and excessive volume levels.

Four categories of components have a direct effect on these factors:

- speakers;
- CD or other electronic media players;
- amplifier, receiver, and equalizer (soft limiter); and
- wireless microphone and microphone mixer.

Selecting the correct components is easier when you understand the elements of a high-quality sound system. However, it is important to seek the advice of individuals and/or companies who are familiar with the specific needs of an aerobic studio when choosing components for your new studio or when upgrading your current system.

Acoustics

Because of the amount of noise and sound that emanates from the activities in physical education and sports, acoustics and sound are of paramount importance in building design. Acoustical treatments in building design are the domain of the acoustical engineer. An acoustical engineer should be consulted when dealing with absorption and reflection qualities of all surfaces within a facility.

Acoustical treatments must enhance sound so that we can hear easily and absorb sound. Background noise, basically unwanted sound that either originates in the teaching station itself or intrudes from another area, must be controlled. Internal background noise might consist of "squeaking" chairs sliding on a floor, reverberation or "echoing" of sound, and reflective sound. All sound travels spherically. When a space is to be acoustically treated, walls, ceilings, floors, and other surfaces within that space must be considered for appropriate materials.

Internal treatments. There are four common modes of internal acoustical treatment of spaces. Using walls and other barriers is one method of controlling sound. Airspace itself is an acoustical treatment. The larger the space is, the farther sound travels and the more it is absorbed. Using soft acoustical materials on various surfaces is a major means of sound control. Acoustical clouds suspended over large, open arenas are yet another means of controlling sound. Extending walls beyond dropped ceilings can afford better acoustical control than stopping internal walls at the dropped ceiling height.

External treatments. External background noise or unwanted sound from outside the teaching space must also be planned for acoustically. Unwanted sound or noise may be transmitted into the room by means of ventilating ducts, pipes, and spaces around pipe sleeves. The transmission of sound through ducts can be reduced by using baffles or by lining the ducts with sound-absorbent, fire-resistant materials. The ducts also may be connected with canvas or rubberized material to interrupt the transmission through the metal in the ducts. Pipes can be covered with pipe covering, and spaces in the pipe sleeves can be filled.

Sound also can be transmitted through the walls, floors, and ceilings. This can be reduced to a desirable minimum by the proper structural design and materials. In conventional wall construction, alternate studs can support the sides of the wall in such a manner that there is no through connection from one wall surface to another. This sometimes is known as double-wall construction. The space inside the walls can be filled with sound-absorbing material to further decrease sound transmission. Sometimes 3 in. or 4 in. of sand inside the walls at the baseboard will cut down the transmission appreciably. Likewise, sound absorption blankets laid over the partitions in suspended ceiling construction can reduce the sound from one room to another.

Machinery vibration or impact sounds can be reduced by using the proper floor covering and/or by installing the machinery on floating or resilient mountings. "Sound locks," such as double walls or doors, are needed between noisy areas and adjoining quiet areas. Improper location of doors and windows can create noise problems. It is imperative to consider the location of the facility itself and also the placement of internal areas of the facility for sound control. Placing physical education and sports facilities in a semi-isolated area of a school helps control acoustics. This same theory needs to be applied internally within the sports facility. The placement of "noisy" areas such as weight training areas, aerobic areas, locker rooms, swimming pools, gymnasiums, and spectator areas must be planned for in relation to quiet areas such as classrooms and offices. It is not good acoustical planning to have a weight room above or next to a classroom. Care must be taken to maintain

acoustical materials. Some paint applications may reduce the sound-absorbent qualities of most materials. Surface treatment for different acoustical materials will vary. The most common treatment of acoustical-fiber tile is a light brush coat of latex-based paint, but most acoustical materials lose their efficiency after several applications of paint.

Exterior treatments. Sometimes the exterior of a space or building must be acoustically treated. If a gym is located on the landing flight path of a local airport, or if it is located next to a fairly steep grade on a major truck thoroughfare, exterior acoustical treatment might be needed. Use the same acoustical principles as inside, with an exterior twist. Keep hard surfaces such as paved areas and parking lots to a minimum. Use shrubbery, trees, and grass wherever possible. Walls, solid fences, berms, and water are all good exterior acoustical items. It is important to plan for acoustics and sound control in a variety of ways. Think spherical, think internal, think external, and think exterior to best acoustically treat a facility.

Many architects and engineers have indicated that acoustical problems can be avoided from the start if sound transmission concepts are kept in mind at the initial planning stage of a recreation facility. Keeping noisy spaces separate from quiet areas is easy to achieve in the initial design phase; correcting problems due to improper space adjacencies is more difficult. Even the best sound-isolating construction techniques cannot completely solve the problems created by improper adjacencies. The final results will always be more acceptable if serious acoustical issues are solved in the schematic design.

Other Electronic Technologies

Electronic Communication

The standard communication tools in sports and recreation facilities include an intercom system and two-way audio systems to various activity and office spaces. Additionally, telecommunication has advanced tremendously, allowing for the integration of telecommunications devices for the deaf (TDDs), text typewriters (TTS) or teletypewriters (TTYs), and faxing capabilities to standard telephone installations.

Audio and visual communication needs for the 21st century require many facilities to be integrated for computerization and satellite/cable television reception. Any space that might use a computer or video connection should be part of this integration. Fiber optics and "wireless" transmission are the current standard for such integration. However, a thorough planning process will also consider future technologies. Minimally, appropriate conduits should be installed during facility construction to afford the broadest range of future choices.

Within spaces, especially those used for instruction, the planning process should also consider the electronic technologies required for distance education, such as two-way audio and visual communication tools (I see you—you see me, I hear you—you hear me), computer links for Internet and computer presentation, conference-call telephones, digital players, LCD overhead projectors, keypads/clickers for student responses, and so forth.

Scoreboards and Electronic Timing Systems

The science and technology of scoreboard design is ever changing, providing for a more satisfying sports-spectator experience. A scoreboard not only provides spectators with game data but also can be configured with a giant video screen and message system and integrated with the facility's sound system. Furthermore, some scoreboards are designed to be used by multiple sports. Large indoor sports arenas are using giant four-sided scoreboards that literally pay for themselves with sponsor advertisement . If timing is your need, recent advances in digital timing systems allow sports races to be judged fairly, regardless of the hundredths of seconds between finish times or the failure of conventional timing equipment.

Elevators and Other Hydraulic Lifts

Elevators and other hydraulic lifts are necessary design features of many sports and recreation facilities. Besides offering users with disabilities federally mandated access to facilities, they enhance the ability of staff to move equipment (possibly reducing the potential for worker-related injury), and they facilitate deliveries.

It is worth noting that in taller and/or less accessible buildings, the elevator industry is beginning to reconsider its views on fire safety and the use of elevators in evacuation. Such a change is not imminent but already exists at a Maryland metro station that is far underground and a tower/hotel in Las Vegas that has limited egress capacity from hotel rooms without the elevators (Lorenz, 2005).

Security

Effective facility security begins with building designs that control access to the facility through a main-desk control area and egress-only doors that do not allow reentry. A number of electronic technologies can further affect the security of a facility, including

- entrance/exit (access/egress) controls and alarms such as card systems, electronically controlled doors and gates, check points with metal detectors (magnetometers), and annunciators (egress door alarms). Card access can also be used to gather meaningful data on the facility's clientele;
- closed-circuit television monitor systems; and
- motion sensor alarms for controlled areas such as pools (sensor detects water motion).

It is important to remember that as electronic technology is applied to security, any power failure will disrupt such systems unless they are backed up by battery or emergency generator systems.

Emergency Alarms

Facility safety begins with smoke and fire and emergency alarm systems that appropriately warn building users in the event of fire and warn facility staff in the event of a life-threatening emergency. Smoke and fire alarms include those that are user activated, smoke or heat activated, and water pressure activated (usually found in wet sprinkler systems). Special alarms for the pool or other exercise/training areas have been designed to notify facility staff in the event of a life-threatening emergency; these are typically staff activated. Weather or disaster notification will usually use an existing intercom system to warn facility users. Emergency alarms, especially those that are designed to warn users, must also be backed up by battery or emergency generator systems.

Emergency Generators

With an increasing reliance upon some of the above electronic technologies and/or the use of arch-supported roofs for indoor sports spaces, power outages will require an emergency generator backup to ensure the safety of facility users and the well-being of the facility. These generators need only to provide minimum levels of power (to be determined by the specifications of the facility) to be effective tools. However, where electric energy is at a premium, some sports or recreational facilities may need to plan on a bank of generators to provide unrestricted energy service. Sport facilities that have fully air-supported ceilings and/or walls require a backup system to ensure the safety of users.

Trends in Electronic Technologies

Illuminated game lines on sports courts and underwater pace lights in swimming pools are two of the more innovative uses of electronic technology, and with laser technology, it is only a matter of time before distances in field events are determined using a laser rather than a tape measure; they are already being used in sports such as golf.

Basic Considerations in HVAC-R

Sports and recreation buildings incorporate a wide variety of HVAC systems. The principal goal of an energy management program is to maximize the efficiency of all systems. *Efficiency* is a term that describes the relationship between energy input and usable energy output (American Society of Heating, Refrigerating, and Air-Conditioning Engineers [ASHRAE], 2006).

Air-Handling Systems

Air-handling systems consist of air-handling units and distribution equipment such as ductwork, dampers, and air diffusers. The typical air-handling unit refers to a ventilation device that, when installed in a building, may serve a number of purposes. The system should provide an airflow with adequate pressure and speed to reach all areas served by the unit; filter and condition the air with cooling, heating, and dehumidification processes; and mix a measured quantity of fresh air with recirculated air. A typical air-handling unit may contain some or all of the following components: fan(s); filters; heating, cooling, and dehumidification coils; germicidal UV air purifier; humidifier; dampers to direct airflow and control the mixing of outside and recirculated air; and control devices to regulate temperature and humidity of the airflow.

Conditioning the Air

Conditioning of the incoming air is generally limited to dehumidification and heating. A room thermostat generally controls the amount of heat required to maintain room comfort. Desiccant systems and heat pipes dry air more efficiently than causing condensation by super-cooling air. Using a desiccant dehumidifier dries air without cooling it, causing the water to absorb to the surface of the desiccant. The desiccant is recharged using either waste heat from the boiler, from a solar collector, or with gas heat that is returned to the space.

The components of an air exhaust system include an exhaust fan, ductwork and grilles, and hoods to capture contaminated air as close as possible to the source. In addition, most exhaust systems incorporate a series of controls to regulate the operation of the fan and its accessories, such as a motorized damper. Energy management action for exhaust systems will depend in part on the area being exhausted.

Fans that exhaust air from locker rooms normally need to operate continuously, especially when athletic equipment needs dried. If this is not the case, then these exhaust fans can be run only when the rooms are occupied.

Heat recovery potential is present in most air-handling systems. However, using the recovered heat by a system must be economically justifiable. Returning the recovered heat to the process from which it came should be the first priority because such systems usually require less control and are less expensive to install.

The hot water heating plant of a building incorporates a number of components that individually are responsible for some form of heat transfer and therefore have their own particular efficiency. Heating systems are made up of three principal components: supply equipment (e.g., boiler), distribution equipment (e.g., supply and return piping); and end-use equipment (e.g., heaters and associated controls).

Boiler efficiency is indicated directly from temperature and composition of flue gases. The latter indicates the air–fuel ratio at the burner, which is the most important parameter affecting combustion efficiency. Maintaining boiler water quality is essential to maintaining high system efficiency. When steam is generated in a boiler, certain impurities (solids) in the water must be purged from the system on a continual basis via an adjustable blowdown valve. Proper adjustment of the blowdown valve must be maintained at all times. Furthermore, ensuring distribution piping is regularly maintained can minimize energy losses in the heating system. Regular maintenance includes an inventory of the system components and documentation of their condition.

End-use equipment in heating systems includes steam and hot water radiators, as well as heating coils in ventilation units. Conditions that result in excessive energy use in these components include valves that leak or are stuck open and faulty controls. These conditions are often associated with comfort problems in the space that is heated. Proper maintenance will avoid excessive energy use by end-use equipment.

Air-Conditioning

All air-conditioning equipment requires regular, planned maintenance to ensure energy-efficient operation. Cooling system maintenance should include periodic inspection of cooling coils (chilled water or direct expansion) for icing or dirt accumulation on the coil. Both will reduce heat transfer rates, reduce airflow to the space, make it difficult to maintain comfort, and waste energy. Cooling system valves and controls should also be inspected periodically to ensure efficient system operation.

Ventilation Systems

Ventilation systems can be large energy users and energy wasters—both directly and indirectly. Energy is used directly in operating fans. Indirect energy use takes place in heating or cooling and dehumidifying the fresh air brought in from outside. Damper condition should be checked periodically because damper efficiency and general condition are directly affected by frequency of use. A damper assembly generally controls the damper unit. A motor mounted at one end of the assembly will control damper positioning. The damper controls how much air is brought in from the outside.

Filter Maintenance

Filter maintenance is another factor that is important in ensuring the energy-efficient operation of air-handling systems. Filter replacement or cleaning should occur on a regular basis according to the rate of the dirt buildup. Clogging of filters does not increase energy use directly. However, a pressure drop increase across a filter due to dirt buildup will result in an airflow reduction and fan power increase. The system cannot operate efficiently with dirty filters.

Other Considerations

Other operating and maintenance energy considerations are discussed next.

Dehumidifier maintenance. Improperly maintained dehumidifiers can increase energy use by maintaining a humidity level higher than required.

Water treatment of HVAC-R systems. An effective water treatment program should maintain a clean system, free of hard water deposits or corrosion products. A water distribution system that is fouled with deposits has a much lower rate of heat exchange and will reduce the energy efficiency of the entire distribution system.

Cooling tower condenser water. The most expensive part of an HVAC-R system to treat is the condenser cooling tower system. A cooling tower has high water losses due to evaporative cooling and requires water makeup to prevent water deposits from forming on the condenser tubes of the chiller. Proper water treatment procedures require the use of water scale control chemicals and corrosion inhibitors.

Domestic hot water systems. Domestic hot water temperatures should be closely monitored to reduce excessive scaling. Systems can be flushed and descaled at regularly scheduled intervals to improve heat transfer at the heat exchanger.

Environmental Climate Control

Environmental climate controls related to HVAC-R affect the quality of work and play environments. Sports and recreation facilities, specifically, must provide an environment where fresh air is exchanged and effectively circulated, where air temperature and humidity are controlled in a manner that promotes good health, and where the air quality is safe.

There are four factors that, when combined, give an optimal thermal environment:
- radiant temperature where surface and air temperatures are balanced,
- air temperature between 64°F and 72°F,
- humidity between 40% and 60%, and
- constant air movement of 20 to 40 linear feet per minute at a sitting height.

These factors must all be considered to achieve an optimal thermal environment. However, they are only part of the planning that must go into providing indoor environments that are technically sophisticated and also enhance user effectiveness, communication, and overall user satisfaction—the best definition of an "intelligent building." Intelligent buildings link technologies such as HVAC, fire detection and alarm, access, security, elevator, and com-munication systems to one computer. Although this section deals specifically with HVAC-R, it is important to consider the advantages of creating the intelligent building with a single computer control. This concept has been implemented in both new designs and retrofits. The key is planning ahead.

Additionally, a number of building design characteristics directly impact the optimal thermal environment in buildings. These interior and exterior characteristics include
- building envelopes that reduce heat loss and gain through insulation, barriers, and thermal mass;
- moisture control through vapor barriers and external shading devices;
- properly glazed windows that have good insulating and glare-reduction properties;
- double- or triple-paned glazed windows that prevent condensation on windows; and
- adequately sized facilities, ventilated, cooled, and designed for easy access, future growth, and reconfiguration, as well as passive heating, cooling, and lighting methods.

There are additional choices to make for building automation and HVAC-R systems, including centralized or decentralized HVAC-R systems, heating systems (such as boilers) and cooling systems (such as chillers and cooling towers), ventilation systems, substation sensing, humidification and dehumidification control, and facility energy management programs such as Night Cycle, Night Purge.

All of this does not negate the need for design planning that includes the choice of heat or energy source: fossil fuels (coal and heating oil) and heat or energy alternatives (propane/natural gas, wood, electricity, below-grade heat pumps, and solar or wind energy). Factors in these choices include geographic location and heat and energy resource availability. Additionally, the start-up or installation costs of some systems are more expensive but cost less to operate and/or maintain over the long term, and vice versa for installation of other systems. If the facility is located in a rural area with clean extended air, make sure that windows can be opened (double hung, slider, hopper, awning, or casement). In polluted environments, such as urban areas, single-hung windows are acceptable.

Propane/natural gas, solar, wind, heat pump, and nuclear power are all considered "clean" sources of heat or energy and are worth thinking about considering the depletion of ozone in the atmosphere from using fossil fuels. These sources of heat or energy may ultimately reduce operating costs, including the "scrubbing" of exhausted air from a building. Finally, the actual selection and type of HVAC-R should consider the economy of operation, flexibility of control, quietness of operation, and capacity to provide desirable thermal conditions.

Air Quality

Facility ventilation is directly tied to the indoor air quality (IAQ). The IAQ is a product of the quality of the fresh air introduced into the ventilation system and the quality of the existing indoor air that is recycled.

Typically, HVAC-R systems recirculate as much conditioned air (warm or cool) as is allowed by health and building codes to maximize energy efficiency and reduce the size of mechanical and electrical equipment. In facilities where health and IAQ issues are paramount (or in facilities where no energy-recovery system exists), as much as 100% of the conditioned air may be exhausted. Such facilities in climates with significant indoor–outdoor temperature differentials in winter and summer can exhaust otherwise reclaimable energy.

Energy recovery in HVAC-R systems involves transferring heat from one air stream to another. In the summer months, intake air at a higher temperature releases heat to cooler exhaust air prior to being mechanically cooled by the air-conditioning process. Conversely, during the winter, intake air is warmed by transferring heat from exhaust air. Approximately 60% to 65% of the available sensible heat may be recovered, whereas latent heat is not recovered.

The air quality issue in sports and recreation buildings has developed into a significant concern for today's building owners and operators. The public now has greater awareness of health-related concerns, and there is increased research documenting these issues. On the other hand, heating and cooling systems that use excess fresh air also require more energy. To compound this problem, there is no single accurate method of measuring air quality, and solutions to air quality problems tend to be building and site specific. The challenge for building managers is to find the optimal levels of fresh air to maintain comfort conditions. Good air quality and energy conservation should be complementary. One should not be achieved at the expense of the other.

Air quality is an evolving issue. Standards and guidelines for air quality in buildings have developed along with an evolving understanding of human requirements for fresh air to support health and of the major air-related contaminants and their effects. ASHRAE was one of the first organizations to establish guidelines for air quality. ASHRAE's research has led to the publication of minimum ventilation rates to maintain the indoor environment within a key range of guidelines.

Air quality is a complex issue that affects occupant comfort, health, productivity, and acceptance of energy conservation measures. Modern building materials contain many new chemicals that can give off gases or vapors such as formaldehyde and radon. Other organic and inorganic chemicals are introduced to recreation buildings through paints, solvents, and photocopiers. Allergens from airborne particles and dust are also present in these environments.

HVAC-R designers and building managers in existing buildings have reduced outside air ventilation rates to lower levels in keeping with energy conservation guidelines. Moreover, outside air quality has generally deteriorated in major cities due to pollution from industrial plants, automobiles, and other combustion-type processes.

Variable air volume systems used in many large spectator facilities often have decreased air circulation rates compared to conventional constant volume systems. Air circulation rates affect the purging of local contaminants, such as cigarette smoke and heat from the activity and spectator areas. Many older buildings are undergoing major retrofits to HVAC-R systems to reduce energy costs. Fans are being modified and generally operated for fewer hours each day. New control strategies call for the conversion from outside air systems to recirculation-type systems with less outside air delivered to the space. This is especially helpful in settings where the outside air is of poor quality.

In older or poorly designed HVAC-R systems that merely recirculate conditioned air without exhausting enough air and/or introducing enough fresh air, the IAQ can become compromised. The IAQ can be managed, even in older systems, if a proactive approach is used to address the IAQ issues. This includes controlling pollution at its source, from both indoor and outdoor sources.

One low-cost way to prevent IAQ problems is to stop potential sources of indoor air pollution where they originate. Known as *source control*, this process manages pollutants by removing them from the building, isolating them from people by using physical barriers, and controlling when they are used. The National Institute of Health (NIH) and ASHRAE have been busy funding research related to IAQ and controlling pollutants at the source. Specifically, the NIH recently funded a study of the CREON2000™ Disinfection Unit. The CREON2000™ uses ultraviolet light to destroy harmful microbes causing allergy, asthma, and illness. Another such disinfecting unit, designed to be placed directly into building ventilation systems, is the Sanuvox™ UV Air Purifier. In one documented application, the Sanuvox™ UV Air Purifier reduced air contaminants by 66% in a southern California classroom. In this case, the UV unit picked up where vacuuming, HVAC-R maintenance, and fresh air ventilation left off, stripping contaminants in the air such as mold spores, bacteria, mildew, formaldehyde, solvents, and viruses.

In 2003, ASHRAE approved funding for eight research projects in the areas of indoor air quality, comfort and health, energy conservation, operating and maintenance tools, and environmentally safe materials and design tools (ASHRAE, 2003).

Generally, comfort is perceived when physical, chemical, and biological stresses are at a minimum. Quality of air and the perception of air quality can be different. The major components influencing each are common:

- physical contaminants in the air,
- chemical contaminants in the air,
- biological contaminants in the air, and
- thermal factors—air temperature and relative humidity, air velocity.

Physical Contaminants

Some of the major physical contaminants are listed below:

Contaminant	Source
Dust particles	Outdoor air
Tobacco smoke	Cigarettes (particulates & vapor)
Asbestos fibers	Asbestos building products
Metallic dust	Building materials
Wood particles	Building materials

The particles of smoke, dust, pollen, and other physical contaminants enter the indoor environment either from outside by infiltration or from activities and processes in the building. The amount of material entering the building from outdoors will depend on the wind velocity and the amount of infiltration. Particles can be generated indoors by smoking, other indoor combustion processes, and existing building materials.

Chemical Contaminants

A number of chemical contaminants can be found in the indoor air of a typical sport or recreation building. These include the products of combustion, namely, carbon monoxide (CO), carbon dioxide (CO_2), oxides of nitrogen (NO_x), and sulphur dioxide (SO_2). These chemicals, in some concentrations, can be found in the indoor air whenever a combustion source is within the building. Ice resurfacers and edgers in ice arenas, carpet cleaning, and forklifts on indoor soccer and field houses, and vacuum systems for cleaning seating capacity venues can contaminate the air with carbon monoxide and nitrogen dioxide fumes. Ozone concentrations can increase due to photocopiers and other sources, such as aerosol spray cans. Cleaning agents can give off toxic fumes. Building materials such as paints and particleboards can add to formaldehyde and other hydrocarbon concentrations.

Biological Contaminants

Biological contaminants are microorganisms that can spread through a facility and be inhaled. Constant temperature levels between 60° and 120°F in stagnant pools of water provide ideal conditions for the growth of microorganisms. These conditions are found in humidifiers, dehumidifiers, and cooling towers, where there is sufficient moisture and appropriate temperature for the growth of bacteria algae and microorganisms. Examples of bacteria-related building epidemics, such as Legionnaires' disease and humidifier fever, have been cited in literature on air quality.

Finding the best solution to an air quality problem in a specific facility requires knowledge of the building and its mechanical systems, as well as its environment and occupancy conditions. As detailed earlier, the design and construction of the building envelope will determine the infiltration rate, that is, the rate of uncontrolled air leakage into the building. In some buildings, infiltration is depended on as a source of supply for makeup air to replace air removed by exhaust appliances. Any change to the air tightness of the envelope will affect the infiltration rate and the amount of fresh air available to the building.

Thermal Factors

Thermal factors affect air quality in two ways. The human perception of air quality control is related to factors such as air temperature, as well as the actual composition of the air. For example, too high a temperature or lack of air movement may create a sensation of stuffiness. Second, the thermal characteristics of the air will affect the actions of contaminants in the environment. For example, excessive humidity will promote the growth of microorganisms. A thermally acceptable environment will minimize physical stress and addresses the following items.

Air temperature. The temperature set by building operation can vary considerably due to temperature stratification within the space, and such variations can affect occupant comfort.

Air velocity. Air distribution systems may create the sensation of drafts or conversely of stuffiness.

Relative humidity. Relative humidity expressed as a percentage varies in the range of 20% to 80% for most buildings. Relative humidity below 20% will result in discomfort for some people.

Static electricity. Static buildup can also occur with low relative humidity. Testing has shown that most people link dryness or perception of humidity level to air temperature.

Air Quality Checklist

There is no single method for improving IAQ. A general checklist follows that will serve as a reference for air quality troubleshooting. As a first step, it is always useful to check air temperatures and comfort criteria in problem areas.

Exhaust re-intake

- Check for recirculation of exhaust air into outside air intake.
- Check outside air intakes at ground level to ensure automobile exhaust or other contaminants are not in-

troduced into outside air intake. Because many sports teams travel by bus, it is important to park buses away from the facility. Motor fumes can be easily sucked into the building by the air handling systems.

- Check exhaust air systems to ensure toilet exhaust is not recirculated to return to air systems.

Avoid exhaust air opening near outside air intakes

- Check proximity of cooling tower to outside air intake. Ensure biological water treatment of cooling tower, especially in summer months.
- Avoid having stagnant pools of water on roof or near outside air intakes.
- Check humidifier pans and sprayed cooling coils for biological contaminants or growths.

Ensure proper water treatment of spray systems

- Check fan coil units for stagnant water in drip pans. Ensure drip pans drain properly.
- Check flooded carpet areas for biological contamination. Change carpet in contaminated areas.
- Check fan rooms for solvents and other chemicals to ensure chemical contamination is not spread by the air handling system.
- Check chemicals used for rug cleaning, and review concentration of cleaning agents used on rugs and floors.

Exhaust at source

- Check for exhaust from high-humidity locations, smoking rooms, kitchens, photocopy rooms, and other process applications.

Dilution

- Check minimum outside air setting, and calibrate for normal occupancy.
- Check ambient air concentrations for CO_2 and other contaminants.
- Adjust fan hours of operation and schedule to suit occupancy.
- Check supply air distribution patterns to ensure adequate flushing of occupied space.
- Check for vertical temperature stratification as evidence of poor air distribution.

Basic Considerations in Energy Management

Over the last decade, energy management has moved from being a one-time activity to an ongoing and essential part of facility planning and management. Furthermore, energy management has become a widely known applied science with new measures, technologies, and analytic approaches. The importance of energy management to facility planning cannot be overemphasized, especially in sports and recreation facilities that consume large amounts of energy.

The long-range forecasts for the world's energy supplies and prices indicate that it is wise to design systems to reduce consumption of energy during periods of shortage and rapidly escalating prices. New technologies and improved heating and air-conditioning equipment show that further savings are possible, even during periods of lower fuel prices.

Next to staffing, utilities normally are the second highest cost of operating sports and recreation facilities. This section will provide an overview of energy management and outline specific aspects of energy management in the building envelope; building operations and maintenance; and heating, cooling, and air handling systems. The chapter looks at how domestic hot water and air quality affect energy consumption and the impact that lighting and building automation systems have on energy management opportunities. Energy management will be addressed, looking at planning and construction issues, as well as maintenance and operating criteria. Finally, the chapter provides reference sources and online sources for the further study of energy management.

In the planning and construction process for sports and recreation facilities, whether for a new building, a building addition, or a major renovation, the owner, the architect, and the construction contractors must resolve thousands of issues. Many of these issues deal with design, selection, and integration of facilities' energy systems (the HVAC-R systems, lighting, and other energy-consuming equipment). Oftentimes, little attention is paid to these issues in the design process and end up being serious and costly mistakes because, over the life of the facility, the energy costs will exceed the initial cost of all the energy systems.

Because many of these issues are technical and involve parts of the facility no one usually sees, energy questions may be mishandled in the design process. This results from design professionals designing the building envelope, HVAC-R, lighting, and other energy-consuming systems independently and, to protect themselves from liability or complaints, typically overengineering these systems. Energy-efficient buildings should be designed by an integrated design approach in which all of the design professionals work together with energy efficiency as one of their goals.

A second reason that energy issues are mishandled in design is that almost everyone makes decisions on the basis of initial cost or first cost rather than on life cycle costs that account for the initial cost and all of the costs associated with operating and maintaining the facility during its useful life. The most cost-effective time to incorporate energy efficiency into a sports and recreation facility is during construction, when the energy savings need only pay back the incremental cost difference between a "regular" system and a more efficient one. Unless the design team evaluates alternative options on a life cycle cost basis, sound decisions cannot be made.

Energy Management as a Process

Initially, energy management was viewed as a one-time application of conservation principles to the building envelope and mechanical systems. Experience has shown that greater savings may be obtained and sustained when energy management is considered to be an ongoing process. It is a process that involves a number of key elements such as

- an assessment of the building and its operating systems;
- a list of appropriate energy conservation measures based on the assessment;
- careful, planned implementation; and
- regular review of actual energy savings.

Once started, energy management is an ongoing process that is integrated with building maintenance and operation and with any changes in building occupancy, envelope, or mechanical equipment. Sports and recreation facilities have major changes in occupancy loads during varying periods of the day and seasons of the year, and understanding these impacts on the mechanical system is a critical step to designing systems. Moreover, these facilities are normally large spaces with big building envelopes containing glass entrances and large roofing structures. Under normal circumstances, these characteristics are not energy efficient.

Energy management as a process also recognizes that buildings are not static. Occupancy changes can affect internal space allocations and patterns of building use, which affect the demands on and performance of mechanical systems. Occupancy codes require a certain number of air changes per hour to satisfy the fresh air needs of the participants and the spectators. These requirements directly affect the HVAC-R systems.

The three major steps involved in energy management are as follows: conduct an energy audit and analysis, implement a strategy, and monitor the results.

Energy Audit and Analysis

Although a simple walk-through audit will often reveal many opportunities for savings, it is recommended that a full energy audit be undertaken. This will serve as the foundation of the implementation program and as a reference point for partial studies that may be required in future years owing to major changes in building occupancy, envelope, or mechanical systems.

A full energy audit is a complete assessment of the building and its energy use patterns. The physical characteristics of the building shell (e.g., walls, windows and doors, roof, floor) and the various electrical and mechanical systems (e.g., HVAC-R equipment, lights, water heaters) are inspected. Utility bills are reviewed to determine actual energy use. If possible, energy use is allocated to each building system separately.

The energy audit also provides the necessary information for designing an implementation program. A list of energy conservation measures is developed based on the energy analysis and target energy use. The list is usually divided into no-cost housekeeping measures, low-cost maintenance, and upgrading and major retrofit or upgrading projects involving considerable capital expenditure. Capital costs and estimated savings for each measure are summarized in the energy audit report. With the deregulation of electricity, numerous energy audit companies are available to work with sports and recreation professionals to design conservation plans for facilities.

Implementation of Strategy

In addition to the building information and recommended measures from the building energy audit, many other practical concerns should be considered when developing the implementation plan. These include existing maintenance programs for envelope and mechanical systems, existing repair and upgrading programs for envelope and mechanical systems, projected plans for changes in building occupancy, projected plans for major repairs or renovations, available funds, and available staff resources for implementation and program management. Implementation of specific energy management measures will proceed according to the implementation program. Key steps in the program are allocating capital funds and staff resources, obtaining estimates and selecting consultants for measures that require professional assistance, assigning a project manager or energy manager to be responsible for implementing the program and monitoring results, and selecting contractors and/or internal staff.

Monitoring of Results

Monitoring an energy management program is essential for measuring results and steering the program with progressive feedback. The simplest monitoring technique involves reviewing energy bills on a monthly and annual basis and comparing them to a previous reference year. However, a more complete monitoring program will include keeping records of factors that affect energy usage. Components of a complete monitoring program include

- measuring energy/usage and costs;
- logging building system performance through indicators such as supply air temperature and boiler efficiency;

- logging weather conditions;
- recording additions or modifications to the building, patterns of building occupancy and use, and occupant comments on comfort;
- recording changes in occupancy patterns and use;
- recording energy management measures as they are implemented; and
- logging maintenance of building equipment and systems.

Energy Accounting

Energy accounting is considered as a means to systematically track and analyze both energy costs and consumption, to better manage and control energy use. In energy accounting, the information gathered through monitoring is used to improve energy efficiency. It involves determining where, how much, and why energy is used. A number of software programs are available to facilitate energy accounting. However, it is important that you purchase software that makes sense for you and/or your organization. Some organizations may choose to contract out this aspect of management, preferring to focus human energy on the organizational programs, leaving the energy accounting to professionals.

Many factors affect building energy use. These include weather conditions at the building site; design, quality, and condition of the building envelope; insulation value of walls and roof; number and size of windows; quality and type of windows; air leakage around windows, doors, and other openings; building mechanical systems; HVAC-R systems and their operation; process activities inside the building such as lighting, hot water, and appliances; maintenance of building equipment and systems; efficiency of systems and components; and patterns of building occupancy and use.

An effective energy accounting system can mitigate or minimize the cost of the system. Some of the most attractive benefits include the following: verifies monthly invoices, pinpoints problem areas, helps manage budgets, monitors energy management programs, justifies energy conservation investments, provides reports to senior management, and provides financing options for energy.

Energy management programs can be financed using a number of options.

Operating funds. Many low-cost/no-cost measures can be funded from existing operating budgets. Energy is an operating expenditure, and energy cost savings can be used to purchase energy retrofits.

Capital budgets. Energy management retrofit programs can be funded from capital budgets.

Leases. Leases can be used to purchase energy management equipment. Lease payments can be designed to be less than the projected energy cost savings.

Energy service agreement. An energy service agreement is a performance contract in which a private company offers to execute efficiency capital improvements in exchange for a portion of the energy cost savings that accrue. Typically, a company enters into a long-term contract and, at its expense, designs, installs, and manages or comanages an energy efficiency system for the facility.

It is important to evaluate the cost and payback period for each measure as it relates to a particular building. What may be a low-cost measure for a large sports facility would represent a substantial investment for a smaller recreation operation. Each situation has to be looked at separately.

Building Envelope

The building envelope consists of the roof, floor, walls, windows, and doors—all parts of the building that enclose the interior building space and separate it from the outdoor climate. The envelope performs several functions. It provides shelter from the elements, lighting (windows), and, in some cases, air changes through natural ventilation (windows) and infiltration. The envelope's success in performing these functions is dependent on the building design, quality of construction, and maintenance of the envelope components.

A building's shape and size will greatly affect its heating and cooling loads. Compact facilities generally require less energy than large seating capacity sports venues that ramble and sprawl all over the site. Proper choice of architectural form and orientation can often reduce energy cost. Large sports facilities should respect the path of the sun and be oriented east–west to minimize solar gain in the summer and maximize solar gain in the winter. Reduced air infiltration and proper analysis for optimal insulation is also critical to study early in the design process.

The role of the mechanical systems and purchased energy is to make up the difference between that which the envelope can provide in occupant comfort and what is required. The quality of the envelope, then, is a major factor in determining energy use for heating, cooling, lighting, and ventilation. Improvements to the envelope can significantly reduce energy demand.

Uncontrolled air leakage through the building envelope is often associated with moisture damage to building components. An added benefit of energy management attention to the envelope is the resolution and prevention of problems affecting the service life of envelope components. It is important to understand the causes of heat loss through the building envelope and to understand the strategies for upgrading the thermal performance of the building envelope.

Energy to heat interior spaces (in winter) or to cool interior spaces (in summer) is lost through heat transfer and infiltration/exfiltration. Heat transfer refers to the movement of heat through walls, windows, doors, roof, or floors whenever there is a difference between the exterior temperature and the interior temperature. Heat transfer occurs through three natural processes: convection, conduction, and radiation.

Convection is the transfer of heat by the movement of a fluid such as air. For example, cool air moving over a warmer surface picks up heat, carries it, and transfers it to a cooler surface. Conduction is the transfer of heat directly through a solid (e.g., wood, brick, drywall). Radiation is the transfer of heat from a surface by electromagnetic waves.

The temperature difference and thermal resistance factored against the square foot area of the envelope determines the amount of heat transferred. Poor thermal performance of the envelope puts greater demand on the mechanical systems for heating and cooling. In addition, cold surfaces or excessive solar gain can create comfort problems and decrease the efficient use of the space. Building elements with poor thermal performance such as single-glazed windows can be the site of condensation that can cause deterioration of surrounding finishes. Thermal weak points in the envelope can also contribute to the defacement and/or deterioration of building components.

During cold weather, warm air rises to upper levels, where it leaks out to colder outside air (exfiltration). The air lost at the top is replaced by cold air leaking into the building at the bottom (infiltration). The building mechanical systems can affect the pattern of infiltration/exfiltration through requirements for the combustion and draft air and by operation of ventilation systems.

There are two basic approaches to saving energy through modifications to the building shell. Infiltration/exfiltration may be reduced by sealing cracks, air barriers, weather-stripping, or adding better fitting windows and doors. Thermal performance may be improved by adding insulation to the roof, walls, or floor or by adding double- or triple-glazed windows. Insulated windows, either aerogel or multiple paned, can prevent conduction of heat through the glass. Low-emissivity (low-E) windows and window films allow windows to reflect heat rather than transmit it, keeping rooms cool in the summer and warm in the winter.

In general, air sealing and other measures that reduce air infiltration/exfiltration should be implemented before adding insulation. The major areas and extent of air leakage can be determined by means of a complete building audit. The techniques used may include a walk-through building audit, a fan-depressurization test, an infrared thermograph scan, and a smoke pencil test. Normally, infiltration and exfiltration should be checked at building joints, windows and doors, mechanical penetration areas, and the top of buildings where the roof structure attaches to the walls. Because sports and recreation facilities are large buildings with roofs spanning long distances, these are important areas to have sealed.

Upgrading the thermal performance of the building envelope can lower demand for heating and cooling. It can also improve occupant comfort and use of space by eliminating uncomfortable drafts and cold spots. Energy conservation measures may also provide effective solutions to serious building damage by correcting thermal weak points that can cause deterioration of building components. A complete energy audit of the building will present a "thermal picture" of the envelope. Furthermore, this will indicate areas of greatest heat loss and cooling load. A thermal picture will be determined by the size and shape of the building, its age, and type of construction. Each part of the building envelope offers unique opportunities and constraints regarding thermal upgrading. The best time to address the thermal performance of a sports facility is during the design phase.

Operation and Maintenance

Proper maintenance is essential to conserving energy in the long term. The building should be designed with future maintenance in mind. Easy access to equipment, having major components of the mechanical and electrical systems labeled and as-built drawings provided are good first steps to making maintenance easier to perform. A manual containing operating instructions and information on all of the components of the mechanical and electrical systems should be given to the owner when the systems are commissioned.

A thorough and well-managed maintenance program will directly reduce energy costs. Equipment that is well maintained operates more efficiently and consumes less energy. If maintenance of HVAC-R or electrical systems is neglected, costs will increase in the long term. This includes the cost of equipment downtime, emergency repair costs, and the increased energy cost to operate the equipment. Energy costs will also increase owing to poor operating efficiencies resulting from neglect.

Good operational and maintenance procedures can complement a well-designed energy management program, specifically as they relate to the following systems: heating, cooling, ventilation, water treatment, and lighting. Energy management must become part of daily operations to be effective. All operating procedures should be energy efficient. Operations logs and well-documented operating procedures are essential ingredients of energy management. Keeping operational logs is one activity that is part of the standard operating procedure for a building. Operating logs perform several functions: They provide a permanent historical record of system performance, ensure that systems are inspected frequently, identify problems by providing historical records of changes in operation and/or energy performance, and provide management programs.

Heat pumps. A heat pump is essentially a refrigeration cycle where the heat rejected at the condenser is used for heating purposes. The total heat delivered to the condenser is the sum of the heat extracted in the evaporator and the heat from the compressor work necessary to compress the refrigerant.

The heat pump must have a source of heat to be cooled in order to work. In residential applications, the source of heat is usually outside air, water, or the ground. In large buildings, the source of heat can be waste heat from lighting in interior building areas or heat from computers. The heating requirement must occur at the same time as the cooling requirement if the heat source is inside the building, or thermal storage must be used to transfer the heat to another time period.

Domestic Hot Water

A hot water plant may include one or several hot water boilers, a heat exchanger to produce domestic hot water, circulating pumps, and control devices. A hot water distribution system, sometimes called a hydronic system, is used to circulate hot water between a boiler and the heat transfer equipment located in the various heated areas of the building. A steam distribution system is used to convey steam from a boiler to the heat transfer equipment.

Domestic hot water systems provide potable water for hand washing, showers, swimming pools, ice resurfacing, and cleaning. Most sports and recreation buildings incorporate some form of domestic hot water heating system. The domestic hot water system is similar to hot water heating systems, except that the heated water is potable and cannot be chemically treated. Cold water is supplied as makeup to this system from the local water utility.

Domestic hot water systems can be subdivided into unitary and central systems. Unitary systems are point-of-use systems with no distribution piping to serve multiple points of use. Unitary systems, or instantaneous water heaters, eliminate long pipe runs and associated line losses. Central systems are more common in sports facilities and incorporate distribution piping to serve more than one point of use. A central domestic hot water system generally includes a hot water generator heated by steam, by natural gas, or by an electric element; a storage tank (frequently integrated with the hot water generator); piping (usually copper pipes); recirculating pump(s); plumbing fixtures such as faucets and showerheads; and control devices that regulate the water temperature and occasionally the water flow to the appliances.

The key energy management measures related to various components of the above systems include
- reducing hot water consumption through the use of restricted water flow showerheads;
- considering separate boiler for domestic hot water heating if domestic hot water is the only summer load for a large boiler;

- stopping circulating pumps 1 hr after occupied periods end to reduce piping losses. Restart the recirculation pumps not more than 1 hr before occupancy periods begin. Computerized energy management systems can be programmed to accomplish these functions based on the activities scheduled in the facility; and
- reducing tank losses of the water heater when hot water will not be used for a period of 72 hr or more. Tanks and lines should be insulated to avoid unnecessary losses.

Water, like energy, is an increasingly scarce and expensive commodity whose use has enormous environmental repercussions. Because the price of water can only go up, the sports facility that takes steps to reduce its water consumption may be less affected.

Large volumes of water are typically consumed by sports facilities for indoor pools, landscaping, and turf maintenance. Artificial snowmaking is another major water consumer. Following are some effective general steps.

Indoor water use. The primary areas of indoor water consumption are washrooms, showers, and laundry rooms. Steps to improve water conservation in these areas include
- instructing and reminding washroom and shower users to shut off taps fully;
- repairing drips and leaks promptly;
- checking that timing cycles are appropriate for the frequency of urinal use for automatic flushing systems—shut them down entirely after hours;
- installing low-flow aerators and automatic shutoff valves on tapes; and
- retrofitting toilets to reduce water consumption, or consider installing "waterless" toilets.

Outdoor water use. Facilities such as golf courses and playing fields spend heavily on keeping their turf healthy and green. Watering during dry spells actually works against the health of the ecosystem as a whole by depleting water reserves elsewhere. Sports facilities can reduce demand for irrigation by encouraging an evolution in the attitudes of users to the point where turf that is less than forest green is acceptable.

Steps that can be taken to reduce outdoor water consumption include
- planting only native vegetation or species suited to the climate;
- limiting watering of turf to playing surfaces that receive heavy use;
- watering only during the evening and overnight to reduce evaporation;
- using trickle or soaker hoses rather than aerial sprinklers; and
- designing parking lots and roadways to allow rainwater to return to the soil, streams, and groundwater.

Lighting

As recent as 2008, lighting costs in sports and recreation facilities accounted for 30% to 50% of total energy costs. When electrical costs were low, little thought was given in building design to the operational costs of lighting systems. Rather, the selection and design of lighting systems were often based on minimizing capital cost. Now, with energy costs significantly higher, owners are paying attention to long-term costs. In 2009, 72 state-of-the-art LED fixtures at approximately 200 W each were installed in the Raymond James Stadium in Tampa, Florida, for Super Bowl XLIII. It was decided later to switch to an LED system and it saved 80% of the energy. Lighting systems in sports and recreation facilities serve five distinct purposes: to provide sufficient illumination to enable occupants to see and play in a safe manner, to illuminate safe pathways for the movement of persons in and out of the building, to complement the architectural and interior design by providing a comfortable and pleasant environment, to deter vandalism (outside lighting), and to enhance or highlight a product or display. A lighting system with higher levels than necessary results in higher up-front costs and higher operating expenses.

A well-designed lighting system should provide adequate and safe levels of light for the activities carried out in a space. Often, when a system is designed, the quantity (illuminance) of light is used as the only criterion for providing suitable lighting. However, recent studies have now found that the quality of light installed is also an important factor to consider when designing or upgrading a lighting system.

Occupant visual comfort and productivity are directly related to the amount of lighting and the way it is provided. Opportunities for reducing lighting energy usage should also be looked upon as opportunities to improve the quality of lighting.

Before an energy management plan or program is developed for a building's lighting system, an analysis of the existing facilities should be undertaken. Information should be collected that relates to the amount of light provided in each area; the type of fixtures and their energy consumption; and the occupant activity for specific lighting areas, including the time period in use.

Once this information is collected, lighting levels can be compared to recommended levels for the activities involved. Opportunities for energy savings can then be identified. They may include reducing power consumption of fixtures through modification or replacement of fixtures or through reduced lighting levels and reducing the operating period of fixtures based on occupant activity. Simply changing metal halide fixtures in a gymnasium to linear fluorescent fixtures can improve lighting substantially and can make that facility safer and more enjoyable to its users (Lynn, 2010). The quality of lighting depends on the following factors, as well as the actual level of illumination: geometry of the space to be illuminated; mounting height of lighting fixtures; light-reflecting properties of the ceiling, walls, and floor; and color rendering of the particular light type under consideration.

Maintaining adequate illumination levels requires effective lighting system maintenance. An effective maintenance program comprises not only lamp replacement but also routine, planned cleaning of lighting fixtures and room surfaces. A regular cleaning and relamping program has definite long-term benefits: More light is delivered per unit cost of electricity, lower wattage lamps can be installed, fewer luminaries can be installed, and overall labor costs are reduced. Note also that induction lights can burn for up to 100,000 hr before replacement, as compared to energy-efficient light bulbs that max out at 12,000 hr (Lynn, 2010).

A final factor to consider before embarking on a lighting energy management program, particularly for large sports and recreation buildings, is the effect of lighting on the HVAC-R systems. The lighting–HVAC-R effect refers to the impact of lighting on the heating and cooling load of a building.

Effectively, the energy consumed for lighting ultimately ends up as heat. This heat can become a significant part of the cooling load of an air-conditioned space. The energy required to air-condition an interior space includes the energy used by the refrigerating equipment (central chiller or rooftop air conditioners). It may also include pump energy to deliver chilled water to the space and fan energy to deliver cool air. These components can be reduced in size if heat output from lights is reduced. Conversely, reducing the energy use of lights increases the heating load of a space in winter because the heating effect of lights is reduced. This lighting–HVAC-R effect in heating and cooling must be calculated when planning lighting measures.

Building Automation Systems

Building automation systems can be included in energy management plans both in the planning and design phases of new facilities and with the renovation of older facilities with operating problems owing to antiquated control systems. Installing a building automation system not only saves money by reducing unnecessary energy consumption but also increases comfort significantly.

The features of an automated control system that can be used in conjunction with an energy management program are sensors to measure the environment, controllers to regulate equipment, and operating equipment. An example of a sensor is a temperature sensor that sends a pneumatic or electronic signal proportional to the temperature back to a controller. Controllers are designed to receive sensor inputs, compare the input to a set point, and send a signal output to a controlled device. The operating equipment is any device connected to and operated by the controller.

Building automation systems include systems that control energy management functions, as well as systems that control other building management functions, such as security (Cohen, 2000). Building automation systems can be classified by the number of control points, the means of control, and the type of data communication used between the controller and the control points.

There are a number of reasons why a building operator or manager might want to incorporate an automated control system into a building: to improve building operation and comfort; to increase building safety or security; to reduce operating costs, including energy costs; or to provide more efficient building management. Following is a brief description of the various control options that can be incorporated into a computer-controlled automated system.

Programmed start/stop. Programmed start/stop is a software-based function that permits the user to schedule starting and stopping of equipment according to a predetermined schedule. In sports facilities when specific occupancy scenarios are known, air handling equipment can be programmed to increase air volumes when spectators are scheduled in the facility and reduce the volumes during nonuse periods. Furthermore, hot water circulating pumps can be programmed to deliver hot water when users are expected to take showers and can be turned off otherwise.

Alarms/monitoring. This type of software-based function signals an alarm or initiates a particular action when an upper or lower limit has been exceeded. Sports and recreation facilities have many entry and exit doors to monitor and control. This type of system can be used to signal an unauthorized entry into a space.

Energy monitoring. This function allows the recording and accumulation of fuel and electricity consumption data, allowing for improved analysis of the consumption rate of fuel and electricity.

Demand control. This software feature reduces electrical power demand by stopping or delaying the operation of certain pieces of nonessential electrical equipment during peak demand periods. Utilities charge a premium to users who consume a lot of electricity at peak periods of time. Staying below this demand level will cut electrical costs all year long because one high-use period sets the rate for the entire year.

Duty cycling. This software executes the stop/start cycles for equipment. One can therefore avoid the simultaneous operation of several loads that do not require continuous operation and limit the energy consumption of controlled equipment.

Optimized stop/start. This type of program function calculates the best time to initiate preheating or precooling of the building.

Optimized ventilation. This software is used to optimize the blending of outside air and return air based on the enthalpy of the two air streams.

Optimization of supply air temperature. This software allows the adjustment of supply air temperature as a function of the heating and cooling loads of the building.

Chiller/boiler optimization. When the cooling system comprises several chillers, this type of function operates the minimum chilling capacity to satisfy the load.

Supply water temperature optimization. This type of control can regulate the chilled water and hot water supply temperatures of the cooling/heating systems as a function of the actual demand of the building.

Temperature setback/setup. Temperature setback/setup type of controls provide scheduling of building space temperatures during unoccupied periods.

Other control options available with building automation systems include controls for exterior and/or interior lighting and security, domestic hot water optimization, cistern flow optimization that modulates water flow to cistern-operated urinals, and options for specialized applications, such as swimming pools and ice arenas. As the technology improves, these systems will change to reflect the additional energy and cost savings available.

6 Ancillary Areas

Jeffrey C. Petersen, *Baylor University*
Rick Gonzales, *University of Wisconsin, Eau Claire*

The primary purpose of any facility constructed for health, fitness, physical activity, recreation, or sport is for users to engage in the activity or event itself. However, the actual use of the gymnasium, weight room, pool, or other activity space is typically dependent upon additional support spaces such as locker rooms, administrative offices, storage spaces, restrooms, and others. In fact, the effective use of activity space can be greatly impacted by the design, quality, and condition of such ancillary spaces. As such, it is vital that these ancillary spaces be properly designed and constructed to enhance the primary use of the overall facility. Actual ancillary space design recommendations for specific facility situations will not be presented in this chapter because each physical activity facility will have unique needs that the professional planning/design team should consider. However, the chapter will include key information and analytical guidelines for the planning process for each of these important common support spaces.

An ancillary space is a space having a secondary or dependent use. In architectural design circles, building code requirements are essential components to ensure the safety of building occupants. Within building codes, the appropriate term that expresses the same thought is *accessory use.*

In a building of any type, there is typically a primary use associated with that building. The concept of primary usage is important as it determines how a building needs to be constructed and who will be allowed to legally occupy and use that building. For example, a simple basketball court without viewing areas would not need fire resistant construction or a sprinkler system to protect the occupants. The introduction of bleachers and the capacity of those bleachers could require fire-resistive construction and/or fire sprinklers. The primary use, the facility area, and the capacity of the occupants are major inputs in determining how a building must be constructed and how it may be used.

It is also possible to have mixed-use facilities. Mixed-use facilities contain more than one primary use. For example, a secondary school facility can include classrooms for teaching activities, offices for the educators, and an attached gymnasium for spectator viewing. In building code terms, this is mixing an educational occupancy, business occupancy, and assembly occupancy. Other mixed uses other than these in the same facility are also possible.

Mixed-use facilities are ideal because they share common areas and place more activities under one roof rather than having separate facilities for each use. They can use available land more readily and reduce construction costs. Whether the facility in question has one or more primary uses, it will always require some accessory use spaces. Even dedicated-use facilities, such as professional sports facilities, can be classified as mixed use. These types of facilities can have a combination of other occupancy uses due to the large size and occupancy capacity of the facility.

From a building code perspective (International Building Code, 2006), the occupancy possibilities include the following:

- Assembly group—the use of a building or structure, or a portion thereof, for the gathering of persons for purposes such as civic, social, or religious functions; recreation, food, or drink consumption; or awaiting transportation.
- Business group—the use of a building or structure, or a portion thereof, for office, professional, or service-type transactions, including storage of records and accounts. Educational occupancies for students above the 12th grade are also included in this group.
- Educational group—the use of a building or structure, or a portion thereof, by six or more persons at any time for educational purposes through the 12th grade.

- Factory group—the use of a building or structure, or a portion thereof, for assembling, disassembling, fabricating, finishing, manufacturing, packaging, repairing, or processing operations that are not classified as a high-hazard group or a storage group.
- High-hazard group—the use of a building or structure, or a portion thereof, that involves the manufacturing, processing, generation, or storage of materials that constitute a physical or health hazard in quantities in excess of those allowed in control areas constructed and located as required.
- Institutional group—the use of a building or structure, or a portion thereof, in which people are cared for or live in a supervised environment, having physical limitations because of health or age are harbored for medical treatment or other care or treatment, or in which people are detained for penal or correctional purposes, or in which the liberty of the occupants is restricted.
- Mercantile group—the use of a building or structure, or a portion thereof, for the display and sale of merchandise, and involves stocks of goods, wares, or merchandise incidental to such purposes and accessible to the public.
- Residential group—the use of a building or structure, or a portion thereof, for sleeping purposes when not classified as an institutional group use.
- Storage group—the use of a building or structure, or a portion thereof, for storage that is not classified as a high-hazard group.
- Utility and miscellaneous group—the use of a building or structure, or a portion thereof, not classified in any specific occupancy group.

From this list, it is important to note that a building used for health, sport, recreation, fitness, and physical activities can potentially have several of the occupancy classifications in large enough areas to warrant the need to be classified as a mixed-use facility. When it comes to facilities that are either new or scheduled to be remodeled, design team members should review the potential implications of various occupancy types and give the owner potential options to reduce construction costs.

Building code exceptions at times may shift an occupancy group from one of the above categories into another category. For example, educational facilities above the 12th grade are classified under the business group rather than the educational group. A competent design professional or designated code official can best classify different uses. These different occupancies are extremely important because they impact project costs, how the facility functions, and the safety and risk management aspects of the facility.

Despite that a building may have a designated primary usage, it is important to note that any health, sport, recreation, fitness, and physical activity building will require

ancillary spaces to function appropriately. For example, a health club or fitness center may require spaces of different types to meet the needs and expectations of its customers. These include, but are not limited to,
- entrance lobbies,
- waiting areas,
- locker rooms,
- massage space,
- athletic training rooms,
- treatment rooms,
- storage areas,
- office spaces,
- meeting rooms,
- file storage,
- mail room,
- maintenance shops,
- laundry room,
- circulation spaces,
- corridors,
- janitor's closet,
- chemical storage,
- trash and recycling areas,
- employee lounge, and
- retail elements (juice bars, concession stands, pro shops, team stores, etc.).

These ancillary spaces are in addition to the primary use spaces that may include, but are not limited to,
- aerobic dance rooms,
- weight rooms,
- aerobic exercise machine areas,
- stretching areas,
- swimming pools,
- gymnasium multipurpose court areas,
- racquetball/squash courts, and
- tennis courts.

In this example, any possible combination of primary use spaces and ancillary use spaces could be selected to create an ideal building. No two facilities are exactly alike, as they should always be designed based upon the users' needs and the goals to be achieved within the facility. The ancillary space requirements for a private health club will differ from the requirements of a college student recreation center or a cardiac rehabilitation facility. The important thing to remember is that the primary activity use will require ancillary space to fully support the primary activities. Minimizing the importance of that ancillary space in the planning process can sharply reduce the overall effectiveness of a facility.

It is easier to plan the types of spaces when a project is in the design phase rather than later. Adding space after a project is complete and in use can be difficult and costly. Sometimes there may be no choice but to deal with space issues after the fact because of less than optimal planning and design.

Within studies of physical activity facilities, ancillary areas typically have been grouped together as the service areas. In 1962, the National Facilities Conference established 11 distinct categories of ancillary space that included dressing rooms, shower rooms, toweling rooms, equipment drying rooms, storage rooms, toilets, first aid rooms, laundry rooms, custodial areas, kitchenettes, and staff/faculty areas. Strand (1988) grouped and categorized the ancillary areas into seven distinct categories in his research involving member schools of the Big Ten Conference. These categories included locker rooms, classrooms, offices, secretarial spaces, storage, laboratories, and training rooms. Petersen (1997) found that the application of ancillary space categories to high school settings had only six primary categories (locker rooms, classrooms, offices, secretarial spaces, storage, and training rooms), as the need for laboratory space was not applicable at the secondary education level.

To consider the design and planning of ancillary spaces, the most common and key ancillary space components will be identified and examined. For the purposes of this chapter, it will include locker rooms, offices, meeting rooms, storage areas, laundry areas, and janitorial/maintenance areas. Athletic training rooms are an ancillary facility component, but this will be covered specifically in Chapter 25. Further consideration for customizing ancillary spaces toward the specific needs of projects in several specialties will be considered including athletics, physical education, fitness clubs, recreation centers, and multipurpose facilities.

Locker Rooms

In most physical activity-based facilities, the locker room is the largest and most complex of the ancillary spaces. The locker room is much more than just a room full of lockers. The locker room fulfills a number of functions related to dressing, storage, personal grooming, social interaction, instruction, safety, and privacy. The most basic components for all locker rooms include lockers, toilets, showers, and grooming stations. Key design factors include the location of the locker room in relation to the activity spaces and arrangement of the locker room components. Whenever a pool or other aquatic venue is a part of the activity spaces, the locker room should be on the same floor level. Figure 6.1 illustrates three basic locker room layouts.

Locker rooms typically fall into three design categories based upon cost, finishes, and features: low, medium, and high end. The low-end locker room typically includes sealed concrete floors, standard metal lockers, basic lighting, non-finished ceilings, and gang showers. The mid-level locker room might upgrade to customized metal lockers, integrated bench systems, showers with tile floors and walls, and finished ceilings. The high-end locker room tends to feature custom wooden lockers, completely tiled

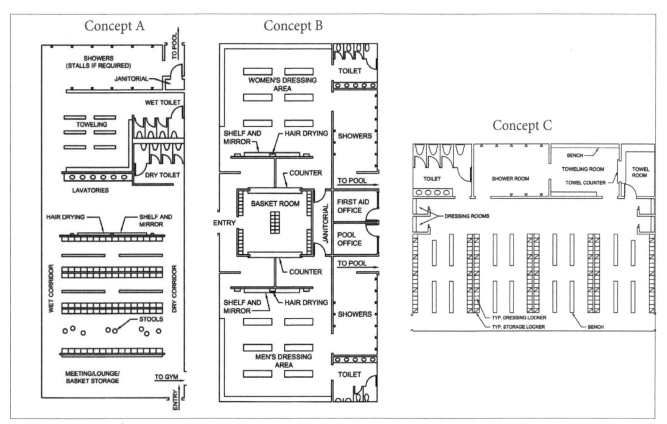

Figure 6.1. **Locker Room Concepts** (*Source:* **Ramsey & Sleeper, 2011**)

floors and walls, carpeted areas, individual showers, solid surface countertops (stone, Corian, etc.), and extra amenities such as saunas, steam rooms, whirlpools, lounge spaces, and televisions (Fickes, 1999). Regardless of the design category and cost, locker rooms have common basic components that need to be carefully planned, for an effective locker room design.

As per Ramsey, Sleeper, and Packard (2004), locker-room essentials include

- fixed benches;
- lockers with raised base;
- locker numbering system;
- provisions for hair dryers (ground fault circuit interrupters);
- mirrors for dressing, shaving, makeup, and so forth;
- shelving for towels, personal storage, and so forth;
- drinking fountains;
- bulletin boards;
- dressing booths;
- clocks;
- door and exit signage;
- a sound system;
- adequate lighting;
- adequate ventilation;
- natural light;
- visual supervision as required; and
- ADA-accessible benches, lockers, showers, and toilet facilities.

Lockers

The lockers themselves are a primary component of the locker room. The lockers provide secure personalized storage space for personal athletic uniforms and gear as well as street clothes. Historically, the primary locker materials were steel or wood, with more recent innovations of plastic laminate and phenolic resin products now in the locker market. Steel lockers still dominate the market at about 70% to 80%, but many have new features such as improved ventilation panels (louvers or mesh designs), antimicrobial treatments, custom and graffiti-resistant paints, and all-welded construction that add to their value. Wood lockers are still the choice for high-cost custom locker applications. The wood is less durable but provides a luxurious appearance. Any type of wood can be used from exotics to oak, but the level of care for wood lockers is much higher. Plastic lockers now available are much more resistant to rust and water damage than the wood and metal materials, and some models are even constructed of recycled materials. Plastic has an advantage over metal lockers in the sound level created during use.

Regardless of the locker material selected, there are many options for the size and configuration of lockers. Depending on the sport or the user's needs, the locker may need to be large for equipment (football, hockey, lacrosse) or it may have more modest space requirements (physical education or soccer). Large single-tier locker systems may be 12 in. to 33 in. wide by 12 in. to 24 in. deep and 60 in. to 72 in. high in standard mass-produced models, with 30 in. being the most typical width of an athletic locker (Dahnert & Pack, 2007). These large, stadium-style lockers often include an integrated seat with storage below, clothing and equipment hooks and hanging bars in the main compartment with storage shelf and possible locking compartments above. Locker configurations may also divide their tiers vertically into two to nine compartments to provide additional locker units in smaller sizes.

New trends in locker designs include Z-lockers that take a two-tier or half locker and notch the dividing panel in the center to provide 8 in. to 24 in. of additional space for hanging clothes such as sport coats, jackets, or longer garments without folding for each of the two stacked half lockers (Dymecki & Stevens, 2007). Extremely small lockers are also available for small items such as wallets, keys, and jewelry. These often come in 4-ft square grids with compartment sizes as small as 3 in. to 4 in. square. These units are useful in applications where facility users are already attired for participation and need minimal secure storage space. In instances where security is of lesser concern, locker units without doors or cubbies can be used for storage in locker room facilities.

Figure 6.2 shows typical locker sizes and most of the possible configurations for doors. Even though many locker configurations are available, there are only two basic types of lockers: those used for storage and those used for dressing. Locking systems for the lockers can vary from the traditional portable combination lock, to built-in keyed/combination systems, to keyless systems such as keypad systems or swipe card systems (Brown, 2008). Each locking system has its own distinct advantages and disadvantages that the planning team should consider.

Determining the total number of lockers to be provided in the locker room is vital to the planning and design process. A peak load of facility users should be determined or projected to provide adequate numbers of lockers for all users. Where total space is limited this may require a mix of locker sizes and configurations to meet user demand. However, locker sizes must still be able to fully accommodate the storage needs of clothing and equipment for the users. Ideally, the number of lockers should exceed the current peak use to accommodate for program growth without the need for immediate facility renovation.

Final selection of lockers should take into consideration a number of factors including cost, appearance requirements, durability and abuse resistance, corrosion resistance, locking systems, size and configuration options, and installation requirements. Lockers should be selected early in the design process to ensure that they are not overlooked and underfunded at the end of the design and building process. Additionally, the specifications for each

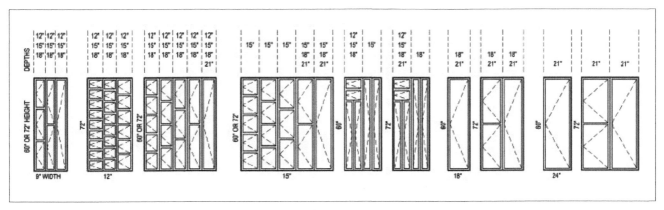

Figure 6.2. **Typical Locker Door Sizes and Configurations** (*Source:* Ramsey & Sleeper, 2011)

locker model installation are important in the planning process. Locker selection and locker room design should also take into account that at least 5% of each type of locker must be accessible to persons with disabilities; these lockers should include easy to operate handles or latches that do not require pinching or grasping to operate and a maximum 54 in. side reach height (LaVoie, 2005).

Showers

A second primary element in the locker room is the showers. The number of showers provided in the locker room and the corresponding capacity of the water heating system are critical to the functionality of the locker room. Cold showers or long waiting lines for shower use will create a negative experience for facility users.

Determining the appropriate number of showers within a locker facility is not an easy task. If usage patterns are known or can be easily projected, then the number of showering stations should be set to meet the peak user demand. The generally accepted ratio of one shower per 20 lockers at times can greatly overestimate or underestimate the true need (LaVoie, 2005). According to the Architectural Graphic Standards (2007), shower facilities located in an area where people have significant time constraints should be sized so there are 10 showers for the first 30 persons and one shower for each additional person. Once a projected peak load and shower number is determined, this information can provide mechanical engineers with the necessary information to determine flow rate and hot water generation capacities needed to properly operate the shower facilities. Innovations such as on-demand tankless water heaters can reduce the total costs in providing hot water as well as reduce or eliminate the dreaded cold shower.

The shower control valve and showerhead are key elements of shower operation and aesthetic appearance. Water conservation can be attained through installing electronic metering valves. These valves can be programmed to set running times from a short number of seconds to a set number of minutes. All shower valves should include thermostatic mixing to control water temperature and prevent scalding (Pfund, 2006). Architectural Graphic Standards (2007) recommends tempering water so that the maximum water temperature cannot exceed 110°F. The showerheads determine the spray patterns provided and also can impact the water usage. Ultralow-flow misting showerheads use little water but also may require longer showering times to remove soaps. High-flow showerheads may provide a luxurious shower experience, but they will cost more in both water and water-heating expenses. Regardless of the shower valve and head selected, the plumbing for the shower should remain accessible for maintenance and repairs without damaging the walls via service panels.

Another key consideration in shower design is the level of privacy desired. The most private of settings may include private individual showers combined with individual drying/dressing areas. A second privacy option would be individual shower with an open drying area. Gang showers provide no privacy for the users but allow many more showerheads or showering stations within a given area. The gang shower may be configured with either wall showers, pedestal showers, or a combination of both. A modification of the gang shower to provide a higher level of privacy is to add partitions or modesty modules. These modesty modules are similar to toilet partitions only shorter. They are added around a prefabricated shower fixture for a lower cost space-saving alternative to full-walled individual shower units. Figure 6.3 displays several possible shower design layouts.

Other important considerations in shower planning include

- providing a drying area(s) adjacent to the showers;
- installing a flush mount hose bib in the shower area for cleaning;
- creating water-resistant ceilings with tile or epoxy paint finishes;

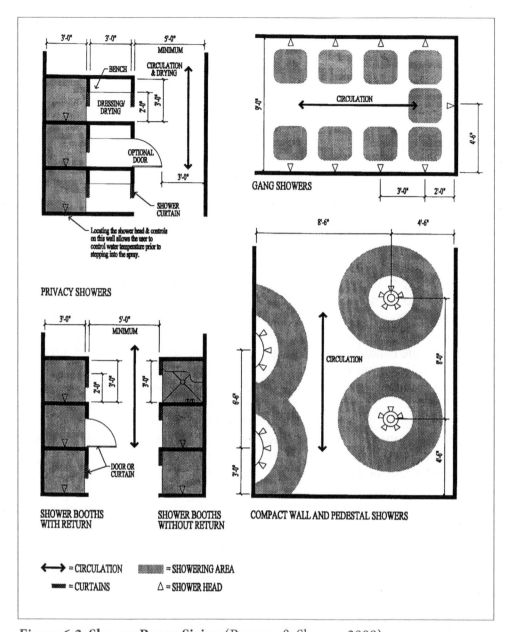

Figure 6.3. **Shower Room Sizing** (Ramsey & Sleeper, 2008)

- setting showerhead heights according to anticipated users with men 6 ft 8 in. to 7 ft, women 6 ft 2 in. to 6 ft 6 in., and children 5 ft 6 in. (from floor to showerhead);
- providing a minimum of 30 in. for each gang shower station;
- creating sloped floors in shower and drying areas to center or perimeter drains;
- installing shower walls and floors that are impervious to water and easily cleaned and maintained such as ceramic tile, stone, or etched terrazzo; and
- considering shower amenities such as towel distribution and collection, soap and shampoo dispensers, shelving, benches, and hooks. (LaVoie, 2005)

Toilets

The location and total number of locker room toilets must be carefully considered. One primary consideration is the wet toilet. If the facility includes aquatic elements, then it is likely that wet patrons will use some toilets. As such, wet area toilets should be provided either in a wet area of the locker room or in a restroom directly connected to the aquatic facility. If wet toilet use is anticipated within the locker room, then it is important to also provide dry toilets in another area of the locker room. Mixing of traffic between wet and dry toilets should be avoided for several reasons. First, no dry person would enjoy sitting on a wet toilet. Second, street shoes in a wet toilet area can lead to slips and falls, and wet bare feet on wet floors soiled by dirt from street shoes is both unpleasant and unsanitary.

The number of fixtures (both water closets and urinals) should be designed to meet the peak demands within a locker room facility. A commonly accepted standard of one water closet per 60 lockers may be adequate for many applications; however, this ratio should be modified as needed to specific needs of facility users (LaVoie, 2005). All toilets should provide privacy for the user; this is typically done with partitions. Selection of partition materials should take into account that most locker rooms have a more corrosive environment than a typical restroom. A growing trend in locker room construction is the creation of individual full-walled toilet rooms for added privacy, each with their own ventilation system.

ADA requirements call for at least one toilet and shower facility per gender that meets these requirements. The required number can increase based on the total number of occupants for a given facility. The primary difference between accessibility standards for lavatories and for vanities is the need for forward approach clearance with knee space. Accessibility standards include requirements for faucets, mirror height, and pipe protection (Architectural Graphic Standards, 2007). The number of specifications that can adequately describe ADA requirements for any facility are extensive and could not be fully presented in this chapter. Additional information is provided in Chapter 4, and it is highly recommended that the reader fully research ADA requirements to the level of detail that this fully deserves.

Grooming Stations/Lavatories

The provision of grooming stations in the locker room complex is the final of the four basic locker room components. These grooming stations may also be referred to as vanities or lavatories. The grooming station will provide users with a location to dry hair, comb hair, brush teeth, shave, apply makeup, wash hands, and perform other related tasks. At a minimum, the dry grooming station will have a mirror, a ground fault interrupter (GFI) electrical receptacle, and a counter or shelf area. A wet grooming station will include a hot and cold water sink, in addition to the dry station elements. A number of additional embellishment options can be added to the grooming stations, such as handheld hair dryers, wall-mounted hand/hair dryers, soap and lotion dispensers, paper towel dispensers, tissue dispensers, waste receptacles, makeup mirrors, scales, and other related items.

Key considerations for the grooming station planning and design include

- the number of stations according to user needs, with typical grooming stations equal to or slightly less than the shower count, with a location along a seam between the wet and dry areas of the locker room not too far removed from locker and changing areas lighting to illuminate both sides of the face and to provide natural coloration such as warm-white fluorescent or incandescent bulbs;
- the addition of at least one full-length wall-mounted mirror; and

- vanity/counter heights of approximately 36 in. for standing use, 42 in. for stool seating, 30 in. for chair seating. (LaVoie, 2005)

Wet/Dry Considerations

The high levels of moisture and water in the locker room areas create a unique layout challenge. The water and humidity can affect the mechanical systems, structural systems, electrical fixtures, and floor and wall finishes. Proper ventilation systems that create negative air pressure in wet areas are one way to combat moisture issues. Second, locker rooms must be designed to minimize the movement between wet and dry areas (Cohen, 1998). Distinctly wet areas of the locker room include the showers, drying areas, and wet amenities such as whirlpools or steam rooms. These wet areas ideally should have a separation or transition area to dry components of the locker room. A drying area placed between the fully wet area and the dry area is one design element to separate the wet and dry locker room elements. Using sloped floors with floor drains is another method to prevent excess water from building up and being tracked into the dry areas. However, wet and dry areas should not be separated by raised curbs as this does not comply with the Americans With Disabilities Act (ADA) accessibility standards. Figure 6.4 depicts wet toilet facilities that have been integrated into the shower drying area.

Drying areas should be sized to be as large as the shower area that it supports. This area should have sufficient drainage, have adequate towel hooks or bars, be constructed of the same water resistant materials, and be designed to contain water from the main locker area.

The mix of wet and dry area concerns makes flooring selection of great importance for the locker room. One key factor in flooring selection is slip resistance. A wet area of the locker room must provide enough traction to reduce or eliminate slips and falls. However, a balance must be maintained in creating high-traction floors. As a floor surface is made more textured for antislip purposes, this rougher surface becomes more difficult to keep clean and can be more uncomfortable to bare feet. Primary floor choices in the locker room include lower cost options such as coated concrete and flow-through interlocking tiles, mid-priced options such as ceramic tile and poured epoxy, and higher end options such as high-grade carpet, porcelain, slate, or marble tile (Popke, 2006a). Figure 6.5 depicts one option for flooring in a shower or drying area.

Size Considerations

The overall size of a locker room must be determined in relation to the number of expected facility users as well as the additional amenities that the users may require. The typical range for locker room square footage accounts for 35% to 60% of total ancillary space within the facility. The determination of the space need for the locker rooms

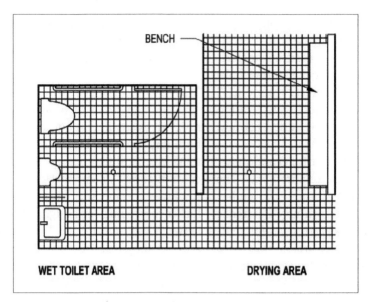

Figure 6.4. **Wet Facilities and Drying Areas** (*Source:* Ramsey & Sleeper, 2011)

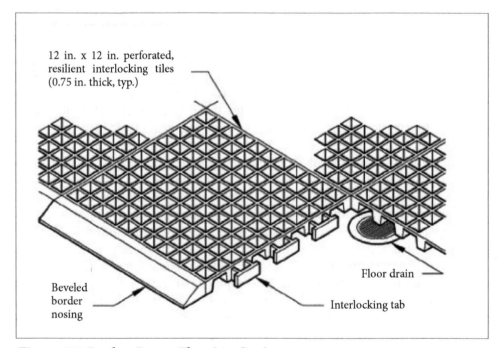

Figure 6.5. **Locker Room Flooring Options** (*Source:* Ramsey & Sleeper, 2011)

should be based upon the peak load expected within the activity areas of the facility. Occupancy levels can be estimated in most applications from the activity area sizes as follows:

- gymnasiums: 12 people per game court,
- racquetball/squash courts: two people per court,
- tennis courts: four people per court,
- lap pools: four people per lane,
- therapy/exercise pools: one person per 50 sq ft,
- group exercise rooms: one person per 45 sq ft,
- fitness floors: one person per 65 sq ft, and

- walking/jogging tracks: one person per 25 linear feet. (LaVoie, 2005)

An additional allowance of 25% to 45% of the above load should account for users waiting to participate and those finished with activity and using shower and dressing areas. The number of lockers provided should meet this predicted demand. For each locker space planned, a total of 7 sq ft to 15 sq ft should be allocated in the locker room area (LaVoie, 2005). In most instances, the size of the locker rooms for both men and women should be the same, and this is vital in educational institutions where Title IX is applicable.

Traffic Flow Considerations

Traffic flow in the locker room complex has two key considerations: first, movement into and out of the locker room and, second, movement within the locker room. The locker room should be located within the facility in an area with direct contact to the activity spaces when possible. When both men's and women's facilities can be located in adjacent areas, the mechanical, janitorial, and special service areas can often be combined. The number and size of entrances and exits will be impacted by building codes, but typically the number of open entrances to the locker room facilities is minimized for security purposes. Main access corridors and doors should be large enough to handle heavy two-way traffic with patrons carrying bags and equipment. When possible, the primary access doors should be held in an open position with door stops or code-approved electromagnetic devices if required for fire suppression measures (LaVoie, 2005). According to the Interior Graphic Standards (2004), locker room entrance and exit doors should have vision barriers. Heavy-duty, moisture-resistant doors at locker room entrances and exits should be of sufficient size to handle the traffic flow and form natural vision barriers. Entrance and exit doors for the locker room area should be equipped with corrosion-resistant hardware.

In Figure 6.6, dimension A should be no less than 36 in., and dimension C should be no less than 42 in. Increases in both dimensions need to be based on the capacity of the locker rooms. Traffic breaks between benches should occur at least every 12 ft. ADA-accessible benches when required tend to be at least 42 in. long, from 20 in. to 24 in. deep, and from 17 in. to 19 in. high. These need to have back support or be affixed to a wall. These benches also need to have a clear floor space for a parallel approach to the end of the bench (Ramsey & Sleeper, 2008).

The movement of facility patrons within the locker room is another major consideration in planning the layout of a locker room. The location of key elements (lockers, showers, toilets, grooming stations, and special amenities) in relation to one another becomes critical to a smooth-operating locker room. The spaces for passage within the locker room, whether in open areas or in corridors, must allow for free and unencumbered movement. Additional consideration for persons with disabilities requires that all passageways be a minimum of 36 in. wide to provide full access (LaVoie, 2005).

The layout of the lockers themselves and their associated benches for changing is a great starting point in locker room traffic flow considerations. Areas for changing clothes should be located out of the main areas of traffic flow within the locker room. Therefore, many locker areas are designed with numerous alcoves to create separate dressing zones and to create additional space for lockers.

Points of access, such as doors or corridors to the locker room, must carefully consider sight lines. Anyone passing by the outside of the locker room must not have a direct view into any portion of the locker room. Planners should not consider a door alone as sufficient to provide privacy in a locker room setting, as high traffic into and out of the facility limits its effectiveness as a sight barrier. In many instances, locker room doors are maintained in an

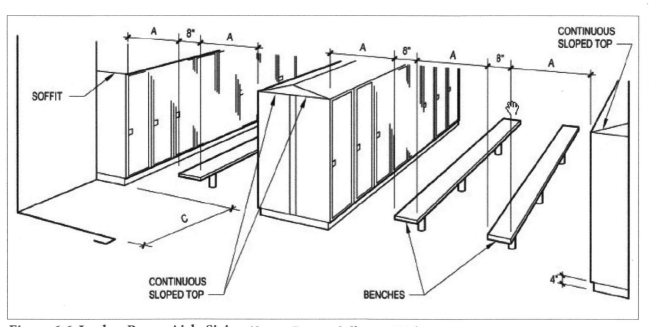

Figure 6.6. **Locker Room Aisle Sizing** (*Source:* Ramsey & Sleeper, 2011)

open position during regular business hours. Typically, a full or partial wall partition is included near all access and egress points within the locker room that will block the view of passersby from the outside.

Locker Room Amenities

Many upscale locker rooms are designed with special amenities to provide additional services to the facility users, such as saunas, steam rooms, whirlpools, or massage areas.

The sauna is typically a small facility designed to provide dry heat at high temperatures. This Finnish form of sweat bathing is used primarily to soothe and relax tired muscles. It has become a popular addition to many locker rooms. As such, the special design considerations for saunas include

- wood-lined walls, floors, and seats, as wood provides less heat conduction than tile or metal for the high temperatures (ranging from 150°F to 190°F);
- use of light woods such as spruce, western red cedar, hemlock, redwood, and aspen reduces sweat staining if combined with regular cleaning and required towel;
- 2 linear feet of bench per person with a typical minimum of 100 sq ft for a group sauna;
- a door that opens swinging out with wooden handles to prevent burns and a glass panel to allow for supervision;
- temperature controls maintained in a lock box or secure area; and
- a self-priming floor drain as the high heat can cause the trap to dry out, allowing sewer gases to enter. (LaVoie, 2005)

A steam room, sometimes referred to as a Turkish bath, is a small high-humidity heat facility. The steam room is typically at a much lower temperature than a sauna (110°F to 120°F) but at 100% humidity. The high humidity levels of the steam bath make these small facilities costly to properly build and maintain. Special considerations for steam baths include

- 2 to 2.2 linear feet of bench space per person or 12 sq ft per person with a steam generator with appropriate capacity for the room volume;
- the steam room interior ceiling sloping at 1:12 to a sidewall or space in the room where users will not be dripped upon by condensing droplets;
- walls, floors, and ceilings that have a totally waterproof membrane, as the high humidity can permeate grout, cement board, and moisture-resistant drywall;
- interior surfaces that are ceramic tile or stone set with thin-set mortar;
- fixtures (hinges, lights, frames, fasteners) that are corrosion resistant;

- doors (preferably glass) that swing out and into an area that will not be damaged by exposure to steam-laden air; and
- maintenance access to the steam generator that is accessible from a mixed-gender corridor so the frequent maintenance will not require closing of the locker room.

The whirlpool is a small communal body of water with a hot temperature (typically 100°F to 104°F) along with air and water jets to create a massage effect for the immersed bather. Roy Jacuzzi invented the whirlpool bath in the 1960s, and it has grown in popularity as a locker room feature. The addition of commercial-grade whirlpools to the locker room areas has become common in many health clubs and fitness centers. The free-standing fiberglass whirlpools designed for residential use are not recommended for application in the facility types included in this text. Considerations for adding a whirlpool to a locker room include

- approximately 10 sq ft to 15 sq ft per person is needed within the whirlpool for space planning;
- interior tub surfaces of tile or stainless steel are most desirable;
- exterior surfaces in the areas surrounding the whirlpool should be tile, stone, aluminum, plastic, or glass to reduce the corrosion from the chlorinated vapors and humidity;
- air-handling systems that will create a negative pressure to surrounding areas to prevent the spread of the corrosive vapors and odors to other areas of the facility are a necessity; and
- at least two sides of the whirlpool must be surrounded by nonslip deck space at least 4 ft wide. (LaVoie, 2005)

Postexercise massage has become a desired amenity at many clubs and spas. A dedicated space for massage directly within or adjacent to the locker room complex is desirable. The massage area should allow for total privacy, as the massage recipient will often only be draped with a towel or sheet. The room should be large enough to include a massage table and have sufficient space for the masseuse/masseur to move around all sides of the table. About 80 sq ft to 100 sq ft should be allocated for a massage area with one station (LaVoie, 2005). Rheostat-controlled lighting that may be adjusted or dimmed is desirable, along with adequate ventilation if aromatherapy is combined with the massage. Separate massage areas may be provided for each gender, but if only one massage area is to be included, it would be desirable to have an access door to the massage area from the men's and women's locker rooms with controls for the sight lines into each locker room.

In addition to these primary locker room amenities described above, many locker room designs may include other auxiliary spaces to meet specific user needs. For example, social lounge space within the locker room, attendant services such as towel service, laundry service or shoe shine, tanning beds or booths, facial rooms, herbal wrap rooms, loofah baths, and private dressing booths have been found within locker room facilities. The facility planning team should thoroughly consider the rationale for inclusion or exclusion of each locker room amenity.

Specialty Locker Rooms

Family locker rooms. The family locker room concept is a small locker room space that allows simultaneous access to both genders with special needs such as

- a mother with a young son too old to enter the women's locker room but too young to be unsupervised in the men's locker room;
- a father with a young daughter too old to enter the men's locker room but too young to be unsupervised in the women's locker room;
- an individual with a disability that requires the assistance of an opposite gender caregiver in the locker room setting; and
- an individual with special privacy needs due to a surgical scar, deformity, or personal preference. (LaVoie, 2005)

Family locker rooms have the same basic components as traditional locker rooms, but their design has changed rapidly over the past 20 years (Bynum, 2007). The family locker room basic elements include private changing rooms, lockers, sinks, toilets, and showers. They may be as simple as a single room with all these elements or more complex with multiple private changing and shower, toilet, and lavatory areas with common coed locker storage areas or other combinations of these components.

Other considerations and features for the family locker room are

- inclusion of ADA-compliant toilet, shower, sink, and locker;
- addition of toddler-sized toilets and a grooming station with a lower sink/counter height;
- inclusion of a diaper-changing station or area; and
- direct access to aquatic attractions within the facility.

The growing popularity of the family locker room concept even has some designers and architects pushing for facilities with a single coed-only locker room. These types of facilities have common locker areas with multiple private shower and changing areas and gender-separate restrooms (Bynum, 2007). In many respects, it is essentially an oversized family locker room. A typical family locker room design is displayed in Figure 6.7.

Staff locker rooms. Those involved in teaching or coaching in the physical activity setting also have need for locker room facilities. In some instances, staff locker storage, shower, toilet, and lavatory/grooming station can be included as a component of the office area, and in other instances, a small separate locker room facility may be needed. In the commercial fitness club setting, staff changing within the main locker rooms can actually displace pay-

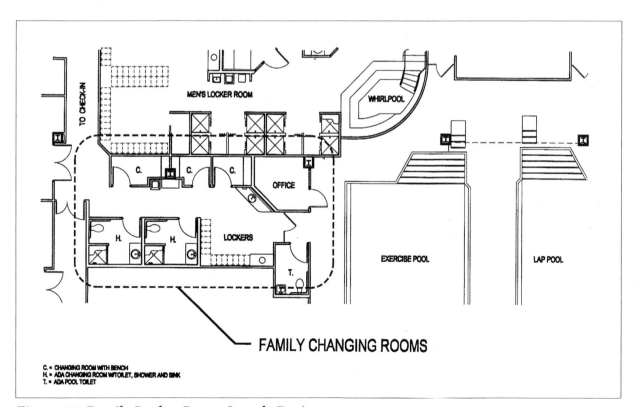

Figure 6.7. **Family Locker Room Sample Design** (*Source:* Ramsey & Sleeper, 2011)

ing customers. The additional cost for separate staff locker room facilities must receive due consideration in the planning process. One effective solution to the staff locker room is the creation of a coed staff lounge (with kitchenette, basic furnishings, and storage lockers) that has a pair of private adjacent unisex changing, shower, and restroom compartments.

Officials locker rooms. Venues designed to host athletic competitions should include a space for contest officials. Game officials will need a secure area in close proximity to the playing court or field. The officials locker room should include enough space to accommodate the entire officiating crew, so the number of officials required for the sports hosted and the number of contests that may be held in a given session should be considered. This facility should provide a space for changing from street clothes to officials' uniforms, storage for clothing and personal items, showers, toilets, and a grooming area with a lavatory. Ideally this space should also allow space for the officials to sit prior to the contest and a secure place to rest during game intermissions. This area should also be capable of being secured from coaches, players, or fans. Additionally, the growing trend of mixed-gender officiating crews may require an additional space for official changing, showering, and grooming.

Express locker rooms. According to an informal fitness center study, from 1993 to 2011, the number of peak-hour users arriving to the facility already dressed and ready to workout rose 60% (International Health, Recreation, and Sport Association, 2012). This growing trend of reduced locker room use in both fitness centers and campus recreation facilities has led to the development of the express locker room. Patrons of express lockers are not in need of shower and changing facilities, but only need a place to store personal belongings (keys, wallet, cell phone) and perhaps a coat and a change of shoes. Express lockers are typically coed and include small lockers (half, quarter-sized, or smaller) for storage and benches. These express lockers are often located outside of the main locker room to reduce the main locker room traffic and increase the privacy for the patrons. A good express locker room location will often be along or close to a traffic pattern between main points of access and primary activity areas. In some settings, the express lockers may be coin-key or swipe card-key operated to provide additional revenue and to avoid the need for users to provide locks.

Offices

The design of commercial office space serves to function appropriately, extend human capacity, and enhance productivity. Office space also serves as an aesthetic image of the company's mission (Interior Graphic Standards, 2004). Offices, regardless of type, must be functional; oth-

erwise, the spaces will not operate as required. It is important to understand how people work so spaces can be designed to meet those operational needs. Table 6.1 identifies a number of key considerations and standards related to office space development. It is also important to consider ergonomics. It is always best to avoid situations that could result in time off for on-the-job injuries and costly claims.

The age of the workforce will impact the habits of those workers. It will also impact the quality of the workplace expectations. Understanding who will most likely work within organizations should also play a part in how the spaces are designed and furnished. Generational trends and their impact on office structure are detailed in Table 6.2.

Interaction and autonomy are the two key factors that must be considered together when understanding an organization's work processes. Space plans have a powerful effect on work processes. Performance is enhanced when space layouts support levels of interaction and autonomy (Interior Graphic Standards, 2004). Figure 6.8 depicts four workspace layout options with the implications of the design related to the workers and tasks.

Back Office vs. Front Office

In sport and recreation facilities, it is not uncommon to have front- and back-office arrangements. Front offices may be used for security or for sales operations. These front-office operations are not to be confused with professional sports' front-office operation, which generally refers to the management of a team or league. Back-office operations tend to be those that are not intended to be as visual. These offices may be where the real work takes place. File storage, cash handling, IT operations, human resources, accounting, and other activities that are not intended to be visible may occur in these offices. Front offices may be more lavish and attractive than back offices.

Administrative and Support Staff

In all office situations, there will be a need for space for key administrative and support personnel. These people handle the day-to-day tasks of filing records, answering phones, greeting guests, copying, mail services, ordering supplies, and so forth. Careful planning must allow for adequate administrative and support space with sufficient space for required storage and for office equipment. These types of spaces may require more power and communication outlets than a typical office space. Photocopiers, fax machines, computers with modems, phones with multiple lines, and other equipment needs will stress the need for greater connectivity.

Sufficient space should be available for copiers. Today, most copiers are leased, and the space allowed for today's leased copier may not be sufficient for the copiers of tomorrow. Larger copy machines may also require a 220-V electrical supply in lieu of the standard 120-V supply. Fax

Table 6.1

Considerations for Development of Workstation Standards

Consideration	Standard
Job Classification or Function	Workstation user and job function: executive, manager, supervisor, professional, technical, or clerical
Work Surface Area	Number and size of work surfaces: primary, secondary, tertiary
Machine use	Amount, types, and sizes of electronic equipment: VDT, PC, printer
Workstation Area	Amount of spaces to be allocated for the individual task
Conference Requirements	Number of guest chairs required
Storage Requirements	Amount and type or unit size of the material to be stored and storage locations (under counter or overhead): letter or legal files, computer printouts, binders, bulk
Configuration	Configuration of work surfaces, primary orientation, and opening for the workstation
Wire Management	Type and location of wire management components: baseline wireway, beltline wireway, grommet locations, clips, or trays
Accessories	Type and number of accessories: tack surfaces, pencil drawers

machines typically operate with analog phone lines. This is important to note, as many offices are being wired for Voice Over Internet Protocol (VOIP). VOIP lines are digital and allow for much greater information and communication capacities.

Office Design Considerations

Offices require three basic but important utilities to function. The first is power, which is required in the right amount and location. The second is lighting. Lighting should be designed to be suitable for the task at hand. Tasks that involve great detail and precision require higher lumens to support that task. Last, a space must be adequately ventilated. People are more capable of reacting to poor power and lighting situations than to conditions of poor ventilation. Ventilation is the key to good indoor air quality and cannot be minimized.

People can be particular about their office requirements. Some people may insist on an outside window or

on being located away from the front door to avoid drafts or away from high-traffic areas to avoid unnecessary noise. It is always a good objective to give people what they want because, if they are happy, it may affect their productivity, but it may not always be possible to be so accommodating. Each building only has so many windows, separate temperature control, offices near the back door, and private office spaces. Situating people will always be a challenge. The best one can probably do is to situate people so the size, configuration, location, and furnishing reflect the contribution that those persons make.

All office space should be sized and furnished based on who will occupy the space and what that person does. High-level administration may require a large office to conduct important business. That important business may include hosting small- to medium-sized meetings. Figure 6.9 depicts a more spacious middle-management type of office that uses 225 sq ft, and Figure 6.10 depicts a much smaller office for a lower level worker who functions in 100

Table 6.2

Work Styles of Americans (LaVoie, 2005)

	Boomers	Gen X	Gen Y
Schooling style/work style	Work alone Structured Unstructured, unsupervised: play with others	Group projects Discussion Team sports for women Mothers worked Computer as a tool	Carefree Need it now Have to be stimulated Cannot amuse themselves Multitask
Thought process	Pen and paper	Personal digital assistant (PDA)	Computer
How they get information	Individual research	Internet	Internet, inquiry
What they do with information	"Power is knowledge"; can be knowledge hoarders	Share info across team and individuals	Team comes first; knowledge resides with the team
What they do if they do not like something	Protest, whine	Drop out, withdraw	Circumvent the rules
How they handle interruptions or noise	Close the door	Put on headset	Not bothered by interruptions—"just one more thing"

sq ft. It is certainly possible to exceed the size of the middle-management type office for a more senior executive, and it is also possible to have useable offices in as little as 64 sq ft. Important office dimensions are detailed in Figure 6.11.

Special consideration should be given to noise control. Offices where confidential information is discussed should be designed to minimize noise transfer. This can be achieved through many different methods. Walls can be insulated, double-paned windows with shades can be installed, ceilings can be insulated, and walls can extend to the underside of the above roof structure. Not all of these are necessary in the same wall; each method is a way to achieve low sound transmission. Controlling sound transmission is important not only for new construction. Existing walls and ceilings can be modified to easily achieve this goal.

Meeting Rooms

According to the Interior Graphic Standards (2011), there are multiple types of meeting, conference, and training (not athletic training) rooms. How rooms of this type are designed should reflect the activities that each room will support. In general, rooms should be designed and furnished to allow for maximum flexibility so the end user is not constrained in how to best use the room. Well-designed training rooms can enhance business operations in dynamic environments, increase workplace diversity, support technology advancements, and help organizations be more competitive. The room types are as follows:

- auditorium—large capacity with fixed seating for 150 or more,
- amphitheater—with built-in work surfaces,
- ballroom—a large capacity meeting room with the potential to serve food,
- boardroom—an upgraded version of a conference room with higher grade finishes and furnishings and seating capacity of 16 to 24,
- large conference room—typically greater than 1,500 sq ft in size and used for formal presentations requiring little audience participation,
- medium conference room—typically 1,000 sq ft to 1,500 sq ft in size and used for interactive group programs,
- small conference room—typically 300 sq ft to 1,000 sq ft in size and used for interactive group programs and small discussion groups,
- breakout room—small discussion area or informal meeting space,
- classroom/training room—varies in size but generally between 300 sq ft and 800 sq ft in size,
- computer training room—workstation configuration, and
- intensive strategy rooms—smaller specialty rooms with high technology requirements and computer capability.

Seating standards for these types of meeting rooms are summarized in Table 6.3.

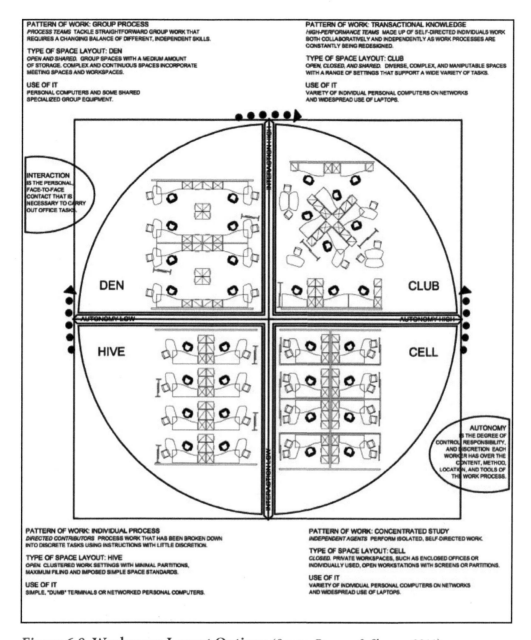

Figure 6.8. **Workspace Layout Options** (*Source:* Ramsey & Sleeper, 2011)

Key design issues that need to be considered when planning meeting rooms include
- adjacencies required,
- traffic flow and circulation,
- whether a lobby or reception area will be required,
- audio/video or other presentation requirements,
- lounge and breakout area requirements, and
- food service needs.

Storage Needs

Room usage, number of occupants, and furniture layout will determine the required room dimensions. Certain dimensions or clearances may be required for specific uses. Room accessories will add functionality. These include

- whiteboards,
- projection equipment,
- projection screens,
- hanging rails system,
- shelving,
- clocks,
- easels,
- lecterns,
- equipment cabinets, and
- serving counters.

Seating comfort for meetings of long duration is critical. Conference room seating types may differ depending on the type of room and function. A related or compatible

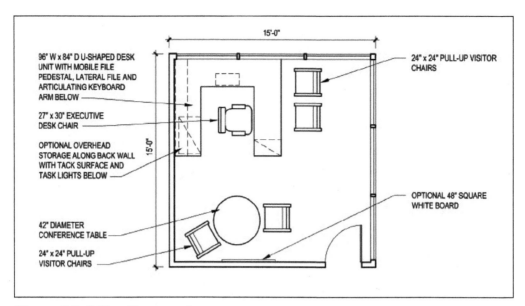

Figure 6.9. **Office Concept A** (*Source:* Ramsey & Sleeper, 2011)

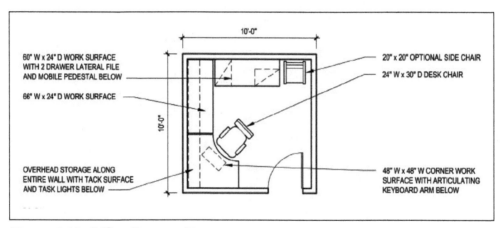

Figure 6.10. **Office Concept B** (*Source:* Ramsey & Sleeper, 2011)

series of seating will unify the image of the conference facility. Considerations when selecting seating for meetings and conferences include

- ergonomics,
- upholstered seat and back cushions,
- chair shape and adjustment features,
- lightweight chairs,
- five caster design, and
- upholstery matching the chair usage and room ambiance.

Meeting rooms often can be modified to function for video conferencing in addition to in-person meetings. Table 6.4 presents basic specifications and applications for video conferencing space.

Team Rooms

Within the athletic realm, team rooms often are multifunctional spaces that combine athletics and academics. Used as a lounge, a bonding place, a "second home," or even a kind of classroom, the team room should provide comfortable seating for individuals and groups, including cable television, a VCR and DVD player, study area with Internet access (often wireless), and storage for reference books and videotapes. Many times, the team room/lounge is used for smaller group meetings, and the locker room is used for larger group meetings.

Both the team room and locker room are key places to use branding, with the logo and team colors on finishes and objects and with appropriate storage and lighting for displays of photographs, awards, memorabilia, and inspirational signs and posters.

Today, there are few, if any, differences between women's and men's locker rooms and team rooms other than those required by a particular sport. The provision of a small private drying/changing space adjoining each shower stall in the women's locker room is becoming a more common amenity in men's facilities as well (Dahnert & Pack, 2007).

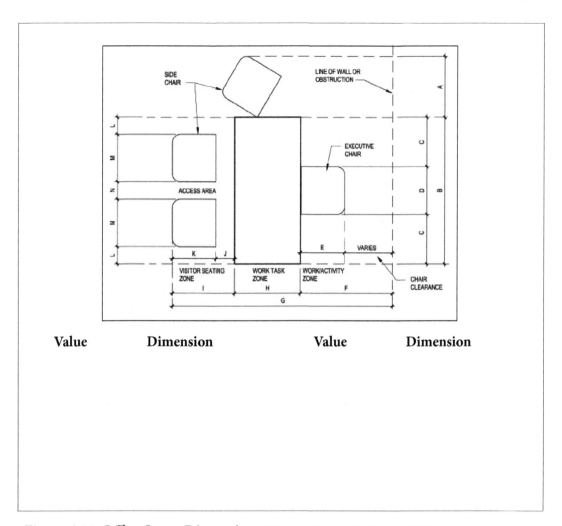

Value   Dimension   Value   Dimension

Figure 6.11. Office Space Dimensions (*Source:* Ramsey & Sleeper, 2011)

Table 6.3

Conference Room Seating Standards (Adapted from LaVoie, 2005)

	THEATER STYLE EXECUTIVE SETUP[1]	THEATER STYLE MAXIMUM SETUP[2]	CLASSROOM STYLE EXECUTIVE SETUP	MAXIMUM SETUP	HOLLOW SQUARE SETUP	U-SHAPED SETUP	CONFER-ENCE SETUP	BANQUET SETUP
Ballroom	14 (1.5)	11 (1.0)	22 (2.0)	18 (1.7)	N/A	N/A	N/A	14 (1.3)
Large Conference	16 (1.5)	13 (1.2)	24 (2.2)	20 (1.9)	40–45 (3.7–4.2)	50–55 (4.7–5.1)	N/A	N/A
Medium Conference	18 (1.7)	15 (1.4)	26(2.4)	22 (2.0)	34 (3.2)	42 (3.9)	40 (3.7)	N/A
Small Conference	20 (1.9)	15 (1.4)	30 (2.8)	24 (2.2)	32 (3.0)	38 (3.5)	35 (3.3)	N/A
Breakout Room	N/A	N/A	N/A	N/A	N/A	N/A	25 (2.3)	N/A
Boardroom	N/A	N/A	N/A	N/A	32 (3.0)	N/A	40 (3.7)	N/A
Amphitheater	N/A	N/A	25 (2.3)	N/A	N/A	N/A	N/A	N/A

Note. Figures represent optimum square feet (square meters) per person.
[1] Executive setup includes executive conference chairs and 24 in. to 30 in. (610 mm to 760 mm) wide tables. [2] Maximum setup includes stacking banquet chairs and 18 in. (457 mm) wide tables.

Table 6.4

Video Conference Room Sizes

Capacity	Room Size (ft [mm])	Applications
1–2	Workstation or desk	Informal meetings Interviews Research Development
2–3	9 x 12 (2,745 x 3,660)	General business meetings Interviews Progress meetings
3–5	11 x 16 (3,550 x 4,880)	General business meetings New business development Group sales meetings Product demonstrations
6–8	15 x 17 (4,570 x 5,180)	General business meetings Branch site meetings Capabilities demonstrations

Storage

The storage space necessary for supplies and equipment is often overlooked in the facility planning process. Examining the programs operating within a facility can determine the storage needs. It is important to gather input from administrators, teachers, managers, coaches, and others who will have to deal with the storage of equipment and supplies.

The arrangement of the storage space should also be considered. One option is to have one large centralized storage area. This type of storage is advantageous to large-scale programs that may have a full-time equipment manager and staff. With this arrangement, it may be easier to control the issuing, returning, and maintenance of equipment and supplies. One possible problem with creating a large centralized storage area is that it may become a target for renovation into a classroom, lab, office space, or other possible uses.

Storage space must be suited for the intended purpose. The storage requirements for boxed files are different than the requirements for large two-person kayaks. Sport and recreation activities may require multiple spaces with each space designed for a specific purpose. Figure 6.12 depicts a basic storage configuration that would be suitable for towels, uniforms, files, or other small- to medium-sized items that can be easily boxed or stacked. The need for storage should never be underestimated.

A second option is to have small, separate storage areas. These storage spaces should be located near the individual team or program activity spaces. An advantage of this system is that individual coaches or program leaders would control their own access to equipment. This arrangement may allow equipment to be stored closer to its point of use. The disadvantage to this system is that control of access to the multiple areas can be difficult to monitor.

In many instances, facilities do not have enough storage space or have outgrown their existing storage space. Using just-in-time purchasing and delivery is one option to reduce the amount of storage space required. For example, rather than ordering and receiving your facility cleaning supplies in bulk for the year, the items could be purchased in bulk but delivered on a monthly or bimonthly schedule. This would reduce the amount of storage space that would need to be dedicated to these types of supplies. This form of purchasing, however, does not work well with large equipment or nonconsumable items.

Regardless of whether the storage space is arranged in a large centralized space or in smaller point-of-use areas, the total amount of space available must be adequate for the proper storage equipment and supplies. Proper storage includes keeping equipment secure and protecting it from inappropriate use or theft. Proper storage is also necessary to reduce liability for the facility operators and owners. In fact, the American College of Sports Medicine's (ACSM) *Guidelines for Health/Fitness Facility Design and Construction* called for separate spaces from activity areas for operational storage (Tharrett, McInnis, & Peterson, 2007). In addition, proper storage includes adequate temperature and humidity controls for equipment that could be adversely impacted by environmental extremes. Using overhead roll-up doors or oversized double doors also can maximize use and access of storage space.

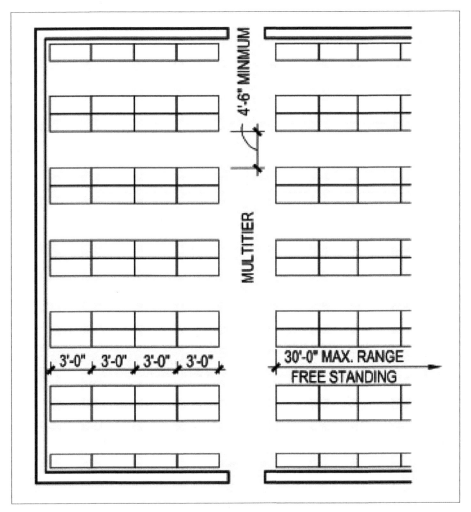

Figure 6.12. **Basic Storage Room Concept** (*Source:* Ramsey & Sleeper, 2011)

How much storage space for equipment is enough? This is a question with no simple answer, but a number of facility studies conducted over time have tried to approach this question in a systematic manner. Some of these studies have relied upon the opinions of expert panels, and others have relied upon data collection from selected facilities and input from facility administrators. Table 6.5 traces the development of these recommendations over a period spanning more than 70 years. These recommendations provide an excellent starting point for consideration of storage space needs. Once an appropriate guideline has been selected for the proper level and facility, then the recommendation for storage space can be tested with the actual and projected needs specific to the programs to be served by the storage.

Laundry

Onsite laundry services can be cost effective if well thought out. Before building an onsite laundry capacity, one should consider many questions:

- Who will operate the equipment?
- How much capacity is required?
- What special construction details will this operation require?
- Will residential equipment suffice, or will commercial equipment be required?

Determining the capacity requirement is an important issue, as it will also lead the operator to the conclusion of whether to purchase residential- or commercial-grade equipment. All washers and dryers are sized by the dry weight capacity of the unit. A washer may be sized to hold 25 lb of soiled towels and linens, but some items may be too bulky to meet the units' actual capacity. Dryer capacity is based on the wet weight of processed items. Because of this, it is typically recommended that the dryer capacity be sized to process about 1.5 times that of the washer(s).

In sizing equipment, one should estimate the desired level of laundry service, the amount of items that require processing, the amount of each item type, which items can be mixed together, and how many hours a day and how

Table 6.5

Equipment Storage Space Recommendations: A Selected Chronology

Date	Researcher(s)	Recommendation	Source & Level
1938	Evenden, Strayer, & Englehardt	400-sq ft apparatus storage room	Expert panel for collegiate facilities
1961	Sapora & Kenney	40% of total activity space dedicated to all ancillary areas including lockers, showers, drying areas, equipment storage, supply rooms, and offices	Research of Big Ten Conference
1967	National Facilities Conference	35% of activity area for all ancillary areas including lockers, showers, drying areas, equipment storage, supply rooms, and offices	Expert panel for collegiate facilities
1968	*College & University Facilities Guide*	250–330 sq ft of storage space for each exercise area	Expert panel for collegiate facilities
1969	Berryhill	35% of activity area space for all ancillary areas including lockers, showers, drying areas, equipment storage, supply rooms, and offices	Research of one high school with expert panel input
1988	Strand	20%–30% of all ancillary space within the facility	Research of Big Ten Conference universities
1989	Walker	20%–22% of all ancillary space within the facility	Research of 18 small colleges from two conferences
1997	Petersen	20%–22% of all ancillary space within the facility	Research of 40 high schools
2007	Petersen	18%–22% of all ancillary space within the facility	Research of 60 high schools

many days a week one plans to operate the laundry. Backup towels or other fabric items should be planned for so one does not run out at the wrong time. If it is preferred not to operate the laundry over weekends or during peak operating hours, then size the inventory accordingly.

Except for commercial operations, it is unlikely that an operation will actually weigh soiled items to achieve maximum water and power consumption efficiencies, but an operation should initially develop rules of thumb for each subsequent operator. Useful rules of thumb could include how many towels of a certain size approximate the load capacity of the washer. These useful rules of thumb

can then be posted for other operators to read and simplify the process.

Commercial equipment requires many construction details that residential units do not require. Heavy-duty washer/extractors spin at high g-forces and can vibrate so much that normal concrete would be pulverized in a short period of time. These high g-forces are necessary to remove water from the washed linens and towels to reduce the required drying time. Reinforced concrete floors with a high design strength can be constructed in new or existing buildings. These washer/extractors also release high volumes of water in short periods of time, so such equipment can easily overwhelm normal-sized wastewater piping. High-capacity trenches tied to a recessed floor drain allow these high volumes of water from rinse cycles to be released without causing backflows and flooding. The actual size of these trenches is based on the amount of water that the washing equipment will release in a given period of time. Commercial dryers can generate more heat than residential dryers and can thus be greater fire hazards. Commercial equipment requires greater air ventilation to offset the increased heat generation and internal humidity levels. In addition to being gas and electrically operated, commercial equipment may also operate using fuel oil and steam if such sources are available. For drying, commercial-grade gas-fired equipment can process about a third more product than steam and twice as much as electric.

Depending on geographic location and the general water quality, water softening may also be required. It may also be necessary to supply compressed air for certain commercial equipment.

Commercial equipment has the ability to process more loads at a higher capacity per hour than residential equipment. Residential equipment is typically not designed as heavy-duty as commercial units. Using any type of residential equipment may also void manufacturers' warranties, so this should always be checked before purchase.

Initial design should plan for maintenance in the laundry area, as significant amounts of lint and other debris can be generated. This can clog exhaust vent piping and waste drains. Removable catch baskets in drains and access hatches in exhaust vent piping should be included in the design. The number of turns in both types of piping should be minimized, and if possible, turns that approach 90° should be avoided. Equipment for service and maintenance should be easily accessible.

In addition to the laundry equipment, it is important to plan for other needs. These needs include areas for folding, cart storage, linen storage, chemical storage, bulletin boards, backup towels and linens, operating instructions, and emergency information. Sample laundry room designs are displayed in Figures 6.13 and 6.14.

There are great advantages to having an in-house laundry facility, but it will come at a high cost for space, for initial cost for equipment, for annual cost to operate, and to staff the equipment. Planners and administrators should carefully analyze their operations to determine whether making such a long-term investment is cost effective.

Janitorial and Maintenance

An effective area for an important duty such as cleaning is typically overlooked in most facilities. Ideally, janitors closets should be situated in a convenient location, be easily accessible, and sized to store all required items, including

- chemicals—some may require separation for safety purposes;
- tools;
- equipment—such as ladders, floor scrubbers, carpet extractors, backpack and upright vacuums, floor buffers or burnishers, and so forth;
- mobile equipment such as man lifts for high ceilings, carts, mobile trash bins;
- recycling bins and storage;
- supplies such as paper towels, toilet tissue, soap, toilet seat covers, and so forth; and
- counter space with electrical supply for battery charging.

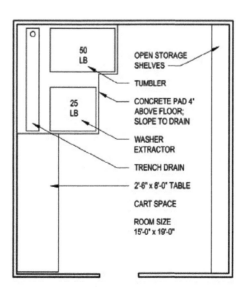

Figure 6.13. **Single Washer and Dryer Laundry Room Concept** (*Source:* Ramsey & Sleeper, 2011)

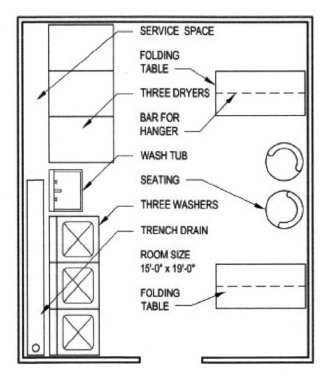

Figure 6.14. **Multiple Heavy-Duty Residential-Style Equipment Laundry Room Concept**
(*Source:* Ramsey & Sleeper, 2011)

Designing a space for work can substantially increase the desired end result in quality. Users of sport and recreation facilities expect a high level of cleanliness in their facilities. Janitorial and maintenance spaces are generally not good candidates for shared use.

Specialization in Ancillary Spaces

Effective space planning is essential for developing support facilities for athletics, recreation, or physical education. Optimal flow of participants between the activity or sport venues, locker rooms, offices, meeting rooms, and other support spaces is crucial. There is no universally accepted layout of these spaces; instead, the ancillary spaces must be laid out in response to the culture of the institution, the user needs, and the existing facility and funding constraints (Dahnert & Pack, 2007). The specialized use may also greatly impact design considerations whether dealing with athletics, physical education, health and fitness clubs, recreation facilities, or any combination of the uses within a given facility.

Athletic Facilities
At the collegiate level, the locker room and other ancillary spaces such as team meeting rooms and training rooms play a significant role in the recruiting process. The design of many athletic locker rooms resembles the high-scale health club locker room and more with plush carpeting featuring team logos, customized wooden lockers, video screen, sound systems, and other amenities. This is especially evident in the major revenue sports of football and basketball at the large college level. Smaller teams may use their locker room facility as a team meeting area, and larger sport programs will often use a separate meeting room (Dahnert & Pack, 2007). In the interscholastic and intercollegiate athletic realm, Title IX requires not only equitable athletic opportunities but also equitable locker space and shower room facilities. To maximize locker room multiuse and efficiency, many new locker rooms are designed with fewer differences for males and females so that they can be used interchangeably based upon the needs of the sport season or competition schedule.

Sport teams such as football, ice hockey, field hockey, basketball, and lacrosse have special locker room requirements. First, the locker sizes for these sports are typically large, stadium-style lockers to accommodate the necessary equipment. The flooring must also be selected to handle the rigors of the footwear requirements. Metal-tipped cleats and skate blades require special surfaces for the safety of the athletes, as well as for the durability of the facility (Cohen, 1998). In some instances, direct outside field access from the athletic locker room is more desirable than requiring athletes to move within halls or corridors to access the locker room.

Physical Education Facilities

Special considerations for school-based physical education focus primarily on the locker room. Physical education locker rooms often include a high traffic flow within the school day and require a high number of lockers or combinations of storage lockers and changing locker systems. Additionally, the school physical education locker room requires a high degree of supervision by the teachers. The layout of lockers and dressing areas and showers should avoid hidden areas where mischief could occur. Teacher offices should include easy access to both locker rooms and activity areas and ideally provide for visual supervision via windows or doors. An additional physical education need is ample-sized and secure storage areas for equipment that is quickly accessible from the activity spaces.

In many secondary-level schools, post-participation showering is not always mandated, and as such, many showers are underutilized and at times not used at all during a typical school day. Due to this factor, the planning team should carefully scrutinize the number of showers provided in the physical education locker room so as not to provide an excess number of showers if the space and funds might be better allocated for other uses.

The amount of space provided for the ancillary facilities should be carefully considered in the physical education setting. Factors such as the overall school enrollment, the number of required and elective physical education classes offered, the size of the teaching staff, the amount and types of equipment used, and the peak load of physical education students should be considered in the planning process. Several studies regarding space allocation have recommended ancillary space guidelines in relation to the percentage of total ancillary space (Strand, 1988; Walker, 1989; Petersen, 1997, 2007). A summary of these ancillary space allocations is provided in Table 6.6.

Table 6.6

Equipment Storage Space Recommendations: A selected chronology

Date	Researcher(s)	Recommendation	Source & Level
1938	Evenden, Strayer, & Englehardt	400-square-foot apparatus storage room	Expert panel for collegiate facilities
1961	Sapora & Kenney	40% of total activiity space dedicated to all ancillary areas including lockers, showers, drying areas, equipment storage, supply rooms, & offices	Research of Big 10 Conference
1967	National Facilities Conference	35% of activity area for all ancillary areas including lockers, showers, drying areas, equipment storage, supply rooms, & offices	Expert panel for collegiate facilities
1968	*College & University Facilities Guide*	250-330 square feet of storage space for each exercise area	Expert panel for collegiate facilities
1969	Berryhill	35% of activity area space for all ancillary areas including lockers, showers, drying areas, equipment storage, supply rooms, & offices	Research of 1 high school with expert panel input
1988	Strand	20-30% of all ancillary space within the facility	Research of Big 10 Conference Universities
1989	Walker	20-22% of all ancillary space within the facility	Research of 18 small colleges from two conferences
1997	Petersen	20-22% of all ancillary space within the facility	Research of 40 high schools
2007	Petersen	18-22% of all ancillary space within the facility	Research of 60 high schools

(Adapted from Walker & Seidler, 1993)

Fitness Clubs

For-profit health clubs, racquet clubs, and fitness centers must maintain a tremendous focus on the overall quality of their facilities in a competitive market. Providing the best activity spaces, ancillary spaces, and customer service in this industry is crucial. Many clubs look to upgrade and provide as many amenities as possible within the ancillary spaces. In some cases, multiple types of locker rooms may be constructed within a fitness club based upon services provided. One type is providing more basic services compared with a second executive or elite level providing maximal levels of amenities and services for a higher membership rate. Depending upon the clientele of the clubs, some facilities may also add an express locker room for those requiring minimal storage and service for the members' activities.

Administrative office space in the fitness setting forms a significant portion of ancillary space. This is due to the various professional staff members included in the fitness setting such as membership sales, fitness programming, management, accounting, human resources, and food/beverage services. In addition to these professional office spaces, a front desk check-in area for all members is required for both management and security purposes. The front desk area should separate the open public spaces from the membership-only area, provide for check-in and validation of membership credentials, control access to the facility, and convey information about programming and facility/service reservations.

The addition of child care ancillary space has become a common element in the health club and fitness center. This space provides an area for the care of small children and allows patrons with children to use the facilities. These areas should include activity space for the children, diaper-changing stations, a restroom for supervised use, and an audio/video system.

Recreation Facilities

The most common recreation facility applications are campus recreation centers in the collegiate setting and community recreation centers in the municipal setting operated in a not-for-profit manner by a city or by a group such as the YMCA/YWCA or a similar organization. The recreation center ancillary space needs are similar in many ways to the for-profit fitness centers and health clubs. However, the level of finishes and amenities provided in most recreation facilities are not as high compared to typical private clubs. Access control within recreation facilities remains important and can be accomplished via a front desk check-in area. The number of lockers typically required can be determined by a ratio of one full-sized day use locker for every 10 members in most recreation and fitness settings (LaVoie, 2005).

Multipurpose Facilities

In many instances, a sport, recreation, or physical activity facility is developed with multiple uses, and when this is the case, the support space design must accommodate the needs of multipurpose use. For example, a high school facility may be used for physical education during the school day, for athletic team use in the after-school hours, and for community recreation use in the before-school hours. These diverse user groups may require different or additional support areas. The locker room needs for a physical education class of 40 students may be far different from the football team of 60 athletes. With proper scheduling, activity space (gyms, courts, fields, etc.) use may not overlap, but often additional support spaces are required in multipurpose facilities. There may be economic advantages to these multipurpose facilities: the facilities are in use for a greater period of time each day and the activity spaces are not duplicated. However, in any multipurpose facility, conflicts for space and time are inevitable. The two areas most common for multipurpose use are secondary-level schools and colleges and universities. To best plan the ancillary spaces for a multipurpose facility, the needs of each user group constituency must be represented in the facility planning, curriculum planning, and scheduling processes. Then the full complement of needed ancillary spaces can be determined before the construction process begins.

7 Graphics and Signage

Michael G. Hypes, *Morehead State University*
Julie Ann Hypes, *Morehead State University*
Mark Cryan, *Elon University*

Signs and signage have been a part of facilities for years. Until recently, signage, or environmental graphics, had been relegated to a backseat in terms of facility planning. Today's large and complex facilities, great numbers of sports facility users, guidelines developed through the Americans With Disabilities Act (ADA) and Occupational Safety and Health Administration (OSHA), and a litigation-oriented society are moving signage to the forefront when planning a new facility. Increasing use of computer technology, the use of electronic signs, and architectural signage will be the basic areas to rapidly develop in the near future.

Revenue-producing signage, such as scoreboards, digital video boards, backlit panels, and rotational signs, is an additional signage category that is growing in prevalence at all sport and recreation levels. These types of signs have become an important design consideration in many settings and can generate revenue to apply toward building construction and operational expenses.

Planning for Signs and Graphics

Have you ever visited an arena, stadium, or convention center for the first time and found that the signs were too small, hard to read, lacking, or obstructed from view? People in that situation experience a high level of frustration, become lost, and eventually stop looking for their destination.

Clear, informative graphics and signs are essential for conveying directional, instructional, or general information to the public. This is especially true in arenas, stadiums, or convention centers that house a wide range of events and attract large crowds.

It has been suggested that when thinking through graphics and signs for a facility, the planners should consider the following key questions during the design phase:

- What will the sign be used for?
- How long will it be used?
- What image is the graphic or sign to depict?
- What is the target audience for the graphic or sign?
- What is the viewing distance for the graphic or sign and the length of time it will take for viewers to read it?
- Where will the graphic or sign be placed and how will it be installed?
- What is the budget for the graphic or sign project?
- Are permits required or restrictions imposed on the sign?
- What other graphics or signs does the facility need?
- When is the graphic or sign needed?

Importance of Signs

Signs are an essential part of a facility and should be an integral part of the planning process in a new facility. Signs have come a long way in the last decade. New materials, colors, and graphics have changed the signage world. Many architectural firms now refer to a signage system as the environmental graphics of a facility. All sports and recreation facilities include a wide variety of signs. It is important to identify facility entrances and to direct individuals to concourse levels and seating sections. Restrooms, concession areas, first aid stations, information centers, locker areas, security areas, and exits must be clearly designated. Information concerning parking area locations must be located near the exits. Traffic flow information must be imparted by external facility signage. The parking area, if large, will need to be sectioned off by effective signs. Elevator and room designation signs must have raised-letter markings for users with visual impairments. The centers of these signs should be placed 60 in. above the floor. Other facility signs should also have raised letters even though at this time this is not an ADA requirement (see Table 7.1).

Table 7.1

Guidelines for ADA Signage

- Pictograms must be placed on a background with a height of at least 6 in. Pictograms must have a text counterpart.
- Raised characters must be at a minimum of ⅝ in. and a maximum of 2 in.
- There are character proportions as well. Letters and numbers must have a ratio of width to height between 3:5 and 1:1 and a stroke width-to-height ratio between 1:5 and 1:10.
- Braille and raised characters have to be raised ⅟₃₂ in., and the font must be either uppercase sans serif or simple sans serif. The font must be accompanied with Braille Grade 2.
- There are requirements for the finish and contrast of the characters. The contrast must be at least 70%, and the colors of the background and characters must either be matte, eggshell, or some other nonglare finish.
- Signage must be mounted at least 60 in. above the floor to the center line of the sign.
- Signage must be mounted and installed on a wall that is adjacent to the door's latch side. If there is no space for that, then the signage needs to be installed on the nearest adjacent wall. Individuals must be able to approach the signage within 3 in. without any protrusions, such as the door swinging or any nearby objects.

Where diverse populations exist, signs must be designed in multiple languages. Using international graphics (or pictograms) can also help in designing signage for multiple languages.

Many sports facilities are large, sprawling, one- or two-floor facilities. If the facilities have been around for a number of years, there is a good chance that additions have enhanced them. Add-ons can create logistic nightmares, and signs become paramount to directing individuals through a facility. It is not uncommon to find sports facilities with interiors of more than 200,000 sq ft. Sports facilities are also among the most heavily used facilities on campuses and related sites. Large sports facilities, such as arenas and stadiums with large numbers of users, call for a well-planned signage system.

Accessible access

Types of Signs

The basic purpose of any sign is to impart information. This information varies with the type of sign used. Five categories of signs are identified for use in facilities:

- warning, danger, caution, and emergency signs;
- notice and standard operational signs;
- directional signs;
- rules and regulations signs; and
- sign graphics.

Even though signage is divided into five distinct categories, the groups overlap. A sign could fall into just one category or it might fall into two or three categories, depending on its purpose and the type of information it conveys.

When signage is developed for a facility or a specific area within the facility, special consideration should be given to the purpose of the signage and the eventual audience for the information. Numerous safety specialists have identified the following issues regarding the communication of hazardous conditions: comprehensibility, readability, and standard phrases.

Comprehensibility refers to the ability of the individual reading a sign to understand the information sufficiently to take the desired action. Comprehensibility is different from *readability* in that the latter is simply a measure of the grade level of the written information and the former is a measure of how well the receiver of the information understood it.

Standard phrases refers to the use of "signal words" in signage. Using the word *danger* indicates an imminently hazardous situation, which, if not avoided, may result in death or serious injury.

Directional signage

This signal word should be limited to the most extreme situations. *Warning* indicates a potentially hazardous situation, which, if not avoided, could result in death or serious injury. *Caution* indicates a potentially hazardous situation, which, if not avoided, may result in minor or moderate injury. It may also be used to alert against unsafe practices.

The population at large may not share the importance that professionals attach to signal words. Many organizations (e.g., American National Standards Institute, U.S. Military) have guidelines for determining what signal words are to be used with specific hazards, and these are usually unknown to the public. The arousal effects of signal words and accepted organizational guidelines need to be incorporated into the design of effective signage.

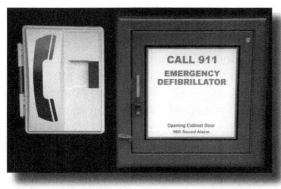

Emergency signage

Designing Signs

If possible, design your signs during the planning process of your building and its surroundings. If you are renovating or making additions to an existing facility, this is a prime time to plan for all new environmental graphics in your complex. Make your signs an aesthetically pleasing part of your facility.

Signs need to be simple and understandable, and they need to attract the facility user's attention. Placement, size, shape, repetitiveness, color, and graphics are important in designing simple, understandable signs that attract a user's attention.

Placement

Signs must attract the facility user's attention. A well-placed sign maximizes its effect on the facility user. Signs need to be placed in the appropriate area and at the appropriate height to have the greatest impact on the user. For instance, a sign reading "No Skateboards Allowed in the Building" will not make its point in the interior of the building. This sign needs to be placed at all building entrances so that a person sees it before he or she enters the building with a skateboard. On the other hand, the sign "No Food or Drink in the Weight Area" needs to be posted outside and inside the weight area.

It is also important to place signs in normal sight lines. Placing signs too high, too low, or off to the side makes them less visible. It is important to remember that sight lines vary according to the user's height. Signs for young users, 6 to 8 years of age, should be placed lower than signs for adults. Individuals in wheelchairs need signs placed in their sight lines.

Signs may be suspended or freestanding on walls, ceilings, floors, columns, or on doors. In some instances, a sign may be on two or more surfaces. It may be partially on a wall and continue onto an adjacent wall or floor. The effect of a sign on multiple surfaces is eye catching, thus attracting attention.

At times, signs must be repetitive within a facility. An example of repetitive signage is in an indoor racquet court battery. If there are eight courts, some signs will need to be repeated eight times, once at each court. An example of repetitive signage is, "Eye Guards Are Mandatory!"

Materials

Signs may be an integral part of the facility as a permanent part of the structure (painted on walls or other surfaces or tiles of different colors that make a sign) or they can be attached to surfaces by a frame or brackets. Architectural or permanent signs are recommended when possible. These signs not only impart information, but also are an aesthetically pleasing part of the structure of the facility. If architectural signage is used and planned for carefully, few signs will need to be added to the facility. It is paramount to plan in advance for successful architectural signage. If mistakes are made in the planning process, they become permanent mistakes, or at the least costly mistakes to overcome. Even with the greatest of planning of architectural signage, some signs will have to be nonpermanent and some signs will have to be late additions. As time and facility use change, signs need to be changed and updated; however, some architectural signage will never need to be changed. Architectural signs are usually made of "like" building material. For instance, a painted wall has a painted sign or an asphalt tile floor has different size, texture, or color inset tiles to form a sign. Signs may be made of wood, metal, tile, paper, glass, paint, plastic, or any combination of the aforementioned items. Signs may be electrified such as lighted signs, billboards, scoreboards, or "running" sign boards. Electrical signs are more expensive than nonelectrical signs. An electrified sign, on the other hand, stands out and attracts attention. Electrical signs must be in a secured location because they are easily broken and are expensive to repair. If electrical signs are to be used, you should plan carefully for electrical outlets or electrical hookups directly in relation to sign placement. Extension cords running from signs to an electrical power source are unaesthetic, unsafe, and unacceptable.

Shape, Color, Size, and Graphics

Signs do not have to be rectangular in shape. Rectangular signs afford maximum use of space if the signs contain only words. Other sign shapes have the ability to be eye catching and/or informational. Take the eight-sided red sign at the end of the street, attached to a metal post, located on the right-hand side of the street. This does not need to be read—the octagonal shape, location, and color indicate stop. Explicitly shaped signs for specific information can be used in facilities to impart information. For example, all pentagonal signs can indicate classrooms, all circular signs can indicate laboratories, and all diamond-shaped signs can indicate offices.

An X-shaped sign in facilities immediately signals *not* to do something ("No Diving," "Do Not Run") just by the shape of the sign itself. The idea of effective sign shapes follows a recent international trend toward standard pictorial signs. Facility signs now must take on and convey a universal message to many ethnic populations. A sign featuring graphics will not alienate a facility's foreign users as much as a sign in English might. Color, such as the red in stop signs, can also be an important aspect of signage design. All signs of one color can indicate storage and housekeeping areas. Color in signs can be used to attract the attention of facility users. Bright-colored signs on a bland wall surface, in most instances, attract attention. A colored sign will attract a user's attention better than a black and white sign. Incorporate color in your signage theme.

Signs vary in size. The size of a sign in itself is a method of drawing the attention of facility users. A small sign indicating exit is easily seen suspended from the ceiling or wall. Sometimes a large sign is needed to house important information and to draw the facility user's attention. "No Lifeguard on Duty—Swim at Your Own Risk" is effective as a large sign. Vary the size of your signs depending upon the information to be imparted, and make use of sign size to attract attention.

The size of a sign's images and print also is instrumental in how the information is relayed. Words and graphics that are too small make the reader work harder and can result in the sign being ignored. Just as some signs can be too wordy or hard to comprehend, too many signs posted in a small area also can create problems. An overabundance of signs may cause the reader to miss a certain sign that has been lumped together in the busy array of other signs. Separating and isolating signs is important to their overall effectiveness (Turner, 1994).

The content and message of a sign must be designed for the educational levels of the individuals using the facility. Content of a sign for a university will read differently than the content of the same sign for an elementary school. In all cases, it is important to keep signs as simple as possible. The simpler a sign is, the easier it is to read and understand its content, thus making the sign more effective.

The old adage that a picture or graphic is worth a thousand words is still accurate for sign design. Using a clown figure to enhance a "No Clowning" sign in a weight area attracts attention to the sign. A facility user's attention is drawn to attractive signs, and adding graphics to signs makes them more attractive. A little humor about a serious matter can help to impart important information to facility users.

Signage and the Three Groups It Serves

Though most signage will be directed at facility users, there are two other groups for whom signage is vital: facility employees and emergency personnel. The litigious society that we live in has placed an increased importance on proper and effective signage in facilities. Effective signage may prevent an injury from occurring or it may be important in defense during a trial. Think of effective signage as both a money saver and a stress saver when it comes to litigation.

Information contained in signage is important not only to the facility users but also to the facility staff. Signs help facility staff acclimate more quickly and more safely to their jobs. Good location, direction, and rules signs help new employees adapt more quickly to a new environment.

Hazardous materials are found in many facility laboratories and swimming pools. Staff must handle biohazardous waste, toxic chemicals and gases, and nuclear contaminants routinely. Signage is paramount in these areas. Signs should first indicate the hazard and second inform the employee how to work safely with the hazard. Containers for hazardous material and waste need effective signage in the form of visible labels. Signage should also be placed in break room and workroom areas to inform employees of various performance and safety requirements.

Emergency personnel are the second group of individuals for whom signage must be well planned. Signs must be planned so that emergency personnel can find their way easily in a complex facility to save lives or deter additional injuries to facility occupants. Emergency personnel should not have to wander around a building before they can complete their jobs. Clear and effective signage in laboratories and pools indicating specifically what hazardous materials were present when an injury occurred can save a life.

Signage Maintenance

Signs placed throughout the facility need to be maintained. If you have electrical signs, you will have to replace bulbs and other electronic components. Most of these signs can be maintained from the front; however, some electrical signs need to be maintained from the rear or from the top. If the electrical signs are small, they will be easy to remove and repair. If the electrical signs are large, heavy, and cumbersome, you need to plan for this in sign placement. A large rear-entry sign can be placed over a planned opening in a wall so that there is easy access for repair work to the rear of the sign without having to remove the sign.

Signs can break. Breakage of signs may be accidental or intentional. Signs in sports complexes take much abuse. Balls hit them; rackets and bats hit them. If possible, place signs out of abuse range. Placing signs higher and in areas away from projectiles and hitting devices will prolong sign life and reduce maintenance costs. Some signs must be placed in harm's way. Polycarbonate sheeting works best for signs that need to be encased or covered with a clear material. Be careful though; the glossy finish of the sign or its covering can create glare problems and take away from the effectiveness of the sign, as well as provide an unwelcome distraction.

Wire mesh (the kind that sometimes covers clocks in school gymnasiums) works as an effective cover on signs whose faces would not be sufficiently protected by plastic sheeting, such as signs that are in the path of balls and other flying objects. If a sign must be covered with a mesh cage, make sure it can still be seen well enough to convey its message (Turner, 1994).

Signs can also be defaced (Sawyer, 2009). By placing signs out of reach, you can avoid some defacing. Use materials in the construction and covering of signs that deter defacing. Polycarbonate sheeting and other slick surfaces will help keep sign defacing at a minimum.

Signs need to be cleaned on a regular basis. Fingerprints, smudges, dust, and other airborne particles need to be removed from signage as a regular routine. Electronic signs need special attention and regular cleaning to ensure that they function at an optimal level. Soiled signage of any type can curtail the amount of information imparted by the sign. Set up a regular cleaning schedule for signage.

Revenue-Producing Signage

Bill Veeck's "exploding scoreboard" at Comiskey Park in 1960 was the first time a scoreboard went beyond simply relaying information. It marked the beginning of stadium signage as part of the game experience. Over the ensuing decades, signage as entertainment has become a standard at virtually every major sporting event.

Add to this the desire of many companies to gain positive brand identification by buying advertising signage in stadiums and arenas (Bellamy, 1998; Hypes, 2009), the constant demand for revenue by facilities and teams, as well as advances in the technology of signage and the dropping prices of such systems (Dahlgren, 2000a; Hypes, 2009), and it is easy to understand the proliferation of venue signage. Electronic displays such as digital video boards have even made their way to the ranks of high school sports facilities, including football stadiums, basketball gymnasiums, and aquatic centers (Popke, 2012a).

Signage has grown in popularity because of the functions it serves: to inform, to entertain, and to promote, as well as to generate sponsorship revenue. Today's large new scoreboards and video boards provide fans a wealth of information. Out-of-town scores, pitch speed, instant replays, and player stats and biographical information are just a start. During breaks in the action, fans can enjoy entertainment such as highlight videos, movie clips, and upbeat music, to name a few. Facilities and their tenants can run television commercials on the big screen, use live shots of sponsored promotions, and run graphics promoting advertisers to generate revenue. Facility operators can even allow fans to take advantage of their mobile devices to post their own photos that can be displayed on the video board. The addition of large video screens also has been found to improve fan satisfaction with the game experience and to increase the likelihood fans will attend future games (Hypes, 2009; Moore, Pickett, & Grove, 1999).

Signage and video displays are also evident in many athletic, recreation, and fitness facilities. These can be as simple as video monitors in fitness centers displaying program information and sponsor messages or as complex as marquee signs promoting the fitness center itself, as well as its programs and sponsors.

The Trend to Digital

Technology has enhanced signage in all of the areas discussed above as well as made it possible to provide signage targeted to a specific market segment. No place is this more evident than in broadcasting. Virtual advertising has been used at sporting events in the United States since the 1990s. Due to restrictive regulations, this format has not been used frequently in a global environment (Sander & Altobelli, 2011).

Virtual advertising involves overlaying an advertisement into a space in the telecast, either over the top of existing ground signage or billboards or in a free space on the field of play or in the crowd (Turner & Cusumano, 2000). This advertising is seen by only the television audience and not the people within the stadium or arena.

Individualizing signage allows for differentiation among a variety of consumer groups at national and international levels. Exposure time and frequency can also be controlled. This type of signage can be an effective communication tool for advertisers, sponsors, and broadcasters of sporting events.

Although there is a variety of types of signage, there is a strong trend away from static or nonmoving signage toward digital signage such as video boards and ribbon boards. This trend has been fueled in part by advances in LED technology that has created clearer, brighter, and easier to see video screens (for more information on LED technology and terminology, see Table 7.2). Initially, digital signage is usually significantly more expensive. Digital signage also has a higher operating cost, such as computer equipment and support as well as staff to program or run the signage during events. There are also planning and design considerations such as locating computer equipment

Table 7.2

LED Technology and Terminology

LED technology has brought improved clarity and brightness to video boards, both indoors and outdoors. LED boards bring HD-level video to the sport setting. Some terminology that is important in understanding this technology is explained below.

LED
A light emitting diode (LED) is a tiny electronic semiconductor that converts electric energy into visible light. The chemical compound used within an LED determines its color, brightness, and power efficiency. Unlike incandescent lamps, LEDs have no filaments that can burn out or fail.

Pixel
Pixel is short for picture element. Pixels are points of light that illuminate together to form letters, words, graphics, animations, and video images. A pixel can be made up of a single LED, multiple LEDs of the same color, or multiple LEDs of different colors. A pixel is the smallest element of the electronic display system that can be individually controlled. It can be turned off or on at various brightness levels

Resolution
Resolution is the basic measurement of how much information a screen shows based on the total number of pixels within the display area and is a significant factor in determining image quality.

Module
An LED module is a combination of parts that forms the building blocks of LED video displays, message centers, and dynamic message signs.

Digit
A digit is a numeric symbol with seven segment bars. Each segment uses discrete LEDs to produce a value between 0 and 9. Scoreboards, timing systems, and price displays use digits to display information.

Viewing angles
LED displays are at their brightest when viewed "head-on" and slowly decrease in brightness as the viewing angle increases. The viewing angles of an LED display—both horizontal and vertical—are the angles at which the intensity has dropped 50% from the direct "head-on" brightness.

Viewing distances
Viewing distances are calculated based on the display type and the distance from the display. Each display will have a minimum and a maximum viewing distance that may vary based on application and intended use. For example, a large character will have a longer viewing distance and a small character will have a shorter viewing distance. Daktronics, a major manufacturer of video and scoreboards, uses 50 ft for every 1 in. of character distance as a general point of reference.

Note. From http://www.daktronics.com/ProductsServices/LED-Learning-Center/Pages/default.aspx

Electronic scoreboard
at Wake Forest

that operates the signage and running data cables to allow computer equipment to communicate with the scoreboard or video board.

Despite these additional costs, the ease of use and flexibility these signs provide outweigh the increased expense for many facility operators. Digital signage changes, so multiple sponsors can be sold the same advertising space. Because it is possible to use moving graphics and sound in some cases, digital signage attracts more attention than static signs, making it more valuable to advertisers and thereby generating more revenue for the facility operator or team (Steinbach, 2008a). Changing the images is also a simple, nearly instantaneous process with no hard cost, whereas changing static signage often requires significant production cost and delay. LED video boards typically use less power and last longer than other types (Dahlgren, 2000b; Hypes, 2009).

Types of Revenue-Producing Signage

Static signage. Some of the earliest revenue-producing signs were simply ads painted onto the wood or brick walls in the outfield of baseball stadiums, the dasher boards surrounding hockey rinks, or other available highly visible spaces at sporting venues. More recent versions of static signage might be printed on vinyl or metal and affixed in place. Many surfaces in sporting venues that once might have been wood or concrete are now covered with padding, such as outfield walls and gym walls behind the end-line of a basketball court. Many of these pads can serve as static signage by being "wrapped" with advertising copy.

On-court or in-ice graphics. This is another form of static signage that provides sponsor value and revenue for facilities and teams. A variety of sticker, stencil, and hand-painted options are available to display a facility name or sponsor name and logo directly on the activity surface.

Banners. Banners are another form of static signage that traditionally has been a way to display advertising signage on a temporary basis. Newer, more durable materials, such as windscreen, have made banner-type signage commonplace in sporting venues, often replacing painted signs or plastic or metal advertising signage. Facility designers can avoid costly, difficult retrofitting of static signage by considering likely sign locations and making allowance for attaching banners. Some banner-style graphics are now produced in adhesive form, allowing signage to be wrapped on concrete columns or affixed to flat concrete walls where no other type of signage can be attached. Floor and stair graphics can also add advertising inventory to otherwise unusable space in concourses and lobbies. Printed on what are essentially large stickers, this type of signage can be created in virtually any size and can display any graphic message, but safety is an important consideration. Floor graphics must be skidproof and must have smooth edges that stay flat to avoid creating a trip hazard. For all types of adhesive signage, care must be taken to ensure that the surfaces underneath are not damaged and that the adhesive can be easily and completely removed.

Examples of electronic and stationary revenue-producing signage at New Bridge Bank Park

Pole banners. Pole banners can be used for decorative or informative purposes. A facility manager can identify a parking lot or simply beautify the facility's grounds through use of these pole-mounted banners.

Sideline frames. This is another type of static signage. Common at soccer stadiums and events, sideline frames feature banner-type signs pulled taut on both sides of collapsible A-shaped aluminum frames. The safest option in this category is signage covering wedge-shaped pads rather than aluminum framing, but the collapsible aluminum frames can be broken down and stored or transported easily, as opposed to pad signs that are bulky and difficult to store or ship. These types of signs are not considered to be part of the facility itself, but allowing sufficient space on the sidelines to allow the display of this type of advertising without affecting player safety may be a worthwhile design consideration.

Menu boards. Another form of static signage that is not typically a part of initial facility design considerations is the use of menu boards. If included during a facility's planning process, menu boards can be backlit with a sponsored panel. They may also be a plastic board with manually changeable letters. Regardless of the type, when concessions facilities in venues are designed, allowances must be made for space to effectively hang such signage where it

is easy for patrons to see. If backlit or digital menu boards are desired, system elements such as electricity and data cables should be considered.

Backlit signs. Backlit signs are a style of static sign that is common in arena and stadium concourses, as well as within the seating bowl of such facilities. These signs, viewed as an improvement on nonlighted signage, are becoming less common as digital signage systems drop in price.

For facility names, including sponsors, and other signage requiring an upscale look, Computer Numerical Control (CNC) signs offer a three-dimensional element that can include separate letters cut to shape and mounted independently or a bronze plaque with raised lettering. In addition to exterior lettering, these types of signs can be affixed on an office wall behind a receptionist station or located to greet or direct visitors as they exit an elevator in a luxury box area. This is typically a higher cost type of signage, but it may be appropriate to some settings.

Scoreboards

The first generation of electronic stadium and arena scoreboards featured digits and message boards composed of incandescent light bulbs, and these are still common today in smaller venues and youth facilities. Simple youth scoreboards can provide basic information to fans and players and can also feature static ad panels or backlit panels. Many youth scoreboards are paid for directly by youth league sponsors such as soft drink makers in exchange for the advertising value.

More advanced scoreboards such as those found in major arenas and stadiums are now usually composed of multiple video boards that can be programmed to look and function like a traditional scoreboard but also have the capability of showing high-definition video and other graphics. Some of the newest facilities in the sport world boast the biggest, most versatile scoreboards ever produced. The Dallas Cowboys' new football stadium features a center-hung scoreboard made up of two video screens that measure roughly 159 ft long x 71 ft high facing the sidelines and two additional video screens measuring roughly 50 ft long x 28 ft high. With a total of just under 13,000 sq ft of screen space, this high-definition board, built by Mitsubishi, is used as a scoreboard and can also play video clips (Fried, 2010).

The additional capabilities of the newer LED-powered boards are attractive to many facility managers, and prices on that type of equipment have decreased in recent years. Despite these factors, the traditional-style scoreboard remains a less expensive option that is a good fit for many community and youth sport settings. In many instances, these boards have a more modern look with the white incandescent bulbs replaced by red LED lights.

Examples of electronic and stationary revenue-producing signage at New Bridge Bank Park

Trivision or Rotational Signage

An early version of changeable signage, the trivision sign, features the ability to display three different advertisers in the same location by simultaneously rotating a row of triangular bars that feature a part of the three different signs on each face. Although the copy or image that is displayed on each of the three faces cannot be changed like digital boards, the fact that the signage has periodic movement means that it will generally attract more visual attention than a simple flat static sign.

This category of signage also includes scrolling rotational signage that has also become common in basketball, where sponsor logos and messages rotate through the same space on a preset schedule. This type of sign is normally heavily padded due to its proximity to the playing surface, and its location must be accounted for in the planning process to provide adequate space and electricity.

Scrolling Message Boards

Any system that displays primarily text, often moving from right to left or top to bottom, is classified as a scrolling message board. Common as part of outdoor marquee signs or scoreboards, these signs can display information in a static format or move constantly or alternate between the two (Schaeffler, 2008).

Video Boards

Large video boards, once commonly referred to as Jumbotrons, have become increasingly commonplace in sports venues. These types of boards have been found to increase the enjoyment of the fans and increase their stated likelihood of attending future games. According to Moore et al. (1999) and Hypes (2009), these also enhance the recall of event sponsors.

One great advantage of video boards is the ability to display so many different types of information: live or recorded video, PowerPoint slides, still photos, computer-generated graphics, and animations. In fact, there is no limit to what can be displayed. The flexibility in how that information is displayed is limited only by the design of the signage system. Many modern signage systems allow for different displays in different sections of the board, also referred to as zones, regions, or tickers (Schaeffler, 2008).

Ribbon Signs or Fascia Ribbon Boards

A new variation on the simple video board, ribbon fascia or ribbon boards are a series of long, narrow video boards that can completely encircle a facility on the fascia or front facing of an arena or stadium's upper deck. Coordinated to function as one unit, ribbon boards have the capability of showing figures seeming to run around the

Example of large electronic media and revenue-producing signage at the Los Angeles Angels park

arena's upper deck or encircle the arena in moving, coordinated graphics that might promote a sponsor, display a player's face, or flash and pulse to heighten the atmosphere for pregame introductions.

Marquee Signs and Other Exterior Signage

Revenue-producing signage is not restricted to the interior of a facility. Many arenas, stadiums, civic center complexes, and other venues include exterior message boards or video screens that can be used to promote upcoming events at the venue and promote facility or event sponsors. These marquee-type signs range from a single-line message board to massive signs with multiple video boards.

Sign Placement

The type of sign is important to facility designers, managers, and advertisers, but the placement is another major factor in the value of the advertising provided. It is also a design consideration that can affect a variety of other elements. The placement and sight lines of certain seating sections may be affected by the placement of courtside or sideline signage. The position of camera locations and permanent signage installations should be carefully considered; better placement of signage can improve the advertising impact (Hypes, 2009; Pope & Voges, 1997) and thereby increase revenue. Stotlar and Johnson (1989) and Hypes

(2009) found that in Division I NCAA basketball venues, signage placement in high-profile areas where spectators are likely to look repeatedly during a contest, such as the scorer's table and the shot clock, was more likely to create recall of the advertisers after the game and increase the sale of products (Hypes, 2009; Stotlar & Johnson, 1989). The LPGA found at an LPGA golf event that over 95% of those surveyed were aware of advertising on the course, with greatest recall for signage near concession locations (Cuneen & Hannan, 1993; Hypes, 2009). Another study found that over 70% of fans surveyed were more inclined to support the businesses that they saw advertised at their school's basketball games (Hypes, 2009). Signage in sports venues can be an effective tool for sponsors, and the placement of that advertising can impact the effectiveness, and therefore the value and price, of that advertising.

Systems Impact

From a mechanical systems standpoint, the trend toward digital signage also means that each signage placement will likely need a source of electrical power and possibly data cables to control the board. Although wireless data transmission has become common, and avoids the cost and trouble of running a data cable, a "hard-wired" connection is generally considered to be more reliable and resistant to outside interference or other technical problems (Steinbach, 2008a).

Miscellaneous Considerations

Signage cost will vary with materials, size, number of signs, and whether the sign is electrical. It is suggested to figure signage cost as a part of the facility construction cost. In some cases, parts of construction costs are bid separately and signage may be bid after the facility is built. This is not recommended. Repetitive signs will reduce costs because more of the same product reduces the cost per sign. The geographic location of the facility will also be a factor in signage cost. It is suggested to purchase high-quality products even though initially these products may be more costly than low-quality products. Over the lifetime of facility signage, quality products cost less.

The geographic location of the sports complex will dictate which and how many languages will be used in signs. Locations of multiple ethnic populations will dictate signage languages. Signs can be affixed to surfaces either permanently or semipermanently. The method of affixing will depend on the philosophy of the design and use of the facility. It will also depend on the longevity of the signage. "Exit" signs, for example, are permanent, whereas rules and regulations signs may change over time. Signs may be attached flat onto a surface or they may extend out perpendicularly or horizontally from a surface.

Protruding signs are sometimes needed for visibility and code adherence. One problem with protruding signs is that they are more susceptible to breakage than flush-mounted signs. Keep in mind that the size and shape of some signs might be dictated by local, state, and federal regulations. Check local fire and building codes to be certain that a particular facility includes all the required signs. Additionally, check with state and national offices for signage needed to meet ADA and OSHA requirements.

In some instances, a one-sided, flush-mounted sign is not sufficient. Signs suspended from the ceiling may impart information on two, three, or four sides. Protruding signs usually give information on two or three sides. As signage is designed, always consider using signs with multiple sides. Some signs will need to be freestanding to be moved from one area to another area of the facility. An example of a free-standing sign is "Caution: Wet Floor." Freestanding signs can take any shape or form; however, the most common is a two-sided pyramid shape.

Sponsorship in sports complexes is common. Sharing a sign with a sponsor is common in athletics (e.g., rolling sponsorship signs). Scoreboards and other signs are either purchased or rented by the sponsor so they can advertise on the sign. This concept of sponsorship can be used for signage in other areas—not just for athletics. Sponsorship or sharing of signage is an important concept and should be studied carefully for all signage in a facility. In any case, both sign sponsors and sports complex directors can obtain mutual benefits by this partnership (Sawyer, 2009; Turner, 1994).

A constantly evolving area in signage design is the use of art graphics in a sports complex. These art graphics or permanently painted or inset materials are designed as integral parts of the facility. Various images can be placed on surfaces in the form of sports art, murals, or basic signage.

These images are color coordinated with the color scheme of the facility. The images can bring life, motion, brightness, and attractiveness to an otherwise plain and dull facility. Currently, there are a number of companies that do art graphic work for sports complexes. Computer imagery is now enhancing the appearance of sports art, graphics, and murals. It is clear the future will bring more dynamic graphics to public assembly facilities.

8 Indoor and Outdoor Surfaces

Hal Walker, *Elon University*

Tony Weaver, *Elon University*

Introduction

Although discussions about indoor surface materials seldom elicit excitement, interest, or enthusiasm among sport, recreation, or facility consumers or operators, choices made in the facility planning and construction process are integral to "facility success" from any perspective. All facets of facility appearance, utility, maintenance, cost, safety, and functionality are impacted by the nature of surfaces in a given facility. Three main categories of indoor surfacing include floors, walls, and ceilings. These surfaces have far-reaching and profound effects on numerous aspects of facility use and care. This chapter will provide useful information to assist in the process of outlining the types of materials available for these surfaces, along with advantages and disadvantages based on use in specific areas. The importance of planning in the selection of surface materials, along with a consideration of individual needs, cost, maintenance, safety, acoustics, and aesthetics, will be addressed in this chapter.

Indoor facility surfaces are generally divided into three distinct areas: service/ancillary areas, the main floor, and office/administrative areas. Planning for and selecting appropriate indoor surface materials, along with proper installation and maintenance over the facility life span, can profoundly impact facility use and costs. Making informed surface choices allows for optimal facility use, enhanced user satisfaction, and reduced incidence of injuries. However, surface options provide a vast and confusing array of choices, with numerous companies touting state-of-the-art textures, materials, colors, and performance characteristics. Yet, of the hundreds of products currently offered on the market, few surfaces are ideal for all activities a typical facility offers. This leads to countless errors in the decision-making process, as it is rare that facility planning takes place with equal participation among all players impacted by this process: owner/funding source, facility manager, maintenance staff, and the end users. There is no "perfect" surface, as the needs and desires of each group can vary extensively. However, communication is critical to selecting a facility surface that effectively meets the demands of the various planning constituents. Available budget, expected activity offerings, life expectancy, performance standards, maintenance costs, risk management, foundation, and climate impact are only a few of the factors that must be considered when making informed facility surface choices. These choices are now impacted by demands for use of green materials, making surface choices extremely complex.

Selection of Indoor Surface Materials

Indoor surface materials must be chosen carefully considering the nature of the facility and the activities that are planned. As mentioned above, the primary surfaces addressed in this section are floors, walls, and ceilings. "When viewed as an essential piece of equipment in a sports facility, the sports floor is the point where the athlete and the activity merge" (Cooper, 2004, p. 4). The following text will outline the types of materials available for these surfaces, their characteristics, and factors to consider when going through the planning and decision-making process.

Generally speaking, the planned activity in a given area should dictate the type of flooring surface used. However, many, if not all, surfaces are used for more than a single purpose. There are three distinct areas of consideration in facilities currently being built. The first of these areas is the service/ancillary areas such as locker rooms, shower rooms, and bathrooms. These areas require surfaces that account for heavy moisture content and "slip and fall" concerns. The second area is the main arena or activity center of the facility. This area tends to encompass the majority of time spent on the decision-making process; however, each area should warrant considerable thought and planning. These central activity areas typically require either a hardwood floor or a resilient synthetic material. Offices, administrative areas, and classrooms account for the third facility location (Flynn, 1993; Sawyer, 2009). Special areas require different materials, layouts, and treatments. For example, basketball courts should be of a nonslip nature, whereas a dance area should have a finished treatment that allows individuals to slide across the floor (Flynn, 1993; Sawyer, 2009). Safety, hardness, absorption, resilience, and lateral foot support are critical in the selection of surfaces for dance floors (http://www.stagestep.com).

Durability, flexibility, and cost are three considerations that have caused synthetic floors to challenge traditional hardwood flooring. Synthetic surfaces take the form of grass or nongrass surfaces. The two most popular synthetic surfacing materials are polyvinyl chlorides (PVCs) and polyurethane. Polyurethane is either poured in place or produced in prefabricated sheets that are adhered on-site, and PVCs are typically prefabricated. The general perception is that polyurethane possesses most of the desirable characteristics sought in a multipurpose facility surface (Flynn, 1993; Popke, 2001; Sawyer, 2009).

Multipurpose approaches are common for many facilities as a variety of activities take place on the same court. Multipurpose courts often "include hardwood, synthetic sheet goods, poured urethane products, and suspended interlocking plastic tiles" (Popke, 2001, p. 47). No surface meets the specific needs of each activity; however, finding the right surface that meets a majority of the user needs is the goal of most facility managers (Kollie, 2004).

There are countless types of wooden floors and many floor manufacturers, and the costs can vary dramatically (Dahlgren, 2000; Sawyer, 2009). Costs also vary extensively among other surface alternatives, such as synthetics and carpets. Varying costs often depend on the materials used, the thickness of the surface selected, and the condition of the existing surface. Thicker synthetic surfaces, for example, although they may absorb more shock and offer greater resilience, are generally more expensive (Flynn, 1993; Sawyer, 2009). Once again, the planned use should be the central factor directing all facility surface decisions.

In the past, the third area—administrative offices and classrooms—has been satisfactorily covered with some type of tile that may include vinyl, asphalt, rubber, or linoleum. Many believe carpet should be considered in some of these spaces. Hard maple floors are generally the most expensive when looking at initial installation; however, over a long period of time, these flooring options become more than competitive when compared with most synthetic surfaces (Neuman, 2003). Unfortunately, many decisions are made based on available finances during initial facility construction rather than the best and most economical surface for

the long term. The cheapest flooring surface option is generally viewed as indoor–outdoor carpeting (Flynn, 1993; Sawyer, 2009).

Floors

Flooring choices are influenced by many factors including cost, maintenance, performance features, aesthetics, and longevity. According to Kroll (2002), flooring choices should be based on "a facility's design, function, and budget." With ever-advancing technology and a variety of factors that contribute to flooring decisions, the large number of options only makes this decision more complicated (Piper, 2003; Steinbach, 2002b). According to Piper (2000), flooring choices are usually made by individuals responsible for design and construction aspects of a project, rather than those who ensure that the surface meets the needs of the end users. Maintenance and operational costs, although commonly the largest facility expense, are often overlooked by concerns of initial financial cost (Piper, 2003, 2000).

Understandably, flooring choices are often made with financial rather than practical decisions. Floors with damaged or worn surfaces are often repaired rather than being torn out and having a new floor installed. Cost management factors often force facility managers "to take the low bid or a Band-Aid approach" to facility flooring repairs and updates (Popke, 2007, p. 57). Carefully consider this decision, as properly installed and maintained floors can have a healthy life expectancy, influencing the real cost of flooring alternatives.

Before factors related to flooring choices are analyzed, various issues need to be considered. According to Viklund (1995) and Sawyer (2009), sport flooring surfaces are categorized as *point-elastic* or *area-elastic*. Point-elastic surfaces maintain impact effects at the immediate point of contact on the floor, with the ball, object, or individual. Area-elastic surfaces allow for dispersion of impact, where a bouncing object or an individual jumping can be felt approximately 20 in. around the point of impact.

Minnée (2012) presented an additional concept known as a *combi-elastic* flooring, which is described by "an area-elastic floor with a point-elastic top layer." This concept describes a point force causing a localized deflection as well as a deflection over a broader space. *Hardness* is another term that describes the nature of a flooring surface and its ability to react to surface contact. The term *hardness* is defined readily in the fields of mineralogy, metallurgy, and engineering. In mineralogy, hardness is defined as the ability of the surface to resist scratching, with a softer surface obviously scratching more easily. This is measured by the Mohs scale, named after Friedrich Mohs, a German mineralogist. In metallurgy and engineering, hardness is determined by pressing a hard material on a given surface,

Point-Elastic Floor

Area-Elastic Floor

Combi-Elastic Floor

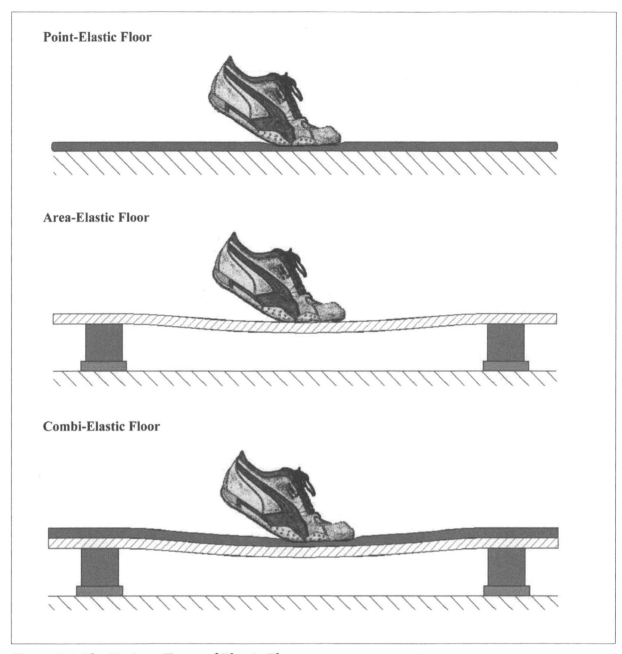

Figure 8.1. **The Various Types of Elastic Floors** (*Source:* www.sportsbuilders.org)

and the size of the indentation made is measured to report the "hardness" of a substance. This is called the Brinel test, named after Swedish engineer Johann Brinel (Williams, 2005, p. 9).

Another internationally recognized standard for sport flooring surfaces is the Deutsches Institut für Normans (DIN). This standard was developed by a testing lab in Germany, establishing minimum standards for flooring (Bynum, 2004a; Cohen, 1998; Kollie, 2004; Sawyer, 2009). "The DIN standard was embraced by manufacturers of wood athletic floors and quickly became the industry-wide benchmark against which all indoor sports floors would

be—and still are—judged" (Bynum, 2004, p. 86). DIN standards are available for minimum levels of shock absorption, ball bounce, deflection, surface friction, and rolling load. These standards suggest a floor must meet the following standards: (a) shock absorption—flooring needs to absorb at least 53% of an object's impact; (b) ball bounce—balls must maintain 90% of their bounce if on concrete; (c) deflection—the point of impact must be a minimum of 3/32 in., and 20 in. from the point of floor impact, the floor must measure 15% or less than the original point of impact; (d) surface friction—these standards vary depending on the nature of the activity; and (e) rolling load—floors need to withstand 367.7 lb of weight (Cohen, 1998). A complete listing of DIN requirements (1991) and the differences between DIN Standard (1991) and Pre-Standard (2001) for area-elastic floors are shown in Tables 8.1 and 8.2 (Bynum, 2004a, p. 88)

European Norm Standards

A more recent standard for indoor sports flooring was released by the European Union in 2006. This new standard is similar to DIN and is now commonly used in North America, as reported by the American Society for Testing and Materials. DIN criteria has provided the benchmark for performance in Europe and North America for more than 20 years. European norm (EN) standards are reported as providing a wider spectrum of performance criteria with many of the familiar DIN criteria). Five factors resulted in this change:

- The creation of EN was multilateral. The DIN measurement was specific to Germany, and the new standard was developed among a more diverse group of European Union members.

- Because DIN was developed for one market, the EN standards represent a wider range of performance values and classifications.

- The EN standard is deemed more consistent by using the same test and evaluation method for all products. The DIN standard uses two versions of testing that provide varied results.

- The EN is now viewed as the "living" standard, and all future research development will focus on improving upon this method.

- The EN standard allows for improvement at all cost levels. Since DIN was created with a single pass–fail approach, it tends to be applied to high-end, high-performance flooring systems only. The new EN standards "provide for a wide range of performance values and classifications" ("Why Switching from 'DIN' to 'EN' Makes Sense in North America," 2006, p. 1).

The EN results in flooring systems being put into various classes to specify the needs and performance expectations of various sport markets. These new standards "allow

Table 8.1

DIN 18032-2 (1991) Requirements

	Area-Elastic	Point-Elastic	Combination
Force Reduction (min.)	53%	51%	58%
Ball Rebound (min.)	90%	90%	90%
Vertical Deflection	Minimum 2.3 mm	Minimum 3.0 mm	3.0-5.0 mm
Area Indentation (max.)	15%	—	5%
Direction I	No limit	No limit	No limit
Direction II	No limit	No limit	No limit
Rolling Load	1,500 N	1,000 N	1,500 N
Slip Resistance	0.5-0.7 mm	0.5-0.7 mm	0.5-0.7 mm

(N = 1 Newton, or the amount of force that causes an object with a mass of 1 kg to accelerate at 1 m/s.)

Table 8.2

Differences Between DIN 18032-2 Standard (1991) and 18032-2 Pre-Standard (2001), Area-Elastic Floors

Criteria	DIN 18032-2 Standard (1991)	DIN 18032-2 Pre-Standard (2001)
Vertical Deflection		
Average (Each Point)	No limit	Minimum 2.3 mm
Area Indentation		
Average (Each Point)	No limit	Maximum 15%
Direction I	No limit	Maximum of 20%
Direction II	No limit	Maximum of 20%
Direction III	Not measured	Maximum of 20%
Direction IV	Not measured	Maximum of 20%
Force Reduction		
Average (Each Point)	No limit	Minimum 53%
Ball Rebound		
Average (Each Point)	No limit	Minimum 90%
Slip Resistance	0.5-0.7 mm	0.4-0.6 mm

specific floors, such as basketball and volleyball courts, to be designed with performance criteria that are more suitable for their intended use (Action Floor Systems, 2012).

Table 8.3

Sports Flooring Safety Standards Released by ASTM

Category	Force Reduction Range	Ball Rebound
1	10%–21%	> 90%
2	22%–33%	> 90%
3	34%–45%	> 90%
4	46%–57%	> 90%
5	> 58%	> 90%

Note. From "New Sports Flooring Safety Standards Released by ASTM for North America," by Tarkett Sports North America, 2012. Retrieved from http://www.tarkettsportsindoor.com/news/new-north-american-sports-flooring-safety-standards-released-by-astm.

Viklund (1995) and Sawyer (2009) discussed the concept of *resilience* when analyzing performance characteristics of various flooring options. Resilience is the shock-absorption ability of a floor based on the amount of force applied to the surface area. For comparison, concrete is a base value with no resiliency (0%). Point-elastic surfaces (synthetics) have a low absorption level (10% to 50%), with most in the 25% to 35% range. Resilience is influenced by both the thickness and the hardness of the floor material, as well as the subflooring under the surface (Sawyer, 2009; Viklund, 1995). When carpet is considered as a surface choice, the quality of the underlay also has a significant impact on the carpet performance and the carpet life. According to Driscoll (2000), "the use of a quality underlay can prolong the life of a carpet from 50% to 75%" (p. 54).

Facility surface choices must also consider the influence of the subflooring material. Flooring characteristics on porous or "floating" surfaces will react differently than others placed on concrete. Flooring choices should be carefully considered based on the subflooring material that is present. The condition of this subflooring can also influence the cost of the project, as this surface may need special preparation for the chosen surface materials to be placed on top. According to Dahlgren (2000a), shock-absorption characteristics of wood floors may be more heavily influenced by the subflooring than the actual surface material itself.

Area-elastic floors also need to be evaluated based on activities planned for the space. *Area of deflection* must be considered with regard to the primary use of the facility surface. Area deflection is the amount of impact that is felt in the vicinity around the points of contact. With area-elastic flooring, it must be decided that the area of deflection will not adversely impact the activities of other individuals concurrently on the surface. According to Viklund (1995) and Sawyer (2009), area of deflection is not a major concern for recreational use; however, it could be a major consideration for competitive or varsity play.

Impact attenuation relates to the result of a body part coming into contact with the athletic surface. Elasticity and point elasticity relate to "how well the floor surface will deform and absorb energy over the area of impact" (Abendroth, 2012, p. 169). Facility surface decisions must be made related to the physical characteristics of the surface for ball bouncing properties as well as the impact on the bones and joints of participants.

Another important consideration for most organizations in making flooring choices is a concept known as the *rolling load*. Rolling load is the capacity of a floor to withstand damage from external forces such as bleacher movement, equipment transport, or similar activities (Viklund, 1995). Any surface used for multipurpose activities must be able to withstand the movement of equipment or materials over the surface area during transition from one activity to another. This concept also applies to the "walk-off" areas that experience heavy use. Even the most durable surfaces over time will deteriorate rapidly under heavy pedestrian or equipment traffic. Mats, padding, or varied traffic patterns can be established by the careful planning of equipment storage areas to extend the life of most facility surfaces. The choices made for the planning of *tare space*, or areas that are not developed for primary activities, may also influence the wear and tear on a floor over the life of the facility surface. Storage and transport of equipment should not be viewed as unimportant in the facility surface decision process, as these can directly influence the deterioration of a surface with heavy equipment and pedestrian traffic.

Although much of the focus on facility surface properties relates to balls, athletes, and moveable equipment, static loads are also important to consider. Portable equipment, once moved, often sits in place for extended periods of time and can permanently alter the properties of a surface. Bleachers, staging, and other loads that may remain in place for extended periods of time should fall within the maximum load guidelines for a facility surface. Maximum load guidelines are measured in pounds per square inch (psi) or newtons per millimeter (metric).

Life cycle costs of a surface are also important to consider when making various flooring choices. Piper (2000) suggested that hardwood flooring is rated for 25 years, as is terrazzo, followed by 15 years for vinyl tile and approximately 10 years for most carpets. It is stressed, however, that these suggested guidelines may not necessarily match individual expectations. A product's *life cycle* may describe how long a product will withstand expected use; however, the aesthetic appearance is also valued by most organizations. For this concept, a product's *attractive life* describes how long a surface will remain acceptable, based on the product's appearance, not its functionality. As a result, organizations should consider the amount of *churn,* which describes the general wear and tear on a given surface, given the expectations for a given location (Piper, 2000). If extensive churn is predicted for a given area, it may not be sensible to place a long-term, high-quality surface that will not remain aesthetic for the life cycle of the product, when compared with its attractive life.

There are a variety of floor surface options that can be used successfully as a main gym floor. Once again, this important surface choice is normally dictated by the primary activity planned for the space. Options for indoor sports flooring are generally broken down into two categories: wood and synthetic. Each surface option has strengths and weaknesses. According to Bishop (1997) and Sawyer (2009), wood flooring with proper maintenance can last 50 years, compared with 20 years for a synthetic surface and 15 years for vinyl tile. Table 8.4 illustrates initial cost, life expectancy, and annual maintenance cost for vinyl tile, synthetic surface, and wood flooring for a 5,000-sq ft gymnasium (Bishop, 1997; Sawyer, 2009).

Vinyl tile floors have a life expectancy of approximately 10 to 15 years, but begin to show their wear after the first few years (Bishop, 1997; Sawyer, 2009). However, newer technology has significantly improved the quality of sheet vinyl and vinyl composition tile, making this flooring choice more aesthetic and more durable (Hasenkamp

& Lutz, 2001). Vinyl floors, however, tend to be very hard and have poor absorption qualities. These characteristics can also lead to athletic injuries if high humidity levels are prevalent or if water spills are not managed properly. Unlike other sport surfaces, which require only washing and damp mopping, vinyl tile floor must be stripped, sealed, and waxed at least three times annually. In contrast, synthetic floors also require regular cleaning, but may require line repainting or a touch-up every 5 years (Bishop, 1997; Sawyer, 2009).

An updated life cycle cost analysis of indoor sports flooring is offered for wood and synthetic flooring options in Table 8.4. Installation and daily, biweekly, quarterly, annual, and major maintenance factors are used to compose an annual cost for each flooring option (Sawyer, 2009).

Hardwood floors are generally designed with intricate subflooring to provide shock absorption and can be expected to last the life of the school. Wooden floors must always be kept clean to provide proper traction. They must also have the lines repainted or touched up and should be sanded down and refinished every 3 years. Synthetic floors do not allow for as much sliding as hardwood floors. As a result, if the activities on the floor involve sliding actions, a wood floor is the better choice. Wood floors can also be designed in a number of ways including subfloor systems, cushioned systems, and spring systems (Flynn, 1993; Sawyer, 2009).

The Maple Flooring Manufacturers Association (n.d.) developed a table below outlining costs and a worksheet for estimating both annual and life cycle costs for a maple strip, PVC sheet, and poured urethane sport floor. See Table 8.5 and Figure 8.2.

Table 8.4

Life Cycle Cost Analysis (Model: 10,000 Sq Ft)

Influencing Factors	Annual Costs		
	Maple	**PVC**	**Poured Urethane**
Total Installed Costs			
(amortized over life expectancy)	$ 2,139	$ 4,333	$ 1,316
Daily Maintenance	$ 2,088	$ 2,088	$ 2,088
Biweekly Maintenance	- - - -	$ 1,848	$ 1,848
Quarterly Maintenance	- - - -	$ 1,230	$ 1,230
Annual Maintenance	$ 2,800	$ 1,966	$ 1,966
Major Maintenance			
(amortized over life expectancy)	$ 845	- - - -	$ 2,566
Life Expectancy	(38 years)	(15 years)	(38 years)
Annual Cost	$ 7,872/year	$11,465/year	$11,014/year

Note. From "Study to Determine Life Cycle Costing for Sports Flooring," by Maple Flooring Manufacturers Association, n.d., retrieved from http://www.maplefloor.org/literature/lifecyclestudy.htm

Table 8.5

Indoor Sports Flooring Life Cycle Cost Analysis

Category	Wood		Synthetic					
Type	Maple	Pre-finished Engineered	Linoleum	PVC	Rubber	Tile	Full-pour Urethane	Pad-and-pour Urethane
Installation costs*	$3,200	$2,368	$1,600-$3,000	$2,600	$2,333-$2,833	$2,750	$3,333-$4,667	$4,333-$5,667
Daily maintenance costs**	$2,088	$2,088	$2,088	$2,088	$2,088	$2,088	$2,088	$2,088
Biweekly maintenance costs**	—	—	$1,800	$1,800	$1,800	$1,800	$1,800	$1,800
Quarterly maintenance costs**	—	—	$1,300	$1,300	$1,300	$1,300	$1,300	$1,300
Annual maintenance costs	$2,800	—	—	—	—	—	—	—
Major maintenance costs***	$1,070	$420	—	$500	—	$250	$350	$350
Life Expectancy (yrs.)	38	38	15-50	25	30	20	15	15
Total annual cost	$9,158	$4,876	$6,788-$8,188	$8,288	$7,521-$8,021	$8,188	$8,871-$10,205	$9,871-$11,205

All surfaces are assumed to be 10,000 square feet.
*Installation costs have been amortized over the expected life span of each surface. **Figures for daily, biweekly and quarterly maintenance represent annual totals, including the cost of labor ($12 per hour) and materials. ***Major maintenance costs have been amortized over the span of 10 years.
Sources: Athletic Business research, Maple Flooring Manufacturers Association

THE FOLLOWING CHART HAS BEEN DESIGNED TO HELP YOU ESTIMATE ANNUAL AND LIFECYCLE COSTS FOR A MAPLE STRIP, PVC SHEET GOODS OR POURED URETHANE SPORTS FLOOR IN ANY FACILITY, BASED ON SQUARE FOOTAGE. TO COMPUTE THE ESTIMATED LIFECYCLE COST COMPARISON OF A SPORTS FLOOR:

1. Enter the square footage of the floor on line one.

2. On lines two through seven, compute the annual costs for each component by multiplying the annual per-square-foot cost by the square footage of your floor.

3. For a total annual cost, add lines two through seven.

4. For a lifecycle cost, multiply line eight by line nine.

	MAPLE STRIP	PVC SHEET GOODS	POURED URETHANE
1. Your floor's square footage	_____ sf	_____ sf	_____ sf
2. Installed cost	x $0.32 = ____	x $0.26 = ____	x $0.33-$0.57 = ____
3. Daily maintenance	x $0.21= ____	x $0.21 = ____	x $0.21 = ____
4. Bi-weekly maintenance	x $0.00 = ____	x $0.18 = ____	x $0.18 = ____
5. Quarterly maintenance	x $0.00 = ____	x $0.13 = ____	x $0.13 = ____
6. Annual maintenance	x $0.28 = ____	x $0.00 = ____	x $0.00 = ____
7. Refinish/resurface	x $0.11 = ____	x $0.00 = ____	x $0.04 = ____
8. Total estimated annual cost for your floor	_____	_____	_____
9. Life expectancy	x 38 years	x 25 years	x 15 years
10. Estimated lifecycle cost for your floor	= _____	= _____	= _____

Figure 8.2. **Life Cycle Cost Comparison Worksheet** *Note.* From "Study to Determine Life Cycle Costing for Sports Flooring," by Maple Flooring Manufacturers Association, n.d., retrieved from http://www.maplefloor.org/literature/lifecyclestudy.htm

As mentioned above, the nature of the subflooring can often be a more significant factor than the actual surface material chosen for a floor (Dahlgren, 2000a; Holzrichter, 2001). Kroll (2002) suggested that cost-cutting processes during the planning phase of building development often alter the subflooring preparation intended for a given flooring option. This in turn may extensively alter the actual performance and longevity characteristics of a chosen surface.

Generally, three types of subfloor constructions are recommended. The first is a suspension floor, which is made out of plywood, foam rubber, or another synthetic material that is available in a variety of patterns. The finished floor rests on top of the subfloor material. The second type of subfloor construction is a spring floor. This involves coiled metal springs, covered by a plywood subfloor, with the finished floor resting on the plywood. The third type is referred to as a padded floor. Padded materials, such as foam or other synthetic or porous materials, are laid over concrete or plywood and then covered with the finished floor (Sawyer, 2009; Stoll & Beller, 1989). As technology and testing procedures for various flooring options continue to develop, manufacturers are paying increasing attention to various floor performance characteristics (Steinbach, 2002b). Steinbach (2002b) described an approach where "strips of foam, as opposed to one solid sheet, can effectively soften a floor" (p. 82). Any number of variables can be altered, resulting in subtle or profound changes in the ultimate performance of the floor. Naturally, the more materials that are needed, along with the cost of these materials, impacts the cost of the flooring choice. Safety should also be considered throughout the decision-making process. In any instance, it is important to be familiar with all these factors such that everyone is aware of the factors involved and their impact on performance, cost, appearance, and life expectancy of the surface chosen.

Synthetic floors remain a popular choice, and they tend to be much softer than wood floors and perform much better acoustically. Wood floors, depending on the effectiveness of their suspension systems, can also have *dead spots*. Dead spots are areas on the floor that can cause objects impacting the floor surface to perform inconsistently. An example would be a basketball that would have a variable bounce due to a change in the characteristics of the floor. Synthetic floors are evenly laid and are less likely to have dead spots; however, inconsistent ball performance can still occur. Quality installation will maximize optimal surface performance with any surface choice. Upkeep of all gym floors calls for constant maintenance. Rubberized synthetic floors, although popular, tend to have higher maintenance costs when compared with wooden floors.

There are many different floor covering options related to sports and recreation activities in today's market. Some examples include ceramic tile, cushioned wood flooring,

and rubber compound flooring. The selection criteria for certain flooring materials should include

- economic feasibility with initial outlay and life cycle costs. Floor covering choices entail much more than the initial up-front cost. Many now realize that the initial cost for materials and installation is only a small component of the total investment needed. Life cycle cost considerations include not only the initial expense and installation, but also the number of years the flooring is expected to last, cost for removal or disposal of the floor, lost revenues during remodeling or replacement periods, and maintenance costs over the course of the surface life (Hard Questions, Critical Answers, 1998);
- ease of maintenance and replacement;
- potential performance capabilities for both intended and possible use; and
- overall compatibility in appearance according to surrounding surfaces and equipment in the facility (Barkley, 1997; Dahlgren, 2000a; Sawyer, 2009).

An important factor that is often overlooked when considering floor options concerns the planned events within the facility. Access to electrical outlets, placement of equipment securing devices (floor plates for volleyball uprights), and tare space necessary for intended spectator traffic and equipment movement are important considerations. If floor plates are to be used, they should be considered early in the process, as well as covered, for ease of maintenance, access, and safety factors. In particular, electrical outlets should be installed in the floor, covered, and flush with the floor's surface, as they are commonly associated with safety issues related to traffic flow. The time spent in preparing a facility for various activities should also be considered. Greater planning for both functional and safety factors can save time (equipment setup and teardown), reduce costs (tape and mats to cover electrical and media system cords), and reduce accidents (tripping over exposed wires and cords).

During surface selection, it is wise to consult other facilities that have similar need and use patterns to explore all flooring options based on performance characteristics. It is also important to consult with individuals who work with and maintain these facilities (maintenance personnel, students, athletes, publics, etc.) because they will likely have a different perspective regarding the suitability of various facility surfaces. The planning team makes the ultimate choice and should consider all factors to make optimal surface decisions.

Although cost tends to be perceived as the overriding factor that drives a facility surface choice, aesthetic factors are being increasingly considered in the decision-making process. Wood flooring, for example, tends to be chosen based on the "quality" or "grade" of the actual wood.

Quality is categorized into first, second, and third grades. First-grade wood has the fewest number of defects and deficiencies when inspected prior to sale. "First grade allows for a very modern, clean and, in some minds, sterile look because it is fairly defect-free. You don't see dark blemishes or a lot of graining" (Dahlgren, 2000a, p. 78).

Wood flooring choices are also made based on color, which once again is influenced by visual appeal. Maple tends to be the industry standard and offers good durability due to a "tight grain and density"; however, the light color also supports its popularity (Dahlgren, 2000a). Second- and third-grade woods tend to offer a darker, more grainy, and "warmer" appearance; however, this choice once again boils down to personal or committee preference. Another consideration that should not be overlooked is the impact of the floor color or aesthetics on the participants and the spectators. A dark or grainy floor, although more appealing to the eye, may be a distraction to participants. As far as performance is concerned, according to Hamar (2000), president of the Maple Flooring Manufacturers Association, "you could blindfold a person and have him dribble a ball on a first-grade floor, a second-grade floor, and a third-grade floor, and he would never know the difference" (p. 84).

A final consideration in the quest for enhancing the visual appeal of a floor surface is achieved by creative efforts with paint, patterns, colors, and contrast. Tiled flooring can easily be created in various patterns and designs that are appealing to the eye; however, during the reconditioning process of a wood floor, alterations in surface applications can create a "new" look with the same "old" floor. Again, these issues need to be addressed by communicating with other facility management personnel and discovering the strengths and weaknesses of the numerous options available before an ultimate decision is made for any facility.

Surface Selection Process

As stated earlier, choosing the appropriate flooring surface is a major decision in either the initial design or the renovation process. Floor materials and maintenance patterns can greatly impact athletic performance, determine how well multiple uses are served, and impact the incidence of sport injuries. Floor surfaces come in innumerable materials, textures, colors, and performance characteristics. Yet, of the hundreds of products on the market, no one surface is perfect for all uses, and there is plenty of room to make the wrong choice (Kollie, 2004; Sawyer, 2009; Viklund, 1995).

A logical and systematic approach should be followed in conducting a search for the appropriate surface. These guidelines will assist in the decision-making process. Viklund (1995) recommended the steps in the following "flooring checklist":

1. Select the room or space to be considered.
2. Prioritize the sports/activities that will occur within the space.
3. Decide whether the preferred floor should be area-elastic or point-elastic.
4. Review the performance criteria for the selected floor type.
5. Test flooring options by reviewing samples and comparing costs.
6. Compare life cycle costs for flooring options.
7. Play on the different surfaces.
8. Check the manufacturers' referenced projects.
9. Make the final decision. (p. 46)

Flynn (1993) and Sawyer (2009) recommended the following steps in the surface selection process.

Definition. Define the characteristics required to meet specified needs (bounce characteristics, sunlight effects, etc.). Many of these questions are addressed by manufacturers in their literature.

Solicitation. Cost should not be a limitation for the initial research and review of possible flooring systems. Request as much information from as many manufacturers as deemed reasonable. Reviewing this information will broaden your knowledge of different systems and be a basis for comparison. Obtain material estimates and project costs from various manufacturers. Manufacturers should also provide references, a list of installers, and the location of like facilities for comparative analysis.

Comparison. After reviewing manufacturer materials and comparing all possible systems, categorize all materials. Categorize information by type and desirable qualities (i.e., natural vs. synthetic, resiliency, initial cost, longevity, safety, aesthetics, and any additional factors significant to your decision-making process). A table that compares the various positive and negative attributes of each surface option is generally deemed helpful in making the right surface choice for your facility.

Visitation. After the field of choices has been narrowed down based on established criteria, perform a site visit for each of the facility surfaces being considered. A closer inspection and discussion with personnel at each facility is also likely to help you make the best choice for your facility. Explore performance and maintenance factors, as initial cost and utility are only two of numerous factors in making a wise surface choice.

Selection. At this point, select a system based upon all research efforts. Consider all performance criteria, and always keep in mind that surface choices are a significant factor in the overall success of a facility.

Quality. A specific surface may be selected; however, there are numerous levels of quality among any number of surface options. Once more, consider the quality of the materials, workmanship, guarantees, facility use factors, and other significant elements when making this important decision.

Manufacturer. Choosing a manufacturer is also important. How long have they been in business? What type of technical support do they provide? What are their methods of quality control, both in the manufacturing process and in the field? What is their reputation? How soon can they provide you with the requested materials? What guarantees do they provide? Many questions should be compiled and asked of each company being considered. Always remember that references are important to obtain; however, do your homework in the inquiry process. Never rely too heavily on references provided by the company being considered, as it will obviously be more than willing to provide positive references for its own work history. Seek out unsolicited references for all finalists in the bidding process followed. It is common in the industry that manufacturers will provide products to clients in exchange for positive reviews.

Installer. The manufacturer should recommend an installer that is familiar with installing its product. Ask questions of the installer similar to those asked of the manufacturer. Another key piece of information is the time frame required for completing the installation. Many jobs are started on time; however, you should seek guarantees for job completion or factor this item into a reduction in cost for jobs not finished when promised. Facility visits and communication with other clients will help you decide upon an installation company.

Maintenance. Maintenance is a considerable portion of the operating budget, and it is important to define exactly what is involved. What type of maintenance is required? How often will the surface need to be refinished, covered, lacquered, replaced, and so forth? Facility planners should

Legend:
● = Above Average
▶ = Average
○ = Below Average
V = Variable
D = Daily
W = Weekly
M = Monthly
Y = Yearly
P = Periodically
S = Semiannually in high traffic areas or yearly in average traffic areas

Material		Strength	Durability	Thermal Insulation	Moisture, oil, chemical resistance	Stain Resistance	Abrasions Resistance / Wearability	Mildew Resistance	Heat Absorption	Limited Application Locations	Sweeping or dust mopping	Vacuuming	Damp mopping	Wet mopping	Scrubbing	Stripping	Dry Cleaning (Chemicals)	Hot water extraction	Waxing	Buffing	Resealing	Regrouting	Sanding & refinishing	Overall Maintenance Ranking
Hard	Ceramic Tile (6"x6"x1/2") Mortar and Grout	●	●	●	V	▶	●	●	○	x	D	x	D	x	S	S	x	x	M	M	x	x	x	High
	Ceramic Tile (6"x6"x1/2") Mastic and Grout	●	▶	●	V	▶	●	●	○	x	D	x	D	x	Y	Y	x	x	M	M	x	x	x	High
	Quarry Tile Mortar and Grout	●	●	●	●	●	●	●	○	x	D	x	D	x	x	x	x	x	Y	Y	x	x	x	Medium
	Exposed Concrete Sealant (2 coats)	●	●	○	○	▶	●	▶	●	✓	D	x	W	Y	x	x	x	x	Y	x	x	x	x	Medium
	Terrazzo (1 3/4")	●	●	▶	●	●	●	●	●	▶	D	x	W	x	Y	x	x	x	x	x	x	P	x	Low
	Epoxy resin	▶	○	●	●	●	▶	●	○	x	D	x	W	x	Y	x	x	x	x	x	x	P	x	Low
	Laminated wood (synthetic core) Vapor barrier & adhesive	▶	▶	●	▶	▶	▶	●	▶	x	D	x	W	x	Y	x	x	x	x	x	x	P	x	Low
	Wood plank (2 1/4")	●	▶	●	▶	▶	▶	●	▶	x	x	D	x	x	x	x	x	S	S	x	x	x	x	Medium
Resilient	Bamboo flooring Vapor barrier & adhesive	●	▶	●	○	▶	●	●	▶	x	x	D	x	x	x	x	x	S	S	x	x	x	x	Medium
	Linoleum (.125")	▶	●	●	▶	▶	●	●	○	x	x	D	x	x	x	x	x	S	S	x	x	x	x	Medium
	Vinyl Compositiion Tile (VCT) Vapor barrier & adhesive	▶	▶	●	○	V	▶	○	○	x	D	x	D	x	x	x	x	x	x	x	x	Y	x	Low
	Vinyl Sheet Vapor barrier and adhesive	▶	▶	●	○	V	▶	○	○	x	D	x	W	x	M	x	x	x	x	x	P	x	x	Medium
	Rubber Sheet (1/8") - Adhesive	●	○	●	●	▶	●	▶	▶	x	D	x	W	x	M	x	x	x	x	Y	Y	x	x	Medium
	Cork (1/8") - Adhesive	○	○	●	▶	○	○	▶	○	x	D	x	W	x	M	x	x	x	x	x	x	x	x	Low
Soft	Carpet tile (18" x 18", 20 oz/syd) Hard back	▶	▶	●	▶	●	▶	▶	●	✓	D	x	D	x	x	x	x	x	x	x	P	x	P	Low
	Carpet tile (18" x 18", 20 oz/syd) Cushion back	▶	●	●	▶	●	▶	▶	●	✓	D	x	D	x	x	x	x	x	x	x	x	x	x	Low
	Carpet (Nylon loop pile 40 oz/syd) Adhesive	▶	▶	●	▶	▶	▶	▶	●	✓	D	x	D	x	x	x	x	x	x	x	x	x	P	Low

Figure 8.3. **Attributes of Various Floor Surfaces** (*Source:* Athletic Business (http://www.athleticbusiness.com/articles/) Moussatche, Languell-Urquhart, & Woodson (2000); www.sportengland.org/facilities__planning/idoc.ashx?docid

not underestimate the expense of properly maintaining facility surfaces and should figure this expense into the overall surface cost and flooring choice.

Kennedy (2000) and Sawyer (2009) recommended that maintenance staff should have a thorough knowledge of the various floor surfaces they are maintaining. Maintenance and cleaning costs account for more than 50% of the total cost of ownership (Piper, 2000; Sawyer, 2009). Cleaning approaches can also vary based on the intended use of the surface. Research by Agron (2001) described an overall reduction in expenditures for both maintenance and operations in elementary and secondary schools. This same author, however, reported an increase in spending for maintenance and operations budgets in higher education facilities. In either case, this concept needs to be factored into the flooring decision process. A less expensive floor may have a limited life span without proper care. The same can be stated for more expensive flooring that requires more specialized care to attain maximal life cycle use.

Moussatche, Languell-Urquhart, and Woodson (2000) provided information that relates life cycle costs with operations and maintenance considerations for hard flooring, resilient flooring, and soft flooring options. As mentioned earlier, the actual cost of the initial flooring is only a portion of the life cycle flooring expense. "Life-cycle cost analysis allows the evaluator to fully examine each alternative and the true service life cost of the material" (Moussatche et al., 2000, p. 20).

Initial cost. What is the "total" initial cost of the system? Make sure no hidden costs will arise later. If two systems are considered similar, yet one is more costly than the other, what is the reason? Is it the quality of the system, materials, or both? Sometimes product name or reputation is a reason for cost inflation.

Life cycle cost. This comparative analysis considers the initial cost, operational costs, maintenance costs, and if necessary, replacement costs during the estimated life cycle. These figures will generate the anticipated total costs. Generally, a higher initial cost system will be comparable in the long run with less expensive systems when all factors are considered.

Bidding. When bidding is required, direct attention toward written specifications to ensure the product and installation methods are accurately described to avoid misunderstandings.

Installation. It is in the owner's interest to require the manufacturer to perform periodic on-site supervision of the installer. This will ensure compliance with the manufacturer's specifications.

Environmental and Sustainability Issues

Environmental factors have become increasingly influential in the construction process for buildings and surfaces. The Leadership in Energy and Environmental Design (LEED) standards influence decisions related to most new product installations. "On the synthetic side, there are a few more options and compositions to consider with an emphasis on green and sustainable design (Catalano, 2012). Joe Covington Jr., president of Covington Flooring Company in Birmingham, Alabama, reported that manufacturers are using less wood by offering thinner strips in their flooring products. This approach saves trees and results in "less material, less freight, and less weight" (as cited in Catalano, 2012). Daniel Heney, executive director of the Maple Flooring Manufacturers Association (MFMA), reported that subflooring products are also changing in content, with the increased use of recycled materials (as cited in Catalano, 2012).

Similar trends are also occurring with the finishes used on wood flooring. Volatile organic compounds (VOC) are being regulated more stringently by the Environmental Protection Agency (EPA), and water-based products are replacing oil-based products, in particular in areas of the United States with stricter laws (Catalano, 2012). These finishes tend to be more extensively impacted by moisture levels, which is pushing manufacturers to experiment with products that counteract this outcome toward becoming greener.

Sustainability efforts related to the "carbon footprint" of the company chosen to install flooring should also be considered. "Action Floor Systems' SCORES criteria (which stands for sustainable construction of renewable engineered surfaces) is another method for documenting sustainability initiatives" (Abendroth, 2012, p. 2).

Risk Management and Safety Considerations

Flooring surface choices clearly need to be assessed based on facility use expectations; however, with liability concerns, surface choices need to be made with extensive consideration of various safety factors. Resiliency, slip, traction, absorption, foot support, activities planned for the space, and the age and ability of the intended users are considerations when deciding upon a flooring choice. Literature supports the notion that a lack of effective communication exists within the process of deciding upon a flooring choice; however, all parties should be concerned about the impact of this choice on risk management outcomes. "Health considerations and their accordant legal and financial liabilities are influencing the selection of sports surfacing" (Cooper, 2004, p. 2). Cohen (2002a) stated, "The distance between the recreation and maintenance professions [is a key factor]" (p. 106). In this article, Cohen discussed that recreation management professionals often have little input into maintenance functions. Maintenance functions are stated as being "dominated by longtime city employees, refugees from other businesses, volunteers and seasonal and part-time workers" (Cohen, 2002, p. 106). Piper (2003) stated that flooring choices are frequently chosen based on aesthetic appearance when new, compared with how they will last through their service life, as well as their resistance to gouging, indentations, stains, rolling loads, acoustics, and slip-resistance characteristics (p. 3).

A device recognized by the ASTM, called a tribometer, establishes the "slip resistance" of various flooring surfaces and footwear (Di Pilla, 2001). Knowing exactly how slippery each floor surface is enables a determination of appropriate activities for this space, possible shoe requirements, and cleaning schedules. A simple change in cleaning materials or application method can impact how slippery the surface will be. Although a comprehensive risk management program can address some of these factors, this issue needs to be considered in the planning process to avoid the resultant risks from slips and falls.

Repairs to surface materials need also consider the impact on end users, as well as the effect on initial manufacturing warranties. Although custodial and maintenance staff may make some repairs, industry professionals may need to make surface repairs to maintain the initial integrity of the facility surface. Facility surface repairs tend not to be repairs that can go on a list of "things to do later," as the use of the facility is dependent on a quick solution. According to Cohen (2000), "each player . . . . is just one misstep from finding that hole, breaking an ankle, and suing you for negligence" (p. 46).

Walls and Ceilings

Walls serve a greater function than providing a divider or perimeter for specific activity areas. Walls function as barriers to sound, heat, light, and moisture. Depending on the location and intended use of the facility, acoustical properties of the material of wall surfaces should be carefully considered as well. Generally speaking, moisture-resistant walls with sound acoustical properties are ideal.

Perhaps one of the most common characteristics of a typical gym is the inability of the various surfaces to absorb sound (Holzrichter, 2001). The acoustical treatments used on walls or within the overhead structures should be high enough so they will not impede the use of wall space or the travel of objects and will not be easily damaged by users. As mentioned earlier with flooring, a trend remains toward greater aesthetic pursuits on walls and ceilings in using colors, pictures, and graphics on these surfaces. Banners, sound panels, and other porous materials can be used to improve acoustical sound properties of a typical gymnasium. Tasteful color schemes can also have a positive psychological value on the participant or spectator, as well as make the environment more aesthetically pleasing (Flynn, 1993; Hasenkamp & Lutz, 2001).

Another wall consideration that has evolved in recent years is padding: how much, how high, how thick, and what material? With lawsuit numbers increasing, the performance of wall padding has earned greater concern by facility architects, planners, and managers. Not only the fact that wall padding is necessary in specific facility locations; but also the effectiveness of this padding in preventing serious injury upon contact. An additional question is, how extensive should efforts be to pad all possible contact zones? Steinbach (2004) described a 1997 accident where an eighth-grade student collided with a padded gym wall during a basketball tryout, resulting in the eventual death of the child.

Walls in the main gym or activity area should have a minimum height of 8 ft and should always be padded for safety reasons. Electrical outlets should be provided every 50 ft and should also be protected by padding (Flynn, 1993; Sawyer, 2009). Small inserts can be cut out of the padding and affixed with fasteners for easy removal and replacement for access to electrical outlets. All padding should be checked regularly, as it can wear and harden with age and contribute to significant injury upon contact. Keep in mind that some unobstructed flat wall space may need to available as appropriate for teaching and/or lecture space. In some cases, all walls should be kept unobstructed; however, this would be based on the specific activities planned for the space (e.g., indoor soccer).

Roof design, local building codes, and the nature of the planned activities should determine ceiling construction. Ceilings should be insulated to prevent condensation and should be the appropriate height to accommodate all planned and future activities. Painted ceilings can also improve the physical look of the facility and enhance light reflection. Bright white ceilings are strongly advised against in areas where light-colored objects are used (e.g., shuttlecocks and volleyballs). It is difficult to visually follow these objects against a bright white ceiling background. A light color is still recommended for ceilings, however, and most facilities find an off-white color to work best. A 24-ft minimum distance (lowest suspended object) is required in any teaching station designed for a variety of activities (Flynn, 1993; Sawyer, 2009). Cohen (2003) suggested 25 ft; however, he also stated that volleyball, which has a minimum ceiling requirement of 12.5 m (37.5 ft), and other planned facility uses may force planners to create greater ceiling heights to accommodate activities such as commencements and concerts. When possible, facility planners should attempt to exceed minimum ceiling heights, as minimum heights can still contribute to game interference, equipment lodging (e.g., shuttlecocks), and greater ceiling fixture expenses as a result of occasional contact with equipment (e.g., volleyballs).

Ceiling height may also impact factors not initially considered when making such choices. Planning for high ceilings may result in alterations of original equipment plans, as "high ceilings might render ceiling-hung basketball standards impractical, necessitating greater storage to accommodate portable backstops" (Cohen, 2003, p. 72).

Acoustical ceiling materials are needed in instructional spaces and in areas with many planned activities. Dropped ceiling panels will require considerable maintenance because they are susceptible to damage by objects or individuals. Because most acoustical instruments are not necessarily made out of the hardest materials, they need to be placed out of range of flying objects. In some cases where there are low ceiling activity areas, dropped ceilings may be equipped with spring-loaded clips that will return the acoustical panel back into place after contact. It should be noted that false ceilings with catwalks above them have been effectively constructed to allow for easier maintenance and the repair of lighting and ventilation arrangements (Flynn, 1993; Sawyer, 2009).

As mentioned earlier, the ceiling should have a minimum height of 24 ft to the lowest obstacle with an off-white color usually being appropriate. A clear span ceiling design without minimum support pillars and substructure girders should be investigated for safety, viewing, aesthetics, and more open and usable space. If equipment is to be mounted or stored in the ceiling area, structural reinforcement may become necessary at these sites (Flynn, 1993). It is important to consider all necessary factors when constructing or remodeling the primary features of a facility.

Once again, the planned use of a given area should guide all planning and material requirements. Moeller stated, "The ceiling is the primary acoustical treatment in the office" (as cited in Roberts, 2000, p. 2). According to Roberts (2000) and Kroll (2003), Noise Reduction Coefficient (NRC) is the capability of a ceiling to absorb noise. An additional consideration is the Sound Transmission Class (STC). This concept measures the effectiveness of a wall or ceiling in blocking sound between offices. Kroll (2003) continued, elaborating on the increased demand for sound reduction within many facilities based on privacy concerns. With the passage of the Health Insurance Portability and Accountability Act (HIPAA), health care providers must make reasonable efforts to respect the privacy of clients. This is particularly true within medical facilities where sensitive material is shared and the ability of a surface to minimize sound deflection is important.

Figure 8.4 provides a guide for floor, wall, and ceiling choices for a variety of rooms within a facility.

Windows

The use and aesthetic value of windows are often overlooked in the planning of indoor facilities, as well as within the process of making surface choices. Windows can provide durable and attractive enclosures, as well as divisions of space within a facility. However, facility planners must keep in mind that windows may face daily exposure to the elements and frequent contact with objects used in the activities planned for the space (Johnson & Patterson, 1997; Sawyer, 2009). Climate is also a consideration when deciding on window placement and use, as it can enhance warming features due to sunlight, which can obviously be a benefit or a detriment depending on the facility's geographical location. Windows can also create glare problems; however, with appropriate placement (northern exposure), they can greatly enhance the aesthetic quality and appeal of indoor surfaces (Holzrichter, 2001; Sawyer, 2009). *Fenestration* is the technical term for the natural lighting created by windows.

According to Piper (1998), the selection process for windows is based on a number of factors, including

- lighting—the three most common ways for controlling the light passing through windows are tinted glazing, heat-absorbing glazing, and low-emissivity coatings;
- keeping the elements out;
- heat loss;
- aesthetics;
- security; and
- view.

Windows are often overlooked when making wall surface choices, but they should be considered in relation to the overall building's aesthetic plan, the regional location of the facility, and the activities scheduled within the facility. Windows also add to the construction costs; however, apart from the impact they may have on the activities planned for the space, they can add extensively to the aesthetic appeal of most facilities.

Lighting

Although not always considered, lighting is an important factor when selecting facility surfaces. With increased efforts to address aesthetics, as well as participant and spectator satisfaction, lighting should be addressed in the planning phase of building construction. Indirect lighting is largely viewed as ideal for most competitive sports and recreation settings. Indirect lighting, however, is heavily influenced by its surroundings. Paint type (flat vs. gloss), paint color, shadows, HVAC, sprinkler pipes, and acoustic strips impact lighting efforts (Cohen, 2002a).

Additional Floor, Wall, and Ceiling Considerations

Floors

Floor considerations include

- an adequate number of floor drains in the proper locations;
- proper floor sloping for adequate drainage (if necessary);
- a water-resistant, rounded base, where the flooring and wall meet in any locker or shower area;

ROOMS	FLOORS							LOWER WALLS								UPPER WALLS						CEILINGS			
	Carpeting	Synthetics	Tile, asphalt, rubber, linoleum	Cement, abrasive, non-abrasive	Maple, hard	Terrazzo, abrasive	Tile, ceramic	Brick	Brick, glazed	Cinder Block	Concrete	Plaster	Tile, ceramic	Wood Panel	Moistureproof	Brick	Brick, glazed	Cinder Block	Plaster	Acoustic	Moisture-resistant	Concrete or Structure Tile	Plaster	Tile, acoustic	Moisture-resistant
Apparatus Storage Room					1	2			1			2	1	C											
Classrooms		2			1							2		1	2				2	1			C	C	1
Clubroom		2			1							2		1	2				2	1			C	C	1
Corrective Room		1			2					2	1				2		2	2	1	2					1
Custodial Supply Room					1			2																	
Dance Studio					1																		C	C	1
Drying Room (equip.)					1		2	2	1	2	1	1					1		1						
Gymnasium		1			1					2	1				2		2	2	1	2	*		C	C	1
Health-Service Unit			1		1							2	1		2				2	1					1
Laundry Room				2					1	2	1	2	2	1	C	*					*			*	*
Locker Rooms		3		3		2	1		1			2	2	3	1	*	1		1	2				C	1
Natatorium		2							1	2	1	3	2		1	*	2	2	1		*	*	C	C	1
Offices	1		3			2						2		1	1				2						1
Recreation Room		2			1					2		2	1		1			2	1	2	*			C	1
Shower Rooms				3		2	1		1				2	1		*	2	1	2	2		*		1	*
Special-activity Room		2			1					2			1		1			1	1	1				C	1

Figure 8.4. **Suggested Indoor Surface Materials** (*Source:* Sawyer, 2009)

- floor plates that are flush-mounted and placed where they are needed;
- the provision of nonskid, slip-resistant flooring in all wet areas (pool, shower, etc.); and
- lines painted as appropriate prior to any sealers being applied. (Patton et al., 1989; Sawyer, 2009)

Walls

Wall considerations include

- an adequate number of drinking fountains, fully recessed into the walls;
- a minimum of one wall of any exercise room that has a full-length mirror;
- "corners" in the shower and locker room areas that are rounded;

Example of properly lined floor

- wall coverings that are aesthetically pleasing, as well as match the decor and color scheme of the facility;
- electrical outlets that are placed strategically within the wall (or floor), firmly attached, and accessible if the wall is protected with padding; and
- in wet or humid areas, materials that should be easy to clean and impervious to moisture. (Patton et al., 1989; Sawyer, 2009)

Ceilings

Ceiling considerations include

- ceiling heights that are adequate for all planned facility activities;
- ceilings, except storage areas, that are acoustically treated with sound-absorbent materials;
- ceilings and access areas that are easily accessible for purposes of routine repair and maintenance; and
- acoustical materials that are impervious to moisture when they will be used in moisture-dense areas. (Patton et al., 1989; Sawyer, 2009)

Service and Ancillary Areas

Locker and Shower Areas

There are numerous options for cost-effective, safe, and easy-to-maintain locker and shower areas. Although the surface choices for these areas have not changed much in the past 20 years, greater emphasis is being placed on voluntary standards such as the LEED Green Building Rating System®. This represents "a measurement of green design developed and administered by the United States Green Building Council" (Popke, 2006a, p. 76). For obvious reasons, locker and shower areas require surfaces that are slip resistant. Slip-resistant surfaces by nature tend to be more difficult to clean. Areas that are more difficult to clean tend to require more chemicals, which opposes the efforts of most environmentally concerned facility operators. Tile, poured epoxy, coated concrete, rubber/vinyl/acrylic, carpet, flow-through tile, and exposed concrete and punched surfaces are the most common wet area floor options, along with various "emerging LEED-compliant possibilities" (Popke, 2006a, p. 77).

Locker area surfaces should possess maintenance ease along with a strong consideration of hygiene factors. All surfaces should be durable and able to withstand excessive moisture and humidity, as well as the accumulation of dirt. Aesthetic appeal once again remains a central issue in facility design within locker room areas, as many participants base their attitudes and opinions about the facility as a whole on their likes and dislikes within the locker room environment. This idea is espoused by Huddleston (2001): "Careful attention to the design and maintenance of locker rooms can greatly enhance a facility's image—and contain its odor" (p. 63).

Locker room areas contain hot and humid wet areas and dry dressing areas, typically within close proximity. Floors in wet areas should always be designed with safety, aesthetics, and maintenance in mind. For obvious reasons, nonslip tile is the best surface for these floors. Because soap and dirt often build up, a beige or brown-colored grout is recommended to keep the tile clean. Some facilities have stopped providing soap as the resultant slips and falls can create legal problems. Frequently wet areas, such as locker rooms, require greater risk management efforts to readily notice problem areas and reduce potential risks (Di Pilla, 2001).

All wet area floors within locker rooms should be pitched away from the dry areas and directed toward a drain. Some alternative sources include epoxy sealants over waterproof sheetrock or concrete block. These surfaces have worked satisfactorily in the past in the dressing room, sink, and common areas. It should also be noted that all corners of these areas should be rounded so moisture cannot penetrate the seams (Patton et al., 1989; Sawyer, 2009). Although many facilities avoid carpeted surfaces within locker rooms, the right carpeting is better equipped to handle moisture than people think, in particular in change areas (Huddleston, 2001). Carpeting is not particularly advised in heavy water areas near showers; however, flow-through flooring has been known to handle heavy water areas. Flow-through flooring allows excessive water to pass through the surface area to the subflooring below, before it passes to the floor drains. As long as this process allows for air circulation and drying of the subfloor system, it can maintain a dry surface and reduce slip and fall occurrences (Huddleston, 2001; Popke, 2006a).

Moisture is clearly the enemy in any building, and even more so where humid or wet areas exist. Precautions during the design process as well as the life span of the facility are important to minimize negative outcomes resulting from humidity, moisture, and microbe growth. Migration of moisture into contiguous areas must also be controlled. Measures must also be taken during the construction process to ensure that all building materials are not moisture damaged prior to installation. An effective and efficient heating, ventilation, and air control system (HVAC) must maintain a balance between humidity control and energy savings (Sawyer, 2009; Straus & Kirihara, 1996).

Prevention is the key to keeping microbiological gardens from growing in your building. Clearly, the most eminent hazard is moisture. Moisture can range from large pools of water from roof leaks or broken water pipes, to invisible rain that is absorbed into building materials, to moisture that condenses on facility surfaces. Dust also serves as a nutrient source for microbial growth. Although chemicals are a common method to combat these problems, moisture is the real culprit and should be the primary focus of effective and routine maintenance procedures (Sawyer, 2009; Straus & Kirihara, 1996).

In drier areas of the locker room, the floor is a major concern for interior decorators and designers. Mildew and mold are constant problems, and the materials should be able to withstand long periods of moist conditions and show little or no signs of delaminating. A 100% nylon carpet is recommended for flooring material in a health and fitness setting. The carpeting provides an aesthetically pleasing appearance and is easily maintained with daily vacuuming and periodic shampooing. It should also be noted that nylon carpets will have a longer life and will be more easily maintained if they are mildew resistant and Scotchgarded (Patton et al., 1989; Sawyer, 2009). Wear tests have also concluded that appropriate cushioning beneath the carpet surface can greatly enhance carpet life, as well as comfort for the participant (Goodman, 2000; Sawyer, 2009).

Wall coverings in locker room areas usually consist of epoxy-coated paint, vinyl, or wallpaper. The chosen material should be strong and not show dirt. Corners and wall-to-wall moldings should also be considered to reduce the amount of black marks and cuts that often appear, typically with heavy use. Ceilings are typically finished with moisture-proof hand-finished paint. As mentioned earlier, acoustical materials should also be used in conjunction with paint to reduce the noise levels that occur in locker rooms (Patton et al., 1989; Sawyer, 2009).

Steam Rooms

Steam rooms require specialized knowledge for construction and care. Building materials used and the planned methods of application are critical to minimizing the maintenance efforts in steam rooms. It is highly recommended to hire a contractor with previous experience in the construction of wet areas when considering steam room construction. The floor surface of a steam room should be covered with a liquid rubber material applied over a concrete slab. A layer of fiberglass fabric is laid over the rubber material followed with an additional coat of liquid rubber. The floor should also slope toward the drain for proper water drainage. This system protects against water leaks and expands with floor movement (Patton et al., 1989).

Steam room walls and ceilings should be covered with a cement building board and fiberglass tape. This wall surface should also be placed on galvanized metal studs or Wolmanized® lumber. It is important to remember to slope ceilings as well to enable moisture to run off rather than drip off. This system has proven to be durable and helps to prevent against rot and mildew. As with other wet areas, the selected tile should be both attractive and durable. A textured nonslip tile should be used on the floors,

whereas many choose to use glazed ceramic tile for the walls and ceilings (Patton et al., 1989; Sawyer, 2009).

Aerobic/Exercise Facilities

As aerobic exercise and other impact activities remain popular in fitness, recreation, and athletic centers across the nation, the effort to reduce impact-related injuries continues. Spring-loaded or "floating" hardwood floors are the most popular surfaces, followed closely by heavily padded carpet surfaces that are sealed and plastic-laminate-bonded to inhibit moisture leaks into the pile textures. This type of flooring allows for regular steam cleaning and avoids the hygiene problems from accumulated perspiration, as with a carpeted and/or padded area. Important considerations are compliance (shock absorption), foot stability, surface traction, and resiliency (energy return). Furthermore, there are synthetic and specially made floors that may be used as alternatives (Patton et al., 1989; Sawyer, 2009). Research on various flooring types should be available from most manufacturers that address the specific needs and demands of the activity you plan to offer.

Finding a balance between all facility surface areas is a considerable challenge for the facility planning team. For example, one of the best shock-absorbing floorings is any type of thick sponge pad. Regular foam may develop dips after prolonged use, but some new synthetics have been specially developed to hold their shape. One such surface is microcell foam, which is available at one fourth of the cost of wood, but it should be noted difficulties may arise with the interlocking sections. These types of synthetic floors are usually soft enough that individual mats are not needed for floor exercises. It should be noted that cleaning may also present unique problems with these floor types. Bacteria growth may also be a problem, in particular if the surface is textured or not properly maintained (Sawyer, 2009; Walker & Stotlar, 1997).

Although the quality of polyurethane surfaces continues to improve, these surfaces are not considered resilient enough by some because they are simply poured directly over concrete. The testing results of a surface may meet the necessary industry standards; however, the surface "hardness" may still be inappropriate for many activities, again due to the nature of the subflooring material. This point was made earlier; however, it is imperative to consider the subflooring material just as vital to the qualities and characteristics of use as the visible surface that is applied, laid, or poured on top. Maintenance issues remain a significant factor, as these surfaces are often plagued with cracking and peeling with age. The life cycle of these surfaces is also much shorter than wood.

Carpeting is relatively easy to install, and newer sport varieties have special shock-absorption properties. These should always be used with foam cushioning and never be applied directly over concrete surfaces. Carpet is versatile, inexpensive, and works well, especially in multipurpose areas. It should be noted, however, that carpets are highly susceptible to staining, can be easily discolored or stretched, and retain odors. The expected lifespan of most carpets is 2 to 4 years, depending on the use, cleaning methods, and quality of the materials.

Historically, wood floors remain a popular choice. Wood is aesthetically pleasing and provides a high degree of flexibility within most multipurpose activity areas. However, wood floors, depending on the subflooring used, are often extremely hard and not resilient enough for high-energy exercise, and excessive humidity can cause the wood to warp (Sawyer, 2009; Walker & Stotlar, 1997).

Strength Training Areas

Another area of continued popularity is the strength training room. The dark and dingy weight rooms of the past are now replaced with colorful new flooring options and light, airy, and open spaces (Steinbach, 2002a). The type of flooring sought depends largely on the nature of the equipment selected; however, the aesthetic appeal is increasingly becoming important in this decision-making process. If a weight area is primarily equipped with machines (Nautilus®, Universal, etc.), an easily maintained durable carpet is sufficient. If the room is dominated by free weights, a resilient rubber surface is recommended—tiled, poured, or prefabricated. Prefabricated options come in the form of sheets or tiles and are simply glued on top of the existing surface or concrete slab.

The desired appearance of the strength training room is important to consider when selecting a flooring material. The level of supervision over these areas is also a factor, as observed participants tend to be less likely to treat equipment roughly and purposely damage equipment or flooring surfaces. Once again, aesthetic appeal is becoming more important, and creative and attractive options are not necessarily more expensive; however, they do take more planning (Hasenkamp & Lutz, 2001; Sawyer, 2009). The color schemes of the walls, equipment upholstery, and flooring must all be coordinated to appeal to the user. Assistance in this area can be provided by consultants or interior designers, and seeking the assistance of these individuals is becoming more prevalent (Sawyer, 2009; Steinbach, 2002a).

Racquetball Courts

The overall playing surface for a racquetball court requires 800 sq ft. Traditionally, racquetball courts are covered with a wood floor surface. Maple floors are attractive, provide favorable ball bounce, and absorb shock to the feet, but there is one disadvantage. When moisture enters the wood, it will buckle the system and cause the floor to swell. This becomes an important factor to note if subterranean facilities are built in areas with porous soil. The only other viable system is a synthetic one. New polyurethane materials have been implemented with satisfactory results. These floors are poured and trawled over the concrete floor slab (Patton et al., 1989; Sawyer, 2009).

The most popular wall systems to choose from are reinforced fiberglass concrete, plaster, panels, poured-in-place cement slab, and shatterproof glass. Before deciding on a wall system, consider material cost, land considerations (moisture and stability), overall appearance, maintenance, and ball action. Plaster is often viewed as a mainstay as it has been around for years, but maintenance costs are usually expensive. Poured-in-place concrete slabs are not often used. The cost is prohibitive, and obtaining a straight wall from a slab that is poured on the ground and then erected is difficult to accomplish. Reinforced fiberglass concrete has a promising future, but many applications have proven inconsistent. Plexiglass walls provide an aesthetic appeal but are too costly for some facilities. Last, the floor system with perhaps the best reputation is a panel system designed from compressed wood. The quality of panel systems varies widely, so facility planning members must carefully select a system with a satisfactory quality-to-price ratio (Patton et al., 1989; Sawyer, 2009).

Racquetball court ceilings are often constructed from the same materials used for the walls. A popular alternative involves a combination of the wall material for the front half of the ceiling and acoustical tile for the back half. The acoustical tile has been found to be successful in deadening the sound of the ball. Another alternative is to use sheetrock covered by paint or a glazed material (Patton et al., 1989; Sawyer, 2009).

9 Landscape Design, Sports Turf, and Parking Lots

Richard J. LaRue, *University of New England*

David A. LaRue, *Landscape Designer*

Thomas H. Sawyer, *Indiana State University*

When the outdoor spaces of sports and recreation facilities, adjacent transitional space, and/or sports fields are planned, the project should include individuals who can lend their understanding and expertise to the process. From a design standpoint, a licensed landscape architect or experienced landscape designer should be employed. If a sports field is the focus of, or is included in, the plan, then an experienced sports turf manager is important to the process. Finally, as all outdoor facilities and spaces require maintenance, a logical planning resource will be the maintenance director and/or an experienced representative of the maintenance staff.

Perhaps the most important individual in the early stages of the planning process is the landscape professional. This person will be invaluable when making decisions related to site selection for the facility and use of all adjacent outdoor spaces.

More than any other major environmental design profession, landscape architecture is a profession on the move. It is comprehensive by definition—no less than the art and science of analysis, design, management, preservation, and rehabilitation of the land. In providing well-managed design and development plans, landscape architects offer an essential array of services and expertise that reduces costs and adds long-term value to a project. A landscape architect has a working knowledge of architecture, civil engineering, and urban planning and takes elements from each of these fields to design aesthetic yet practical relationships with the land. Members of the profession have a special commitment to improving the quality of life through the best design of places for people and other living things (American Society of Landscape Architects [ASLA],n.d.)

Sports fields are truly unique facilities. When natural turf is selected, a sports turf specialist is needed to oversee the development of a total field management program (Lewis, 1994). Lewis (1994) suggested that a comprehensive program should include (a) selecting an adapted grass or grass blend for the locality, (b) mowing this selected grass at proper height and frequency, (c) fertilizing at the proper time and rate according to the turfgrass growth, (d) irrigating as needed to encourage establishment and to reduce stress periods, (e) aerating to relieve compaction or dethatching according to the turf and the amount of play, and (f) using the appropriate preemergence and postemergence herbicides. The goal is to produce a vigorous turf that will be competitive to the weeds.

Such a program will be served by the design of the field, including irrigation and drainage, the choice of grass, and so on. Careful consideration involves knowing the grass and soil makeup, need for aeration, fertilization, topdressing, seeding, and, later, weed control.

Parking lot design is related to the planning process. A successful parking facility can present an important and positive first image for visitors to the sports or recreation facility.

Finally, as the ultimate success of the facility planning process is often measured years later, it is important to consider those aspects of groundskeeping and parking that will be predetermined in the design of the fields and other outdoor spaces. Specifically, the labor and equipment required to maintain these spaces can be controlled with a carefully prepared design. The life expectancy of both green and hard goods is directly related to the level of quality afforded. Management of money and resources (capital expenditures, debt load, salaries and wages, existing equipment vs. new equipment, etc.) begins with the planning process and the investment decisions made prior to plan implementation (Sawyer, 2009).

In summary, the planning process must include consideration of the facility and the adjacent outside or transitional space. Furthermore, the planning process will benefit from the expertise of a registered landscape architect or experienced landscape designer, an experienced sports turf specialist (if planning a formal play space), an experienced parking lot consultant, and a representative of the facilities maintenance staff. The quality of the planning process will be measured against the ability of the facility and all aspects of the plan to meet the goals described in the facility's case statement or building program document.

Landscape Design: Aesthetics, Function, and Safety

Frequently, when money is tight and/or the facility costs exceed expectations, careful development of the adjacent outdoor space is often ignored. Experience has demonstrated that this is shortsighted, as there are essential components that must be considered exclusive of selecting a site of a facility. The design of this transitional space, whether for an indoor or outdoor facility, should consider

- the aesthetics of the space relative to all adjacent facilities,
- the functional characteristics of the space relative to adjacent facilities, and
- the safety of users (including accessibility) within the space and relative to adjacent facilities

Aesthetics

The basics of aesthetics in landscape design are sight lines that bring focus to the important features of a facility or space, how the space or spaces are used (especially spatial relationships), and the ability of the finished product to enhance the quality of the experience for the users.

Annuals commonly used in landscaping. A good landscape needs anchor plants: trees, shrubs, and perennials that provide color year after year. However, to keep the landscape lively and fresh year to year, you should mix in new and different annuals each season.

The annuals need to be selected based on the type of exposure in which they will be growing: sun or shade, cool or hot weather, and humid or dry conditions. The top 10 annuals for landscaping are

- impatiens (shade),
- petunia (sunny),
- angelonia or summer snapdragon (full sun),
- geranium (sunny),
- vinca (sunny),
- pentas or star cluster (sunny),
- viola (sunny, cool),
- begonia (shade),
- ornamental millet (sunny), and
- marigold (sunny). (Atchison, 2003)

An example of an aesthetic use of flowers and foliage

Function

There are critical components to a comprehensive design related to function. The way the implemented design reacts to natural and man-made stresses is indicative of the time and resources invested during the planning process. Furthermore, the long-term demand for maintenance will also be affected by the design. However, not to be left out as an important element of the design process is the way the design serves the facility program and the users' needs.

In addition to the characteristics described above, site selection is an important part of function for an outdoor facility and should also include

- the orientation of play spaces with respect to the sun angle and prevailing wind direction,
- the topography of the developed and undeveloped outdoor space,
- the existing and necessary surface and subsurface irrigation and drainage,
- the appropriate use of natural and man-made barriers,
- environmental concerns, and
- the minimization of normal wear and vandalism. (Macomber, 1993; Sawyer, 2009)

Safety

It is critical that the planning considerations for safety result in a landscape design that manages the risk of all adjacent outdoor spaces so that all foreseeable user accidents or injuries can be avoided. This safety and security plan should include

- signage in large lettering that clearly identifies pedestrian and vehicular paths, facilities, right-of-way, accessible parking, no parking, fire zones, and other user-friendly restrictions or expectations;
- perimeter fencing or appropriate use of natural barriers;
- programmable and/or light-sensitive night lighting;
- pedestrian and vehicular circulation that is easy to maintain and has reasonable and unobstructed views of cross traffic at every intersection;

- smooth (yet skid-resistant) pavements and other path or road surfaces;
- bollards (permanent and removable barriers) restricting vehicular travel on pedestrian paths; and
- surveillance.

Surface and Subsurface Irrigation and Drainage

An effective landscape design will consider the operation of surface and subsurface irrigation and drainage. Not having enough moisture can be deadly to grass and plants. Too much moisture and no way for the water to drain can also drown plants and fields. When rain does not come, appropriate irrigation must be available. Irrigation planning is both an art and a science. There are extraordinary examples of how, after large amounts of rain and subsequent flooding, the drainage of a sports field has allowed a contest to be held in an amazingly short time (Sawyer, 2009; Smith, 1998; Tracinski, 1998).

Irrigation
The principle of "deep and infrequent" watering remains the norm. This practice over the years has proven to be the most effective method. The physical properties of the soil must be considered in planning any watering program. For example, a clay soil will not accept as much water as a sandy soil and will require lighter, more frequent irrigation.

Most turfgrasses need at least 1 in. to 1.5 in. of water per week during the growing season to support turf growth (Puhalla, Krans, & Goatley, 2010). The best time to irrigate turf is in the early morning hours, just prior to or after sunrise. This eliminates interference with use, reduces disease incidence, and increases the amount of water placed in the soil for plant use.

Irrigation on a baseball field

Two basic types of irrigation systems are available for use: portable irrigation and installed irrigation. Portable irrigation systems include traveling irrigators (i.e., rotating sprinkler attached to a hose, propelling itself along a wire), quick coupler systems (i.e., systems are made up of a series of underground pipes with quick couplers permanently installed flush with the ground), and rain guns (i.e., a huge impact-type sprinkler that is used to irrigate a large turf area).

The price for installed systems is decreasing, and the reliability of operation is increasing. Automatic systems save maintenance labor costs when compared to portable systems and provide for a more even distribution of water.

Drainage
Whether designing a drainage system for a new field or for an existing field, some questions need to be answered:
- How quickly should the field be returned to playable condition after a rainstorm?
- In what climate is the field located?
- Is the field designed for amateur or professional use?
- What kind of flexibility will there be in rescheduling?
- Will the field have a crown or will it be flat but sloped?
- Will the field have a dense, clay-like soil or a sand soil?
- Will the collection system be shallow or deep?
- Will there be a single- or multilayered filter system?

Most landscape architects will use the following rule of thumb relative to drainage: Whether designing a single field or a multifield complex, landscape architects keep in mind that each field should be designed and constructed as an individual drainage unit. A well-designed drainage plan will install interceptor drains to isolate water, cuts and fills, catch basins, swales, and French drains.

Furthermore, Puhalla, Krans, and Goatley (2010) suggested field designs for surface drainage fall into one of two categories: crowned or flat. The typical percentage of slope for a sports field runs between 1% and 1.75%.

The most common type of crowned field is a football field (see Figure 9.1). However, now that many football fields are also used for soccer, they have become flat fields because the soccer field overlaps the football field. Most soccer fields are often designed using a lower percentage of slope and installed drain systems are usually added (see Figure 9.2).

Most flat fields need an installed parallel or grid drainage pattern, and crowned fields typically have a herringbone pattern (Breems, 2001). In either case the drainage pattern should extend at least 15 ft beyond the playing surface on all sides. Be certain that the field records indicate it is a flat, sloped, or a crowned field. Otherwise, 10 years after initial construction, some well-meaning person might try to "recrown" the field, causing a real mess. The collection system should be located near the surface of the

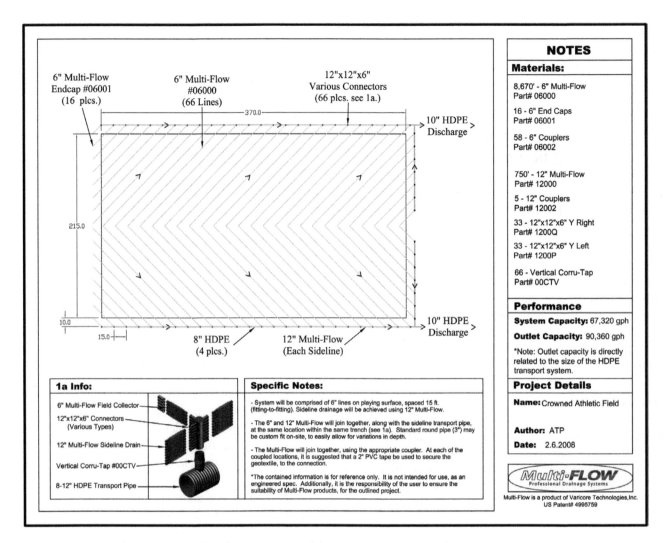

NOTES

Materials:

8,670' - 6" Multi-Flow
Part# 06000

16 - 6" End Caps
Part# 06001

58 - 6" Couplers
Part# 06002

750' - 12" Multi-Flow
Part# 12000

5 - 12" Couplers
Part# 12002

33 - 12"x12"x6" Y Right
Part# 1200Q

33 - 12"x12"x6" Y Left
Part# 1200P

66 - Vertical Corru-Tap
Part# 00CTV

Performance

System Capacity: 67,320 gph

Outlet Capacity: 90,360 gph

*Note: Outlet capacity is directly related to the size of the HDPE transport system.

Project Details

Name: Crowned Athletic Field

Author: ATP

Date: 2.6.2008

Multi-**FLOW**
Professional Drainage Systems

Multi-Flow is a product of Varicore Technologies,Inc.
US Patent# 4995759

1a Info:

6" Multi-Flow Field Collector
12"x12"x6" Connectors (Various Types)
12" Multi-Flow Sideline Drain
Vertical Corru-Tap #00CTV
8-12" HDPE Transport Pipe

Specific Notes:

- System will be comprised of 6" lines on playing surface, spaced 15 ft. (fitting-to-fitting). Sideline drainage will be achieved using 12" Multi-Flow.

- The 6" and 12" Multi-Flow will join together, along with the sideline transport pipe, at the same location within the same trench (see 1a). Standard round pipe (3") may be custom fit on-site, to easily allow for variations in depth.

- The Multi-Flow will join together, using the appropriate coupler. At each of the coupled locations, it is suggested that a 2" PVC tape be used to secure the geotextile, to the connection.

*The contained information is for reference only. It is not intended for use, as an engineered spec. Additionally, it is the responsibility of the user to ensure the suitability of Multi-Flow products, for the outlined project.

Figure 9.1. **Grid Drainage Plan for Sports Field Drainage** (*Source:* Puhalla et al., 2010)

field. The deeper the collectors are located, the slower the drainage will be. The system that is submerged 6 in. with sand located above and around the collectors is fast and efficient (Breems, 2001).

Finally, a multilayered filter system protects the collectors from failure due to binding and guarantees a long life. A fabric filter prevents the core from filling with fine sand and silt. A 3.5-oz to 4-oz needle-punched geo-syn-

thetic fabric does a fine job. An inch or two of very coarse sand surrounding the fabric will prevent the fabric from blocking. As the water passes through, the sand particles of clay and silt are arrested before they reach the fabric filter (Breems, 2001).

Trends and New Technologies in Landscape Design

Finally, the planning process will consider new trends or cutting-edge technologies in the design of outdoor spaces. Consider making a significant investment in all aspects of the planning process to reduce short- and long-term mistakes. Once the plan is implemented, the success of the planning process will be easily measured in its ability to meet the needs of the facility program. Include the right people in the planning process. The experts are easy to remember. However, user input is also critical to promote inclusion and a sense of ownership in the pro-

Drainage culvert

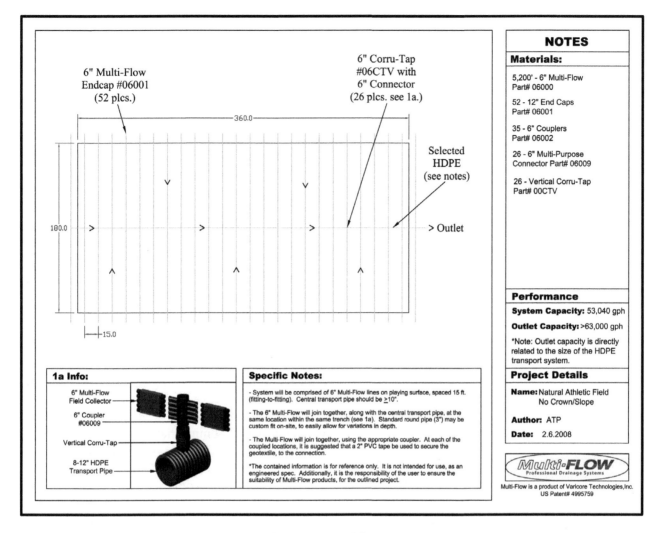

Figure 9.2. Herringbone Drainage Plan for Sports Field Drainage (*Source:* Puhalla et al., 2010)

cess. Users include the people who will manage the facility and outdoor spaces as well as those who will participate in facility programs. An appropriate number of such people will help build goodwill and, more important, should serve the planning process effectively because of their unique "user" viewpoint. The long-term reality of maintenance and the cost of labor, materials, and equipment demands that landscape designs provide for minimal maintenance. A landscape architect or experienced landscape designer as well as a representative member of the groundskeeping staff should provide the expertise to design minimal maintenance into the outdoor spaces. Finally, the planning process should consider sustainability and future implementation of the design, when it comes to the level of quality selected in green and hard goods. Experience tells us that when purchasing such goods, the better the quality, the better the satisfaction.

Trends and new technologies in turf management are often made available by academics who are committed to this aspect of venue design and management. An excellent source of such information can be found at http:// turfgrass.hort.iastate.edu/extension. Articles specific to athletic fields and made available by Dr. David Minner of Iowa State University at this website include

- *Infield Skin Testing;*
- *Athletic Field Generic Football Field Maintenance;*
- *Athletic Field Procedure for Selecting a Sand Rootzone;*
- *Athletic Field Coring and Topdressing Table;*
- *Athletic Field Poa Annua Control;*
- *Athletic Field Safety and Maintenance Checklist;*
- *Athletic Field Evaluation and Traffic Survey;*
- *Athletic Field Construction, Renovation, and Maintenance Costs;*
- *Athletic Field Management—Tips for a Limited Budget;*
- *Athletic Field Gypsum?;*
- *Athletic Field Liability Signage;*
- *Athletic Field Care Tips;*
- *Athletic Field—Selecting Bluegrass Varieties;*
- *Athletic Field Pre-Germinated Divot Mix;*
- *Athletic Field Seeding Schedule;*
- *Athletic Field End of Season Practices; and*
- *Grass System Response to Traffic and Recovery.*

Additionally, at this same website Dr. Minner includes scholarly articles related to turfgrass and golf courses.

Sustainable Landscapes

Planners and designers of landscapes should always consider ways to make the design responsive to the environment.

Sustainable landscapes are responsive to the environment, regenerative, and can actively contribute to the development of healthy communities. Sustainable landscapes sequester carbon, clean the air and water, increase energy efficiency, restore habitats, and create value through significant economic, social, and environmental benefits. (ASLA, n.d.-b, para. 1)

When planning landscapes the planners and designers need to be concerned about green building technologies.

Green building technologies like site planning, tree canopy coverage, and green roofs, have positive impacts on communities and the environment, including reduction of stormwater runoff, improved air and water quality, mitigation of urban heat island effect, and energy savings. ASLA supports efforts to encourage the use of these technologies and other design techniques that will create more sustainable communities. (ASLA, n.d.-a, para. 1)

Sports Grasses and Turfs

Characteristics of Turfgrasses Commonly Used for Sports Turfs

Puhalla et al. (2010) suggested there are 11 grass varieties commonly used as turfgrasses. However, of these species, only five are widely used in sports turf situations: Bermuda grass, Kentucky bluegrass, tall fescue, perennial ryegrass, and creeping bentgrass. There are two other grasses that are sometimes used: buffalo grass and zoysiagrass.

Furthermore, Puhalla et al. (2010) indicated Bermuda grass (monostand) is planted and maintained alone except when overseeded with perennial and annual ryegrass for winter play. Tall fescue, perennial ryegrass, and Kentucky bluegrass are planted and maintained as either monostands or in combination with other cultivars (polystands). Creeping bentgrass is usually planted as a monostand.

Turfgrass selection is usually based upon weather zones (i.e., warm, transitional, or cool). In warm weather zones (southern states across the United States), sports turf is generally dominated by Bermuda grass because it flourishes in the hot summers and mild winters and can withstand occasional summer dryness without damage.

In the transitional zone, tall fescues and specifically developed Bermuda grass dominate fields. Finally, in cold zones (northern states across the United States), Kentucky bluegrass and perennial ryegrass predominate, and a mixture of those species is probably the most popular sports turf (Puhalla et al., 2010). "Both types tolerate the cold northern winters adequately, and the mixture allows for the aggressive spreading and recovery characteristic of Kentucky bluegrass, along with the stability and wear resistance of perennial ryegrass" (Puhalla et al., 2010, p. 8).

In some very dry climates where pure water is not available or cannot be used to irrigate turf fields, some turfgrasses have been designed to tolerate a blend of saline and freshwater. For example, in Dubai, United Arab Emirates, the five primary sport clubs have turf fields that are maintained in excellent condition using partially saline water and a carefully managed selection of turfgrasses, throughout the dormant (summer and winter) and growing seasons (spring and fall). The balance is likely an annual ryegrass overseeded in the late spring for the summer months (hottest and driest); and when the fall comes, the annual ryegrass dies, making way for the overseeding of Bermuda grass or Seashore Paspalum.

The National Turfgrass Evaluation Program (NTEP) tests hundreds of commercially available cultivars and experimental entries of turfgrass annually. Researchers conduct these tests at universities in 40 states and a few Canadian provinces. Data from each year are summarized and published at http://www.ntep.org and also in CD-ROM format. Go to the website, read the disclaimer at the bottom of that page, then click enter. This will take you to the main page (http:www.ntep.org/contents2.shtml). To find a grass species, simply click on the link in the yellow box, "All NTEP Reports—Select a Turfgrass Species."

Portable Grass

During the 1990s, Popke (2000) indicated a number of natural-grass suppliers (e.g., GreenTech® Inc.-ITM turf modules, Hummer Turfgrass Systems Inc.-Grasstiles™, the Motz Group-TS-II™, Desso DLW Sports International-DD GrassMaster, SportGrass® Inc.-SportGrass system, Southern Turf Nurseries-STN 2000, Thomas Brothers Grass, a division of Turf-Grass America Co-SquAyers, Southwest Recreational Industries Inc.-AstroGrass®) became responsive to facilities' needs for a more durable natural grass product.

The suppliers began to use (a) portable grass that unrolls as a cover for concrete floors and parking lots, (b) grass tiles with roots that are reinforced and stabilized with synthetic fibers, and (c) systems that mix grass with synthetic fibers woven or stitched into a backing. These renewed processes allow sections of worn surface (e.g., golf tee-boxes, areas in front of a soccer goal, middle sections of football fields) to be replaced without tearing up the entire area and the entire surface can usually be removed or installed in less than 24 hr. All of the systems claim to be able to better reinforce the root zone and extend usage.

Often, with these portable systems, grass is grown in trays that allow for drainage and air movement. Synthetic reinforcements play a role in several portable grass surfaces and are considered 100% natural by their suppliers. This can be said because the majority of the additional synthetic material is inserted below the grass surface for root reinforcement and additional wear resistance. However, a better term might be *hybrid*.

Some of the hybrid systems are a combination of sand-filled, fibrillated synthetic tufts and a dual component backing of biodegradable fibers and plastic mesh. The matrix shelters the vegetative parts of the grass plant that are essential to rapid growth and recuperation while the grass roots intertwine with the tufts and grow down through the plastic mesh. If the turf canopy wears away, the sand-filled synthetic matrix continues to provide a consistent playing surface. There are a few systems that do not use a cloth backing. Instead, they train the roots to grow on top of a plastic barrier, similar to roots in a potted plant.

A Kinder, Gentler Synthetic Turf

Popke (2000) described three new kinder, gentler synthetic turfs: Astroplay®, Fieldturf™, and Sofsport™. These synthetic surfaces have been designed to reduce injuries to players. The new synthetic surfaces blend and tuft polyethylene and polypropylene fibers into a permeable surface backing. Each synthetic grass fiber is placed to create a pattern of natural grass. The fill is made from sand and ground rubber, which surround each fiber much like soil holds a blade of grass. One supplier does not use sand, but rather uses a combination of rubber and nylon fibers mixed with longer polyolefin strands. This combination enhances drainage, reduces compaction, and adds resilience.

On July 30, 2008, the U.S. Consumer Product Safety Commission (CPSC) released its evaluation of various synthetic turf fields with regard to lead exposure:

> CPSC staff evaluation showed that newer fields had no lead or generally had the lowest lead levels. Although small amounts of lead were detected on the surface of some older fields, none of these tested fields released amounts of lead that would be harmful to children. (p. 12)

Though the bottom line was that the amount of lead exposure that older artificial turf fields may release was not found to be significant, older fields may need to be tested, and participants should wash their hands after playing on these fields.

The debate continues regarding the pros and cons of synthetic turf versus natural grass. The positive aspects of synthetic turf include lower maintenance costs, pesticide-free, increased playability, and fewer injuries. However, the negative aspects have not all been mitigated over time. They include heat hazard, the presence of chemicals beyond lead (including zinc), an increased risk of MRSA when skin makes direct contact with the turf and causes skin lesions, and the possibility of an adverse effect on asthmatics because of the dust caused by ground-up tires.

Synthetic turf requires regular cleaning to ensure that bacteria does not grow on the field and especially along the sidelines (where players gather). Another caution to take with synthetic turf (and perhaps turfgrass fields as well) is to test fields that have been flooded with a combination of rainwater and sewer systems overflow for coliform and other bacteria. Especially on synthetic turf fields, coliform can be a hazard to players who suffer skin abrasions. Under these circumstances, the field will need to be cleaned and retested to ensure the safety of participants.

As synthetic turf becomes more popular, research laboratories such as the Missouri Turf Research Center and the Center for Turfgrass Sciences at Penn State will continue to provide important information for owners and prospective owners regarding health and safety-related developments of synthetic turf fields.

Groundskeeping: Management, Maintenance, and Equipment Planning Responsibilities

Appropriate to the review of groundskeeping management, maintenance, and equipment are three concepts related to success in these areas: time management, money and resource management, and machinery and equipment management. The responsibility for planning related to groundskeeping should be shared by a seasoned member of the groundskeeping staff. Efficient use of staff time can be facilitated in a properly planned landscape design. A significant aspect of the plan will be reducing labor as it relates to maintenance. If, by design, you reduce the employee labor required, you are managing time more efficiently. Second, if you demand quality green goods when installing your landscape design, then the money and resources for your project will be managed more efficiently. Finally, if your planning process includes a design that can be maintained with existing equipment, you are taking responsibility for the future without ignoring the reality of the present. Groundskeeping management must be considered when designing your landscape. Few people can better assist you with this planning than a knowledgeable representative of your groundskeeping staff.

Topdressing a Baseball/Softball Field

Topdressing describes the application of a structural material to the top layer of turf. According to Wilkinson (2002), a structural material is one that is not solubilized rapidly in water (e.g., soil conditioners, sand, and soil). Topdressing benefits the field in three ways: (a) improves the quality of the turf surface, (b) protects the turf crowns, and (c) improves the soil's porosity and reduces the organic thatch. Most baseball and softball fields can be improved by topdressing. Both the skinned and turf areas can benefit.

The skinned area of a baseball or softball field is often built using heavy-textured clay, and a soil clay amendment is worked into the top few inches to achieve a desired surface (Wilkinson, 2002). The surface of the skinned area should be almost 100% soil clay amendment. The surface should be topdressed once or twice a month, depending on usage. The soil amendment should be spread uniformly and raked into the top inch of the soil. Using ceramic conditioners will dry out the skinned area and cause it to harden and crack. A great deal of water will need to be used to achieve a great playing surface.

Topdressing a baseball or softball turf can help the turf and produce a great playing surface. A turf area should not be topdressed with a structural material containing more than 40% ceramic conditioner (Wilkinson, 2002). The more clay soil amendment that is added, the greater the chance is of stressing the turf. The recommended mixture for topdressing is 30% or less ceramic conditioner to 70% or more natural soil in which the turf is growing. If the field was built with sand, then add 30% soil amendment to the same kind of sand. For single application of topdressing, add enough to achieve a layer ⅛ in. thick or less (Wilkinson, 2002).

How to Select a Field Cover

Field covers keep fields dry, reduce the risk of rainouts, increase turf enhancement, and lend themselves to great advertising and sponsorship arrangements. The advertising dollars should be spent on the cover for the tarp when it is rolled up. More people will see the advertisement, and it is easier to place logos on the cover for the rolled-up tarp than it is to place logos on the actual tarp material. The color of covers can play an important role in turf management. Tests conducted by several turf specialists found that certain colors of covers can positively affect turf development.

- White–silver combination with white side exposed to the sun, on average, has 14°F less heat build-up under the cover than other color combinations. This color combination would be appropriate for southern climates.
- Black–silver combination with black side exposed to the sun draws more heat to the turf surface. This combination would work well in northern climates.
- Orange–white combination allows light penetration and enhances turf development. This combination would be appropriate for northern and southern climates.

Both woven polyethylene and vinyl provide a good cover. The common differences between polyethylene and vinyl are outlined in Table 9.1.

Field Traffic

A frequent concern for turf managers relates to field traffic (number of events per field, per year). According to Minner (2004) and Sawyer (2009), on average, an individual field receives 125 events per year. A field receiving over 79 events may not be able to recover to an acceptable level. Most turf managers felt they could maintain an acceptable field if the annual event schedule was less than 64 events.

However, this is not a definite maximum. Some programs cannot even tolerate 64 events, and others, because of proper management, have tolerated many more. There are a number of variables regarding field tolerance, includ-

Table 9.1

Comparison of Polyethylene and Vinyl Covers

Characteristic	Polyethylene	Vinyl
Weight	1/3 lighter	1/3 heavier
Price	1/2 less in cost	1/2 more in cost
Color	fewer choices	greater choices
Snow removal	not as durable	more durable
Wind	less effective	more effective
Joining sections	Velro®	plastic zipper

(*Source:* Puhalla et al., 2010)

ing "warm/cool season climate, soil type, grass selection, irrigation, cultivation, seeding/sodding renovation, etc." (Puhalla et al., 2010, p. 38).

Minner (2004) recommended that turf managers begin collecting their own data (specific information reflecting field activity and performance) to use when making important field-use and planning decisions. "Without this type of data, it will be difficult to limit field-use or to plan the appropriate number of fields when building for future growth" (Minner, 2004, p. 38).

Combining field performance information with accurate field use records on a person per hour or field per hour basis will give the turf manager the best decision-making data from which to work. When organizations do not allow for reasonable field usage, Minner (2004) suggested that an appropriate amount of funding be channeled to grounds management to offset field damages from high use. In cases of extreme field activity, there may be no level of funding that will keep the fields from wearing out and your only recourse is to close the fields for revegetation (Minner, 2004).

Rotational Field: A Relatively New Concept

As the interest in team sports, such as soccer, continues to grow at all levels, the demand for time on traditional playing fields is escalating. Daily team practices, eight- to 10-game weekend schedules and pickup games when the fields are not in use are becoming common. Bob Stienhaus, president of Pioneer Fields (Pittsburgh), and fellow founder Matthew Butch have come up with a practical solution for preserving natural turf fields that requires less maintenance and provides for safer, year-round play. The concept is a rotational athletic field.

The design concept incorporates a rectangular athletic playing field fitted within a substantially circular turf area. The uniquely graded circular area can essentially be scaled to fit any size rectangular playing field (e.g., football, field hockey, lacrosse, or soccer) with some buffer space. The playing field rotates at select times throughout the season of play to limit the amount of play in high-traffic areas or to avoid damage or unsafe turf. The rotation schedule can range from daily, such as following a rough game in heavy rains, to just three times a year for seasonal play and seasonal turf repairs.

Winter Management in Preparation for Spring Sports

Developing an appropriate plan for fall maintenance of sport fields will likely improve the quality of the fields for spring use (McKenna & Goatley, 2009). This plan includes fertilization in high-use areas that is specific to the type(s) of turfgrass(es). Aeration, topdressing, and seeding are also recommended. Turf blankets (breathable covers) have been shown to extend field use in the fall as well as

enhanced "greenup" in the spring (Goatley, Maddox, Lang, Elmore, & Stewart, 2005).

Additional challenges include

- implementing proper pest management (pesticides must be properly applied);
- avoiding any kind of traffic on the field, especially "concentrated" traffic during the late fall and early winter when turfgrass growth is limited;
- rotating use between fields (e.g., practice and game fields or between multiple practice fields); and
- rotating the field orientation during practice (e.g., using those areas that normally get less traffic—you'll need portable goals or markers).

Chemical Handling and Storage, Legal Aspects, and Recommendations

Besides the Chemical Hazards Act managed under the Occupational Safety and Health Administration (OSHA), both state and federal regulations govern the handling of many of the chemicals used in weed control, insect management, and fertilization. The Chemical Hazards Act requires the employer to properly warn and protect employees using such chemicals. All chemical manufacturers must ship hazardous chemicals with Material Safety Data Sheets (MSDS), which should be kept on file for employees and specifically outline the guidelines for proper use of their products. Posting reentry signs is a must when chemicals have been applied to fields where teams might be exposed by using the field prior to the specified reentry time following a chemical application.

Other government regulations require groundskeeping staff to be certified in the proper application and handling of chemicals. It is the responsibility of the groundskeeping staff to be knowledgeable in the use and handling of these chemicals and associated equipment. With a knowledgeable resource on the planning committee, the facility can provide for proper storage of chemicals and cleanup of chemical application equipment used in groundskeeping.

Lining Athletic Fields

Steinbach (2000) suggested the primary concern when marking grass fields is to keep the turf in good growing condition. Water-based paints are the preferred choice. Chalk (e.g., limestone or marble) is less friendly to turf due to the accumulated buildup that blocks water's movement to the grass root system. The best paint contains a higher concentration (1 to 2 lb per gallon) of titanium oxide (TiO_2), which brightens the paint. The other common ingredient is calcium carbonate ($CaCO_2$), a paint filler. Colored paints will have a higher amount of calcium carbonate. White paint can be diluted up to 9:1, but colored paints can only be diluted to 1:1. Too much calcium carbonate makes playing fields abrasive, and it can kill the turfgrass.

The following are a few painting tips provided by Mike Hebrard, owner of Athletic Field Design:

- Make an enlargement of the logo to be painted using the grid method, and then draw a series of lines in a graph format on the logo at a workable uniform spacing. Layout the size of the logo, converting inches to feet, and mark dots on the grass at the edges of the design. Use an inverted spray chalk to do the initial layout. Repeat the graph, using string and long nails, going back and forth until the graph is complete. By looking at the drawing, note where each line crosses a grid and duplicate it on the grass by painting a line, gradually connecting the shape of the logo. Use inverted aerosol cans to differentiate colors and features. Once the logo has been completed, you can brighten it using an airless sprayer.

- The most popular method of painting on athletic turf is the stencil on a heavy plastic sheet or tarp. Stencils are readily available from most athletic paint suppliers. After use, fold up the stencil and put it into a marked duffle bag to store and identify its contents.

- The key to painting dirt is to have it moist enough to take the paint, much like staining wood. If it is too wet, the paint will bleed into the other colors. If it is too dry, the paint will not be very bright and will wear off quickly.

Example of a lined football field

Parking Lot Design

Facilities managers are being challenged to develop fair and customer-focused parking strategies, prioritize the use of decreasing parking resources, understand the explosion in parking technology, provide cost-effective parking solutions while catching up with deferred maintenance, address the widely held perception that safe and convenient parking can only be provided next to the front door, and provide adequate accessible parking spaces for the size of the lot (see Table 9.2).

Table 9.2

Number of Accessible Parking Spaces Required Under Federal Law

Total Parking in Lot	Required Minimum Number of Accessible Spaces
1–25	1
26–50	2
51–75	3
76–100	4
101–150	5
151–200	6
201–300	7
301–400	8
401–500	9
501–1000	2% of total
1,001 and over	20 plus 1 for each 100 over 1,000

(*Source:* Access Board, 2008)

The traditional parking paradigm must be expanded to meet the planning challenge. In the past, planning focused on the number of vehicles within given parking parameters. However, as the number of available sites decreases and the cost to develop and operate parking facilities increases, communities are demanding more cost-effective solutions.

Ideally, the parking design should be incorporated into the overall landscape and building design, especially in terms of aesthetics, function, and safety. However, there are additional design options to consider including function, aesthetics, and safety.

Function

Will parking discriminate against users who arrive later in the day? Do plans include large and visible signage so that users understand all allowances and restrictions? Is there adequate parking?

Will the facility require a parking garage? Can users exit the parking areas in a timely fashion? In the past, planning focused on the number of vehicles within given parking parameters. The new focus should be on consumer needs. Planners and facilities managers should move away from the traditional parking paradigm to one that is consumer oriented.

The traditional parking paradigm. Considerable energy has been focused on the management of vehicles and pedestrians within the boundaries of parking areas. Traditional parking technology contributed to this planning focus, with the "pay-on-foot" approach in parking structures, central pay stations in surface lots, "smart cards," debit cards, proximity cards, and so on. Planners are bombarded with issues, concerns, and solutions within the parking space boundaries. Traditional master planning guidelines for sports and recreation venues have also contributed to this planning focus.

Kirkpatrick (1997) and Ben-Joseph (2012) suggested that many planners have successfully implemented a pedestrian orientation to the recreation and sport environment, resulting in parking located at perimeter or off-site locations. This approach has increased the need for transportation.

Yet, the planning focus has remained within the boundaries of the parking areas as planners have attempted to match and manage the vehicle demand to the space available. Over the years, many strategies have been developed to manage the increasing demand for limited parking space.

Parking planners have matched various forms and combinations of reserved parking, zoned parking, and open parking to the specific community culture. But the planning focus has remained directed at single-occupant vehicles within designated parking boundaries. Regardless of the system used to manage vehicles within designated parking boundaries at perimeter locations, customer dissatisfaction with parking systems increased dramatically. Customers lamented that convenient parking space was not available and that the cost of parking was rising. At the same time, many facility managers were faced with deferred maintenance, escalating costs to operate and maintain a parking system, and increasing customer demand for a decreasing supply of parking.

The following factors contribute to the increasing customer and administration dissatisfaction with parking systems that traditionally were perceived as successful:

- New parking structures are costly to build.
- Costs to maintain structures are escalating.
- Surface lots are costly to build.
- Costs to maintain core area surface lots are escalating.
- Deferred maintenance is adding up for many older structures and surface lots where security, aesthetics, and quality construction may not have been a priority in the past.

Thus, it can be seen that costs to build, repair, and maintain parking structures and surface parking lots are escalating. At the same time, customers are not willing to absorb these additional costs by paying higher parking rates, especially when a perceived value may not be present.

A parking paradigm shift: Customer-oriented parking. Planning that traditionally started once a vehicle reached a parking area now encompasses options for getting from home to the sports and recreation venue. This has become necessary because

- many sports and recreation venues cannot cost-effectively operate and maintain the traditional expansion of surface lot and structure parking,
- the customer or participant is typically not willing to pay the increasing cost, and
- the traditional parking planning focus of one vehicle per person no longer meets the diverse needs of all customers.

The customer-oriented parking paradigm requires that planners understand and know the customers to meet their needs and provide a better service. The parking menu should reflect choices in terms of cost to convenience. For example, parking options might include

- reserved space or parking area;
- core area parking;
- perimeter area parking;
- designated motorcycle parking in the preceding four areas if demand requires;
- car pool/van pool parking in the first four areas above if demand requires it;
- bicycle parking, which might include bicycle storage lockers and the traditional hoop;
- shared parking resources with the surrounding community, such as with park-and-ride programs;
- economic incentives provided to promote shared bus services with the surrounding community; and
- walking as a parking option that needs only to be promoted. Typically, implementing many sports and recreation venue master plans has resulted in a pedestrian orientation to the venue where special attention has been focused on providing appropriately placed sidewalks (7 ft or 8 ft wide for snow removal, which is also a good width for group walking) with excellent lighting, an effective emergency telephone system, and beautiful grounds.

Another key to success is the flexibility of a parking system to provide multiple options to fit diverse lifestyles.

Parking systems. Parking administrators have matched various forms and combinations of reserved parking, zoned parking, and open parking to their specific recreation and sports and cultures. Kirkpatrick (1997) and Ben-Joseph (2012) suggested the following advantages and disadvantages of each form:

- Reserved parking is typically the most expensive option with the lowest occupancy. As space constraints continue to grow with the projected decrease in core area parking, it may be increasingly difficult to provide reserved parking for large numbers of people.
- Zoned parking typically restricts parkers to an area close to their work site. The occupancy rate is generally higher than that for reserved parking. As core area parking space continues to decline, the demand typically exceeds the supply.

- Open parking, commonly referred to as "hunting license" parking, provides a system of parking on a first-come basis and has the highest occupancy rate. However, as the demand for parking increases, the level of frustration grows, as customers perceive wasted time in hunting for a parking space.

Parking options. The following menu of seven parking options is listed, in order, from the most expensive to the least expensive:

1. Reserved space or area is usually the most expensive and has the lowest occupancy rate. If the demand exceeds the supply, the challenge may be to develop criteria for eligibility that customers perceive to be fair.
2. Core area parking typically provides parking within a reasonably short walking distance to most recreation or sports activities.
3. Perimeter parking generally provides parking that requires a longer walk or a short bus ride to most recreational or sports activities.
4. Motorcycle parking that typically cannot be used for vehicle parking may be promoted for motorcycles because motorcycles require less space than cars, and a lower rate can be charged, whether in a reserved area, core area, or perimeter area parking location.
5. Car pool/van pool programs are a cost-effective approach for those who are willing to contend with the perceived inconvenience of organizing. Payment choices could be offered depending on whether reserved, core area, or perimeter parking is used.
6. Bicycle parking could be offered, from the traditional hoops to bicycle lockers. Because many bicycles are expensive, the provision of lockers may promote the use of bicycles over vehicles. Attended bike corrals are also becoming more available.
7. Park-and-ride lots may provide an opportunity to share resources with the surrounding community, to reduce operating costs, to take advantage of parking space that may be underused, and to address a unique need of commuting participants.

Finally, flexibility must be built into the parking system to provide customers with easy access to multiple parking options based on their own unique needs.

Parking technology. Like many fields of endeavor, the parking industry is experiencing an explosion in technology. Extensive amounts of data may be tracked and monitored. However, implementing such technology may be costly. The initial task is to identify the information that is essential to managing a successful parking system. The typical challenge is to fund only the hardware and the software that are actually needed but with expansion capabilities for future growth. Effective strategic planning, together with a total quality management approach, will help to identify the likely future direction for use of emerging parking technologies.

The following are examples of available parking technologies:

- Equipment to monitor parking structure activity. Typically, this involves a chip in a card or on a permit or sensors installed in the pavement. For enforcement purposes, gate equipment may be used. Types of information that may be monitored are as follows:
  — Number and time of entry/exit
  — Occupancy trends
  — Use by permit type such as student, client with disability, or guest
  — Amount of parking used per parker
  — Identification of maintenance needs such as a gate remaining open
  — The system may include a "Parking Available/Full" sign at the entrance for customers' convenience. If the system operates close to full occupancy on a daily basis, all structures may be networked so that if a particular structure is full, a message sign will direct customers to the next closest structures that have parking available.
- Central pay stations may be used in structures or surface lots. Individual parking meters are eliminated, and customers are directed to a central location to pay. Advantages for the customer are that a parking receipt is provided and dollar bills may be used, eliminating the need to carry a large number of coins. Advantages operationally are that (a) enforcement will pull a tape at the central pay station to quickly identify vehicles whose time has expired, (b) collection time is saved because collection occurs at one location, and (c) audit control is simplified because a tape is provided that identifies the amount of revenue being collected. If multiple locations are added, central pay stations may be networked to an administrative location for on-time identification of all activity in total or per lot. For example, data could include occupancy, percentage of illegal parkers, and/or revenue collected.
- Debit card systems allow the parker to add value to a card from a central location or multiple locations and pay only for actual time parked. Debit card capability may be added to many systems such as central pay stations or individual parking meters. The key advantage to the customer is convenience (i.e., not having to carry change). Advantages operationally are that revenue is collected up front, collection costs are reduced, and audit control is simplified.

Referencing the above examples, astute questions must be asked to determine the minimal level of hardware and software needed to operate an effective parking system;

however, there must be an understanding of future directions to ensure that the system can be expanded.

For example, in monitoring structure activity, is it necessary to know parking use per customer, or is overall occupancy and identification of peak use enough information to operate a parking system successfully? Networking parking structures with a message sign may be costly. Is the cost worth the customer service? Networking multiple central pay station locations provides extensive information at a glance. Does the need for quick information justify the cost of networking and staff time to track and monitor data? Debit cards are a customer convenience. Careful planning must be done to determine whether one solution is better than other options.

Aesthetics

The first experience people have at the facility will likely come when they park their vehicle and approach the facility on foot. What are the sight lines, the use of space, and the placement of parking to the facility that make this experience inviting? Can parking be distributed in a way that avoids a large "car-lot" look? Are there natural and man-made barriers that can enhance the aesthetics of the parking space(s) without compromising safety?

Image of the parking facility. The parking environment can influence a visitor's first impression of the facility. Many factors will contribute to a positive image. Key factors are the level of maintenance, lighting, signage, and the perception of safety.

Level of maintenance. An appropriate level of maintenance must be established in the following areas:

- landscape care;
- striping;
- miscellaneous painting such as pavement arrows, objects of caution, structure railing, stairwells, and lobby areas;
- sweeping;
- pavement cleaning, such as of oil spills;
- relamping and cleaning of light fixtures;
- pavement care such as repair of potholes and cracks;
- replacement of faded, damaged, or missing signs;
- structure window washing;
- trash removal; and
- snow removal. (Ben-Joseph, 2012)

Ideally, maintenance should be scheduled during times of low occupancy. However, when this is not possible, prior notification of any closure should be provided for good public relations.

Lighting. Many customers associate safety with lighting level. Incorrect lighting, particularly in parking structures, can create a variety of problems including shadow zones, sense of insecurity, reduced visibility, loss of direction, and even a sense of claustrophobia. Planners have to be sensitive to the correct illumination, uniformity, color of light, surface colors, and reflectance.

Signage. Most successful signage systems are those that provide as little overall signage as possible. The following guidelines will contribute to a successful system:

- Letter size and wording should be standardized throughout the system.
- Warm and fuzzy wording will contribute to a friendly image. For example, "Please Drive Slowly" rather than "Drive Slowly" may go a long way toward achieving customer cooperation.
- Sign locations should be standardized as much as possible. Customers typically learn where to look for directional signage.
- Signage should be coordinated with lighting locations to further enhance signage visibility.
- High-pressure sodium lighting will distort many colors. If color-coding is used as a level indicator, colors should be selected that will not be distorted. For example, red will appear brown, but yellow will not change in appearance.
- Typically, a successful directional system will incorporate multiple approaches. For example, some customers will remember colors better than the printed word. A level or area indicator sign may include the number 2 above the written word *TWO* against a blue background. Such a sign includes numerical and written identifiers as well as color-coding.
- Traditional colors such as red, brown, yellow, and blue will probably have a higher recognition level than trendy colors such as mauve, taupe, coral, and cinnamon. Some customers may not know the name of such colors to use when asking for directions.
- Signage located around the perimeter of a surface lot rather than within the parking lot will provide ease of snow removal and sweeping.
- Information panels, campus directories, and "you-are-here" maps should be clustered in pedestrian areas such as structure elevator lobbies and bus pullouts.
- Standardizing signage, maintaining an inventory, and fabricating and installing in-house typically will provide faster service and a more cost-effective approach.

Funding of the Parking System

Ideally, a parking system should be self-supporting. Typical funding sources include

- permits,
- metered parking,
- designated visitor parking,
- parking for special events, and
- parking tickets.

Budget for the Parking System

Assuming that the parking system is self-supporting, rates should be set to fund the following components annually:

- administration,
- maintenance,
- repair and renovation,
- deferred maintenance,
- new construction,
- a reserve for new construction, and
- alternate transportation options.

As the annual budget is itemized for projected expenses and revenue, it is helpful to attach an explanation for each item. For example, why is permit revenue expected to increase/decrease or why are utility costs expected to increase/decrease? This information may be invaluable in the future for projecting trends.

Safety

The safety and security of users is the most important characteristic of parking design. Will facility users circulate between the facility and parking areas secure in the knowledge that they will be safe and their vehicle will remain intact? Will the location of the parking areas mandate use of perimeter fencing? Can pedestrian paths be designed that allow users to avoid walking in vehicular areas in the parking lot? Are permanent or removable bollards required to manage vehicular traffic on pedestrian paths? Is lighting adequate for user safety and security at night?

How will surveillance in the parking areas be managed: using closed-circuit cameras or parking attendant(s)? Will the parking areas have emergency telephone towers or call stations? And, if the lot is gated, will the entrance use pedestrian-safe, one-way traffic controllers with below-grade spikes?

The parking area should be controlled and monitored for safety. This will require a number of important decisions to be made, including

- type of parking systems (e.g., ticket and ticketless—magnetic stripe, microwave, etc.),
- type of dispensers (e.g., machines, meters, cards, or tags), and
- using a van or shuttle system.

Additional action may be needed to combat a past stereotype that parking structures or areas are not safe. Some strategies to consider include

- installing an emergency telephone system, highly visible, in standard locations;
- adding glass panels in stairwells to increase visibility;
- installing closed-circuit televisions (CCTV) that are part of an active surveillance program;
- adding parking attendants during evening hours;
- providing security personnel walking or driving through the structure at random times;
- increasing lighting levels;
- publishing and posting procedures to enhance user safety awareness; and
- establishing safety programs such as escort services.

Section II

Field and Court Specifications

Section 11

10 Indoor and Outdoor Courts

Bernie Goldfine, *Kennesaw State University*

Indoor and outdoor courts are popular competition and recreation venues. These venues are continually being modernized and improved. In this chapter, a discussion of the most popular courts will outline important considerations for planners developing new facilities.

Note: Field diagrams and specifications can be found at http://www.athleticbusiness.com/specifications/

Tennis Courts

Layout, Orientation, Dimensions, and Fencing

Tennis was first played in the United States during the mid-1870s. At that time, the game was slow-paced and was played on the grass lawns of houses and parks. The game has now changed to a fast-paced athletic sport. As tennis has changed, so too have the courts on which it is played. Today's outdoor courts are laid out in a manner that minimizes the effects of wind, sun, background vision, and the lay of the land. Tennis courts are constructed of grass, clay, soft and hard composition, asphalt, concrete, and various synthetic materials. Many other features such as accessibility, storage, parking, lighting, and fencing need to be carefully planned for indoor tennis court construction.

In the construction of outdoor tennis courts, prevailing winds must be accounted for in the planning process. If prevailing winds exist, courts should be placed near natural barriers, such as woods or hills that act as windbreaks. If no existing barriers are in the area of court construction, a thick stand of staggered trees can be planted to serve as a barrier.

Alternatively, if existing buildings are near the construction site, they may be used as a wind barrier. Visual background must be planned for in the layout of tennis courts. The background at both ends of the courts should be natural grass, shrubs, woods, or other natural landscaping. Roads, parking areas, and pedestrian high-traffic areas are not acceptable at the ends of tennis courts. Too many objects moving in front of the tennis player causes lapses in concentration and makes play more difficult. If busy areas must coexist with tennis courts, they should be at the sides of the courts. Furthermore, tennis complexes should not be placed too far from the remainder of the sports complex or center campus. The more removed the courts are, the more difficult user access will be. Court layout must also meet Americans With Disabilities Act (ADA) requirements (see Chapter 4) for all users with disabilities.

The contour of the land for proposed tennis court construction also needs careful thought. It is much cheaper to construct tennis courts on flat land than on rolling terrain; it is less expensive in terms of both earthmoving and drainage concerns. If courts must be on rolling terrain, they should be laid out with the minimum of cost for earthmoving and drainage. Also, hills should serve as natural barriers when possible.

Outdoor tennis court planning must also include the sun, which can create visual problems for the tennis player. If tennis courts are to be used mostly between April and October, they should be aligned north to south on the long axis of the court. If courts are to be used year-round, the long axis should be northwest to southeast at 22° off true north. These orientations minimize the amount of sun-related visual problems for tennis players (Francesconi, 2012).

If courts are nonporous, provisions must be made for the drainage of water off the courts. Courts may be sloped from 0.5% to 1.5% depending on the type of surface. Any slope greater than 1.5% can be visually detected by the players and is not acceptable. Courts may be sloped side to side, end to end, center to end, or end to center. If only one individual court is constructed, either a side-to-side or an end-to-end slope works well. If a battery of courts is constructed, the slope should be dictated by the fastest way to drain the most courts. For example, if five courts were built side by side, an end-to-end slope would be best because all courts would drain and dry simultaneously. If a side-to-side slope were used, the courts on the upper end of the slope would dry quickly, but the last few courts would retain water for a much longer period of time because the water from the upper end slope courts would have to drain across the courts at the lower end of the slope (Francesconi, 2012).

Center-to-end and end-to-center slopes are least desirable. When these types of slopes are used, the water remains on the court and court perimeter-playing surface much longer than when side-to-side or end-to-end slopes are used. Additionally, an end-to-center slope requires drains at or near the net. Drains on the court itself are not desirable.

When slopes are planned for use, natural drainage basins should be used when possible. Thus, if a small creek basin or lower land is adjacent to the court area, it is worthwhile to slope courts to these areas to limit artificial drainage and minimize drainage costs.

As outdoor tennis courts are planned, the size of the courts and the perimeter space around the court need careful attention. A singles court is 78 ft long x 36 ft wide. Including perimeter space, the minimum size for one doubles court would be 122 ft x 66 ft. These dimensions give minimum safety between the court and the fencing on the sides and the ends of the court (Francesconi, 2012).

The minimum distance between side-by-side courts is 12 ft. The minimum distance between the court sideline and the side fence is 15 ft. Finally, the minimum distance between the court baseline and the end fence is 24 ft (Francesconi, 2012). The shortest distance is between courts because a player has open space (the adjacent court) in which to run in order to retrieve a ball. There is more distance between the sideline and the side fence because players can run into the fence. Finally, the baseline distance is the greatest because this area is essentially a part of the playing area even though it is not a part of the actual court. Figure 10.1 illustrates these minimum distances as well as the dimensions of a tennis court. Tennis courts should be enclosed with chain-link fence. The fence can be either 10 ft or 12 ft high.

The 12 ft high fence is more expensive than the 10 ft high fence; however, those additional 2 ft of fencing keep in a significantly greater percentage of balls (Francesconi, 2012). Chain-link fence comes in a No. 6 or No. 9 gauge. The No. 6 gauge is thicker and thus more costly. Either gauge is acceptable. Fence is also available with a polyvinyl chloride (PVC) plastic coating (most often green). Coated fencing is more expensive; however, in addition to its aesthetic qualities, it does not rust like galvanized fencing will.

Line posts that hold the fencing must be no farther than 10 ft apart, and all corner and gateposts should be stabilized by cross braces. All line posts should be embedded at least 3 ft into the ground. If a windscreen/visual screen is attached to the fence, all line posts should be embedded in a concrete footer.

Adequate gates should be placed throughout the tennis court complex. These gates need to meet the needs of instructors and players. Each set of courts in a complex must have an external gate and an internal gate. Gates are expensive, but compromising on the number of gates will compromise accessibility to the courts, both internally and externally.

Types of Courts

Courts are classified as either porous (those that allow water to filter and drain through the court surface itself) or nonporous (those that do not allow water to penetrate the surface). The sloping as previously mentioned is for nonporous courts but is sometimes used in porous courts to carry penetrated water into the subsurface drainage system. Clay, grass, soft composition (fast dry), porous concrete, and various synthetics are porous courts. Concrete, asphalt (cushioned and non-cushioned), hard composition (liquid applied synthetic), and various synthetics are nonporous courts. As a group, asphalt courts are composed of asphalt plant mix, emulsified asphalt mix, plant and emulsified mix, asphalt penetration mix, and asphalt bound system (cushioned; U.S. Tennis Association [USTA], 2012).

In 2010, the International Tennis Federation (ITF) launched the Court Classification Scheme, through which courts are assessed in terms of their surface pace rating. Each surface receives a pace rating that categorizes it as slow (Category 1), medium (Category 2), or fast (Category 3). This classification also aids tournament organizers in determining whether to use fast-paced (Type 1) or slow-paced (Type 2) balls. This means that a classification once gained is good for three years before reclassification. (http://www.itftennis.com/technical/equipment/courts/class)

Numerous items must be considered when selecting the appropriate type of court: initial cost, cost of upkeep, amount of use, area of country, maintenance personnel needed, type of players, level of competition, and age of players.

Clay, grass, and soft composition courts are much easier on the legs of players and allow for a much slower ball bounce than other courts. These courts are superior for young players, beginning players, and older players. However, they need a high level of maintenance, which is costly in both materials and personnel. Clay courts must be leveled, must have clay added periodically, require watering, and must be kept free of vegetation. Soft composition courts must be rolled, require watering, and need to have screen and base components added often. Grass courts are similar to golf greens and need daily maintenance.

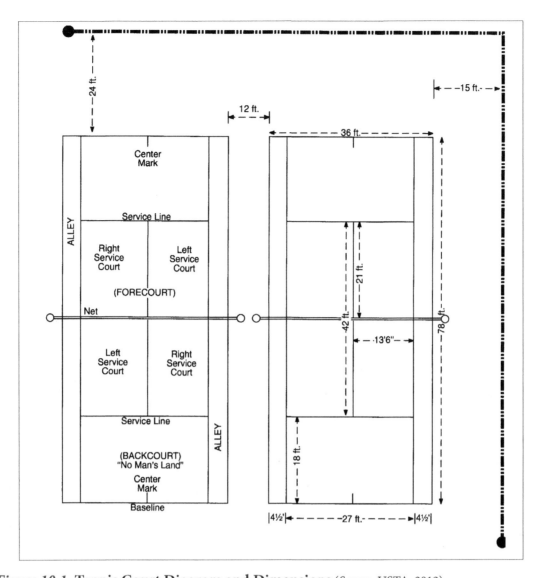

Figure 10.1. **Tennis Court Diagram and Dimensions** (*Source:* USTA, 2012)

Additionally, grass courts that receive heavy use should be alternated daily. That is, a court used on Monday should not be used again until Wednesday. Consequently, more court space is necessary for heavily used grass courts. Grass courts give a skidding ball bounce, and sometimes an erratic bounce, because of small divots, excessive wear, and taped lines. Overall, clay, grass, and soft composition courts are recommended for commercial clubs where the cost of upkeep can be packaged into member fees. They are not recommended for schools and recreation programs because of upkeep costs.

Asphalt, concrete, and hard composition courts need less maintenance but provide a faster ball bounce and cause more stress on the legs of players. Of the three types, asphalt courts are the most inexpensive to construct and hard composition courts are the most costly. Hard composition courts take a few months to cure and harden, and they should not be used until they cure completely. Hard composition courts can be constructed with multiple layers of cushioning material. The more layers that are in the courts, the greater the resiliency of the surface will be; however, each additional layer of cushioning increases the cost. Hard composition courts are smoother than concrete or asphalt, and therefore they cause less wear and tear on balls, shoes, and rackets. Asphalt, concrete, and hard composition courts are recommended for schools and recreation programs. Hard composition is the optimal choice of the three.

Numerous synthetic court surfaces are available. If synthetic outdoor courts are to be constructed, users should be consulted to determine the advantages and disadvantages of such courts for players and owners. Also, product descriptions of the material should be studied carefully to determine which synthetic surface best meets the specific needs of the court under construction.

Regardless of the type of court surface, it is paramount that a tennis court construction firm be employed to build the court(s). A local construction firm with no tennis court-building experience should not be permitted to construct the courts. Typically, a builder inexperienced in tennis court construction does not have the expertise to properly build tennis courts. This lack of expertise results in the use of poor construction techniques; more important, it ultimately results in premature (and costly) repairs and renovations.

Costs for an outdoor surface and base vary depending upon the number and size (i.e., youth to championship) of courts, the geographic location, and the amount of earthwork and drainage required. There are three basic types of courts commonly used: (1) asphalt with a cost ranging from $40,000 to $60,000; (2) synthetic with a cost ranging from $55,000 to $75,000; and (3) posttension concrete with a cost ranging from $100,000 to $125,000. There will be additional costs for fencing ($7,500 to $12,500); lighting ($10,000 to $15,000); and ancillary areas such as bleachers, storage, concession area, restrooms, drinking fountains, and so forth ($50,000 to $75,000; USTA, 2012).

All tennis courts should have sufficient secured storage areas constructed on a concrete base adjacent to the court complex. The size of the storage area is dictated by the amount and type of equipment to be stored in it, for example, ball hoppers, tennis rackets, fanny packs, ball-throwing machines, and other teaching equipment. The storage area must be waterproof and include shelving, bins, racks, and hook.

If maintenance equipment is needed at the courts, a separate storage area must be built for appropriate machines, rakes, hoses, screens, and materials. Parking areas need to be built in close proximity to the court complex. The size of the parking area is dictated by the maximum number of user vehicles for the complex in addition to sufficient space for spectator parking. If the tennis complex is lighted, the parking area should be illuminated with high-pressure sodium lights.

Night outdoor tennis is popular in many areas of the United States. The recommended surface lighting level for recreational tennis is 38 foot-candles and for tournament tennis is 63 foot-candles. Lighting tennis courts is a necessity in some areas. Information as to the number of light standards and how much light will be needed for the complex can be obtained by consulting the local electric company and a manufacturer (e.g., General Electric). A number of outdoor sports lighting companies install quality tennis court lighting systems. If the cost of ongoing high electric use is of concern, coin-operated light boxes can be installed to defray the electricity cost (Francesconi, 2012).

Although lighting may be optional, water must be provided at each court complex. One water fountain (refrigerated) and one hose connector are recommended for each set of four courts. Electrical outlets must be provided for each court and for any electrical maintenance equipment. All outlets should be located in the fence area and at the storage areas.

Benches need to be provided outside the fencing for those awaiting an empty court. Unobstructed spectator seating should be provided as close to the courts as possible if tournaments or instruction are to be provided on the courts. Courts used for tournaments and high-level competition also require scoring equipment, officials' seating, tables, benches, concession areas, and a protected area for videotaping.

Finally, court surfaces can be a variety of colors. Synthetics can be found in any color, whereas most nonporous tennis courts use a contrasting red and green color scheme. Several factors should be considered when deciding on court colors, including the effect of color on perception of the ball, how well a color scheme masks or highlights wear and stains, and the color's compatibility with its surroundings. From the ball perspective, single-colored courts are easiest on participants' eyes because multicolored courts promote eye fatigue as one's vision changes focus from light to dark areas. A subtle difference between actual court coloring (within the lines) and surrounding court coloring (e.g., light green inside the lines surrounded by dark green) allows for similar reflectivity level and subsequently less eye fatigue. As far as a court's ability to hide stains or wear marks, darker colors are advantageous. It should be noted that a variety of colors are available for tennis courts from traditional green to the much-publicized purple courts with which the Association of Tennis Professionals (ATP) experimented during the Men's Tour of 2000. Choosing a color that is in harmony with the surrounding vegetation (e.g., green courts in an area surrounded by lush green vegetation) provides a nice aesthetic appeal (Jones, 1990).

Indoor Tennis Courts

Indoor courts can be practical for tennis. Because the weather can affect the ability to play, tennis is a seasonal sport in many parts of the United States. Consequently, indoor courts meet a specific need in certain regions.

The number of courts to be enclosed depends on the number of users and the amount of money available for construction. The type of enclosure varies greatly from complex to complex. Prefabricated steel buildings, air structures, tension membrane structures, and standard brick-and-mortar buildings have all been employed successfully. Using combination structures has some advantages. A translucent tension membrane that allows light onto the courts combined with a turnkey or one standard structure can save roofing costs as well as electricity costs during the day.

Lighting should be indirect so that the tennis ball is not lost in the glare of lights. The background at the end of the courts should be plain. Traffic patterns need careful planning to ensure they do not conflict with play on the courts. Netting must be used between courts because fencing does not exist, and the ceiling height needs to be a minimum of 30 ft. Most indoor court surfaces are synthetic. As with outdoor courts, indoor courts should plan for storage, parking, water fountains, electrical outlets, seating, concessions, officials' needs, videotaping, and locker and shower facilities.

Tennis Courts for Junior Players

Smaller courts and their justification. There has been an impetus to teach younger children (aged 5–10) the game of tennis, in a systematic progression of court sizes, rackets, and balls, scaled down to an appropriate level for each age group (Tennis Canada, year; Tennis Professionals Association, 2012). This system of teaching has been imported from European countries such as Belgium and Switzerland, where it was used to successfully develop high-profile players such as Justine Henin-Hardenne and Roger Federer. The USTA has implemented these changes in their youth programs designed to make the sport of tennis easier to develop a relatively higher degree of mastery than on traditional courts for children under age 13 years. The program entails play on smaller sized courts, with lower compression balls, as well as smaller rackets, the later change being applicable to players in the 10 years and under (U-10) age category. For purposes of this book, the following discussion relates only to changes in court dimensions. It should be noted that other sports have a longer history of modifying their court, field, or standard dimensions for young children (e.g., soccer, baseball, and basketball).

The USTA's initiative relative to the U-10 children is called the QuickStart Program. Regarding younger children (aged 8 years and under, U-8), since January 2010, all sanctioned events have been played on smaller tennis courts measuring 36 ft x 18 ft. Such courts can be built on a stand-alone basis (specifications can be found at http://assets.usta.com/assets/1/15/36%20Permanent%20 Court%20Details.pdf) or integrated into existing regulation 78-ft tennis courts using portable net standards. In fact, as many as four of these U-8 courts can be converted across a 78-ft court on a 56 ft x 114 ft footprint, as illustrated in this USTA specification diagram: http://assets.usta. com/assets/1/15/78%20Court%20Conversion%20To%20 Four%2036%20Courts%20(114%20x%2056).pdf. As of January 2012, children who are 9 and 10 years old (U-10) playing in USTA-sanctioned contests use courts measuring 60 ft long x 36 ft wide. As with U-8, these courts can be built on a stand-alone basis (http://assets.usta.com/assets/1/15/60%20Permanent%20Court%20Details.pdf) or be lined up on existing courts. However, it is essential that if U-8 or U-10 courts are lined on existing 78-ft courts, the lines should be textured and blended (i.e., they should be from the same color family as the existing 78-ft court; e.g., lighter blue lines painted on a light blue court surface) and terminate 3 in. from the existing 78-ft court lines. Grants

for court construction or the painting of permanent lines on 78-ft courts are available through the USTA (2012).

Paddle Tennis

Dimensions

Paddle tennis courts are 50 ft long x 20 ft wide. The safety space or unobstructed area should be a minimum of 15 ft behind each baseline and 10 ft from each sideline or between each adjacent court. As Figure 10.2 shows, service lines for each side of the court run the entire width of the court, parallel to and 3 ft inside each baseline. The center service line extends from the service end line, down the middle of the court. The service boxes, therefore, are 22 ft long x 10 ft wide (U.S. Professional Tennis Association [USPTA], 1996).

Paddle Tennis Web

An optional restraint line extends the width of the court, 12 ft from the net. These restraint lines are used in doubles play only. All dimensions for paddle tennis court markings are to the outside of the lines with the exception of the center service line, which is divided equally between service courts.

Miscellaneous Considerations

Paddle tennis net posts are located 18 in. outside of each sideline and are 31 in. in height. Unlike tennis court nets, the paddle tennis court net is strung taut so that the height measures the same (31 in.) at each post and in the middle of the court. Court surfaces are concrete or asphalt, but competition can also take place on hard-packed sand (USPTA, 1996).

If construction of stand-alone paddle tennis courts is not an option, paddle tennis court markings can be su-

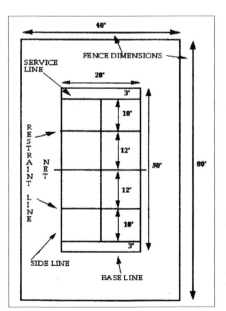

Figure 10.2. USPTA Official Paddle Tennis Court Dimension With Restraint Line

perimposed on a regulation tennis court by using chalk or tape or by painting lighter colored lines and the net can be lowered to the proper height.

Pickleball

Described as a mixture between tennis, ping-pong, and badminton, pickleball has been popular among seniors for the last 50 years and is growing in popularity among younger players. According to the USA Pickleball Association (USAPA, as cited in Ramirez, 2012), pickleball is one of the fastest growing sports in the United States, with over 100,000 players active in the sport on 2,000 courts nationwide.

Dimensions

Pickleball courts are rectangular, measuring 20 ft wide x 44 ft long for singles and doubles matches. The minimum required playing area is 30 ft x 60 ft; however, the preferred dimensions are 34 ft x 64 ft. The service boxes measure 15 ft long x 10 ft wide, but they do not extend all the way to the net. Instead, the service boxes end 7 ft from the net. This 7-ft buffer area from the net, on each side of the court, is considered the non-volley zone.

The net posts are 36 in. high, as is the net at this point, whereas the net height should measure 34 in. at center court. A center strap can be placed at the center of the net to enable the net to be adjusted to 34 in. Recommended placement for net posts is 12 in. from the sidelines.

Paddle

Dimensions

The sport of paddle is played in approximately 15 countries including the United States. A paddle court is 65 ft, 7 7/16 in. (20 m) long x 32 ft, 9 ¾ in. (10 m) wide with a plus or minus 1% tolerance level. The net, which divides the court in half, extends to the perimeter fence where it is anchored to the two center posts of this fencing or to an independent anchoring system. Regardless of the anchoring system, the net must coincide with the perimeter fence.

The net measures 37 7/16 in. (0.95 m) at the posts and is 2 in. lower at the center of the court (35 7/16 in. or 0.90 m) where it is held down at the center by a central belt that is 2 in. wide (American Paddle Association, 1996).

The service lines for each side of the court run parallel to the net and are placed 22 feet, 9 ½ in. (6.95 m) from the net. A central service line, 2 in. wide, runs perpendicular to the net. This line bisects the court, dividing it into equal service zones on both sides of the net. Each service zone measures 22 ft, 9 ½ in. long x 16 ft, 4 ⅞ in. wide. All measurements for the court markings are made from the net or center of the central perpendicular service line (APA, 1996).

The paddle court (Figure 10.3) is completely enclosed by back walls, sidewalls, and fencing on the remaining sideline areas. The back walls at the end of each court measure the width of the court (32 ft, 9 ¾ in.) and are between 9 ft, 10 ⅛ in. (3 m) and 13 ft, 1 ½ in. (4 m) in height. The partial side or "wing walls" extend 13 ft, 1 ½ in. (4 m) from

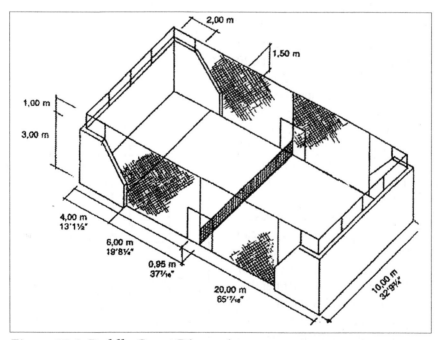

Figure 10.3. **Paddle Court Dimensions** (*Source:* World Paddle Association, 2012)

the back walls. The wing walls decrease in height from 9 ft, 10 ⅛ in. (3 m) to 5 ft (1.5 m) beginning at the wing wall's midpoint (6 ft, 6 ¾ in., that is, 2 m from the junction of the back and wing walls) to the end of the wall. This decrease in height on the wing wall should be at approximately a 38° angle. The remainder of the court perimeter is enclosed with a wire fence measuring 13 ft, 1 ½ in. (4 m) in height from the court surface (APA, 1996).

Miscellaneous Considerations

Paddle court surfaces vary from hard courts to artificial grass. The sport can be played on outdoor and indoor courts. If played indoors, however, courts must have a minimum ceiling clearance of 25 ft.

Back walls and partial sidewalls consist of stucco, concrete, or glass and/or a blindex material that provides for optimal spectator viewing of the court from all surrounding areas.

Portable courts (not inclusive of surfacing) are available for purchase for approximately $32,500.

Platform Tennis

Dimensions

A platform tennis court is 44 ft long x 20 ft wide. The entire platform surface is 60 ft x 30 ft, which allows for 8 ft of space beyond each baseline and 5 ft of space between each doubles sideline and the fencing. All court markings are 2 in. wide, and measurements are to the outside of the lines except for the center service line, which is equally divided between the right and left service courts. Service lines running parallel to the net are 12 ft from the net, and doubles alleys are 2 ft wide.

Net posts are located 18 in. outside of the doubles sidelines, and the net height is 37 in. at the posts and 34 in. at the center of the court. Fencing, which measures 12 ft in height, is 16-gauge hexagonal, galvanized, 1-in. flat wire mesh fabric.

Miscellaneous Considerations

The total area needed for construction of a platform tennis court is 2,584 sq ft (68 ft x 38 ft). This allows for the foundation beams at the corners and at the locations of the uprights (Figure 10.4). Specifications for a platform tennis court typically call for 4 in. x 6 in. foundation beams across the base of the platform. It is recommended that wood beams be waterproofed with creosote. Each beam rests on four evenly spaced concrete blocks; the blocks should be placed such that the beams rest 4 ft apart (measured from center to center). The foundation beams at the corners and at the locations of the uprights must project far enough to afford a base for the outer support of the uprights. The deck surface should be constructed of Douglas fir planks measuring 2 ft x 6 ft. The planks should be laid ⅛ in. to ¼ in. apart to allow for drainage. The corner uprights and the intermediate uprights must measure 12 ft from their base (i.e., the deck surface) to their top. The corner uprights should be constructed of 4 in. x 4 in. beams; the intermediate uprights should measure 2 in. x 4 in.

The construction of the backstop is a detailed procedure. Top rails are bolted horizontally to the insides of

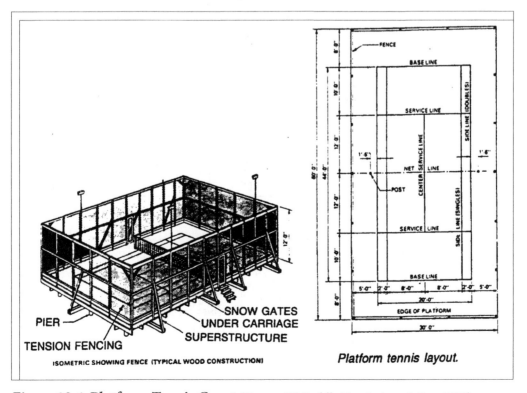

Figure 10.4. **Platform Tennis Court** (*Source:* US Paddle Tennis Association, 2012)

the tops of the uprights and measure 2 in. x 4 in. along the sides. Therefore, the rails to which the wire fabric is attached project inside the uprights by 4 in. at the ends and 2 in. at the sides. All of the space around the platform is covered by wire except 12-ft openings in the center of each side, at least one of which is closed with either netting. This closure is for containing errant balls. All wiring should be attached vertically on the insides of the uprights and stretched in 6-ft widths from the top down to the tension rail below.

Badminton

Dimensions

A badminton doubles court (Figure 10.5) is 44 ft long x 20 ft wide; a singles court is the same length (44 ft), but 3 ft narrower (17 ft). All court markings including the center service line, short service lines, and doubles long service lines are marked in yellow or white and measure 1 ½ in. wide. All dimensions are measured from the outside of the court lines except for the center service line, which is equally divided between service courts.

A net that is exactly 5 ft above the ground at the center of the court and 5 ft, 1 in. at the net posts bisects the court laterally. The net posts are placed directly on the doubles sidelines. However, when it is not possible to have the posts over the sidelines, this boundary should be marked with a thin post or strips of material attached to the sideline and rising to the net cord. The safety distance or unobstructed

space behind the back boundary line should measure 8 ft behind and 4 ft to 5 ft outside of each sideline or between courts.

Miscellaneous Considerations

Ideally, ceiling clearance for indoor badminton should be no less than 30 ft over the entire full-court area. This is the standard for international play. However, a 25-ft clearance is the recommended minimum and is sufficient for other levels of play.

Basketball

Dimensions

Indoor and outdoor basketball courts vary in size depending upon the level of competitive play. It is recommended that courts for junior high, high school, and recreational play be 50 ft wide x 84 ft long. Competitive collegiate and professional basketball require a 50 ft x 94 ft court. Regardless of the level of play, a 10-ft unobstructed or safety space is highly recommended, especially considering today's game and the increased size of the players. However, the collegiate (NCAA) and high school (NFHS) rule books require a minimum 3-ft safety buffer but suggest preferably it be 10 ft (see Chapter 2). However, if a court is constructed with less than 10 ft of safety space, wall padding should be installed the entire distance of the wall that parallels the end line. Another important safety consideration concerns glass or windows that are part of the

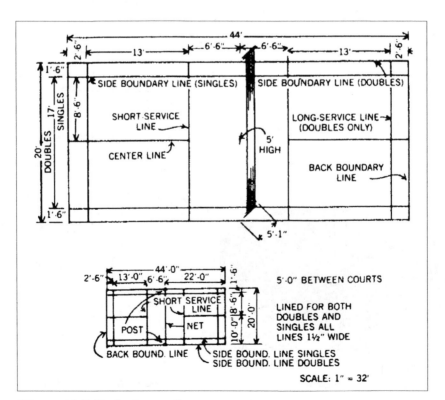

Figure 10.5. **Badminton Court** (*Source:* USA Badminton Association, 2012)

surrounding basketball gymnasium. All glass and windows should be shatterproof safety glass. Finally, in a gymnasium setting, especially where other sports can be played, a height clearance of 30 ft is strongly recommended, but a minimum clearance of 23 ft is imperative.

Concerning the size and colors of the lines, several guidelines should be kept in mind:

- All lines must be 2 in. wide, except for the neutral zones.
- The color of the boundary lines should match the midcourt markings.
- The color of the lane space and neutral zone markings should contrast with the color of the boundary lines. (NCAA, 2000)

The 3-point arch measures 19 ft, 9 in. from the center of the basket for high school. Starting in the 2008–2009 NCAA collegiate basketball season, the college men's 3-point line was moved back 1 ft from this 19 ft, 9 in. standard to 20 ft, 9 in., and in 2012, the college women's 3-point line was also moved back to 20 ft, 9 in. Therefore, where collegiate men's and women's basketball teams share a court, two separate 3-point lines are no longer needed (Johnson, 2011). This decision was the first modification of the 3-point shot since it was first established in the 1986–1987 season.

Miscellaneous Considerations

Collegiate competition requires backboards that are transparent and measure 6 ft horizontally x 4 ft vertically. The backboard should have a 2-in. white-lined target centered behind the goal. This target should measure 24 in. horizontally x 18 in. vertically. The backboard should also have 2 in. thick gray padding on the bottom and up the sides for the players' protection. Attached to the backboard is an 18-in. (inner diameter) bright orange ring mounted parallel to and 10 ft above the floor. Although the standard height for a basketball goal (from rim to floor) is 10 ft, adjustable standards that allow the rim to be set at the standard height or lower (i.e., as low as 8 ft) provide opportunities for young children to practice shooting at a goal that is more age appropriate (NCAA, 2000).

The gymnasium flooring is an important consideration. It is imperative that the flooring provides sliding characteristics (the surface friction of a finished floor) and shock absorption that conform to criteria established by the Deutsches Institut für Normung (DIN) standards to minimize the possibility of participant injury. Also, the flooring should provide adequate ball bounce or deflection as prescribed under the DIN standards. A final consideration is the placement of padding in appropriate areas, such as the wall directly behind each basketball backboard, especially if the distance between the backboard and wall is less than 10 ft.

Outdoor basketball courts should run lengthwise in approximately a north–south direction. Proper drainage can be ensured by slanting courts from one side to the other allowing one inch of slant for every 10 feet of court. If a backboard is mounted on an in-ground pole, the pole should be padded. Additionally, the pole should be off the playing court and the backboard should extend at least 4 ft onto the court. The buffer or safety zone (unobstructed areas) should be 10 ft at the ends and 3 ft to 10 ft on the sides. Fencing is not a necessity; however, if finances allow, anodized aluminum chain-link should be used. The fence height should be a minimum of 10 ft. The fence posts should be placed 6 in. to 1 ft inside the hard surface, and the fence fabric should be affixed on the inside of these supporting posts. Posts should be mounted in concrete such that 35% to 40% of the length of the pole is above the surface. Gates or fences should be constructed large enough to allow maintenance equipment to be brought into the court areas.

Volleyball

Dimensions

Although volleyball courts within the United States traditionally measure 30 ft wide x 60 ft long, the United States Volleyball Rules (USAV, 2012)—which are those of the International Volleyball Federation—call for the court to measure 59 ft x 29 ½ ft (18 m x 9 m; Figure 10.6). Notably, all court dimensions are measured from the outside edge of the lines, and all court lines should be 2 in. (5 cm) wide (USAV, 2012).

A minimum of 6 ft, 6 in. of safety or unobstructed space should surround an indoor court; however, the ideal situation is to provide at least 10 ft from the sidelines and 13 ft from the end lines (NCAA, 2012).

Ceiling clearance is a critical issue. Although United States Volleyball Rules (USAV, 2012) call for a minimum of 23 ft (7 m) of unobstructed space as measured from the floor, 30 ft of overhead clearance is highly recommended. Figure 10.6 provides a detailed display of volleyball floor markings. Notably, in recent years, the service zone has been extended the full width of the court as a result of a rule change permitting players to serve anywhere behind the end line.

Net Height

The volleyball net height is 7 ft, 11 ⅝ in. (2.43 m) for men's competition and 7 ft, 4 ⅛ in. (2.24 m) for women's competition, as measured at the center of the playing court. The two ends of the net, directly over the sidelines, must be the same height from the playing surface and may not exceed the official height by ¾ in. (although a constant height is far more desirable). The net height may be varied for specific age groups in the following ways:

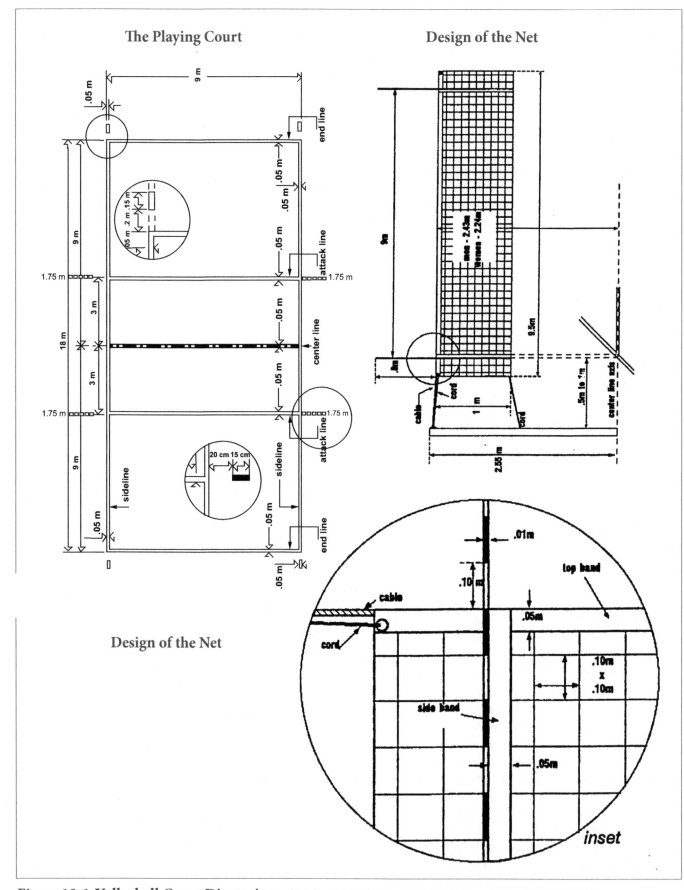

Figure 10.6. **Volleyball Court Dimensions.** (*Source:* United States Volleyball Association [USVB], 2012)

The net itself is 39 inches wide and a minimum of 32 feet long. The posts (supporting standards) are fixed to the playing surface at least 19 ½ inches to 39 inches from each sideline. Two white side bands, two inches wide and 39 inches long, are fastened around the net vertically and placed perpendicularly over each sideline. Six-foot-long antennas are attached at the outer edge of each side band and extend 32 inches above the height of the net. (USAV, 2012)

Miscellaneous Considerations

One of the most important safety factors is to provide poles that are sunk directly below floor level in sleeves or that telescope up from below the floor. Volleyball standards/poles that are on mounted or weighted bases are extremely hazardous. Likewise, volleyball net systems that rely on guy wires are not desirable. If wires are part of an existing volleyball net system, they should be clearly identified and padded. Furthermore, volleyball posts should be padded to a minimum height of 6 ft and all official stands should be padded.

Ideally, in a facility built primarily for volleyball, the walls (particularly those behind each end line) should be painted a color that provides contrast to the color of volleyballs, which are generally white. This contrast in color allows participants to more easily track the flight of the ball during play.

Additionally, the ceiling color should be off-white or another light color that provides a contrasting background for players attempting to follow the flight path of the volleyball.

Light fixtures need to be placed at least as high as the lowest ceiling obstructions to avoid shadowing effects. Also, lighting needs to be bright (a minimum of 27.9 footcandles, measured at 1 m above the playing surface). The lights, however, should not be closely grouped because they would create a blinding effect for participants (USAV, 2012).

Outdoor Sand Volleyball Court Guidelines

The dimensions for an outdoor sand court are identical to indoor volleyball court dimensions (i.e., 59 ft [18 m] long x 29 ft, 6 in. [9 m] wide as measured from the outer edge of the boundary). However, in 2002, the Fédération Internationale de Volleyball (FIVB), the world governing body, approved the reduction of the dimensions of the two-person outdoor sand volleyball court. Doubles sand volleyball is now played on a smaller court 16 m long (52' 5 and 59/64") x 8 m wide (26' 2 and 31/32'), that is, the court is about 6 ½ ft shorter and 3 ¼ ft less wide than the traditional indoor court or the 4 to 6 person outdoor court.

Ideally, the court should be constructed with the net running in an east–west direction so that the morning and evening sun does not face directly into the eyes of one team. Outdoor courts should provide a minimum of 9 ft, 10 in., or 3 m, of free space that is composed of sand and surrounds the court area.

In other words, the complete sand area should measure a minimum of 80 ft long x 50 ft wide. For professional competitions, the court should be centered on an area 93 ft long x 57 ft wide. Standard net heights are the same as for the indoor game: 7 ft, 11 ⅝ in. (2.43 m) for men's and coed play and 7 ft, 4 ⅛ in. for women's and reverse coed play. Children aged 10 to 16 may have the net height adjusted according to the standards listed above regarding indoor volleyball net adjustments (USAV, 2012).

Boundary lines are brightly colored ¼-in. rope or 1 ½-in. webbing tied to the four corners with buried deadpan anchors. No center line is required for outdoor play, but approximately 14 ft of rope will be needed beyond the 177 ft total necessary for court lines to anchor the corners (USAV, 2012).

Net supports should be made of metal, wood, or other material that will withstand tension. The supports should be about 14 ft long and should be buried 5 ft deep using a concrete footing unless the soil is solid, in which case packing in and washing the soil should suffice. These support standards should be set 39 in. (1 m) from the boundary of the court. Any less space will leave insufficient room for the full net and adjusting cables (USAV, 2012).

Suggested specifications for different net supports are as follows. Metal net supports should be 4-in., diameter schedule 40, galvanized steel pipes. Round wood poles should measure 8 in. in diameter and should be made of treated, weather-resistant wood. Square wood supports are not recommended because of the potential for participant injury on corner edges. In all instances, padding the support poles is an important safety measure. If the support does not have equal sides, the narrower side should be the net anchor side (facing the court; USAV, 2012).

Hooks, hook-and-eye hardware, and any winch hardware (padded) are necessary to attach the net to the standards. One way to provide for total adjustability of net height is to have four metal collars made that have loops for attaching the net (i.e., the top and the bottom of the net on both sides) that can slide up and down the poles. Holes can be drilled into the collars and set screws can be inserted that can be tightened with an Allen wrench. Finally, the net should be 10 m in length with a cable top, but strong rope such as Kevlar® also works well. However, the effort of fashioning this system can be avoided by purchasing outdoor standards now available from a variety of vendors.

Actual sand court construction should start with the excavation of the area with a front-end loader. The court area should be excavated between 2 ft and 3 ft in depth. In low-lying areas, such as the shoreline areas of Florida, the court should be excavated only 6 in. to 8 in. This will yield an elevated court rather than one that is flush with the ground. Also, the dirt that is excavated should be used to create a slight slope up to the court.

The court perimeter edges can be contained to keep dirt and grass from leaking into the court. Lawn edging material or rubber handrail material from escalator companies seated atop 2 in. x 6 in. wooden boundaries is a good method of providing perimeter boundaries. If railroad ties or similar materials are used, the top edges should be padded to minimize injury potential (USAV, 2012).

Drainage of the court under the sand is important. Installing leaching pipe on the standards with a slant of 14° is highly recommended for a good permanent court. Perforated pipe (approximately two rolls of 250 ft) can be laid perforated side down with the open end at the low point of the court. Each section of the pipe should be wrapped with a flex wrap or "handicap wrap," which can be purchased at plumbing supply houses. This wrap prevents sand from filling up the pipes. Finally, the drainage points should lead away from the court at the lowest point (USAV, 2012).

The next step is to set the standards in concrete. Poles should be set at a slight angle outward from the court to allow for bending caused by eventual net tension. To allow for ease of maintenance or replacement, steel poles should be seated in steel sleeves so that they can be easily removed.

Small, pea-sized gravel used for drainage (#56, #57, #2, or #3) should then be placed over the drainage pipe to a depth of about 1 ft. Approximately 2,600 cu ft (110 tons) of this gravel is necessary. Plastic landscaping or ground stabilization filter fabric (a woven polyblend that will not deteriorate easily) is placed over the gravel to prevent the sand from washing through (USAV, 2012).

The final step in sand court construction is depositing the sand. A good court requires an investment in good sand. Sand comes in a variety of grades; some types are very "dirty" and unsuitable for a court. Washed beach (dune), washed plaster, washed masonry, or washed river sand are the most desirable types of court sand. The most highly recommended sand is silica sand regionally available by contacting Best Sand. This sand should be deposited and raked level around the court; it should measure 1 ft to 2 ft in depth. The minimum recommended depth of the sand is 19 ½ in. In essence, a sand court requires approximately 5,200 cu ft (205 tons of washed sand). The final price tag for the construction of a good sand volleyball court will range anywhere from $12,000 to $20,000 (USAV, 2012).

Finally, it is important to point out that two-person women's sand volleyball is an emerging sport in the NCAA and, as of August 2012, has 20 collegiate teams competing from around the United States. Once the sport reaches 40 programs, it will move from the Emerging Sports List to the full NCAA sponsorship with a championship (American Volleyball Coaches Association [AVCA], 2012). The current trend is resulting in the construction of a large number of sand courts on college campuses around the United States. The AVCA (n.d.), the primary collegiate volleyball governing body, has published specifications for courts including (a) two courts are required for competition, but three courts are recommended to conduct an NCAA match; (b) when courts are built adjacent side to side, 6 m (almost 20 ft) of free space is recommended, whereas if adjacent courts are built end line to end line, the free space should measure at least 9 m (approximately 30 ft); and (c) sand depth on the court should be at least 18 in. and 12 in. on the free space surrounding the court.

Racquetball, Handball, and Squash Courts

Dimensions and Design Considerations

Four-wall courts for squash and handball have been in sports facilities for over three quarters of a century. Originally, these courts were made from Portland cement with smaller than normal doors.

Paddleball and racquetball were first played on these courts in the late 1950s and early 1960s. Today's courts are designed for racquetball, handball, and squash even though other activities may also be played in these enclosed four-wall courts (such as walleyball and Bi-Rakits). Today's state-of-the-art courts are constructed of laminated panels and/or tempered glass. In the planning of four-wall courts, teaching, competition, accessibility, and amenities need to be considered (USSRA, 2012).

The recommended four-wall racquetball/handball court is 40 ft long x 20 ft wide with a front wall and ceiling height of 20 ft and a back wall at least 14 ft high (Figure 10.7). The lower back wall provides a space for a viewing or for an instructional gallery, which may be open with a 3 ft to 4 ft high railing. Clear polycarbonate sheeting should be placed under the railing for seated viewing purposes and safety. The gallery may be totally enclosed with clear polycarbonate sheeting and a small 4-ft square open window. An open gallery is recommended for communication purposes between instructors/officials and the players. However, an open gallery poses the risk of spectators being hit by a ball; therefore, appropriate signage should be posted to indicate this hazard. Squash is becoming popular in some regions of the United States. The international singles squash court is 21 ft wide x 32 ft long (Figure 10.8). The old North American standard of an 18 ft, 6 in. wide singles squash court is no longer acceptable and should be avoided.

North American doubles squash is played on a larger court measuring 25 ft wide x 45 ft long (Figure 10.9). Squash court wall heights vary compared to the standard 20-ft racquetball/handball wall heights (U.S. Squash Association, 1997).

When more than a single battery of courts is to be constructed, the batteries should be arranged so a corridor approximately 10 ft wide x 12 ft high separates the back walls of each. Courts should be located in the same area of the facility rather than spread out. Courts should be placed on adjacent walls rather than on opposite walls to achieve close proximity, thereby aiding in quality instructional time. Corridors and galleries should be illuminated with indirect light. The minimum number of courts for schools should be dictated by maximum class size and total student enrollment. Normally, no fewer than six to eight courts are recommended, which can adequately handle 15 to 20 students at a time. The number of courts for clubs and private usage is determined by the number of users and by the popularity of racquetball, handball, and squash in any given area.

Walls may be constructed of hard plaster, Portland cement, wood, laminated panels, or tempered glass. Laminated panels and tempered glass are recommended. The panels are 4 ft x 8 ft particleboard or resin-impregnated Kraft papers covered with a melamine sheet. The panels come in different thicknesses, from $^{13}/_{16}$ in. to 1 $^{1}/_{8}$ in. The thicker the panel is, the truer the rebound action of the ball will be; however, the thicker panel is also more expensive. Panels are mounted on aluminum channels or metal studs. Screws that hold them to the wall superstructure are inset and covered with a plug.

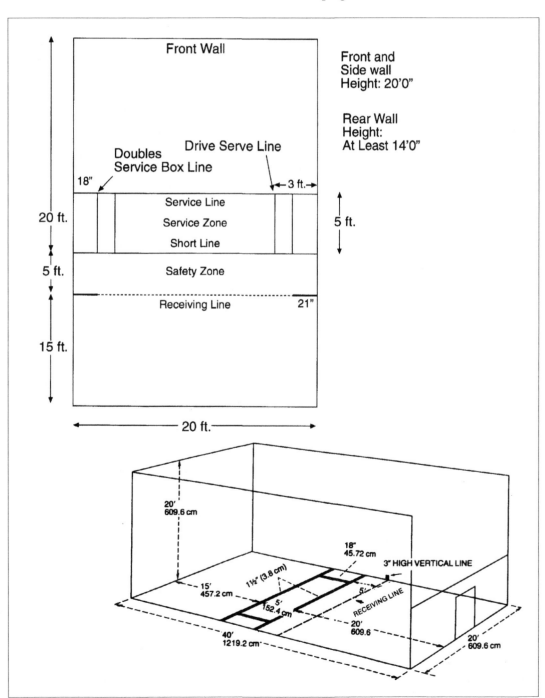

Figure 10.7. Four-Wall Handball and Racquetball Courts and Dimensions (*Source:* U.S. Racquetball Association, 2012)

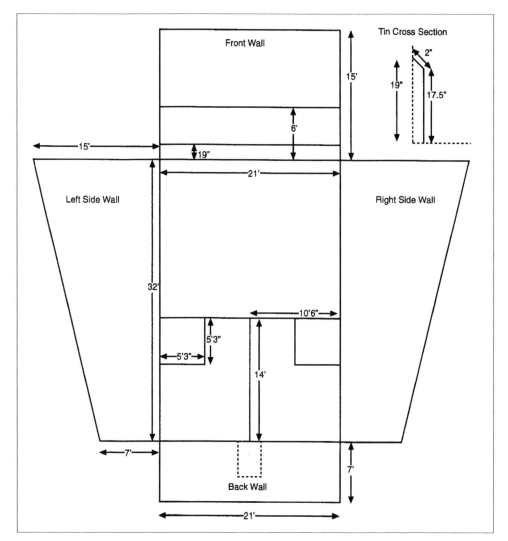

Figure 10.8. **Singles Squash Court** (*Source:* U.S. Squash Association, 2012)

This creates a monolithic surface for the walls. The panels have a high life expectancy and are easily maintained. Glass walls of ½ in.-thick tempered, heat-soaked glass is ideal but expensive. All courts are recommended to have the minimum of glass back walls, and one court should have an additional glass sidewall. This will offer good instructional and spectator viewing (Figure 10.10). Finally, one-way glass, which provides spectator viewing but appears to be a solid surface to participants within the court, is a relatively new innovation.

If glass walls are used, spectator and instructional viewing areas should be planned for carefully. These areas usually are stepped with carpeted risers along the sidewall or back wall of the court. A built-in, two-way audio system should be used for this court. Carpet color should not be totally dark and definitely should not be blue or green because ball visibility through the glass walls is obscured with dark colors as a background. Courts with two glass sidewalls, those with glass sidewalls and a glass back wall, and all-glass wall courts are superior to other courts; however, their cost is prohibitive in most facilities.

Doors are standard size and are placed in the middle of the back wall, not in the corners of the court. The corners are crucial real estate in intermediate and advanced racquet sports, so doors that can cause "untrue" bounces should not be placed there. Door handles should be small and recessed, and all door framing should be flush on the inside of the court. Doors should open into the court, and there should be no thresholds under the doors.

Floors should be hardwood, as in standard gymnasium construction. The more sophisticated the floor system is, the more costly it will be. Resilient wood floors play differently than more rigid system wood floors, but they are more expensive. Any good hard maple floor system is acceptable. Floors should be flush with sidewalls so that no joint is evident. Joints collect dirt, dust, and debris and are a maintenance nightmare. Floors should be resurfaced as needed with a high-grade finish. When floors need refinishing, they become slippery and can be dangerous. The amount of use, the types of shoes worn during play, and the amount of dirt and grit brought into the courts on shoes will dictate how often refinishing is needed. Floors should

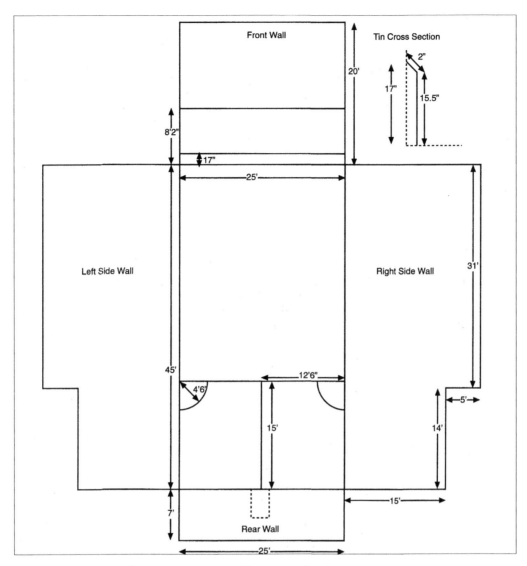

Figure 10.9. **North American Doubles Squash Court** (*Source:* U.S. Squash Association, 2012)

be cleaned with a treated mop daily or as needed. Synthetic floors should not be used in racquet courts because they create too much friction and do not allow feet to slide, which is needed for effective and safe racquet sports.

Court line markings should be a light color, rather than a dark color such as blue or black, which helps the participants' visual acuity in following a dark ball across lighter lines. Off-white, light pastel yellow, or light gray lines are best. Squash lines are red.

For racquetball and handball courts, the first 12 ft of the ceiling from the front wall should be devoid of heating or ventilation ducts. This portion of the ceiling must be hard and compatible to the wall surfaces for ball rebounding. Lighting and any other fixtures in the ceiling must be totally flush. The rear 8 ft of the ceiling is not as crucial because this part of the ceiling is seldom used in play.

The ceiling is not used in squash, but it should still be made of an impact-resistant material in case errant balls hit it. Panels or Portland cement would be good for the front 12 ft of the ceiling. If walleyball is to be played in the court, the ceiling must be strong enough to absorb the impact of the volleyball. Panels, but not Portland cement, work well in courts.

Lighting, Acoustics, and Ventilation

All lighting must be flush with the ceiling. Lights should illuminate all portions of the court equally; therefore, they should be spread throughout the ceiling. Shadows and low-light areas are not acceptable in these courts. Light accessibility for changing bulbs must be planned carefully. Because there is normally a battery of courts, the chore of changing light bulbs is magnified by the number of courts needing a bulb-changing system. The best light bulb-changing method for courts is to have a crawl space above the ceiling. This enables maintenance personnel to change bulbs from above. This system eliminates the need to use cumbersome hydraulic lifts and/or A-frame ladders (U.S. Racquetball Association, 2012).

A metal halide system of lighting is recommended. Metal halide lights give the most light at the least cost. Metal halide bulbs also have a long life expectancy. However, to garner cost savings and longevity, the court lights must be on at all times. Turning these lights off and on causes a delay (about 6 to 8 min) for the bulbs to obtain full brightness. Turning halide lights off and on also increases the cost of lighting and decreases bulb life expectancy. Metal halide lights should be controlled from a central console, not at each court.

If single courts are not used often, a recommended method of turning the lights on and off is to install switches that are activated by opening or closing the door to the court. This method requires a metal halide lighting system. When the door is closed, lights in the court will turn on. When the door is opened, the lights will turn off automatically, leaving only the night light to burn continuously. Usually, a 2-min to 3-min delay occurs before the lights go off after the door has been opened, preventing a disruption of lighting during the brief time it takes for players to exit or exchange the court.

A relatively new concept uses an annunciator (an electrically controlled signal board) to indicate to the building reservation/control center which courts are occupied at any time. Lights on the signal board are activated by the trip switch on each door as it opens or closes. When lights are continually turned off and on, incandescent bulbs work fairly well. Fluorescent lights should not be used in racquet courts because they tend to flicker and can cause visual acuity problems during play. If walleyball is to be played in the court, stronger light shields and light fixtures will be needed to absorb the impact of a volleyball.

Court walls and floors are hard surfaces, and much sound reverberates in the courts. For non-glass court surfaces, acoustical treatment is important within the surfaces. Insulation in the walls and ceiling will buffer sound within a court and also between courts. The rear 8 ft of the ceiling should be constructed of acoustical tiles because this area is seldom used in racquetball and handball and never used in squash. Although these tiles provide minimal acoustical treatment, it is important to attempt to control sound, and they should be considered in each court. If walleyball is played in a court, soft acoustical treatment cannot be installed on the ceiling.

Ventilation should be provided by air-conditioning. The ventilation of each court is important so that moisture does not build on wall surfaces and make the courts unplayable. Ample air circulation and air dehumidification are major concerns in the ventilation of the courts. Only air-conditioning can provide circulation, cooling, and dehumidification. To minimize the potential for moisture, courts should not be built underground with walls exposed to external moisture. Moisture and/or condensation can easily intrude to the interior wall surfaces of the courts.

If courts must be built underground, extra waterproofing needs to be completed in this portion of the facility.

All vents for air circulation should be located in the back 8 ft of the ceiling for racquetball and handball (Sawyer, 2009, but squash courts may have vents anywhere in the ceiling. The temperature of each court should be controlled by an individual jar-proof, flush thermostat that is preset and tamperproof.

Miscellaneous Considerations

Small storage boxes should be built flush with wall surfaces into sidewalls near the back wall of each court to house valuables and extra balls. The door to this storage box should be constructed of clear polycarbonate sheeting. Storage areas for students' coats, books, and other gear should be provided in an area near the courts. Extra storage must be provided for rain gear and winter gear where applicable.

Secured storage for racquetball rackets, handball gloves, squash rackets, eye guards, and balls should be provided near the court area.

All courts should have joints, seams, doors, vents, lights, and corners flush with the surrounding surface. Any unevenness in a court will cause untrue ball rebounds, which are unacceptable in court games. Each court should be equipped with a two-way audio system. Access to this system should be housed in the central console. This audio system can be used to make announcements, provide music, and facilitate instructional purposes between the court user and the instructor.

Effective external signage is important for all courts. Signs for court rules need to be posted near each court entrance. Rule signs such as "Eye guards are mandatory" and "Only non-marking athletic shoes may be worn in courts" are typical for racquet courts. Other signage includes the designation of a challenge court(s) with rules and a daily sign-up sheet. Courts also must be numbered, and a visible wall clock near the courts is important.

Courts and galleries should be accessible to individuals with disabilities. Doors should be wide enough for wheelchair passage and have no barriers such as thresholds or steps at access points. Additionally, the court's location within the sports facility and a route from adjacent parking areas must be free of barriers.

University courts should be built at a location with easy access from all points on campus, and ample parking in close proximity of the courts should be carefully planned. Within the sports complex, the courts should be located near the console control area.

In any facility, all courts need to be situated near refrigerated water fountains. In a commercial court complex, an area close to the courts must be designated for a pro shop. This area needs to be large enough to accommodate the types of equipment and apparel to be sold. The pro shop area must also be able to be secured by either lockable doors or a metal mesh gate because it will not be staffed during all operation hours of the court area.

If courts and/or galleries have hallway access, the hallway must have a ceiling height of 12 ft. A lower ceiling height lends itself to damage from individuals jumping up and hitting it with their rackets. Light shields in these hallways should be flush with the ceiling to deter breakage. Skylights above the court ceiling height, in gallery areas only, add a nice aesthetic touch. Using a translucent glass or polycarbonate sheeting in skylights will alleviate glare problems.

Movable metal "telltales" can be installed across the front of handball and racquetball courts for use in squash instruction. However, the courts are racquetball sized, not squash sized. The floors, walls, ceilings, lighting, heating, and ventilation of squash courts are similar to those of four-wall racquetball and handball courts.

One court at any instructional facility should be a permanent teaching court. There should be a 3 ft x 3 ft front wall viewing and videotaping square. This "window" should be covered with a single sheet of clear polycarbonate sheeting. The window should be 3 ft or 4 ft high from the floor and closer to one side or the other of the front wall. Access to this window from outside the court must be provided. There should be a small lockable area behind the viewing window, preferably 5 ft x 5 ft with a ceiling height of 8 ft. An adjustable-height table and chair need to be in this small room, and a small area for storage of a portable video camera, videotapes, and speed gun should be provided there as well.

The teaching court also needs two flush covered electrical outlets for power sources. A multimedia projector and a video camera should be mounted within the back wall. Both projector and camera need to be protected with a clear polycarbonate sheet. A lockable, flush console should be built into a sidewall to house a laptop computer and VCR. This setup allows for viewing via slides, videotapes, television, and computer. None of this high-tech equipment ever needs to be moved into or around the courts.

Polycarbonate mirrors, each section measuring 6 ft long x 6 ft high, should be placed flush on two adjacent walls. The back wall and a sidewall work best for the mirrors. Mirrors are great instructional tools because they allow the students to view themselves.

Foot templates for various movement patterns should be permanently placed on the floor. Different colors may be used along with arrows to indicate foot movement direction. Ball-flight path patterns should be painted on the floor, and flight paths for a down-the-wall passing shot and/or a cross-court passing shot should actually be templated onto the floor. Again, different colors should be used for different ball paths. An elliptical circle 6 ft wide

x 4 ft deep should be painted and labeled "center court" in the center area of the court. An area 3 ft square also needs to be painted and labeled in each back corner. The back corners and center court are the two most important areas in racquet courts.

Targets of varying size and height should be placed on both the front wall and sidewalls to serve as aiming points for various shots. A few targets also need to be placed on the ceiling near the front wall as ceiling shot templates for racquetball and handball. Skill templates such as "Be Patient and Play the Ball Low" and "Culminate All Sources of Power at Ball-Racquet Impact" should be placed in a few selected areas of the court. These become constant visual educational reminders for students.

Ideally, the teaching court should have one glass sidewall and a glass back wall. A glass back wall alone will suffice. A two-way communication system must be in place for the instructor when in the court to be able to talk to students outside of the court and vice versa (see Figure 10.10).

Good court construction is paramount for teaching, competition, safety, and maintenance. All court surfaces must be flush. The activity that is played in the court will be a determining factor in the size of the court and the materials used in court construction.

Indoor Soccer

Variations of indoor soccer are referred to herein. Indoor soccer has gained increasing popularity in the United States because it allows for year-round participation in the sport.

Dimensions

The *Official Rules of Indoor Soccer: Amateur and Youth Edition* (U.S. Indoor Soccer Association, 2011) specified that the field of play should be adapted to the size of the facility, with the dimensions measuring 140 ft to 190 ft long and 60 ft to 90 ft wide. However, standard dimensions are 180 ft x 75 ft, with corners rounded in the arc of a circle having a 28-ft radius (U.S. Indoor Soccer Rules, 2011–2012). The field of play should be enclosed by a perimeter wall measuring 4 ft to 12 ft in height (with the standard being 8 ft), which is part of the playing surface. The perimeter wall should be 2 ft above the crossbar of the goals and 4 ft along the team benches.

Each goal adjoins the perimeter wall at the center of each end of the field and is made up of two upright, tubular goals, 12 ft to 14 ft apart (measuring in the interiors, i.e., their points), and affixed to a horizontal crossbar, which is 6 ½ ft to 8 ft high. The dimensions for a standard goal are 12 ft high x 6 ½ ft high (U.S. Indoor Soccer Rules: The Official Rules of Indoor Soccer, Youth and Amateur Edition, Appendix A).

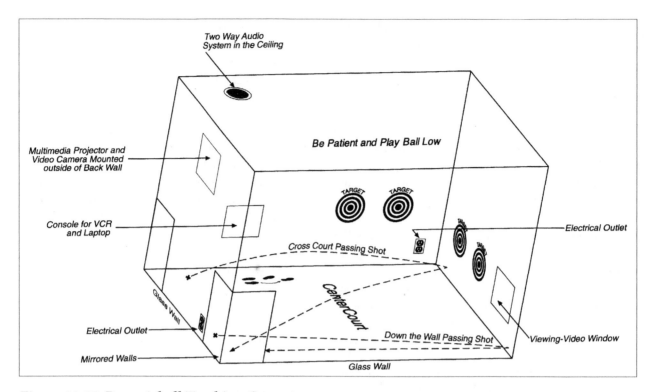

Figure 10.10. **Racquetball Teaching Court** (*Source:* U.S. Racquetball Association, 2012)

The line markings for indoor soccer are 4 in. wide and include

- a halfway line that runs parallel to the goal lines and divides the field into two equal halves;
- a center mark that indicates the center of the field of play is 9 in. in diameter;
- a restart mark that marks the center of the field of play 50 ft from each end of the field;
- red lines located 50 ft from the goal lines running parallel to them, extending through the restart marks and up the perimeter walls;
- goal lines that indicate the boundary of each goal that are drawn between the goalposts;
- corner marks that are 9 in. in diameter and are located 3 ft within the perimeter wall, situated beneath each corner flag at the end point of each touch line;
- touch lines that are made up of 3-ft dashes separated by 1-ft spaces and are 3 ft within the perimeter wall along the length of the field between corner marks;
- a penalty arch surrounding each goal within the field. The standard dimensions for the penalty arch consist of two 20-ft lines drawn at right angles to the goal line, each extending from the perimeter wall 8 ft from the nearer goalpost. A semicircle with a 15-ft radius that connects the lines' end and extends farther into the field of play completes the penalty arch. As an alternative, the arch may measure up to 30 ft wide and 25 ft long, with the end of each length connecting to the semicircle at right angles;

- free kick marks, measuring 9 in. in diameter, mark the top of each penalty arch;
- a 15-ft mark, which is a line 1 ft long x 2 in. wide and drawn parallel to the goal line is centered within the penalty arch 15 ft from the free kick mark; and
- a referee crease, which is a semicircle (with a 15-ft radius), extends to the perimeter wall at the center of the field and across from the team benches or wherever the official scorer's table is located. (U.S. Indoor Soccer Rules: The Official Rules of Indoor Soccer, Youth and Amateur Edition, Appendix A)

Team benches are located on each side of the halfway lines along one of the field's lengths and are separated from each other. Penalty areas are located directly across the field from the team benches, just beyond the perimeter wall, on each side of the referee crease.

A diagram of an official indoor soccer field can be found at http://www.usindoor.com/docs/rules_summary.pdf (U.S. Indoor Soccer Association, 2009, p. 17).

Shuffleboard

Dimensions

The actual playing area of a shuffleboard court is 39 ft long x 6 ft wide (Figure 10.11). However, the area outside the court markings includes a 6 ft, 6 in. standing area at both ends of the court and a 2-ft area adjacent to the sideline boundaries. Thus, the entire area for a shuffleboard court should measure 52 ft long x 10 ft wide.

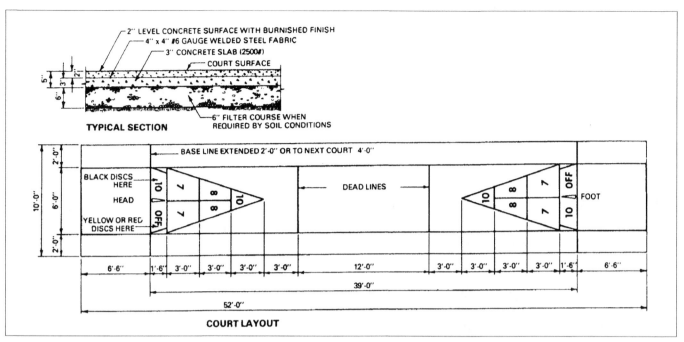

Figure 10.11. **Shuffleboard Court** (*Source:* USA National Shuffleboard Association, 2012)

Lines painted with a black dye, white road paint, or white acrylic stain mark off the shuffleboard court. The lines measure from ¾ in. to 1 in. wide. The baselines extend to adjoining courts or 2 ft beyond the sides of the court.

The separation triangle in the 10/off area measures 3 in. at the base and extends to form a point in the direction of the scoring area. The outline of the legs of this triangle is ¼ in. wide, with a clearance of ½ in. at both the point and the base. Finally, the base of the separation triangle is not marked.

Miscellaneous Considerations

Outdoor shuffleboard courts should be oriented north–south and must be constructed on a level area. A smooth playing surface is essential; therefore, the surface of an outdoor court is typically concrete or asphalt. Furthermore, the courts should be developed over a well-drained area. For proper drainage, a depressed alley should be installed between and at the sides of all courts. The alley must be 24 in. wide and must slope from both baselines toward the center of the court. To ensure proper flow of rainwater, the alley should descend 1 in. in depth during the first 6 in. in length (moving along the alley from each baseline toward the center of the court) and gradually increase in depth to at least 4 in. at midcourt where a suitable drain should be installed. The court can be lit using a 20-in. hinged pole with a 1,500-W quartzite floodlight. This pole should be erected outside the courts next to the scoreboard or benches at the base of the courts. Overhead lighting is also an option in recreational areas. Frequently, 2 in. x 2 in. backstops are installed (in a loose fashion) to prevent discs from rebounding back onto the court.

Indoor shuffleboard courts must also be constructed in a level area. Reinforced concrete or any reasonably smooth surface is sufficient. Portable courts are available from vendors.

Croquet

Dimensions

The two most common forms of American croquet are six-wicket croquet (Figure 10.12) and nine-wicket croquet (Figure 10.13). Dimensions, configurations, and layouts are different for each game and are described separately.

The standard croquet court for American six-wicket croquet is a rectangle measuring 105 ft (35 yd) long x 84 ft (28 yd) wide. Boundary lines should be clearly marked, the inside edge of this border being the actual court boundary. If the area is too small to accommodate a standard court, a modified court may be laid out in accordance with the same proportions as a standard court (i.e., five units long by four units wide; for example, a court could be 50 ft long x 40 ft wide). In fact, in instances where the grass is cut high or beginners are competing, a smaller court such as a 50 ft x 40 ft court is more desirable (U.S. Croquet Association [USCA], 2012).

The stake is set in the center of the court (see Figure 10.12). On a standard full court, the wickets are set parallel to the north and south boundaries, the centers of the two inner wickets are set 21 ft to the north and south of the stake, and the centers of the four outer wickets are set 21 ft from their adjacent boundaries. On a smaller modified 50 ft x 40 ft court, the corner wickets are 10 ft from their adjacent boundaries, and the center wickets are 10 ft in each direction from the stake (USCA, 2012).

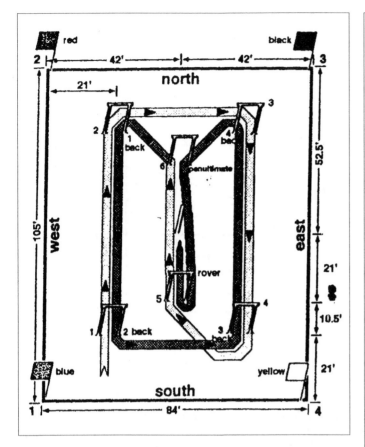

Figure 10.12. **Six-Wicket Croquet Layout** (*Source:* U.S. Croquet Association, 2012)

American nine-wicket croquet is played on a rectangular court that is 100 ft long x 50 ft wide with boundaries, but marked boundaries are optional. However, a court may be reduced to fit the size and shape of the available play space. If the court is reduced, a 6-ft separation should be maintained between the starting/turning stake and the adjacent wickets (USCA, 1997).

Miscellaneous Considerations

For further information regarding the construction of courts, rules, or equipment, contact the United States Croquet Association. Their contact information can be found at http://www.croquetamerica.com.

Fencing

Dimensions

The fencing court (Figure 10.14) is referred to as the foil strip or piste and is constructed of wood, rubber, cork, linoleum, or synthetic material such as plastic. The strip is from 5 ft, 10 in. (1.8 m) wide to 6 ft, 7 in. (2 m) wide and 45 ft, 11 in. (14 m) long. The strip markings include seven lines that cross the width of the entire strip: one center line; two on-guard lines, one drawn 6 ft, 7 in. (2 m) from each

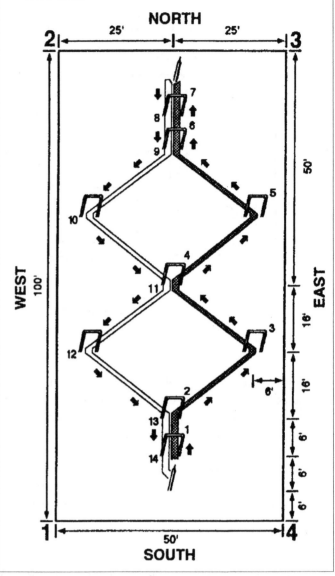

Figure 10.13. **Nine-Wicket Croquet Layout** (*Source:* U.S. Croquet Association, 2012)

side of the center line; two end lines at the rear limit of the strip; and two warning lines marked 3 ft, 3 in. (1 m) in front of the end lines. Portable strips are also an option for those wishing to avoid permanent floor markings. Finally, ceiling clearance should be a minimum of 12 ft.

Miscellaneous Considerations

For electric foil and épée, a metallic piste must cover the entire length of the strip, including the extension areas. Electrical outlets and jacks should be located at the ends of the strips to provide power for electrical equipment. For safety, any rackets for mounting fencing targets should be either recessed flush with the wall or fastened to the wall at least as high as 7 ft.

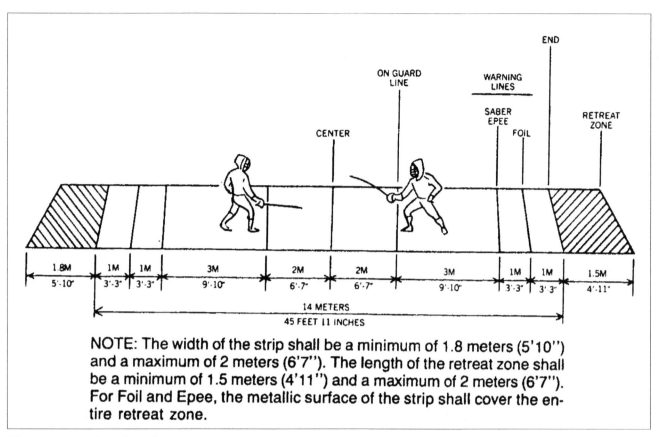

NOTE: The width of the strip shall be a minimum of 1.8 meters (5'10")
and a maximum of 2 meters (6'7"). The length of the retreat zone shall
be a minimum of 1.5 meters (4'11") and a maximum of 2 meters (6'7").
For Foil and Epee, the metallic surface of the strip shall cover the entire retreat zone.

Figure 10.14. Fencing Court (*Source:* USA Fencing, 2012)

Field Spaces

Thomas H. Sawyer, *Indiana State University*
Tonya L. Gimbert, *Indiana State University*

Sports fields generally require the largest amount of space in an outdoor complex. The activities that can be conducted are varied and require a variety of sizes. Additional acreage is required for spectators, officials, service personnel, and service areas (e.g., concessions, restrooms, equipment storage, scoreboards, press box, parking lots, picnic areas, batting cages, bull pens, playground areas).

The usability of the areas, particularly at night and after inclement weather, often requires substantial support utilities, such as communication, drainage, irrigation, lighting, security, and sewer systems. Furthermore, the surface material, synthetic or natural, and its substructure systems are also critical.

The various sports field venues that are highlighted in this chapter include baseball and softball, cricket, croquet, field hockey, football, lacrosse, rugby, and soccer. The beginning of the chapter will highlight common planning challenges for all fields, and the latter portion will cover specific needs for the various fields.

All fields must have adequate seating for spectators. Numerous types of seating are available, from concrete stands, to steel or wood bleachers of various heights, to portable aluminum bleachers. The seating has changed from 18 in. wide to 20 in. to accommodate the spectators' larger backsides. Many of the seats are fiberglass rather than wood, and some are aluminum. The seats are contoured for greater comfort, and some areas have soft theater seating. The choice comes down to the size of the purchaser's pocketbook.

The planners need to consider the following safety suggestions when developing seating for spectators for outdoor events: (a) conforming to Americans With Disabilities Act (ADA) guidelines (see Chapter 4); (b) conforming to U.S. Consumer Product Safety Commission guidelines to provide railings for each side and the top row to prevent falls; (c) closing areas under each row of seats to prevent children from falling through or climbing; (d) enclosing the structure to gain space for storage, concessions, or restrooms and at the same time prevent children from playing under the bleachers; and (e) providing aisles with railings for ease of accessing seating.

Note: Field diagrams and specifications can be found at http://www.athleticbusiness.com/specifications/

Planning Checklist for Fields in General

According to Flynn (1985) and Sawyer (1999, 2002, 2005, 2009), field planners should use the following checklist when designing field spaces:

- Define the use of the field complex (i.e., single- or multiple-sport users; youth, adolescent, or adult; amateur or professional).
- Pay careful attention to slope on fields to encourage proper and adequate pitch for drainage.
- Ensure subdrainage requirements are met, the type as well as placement of drainage outlets is well out of the playing area, and swales are beyond safety or buffer zones.
- Make sure fences on the perimeter are offset beyond safety or buffer zones. The height of the fence should be consistent with the ASTM standard (i.e., at least 8 ft) for the type of activity. Fences should be flexible, resilient, and padded. Furthermore, ensure that fences are placed in front of players (i.e., dugouts and field-level shelters) and spectators. The fence should be sturdy enough to attach a windscreen or sunscreen. Finally, the mesh on the fences should be of a size to discourage climbing and the top should have knuckled mesh.
- Provide gates for security and for service of different practice areas and game areas.

- Design warning tracks to provide advanced warning of perimeter barriers, and ensure they are wide enough and of appropriate material to meet ASTM standards.
- Ensure that light poles, fence poles, and foul poles are not in the field of play and are padded.
- Plan that mowing or maintenance strips along fences are provided so they are not hazardous.
- Place all shrubs and tree plantings well outside the playing area.
- Ensure that the turf (artificial or natural) is suitable for different weather conditions (i.e., hot, cold, dry, or wet).
- Install the scoreboard well outside the playing area and its fence line.
- Design the irrigation system so that it will not interfere with play and that all valves, distribution boxes, and other fixtures are well outside the field of play.
- Make sure that vehicular and pedestrian traffic flow patterns prevent conflict and interference and that bike and vehicle parking is marked and controlled.
- Ensure that emergency call stations are placed at strategic locations and emergency vehicle access is available for immediate response to all areas.
- Plan the field area so that hazards are not nearby (e.g., major highways, railroad tracks, waterways, culverts, ravines, industries, woods, uncut roughs, and utility lines).
- Create the field area so that security vehicles have easy access and surveillance during game time as well as other times.
- Understand the importance of field orientation relative to the movement of the sun and prevailing wind patterns.
- Configure spectator seating to ensure the best viewing of the game as well as easy access and exit.
- Ensure each activity space has the appropriate safety or buffer zones.
- Review the plan to ensure that the field dimensions are accurate and meet the specified association rules for the level of play.
- Configure all field spaces to include metal sleeves for goalposts, goals, and flags.
- Encourage the owners to ensure that regular maintenance and inspections are done to eliminate ruts, ridges, and depressions in the fields after use; remove debris and rocks from the playing area as well as safety zones; ensure all hooks on goalposts, foul line posts, and fencing are recessed; eliminate sharp edges on posts, rails, and welds; and make sure benches, seats, and bleachers are protected by screening or barriers.
- Create backstops that protect players, spectators, and other game personnel from injury from errant balls or bats.

Safety and Fields

The owner of a potential sports field property must apply the sound and proven guidelines for planning a facility that are outlined in this textbook to reduce the athletes' exposure to risks (see Chapter 2). The planning process should include an analysis of the causation of injuries.

The size of the field area is critical. According to Flynn (1985) and Sawyer (1999, 2002, 2005, 2009), neither athletes nor spectators should be exposed to any of the following hazards, and planners need to consider each concern when selecting a location for a field:

- Streets should not be located any closer than 100 yd to a facility and should be fenced off.
- Railroad tracks, like streets, should not be any closer than 100 yd to a facility and should be fenced off.
- Watercourses, man-made culverts, or natural stream ways can contain deep, fast-moving water that can trap or entangle people who slip, walk, or slide into them. They should not be any closer than 100 yd to a facility and should be fenced off.
- Trenches or gulleys can be hazards that hold deep muck, hidden snakes, other reptiles, or rodents or that contain wires, quicksand, or reinforcing rods that can pierce or entrap a person. They should not be any closer than 100 yd to a facility and should be fenced off.
- Settlement ponds or basins can contain toxic liquids, silt, or flammable materials and should not be any closer than 100 yd to a facility and should be fenced off.
- Storage yards, with old concrete or other culvert pipes that can roll and crush; junk cars and machinery that can cut or pierce; old wood and metal junk piles; and hazardous drums of liquids (e.g., lead paint, paints, sealants) or acids that can explode or burn should not be any closer than 100 yd to a facility and should be fenced off.
- Climatic noise, odors, smoke, and dust should be avoided.
- The protective perimeter of the area should consist of fencing to keep spectators away from the area of play and to keep players within the play area.
- The area must not consist of soils that are toxic, poor draining, decaying, or of poor structure. They should be free of debris and glass.
- The field space should be located in an area that has no other activity spaces in close proximity to protect the athletes and spectators.
- The visibility of the entire area should accommodate foot and vehicle security.
- The area should be illuminated at critical times to facilitate supervision and security.
- The multipurpose fields that are used for baseball or softball as well as soccer, field hockey, or football

should not have ruts that create dangerous high-speed bounces of the ball on the playing surface.

- The games of baseball and softball have three major concerns for spectators and parking areas: foul balls, home runs, and overthrows as well as overruns which are likely in all field sports.
- The participants' age, gender, skill levels, and/or experience must be considered in creating facilities for all participants.
- The area must be accessible to participants and spectators with disabilities.
- Concealment areas caused by shrubbery or tree canopy or adjacent structures should be eliminated to deter improper activity.
- The public comfort for players and spectators must include restroom facilities close to supervised areas, properly designed and positioned litter containers, benches, drinking fountains, and walkways.
- The safety or buffer zone around the field and its appurtenance and equipment must be large enough to keep players from hitting stationary objects along its perimeter and, if existing, such objects should be padded.
- The padding or other accepted proven safety precautions, such as releasable or yieldable devices for outfield fences, stanchions, barriers, and other perimeter containments, must be used, and/or sufficient buffered perimeter areas should be used.
- The safety glazing of nearby windows, observation panels, and doors is a necessity.
- The relationship of fields and appurtenance among facilities should be harmonious and complementary in encouraging and facilitating play.
- The traffic flow of users from one field or appurtenance to another should be designed to be safe.
- The durability and maintainability of the types of appurtenances within and adjacent to the field must be considered.
- The pedestrian, player, and spectator traffic around the activity field is important. The field must be located so that there is no interference with the traffic of people, buses, automobiles, service vehicles, vendors, and bicycles. Pedestrian traffic should be routed to have easy access to comfort stations, security, refreshments, lockers, and other related facilities.
- The automotive and service (e.g., lawn mowers, maintenance vehicles) driveways should not bisect or parallel open play or human access areas.
- Immovable barriers should be installed to separate automotive traffic routes from activity areas.
- Maintenance vehicle access to fields should have the correct subbase and surface materials installed to limit wear and irregular surfaces.

- The utility lines, above, on, or below ground, should be positioned so as not to interfere with players, the game, or spectators, or accessible to contact with any person.
- Storm drains are frequent hazards, often within the field limits or directly adjacent to them. Players can have their feet entrapped by such street-sized drains. They should be located at least 5 yd from the play line.
- Irrigation heads for pop-up or quick-couple sprinklers can cause tripping if not designed properly. They should be recessed as per manufacturers' guidelines.
- Relocatable aluminum irrigation pipes and sports equipment left on the field are also hazardous and should be properly stored and secured.
- Power lines, poles, transformers, and control panels must not be in proximity to playing and/or spectator areas. They should be in remote and inaccessible secure locations.
- Fire hydrants, hose bibs, and drinking fountains must not be placed in the vicinity of the area of play.
- The buffer/safety zone for outdoor fields is 10 yd. When there are multiple fields in a field complex, the distance between parallel fields should not be less than 10 yd on each side of the field. Bleachers should not be any closer than 10 yd from the sideline or end zone.

The types of turf that are used on sports fields are synthetic and natural turf. (See Chapter 9 for a complete discussion on natural turf.) From the 1960s to the late 1980s, many natural turf fields were converted to synthetic turf fields. The conversions were intended to reduce the cost of maintenance and to provide flexibility to sports schedules without concern about the wear and tear that occurred on natural turf fields being used by numerous sports teams. Conversions back to natural turf through the 1980s and 1990s were prompted by the increase in athletic injury related to synthetic turf. In 1988, the next generation of synthetic turfs, which replicate a natural grass surface, began to appear. This product is durable, cost efficient, and consists of a sand and rubber infield system that has reduced sports injuries related to synthetic fields.

Type of Surfaces

Bioengineered Surface

Synthetic materials can be soft or firm. They can be piled, turfed, graveled, or smoothed. They can be rolled or poured, paneled, or sprayed. The ingredients of the turf can be rubber, polymer, pigment, polyvinyl chloride (PVC), thermoset, thermoplastic, and a host of other new high-tech materials. Synthetic products have substrates that are also of varied ingredients.

Synthetic turf is attractive to players for a number of reasons, including that the surface and footwear interact well for better footing, the surface stays in place, it is resilient, balls bounce well, the surface dries rapidly, and it has a cooling effect. It also has distractions for players, including that the surface has little resiliency, balls respond inconsistently, the surface affects the speed of the ball (making it faster), and the surface is hot on hot days.

Attractions for operators include that the surface is repairable, is picturesque, is portable, is durable, is stable, is paintable, and drains rapidly. However, the greatest detraction of synthetic surfaces for the operator is life of the surface, which is approximately 15 years.

Sports Field Lighting

Lighting (illumination) is critical to safety and revenue generation (see Chapter 5 for detailed information). The illumination level for baseball and softball is 20 foot-candles for the outfield and 30 foot-candles for the infield. The lighting for other team sport fields (e.g., field hockey, football, lacrosse, rugby, and soccer) is a minimum of 30 foot-candles. If sporting events are to be televised, the lighting requirement will be much different. However, if this happens only occasionally, portable lighting companies can be hired to provide additional lighting requirements. The air should be monitored for contaminants that can cause the reflector surface to change by increasing diffusion and decreasing total reflection. This results in less total light energy leaving the face of the light with less lumens. There should be no shadows on the field that create unsafe catching, and there should not be any glare or irregular bright patches. All stanchions or poles must be outside the field of play.

Sports Field Orientation

There are various thoughts about the orientation of baseball and softball fields. It depends on where the field is and the time games are to be held. One school of thought is that the back of home plate should be set to point south to southwest or have the baseline from home plate to first base run in an easterly direction. The theory is for the batter to look into the sun, which implies the catcher as well. Another thought is for the batter to look away from the sun. Presently, the orientation is probably the least of the safety problems. However, because the batter and catcher or pitcher is in the most hazardous position, the orientation should still be considered. A line through these positions would be the axis for orientation for either position. After locating the axis, locate the sun's position at sunrise, early morning, late afternoon, and sunset. Establish an orientation for the field that avoids the batter and catcher or pitcher from facing directly into the early morning or late afternoon sun.

Furthermore, all new fields should be oriented with consideration to the following factors: protection of play-

ers, comfort of spectators, season of use (February–June), latitude (north to south), east–west geographical location within time zone, prevailing winds, daylight saving time, background, and obstacles or barriers. In general, those considerations will lead to home plate being located in the southwest corner of the field, and a line drawn through home plate, the center of the pitcher's plate, and out to centerfield will extend to the northeast.

All other fields should run north to south to avoid the direct movement of the sun from east to west. However, if all contests are played in the evening after sundown, the sun does not become a factor.

Sports Field Fencing

Generally speaking, fields should be fenced to protect the field, athletes, and spectators. The height of the fence ranges from 4 ft for youth fields to 8 ft for interscholastic, intercollegiate, and professional fields. A number of fields have 6-ft fences, which is acceptable but not ideal. All fences less than 8 ft high should be covered with a brightly colored vinyl protector with or without padding. The fence should be sturdy enough to withstand an athlete's weight and to serve as a windscreen.

Baseball and Softball Fields

The fence height should start at 8 ft as it leaves the backstop around the circumference of the field, including in front of the dugouts. The fencing should be attached on the field side of the poles, with all attachments and prongs on the outside of the fence. The fence should be stretched down from the top to the tension rail on the bottom. The fence is meant to protect players as well as spectators. It should be no closer than 30 ft to the sidelines or foul lines but preferably will be 50 ft to 75 ft away.

Sports Field Drainage and Irrigation

A properly constructed sports field has a good drainage system (see Chapter 9) so play can resume after a short waiting period and so the turf is not destroyed when played upon in a wet condition. Turf that is too wet or too dry will be compromised. The subsoil of the field should be composed of sand (80% to 90% sand base) to improve the speed of drainage. The playing field should be crowned to allow the heavy rainwater that cannot be absorbed to drain to the sidelines. The slope on either side of the crown should not exceed ¼ in. per foot toward the sideline drainage area. The sideline drainage area should be at least 5 yd from the playing field, contoured, and sloped to catch the runoff to direct it to large drains that are approximately 20 yd apart along the sidelines. These drains should be approximately 15 ft to 20 ft deep with a 3-ft to 5-ft diameter filled with gravel and covered with a metal grate. Marketers always say the key to sales is "location, location, location."

The key to a great field is drainage, drainage, drainage.

Irrigating a field is important in dry climates. There are basically three types of irrigation systems available for fields: underground with sprinkler heads throughout the field space, underground with sprinkler heads on the perimeter of the field, and aboveground with portable piping and sprinkler heads or hoses. The latter option is labor intensive and requires a lot of equipment storage. The other options are the most convenient and least labor intensive.

The planners of the irrigation system need to consider the following: (a) the safety of the participants (i.e., perimeter or within-field sprinkler layout); (b) type of sprinkler heads; (c) the watering pattern layout (i.e., the number of overlapping zones needed, based on the available water pressure, to reach all areas of the field evenly); (d) the source of water (i.e., wells with a pumping system or government or private water company); (e) a timing system; (f) a plan for winterizing in climates that have temperatures below freezing; (g) tie-ins for drinking fountains and hose bibs; and (h) the possibility of a liquid fertilization option.

Sports Field Service Areas

Sports field service areas include concessions areas, press box, restrooms, scoreboards, and storage. These areas are important to spectators and support staff. If the service areas are well designed and maintained, they will increase fan loyalty.

Concessions Area

The concessions area should be centralized ideally behind home plate, especially in multifield complexes as shown in Figure 11.1. The area can be constructed from wood or concrete block. It should have plenty of counter space for preparation of products and to service the patrons. The floor should be concrete with numerous drains. There should be at least one double sink and ample cabinet space for storage. The area should have numerous electrical outlets and ground fault interruption (GFI) outlets

near water sources. The lighting should be fluorescent. The equipment in the area should include refrigerator, freezer, stove top with at least four cooking elements, microwave, popcorn popper, hot dog cooker/warmer, coffeemaker, soda fountain, ceiling fans, shelving for merchandise, sign board for advertising, and cash register.

Press Box

The press box is important for the press, scouts, scoreboard operator, and those filming games. The press box should be located higher than the highest part of the bleachers. The size will depend on the number of users. It should have an unobstructed view of the playing field. The following should be available for the press:

- a table to write on or broadcast from;
- comfortable chairs;
- phone hookups;
- computer hookups;
- electrical outlets;
- refrigerator;
- coffeemaker;
- separate areas for press, radio announcers, scorekeeper, public address (PA) announcer, coaches, and scouts; and
- an area above the press area exclusively for filming games. These facilities are generally constructed of wood with fluorescent lighting.

Restrooms

Numerous restrooms need to be provided, preferably not portable. The number of facilities for women should be twice as many as that provided for men. Each restroom should provide changing areas for babies, with adjacent waste disposal units. Each restroom area should be accessible, or at least an appropriate number of restrooms need to be accessible and so labeled. These facilities are generally constructed of concrete block with concrete floors with drains for cleaning. The lighting should be fluorescent. The rooms should be adequately ventilated.

Scoreboards

There are a number of reliable scoreboard companies. The planners need to consider what the function of the scoreboard will be—to depict score and time remaining only or to provide entertainment and information as well.

Scoreboards can be simple or complex in nature. The planners need to consider what they want the scoreboard to depict before determining the type of scoreboard to be purchased. The choices include the score; periods or innings; injury time or penalty time remaining; times and places by lanes; diving score by judge, degree of difficulty, total points scored, ranking after x number of dives; balls, strikes, outs; roster; players' vital statistics; advertising; PA system; multiple functions for various sports using the

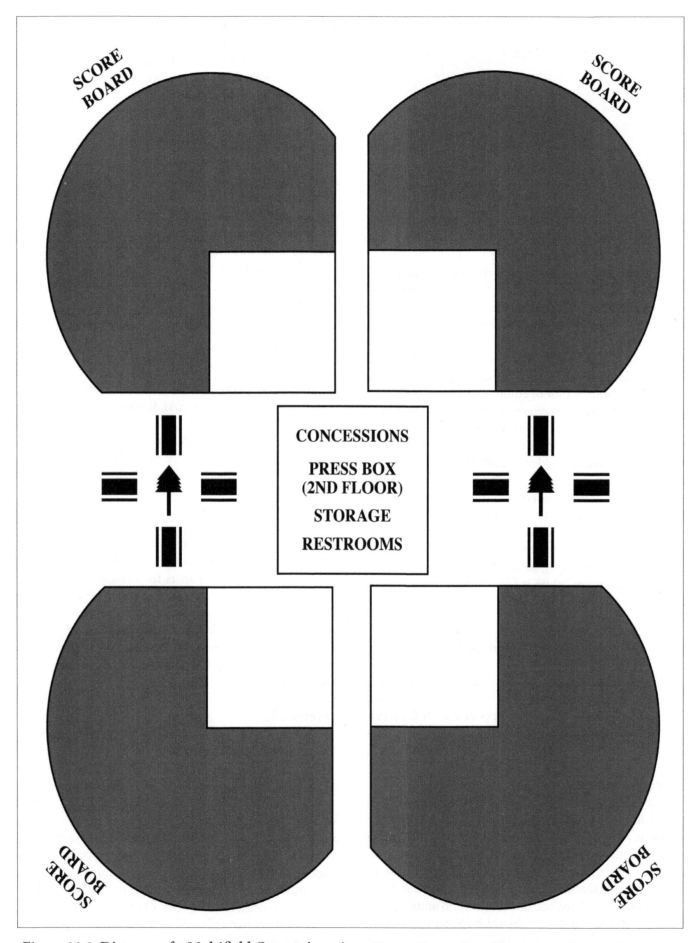

Figure 11.1. **Diagram of a Multifield Concessions Area** (*Source*: Meghan Rosselli)

field complex; close-ups of players and spectators; time of day; scores from other games; and much more depending on the planner's imagination.

Storage

As is true with indoor facilities, outdoor facilities never have enough storage. The planners need to consider what items need to be stored. These include various types of riding lawn mowers; push mowers; tillers; weed eaters; shovels, rakes, and hoes; utility vehicles; irrigation pipes; hoses and sprinkler heads; field liners; goals; field flags; benches; waste containers; protection screens; pitching machines; tarps; fertilizers, insecticides, and talc; paint; chains, yard markers, and padding for goalpost for football; and much more.

Storage areas generally are constructed out of concrete blocks with concrete floors and an appropriate number of drains for cleaning. The space should have fluorescent lighting with an adequate number of electrical outlets. There should be a separate work area with a workbench and an adequate amount of storage with shelving. The entrance should be an automatic roll-up door at least 8 ft high. The ceiling height should be at least 10 ft. The voids under bleachers should be enclosed (these spaces make inexpensive storage areas). The space for chemical storage must meet Occupational Safety and Health Administration (OSHA) guidelines.

Baseball and Softball Fields

Baseball and softball facilities are important aspects of sport in public schools (Grades 5 to 12), colleges and universities (varsity competition as well as recreation), community recreation programs, Babe Ruth Leagues, Little Leagues, Miss Softball Leagues, corporate recreation programs, and military recreation programs. The space re-

quirements for these spaces vary (see Table 11.1)

Due to the alarming number of injuries reported to the U.S. Consumer Product Safety Commission, safety is a principal concern. This concern places pressure on field operators, turf managers, maintenance managers, and others to have a safe playing field. A "field of dreams" is created from a consistent set of proven guidelines and safety standards to ensure consistency around the country. It is important for the planners to be aware of the field specifications described in the various rule books that govern these two sports (e.g., National Federation of High School Activities Association, National Collegiate Athletic Association, National Intercollegiate Athletic Association, National Junior College Athletic Association, National Softball Association, American Softball Association, United States Softball Association, United States Fastpitch Association, Softball USA, International Softball Federation, National Association for Girls and Women in Sports, Little League Association). These rule books are the gospel in regard to the specific dimensions for the fields, and most rule books are revised annually.

Common Design Errors With Possible Solutions

There are four common design errors that planners need to avoid when designing baseball and softball fields: incorrect field contours, failure to isolate fields as drainage units, insufficient clearance around the field, and failure to provide sufficient access. Each of these will be discussed below with possible solutions offered.

Sports field contours are expressed as percentage of slope. Incorrect field contours are those that are less than 1% or more than 2%, except for infields, which should have a .5% slope. According to Puhalla, Krans, and Goatley (2002, 2010), the preferred slope for grass sport fields is 1.25% to 1.75%. The optimal slope for skinned areas should be .5% to 1.75% . The infields of baseball and softball fields

Table 11.1

Space Requirements

Type of Field	Distance to Center Field Fence (ft)	Acres	Sq Ft
Baseball:			
90 ft Bases	400	4.5	195,000
80 ft Bases	315	2.8	123,000
70 ft Bases	75	2	90,000
60 ft Bases	215	1.5	64,000
Softball:			
65 ft Bases	75	2.4	105,000
60 ft Bases	200	1.4	60,000

(*Source:* Puhalla et al., 2002, 2010)

should be the highest point to enhance surface drainage. Finally, a field with a 1.5% slope should be graded evenly with a 1½ ft difference in grade over a span of 100 ft.

No field should be expected to drain away more water than which falls on it. Planners need to be careful not to isolate fields as drainage units. Even if a field is built with correct contours, water running onto the field from another field or an adjacent area can seriously compromise playability in rainy conditions, according to Puhalla et al. (2002, 2010). The preferred design isolates each field as an individual drainage unit by using swales and/or catch basins around the field or by making the field higher than its surroundings.

According to Puhalla, Krans, and Goatley (2003), fields that are designed or constructed with insufficient clearance will have inherent problems: out-of-bounds areas may be too small for the safety of players, spectator areas may be cramped or unsafe, and surface drainage around a field may not work as intended. The designers should consider space requirements in the planning stages. Making sure enough space is available around each field before construction begins will prevent water from being locked in by other fields, parking lots, roads, buildings, and the like.

According to Puhalla et al. (2002, 2010), a well-designed sports field includes access roadways for players, spectators, maintenance equipment, and heavier renovation equipment (e.g., large trucks, tractors).

Bases

The base areas must be level, with all irregularities eliminated. The type of base used in either baseball or softball varies, and the rule books stipulate what types are permissible. The planner should contact the ASTM International for detailed information regarding the appropriate standards for bases. Presently, the ASTM F08 Committee on Sports Equipment and Facilities is establishing standards and classifications for bases.

Bases are intended to be a reference point on baseball and softball fields. They are integral to the game. There are four types of base designs used: permanent or stationary bases, modified stationary bases, release-type bases, and throw-down bases. The type of base usually refers to how the base is secured to the playing field or its function.

Stationary base. This base uses a ground anchor permanently installed in the playing field. The anchor measures either 1 in. or 1 ½ in., installed a minimum of 1 in. below the playing surface. The base is designed with a stem that fits into or over the ground anchor and holds the base securely in place.

The base should be constructed of permanently white material, which can be rubber, polyvinyl, polyurethane, or other synthetic material to increase service life. The base top should have a molded tread pattern to increase player traction and reduce slippage. Base size and color should conform to individual governing organizations.

Permanent or stationary bases can be used on fields by players with more advanced or higher skill levels only after (a) the players have been thoroughly warned that they can be seriously injured for life if they make a mistake in judgment or miscalculation and (b) they have been made thoroughly aware of other options (e.g., the tapered side base or low silhouette that tapers to the ground, eliminating impact of a sliding player against a vertical surface and uses that momentum to slide over the base). Bases are the number one cause of injuries to ankles and other body parts, especially stationary, modified stationary, and poorly designed release-type bases.

Modified stationary base. The flexible base is a one-piece base that uses a fixed-anchor system for secure placement. It is constructed with interdependent ribs that allow the base to compress and absorb energy generated by a sliding player. The cover flexes inward and downward but does not release.

The strap-down base or tie-down base must be held in place by four spikes inserted into the ground. Straps attached to the base are inserted through loops in the spike head and tightened down. The base is constructed of vinyl-coated nylon or canvas filled with a foam or other resilient material. If installed properly, a portion of the base will remain somewhat stable. However, it has a tendency during play to loosen and move. This style is low cost relative to other base styles, which accounts for its popularity.

Release-type base. The release-type base is designed to reduce the chance of injury to a sliding player by releasing from its anchor system on the impact of a hard lateral slide. The release base must use a permanent ground anchor securely positioned below ground for installation. There are two-piece and three-piece designs. The release-type must not expose hidden secondary hazards after the primary aboveground base portion releases.

Throw-down base. This base is a thin square, sometimes using a waffle design on the bottom, usually constructed of canvas or synthetic material with little or no padding. It is not physically attached to the playing surface and therefore is dangerously subject to moving when a player steps on or rounds a base. Throw-down bases are not recommended for teaching basic skills in a gym, such as in a physical education class.

Specialized bases. The flush or recessed base (except home plate, which is mounted flush with the playing field) is usually not considered for the following reasons: (a) it is difficult to keep the base visible and clean, (b) it is difficult for the umpire to make a call at the base when the base is not visible, (c) it changes the nature of the game, and (d) it is not widely used.

Double first base. The double first base uses a securely positioned ground anchor system. The base is designed to reduce or eliminate the contact between the first baseman and base runner. It is a unit equal in size to two bases side by side, one-half white and mounted in the normal first base position, and one-half colored, and mounted in foul territory.

Home plate. The home plate, batter's box, and catcher's box and their correct dimensional size and positioning must conform to the game and the rules of the appropriate governing body. The area should be well compacted, properly tapered, and level, with no irregularities. The plate must be firmly anchored, and any undermining or ruts must be corrected before play begins.

The home plate is a reference point on the playing field. It establishes the horizontal limits of the strike zone used by the umpire in calling balls and strikes. It is imperative that all home plates have a white surface that measures 17 in. x 8 ½ in. x 8 ½ in. x 12 in. x 12 in. flush with the surrounding playing surface. Furthermore, all home plates must have a peripheral black bevel that does not exceed 35°. The outermost edge of the bevel must be sufficiently below the playing surface. It does not matter how the plates are field mounted as long as they remain flat and flush with surrounding playing surfaces with no sharp corners or sharp nails exposed.

There are four styles of home plate, including buried, staked, anchored, and throw down.

Buried. A rubber or synthetic plate 2 in. or more thick is buried, and the uppermost white surface is installed flush with the playing surface. It can be mounted in a concrete subbase to provide greater leveling stability.

Staked. A rubber or synthetic plate ¾ in. to 1 in. thick has an installed white surface flush to the playing surface. It can be mounted in a concrete subbase for better anchoring.

Anchored. A rubber or synthetic plate has a stem built into the bottom that fits into a permanent ground anchor. The uppermost white surface must be installed flush with the playing surface.

Throw down. A rubber or synthetic thin mat, sometimes using a waffle design on the bottom, is laid down on the playing surface and is not mechanically held in place. Throw-down home plates are not recommended for teaching basic skills in a gym, such as in a physical education class.

Skinned Infield

With an eye to player safety, begin the outfield slope 20 ft back into the outfield, lessening the transition from the infield to outfield (this is for both synthetic and natural fields). The infield slope should be established at 0.5% and the outfield slope at 1.3% all the way around to further speed drainage. The infield should be an 80:20 premixed sand-to-clay material at a depth of 3 in. . The demarcation between skinned area and turf must be smooth and firm. The skinned areas must maintain the proper pitch to eliminate puddling and erosion. Irregular clumps of turf, uneven edges, and undermining of skinned materials are among the causes of ankle and leg injuries in the game.

Skinned areas could be just cutouts around the bases, home plate, and pitcher's mound or could include baselines or the entire infield area. In all cases, the skinned areas must be continuously inspected and groomed. All irregularities must be eliminated, particularly around bases where sliding grooves the area.

Clay is most often used for a skinned area; however, other materials and mixes of materials have been used depending upon local sources and preference. Most fields should be designed to be playable within 15 min to 20 min after rain. A higher percentage of sand may be needed to achieve that without underground drainage.

Turf Infield and Outfield

Chapter 9 discusses natural turf and irrigation concerns. However, it needs to be noted here that natural turf in the infield and outfield should be Tifway™ Bermuda grass. It should be overseeded (see Base Paths) with Topflite™ perennial ryegrass. Table 11.2 displays the square footage of the skinned area and the grass area for common-sized baseball and softball fields, including foul territory.

Pitcher's Mound

The pitcher's mound and its plate must meet the requirements of the game's governing body. The height of the plate, the pitch of the slope within the circle toward home plate, the radius of the circle, and the level plate length and width size are critical to safety in any type of designated and designed field and must be checked and maintained before any game.

Base Paths

A regular maintenance concern is the rutting of the base path. Like the infield, the base path should be free of ruts and irregularities on the surface. Periodically hand rake the base paths between first base and second base and second base and third base to identify low spots. The

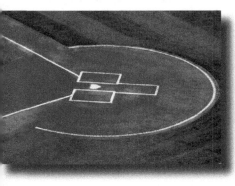

Example of the markings of a home plate area

Table 11.2

Square Footage of Skinned Area and Grass Area

Type of Field	Distance to Center Field Fence (ft)	Skinned Area (sq ft)	Grass Area (sq ft)
Baseball:			
90 ft Bases-95 ft Arc			
With Grass Infield	400	11,500	120,500
With Skinned Infield	400	8,300	113,700
80 ft Bases-80 ft Arc			
With Grass Infield	315	8,400	74,500
With Skinned Infield	315	13,650	69,250
70 ft Bases-70 ft Arc			
With Grass Infield	275	6,800	53,550
With Skinned Infield	275	10,700	49,650
60 ft Bases-60 ft Arc			
With Grass Infield	215	3,850	39,500
With Skinned Infield	215	6,700	36,650
Softball: (Skinned Infield)			
65 ft Bases-65 ft Arc	275	9,300	61,450
60 ft Bases-60 ft Arc	200	8,350	31,500

(*Source:* Puhalla et al., 2002, 2010)

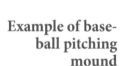

Example of baseball pitching mound

Base path

base paths between home plate and first base and first base and third base can be composed of clay and sand like the infield or of natural turf or synthetic material. If the base path is composed of natural turf, it should be overseeded with Topflight™ perennial ryegrass prior to the season, periodically during the season, and at the conclusion of the season, as well as in early fall.

Prior to overseeding in the early spring and early fall, the area should be aerated then dethatched to provide good seed-to-soil contact. The seeded area should be fertilized first with 10-10-10 fertilizer, and 1 month later with a slow-release 30-16-10.

Warning Track

Warning tracks are playing surfaces located on the margins of the playing area for the purpose of providing a warning to the player that he or she is approaching a hazard (commonly a fence) or out-of-bounds area. To provide for an effective warning track surface, the warning track must be constructed and maintained in such a manner so that the player can sense the change in texture from the regular playing surface and the warning track without having to look. This feature is important because the player is often visually focused on the ball during play and would not be looking at the ground as he or she is running toward the warning track. The warning track must also be constructed and maintained in such a manner that the warning track itself, or the surface transition, does not pose a hazard to the players.

The warning track areas of sports fields should provide a uniform surface with good footing. The change in surface texture of the warning track from the surrounding playing surface must contrast enough that the player can sense the change without looking. Most often, warning track surfaces are devoid of turf or other vegetation. However, turfed warning track areas may be used in instances where such purpose is to "warn" the player of an impending hazard where the primary playing surface is a skinned area. This may be the case in softball where the entire infield playing surface is a skinned area and a turfed warning track is used along the first base and third base fence lines. Undulations, rough surface, hard or soft surface, weeds, stones, debris, wet spots, and so forth detract from a good, safe warning track. The safety and effectiveness of the warning track is largely affected by construction and maintenance procedures.

During construction, factors such as the physical and chemical properties of materials used in the area; freedom from stones, sticks, and other debris; and surface drainage and internal drainage should be considered. The surface elevation should also be considered so that a drastic change is not produced by the transition from the playing surface to the warning track area that may create a tripping or falling hazard.

Maintenance practices that influence the playability of the surface include edging, dragging, rolling, watering, vegetation control, and removal of stones and debris that may adversely affect play and safety.

The warning track and/or buffer zone should be equal in width to 5% of the distance from home plate to the deepest part of the playing field and should completely encircle the field (see Table 11.3). Any edge between the track and the turf should be smooth and even.

Guidance on construction and maintenance of warning tracks. A safe and functioning warning track can prevent serious injury to baseball and softball players, as well as participants in other sports. A new guide created by ASTM International's Committee F08 on Sports Equipment and Facilities addresses the issues involved in building and maintaining warning track areas.

Subcommittee F08.64 on Natural Playing Surfaces (2012) created *F 2270 - 12: Standard Guide for Construction and Maintenance of Warning Track Areas on Athletic Fields* to provide guidance in selecting the materials with which to build a new warning track or to recondition an older track and to advise on management practices to best maintain a warning track.

Warning tracks are particularly important in baseball and softball because players frequently run with their eyes focused high in the air on a fly ball. To avoid slamming into a fence or wall, players depend on being aware of the approaching hazard by sensing the difference in surface texture as they run from the field onto the warning track. However, the warning track needs to be built and maintained so that neither the warning track nor the transition from field to track poses a risk of injury to players.

Guide F 2270 (ASTM F 2270, 2012) deals with construction issues such as physical and chemical properties of materials used in the area; freedom from stones, sticks, and other debris; and surface and internal drainage, among other considerations. The standard also focuses on maintenance issues such as edging, dragging, rolling, watering, vegetation control, and removal of stones and debris.

Backstop

The backstop is a key element of a field for safeguarding the players and spectators. The basic purposes of the backstop include keeping the ball within the playing area, protecting the spectators, safeguarding others involved in the game (e.g., batters in the on-deck circle, bat persons), and protecting nearby activities from conflict with pop-ups (e.g., adjacent ball fields, concessions areas, restrooms, parking areas).

Table 11.3

Recommended Warning Track Dimensions

Distance From Home Plate to Backstop[a]	Foul Territory[b]	Outfield Fence
25 ft	8 ft	12 ft
30 ft	10 ft	12 ft
40 ft	12 ft	15 ft
50 ft	15 ft	15 ft
60 ft	15 ft	15 ft

[a]The distance from the foul lines to the dugout is the same. [b]Includes backstop fence and foul line fence.

According to Flynn (1985) and Sawyer (1999, 2002, 2005, 2009), when designing the backstop, the planners should consider

- using small mesh to discourage people from climbing the structure;
- ensuring the parking and traffic areas are not close;
- installing a double mesh to prevent fingers, faces, and other body parts of spectators from being crushed by errant balls or thrown bats;
- keeping the mesh free from barbs or penetrating parts to ensure safety for players and spectators;
- ensuring the distance between home plate and the backstop is not less than 25 ft but preferably 60 ft to ensure player safety;
- using ground materials of either (a) turf with an appropriate warning track composed of clay or crushed granite (M-10) or crushed brick or (b) no turf with either clay or crushed granite (M-10) or crushed brick; and
- ensuring the height of the backstop is at least 18 ft, preferably 20 ft, with a 4-ft to 6-ft overhang at the top with a 45° angle.

The most frequently used backstop consists of three 12 ft wide panels that are 18 ft to 20 ft high and covered with a 1 ½-in. galvanized wire mesh material. These panels can be made of steel, aluminum, or wood. One panel is placed directly behind home plate and the other two on each side flaring at 30° with the center panel. The fencing on either side of the side panels should gradually taper down to 8 ft behind the players' bench area to provide greater protection for the spectators in bleachers on the other side of the fence. The top of the backstop will have three panels, 4 ft to 6 ft x 12 ft, attached to the upright panels and positioned at a 45° angle to contain errant balls. This overhang will be covered with the same material as the uprights.

Players' Bench Area

There are two types of players' bench areas commonly constructed for baseball and softball: dugouts and field-level shelters. The safer of the two is the dugout, but it is also the most expensive to construct. The dugout is usually 4 ft deep, constructed of poured concrete and concrete blocks with drains to remove water quickly. It has an elevated players' bench area, entrance to locker rooms (if in a stadium complex), drinking fountain, communication system, bat rack, other storage space, lights, and electrical outlets. Recently, to better safeguard the players, either shatterproof plastic or wire mesh has been installed to repel errant balls and bats. The roof is constructed so as to discourage people from sitting or climbing on it.

The field-level shelter is at field level with a poured concrete floor and concrete block walls. It has a wire mesh fence at least 6 ft high to repel errant balls or bats. The space should have a bat rack, communication system, a drinking fountain, additional storage, lights, and electrical outlets. The roof should be constructed to discourage sitting and climbing.

Batting Cage

The batting cage should be located outside the fenced playing field. It should be constructed of steel, aluminum, or wood. The minimum size for one batter should be 10 ft wide, 100 ft long, and 10 ft high. If more than one batter is going to be hitting, then the cage needs to be wider (i.e., 10 ft wider for each batter) with a separating mesh curtain. The space must be completely covered by mesh netting to protect other players and spectators. There needs to be a source of electricity and numerous GFI electrical outlets. The floor surface should be similar to home plate for the batters and natural mounds for the pitchers.

Bull Pen

Bull pens should be located either down the first- and third-base lines into the outfield area or in right and left center fields. These areas should be protected from errant balls and the spectators. The area behind the catcher should have a protective fence to protect the spectators. Pitching mounds should be exact replicas of the actual playing field mound. There should also be a home plate area. Finally, benches should be available for the players.

Field Size

The area required for a baseball or softball field will vary from 260 ft to 460 ft depending on the level of play anticipated. Because baseball and softball are now often scheduled on the same fields, the age group and type of activity govern the field size. It is recommended that if multiple age groups are to play on a field, it should be sized for optimal use. Many fields have been planned for a size for high school play only to have young adults scheduled for the same field. This creates numerous incidents with players colliding with obstacles or other players. Ideally, if funding is available, there should be separate facilities for the various age groups.

It is common to see multifield complexes for baseball, softball, and combination baseball and softball. The most common multifield complex contains four fields. If one were to view the complex from an airplane, it would resemble a wheel with four spokes coming from a central hub.

The central hub (see Figure 11.1) would contain a two-story building with each side facing a different backstop and field. The first floor would contain a concession area, restrooms, storage for game and maintenance equipment, and a first aid space. The second floor would have four large screened windows, four scorer tables, four scoreboard controls, a communication center, and field light controls. The pathways leading to the various fields would contain either crushed granite (M-10) or crushed brick. The parking area would be located at least 100 yd from the nearest outfield fence. All fields would be lighted.

Field Hockey, Football, Lacrosse, and Soccer Fields

Fields for field hockey, football, lacrosse, rugby, and soccer have a number of common requirements. For example, a drinking fountain should be available for each team to use near the team benches. A utility structure should be placed at midfield, set back from the field 25 ft, to store equipment and house the scorer and controls for the field lights and scoreboard. Shade must be available for the teams at halftime, preferably from a deciduous tree grove at either end or side of the field and about 25 yd away from the playing field.

Field Hockey

This sport needs sleeves in the ground for corner flags and goalposts. Official rule books can be purchased from the NCAA or National Association for Girls and Women in Sports (NAGWS); rules are revised annually.

Football

There should be sleeves in the ground for the end zone flags. The goalposts (usually a single pole with uprights) need to be centered and secured at the end line. Official rule books can be purchased from the NCAA; rules are revised annually. Planners should review carefully ASTM International's publication *Safety in Football.*

Lacrosse

There should be sleeves in the ground to hold the goals. Official rule books can be purchased from the NCAA or NAGWS; rules are revised annually.

Soccer

Sleeves in the ground are needed for the flags for the corner kick area, substitute area, and the goalposts on the end line. Tie-down hooks should be inserted at least 1 ft into the ground for securing the nets to the ground. There should be a drinking fountain available for each team to use near the team benches. Official rule books can be purchased from the NCAA; rules are revised annually.

Rugby

The following text relating to rugby has been adapted from http://rugby.isport.com/rugby-guides/rugby-field-dimensions

The rugby field, or "pitch," is comparable in size to a soccer (or football) field. Although both Union and League rugby fields are similar in size, they have distinct markings.

Union Rugby

Because the grounds on which many fields are located vary from place to place, there are a set of minimum and maximum size requirements rather than exact specifications. The level of play also plays a role, as youth players will not play on the same-sized field as adult players.

Dimensions. The playing area length—the length of the field not including the in-goal areas—is not to exceed 100 m, and the in-goal areas must be between 10 m and 22 m deep. With that, the total field length must be between 120 m and 144 m, and the field must be no more than 70 m wide. Also, the playing area is defined by the dead-ball lines, touch lines, and touch-in-goal lines.

Markings. The markings used are the biggest difference between Union and League fields, in that Union games require many more types of markings.

Boundary lines. *Touch line (2x).* No more than 100 m, these lines run lengthwise down both sides of the pitch perpendicular to, and at the ends of, both goal lines.

Goal line (2x). No more than 70 m, these lines run widthwise down both sides of the pitch at both ends of, and perpendicular to, the touch lines.

Dead-ball line (2x). The same size as the goal lines, these lines sit between 10 m and 22 m behind each goal line.

Touch-in-goal line (2x). These lines perpendicularly connect the touch lines and dead-ball lines. Their length depends on the size of the in-goal area.

Position lines. *5-meter line (2x).* Two lines of six 1 m hashes that run parallel to, and exactly 5 m in from, both 5-meters-indicated lines and between both touch lines, placed 5 m and 15 m from each touch line and in front of both goalposts.

10-meter line (2x). Two lines with small hashes that run perpendicular to both touch lines exactly 10 m on either side of the halfway line.

22-meter line (2x). Two solid lines that run perpendicular to both touch lines exactly 22 m in from both goal lines.

5-meters-indicated (2x). Two lines with small hashes that run parallel to, and exactly 5 m in from, both touch lines and between both goal lines.

15-meters-indicated (2x). Two lines of 1 m long hashes that run parallel to, and exactly 15 m in from, both touch lines and between both goal lines; lines go solid between each end's 5-meters-indicated line and goal line. One line, .5 m long, placed at the exact center of, and perpendicular to, the halfway line.

Halfway line. A solid line that runs through the exact middle of the pitch perpendicular to both touch lines.

Equipment field markers. There are 14 marking flags (seven on each side of the field) that are used to determine general position on the field. These flags must be at least 1.2 m high and sit at least 2 m away from the field at each end of both in-goal lines, both touch-in-goal lines, both 22-meter lines, and the halfway line.

Uprights. The top edge of the crossbar must be exactly 3 m from the ground. The goalposts attached to both ends of the crossbar must be at least 3.4 m high and spaced exactly 5.6 m apart.

Uprights pads. Though technically optional, most teams will secure a foam pad around the bottom support of each upright to prevent players from injuring themselves when coming into contact with it. The only stipulation regarding this pad is that the distance from the goal line to the external edge of the padding cannot exceed 300 mm.

Ball. A Union ball must meet the following requirements:

- It must be oval and made of four separate panels.
- It must be between 28 cm and 30 cm in length.
- Its end-to-end circumference must be between 74 cm and 77 cm.
- Its circumference at the widest point must be between 58 cm and 62 cm.
- It must weigh between 410 g and 460 g and support air pressure between 9 ½ lb and 10 lb per square inch.

League Rugby

Though the fields that Union and League rugby use are similar in size, there are several differences in layout and markings. Here is a breakdown of the more distinguishing characteristics of a League rugby field.

Dimensions. Much like a Union field, a League field's specifications regarding are a combination of exact requirements and flexible size criteria. The playing area (the field between both goal lines) is exactly 100 m long and exactly 68 m wide. The in-goal areas must be between 6 m and 12 m deep, which are slightly smaller than Union areas. As a result, the total pitch length must be between 112 m and 122 m long.

Markings. Although Union and League fields share several markings, the League field is much closer in style to an American football field. This is most predominant in the use of solid lines running the width of the field at exact 10-m intervals, much like the yard lines found on an American football field.

Boundary lines. *Touchline (2x).* These lines are exactly 100 m, run lengthwise down both sides of the pitch perpendicular to, and at the ends of, both goal lines; these lines are white and 15 cm wide.

Goal line (2x). These lines are exactly 68 m, run widthwise down both sides of the pitch at both ends of, and perpendicular to, the touchlines; these lines are white and 15 cm wide.

Dead-ball line (2x). These are the same size as the goal lines, sit between 6 m and 11 m behind each goal line (depending on the size of the in-goal area); these lines are white and 15 cm wide.

Touch-in-goal line (2x). These lines perpendicularly connect the touchlines and dead-ball lines. Their length depends on the size of the in-goal area; these lines are white and 15 cm wide.

Position lines. Two broken lines run between both goal lines, at 10 m and 20 m in from both touch lines. These lines are 10 cm wide, white in color, and each segment of line must be no more than 2 m apart. A series of solid lines run perpendicular to the touch lines exactly every 10 m from the goal lines; these lines are white and 15 cm wide.

These lines are also numbered; starting from both goal lines and moving toward the middle of the pitch, the first line is marked 10, the next 20, and so on until both sides meet at the middle line, the 50. The numbers are 2 m high and are white with a red outline.

Of these numbered lines, both 40-meter lines are to stand out from the others so the official can ensure a kick-off has traveled at least 10 m.

Equipment field markers. Aside from the numbered lines, the only markers that run every 10 m are two posts that reside at both ends of each in-goal line, where they meet the touch lines. They must be at least 1.25 m in height and made of a flexible material so that if a player runs into one, he or she will not be injured.

Uprights. The base of the uprights is made up of two posts exactly 5.5 m apart and connected by a crossbar that's exactly 3 m from the ground. Both posts are at least 16 m in height. However, they are considered to continue upward indefinitely.

Upright pads. Though optional, most teams wrap the bottom of each upright post with some kind of protective foam padding.

Ball. A League ball is close in size and shape to a Union ball, though a League ball is slightly smaller, skinnier, and the ends are slightly pointier. A professional ball is to be 27 cm long and 60 cm in circumference at its widest spot. It should also weigh between 383 g and 440 g.

Cricket Field

The following text relating to a Cricket Field is adapted from http://en.wikipedia.org/wiki/Cricket_ground

A cricket field consists of a large circular or oval-shaped grassy ground on which the game of cricket is played. There are no fixed dimensions for the field, but its diameter usually varies between 450 feet (137 m) to 500 feet (150 m). Cricket is therefore one of only two major sports (with baseball) that does not define a fixed-shape ground for professional games. The cricket ground can vary from being almost a perfect circle to being an extremely elongated oval. On most grounds, a rope demarcates the perimeter of the field and is known as the boundary.

The ICC Standard Playing Conditions define the minimum and maximum size of the playing surface. Law 19.1 of ICC Test Match Playing Conditions states:

> The playing area shall be a minimum of 150 yards (137.16 metres) from boundary to boundary square of the pitch, with the shorter of the two square boundaries being a minimum 65 yards (59.43 metres). The straight boundary at both ends of the pitch shall be a minimum of 70 yards (64.00 metres). Distances shall be measured from the centre of the pitch to be used. In all cases, the aim shall be to provide the largest playing area subject to no boundary exceeding 90 yards (82.29 meters) from the centre of the pitch to be used.

In addition, the conditions require a minimum 3-yard gap between the "rope" and the surrounding fencing or advertising boards. This is to allow the players to dive without hurting themselves.

The conditions contain a grandfather clause that exempts stadiums built before October 2007. However, most stadiums that regularly host international games easily meet the minimum dimensions.

It is worth noting that based on these guidelines, a cricket field must have at least 16,000 square yards ([150+3+3]/2 [70+70+3+3-22/2]/2 pi) of grass area. A more realistic test-match stadium would have more than 20,000 square yards of grass (having a straight boundary of about 80m). In contrast, an association football field needs only about 9,000 square yards of grass, and an Olympic stadium would contain 13,500 square yards of grass within its 400m running track, making it impossible to play international cricket matches unless the stadium was specifically built for cricket. However, the Stadium Australia which hosted the Sydney Olympics in 2000 had its running track turfed over and 30,000 seats removed to make it possible to play cricket in the stadium, at a cost of $80 million. This is one of the reasons cricket games generally cannot be hosted outside the traditional cricket playing countries, and a few non-test nations like Canada, the UAE, and Kenya that have built test-match standard stadiums.

The Pitch

Most of the action takes place in the centre of this ground, on a rectangular clay strip usually with short grass called the pitch. The pitch is 22 yards (20m) long.

At each end of the pitch, three upright wooden stakes, called the stumps, are hammered into the ground. Two wooden crosspieces, known as the bails, sit in grooves atop the stumps, linking each to its neighbor. Each set of three stumps and two bails is collectively known as a wicket. One end of the pitch is designated the batting end where the batsman stands and the other is designated the bowling end where the bowler runs in to bowl. The area of the field on the side of the line joining the wickets where the batsman holds his bat (the right-hand side for a right-handed batsman, the left for a left-hander) is known as the off side, the other as the leg side or on side.

Lines drawn or painted on the pitch are known as creases. Creases are used to adjudicate the dismissals of batsmen and to determine whether a delivery is fair.

12 Bleachers

Michael G. Hypes, *Morehead State University*

Bleachers and grandstands are part of almost every sports facility. It has been estimated that approximately 60,000 facilities have bleachers in the United States (US-CPSC, 2000). This number includes school facilities, sports facilities, state and local parks, and fitness and recreation centers. Providing safe bleachers and grandstands has prompted the passage of the Minnesota Bleacher Safety Act (2000) and the development of the U.S. Consumer Product Safety Commission's (CPSC, 2000) *Guidelines for Retrofitting Bleachers.*

Types of Bleachers

Bleachers are structures designed to provide tiered or stepped seating and are available in various sizes and configurations. The bleacher system normally consists of a series of seat boards and footboards, generally without any type of backrest. A grandstand is nothing more than a bleacher with a roof attached. The type and number of bleacher components are dependent upon the activity, space requirements, number of spectators, and available financial resources. Bleachers can be classified into one of four basic categories: permanent or stationary bleachers, portable or movable bleachers, telescopic or folding bleachers, and temporary bleachers.

Permanent or Stationary Bleachers

Permanent or stationary bleachers are typically large units that will remain in the same location for the life of the facility. Permanent bleachers can be made of metal or concrete and are usually secured to the ground by an anchor. If they are made of metal, exposure to the sun can create extremely hot conditions that could cause burns.

Portable or Movable Bleachers

Portable bleachers are usually smaller units and are constructed of lightweight materials. Such bleachers will have skids or a wheel system that makes them easy to relocate from one site to another.

Permanent bleachers

Telescopic Bleachers

Telescopic bleachers are typically found in gymnasiums where space is at a minimum. These bleachers can be either pushed in or pulled out for spectator seating. When closed, this type of system takes up relatively little space and can function as a divider.

Temporary Bleachers

Temporary bleachers are typically stored in pieces or sections and then constructed together for use during special events (e.g., golf tournaments, parades, circuses, inaugurations). After the event, the bleachers are then disassembled and stored until needed the next time.

Portable bleachers

Bleacher Components

As mentioned above, all bleacher systems have common elements. These common elements include footboards, seat boards, risers, and guardrails.

Rails are used as a safety feature. They provide security while entering or exiting the bleachers. There are a variety of styles that will minimize the exposure to injury. Folding rails are ideal for recessed areas and other obstacles. Rails should be lightweight for easy setup and takedown yet strong enough to provide adequate support. Guardrails should extend 42 in. above the lowest surface of the leading edge of the bleacher component (i.e., footboard, seat board, or aisle). Risers and footboards are typically aluminum and should be weather resistant for outdoor use. Seat boards can be aluminum or vinyl-covered metal. Indoor bleachers may have risers, footboards, and seat boards made of wood. It is desirable to mark the edges of treads so that they can be distinguished.

Plans for bleachers should consider any gaps or openings that will be in the final product. Any opening between the components in the seating, such as between the footboard, seat board, and riser, should prevent passage of a 4-in. sphere where the footboard is 30 in. or more above the ground and where the opening would permit a fall of 30 in. or more.

Bleachers usually come in 4-row to 52-row systems. Local and state building codes should be consulted when planning bleachers. Table 12.1 provides generalized seating capacity for various types of bleachers. Telescopic or pull-out bleachers should have a wheel or channel system to prevent damage to the floor surface. In addition, these systems are best used if they are automated. Electrical systems allow the telescopic bleachers to open or close with the turn of a key. This type of system allows the user to open entirely or partially a section of bleachers without having the section get out of line or be damaged. With any mechanical system, a manual override is suggested. For bleachers already installed that do not have an automated system, there is equipment (such as a portable power system) that is easily handled for convenient movement of bleachers.

The power or automated system
- provides the ability to open and close bleacher systems quickly and correctly,
- omits and/or reduces maintenance costs,
- solves the problem of broken board ends from manual operation,
- adds stability to the gym bleachers by attaching all sections together to operate as one system,
- omits manual operation by unauthorized personnel, and
- reduces liability exposure on gym bleacher equipment.

Codes and Regulations

Several agencies/organizations have developed codes and/or standards for the construction of bleachers. These organizations include
- International Building Code (IBC) of the International Code Council (ICC),
- National Building Code (NBC) of the Building Officials and Code Administrators (BOCA),
- Standard Building Code (SBC) of the Southern Building Code Congress International (SBCCI),
- Uniform Building Code (UBC) of the International Conference of Building Officials (ICBO), and
- National Fire Protection Association (NFPA).

Table 12.2 provides a summary of current industry codes and standard requirements for guardrails and openings in bleachers. In addition, state and local codes adopt and modify these codes to develop policy for constructing new bleachers. The local building inspector should be consulted early in the planning phase to avoid expensive and time-consuming errors in the construction of a bleacher system.

2001 Minnesota Building Codes and Standards Division Requirements

States such as Minnesota develop their own policies regarding construction. The Minnesota Building Codes and Standards Division reviewed the Uniform Building Code, International Building Code, and the National Fire Protection Association Life Safety Code in developing Policy PR-04 (3/00). Under Minnesota law, reviewing stands, grandstands, bleachers, and folding/telescopic seating, whether indoors or out, must be designed, constructed, and installed in accordance with the applicable provisions contained in the Minnesota State Building Code (Minnesota Building Codes and Standards Division [Minnesota], 2001).

This policy addresses the following areas of concern with regard to bleachers and grandstands:
- press box construction,
- number of seats to an aisle,
- required plumbing fixtures,
- aisle width,
- accessibility,
- foundations, and
- use of space below bleachers/grandstands.

Press Box Construction

According to UBC Section 303.2.2.3, combustible non-rated A-4 occupancies are limited to a height of 20 ft above grade. Except for the press box located on top of most school grandstands serving ball fields, most grand-

Table 12.1

Sample Number of Bleacher Seats Based on Length and Number of Rows

Length in Feet	4 Rows	7 Rows	10 Rows	13 Rows	16 Rows
18	48	84	120	156	192
36	96	168	240	312	384
54	104	252	360	468	676
72	192	336	480	624	768
90	240	420	600	780	960
108	288	504	720	936	1,152
126	336	588	840	1,092	1,344
144	384	672	960	1,248	1,536
162	432	756	1,080	1,404	1,728
180	480	840	1,200	1,560	1,920
198	528	924	1,320	1,716	2,112
216	576	1,008	1,440	1,872	2,304
234	624	1,092	1,560	2,028	2,496
252	672	1,176	1,680	2,184	2,688
270	720	1,260	1,800	2,340	2,880
288	768	1,344	1,920	2,496	3,072
306	816	1,428	2,040	2,652	3,264

Length in Feet	19 Rows	22 Rows	25 Rows	28 Rows	31 Rows
18	228				
36	456				
54	684	792	900		1,008
72	912	1,056	1,200	1,344	1,488
90	1,140	1,320	1,500	1,680	1,860
108	1,386	1,584	1,800	2,016	2,232
126	1,596	1,848	2,100	2,352	2,604
144	1,824	2,112	2,400	2,688	2,976
162	2,052	2,376	2,700	3,024	3,348
180	2,280	2,649	3,000	3,360	3,720
198	2,508	2,904	3,300	3,696	4,092
216	2,736	3,168	3,600	4,032	4,464
234	2,964	3,432	3,900	4,368	4,836
252	3,192	3,696	4,200	4,704	5,208
270	3,420	3,960	4,500	5,040	5,580
288	3,648	4,224	4,800	5,376	5,952
306	3,876	4,488	5,100	5,712	6,324

Press box in a permanent bleacher setting

stands are built of noncombustible construction. These noncombustible bleacher structures are permitted to be at least 40 ft in height. However, press boxes are typically built with combustible construction materials (wood framing). This results in classifying the entire structure as combustible, therefore severely limiting the maximum permitted height of noncombustible grandstands with combustible press boxes to 20 ft (Minnesota, 2001). Minnesota derived the following alternative to part of UBC Section 303.2.2.3. Press boxes located atop open-air bleachers may be built of combustible construction as long as other components of the bleacher system are of noncombustible construction.

Table 12.2

Overview of Building Codes and Standard Requirements

2000 International Building Code (IBC) of the International Code Council (ICC)
Guardrails
- Required on open sides more than 30 in. above grade.
- Guardrails must be at least 42 in. high, vertically measured from leading edge.
- Guardrails shall have balusters to prevent passage of 4-in. sphere through any opening up to a height of 34 in.
- From a height of 34 in. to 42 in., should prevent passage of an 8-in. sphere.

Openings
- Where footboards are more than 30 in. above grade, openings between seat and footboard shall not allow passage of a sphere greater than 4 in.
- Horizontal gaps shall not exceed .25 in. between footboards and seatboards.
- At aisles, horizontal gaps shall not exceed .25 in. between footboards.

1999 National Building Code (NBC) of the Building Officials and Code Administrators (BOCA)
Guardrails
- Required along open-sided surfaces located more than 15.5 in. above grade.
- Guardrails should be at least 42 in. in height measured vertically above leading edge.
- Open guardrails shall have balusters of solid material that prevent passage of 4-in. sphere through any opening.
- Guardrails shall not have an ornamental pattern that would have a ladder effect.

Openings
- Openings between footboards and seat boards should prevent passage of 4-in. sphere when openings are located more than 30 in. above grade.
- Horizontal gaps between footboards and seat boards shall not exceed .25 in.

1997 Standard Building Code (SBC) of the Southern Building Code Congress International (SBCCI)
Guardrails
- Located along open-sided walking surfaces and elevated seating facilities that are located more than 30 in. above grade.
- Guardrails shall not be less than 42 in. vertically from leading edge.
- Open guardrails shall have intermediate rails or ornamental pattern to prevent passage of 4-in. sphere through any opening.

Openings
- There shall be no horizontal gaps exceeding .25 in. between footboards and seat boards.
- At aisles, no horizontal gaps should exceed .25 in. between footboards.

1997 Uniform Building Code (UBC) of the International Conference of Building Officials (ICBO)
Guardrails
- Perimeter guardrails shall be provided for all portions of elevated seating more than 30 in. above grade.
- Guardrails shall be 42 in. above the rear of a seat board or 42 in. above the rear of the steps in an aisle.
- Open guardrails shall have intermediate rails or ornamental pattern to prevent passage of a 4-in. sphere.

Openings
- The open vertical space between footboards and seats shall not exceed 9 in. when footboards are more than 30 in. above grade.

2000 National Fire Protection Association (NFPA) 101 Life Safety Code
Guardrails (applies to both new construction and existing installations)
- Guardrails are required on open sides more than 48 in. above adjacent ground.
- Guardrails must be at least 42 in. above the aisle or footboard or at least 36 in. above the seat board.
- Guardrail is exempted where an adjacent wall or fence affords an equivalent safeguard.
- Openings in guardrails cannot allow passage of 4-in. diameter sphere.

Table 12.2 (cont.)

Openings (applies to both new construction and existing installations)
- Vertical openings between footboards and seat boards cannot allow passage of 4-in. diameter sphere where footboards are more than 30 in. above grade.
- Openings in footboards cannot allow passage of .5-in. diameter sphere.

Inspections (existing installations)
- Annual inspection and maintenance of bleacher/grandstand or folding/telescopic seating required to be provided by owner to ensure safe conditions.
- Biennially, the inspection is to be performed by a professional engineer, registered architect, or individual certified by the manufacturer.
- Owner required to provide certification that such inspection has been performed as required by authority having jurisdiction.

Note. Modified from *Guidelines for Retrofitting Bleachers,* by U.S. Consumer Product Safety Commission. Bethesda, MD: USCPSC.

Number of Seats to an Aisle

Prior to the 1997 edition of the *Uniform Building Code,* the number of seats without backrests between any seat and an aisle could not be greater than 20, for a total of 42 seats in a row with aisles at each end. In general, this is what the bleacher seating industry has used as a standard for the manufacture of their products for years. Now both the 1997 UBC and 2012 IBC only permit a maximum of 14 seats per row with the typical 12-in. wide aisle accessway. In contrast, for indoor bleachers the 1997 UBC permits nine seats between any seat and an aisle, for a total of 20 seats in a row. This is less restrictive than that permitted outdoors. The maximum number of seats permitted between the farthest seat and an aisle in bleachers is 20 in outdoor bleacher seating (Minnesota, 2001, 2012).

Required Plumbing Fixtures

Minimum numbers of water closets and lavatories are to be provided for all buildings and structures including exterior assembly areas, such as bleachers and grandstands. The Standards Division recognizes either of the following to satisfy this requirement:
- permanent fixtures located either on-site or available in an adjacent building or
- portable temporary fixtures that are available on-site when the bleachers are in use.

The use of portable fixtures as acceptable modifications is based on the concept that outdoor bleachers are seasonal in nature. Last, the ratio of water closets for women to the total of water closets and urinals provided for men must be at least 3:2 in accordance with the Minnesota Building Code (1300.3900).

Aisle Width

The Standards Division identified two methods for determining aisle width. Method A identifies that aisles are neither required to be more than 66 in. wide nor considered a dead-end aisle when the following are satisfied:
- the seating is composed entirely of bleachers,
- the row-to-row dimension is 28 in. or less, and
- front egress is not limited.

Method B is based on IBC Section 1008.5.3. The clear width in inches of aisles shall be not less than the total occupant load served by the egress element multiplied by 0.08 where egress is by aisles and/or stairs. The multiplier is 0.06 where egress is by ramps, tunnels, corridors, or vomitories (Minnesota, 2001).

Accessibility

Bleacher seating structures complying with the Minnesota Accessibility Code require
- exterior access to elevated seating areas in exterior bleachers must be accessible by a route having a slope not exceeding 1:20 and a width not less than 48 in.,
- locations for wheelchairs are provided in the number and location required, and
- alterations to existing bleacher seating facilities comply with the Minnesota Bleacher Safety Act. (Minnesota, 2001)

Foundations

A foundation plan must be prepared by a Minnesota Licensed Engineer for all open-air bleacher and grandstand facilities. This does not apply to portable bleachers of five rows or less (Minnesota, 2001, 2012).

Use of Space Below Bleachers or Grandstands

Spaces under a grandstand or bleacher shall be kept free of flammable or combustible material. Storage is permitted under bleachers, provided it is separated with fire-resistive construction (Minnesota, 2001, 2012).

U.S. Consumer Product Safety Commission Guidelines

The CPSC developed *Guidelines for Retrofitting Bleachers* as a result of a petition by Representatives Luther and Ramstad of Minnesota in 1999. This petition led to the adoption of the first bleacher safety law at the state level. A summary of the CPSC's retrofit recommendations is found in Table 12.3.

Table 12.3

Summary of Retrofit Recommendations

- Guardrails should be present on the backs and portions of the open ends of bleachers where the footboard, seat board, or aisle is 30 in. or more above the floor or ground below.
- The top surface of the guardrail should be at least 42 in. above the leading edge of the footboard, seat board, or aisle, whichever is adjacent.
- When bleachers are used adjacent to a wall that is as high as the recommended guardrail height, the guardrail is not needed if a 4-in. diameter sphere fails to pass between the bleachers and the wall.
- Any opening between components of the guardrail should prevent passage of a 4-in. sphere.
- Any opening between the components in the seating should prevent passage of a 4-in. sphere where the footboard is 30 in. or more above the ground.
- The preferable guardrail design uses only vertical members as in-fill between the top and bottom rails. Openings in the in-fill should be limited to a maximum of 1.75 in. If chain-link fencing is used on guardrails, it should have a mesh size of 1.25-in. square or less.
- Aisles, handrails, nonskid surfaces, and other items that assist in access and egress on bleachers should be incorporated into any retrofit project where feasible.
- The option of replacing as opposed to retrofitting should be considered.
- Retrofitting materials and methods should prevent the introduction of new hazards, such as bleacher tip-over, bleacher collapse, guardrail collapse, or contact/tripping hazards.
- Bleachers should be thoroughly inspected at least quarterly by trained personnel, and problems should be corrected immediately. Maintain records of these actions.
- Bleachers should be inspected at least every 2 years and written certification should be obtained that the bleachers are fit for use. A licensed professional engineer, registered architect, or company that is qualified to provide bleacher products and services should conduct inspections.
- Keep records of all incidents and injuries.

Note. Modified from *Guidelines for Retrofitting Bleachers,* by U.S. Consumer Product Safety Commission, 2010, Bethesda, MD: USCPSC.

Section III

Recreational Spaces

Aquatic Facilities

Leland Yarger, *Ball State University*

Steven Dalcher, *Water LLC*

Facilities with water venues have specialized issues. Specific issues range from design, to construction, to the operation of the assets. A failure at any point can result in additional expenses and, more important, potential for loss of life. Safety concerns are threaded throughout this section because of the critical nature of this planned environment.

The first city pool in the United States was established in 1887 at Brookline, Massachusetts (Gabrielsen, 1987). Pools of this era were referred to as "baths" and were simply filled with water and periodically drained. These baths were not sanitized or filtered as required by today's health codes. Compared to these baths, today's pools require the professional aquatic community to maintain water quality and keep water safe. Disease transmission is rare in the properly planned, designed, and managed aquatic facility.

In this chapter, we discuss a brief history of aquatic facilities and how planning, construction, and operations directly affect aquatic facility design. We identify a collection of aquatic books throughout this chapter that provide additional information and will be of great use to the aquatic facility manager. As with any profession, aquatics has many resources, such as this text, that supervisors of aquatic assets should use. This chapter will enhance the manager's ability to limit personal and organizational liability, contribute to a cost-effective facility, and increase patron and staff safety.

History and Trends

From the late 1800s to the early 1950s, pools gained popularity, and by the end of this period, there were approximately 184,200 pools in the United States (Aquatics International [AI], 2003). In the 1920s, the United States saw a surge in aquatic recreation activities and the use of naturally occurring springs as resort spas. These resort spas were widely visited and renowned. Like the early baths, the spas were not sanitized and did not have a process of mechanical water exchange. Subsequently, there were health issues and cases of disease transmission. The onset of the Great Depression caused most of these American resorts to fall into financial ruin like many other areas of society during this time frame.

In the years following the Great Depression, growth in swimming and pools continued. After World War II, there was an industrial boom in the United States. This boom in growth was not limited to industry; substantial increases in public pool construction happened as well. The standard swimming pool, in both residential and public facilities, was the generic "box" of water. These pools were typically rectangular shaped, shallow, and 3 ft deep to about 10 ft deep in the pool basin. Pool decks were generally small and recreational activities were sparse. Pools were a place to simply cool off or swim laps. In 1975, the White House even added a swimming pool. Aquatic facilities began to represent the status of well-to-do communities and families (AI, 2003).

Many of the standard "box" pools are still in use today at community centers, YMCAs, YWCAs, parks and recreation departments, and schools and universities. These pools are of significant note because they are nearing the end of their useful life and, in many cases, have become maintenance nightmares for the owners. These early pools had 50-year life expectancies. Today, new construction companies typically plan to build for a 20-year life expectancy for aquatic facilities. Considering the enormous capital expense involved, this life expectancy of only 20 years seems shortsighted and foolhardy.

As knowledge increased about the potential for disease transmission in pool water, the practice of unfiltered swimming pools gave way to chemically treating and mechanically filtering the swimming pool to clean the water and reduce the risk of waterborne illness. Proper planning, design, and management considerations include understanding the demands placed upon the facilities water and ensuring that filtration, sanitation, and monitoring happen 24/7.

Generally, pool water is extremely safe; take a moment to reflect upon other bodies of water such as oceans, lakes, rivers, and ponds that people enjoy. Consider all of the creatures that live in and around these waters. The children's book *Everybody Poops* comes to mind when we think about water quality in these locations. Rarely do we hear of massive outbreaks of sickness or even death in these waters. Because we do not control the open bodies of water the way that we can control the water in pool basins, this simple fact goes unnoticed. Pool water should meet higher standards for obvious reasons; however, proper pool management frequently is poorly understood and often overlooked, especially in seasonal community pools. Consider that water venues are visited about 301 million times per year. During an 18-year period, the Centers for Disease Control and Prevention reported that the most common Recreational Water Illnesses (RWI) resulted in 19,000 people becoming ill. This equates to one illness in 341,232 visits (Otto, 2006).

In recent years, swimming has consistently ranked second only to fitness walking as the most attended physical activity/sport according to the National Sporting Goods Association (year). With the high volume of people seeking aquatic recreation, aquatic facilities must ensure that sanitation of their facilities is consistently at the highest level. The implications for unkempt facilities due to poor design or management can be costly to owners and operators. Health departments are the common enforcement group that inspects and investigates facilities and water quality.

In the late 1970s, theme parks joined in on water attractions, starting the water park craze. These facilities had high-energy water rides and attractions that drew patrons from hundreds of miles. The water parks created a new vacation activity, and some water parks can take multiple days to experience all of the attractions. Water parks are even more popular today, and new attractions are created each year. Some of these new attractions even defy grav-

Water theme park

ity, and uphill waterslides have gained popularity recently. From 2000 to 2006, research showed that the indoor water park industry grew eightfold (Inter, 2007).

In the 1990s, municipalities, hotels, and smaller organizations with pools decided to cash in on the theme-style water attractions. The potential revenue from providing mini-vacations to regional residents has become popular. Aquatic facilities in some locales have morphed into mini-water parks/leisure facilities that boast multiple smaller attractions. Instead of the five-story water park waterslide, smaller versions of these types of slides are placed indoors. Some slides have music and visual displays in the slides to further entertain riders. This trend is still growing today, and planners have limitless ideas for rides and interactive structures.

There are in excess of 7.2 million pools in the United States today (AI, 2012). Granted, many of the pools are at residential properties. Public pools are under more pressure to provide recreational, educational, and athletic opportunities to offset operational costs. As such, aquatic professionals are hired to manage public facilities to reduce risks to the organization. Organizations that have had serious incidents understand that significant financial and human losses are possible due to negligence. The aquatic professional must be involved with the aquatic facility design and policy development. Aquatic operations have specific education and certifications requirements. A professional with this knowledge can provide an aquatic facility growth in a safe and successful process.

Planning

What Kind of Facility?

The first step is to decide what the facility will be used for and to identify services and programs that will be offered. Will staff training be conducted at the facility, and what requirements will this entail? These questions must be understood and answered prior to the facility design process. Unfortunately, many times this process is not followed, and a pool is designed without this information, which invariably leads to disappointment and a facility of limited use.

Today, across the nation, we find aquatic facilities that represent a wide range of aquatic venues. Facilities range from indoor and outdoor traditional pools as defined earlier in this chapter, to water theme parks, splash pads, wave pools, flumes/water treadmills, waterslides, rehabilitation pools, spas/hot tubs, water playgrounds, diving wells, Olympic-style competition facilities, simulated waterfronts, wave/surf machines, lazy rivers, rapids, water rides similar to roller coasters, and a variety of interactive attractions based around water attractions.

The number one priority for planning a facility is functionality, which must always precede aesthetic appeal.

Architects strive to create unique designs for facilities to become icons. This philosophy of creating landmark icons is fine as long as the facility can serve the organizational mission.

Another major decision is whether to have an indoor or outdoor facility. This answer depends upon facility use, percentage of the year open, local climate, and obviously the cost to build and maintain the facility. Facility types are broken into general groups in the following paragraphs to help you determine what you need and what specific design/operational considerations should be understood.

Competition

The competitive section that follows requires that facility planners review the specific aquatic design requirements for the sanctioning bodies in which the participants will be competing. These sanctioning bodies include United States Swimming and Diving, National Collegiate Athletic Association (NCAA), United States Masters Swimming, Fédération Internationale de Natation (FINA), and the Amateur Athletic Union (AAU).

Lap Pools

The standard competitive lap pool is typically designed with competitive sanctioning body requirements in mind. Standard lengths of 25 yd, 25 m, or 50 m are the norm depending upon the sanctioning body of the competitive events that will be held. These sanctioning bodies define pool depth, lane width, starting block specifications, as well as a host of other specifications, including lighting, markings, and stanchions, to name a few.

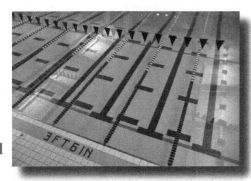

Lap pool

Diving Wells

As with competitive pools, diving wells have specific dimensional requirements set forth by sanctioning bodies. Bathing code requirements and specialty equipment must also be considered, which sanctioning bodies do not always discuss. These include bubbler systems, rope and harness systems, trampolines, and land-based springboards with crash pits. A bubbler system allows divers in training a softer water entry due to bubbles breaking the surface tension of the water. Rope and harness systems allow a

diver to be belayed by an assistant to arrest his or her fall over the water, over a trampoline, or over a crash pit when the diver attempts new or complicated skills during training sessions.

Springboard and diving well

Springboards

Commonly referred to as diving boards, the springboard is common to many facilities and generally is considered safer than a waterslide. Not only should bathing codes be reviewed for proper installation, but also guidelines produced by the sanctioning bodies must be considered if competition is desired. Commonly, 12 ft of water depth is needed under the 1-m diving board, but this is not a universal requirement. Many state laws vary from this requirement. The owner must decide what the springboard's purpose will be—competition, instruction, and/or recreation at the local, state, regional, national or international level. Many details for diving boards and diving standards are required to be observed, especially for competitive use. A useful text, *Official Swimming Pool Design Compendium* (National Swimming Pool Foundation [NSPF], 1997), provides regulations from governing competitive bodies that include design drawings.

For springboards, the fulcrum or pivot point should be locked in the full forward position during recreation use times. The fulcrum provides trained divers the ability to generate great amounts of lift when they press the board during the approach of the dive. Inexperienced recreation divers can easily hurt themselves by using the springboard with the fulcrum in the rear position.

If a pool is considered that does not have a separate diving well that can maintain a warmer water temperature, a hot tub dedicated for competitive divers might also be considered in the facility design.

Competitive swimming and diving pool resources include the local/state high school athletic association, AAU, NCAA, USA Swimming, and FINA.

Recreational

The recreational facility's primary focus is on family and individual recreation opportunities. Thirty years ago, this meant open swim, often with one or two lap swim lanes. The children would play in the shallow water or off the diving boards while the adults often talked or swam laps.

Today, with the advent of many interactive aquatic assets, the recreational facility can provide attractions for all ages, including

- age-appropriate water playgrounds,
- diving boards,
- waterslides,
- bubble benches,
- climbing structures,
- wave pools,
- zero-depth entry pools/simulated beaches,
- surf machines,
- water basketball,
- water volleyball,
- water obstacle/confidence courses,
- water polo,
- various land activities,
- group spas or baths,
- tanning booths,
- individual hot tubs,
- moveable bulkheads, and
- moveable floors.

Many items on this list require specific design considerations dealing with additional space and construction depth. The simple ability to make the water temperature comfortable may be one of the most fiscally challenging prospects.

Special attention should be given to the sanitation and filtration systems of warm water (85°F+) basins. For example, a typical small hot tub with minimal users has a sanitation load similar to a normal-sized pool at maximum capacity. Any hot tub or spa installed for use in aquatic facilities should be specifically designed for commercial use and operation. Failure in oversight here can lead to waterborne illness and disease transmission to many patrons.

Recreational facilities are attractive to parks and recreation departments, YMCAs, hotels, resorts, and private clubs. Park departments and hotels are cashing in on the mini-water park concept. Nationwide, mini-water parks provide vacation opportunities with exciting attractions such as waterslides and wave pools. The following recreational pool references provide guidelines for many of the areas listed in this section: NSPF, YMCA of the USA (YMCA), National Recreation and Park Association (NRPA), National Intramural Recreational Sports Association (NIRSA), and the Association of Pool and Spa Professionals.

Health and Fitness

Water fitness is often viewed as simply lap swimming and water exercise. In today's world, however, water fitness can include mobile and stationary exercise venues that may be both land and aquatic based. If the primary users are health and fitness clients, the facility may also have large areas of chest-deep water and large deck areas. Both of these areas may have equipment similar to what is found in the traditional land fitness room. There may be multiple workout stations and a staff of personal fitness trainers as well as water aerobics instructors. Depending on the age, flexibility, and health conditions of the clients, factors such as water depth, water temperature, and the types of pool access fixtures will vary. Arthritic participants make good use of stairs, ramps, and zero-depth entry into warm water (88°F+) pools. Newer aquatic fitness facilities sometimes include flumes and water treadmills. The flume allows a relatively small area for the individual to swim in place against a pump-generated current. This allows trainers to evaluate the swimmer's cardiovascular, respiratory, and kinesthetic techniques in a tightly controlled environment. The water treadmill (like a land treadmill) is similar to the flume in that the water resistance while using the treadmill allows trainers to closely monitor land athletes in a therapeutic warm water environment.

Multipurpose Facilities

Today, the multipurpose aquatic facility allows for a host of recreational, instructional, and athletic activities to take place in the same facility. Many times, a variety of activities can even take place at the same time in a well-planned facility. The purpose of this section is to look specifically at multipurpose aquatic facilities versus the multipurpose recreation center.

Pool temperature and sanitation are the two biggest problems if a one-basin multipurpose facility is considered. The sanitation problem for a single body of water comes primarily from accidental fecal release by a child. The treatment process is lengthy and thus closes the body of water to all patrons. This can literally bring facility operations to a complete halt. Multiple basins and sanitation systems are a better choice. If there is a fecal accident in one basin, it can be closed and treated, and other pools can

Recreational waterslide

still be used as long as they have independent sanitation and filtration systems.

Pool temperature on a one-basin multipurpose facility will create the most complaints and safety issues. The water temperature varies dramatically for different programs. For example, recreational swimmers and learn-to-swim participants enjoy water close to 85°F, therapy and rehabilitation patrons use water temperature of 88°F+, and competitive swimmers use 77°F to 79°F water so that they do not experience heat exhaustion.

It is not realistic or cost effective to raise and lower the water temperature for each group using the facility. Separate pool basins are the solution to this problem. Many facilities also worry about closure due to equipment wear. These facilities often install redundant systems for heating, water circulation, and filtration. This will allow an operator to correct operational malfunctions without closing the facility.

There is a growing trend to include recreation aspects into all facilities. This provides new facilities with a multipurpose aspect and hopefully provides the owner higher usage and revenue opportunities. Current high-excitement trends include stationary wave generators to surf or bodyboard in place, a variety of interactive attractions and play structures, slides of many shapes with the ability to even ascend similar to theme park roller coasters. Some of these high-excitement fixtures require significant floor space, vertical clearance, as well as extra staff. The typical high bather loads may require additional filtration and sanitation system capacity to ensure proper sanitation. One result of the new facility concepts include mechanical space requirements that are far larger than the typical rectangular pools from the 1950s to 1970s. This area is frequently overlooked in the initial design and creates myriad headaches. Adequate space must be allotted for all water and air-handling equipment and laid out so that ease of access is implemented, as this type of equipment is frequently serviced and poorly planned equipment rooms create safety and operational issues of high magnitude.

When designing the multipurpose aquatic facility, consult the guidance/requirements of ruling agencies. The following list provides suggestions for the types of assets considered:
- Waterslides: World Waterpark Association (WWA)
- Hot tubs/spas: NSPF, YMCA, NRPA

Training/education
- Lifeguard training: American Red Cross (ARC), American Safety and Health Institute, Ellis and Associates, National Aquatic Safety Company, United States Lifesaving Association, YMCA
- Swimming lessons: ARC, YMCA, Ellis and Associates, Starfish Aquatics
- Canoe and kayak: American Canoeing Association, ARC

Lifeguard on duty

- Scuba: National Association of Underwater Instructors, Professional Association of Diving Instructors, Scuba Schools International, Scuba Diving Institute, Handicapped Scuba Association, International Association of Nitrox and Technical Divers
- Pool operations: NRPA's Aquatic Facility Operator, NSPF's Certified Pool-Spa Operator, YMCA's Pool Operator On Location

There are many documents and texts produced by the groups listed above that should be reviewed for compliance. The depth and scope of the recommendations from these groups is comprehensive and should be given lengthy study.

Instructional
For structured activity classes, it is crucial to understand the training requirements for courses. For some swim instructor classes, there are swim tests with standard pool lengths. The height of participants must also be accounted for; adults generally see shallow water as 4 ft deep or less. Children in 4 ft of water may have the water line at their eyes. Anyone standing with the water at eye level and just learning how to swim will be uncomfortable; therefore, this would be a poor learning environment.

Facilities designed for the educational focus must pay attention to training agency standards and curricular requirements to be fully functional. Agencies that offer certification-based programs must comply with the training standards or risk serious liability consequences. Aquatic facilities can offer a host of educational opportunities including
- learn to swim (all ages),
- CPR and first aid courses,
- lifeguard training,
- junior lifeguard courses,
- canoeing,
- kayaking,

- competitive swimming,
- scuba diving,
- springboard or platform diving,
- synchronized swimming,
- water aerobics,
- water survival,
- biomechanics of swimming and diving,
- fitness swimming,
- water rehab/therapy instruction,
- swimming instructor class,
- watercraft safety,
- residential pool safety,
- pool operations/facility management, and
- water polo.

Athletic

Many of the educational activities offered above translate into athletic opportunities—competitive swimming opportunities from youth-aged group swim and diving teams, masters teams, to high school and collegiate swim teams. Depending upon local demand, synchronized swimming and water polo can also provide additional athletic opportunities.

Legal Considerations

Federal Law

In 2008, a new federal law titled the Virginia Graeme Baker Pool and Spa Safety Act (H.R. 6-303 to 309, Title XIV – Pool and Spa Safety) passed. This law impacts existing and new aquatic facilities. The law requires that all public pools have a main drain cover that complies with ASME/ANSI A112.19.8 (Robledo & Kozen, 2008). The intention of this law is to prevent entrapment of body parts by the suction created by circulation or feature pumps. This is the first federal law of its kind that specifically addresses design and operational safety for aquatic facilities. Past cases of entrapment have included drowning because of the suction holding people underwater and evisceration from the suction forces created. At the time of this publication, some aquatic facilities are still attempting to comply with this safety act. Many manufacturers have had to recall drain covers because they did not meet the requirements in this act. Seek out compliance guarantees from vendors to ensure that your facility is financially and legally protected.

Basin Accessibility

Compliance with the *ADA and ABA Accessibility Guidelines for Buildings and Facilities* (Department of Justice, 2010) is recognized at non-aquatic facilities but is frequently overlooked at aquatic facilities in the early stages of planning. The current ADA requirements have additional aquatic-related guidance and must be reviewed for both new and existing facilities. ADA requirements are enforced through the Department of Justice (DOJ). Most construction codes for pools require at a minimum vertical pool ladders to enter and exit the pools; these do not meet accessibility guidelines. These vertical ladders are not user friendly to many pool participants. If your facility has an older population, heavier weight population, arthritic participants, population with physical disabilities, or the very young, consider the alternatives below.

Stairs. Stairs into pools are probably the most common accessible entry fixtures and have been built into basins during the last 20 years. Stairs must have handrails, and the step surfaces must be slip resistant with 1-in. tile or other nonslip surfaces. Fiberglass stairs can also retroactively be added to a facility for minimal cost and removed when not needed.

Transfer tiers. The use of transfer tiers can help many participants in wheelchairs enter the pool by themselves or with minimal assistance. A transfer tier is simply a seat or high fixed step that a participant can roll up to on the deck next to the side of the pool. When the participant is seated in his chair, he can slide over onto the tier and swing his legs into the water's edge from the tier.

Zero-depth entry. The typical gradual beachfront entry closely resembles the zero-depth entry pool. The typical depth change at the zero-depth entry point is 1 in. depth for every 12 in. to 20 in. of distance. Some state codes specify the minimum change in depth for zero-depth entry points. Zero-depth systems can also retroactively be added to a preexisting pool at substantial additional cost.

Ramps. Portable and fixed pool ramps may also enhance accessibility and provide new freedom to participants with limited mobility.

Lift chairs. Both fixed and portable lift chairs can provide access to the pool basin and often require manual, hydraulic, or electrical input for operations.

Accessible chairlift

State and Local Law

Most states have construction code that is required for swimming facilities. The aquatic professional will provide valuable insight for planning to meet the state construction and operation requirements. Along with construction code, most states have bathing or operational code for public pools. These laws mandate everything from lighting requirements to staff and equipment required at the facility.

Specific examples of state operational requirements that affect the design and operation of aquatic facilities are outlined below:

- Indiana administrative code specifies that one lifeguard is required for each public pool that has a pool surface area that exceeds 2,000 sq ft. Additionally, one lifeguard must be on duty for every 75 people and additional guards for each additional 75 bathers (IAC 410.20.1-5, 2008)
- The Florida Department of Health (2004) specifies that a certified pool operator must be on duty whenever the pool is open.

If the state has no requirements, then the supervisor must rely on other codes, industry standards, and recommendations. Additional codes include county and municipal requirements that are often more rigorous than state codes. Other standards often come from building construction codes and requirements from a variety of groups, including American National Standards Institute, American Society of Mechanical Engineers, ASTM International, National Fire Protection Association, National Electrical Code, National Science Foundation, and Underwriters Laboratories. Recommendations also come from a variety of sources such as the Association of Pool and Spa Professionals, NSPF, YMCA, Centers for Disease Control and Prevention, Consumer Product Safety Commission, ARC, and a variety of professional texts. Owners have a professional responsibility to follow standards recognized for safe operation of certain types of facilities to protect patrons. If laws in your state do not address professional standards, then refer to texts including *Aquatic Facility Management* (Fawcett, 2005), the second edition of *The Complete Swimming Pool Reference* (Griffiths, 2003), the *NIRSA Aquatic Directors Handbook* (NIRSA, 2001), *Swimming Pools* (Gabrielsen, 1987), *YMCA Aquatic Management* (YMCA, 2003), as well as a variety of pool operations and lifeguard certification texts. This collection of material constitutes knowledge that is commonly referred to as professional standards or practices.

Industry Practice

The aquatic professional will be a great asset in the design and construction phases. Consideration should also be for delays that occur in construction. When construction is delayed for weather or other issues, the aquatic professional can work on the standard operating procedures (SOPs) and emergency action procedures (EAPs). This prior planning is crucial for the opening of any new facility.

Industry practice also refers to common procedures that veteran aquatic professionals have learned over the years that may not be reflected in industry literature. This knowledge and experience is invaluable when setting up a new facility. It may limit the potential for negligence and thus reduce financial losses.

Training agencies for some programs have specific facility design requirements for certain certification programs. If the facility is built ignoring these facts, it can create an operational nightmare. For example, there are pool depth requirements to train and certify lifeguards by some agencies, such as the ARC, which requires 7 ft to 10 ft of water depth to retrieve a 10 lb diving brick during a swim test (ARC, 2007). If the facility does not meet these requirements, the ability to train lifeguards in-house will be greatly hampered.

Training agencies often have additional mandates that affect staffing at facilities. All major lifeguard training agencies in the United States require that two lifeguards perform spinal injury rescues in the water and also require two persons be used for victim removal from the water. A facility planned for one lifeguard-only operations clearly violates this standard and thus creates an unsafe position for the guard and sacrifices patron care to save a few dollars. A single basin with few swimmers may warrant only one guard actively watching the swimmers, but a second guard must be immediately accessible with a moment's notice in an emergency.

Facility owners rarely wish to spend the time learning a new profession and therefore hire an aquatic professional to understand the legal obligations that the facility should follow to prevent negligent actions or inactions at their facility. Ignorance of laws or professional standards will not protect from negligence-based lawsuits. The importance of hiring a qualified and experienced aquatic professional before starting the design of an aquatic facility cannot be overemphasized.

Emergency Management Design Considerations

Designed for Immediate Emergency Care for Patrons

Lifeguards are considered by most training agencies to be first responders. As such, the lifeguards need immediate access to the tools with which they are trained to provide care, including automated external defibrillators (AEDs) and emergency oxygen. The facility must be well planned to house these items along with other equipment so that rapid access can be provided to the victim in need of care.

The well-planned facility will also address emergency entrance and egress routes to facilitate rapid transfer of patient care from facility staff to emergency medical services (EMS). Research has shown that if an AED is used for a cardiac victim within the first minute of arrest, there is about an 85% rate of survival (Law-Heitzman, 1998). For each minute that AED care is delayed, the chance of survival decreases 7% to 10%. On-scene emergency oxygen is recognized by many training agencies as beneficial to patients in almost every emergency care situation. Emergency oxygen care has a long, confirmed useful history in the scuba diving community. In January 2003, the YMCA mandated that lifeguards must have emergency oxygen certification prior to being hired at all YMCAs. Given the potential benefit to the victim, it is reasonable for properly trained first aid providers to give emergency oxygen when it is available (American Safety and Health Institute, 2007).

Using both an AED and oxygen can significantly aid in the favorable resuscitation of near-drowning victims. AEDs and oxygen require scheduled maintenance and record keeping. AED batteries and defibrillation pads have expiration dates. Oxygen tanks must be verified each shift as being full and ready to use. AEDs are electronic; operational tests vary from each of the manufacturers. These checks are critical if the units are to be functional when they are needed.

Medical Emergencies

Along with on-scene care, the design team must consider EMS provider access to a patron in need. There must be a point of rapid access to the victim who needs EMS care. Careful planning and design can save time that the victim desperately needs for treatment in emergency care. When the facility is being planned, consider dedicated pool area emergency evacuation points. This consideration is generally automatic for fire concerns but often forgotten when it comes to emergency medical care. If a patron has a heart attack, how will he be moved to an arriving ambulance quickly? Can the ambulance drive onto facility grounds? What does the local EMS service recommend? What do facility staff do on-site to enhance victim care? This should be discussed in planning and operational meetings early on.

The most common care provided at aquatic facilities is general first aid. Often, scrapes, cuts, and bruises happen even in well-managed facilities. Therefore, the facility must ensure that it has all of the emergency care equipment and supplies the lifeguards are trained to use. A dedicated area or room for these activities can greatly influence patron care and provide some privacy for the injured person.

Fire Emergencies

Aquatic facilities, like other facilities, are required to account for fire emergencies. The construction and operational codes dictate fire alarms, extinguishers, signage, and exits. Typically the NFPA (National Fire Protection Association) standards guide these codes.

Specific fire concerns that often get overlooked are the chemicals to be stored at the facility for water balance and treatment. The chemical rooms should display hazardous material placards that assist first responders in the evacuation and control of chemical-related emergencies. It should be noted that some chemicals can react violently with organic materials.

Patron care by facility staff and equipment assets can mean the difference between life and death. These considerations must be planned for in the initial design and construction. Proper planning and coordination with the local fire department representatives can enhance the facility response in fire emergencies.

Lightning and Severe Weather Planning

Both indoor and outdoor facilities should consider the risks involved with lightning. Safety experts say that pools should be cleared for 30 min. from the sight or sound of lightning. Some state laws are specific about the legal requirements for the operation of public pools when lightning is in the area. Some codes require pool closure for lightning even at indoor facilities.

There are now lightning predictors available that can alert the facility to atmospheric conditions that are conducive for producing lightning. This investment especially at outdoor facilities can save lives and take the guesswork out of facility closure criteria.

Due to current safety concerns for staff and patrons, a large reinforced interior "safe" room on the first floor or below grade should be considered for the immediate cover for facility users. The safe room may also be useful in the event that a person threatens violence; those seeking a secure location may be able to quickly flee to this location in such an emergency. This room can also double for a training/meeting area or reserved space for events or parties.

Construction Issues

There are many important construction issues for swimming pools, and the requirements often vary from state to state. This section will identify specific issues that are significant to all aquatic facilities.

Preconstruction Through Operation

Proper planning and anticipated growth for future needs during the planning phase can greatly reduce costs to expand later or correct preventable problems. The single largest impact for aquatic facility design lies with understanding the operational requirements for the facility. Having the input of an aquatic professional who is working for the organization's interests is critical. End use of the facility once it is complete drives the design and construction. The aquatic professional understands construction and operational codes as well as the industry standards. Things that appear to simply be management concerns, prior to facility construction, are in fact paramount to the lawful, successful, and cost-effective operations of the aquatic facility.

Operations that significantly affect annual budgets include staffing, heating, cooling, chemicals, and electrical costs. Poor planning can easily double or triple the expenses of any one or all of these areas. The aquatic professional should be one of the project managers during the aquatic planning, design, and construction phases to reduce the potential for major problems later. This professional should have experience ranging from programming, to operations, and obviously to construction of swimming facilities. The initial cost to hire this individual is minimal in the long run. This person should report to the parent organization and not be tied to the consultants, engineering firm, or construction company or be related to the company building the facility.

Facility Longevity

The new aquatic facility is a substantial investment, and the construction methods should represent a 50-year-plus life span for the facility. Contractors who do not plan for these terms should be avoided, or substantial maintenance costs could be realized.

In the planning phase, determine what the organizational goals are for the facility. There may be primary users and then secondary users. After all, there are constant costs whether there are no swimmers or 100, so schedule the facility use as close to 24/7 as possible to get more bang for the operational buck. These constant financial costs include filtration, electrical, chemicals, and heating.

What is the purpose of the facility, and who will it serve? Will the facility be self-supportive financially? Calculate costs and revenue projections to justify them in the main project. Failure to plan for the 50-year life span can significantly reduce revenue and lead to added annual expenses due to renovation costs within the first couple of decades.

Exact specifications must be expressed in the scope of work for the bidding process. Failure to specifically identify things such as basin dimensions and depth can create a facility of limited use. Oversight in this area can limit programming, create safety hazards, and prohibit the ability to conduct staff certification training. If forward planning is only conducted for the next year to next 5 years, the facility may quickly become less than functional after construction is finished. Never build to minimum standards; seek out preferred standards so that the facility does not become immediately obsolete.

Site Survey

Evaluation of the future site of the pool basin is important because of the depth of excavation needed for pools. Core samples must be taken so that building cost can be estimated accurately. This is because excavation of soft soil is much easier and less expensive than digging through rock. Oversight here leads to additional cost and longer construction time for the project.

Another critical aspect for the site is locating the site away from major streets and highways. Children commonly trek to the pool and play around the facility; speeding traffic and children playing is a combination for disaster.

The site elevation should be analyzed to verify that the facility will not flood with regular precipitation. If the facility is prone to flooding, plan for frequent pool closures. It can take weeks to get the pool chemically rebalanced once dirty runoff or groundwater enters the basin.

Compaction of Soil

Another site preparation concern specific to aquatic facilities is the importance of proper soil compaction prior to the placement of footers, floors, and walls. Consider the weight of the structures, and then consider the volume of water to the basins. At 8.3 lb per gallon of water, consider that the typical 25-yd, 3 ft to 10 ft deep competition pool holds about 150,000 gal or 1,245,000 lb of water. This weight on improperly compacted ground can lead to subsidence, or the sinking of the basin. This sinking can lead to structural damage, broken plumbing, and leaking water from the basin.

Basin Construction

There are many choices for pool basins, including the traditional concrete/reinforcing bar, metal (aluminum and PVC laminated stainless steel), and reinforced fiberglass. Often a concrete basin will be lined with tile, gunite, stone aggregate, PVC, painted with epoxy or polyurethane coatings.

Depending upon the pool use, some surfaces can be expensive to install. For example, a competitive lane line on the pool bottom is easy to install in both PVC and tile, but a stone aggregate would be more expensive. This is also true for the basic cost of the materials. A painted concrete basin is often the least expensive but also has the shortest life span. Concrete, tile-surfaced basins are expensive but generally give the longest life. Aggregates are typically the most expensive but provide better durability than painted surfaces.

Most bathing codes require a gutter system for pool water surface skimming. Like pool basins, gutter designs are available in many types of materials. Select a gutter system that is flush and virtually unseen by patrons or traditional open gutters with a variety of volume capacities. Often gutters will also perform overflow duties similar to that of a surge or balance tank. This is so water displaced by swimmers is not lost but relocated until the swimmers leave the pool basin.

As pools age and repeatedly flex, some basins require painting, grouting, or sealer. If painting is needed, ensure that appropriate surfaces are nonskid and that epoxy or polyurethane-based paints are used. These paints cost more but are more resistant to chemicals and are less likely to flake off in only one season.

Hydrostatic Pressure

Hydrostatic pressure is simply water pressure exerted upon an object. The installation of hydrostatic pressure relief valves must be mandated during initial basin construction or verified as present and operational during basin repairs and renovations. The valves are placed in the deepest main drain sump or sumps in each basin. These valves automatically relieve water pressure that can be under the pool due to a shallow water table or flooding. If the pool is drained without operational hydrostatic relief valves, the pool can literally float out of the ground like a boat. Many home pools and a few public pools have been destroyed when the pool was drained due to this hydrostatic pressure. This damage arises from a lack of relief valves or the failure of the valves. The pressure can become so great that the basin floats, breaking pipes and damaging the foundation soil. Once this happens, there is no putting the pool back together.

Deck Surfaces

A variety of construction materials are available for pool deck construction. The absolute best nonslip, attractive, and long-lasting surface is 1 in. x 1 in. tile. These small tiles are expensive but satisfy so many desired needs. The state and local bathing and construction codes must be reviewed so that colors selected are not prohibited by law.

If selecting some other deck or basin materials, the planner should seek out solid references and warranties for the product being considered. A less expensive alternative is not less expensive if it needs repair frequently or replaced all together in a few years.

Broomed concrete is often chosen at outdoor pools because it is inexpensive. When the deck is poured, the surface is broomed or power troweled to leave striations in the concrete surface to act as a nonskid surface. Be aware that after a season of operation, the concrete may need to be resurfaced or it may become extremely slippery.

Tiles larger than 1 in. x 1 in. should be avoided due to the limited contact resistance from larger tile with the bottom of wet feet. Slip and fall injuries can lead to serious legal problems. Other deck surfaces include PVC liners or removable plastic walkways that sit on top of concrete decks.

Facility Sanitation

Planning for the long-term maintenance of the facility is important to keep operational costs manageable and patrons safe. Anything that is on the deck typically ends up in the pool. This includes algae that grows in puddles in the parking lot, sidewalks, pool decks, and locker areas. Of even more concern is the variety of bacteria and viruses that can live and multiply in water. The big three for pools include *E. coli*, *Giardia lamblia*, and *Cryptosporidium*. Failure to conduct normal maintenance can result in costly repairs or worse in the growth of a variety of contaminants. Due to this growth, locker and bathroom decks must be sanitized with a 5% bleach solution daily (YMCA, 2003). This solution must be made fresh before each use. The pool deck should be hosed off daily and sanitized weekly. This practice reduces the spread of bacteria and viruses and allows the pool sanitizers to work more effectively, providing better water quality. A scum line in a pool is similar to a dirt and oil ring found after taking a bath in a tub. Enforcing that all patrons take showers and daily deck sanitation will reduce this deposit and lessen chemical treatment costs overall.

A big part of pool sanitation involves not allowing street shoes on deck. Consider shower entry points that prevent people from entering the pool deck dry; showers with automatic motion sensors can ensure that anyone entering the pool is showered. This will reduce the amount of body debris introduced into the pool as well as deter patrons from wearing street clothes on deck. Showers placed with these sensors will also reduce water consumption and heating costs for the water.

Water Quality

The water quality of the pool is a direct result of the proper design, planning, management, and dedication by staff at the facility. Water quality must comply with federal, state, and local guidelines. In addition to these laws, the industry has commonly accepted practices that can be found in texts/certification programs such as the NSPF's Certified Pool Operator, NRPA's Aquatic Facility Operator, and YMCA's Pool Operator On Location. These three programs account for the vast majority of pool operators trained and certified in the United States. Proper water chemistry is so important that some states require certified pool operators to be at the facility at all times when public pools are in operation. In our opinion, having a qualified pool operator on staff should be required.

The physical treatment of pool water happens through circulation, filtration, and sanitation. These systems must be designed to operate 24/7. The circulation/filtration systems most commonly found in commercial pools are pressure or vacuum sand or diatomaceous earth (DE) combinations. DE has the ability to filter down to about four microns, whereas the best sand filters down to about 25 microns. Thus, if filming or other photography will be a regular part of the facility operations, DE filters should be considered carefully for crystal-clear water quality.

The sanitation or treatment of pool water is possible through many methods. With the proper planning and appropriate staff training, all are safe. Chemical treatment is the most common method for water treatment in pools. The four dominant chemicals used are tablet chlorine, gas chlorine, liquid chlorine, and bromine. Bromine is preferred for high water temperature applications such as hot tubs. Tablet chlorine comes in many compositions, the most commonly used being calcium hypochlorite, at about 65% chlorine. Chlorine gas is the most potent form at 99%, but many municipal codes forbid its use due to the risk of chlorine gas poisoning from accidental exposure. Liquid chlorine is common but degrades rapidly, and even at its most concentrated, fresh solution is only about 15% chlorine.

Other methods of treatment of pool water during the past 15 years include ultraviolet light chambers (UV), ozone generators, chlorine generators, and non-chlorine sanitizers. Codes vary from state to state, and some methods may not be recognized by some states. Both UV and ozone systems primarily treat the water in the circulation system plumbing, but have limited or no effect on the water in the basin. Chlorine generators make chlorine on-site in the pool system. In low bather load pools, the chlorine generators work well, but often are not correctly sized for heavy-load situations and may need alternate methods of treatment if not properly planned for. Some facilities have begun to use non-chlorine chemicals such as potassium monopersulfate with their chlorination systems to reduce combined chlorine levels. Other non-chlorine oxidizers include sodium percarbonate and hydrogen peroxide.

Chemical Control and Feeding Systems

Water management systems are commonly installed, and in some codes, certain automated systems are required to add chemicals to the pool while swimmers are present. In many state health codes, chemical additives cannot be manually added to the water while bathers occupy the pool. Today technology allows the ability to monitor and make changes to the water quality off-site. Some of the automated systems also retain electronic reports of minute-by-minute water samples, allowing owners to validate proper water quality around the clock.

It is foolhardy to ignore these systems. The alternative to these systems means hiring someone to test, analyze, and adjust the water quality every moment that the facility is open. To do so is akin to having central air in your home with no thermostat and attempting to keep the house at exactly 78°F.

The most rudimentary systems allow the monitoring and automatic adjustment of pH and chlorine. Advanced systems can include monitoring of alkalinity, hardness, temperature, combined chlorine, and the saturation index.

Dangerous Rooms

Ensure that chemical and mechanical rooms are secured whenever staff are not in these areas. This prevents patrons from inadvertently entering a room with hazardous items. Additionally, pool chemicals that are unsecured may make a tempting invitation to young children, as some chemicals can look like "little white mints." If the chemicals are ingested, the result could be fatal.

Pool Design Supervision Issues

Designed for Direct Supervision

The direct supervision of patrons in the facility is a key factor to reducing submersion (drowning) incidents. To do this effectively, lifeguards need training on how to watch patrons and supervisors must employ a variety of techniques. Facilities must also consider this job during the design and planning phase. If a large basin is designed, then elevated lifeguard stations should be considered. The elevated station allows guards an unobscured view of the pool bottom despite the viewing angle or glare from the water. The elevated station also enhances perceived authority over the facility. Guard stands must have an unobstructed view of the area supervised. Support columns for the roof must not be placed in a manner that disrupts a lifeguards full view of the observation area.

Facilities, both indoor and outdoor, must carefully consider the position of the facility in relation to the sun. The ability for staff to properly supervise the patrons in the water attractions can be seriously impacted by glare from the sun. In outdoor pools this means pool shape and guard towers must be carefully planned so that glare is kept to a minimum or staff have multiple stations from which to select during the course of the day. Indoor pools should consider ways to limit direct sunlight. Use reflected lighting methods to reduce lighting costs and maintain an observable body of water.

Lighting

Planners should consult their state and local bathing and construction codes because often lighting requirements are specific for pools. Like external natural light, artificial pool lighting is a serious proposition when selecting lighting. Lighting fixtures and replacement bulbs are expensive, so consideration of things such as bulb placement, operational hours, replacement costs, and effects of water or humidity on the system should be addressed.

Bulb life may help determine long-term costs, and access to a burned-out bulb should be considered. Will special equipment or lifts be required? These types of considerations can significantly increase costs while degrading function. Determine how long the bulb will provide x number of lumens or candle-feet of light when new. How about after 1,000 hr of operation? What is the kilowatt-hour electrical consumption for the proposed systems?

Also decide whether underwater basin lights or whether overhead systems are sufficient for your facility. Is there an emergency lighting plan if power to the facility is suddenly lost? Again, the bathing code for the facility area must be addressed before any decision is made.

Drowning Prevention

Drowning prevention must be designed into the facility to help staff provide a safe environment. Currently, new technologies may be able to assist facility staff through drowning detection systems. One system named Poseidon is about a decade old and has a proven track record to help save lives at indoor facilities. This computer-based system uses a series of cameras to evaluate swimmers and determine when someone might be in trouble. This system does not replace lifeguards; it does provide another set of "eyes" (cameras) on the water, so to speak.

Access Points

When new aquatic facilities are designed, a simple oversight can lead to tragedy. Placing entry points to the pool deck in relation to where the deep water of the pool is located is important. Locker rooms that enter the pool area next to a diving well or water deeper than the average swimmers height are "asking" for patrons to immediately enter water over their heads, and those with poor swimming skills find themselves in trouble. Make sure that pool deck entrances are at a shallow area of the pool basin.

Physical Security and Safety

The organization should give special consideration for the security of the facility outside of operational hours. The design can help staff quickly determine that the facility is secure and that no person can gain easy access at closing or during the night. All windows, doors, gates, and vents should be verified as secure at closing each day, and an alarm system should be considered to prevent unauthorized entry and use. Trespassers should be prosecuted immediately. A swift punishment may deter others thinking about unauthorized entry into the facility. Failure to prosecute may help make a case against the facility as an attractive nuisance. By building an inviting facility with little thought for securing it, an organization may find itself in legal difficulty.

Operational Security

Facilities should consider single points of access to the facility for normal operations. This will limit the staff needed to control facility use and observation. Systems such as floor-to-ceiling turnstiles with swipe card readers should be considered to control access and speed patron entry and egress for the facility. The theft of both facility items and patron property may be reduced by using turnstiles. A main operational desk can be located in the lobby just prior to the turnstiles, allowing for monitoring of patron entry. This also means that "one-stop shopping" can happen in this location. From program registration, to memberships, to concessions and pro shop sales, this location can control it all. With a limited number of staff, security and services can happen from this central location.

Fences

Fencing is often used as an inexpensive barrier device when long distances must be covered, especially at outdoor facilities. Consider how the fence will be used, and pay close attention to ensuring that climbable opportunities are not created by the design. This situation happens at 90° corners; the fence becomes an easy way in due to the corner support poles. Consider sweeping, rounded corners to make turns in the fence.

The fence itself should not allow a 4-in. disk to pass through the gaps; for chain-link fencing, the mesh should not exceed 1 ¼ in. (NSPF, 2012). Ideally, a square, non-climbable fence that is at least 8 ft tall will be a better barrier than traditional chain-link fencing. Consider the fence around tennis courts; it has 2-in. holes, is 10 ft tall, and is used to keep balls in the court. Is it more important to keep a ball in a tennis court or keep children out of an outdoor pool after hours?

Other Aquatic Design and Operation Concerns

Air Quality

The air quality at indoor pools has a serious effect on the water quality, staff health, patron health, and facility structural longevity. Air quality is not just heating and cooling; it also includes dehumidification and the reduction of chloramines in the air.

The air temperature at indoor pools should be 3° to 5° higher than the water temperature for bather comfort. This temperature may be addressed by local bathing codes and/or health codes. If people complain about the water temperature being too cold, they typically are uncomfortable because the air temperature is too warm, thus making the water feel colder. Do not regularly change the water temperature; it will not solve the problem, and it will cost dearly in heating expenses.

Staff will see the consequences of poor air quality when they contract breathing problems such as lifeguard lung, which is common to pools with poor air quality. Worse yet, staff or patrons who have mild asthma may have elevated effects because of the poor air quality. This could mean increased EMS visits to your facility when people fall ill.

The fence in the foreground is decorative and may prevent toddlers from entering the pool areas, but adults can easily circumvent it.

Serious research and consultation about aquatic facility air quality can ensure a facility has a long life and patrons will enjoy using the attractions.

Rooms at the Facility

The usable spaces described below should be considered for every well-designed aquatic facility.

Guard office. This is where staff store rescue equipment, records/reports, and their on-duty personal items such as uniforms, pocket masks, whistles, and eye and skin protection. Other testing and monitoring equipment may also be kept within this area.

Main office. This room will be the central point of access for entry and information for the facility and should include the pro shop and concession activities.

Pool mechanical room. This room will house the circulation, filtration, and pool water heating systems. Sufficient room is needed around each piece of equipment to monitor and maintain the equipment. Computer control systems for chemicals should also be in this room for a longer operational life.

Chemical feed room. This room will have only the chemical feed systems due to the caustic nature of pool chemicals. Only pool chemicals should be stored here; the only mechanical equipment should be the chemical feeders.

Electrical room. A dedicated electrical room that feeds the electricity to the facility will be distributed from this point.

Custodial room. This room should provide the needed area to store cleaning equipment and supplies to maintain the facility.

Locker rooms. The locker rooms should provide a changing area, toilets, and showers typical to any bathing facility.

Storage. There is never enough storage, so anticipate future programs and operational storage needs for this space.

Class/meeting room. To conduct staff training, classes with land-based components (such as CPR and first aid) as well as a room for pool parties or other programming should be considered.

Pool Utilities and Green Facilities

With any facility, heating, ventilation, and air-conditioning (HVAC) are common issues. In aquatic facilities, heating, cooling, and dehumidification become critically important for both patron comfort and facility longevity. There is substantial cost in proper aquatic facility air quality and control systems; this cost can be further increased by shortened facility longevity due to ignoring these issues. Serious consideration must be given not only to the purchase price of air quality systems but also to operational and maintenance expenses. These systems must not only effectively control the pool area humidity but also account for fresh air exchange and reduce the off-gassing of pool chemicals into the air. Failure to consider these issues can result in a nonfunctional facility that has a dramatically shortened useful life span. The American Society of Heating, Refrigerating, and Air-Conditioning Engineers (ASHRAE) created standards in this area that should not be overlooked.

Today more than ever, people and facilities must consider "green" facilities. Solar heat can reduce the amount spent on electrical or gas heating. Solar heating can supplement pool heating but cannot be consistently relied upon to bring the water temperature to the ideal range by itself, except in tropical climates. Another option to reduce the heating expenses is geothermal heating. Geothermal heating allows the facility to use the warmer ground temperature water rather than cold tap water thus bringing it to ground temperature prior to electric or gas heating to the desired level. This works in the reverse in the summer; the water can be cooled in the summer months as needed. Wind and photovoltaic electrical generation can offset some of the facilities' costs as well. Large wind generators, similar to windmills of the past, in some regions of the country may be able to generate more power than the facility can use. Photovoltaic cells may be placed on the roof of the pool area along with solar thermal heating plumbing to reduce both electrical and heating expenses.

Simple solutions such as the color of the exterior roof surface (i.e., a light color vs. a dark color) can reduce cooling costs dramatically. Exterior air-conditioning units should be a light color, preferably shaded, protected, and regularly inspected for damage and debris. Insulate all exterior ceilings, walls, as well as pool walls if a gallery is present. The gallery or hallway/crawl space under the deck that surrounds the pool allows for easy plumbing repairs and provides access for underwater filming/instruction. The photo below shows the plumbing, a video camera, and underwater windows. Also note the insulation on the ceiling. This facility has radiant deck heating in the concrete just under the tile pool deck surface. The insulation helps keep the heat in the deck as warm water heats the deck and the facility is heated by the rising warm air in contact with the deck surface.

Outdoor pools should have pool covers to reduce water loss through evaporation. The covers can also retain heat on cool nights, thus reducing heating costs. Pool cover auto-retracting systems can be built into the design of the basin during construction. External units can be purchased after construction, but wear and tear can be excessive if staff do not receive proper training on proper handling and use of the covers.

14 Playgrounds

Donna Thompson, *University of Northern Iowa*

Susan Hudson, *University of Northern Iowa*

Playgrounds are an essential part of children's play. These play sites can be found in a variety of settings, including public parks, schools, child care centers, apartment complexes, churches, and commercial establishments. Whatever their settings, playgrounds should have certain elements in common:

• the fostering of a child's physical, emotional, social, and intellectual development and

• the provision of age-appropriate equipment to meet children's needs.

The word *playgrounds* in this chapter refers to designated areas where stationary and manipulative play equipment is located to facilitate a child's physical, emotional, social, and intellectual development. These areas employ

• the use of proper surfacing under and around equipment,

• the placement of equipment that allows for easy supervision by adults, and

• the regular maintenance of the equipment and the environment.

This chapter will review trends in playground design; general planning considerations; specific planning steps; installation of the equipment and the surfacing; and ongoing maintenance, repair, and inspection procedures.

General Planning Considerations

Playground Guidelines and Standards

During the 1970s, in response to consumer interest and complaints, the U.S. Consumer Product Safety Commission (CPSC) initiated a process to develop safety guidelines for playgrounds. The first guidelines were produced in 1981. The guidelines came in two handbooks—one designed to give general information to the public, the other

to give technical assistance to the manufacturers of playground equipment. These guidelines were revised in 1991 and merged into one handbook for public use. In 1988, the American Society for Testing and Materials (ASTM) accepted responsibility for creating a standard based on the refinement of the technical specifications for playground equipment.

The CPSC has maintained its involvement with the technical standards for public use by assisting the ASTM with further development and refinement of these specifications. As a result of these efforts, the first voluntary standard for the playground industry was developed in 1993. This standard, known as F-1487-93 (Standard Consumer Safety Performance Specification for Playground Equipment for Public Use), provided technical specifications for playground equipment, use zones, prevention of entrapments, and maintenance. The standard was revised in 1995, 1997, 2001, and 2007. A surfacing standard was created in 1991 (F-1292-91). This standard provided for the testing of the impact attenuation of playground surfacing. Specifically, it provided the methodology to assess the amount of surfacing necessary under and around playground equipment to prevent fatal head injuries of children who may fall to the surface off the equipment. This standard has been revised five times (1993, 1995, 1996, 2004, and 2009).

Both the ASTM standards and the CPSC guidelines (which were revised again in 1994, 1997, 2008, and 2010) have been instrumental in creating safer play environments for children by providing design criteria for surfacing and equipment. Together, they are essential documents needed for designing playgrounds. They were signed into law in 2010 by the attorney general and went into effect in March 2011.

A third guideline now influencing the playground design comes from the U.S. Access Board. In November 2000, the U.S. Department of Justice published the Access Board's guidelines regarding the interpretation of the

Americans With Disabilities Act (ADA) and public playgrounds. These guidelines address issues of accessibility to and from play equipment as well as the use of the play equipment by children with disabilities. All new public playgrounds, including those found in schools and community parks, should conform to these guidelines. If major renovation is done on existing playgrounds, then they also need to comply with the guidelines. In addition, whether new or old, public-use playgrounds need to provide access to and from the play equipment as mandated in the ADA regulations passed in 1991.

Safe playground designs include four major elements:
- the placement of equipment and support structures (e.g., benches), which facilitate the supervision of children in the play area;
- the proper positioning of age-appropriate equipment to promote positive play behavior;
- the selection of appropriate surfacing that will absorb the impact of children falling from the equipment; and
- the consideration of equipment and surface maintenance issues that contribute to the development of safe playground environments.

Supervision Design Considerations

Supervision requires individuals to be able to see and move through the playground area; therefore, design considerations for supervision include age separation of equipment, use of signs, open sight lines, and zones for play.

Age Separation

It is important to divide the playground area into sections appropriate for different ages of the users. ASTM standard F-2373 was developed in 2008 for children aged 6 months to 23 months. Therefore, play equipment found in the play area should be separated into three distinct zones for children aged 6 months to 23 months, aged 2 to 5, and aged 5 to 12.

Mixing the three distinct types of equipment means that the supervisor will have a difficult time guiding children to use the equipment appropriate for their developmental age level. (A more complete discussion of this can be found in the Age-Appropriate Design Considerations section of this chapter.)

Use of Signs

Signs can provide information to adults concerning both the age separation of equipment and the need for supervision. Signs provide adults with a clear indication as to which age group should be on the equipment. It also reminds adults that the equipment will not supervise the children. This is an important consideration for schools whose playgrounds are used before and after the organized school day and in public parks where no formalized supervision is in place. It provides a "good faith" attempt by a sponsoring agency to promote safe supervision practices.

Open Sight Lines

Open sight lines refer to several angles of visual access for the supervisor. Sight lines must occur through equipment and through natural vegetation. Furthermore, sight lines for play structures should allow visual access to all points of the age-appropriate design. While in older structures sight lines should come from at least two directions on the play structure's overhead ladder (Bowers, 1988, p. 42). Essentially, the supervisor's response to emergencies is dependent upon his or her "ability...to approach the structure and get to all the events to provide assistance" using the routes implied by the sight lines (Bruya & Wood, 1997, p. 14).

Zones for Play

Play sites should also be divided into zones for different activity types. Two types of zones to which the designer should pay attention are activity zones and use zones. Activity zones describe the type of play behavior in which children might engage given the space and equipment that is present. Examples of activity zones include areas for social/dramatic play, fine motor play, gross motor play, and quiet play.

Use zones refer to the safe areas around equipment that need appropriate surfacing. Use zones will be further discussed in the Considerations for Proper Surfacing section.

Age-Appropriate Design Considerations

Playgrounds should be designed according to the characteristics of the intended user. Therefore, age-appropriate design considerations include selection of the correct size of equipment for children, developmental needs of children, and the physical layout of equipment to support positive play activities.

Correct Size of Equipment

Size of equipment refers to height, width, and bulk. The *height* of the equipment includes the overall distance from the top of the equipment piece to the surface. It also includes the space between various components, such as steps and platforms. Because 70% of reported playground injuries involve falls to surfaces, the height of the equipment becomes a critical factor in designing a safe playground. Experts have suggested that equipment for preschool children be no taller than children can reach. Maximum height for most equipment for school-aged children should be 8 ft (Thompson & Hudson, 1996).

Width of platforms should also allow children to make decisions about how to get on and off equipment safely. A child standing on top of a 6-ft slide should have sufficient room to turn around and climb back down the ladder if he or she decides not to slide down.

Bulk is the relationship between the thickness of the material and the grip size of a child's hand. All handrails, rungs, and other components that children grasp should be between 1 in. and 1 ½ in. in diameter.

Developmental Needs

Developmental needs of children are also a factor in age-appropriate design. Children grow and develop by stages. The thinking ability of a 3-year-old is much different than that of a 7-year-old. Preschoolers are physically smaller than school-aged children. It is important to consider the developmental needs and abilities of children in planning and designing age-appropriate playgrounds. These needs and abilities include

- physical (i.e., strength, grip, height, and weight),
- emotional (i.e., risk-taking and exploration),
- social (i.e., cooperation, sharing, and accepting),
- intellectual (i.e., decision-making, inquisitiveness, and creativity), and
- accessibility (i.e., mobility).

These needs and abilities apply to all children. As previously mentioned, even children with limited physical, emotional, social, and intellectual capacities and/or mobility have the legal right to use public play areas. Thus, the designer needs to design for the composite "typical/atypical" child if the playground is to be one where all children can interact successfully.

Physical Layout of Equipment

The physical layout of the playground pieces can limit or enhance the play value and safety for children. An interconnected play area is one in which easy movement throughout the play structure is developed through the inclusion of alternate routes of travel (Bowers, 1988). Shaw (1976) investigated interconnection between parts of the structure that he called the "unified play structure." As a result of the Creative Learning Project, he determined that overall use patterns decreased for separate play modules when compared to the "unified" play space. Thus, unified or interconnected play elements in a play space increased overall complexity. A 2004 study by the National Program for Playground Safety found that over 95% of all school and park playgrounds now have composite structures.

Although composite structures increase the complexity of the play space, they also can cause a safety problem if not carefully thought out. Over 84% of park playgrounds now have composite structures that they claim are appropriate for ages 2 to 12 (Hudson, Olsen, & Thompson,

2004). What this means is that the interconnections of these structures are allowing 2-year-olds up to heights and on equipment not designed for their developmental abilities. Planners need to understand that one size does not fit all. If composite structures are used, they should be clearly labeled for the age group for which they are designed—either ages 2 to 5 or ages 5 to 12. Having a composite structure for ages 2 to 12 is inappropriate and goes against the ASTM standards and CPSC guidelines.

Community playground

Considerations for Proper Surfacing

Surfacing is the third important general design element. Factors that need to be considered include how much fall protection is required, accessibility, maintenance, management requirements, and costs.

Adequate Fall Protection?

For the prevention of life-threatening injuries, adequate fall protection needs to be present. The National Program for Playground Safety (NPPS) has developed a safe surface decision-making model to help individuals determine whether a playground surface will meet the criteria of adequate fall protection. As can be seen in the model outlined in Figure 14.1, four decisions are involved in selecting surfaces that will provide adequate fall protection. These include the selection of suitable materials, the height of the equipment, the depth of the materials, and adequate coverage in the use zone.

Selection of Suitable Materials

According to the CPSC (2010), a number of materials can reduce the risk of life-threatening injuries. Acceptable materials include sand, gravel, wood chips, engineered wood fibers, shredded rubber, and synthetic surfaces. Hard materials, such as asphalt and concrete, are unacceptable surfaces under playground equipment. Similarly, earth surfaces such as dirt, soil, grass, and turf are unacceptable because their shock-absorbing properties vary depending on wear and climatic conditions (CPSC, 2010).

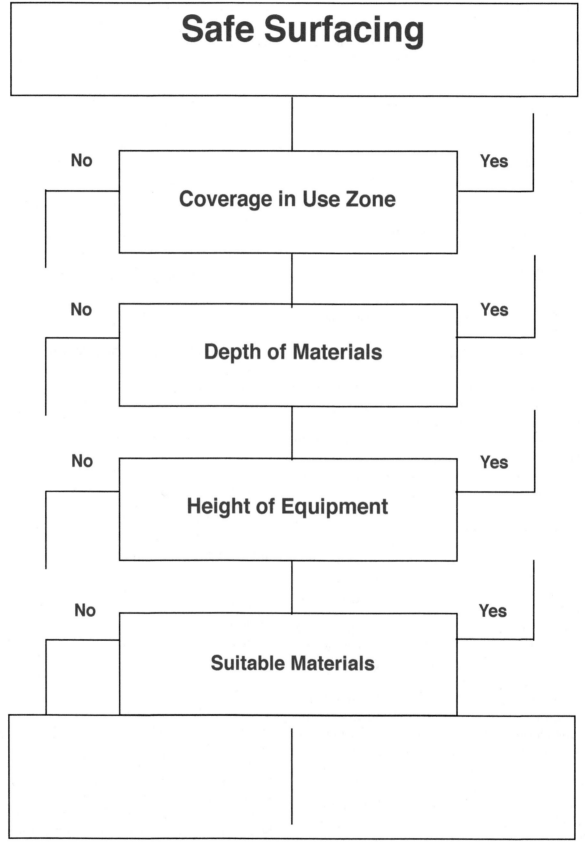

Figure 14.1. Safe Surfacing Decision-Making Model

Height of the Equipment

Equipment height affects the choice of shock-absorbent surfacing in two ways. First, some surfaces, such as pea gravel, provide shock absorbency protection for limited heights (e.g., 6 ft in the case of pea gravel). Second, currently no surface over 12 ft has been laboratory tested. Thus, to date, no one can guarantee the shock-absorbency characteristics for equipment over the height of 12 ft. Because research studies have indicated that equipment over 6 ft in height has doubled the injury rate of equipment under 6 ft, the NPPS (2008) recommended that the height of playground equipment should not exceed 8 ft for school-aged children and 5 ft for preschool-aged children.

The CPSC (2010) recommendations for the fall heights for various pieces of playground equipment are as follows:

- Climbers and horizontal ladders—the maximum height of the structure.
- Elevated platforms including slide platforms—the height of the platform.
- Merry-go-rounds—the height above the ground of any part at the perimeter on which a child may sit or stand.
- Seesaws—the maximum height attainable by any part of the seesaw.
- Spring rockers—the maximum height above the ground of the seat or designated play surface.
- Swings—because children may fall from a swing seat at its maximum attainable angle (assumed to be 90° from "at rest" position), the fall height of a swing structure is the height of the pivot point where the swing's suspending elements connect to the supporting structure.
- Slides—CPSC has no recommendations concerning slide height. Research has shown that equipment higher than 6 ft has double the injury rate than equipment at lower heights.

It should be noted that equipment that requires a child to be standing or sitting at ground level during play is not expected to follow the recommendations for resilient surfacing. Examples of such equipment are sandboxes, activity walls, playhouses, or other equipment that has no elevated designated playing surface.

If the surface does not meet minimum standards for shock absorbency, then it should not be used. Minimum standards are determined through testing procedures as stated in the ASTM F-1292 standard for playground surfacing. However, because of time and cost constraints, many consumers cannot afford to perform this testing. Consequently, as a public service, the NPPS conducted testing of five common loose-fill materials: pea gravel, sand, wood chips, shredded rubber, and engineered wood fiber. The results are provided in Table 14.1. The chart reports the heights at which a life-threatening head injury would not be expected to occur for compressed loose-fill materials at three different depths. As can be seen in Table 14.1, 12 in. of compressed sand, wood chips, shredded rubber, and engineered wood fiber can provide shock absorbency for equipment up to 8 ft in height. In contrast, the maximum height for 12 in. of pea gravel is 6 ft. The depth of any loose-fill material could be reduced during use, resulting in different shock-absorbing properties. For this reason, a margin of safety should be considered in selecting a type and depth of material for a specific use. When loose-fill materials are used, it is recommended that there be sections of containment around the perimeter of the use zone (CPSC, 2010; see Table 14.1).

Table 14.1

Playground Surface Materials

Height of Equipment	Pea Gravel 6"	9"	12"	Sand 6"	9"	12"	Wood Chips 6"	9"	12"	Shredded Rubber 6"	9"	12"	Engineered Wood Fiber 6"	9"	12"
1'	Y	Y	Y	Y	Y	Y	Y	Y	Y	Y	Y	Y	Y	Y	Y
2'	Y	Y	Y	Y	Y	Y	Y	Y	Y	Y	Y	Y	Y	Y	Y
3'	Y	Y	Y	Y	Y	Y	Y	Y	Y	Y	Y	Y	Y	Y	Y
4'	Y	Y	Y	Y	Y	Y	Y	Y	Y	Y	Y	Y	Y	Y	Y
5'	N	Y	Y	Y	Y	Y	Y	Y	Y	Y	Y	Y	Y	Y	Y
6'	N	N	Y	Y	Y	Y	Y	Y	Y	Y	Y	Y	Y	Y	Y
7'	N	N	N	Y	Y	Y	N	Y	Y	Y	Y	Y	Y	Y	Y
8'	N	N	N	Y	Y	Y	N	Y	Y	Y	Y	Y	N	Y	Y

Note. Based on depth test results conducted by NPPS or manufacturers' literature. The loose-fill results are based on materials tested in a compressed state. Y = Yes, it did meet CPSC recommendations for this critical height. N = No, it did not meet CPSC recommendations for this critical height.

Coverage in the Use Zone

The final element that helps decide if the appropriate surface is present is the determination of the placement of the surfacing under and around playground equipment. *The Consumer Products and Safety Commission Handbook for Public Playground Safety* (USCPSC, 2010) defined these areas as use zones. Table 14.2 presents the requirements for use zones as outlined in the CSPC handbook.

Table 14.2

Use Zones for Equipment

Equipment	Use Zone Requirement
Stationary equipment	Six feet on all sides of the equipment.
Slides	Six feet on all sides. Four feet plus the height of slide in front of slide chute.
Swings	Six feet on each side. Twice the height of the swing beam in front and back of swing.

The basic use zone is 6 ft. However, because children move off swings and slides in different ways than onto other equipment, the use zone is expanded to provide a larger safety zone. For instance, if a swing beam is 8 ft high, then the use zone extends 16 ft in front and 16 ft in back of the swing beam to accommodate children who might jump out of the swing seat while in motion.

Accessibility

The second characteristic that needs to be considered in selecting surfacing is that of accessibility. According to the ADA of 1991, discrimination on the basis of disability in public accommodations is prohibited. The entire playground area does not have to be accessible, but an accessible pathway must be available to accessible playground equipment. Therefore, a pathway made of an accessible surface material must be provided. At this time, the testing of loose-fill materials for accessibility is still in process. However, it is well accepted that sand and pea gravel are not accessible surfaces. Until more testing is done, the only materials that are generally considered accessible under certain conditions are wood fibers and unitary materials, both of which are commercially available. According to a U.S. Department of the Interior advisory, uniform wood fibers tend to knit together to form an accessible surface, but other wood materials (wood chips, bark, mulch, etc.) do not.

Maintenance

The third characteristic, which is often ignored during the selection process, is the maintenance requirements that various surfaces need so that the shock-absorbency characteristics are properly retained. Three elements that should be considered in this area include environmental conditions, soil conditions, and management requirements.

Environmental Conditions

Environmental conditions such as strong winds, rainy weather, high humidity, freezing temperatures, and so forth may influence the appropriateness of the type of surfacing selected. For example, strong winds can erode organic loose-fill materials and sand, so they must be replenished often. Wind and dirt tend to form a hard pan or crust in pea gravel that needs to be broken up periodically. When wet, sand tends to stick together and becomes almost rigid. Some types of unitary materials are susceptible to frost damage. Thus, the climatic conditions of the playground must be considered when selecting a surface material (Mack, Hudson, & Thompson, 1997).

Soil Conditions

Playgrounds located over poor soil will not drain well, causing pooling of water under equipment. In some areas of the United States, the shrink/swell characteristics of clay soil can loosen the foundation of play equipment. Shrink/swell conditions can also cause sinkholes under playground surfaces. This problem can easily destroy a poured-in-place or other unitary surface. Check with the local soil conservation district or a county extension agent to check the suitability of the soil for playground development.

Finally, the designer must pay attention to the drainage of the site. Normally, water should run away from the playground. This might mean that the area around the equipment will need to be slightly raised. Because drainage is also dependent on soil type, as mentioned above, the soil composition should be checked prior to installing equipment. The designer should also be aware of what might drain into the playground area. For instance, if a parking lot is located above the play area, grease, oils, and even gasoline may be washed into the play area during a rainstorm. Good drainage at and around the site will help to avoid problems.

Management Requirements

Consideration must be given to how the area will be managed. A site that will have high traffic use will require a surface that will be durable without frequent maintenance. Rubber tiles or poured-in-place surfaces, although initially high in cost, may be more appropriate for these types of areas. Loose-fill materials would be more easily displaced, which would impact the overall safety of the site.

However, in areas that have controlled use, loose-fill materials may be appropriate. Maintenance costs and the needs of surfacing materials vary greatly, with loose-fill materials tending to have much higher maintenance needs. In high-use areas, loose materials may need to be raked daily to replace materials that have been pushed or kicked away. Loose-fill materials need to be regularly inspected for protruding and sharp objects such as glass, pop tops, sharp rocks, and metal objects. These surface materials may also have to be tilled periodically to loosen compaction. Sand should periodically be turned over, loosened, and cleaned. Additionally, loads of loose material may need to be added on an annual or semiannual basis to keep the surface at an appropriate depth.

While not as time consuming, unitary materials such as rubber mats, tiles, and poured-in-place surfaces also have maintenance needs. Repairs may need to be made to gouges, burns, and loose areas. Unitary materials may also need to be swept frequently to prevent sand, dirt, rocks, or other loose materials from becoming a slip hazard. Finally, rubber surfaces must be washed occasionally to remove spilled beverages, animal excrement, and other foreign matter.

Costs

Cost factors of the surfacing material should be prorated over the life expectancy of the playground. Materials with low initial cost include sand, pea gravel, wood chips, and bark mulch. However, you should also consider the replenishment costs of these materials. In addition, some method of containment is needed and the materials cannot be installed over existing hard surfaces such as concrete and asphalt.

Materials with medium initial cost include wood fiber and shredded rubber. Some of these materials are easily installed and others require professional installation. They may also require a drainage system. Like other loose-fill materials, these materials require some type of containment and they cannot be installed over concrete or asphalt.

Unitary materials such as poured-in-place surfaces, rubber tiles, and rubber mats have a high initial cost when compared to low-cost loose-fill materials. Poured-in-place surfaces are usually the most expensive with a cost 10 to 15 times higher than common loose-fill surfaces. Rubber mats and tiles typically cost 6 to 12 times that of the cheaper materials. Installation and site preparation costs should also be considered because these materials must be professionally installed. Unitary materials also require a hard base. If the existing surface is not concrete or asphalt, then a subsurface must be installed prior to the rubber surface. However, if the current surface is concrete or asphalt, installing a rubber surface will avoid the costs of excavating and removing the existing surface.

Equipment and Maintenance Considerations

Considerations about maintenance have to be part of the initial planning process. A poorly built playground is difficult to maintain. Providing good upkeep for a safe play environment begins with planning the playground site. Factors that need to be considered regarding this area include preplanning, materials, inspection, maintenance, and environment.

Prior to the installation of equipment and surfaces, a proper site analysis needs to be conducted. A site analysis addresses natural, manufactured, and aesthetic elements that may affect playgrounds. All of these items will be discussed in greater detail in the next section.

Materials

There is no perfect material for playground equipment. Without good maintenance, wood will splinter, metal will rust, and plastic will crack. A good maintenance plan should be based on

- instructions received from the designer/manufacturer,
- materials used for equipment and surfaces,
- age of the equipment and surfaces,
- given frequency of use on the equipment and surfaces, and
- environmental factors at a specific location.

Be certain that all instructions from the designer/manufacturer are retained in a file and that the schedule of maintenance is followed. Remember, any modification, deviation, or change from these instructions means that liability issues will reside with the agency, not the designer/manufacturer.

Inspection

Inspect all materials prior to installation. Wood products are aesthetically pleasing but will weather faster than metal or plastic. Plastic materials may not be appropriate in areas of great temperature extremes. Metal materials also tend to absorb heat and cold, which can cause problems in hot and cold climates.

Even newly installed playgrounds should be inspected for hazards. Just because a playground is new does not mean that problems cannot occur. This is especially true if the equipment was installed improperly or the overall design and placement of equipment is faulty. On the other hand, older playgrounds need more regular inspections simply because parts may wear out due to age.

Maintenance Schedule

A well-used playground will need more frequent maintenance than one that is used less often. This is especially true with playgrounds that have loose-fill materials as the surface under and around playground equipment. An agency that schedules only one refilling of these materials a year may find that over half of its playgrounds are unsafe due to the high usage. Each play area may have its own use cycle, and the maintenance schedule should reflect this.

Environmental Factors

Finally, the environmental factors at a specific location determine the required frequency of maintenance. A playground that is located near a shady grove of trees may need to be inspected more frequently because of materials left on the surfacing (e.g., leaves) or other hazards (e.g., overhanging limbs). A playground that is in a wide-open area and exposed to the elements may also experience greater maintenance needs.

It is evident that to maintain a safe playground environment, maintenance practices and procedures need to be thought about at the beginning of the design process. It is also important that these practices and procedures be continually revised and improved.

Specific Planning Steps

The actual planning and design of a playground is accomplished in four distinct phases: site analysis, preliminary design, equipment and material selection, and final design.

Site Analysis

Site analysis involves the gathering of information and data about the playground site and adjacent properties. "The purpose of site analysis is to find a place for a particular use or find a use for a particular place" (Molnar & Rutledge, 1986). One of the first steps that should be taken during the site analysis is an on-site visitation. Personal site visits enable the planner to see how the area is used and how it relates to surrounding land uses (Illinois Park and Recreation Association [IPRA], 1995). It allows the planner to mentally visualize the space available for the project. During the site analysis, step information about environmental elements, manufactured elements, and hazardous conditions is gathered and analyzed.

Environmental characteristics. Environmental characteristics that should be considered during the site analysis include soils and geology, drainage, topography, vegetation, and other physical characteristics that may impact the development process.

Soils and geology. Soil type is important because it is directly related to drainage. The playground should be constructed on well-drained soils. A playground constructed on poor soil will be subject to water pooling or standing. Poor soil also tends to erode the foundations of the equipment and cause other problems of equipment stability.

Drainage. In general, water should drain away from the playground. As mentioned earlier, the play area may

need to be slightly elevated to accomplish this. Remember that construction of the playground and/or surrounding areas may alter the water movement patterns on the site. If there are questions about preventing or solving water problems, a good source is the local office of the Soil Conservation Service (SCS).

Topography is concerned with the general lay of the land. Playground developments work best within a range of slopes. As a general rule, slopes around and beneath playgrounds should conform to the following guidelines (IPRA, 1995):

- Slopes between 1% and 4% are most suitable for playgrounds (a 1% slope falls 1 ft for every 100 linear feet).
- Slopes less than 1% may result in drainage problems.
- Slopes greater than 4% may require site modifications to install and level the equipment.

In addition, slope is an important consideration in providing equal access into the playground for everyone regardless of physical capabilities. The accessible route into the playground must have a maximum slope of 5% (1 ft of fall for every 20 linear feet) and a maximum cross slope of 2%.

Vegetation. Vegetation is another environmental consideration in playground design. Shade should be an essential ingredient for every playground. If trees are not present, it may be necessary to provide man-made shade, such as the placement of shelters. Although trees planted along a western and southern exposure may provide the necessary shade, caution must be taken to ensure that overhanging limbs do not interfere with play activities. "In particular, trees planted inside the playground must be carefully located because they may be used for climbing" (IPRA, 1995, p.13). In addition, avoid planting trees and shrubs that are messy or likely to attract stinging insects such as bees.

Other considerations. Other environmental considerations include sun orientation, wind patterns, climate, and animal control. Slide surfaces tend to absorb heat and therefore should not be placed on a western exposure. The best orientation is north. However, if this is not possible, then natural or manufactured shade needs to be provided.

The direction of the prevailing winds should also be determined. If at all possible, the playground should not be located downwind from open fields, farms, or areas such as unpaved roads where dust from these sites will blow directly into the play area. In addition, if an area is susceptible to strong winds on a routine basis, some type of windbreak should be created (Thompson, Hudson, & Olsen, 2007).

Climatic conditions that affect playground equipment and surfaces include heat and cold, humidity, and precipitation. As mentioned earlier, temperature extremes directly influence the different materials used for equipment and surfacing. In addition, humidity may affect certain loose-fill surfaces, as well as cause the surfaces of equipment to become slippery and hazardous. An area that has constant precipitation may need to have a cover over the equipment as well as excellent drainage.

Manufactured elements. The second factor to consider in the site analysis is manufactured elements. These include utilities, roads, buildings, adjacent land use, accessibility, and other considerations that could affect or be affected by the playground.

Utilities. As a general rule, playgrounds should not be constructed under utility lines. Also pay attention to unused utility easements. There might be a temptation to use these seemingly open areas, but nothing can stop a utility from using the easement at a later date for power lines. Another utility consideration is the support structures that may be found near the playground site. Power poles and towers can constitute an attractive nuisance in the play area. In addition, guidewires or other supporting cables on these utility structures can create a hazard for children in the area.

Roads. The playground should be located far enough away from roads and parking lots that moving vehicles do not pose a hazard for children. A barrier surrounding the playground is recommended if children may inadvertently run into a street. If fences are used for such barriers, it is recommended that they conform to applicable local building codes (CSPC, 2010). In addition, ASTM has developed a specific standard for fencing around playgrounds (ASTM 300).

Buildings. Proper use zones need to be maintained in relation to any buildings or structures that may be present on the site. For example, a school playground should be located far enough away from the school buildings so that a child on a climbing structure would be in no danger of falling off the play equipment into the building. In addition, close proximity of the playground to windows may encourage vandalism problems.

Adjacent land use. Neighboring land uses need to be considered because they may affect or be affected by the playground (Hudson, Thompson, & Olsen, 2008). Railroads, freeways, landfills, streams, and rivers may contribute to a hazardous environment for children. The long-term effects of some of these items (e.g., waste dumps) may not be determined for years. On the other hand, the location of the playground itself may be seen as a less-than-desirable element within the neighborhood environment. Some people may be upset by the perceived increase of noise, vandalism, and traffic they assume a playground will attract.

Accessibility. Accessibility to and from the site is also a consideration. How will project users get to the playground site? Will it involve children arriving on bicycles, walking, or being brought by cars? The answers to these questions will determine the need for bicycle racks, pathways, and parking lots.

Other considerations. Other considerations may include sources of noise such as airports, railroad lines, roadways, heavy machinery, and factories that can detract from the recreational experiences of playground users. Odors from factories, sewage treatment facilities, and stagnant ponds can have the same effect. Locating a playground adjacent to such detractors should be avoided (Hudson et al., 2008).

Hazardous conditions. A variety of hazardous conditions must be considered before determining the site location of the playground. These include visibility and security, crossings, water, and mixed recreation use zones.

Visibility and security. Visibility and security are primary considerations. Large shrubs (above 4 ft in height) should not be planted around a playground because they inhibit the ability to observe children at play. In addition, as already mentioned, low tree branches (below a height of 7 ft) should be removed to prevent climbing. Trees that will be seriously affected by the development of the playground should also be removed before they create a hazardous situation.

Crossings. Children should not be required to use unprotected crossings to reach playgrounds. Railroad tracks are a similar hazard. Fencing or natural barriers may be necessary if alternative solutions are not feasible (Hudson et al., 2008). Another traffic consideration can occur around schools and child care centers where delivery truck routes may pose a potential hazard for children going to and from the play area. Special care should be given to be certain that these routes do not intersect the play area and are not located nearby.

Water. Water is another site element that may pose a hazardous situation. Children are attracted to ponds, streams, and drainage ditches. Cement culverts or ditches are especially dangerous because their smooth sides may not allow a child easy escape in case of a flash flood. Signage alone will not stop children from trying to incorporate these areas into their play behavior.

Mixed recreation use zones. Mixed recreation use zones can also produce hazardous situations. A soccer field or baseball diamond located too close to a playground is a safety concern because of the chance that errant balls may enter the play area and injure playground users. Locating a playground adjacent to basketball courts, tennis courts, and other similar recreation facilities can also create conflicting access patterns and users.

Preliminary Design

The preliminary design phase is where information about the activity, user, site, and necessary support factors are analyzed and alternative solutions are evaluated. At the end of this step, the actual schematic plans will be developed.

Activity information. What is the purpose of the playground? This fundamental question needs to be answered in terms of performance objectives rather than physical objectives. For instance, if you answer this question by saying the purpose of the playground is to provide slides, swings, and climbing apparatus, then you will limit the possibilities of the play behavior of children. On the other hand, if you answer this question by looking at what children should be able to do, then a different design may result. The philosophical basis for the existence of the play areas must be reflected in the answer to this question. For example, in a school setting, the purpose of the playground should be tied to the educational goals of the total curriculum. Thus, the playground may be designed so that it contributes to a child's understanding of math, language arts, science, and physical education. In a park setting, the playground may reflect the extension of school goals as well as emphasize the physical, emotional, social, and intellectual development of a child. In a child care setting, the play areas should reflect the growth and development of the different ages of young children (Hudson et al., 2008).

Once the philosophical question about the purpose of the playground is answered, the next step is to decide what experience opportunities should be provided. Experience opportunities are ways that the child will participate in the playground experience. Four different experience opportunities are usually present in the playground environment: basic ability level, skill improvement, program participation, and unstructured participation.

Basic ability. This is especially important in planning play environments for young children. Children develop in different stages. For instance, in terms of access on play equipment, ramps provide the easiest way for a small child to get onto equipment, followed by stairways, stepladders, rung ladders, and climbers. Thus, if you wanted to provide basic skill level opportunities, the design of the play structures would incorporate a variety of ramps and small stairways and be built fairly low to the ground.

Skill improvement. This allows for children to develop their abilities in incremental steps. For instance, at age 6, children do not have the upper body strength to control their bodies on overhead ladders. Some intermediate type of equipment is needed between a 6 ft long and a 20 ft long overhead ladder so children can build up the muscle strength and endurance needed to master the higher and longer apparatus without the fear of falling.

Program participation. A playground developed on a school site should be designed to complement the academic offerings of the curriculum. Thus, the design of this playground should have specific equipment pieces and shapes that would supplement the academic program (math, science, art, etc.).

Unstructured participation. In unstructured participation, children are free to roam, explore, discover, and play. Again, this type of experience opportunity demands specific design considerations, including placement of equipment, open sight lines, and easy access.

Not all playgrounds have to emphasize the same experience opportunities. However, if the designer/planner fails to recognize which opportunities should be present, the playground may become only an area where equipment is randomly placed.

User information. A brief profile of the intended users is an important aspect of the planning process. Such a profile should include the age distribution of the intended users, developmental and skill levels, known disabilities, and participation time patterns. In addition, information about participation rates per activity period is necessary to determine the design load of the area in terms of needed equipment units, support areas, and services. Seasonal, monthly, and weekly peak participation periods may be additional planning factors in terms of maintenance and operational considerations.

Site factors. A third consideration in this preliminary design stage is the resource and facility factors that are directly related to the site development. Special requirements, such as the spatial size for the playground area, need to be noted. Preliminary layout of equipment on a grid will allow the planner to visualize traffic flow on and off equipment, relationships of equipment pieces with one another, and space requirements for use zones (Hudson et al., 2008). Other special requirements may be the location of items such as tree limbs, power lines, and telephone wires that can infringe on air space and cause a hazardous situation.

The solar orientation of the space in relation to the placement of equipment is also an important factor. The primary consideration should be to minimize glare and sun blindness during play and avoid hot surfaces on the equipment.

Necessary support factors. Items that are auxiliary to the playground but support the area also need to be considered during this preliminary design stage. These items enhance the aesthetic appearance of the area, contribute to the safety of the children, and provide amenities that create an overall positive experience. Trees, bushes, and other vegetation may need to be planted to provide shade and/or avoid a stark appearance of the playground site. Fencing may be added to keep children safe during play and keep out unwanted animals during other times of the day. Benches, water fountains, and shelter areas may provide children and adults with areas to relax and refresh during their visit to the playground. These support factors and others such as bicycle racks, trash and recycling cans, and security lighting will not suddenly appear unless they are planned for in the preliminary design stage. Furthermore, if they are added later, their placement may not be in congruence with the overall design of the area.

Equipment and Material Selection

Equipment for playgrounds should be designed for public use; be durable; and meet requirements for insurance, standards, warranty, age appropriateness, and use. Any equipment purchased should conform to both CPSC guidelines and ASTM standards F-1487 and F-2373.

Product Compliance

Always require a certificate of compliance with the CPSC guidelines and ASTM standards from the manufacturer prior to the purchase of the equipment. The same type of compliance with ASTM F-1292 should be secured for any surfacing material. If a manufacturer is unable to produce such documentation or will only provide oral assurances of compliance, equipment should be purchased elsewhere (Thompson et al., 2007). In addition, be certain that any equipment purchased for public-use playgrounds is designed for that purpose. Many times, people with good intentions but limited funds will purchase equipment intended for home use and place it in a public setting. This equipment is neither durable nor strong enough to withstand the constant, heavy use that is found in public sites. In addition, the standard for home-use equipment is different than that for public-use equipment.

Product Materials

Playground equipment is usually made out of one of four types of materials: wood, steel, aluminum, or plastic. Each material has its own advantages and disadvantages.

Wood. Wood must be treated to prevent rotting by weather or insects. This is especially true when wood is in direct contact with the ground. Any chemical wood preservative used must be approved for contact with humans. Wood is also subject to splitting and checking, which may eventually weaken the structure. Watch out for evidence of splitting in new wood, especially pieces used as support beams and poles. Sanding and other treatments may be required to avoid injuries from splinters. Although aesthetically pleasing, wooden pieces usually have a life span of only 10 years (Thompson et al., 2007).

Steel. Steel equipment pieces should be galvanized and have a protective coating that inhibits rust such as powder coating and painting. Any paint used should not have lead as a component. It should also be noted that scratches and construction defects are subject to rust. Steel also can heat up to dangerous levels with direct exposure to sunlight. On the other hand, steel equipment pieces are durable and have a long life span.

Aluminum. Aluminum components are rust resistant and offer lightweight installation. Aluminum is sometimes more costly at purchase; however, the reduced maintenance is often worth the extra cost. Shipping charges will be reduced because of the lighter weight. Like steel, aluminum can heat up with direct exposure to sunlight.

Plastic. Plastic can be molded, cut, or formed into a wide variety of shapes for playground use. Because of this, it is a favorite material that many playground manufacturers use. However, most plastics do not have the strength of natural lumbers and metals and can sag and bend. It is recommended that ultraviolet (UV) light inhibitors be added to the plastic to extend the life expectancy and color. Plastic components must meet safety standards (Hudson et al., 2008).

Purchase Factors

Consider at least five factors prior to purchasing equipment or surface materials. These include product liability insurance, compliance with standards, product warranty, age appropriateness, and public-use equipment.

Product liability insurance. Product liability insurance protects the buyer against any accident caused by the design of the equipment. However, if the buyer alters or modifies or fails to maintain the equipment properly, the insurance will not cover the agency. The equipment vendor should furnish the agency with certificates of insurance and original endorsements affecting the coverage. As with all documentation, insurance coverage should be in writing and on file.

Compliance with standards. Compliance with standards should also be documented and on file. Do not buy equipment that does not meet CPSC guidelines and ASTM standards F-1292 for surfacing and F-1487 and F-2373 for equipment. In addition, a certification of proper installation should be obtained from the manufacturer or his or her representative following the final inspection. Once the manufacturer agrees that the playground is in conformance with its installation recommendations, ask for a sign-off letter stating the date of inspection. Make sure that you keep this document on file. It is extremely important should an injury occur due to improper design or installation.

Product warranty. Product warranty simply provides the buyer with the length of time for which products are protected against defects. Many times, the product warranty is a good indication of the product's life expectancy. Again, any modification or repair made without conformance to the manufacturer's guidelines will nullify most warranties.

Age appropriateness. The equipment manufacturer should be notified in writing of the ages of intended users to ensure that age-appropriate equipment is provided at the time of purchase.

Public-use equipment. Public-use equipment is the last item to consider. Not all pieces of equipment are recommended for use in a public playground. The following is a list of equipment to avoid, primarily because the items fail to meet safety guidelines:

- spinning equipment without speed governors,
- tire swings that do not meet requirements for clearance,
- seesaws that do not meet current safety standards,
- heavy swings (metal, wood, animal-type),
- ropes/cables that are not attached at both ends,
- swinging exercise rings and trapeze bars,
- multiple occupancy swings,
- trampolines, and
- homemade equipment.

Final Design

At this stage, it is time to put all the components together in a scaled schematic drawing that shows layout, use zones, site amenities, access points, and other construction details. Accessible routes to the equipment must also be present.

The easiest way to begin this process is to use cutouts or round bubbles to represent the actual equipment and to place these items on a scale grid plan. In this way, it is possible to visualize how the equipment pieces fit together and where potential conflicts of use may arise. Any moving equipment, including swings, should be located away from other structures, preferably at the edge or corner of anticipated traffic patterns. In addition, infants (6 months to 23 months) must be separated from preschool (aged 2 to 5) equipment and from school-aged (aged 5 to 12) equipment.

All equipment has space requirements. Moving the cutouts or squares around can confirm that the use zones of the various equipment pieces do not overlap. Remember that these use zones are minimum guidelines. The authors have seen several instances where slide exits were placed directly in front of swing sets. Although the proper use zone was in place, exuberant children who jumped out of the swings landed directly in front of or to the side of the slide. Of course, the best way to avoid this situation is not to place these two activities near one another.

As mentioned earlier, site amenities should be part of the planning stage. Make sure that the scaled drawings include the placement of benches, bicycle racks, trash cans, and so forth. If these items are not included in the drawings, they might be haphazardly placed later at inappropriate spots.

Before finalizing the drawings, be certain that you have considered traffic flow patterns on and off equipment and general access to the area. Every playground should have at least one accessible route to the equipment that will permit children with disabilities the opportunity to be in the playground area and interact with others. Although the ADA regulations have not been finalized, it is important to understand that just getting to the equipment will not be enough to satisfy the law. Once at the equipment, children with disabilities should be able to access at least some of the equipment, as well as interact with their nondisabled counterparts. Consult the U.S. Access Board for further information on this subject.

Installation

Installation of equipment is important to the overall planning process. If equipment and surfacing are installed improperly, the safety of the total play environment will be jeopardized. When installing equipment and surfacing, consider these three factors: planning of the installation, actual installation of the equipment and surfacing, and liability issues related to the installation.

Planning of the installation. Five items need to be considered during the planning of the installation process: the manufacturer of the equipment, the manufacturer of the surfacing, the materials needed, who will perform the installation, and budgetary factors

Manufacturer of the equipment. This business must be selected carefully. The decision about which manufacturer to use should be made on the basis of the planning committee's criteria. It is critical that the manufacturer decided upon produces equipment that meets the ASTM F-1487 or F-2373 current standards and the CPSC guidelines. After tentatively selecting the manufacturer, the planning committee should talk with others who have purchased equipment from the potential vendor and check the company's competency. The committee should also find out whether the equipment installation process was understandable and reasonable and, most important, how the equipment held up after being installed.

Manufacturer of the surfacing. As with the equipment manufacturer, the surfacing manufacturer should also be selected with care. Again, any decision should be based on the criteria established by the planning committee. The surfacing manufacturer must be able to provide testing data from an independent laboratory to show the depth of the product needed proportionate to the height of the equipment purchased. The testing procedure used must be based on the ASTM F-1292 current standard. In addition, it is a good idea to talk with others who have dealt with the prospective manufacturer to determine the company's competency and service record.

Materials needed. A third item that needs to be considered in the planning process for installation is the materials needed. It is easier to obtain materials in some areas of United States than in others. This will affect their costs. Weather factors have been previously discussed; however, the time of year that installation will occur also needs to be considered. This is especially critical in relation to surfacing and the setting of cement for footings. It is also a consideration for the drying time of preservatives on wood products.

Who will perform the installation? Determining the actual installer(s) is the fourth factor. It is possible to use an installer the company recommends. If that is the decision, the installer should be trained by the company or be a certified installer the company recommends. A trained installer adds to the overall cost of the equipment. Thus, many times, in an effort to reduce costs, the purchaser will decide to use in-house agency personnel to install the equipment and surface. If this method of installation is selected, it is important for liability protection to have a company representative observe the actual installation process or direct the process. Either way, an agency should have the company sign off that the installation process has met the company's specifications (Hudson et al., 2008).

Budgetary factors. The budget for installation is the last item that needs attention. The budget will be determined by the cost factors associated with whom does the installation, the materials needed, and the time it takes to perform the installation. Cutting costs on installation is many times a shortsighted cost savings. As mentioned before, if the equipment is not properly installed or poor materials are used, the playground will cost the agency more money in the long run due to increased maintenance and liability issues.

Installing the equipment and surfacing. Four factors should be considered in relation to the actual installation of the equipment and surfacing: manufacturer's instructions, coordination of the installation, time needed for installation, and manufacturer sign-off.

Manufacturer's instructions. According to ASTM F-1487, the manufacturer or designer must provide clear and concise instructions and procedures for the installation of each structure provided and a complete parts list (ASTM F-1487-07, 2007, or F-2373-08, 2008). It is important that these procedures be followed during the installation process. In addition, these instructions should be filed in case liability issues arise concerning the proper installation of equipment (Thompson et al., 2007).

Coordination of the installation. The next step is to coordinate the installation process. Four potential groups need to interact with one another during installation. These groups include the manufacturer, the owner of the site, the organizer for the personnel who will perform the installation, and the vendors from whom products will be purchased.

Time needed for installation. Time is also an important issue that needs to be considered. In particular, the amount of time needed for the installation will influence the number of people involved in the actual installation process. It must be determined whether the community will tolerate weekend installation or whether the work must be done during usual work hours or in the evenings. If installation takes an extended period of time, protecting children from using partially built structures is a priority.

Manufacturer sign-off. After the installation has been completed, the agency should have the manufacturer of the equipment and surfacing sign off that both items were installed according to specifications. This ensures that the structures and the surfacing are safe for children to use (Hudson et al., 2008).

Liability issues. Because we live in a litigious society, it is important to protect the agency from being sued. Following appropriate procedures will not prevent lawsuits, but it may reduce the amount of financial responsibility that is imposed if a suit is upheld. However, the most important point to remember about following proper installation instructions is not the liability issue, but rather the safety issue. By following manufacturer's instructions, the agency is proactively trying to reduce the potential for children being injured on the playgrounds.

An agency should be concerned with four liability issues regarding the installation of equipment. According to Clement (1988), these are manufacturer's specifications, manufacturer's recommendations, the posting of manufacturer's warnings, and the importance of following manufacturer's instructions.

Manufacturer's specifications. It is critical that the agency be certain that the installer follows the manufacturer's specifications for installation. The responsibility for this falls on the manufacturer if the company performs the installation. If the agency does the actual installation, it assumes the liability and the burden of proof regarding the following of proper procedures.

Manufacturer's recommendations. Any recommendations the manufacturer makes must also be followed. For example, to properly deal with the impact attenuation of a surface, it may be recommended that pea gravel be separated from a wood product by use of a fabric. Once the materials are installed, it is the agency's responsibility to see that such a separation is continued. Other recommendations might include that bushings on swings be checked annually for wear or that wood products be covered with a preservative on an annual basis. In each of these cases, it is imperative that the agency follows the manufacturer's recommendations (Thompson et al., 2007).

Posting of manufacturer's warnings. The agency must post the manufacturer's warnings that are included with materials. Many manufacturers now place labels on equipment that suggest ages for which the equipment is designed or the proper depth for loose-fill surface materials. In cases where warnings accompany playground equipment, the agency is responsible for replacing the warnings if they become illegible, are destroyed, or are removed. Diligence on the part of the agency in regard to the posting of the warning label will inform adults about ways to prevent a child from being injured.

Following manufacturer's instructions. Last, following manufacturer's instructions is extremely important in the installation of equipment. These instructions should include the proper use zone placement of equipment, the installation of the equipment at the proper depths, the correct method of mixing adhesives for surfacing materials, the correct proportions for mixing cement with water, and the use of proper tools to lock joints of structures. The agency may need to be able to provide evidence that such procedures were followed. As adults work with installation, they can conclude that they are dealing literally with the dirt of responsibility, the grit of reality, and the grind of responsibility.

Ongoing maintenance, repair, and inspections. The playground area should be perceived as an environment for play that contains many elements including playground equipment (Hendy, 1997). Parking lots, sidewalks, field areas, seating, shelters, and restroom facilities are only a few of the amenities that complement many playground areas. These amenities require maintenance as well. To ensure proper long-term maintenance, a comprehensive program must include the total playground environment, not just the equipment.

Maintenance. The basic function of maintenance is to ensure the safety of users by keeping the playground area and equipment in a safe condition. Maintenance also keeps the equipment functioning efficiently and effectively. A track ride is not much fun if the bearings are worn and the mechanism will not glide easily. Maintenance is also performed to keep the area hygienic. An area that is well maintained remains aesthetically pleasing.

Repair. A safety audit should be performed when new equipment is purchased and installed to verify that the equipment and installation are consistent with the standard of care set forth by the agency and the manufacturer. The audit will not need to be repeated unless the standard of care changes, the equipment is heavily vandalized, or a natural disaster impacts the equipment.

Inspections. There are basically two types of maintenance inspections that are performed on playground equipment: seasonal (periodic) and daily (high frequency). A seasonal or periodic inspection is one performed two to three times a year. This is an in-depth type of inspection to evaluate the general wear and tear on the equipment. A daily or high frequency inspection is done routinely to identify rapidly changing conditions due to weather, vandalism, and sudden breakage. It also identifies surfacing problems typically associated with loose-fill surfacing materials.

There is no magic formula for determining the frequency necessary to perform each type of maintenance inspection. How often the playground is used and by what age group are two common considerations that will determine frequency of inspection. The vandalism rate in an area will also dictate the timetable chosen to inspect the playground.

The nature of the area and the environment will influence the need for playground maintenance. The soil type and drainage conditions, as well as other geographic and climatic conditions, will also influence inspection frequency.

Record keeping. Inspections, repairs, and maintenance should be recorded regularly. In addition, the agency must establish a system of work requests that will enable maintenance staff to expedite the ordering of replacement parts and repair services. As part of the overall comprehensive program of playground maintenance, documentation of all inspections and maintenance procedures is important. A fail-proof follow-up system must be established that enables a supervisor to review the inspection forms, noting

- who performed the inspection;
- items that were corrected on-site at the time of inspection;
- hazards that need to be corrected;
- work orders that were issued;
- purchase orders for equipment services or replacement parts;
- when equipment, parts, or services were supplied or rendered;
- when repair work was completed;
- who performed the repair work; and
- final approval from the supervisor.

Designing Facilities for Parks and Recreation

Kimberly J. Bodey, *Indiana State University*
John H. Pommier, *Indiana State University*
Thomas H. Sawyer, *Indiana State University*

Park and recreation departments aim to build communities and connect citizens through leisure, fitness, and education opportunities. Recreation centers may improve the quality of life for patrons as well as entice new businesses and create jobs in the local area. Park and recreation facilities experience a multitude of trends that impact the planning process. Although planning principles do not typically change, inputs to the planning process are undergoing substantial change.

The last decade may be characterized by a variety of trends, including

- changing participation rates in existing recreation and leisure activities;
- expanding new recreation activities, such as in adventure recreation and exergaming;
- a greater recognition of how cultural and ethnic background impacts the type of recreation and recreation facilities;
- a greater understanding and recognition of women's needs in recreation;
- a changing population and household composition;
- marked increase of health-associated concerns;
- dramatic innovations in leisure equipment technology;
- the impact of electronic media and burgeoning electronic marketplace;
- changes in world energy and the growing green movement;
- changes in regional economies;
- increased demand for sustainable operations;
- unstable political environments; and
- the slowdown of the economy and resultant impact on recreation facility development, construction, and services.

Facilities and open spaces must clearly be conceptualized and designed to accommodate the dramatic changes occurring in America. The public will need to continue its involvement in the planning process.

General Planning Issues

A Master Plan Concept

The planning process, regardless of the size of the community involved, typically occurs at three levels. First, there must be a master plan conceptualized at the policy-making level. Second, there is a concept plan that deals with physical matters in that it is site specific and incorporates factors associated with layout, facility relations, construction, and landscaping. Third is the planning stage, which focuses on operation and maintenance for facilities, parks, and open spaces. All three levels are critical to sound planning (see Chapters 3 and 4); however, the master plan level is the most important because it is at the policy-making level where critical initial decisions are made that guide and control all future decisions at the second and third levels of planning.

Community Involvement

Plans for new recreation, park, and open spaces and proposed improvements to existing facilities and areas must reflect, as suggested within the master plan concept, the wants and needs of the community. Public cooperation and involvement in the initial planning stages will strengthen community interest, both politically and financially. There are many ways to involve the public in the planning process. One is the public meeting. Although time consuming, a series of well-organized public meetings is an effective means to present proposed plans and receive necessary feedback. Public meetings are effective in bringing moderate-sized groups of people together; however, even well-planned meetings typically do not draw large crowds. In many communities, large crowds are generated by controversy over proposed planning.

Although the public meeting has been a marginally successful method in the past and should not be discarded, it cannot be the only method. Other methods of involving the public are also effective and may provide useful information. These include face-to-face focus groups (e.g., small groups of eight to 12 purposefully chosen people from the community), individual interviews with key informants, and presentations to service clubs, religion-based organizations, or special interest groups. Increasingly, administrators have relied on social networking sites to promote availability and access to online forums frequently housed on the agency's homepage.

A survey of leisure behavior and attitudes can be useful in determining the needs and desires of the people within the planning area. Surveys can be conducted by mail, phone, or Internet. Conducting a successful survey requires a carefully constructed process, and even then many people may be wary of responding. Surveys can be costly and, if not well constructed, might not provide usable information for the agency. Using consultants in the process is strongly encouraged.

Another method used to strengthen proposals is interagency agreements for shared use and funding of facilities. Also, cooperation between community agencies and organized groups facilitates planning, promotes financial considerations, and ensures community involvement.

Rebuild or Renovate?

Facility planners are increasingly faced with the question of whether to rebuild or renovate older recreation space, infrastructure, and design. Decision making is largely based on an assessment of what the community would like to change. Consider two types of obsolescence: physical and functional. Physical obsolescence pertains to problems related to layout, ventilation, floors, lighting, or meeting current standards and codes to manage the facility. Functional obsolescence simply means patrons do not enjoy the activities the facility has to offer. To manage functional obsolescence, planners must ask the question, what can be done to increase the recreational values of this facility? To a large extent, the answer lies in understanding community demographics and preferences. There is no one-size-fits-all design. Every facility must be tailored to fit the unique needs and wants of the intended users.

Planning Considerations for Urban Areas

Rapidly growing urban population centers have placed open space at a premium. This has led to growing public concern about recreational facilities and services. The following factors must be considered when planning recreational facilities within congested urban areas:

- Declining availability of open space and limited economic resources make it essential that multijurisdiction government agencies cooperate in planning facilities areas. Recreational use of public housing facilities, the presence of social and health care programs in recreation centers, and parks and trails jointly administered by multiple jurisdictions are a few examples of ways in which the public can maximize facility use.
- Multiple and not necessarily compatible uses of facilities, both public and private, should be considered. For example, if properly planned, the parking lot of an industrial plant can be used for recreation activities on evenings and weekends with little or no additional cost.
- The mobility of people in dense urban areas is often restricted. Therefore, facilities must be easily accessible to the people by sidewalks, bike paths, bus and train routes, and so forth.
- All facilities and associated elements need to meet the requirements of the Americans With Disabilities Act (1990).

Multiple-Use Facilities

Planning facilities for multiple uses is a major consideration in establishing recreation areas. Multiple-use facilities require space that can accommodate varied activities for all user groups during various times of the day, week, month, season, or year. The traditions of seasonal activities have lessened. Technology allows most weather-dependent activities to be conducted year-round (e.g., video golf). Furthermore, single sports have developed year-round training programs and competitive participation opportunities (e.g., summer basketball league). Facilities that are planned to accommodate a single use become an expensive investment if allowed to stand idle much of the year. Evolving recreation preferences require that indoor and outdoor areas not be restricted with permanent spatial and architectural fixtures designed for specific activities in a set period of time. There must be flexibility built into indoor and outdoor facilities.

The character and location of the population are constantly changing. The ethnic, socioeconomic, and demographic features such as family makeup can vary within neighborhoods. With today's mobile population, a community facility that is planned on the basis of a static population soon has many obsolete features. Yet failing to plan for a neighborhood's ethnic and cultural foundations also means the facilities may not be used to meet user needs and wants effectively. Only in recent years have recreation and park planners realized that recreation patterns are strongly affected by ethnic background and culture. Understanding these cultural impacts allows planners to develop facilities that meet specific needs and wants and can be adapted for different populations.

Eliminating Architectural Barriers

It is essential that all recreation facilities be designed to serve people with disabilities. Therapeutic recreation services for people with disabilities need to be considered in the planning process to ensure that activities and facilities will serve them. Guidelines for eliminating architectural barriers are detailed in Chapter 4.

Green Design

There are many positive outcomes related to green design. Green design protects the planet and reduces a facility's operating costs through energy efficiency and water conservation and promotes occupant health and productivity through improved air quality. Moreover, green design enhances a building's marketability and helps to create a sustainable community.

The USGBC's Leadership in Energy and Environmental Design (LEED) rating system is the known standard for designing, constructing, and operating green facilities. Specifically, being "green" means those design and construction practices significantly reduce or eliminate the negative impact of buildings on the environment and occupants in five areas: sustainable site planning, safeguarding water and water efficiency, energy efficiency and renewable energy, conservation of materials and resources, and indoor environmental quality. As with any facility plan, green design does not have a one-size-fits-all approach. Trade-offs exist that must be considered in relation to resource availability and community needs and wants. However, the capacity to select materials that meet LEED criteria is made easier by the availability of certification programs and online product directories administered by unbiased organizations.

Many new construction projects consider LEED certification, but administrators may not follow through because of the additional architect-based fees (e.g., permits) that are affiliated with LEED certifications. Fees will typically amass an additional 10% (or greater) expense of the total construction cost (i.e., $50 million project would encumber an additional $5 million expense for the potential LEED certification). Materials and construction costs are typically not the primary deterrents; therefore, projects are completed in a "green" fashion by being constructed within LEED-certified parameters. These projects are referenced as "LEED certifiable."

Indoor Recreation and Community Centers

Neighborhoods, quadrants, communities, and cities form the basic units for planning facilities, programs, and activities. The park and recreation agency, to plan and manage its services properly, establishes its facilities, programs, and activities given the demands of its designated service populations. The larger the planning and managing agency is, the broader the population groups with which the agency will be concerned.

Authors and organizations have historically provided classifications for types of recreation facilities based on service areas. Some larger communities have created their own standards for recreation facilities. Yet there remains no commonly accepted standard for the number of people a recreation center should serve or what should be contained in a recreation center. Even with this knowledge, common terminologies for recreation centers can be suggested. Recreation planners have learned that communities have different expectations for services, and the cookie-cutter approach used in the 1960s and 1970s has given way to unique facilities designed to meet community members' desires. Recreation centers should be planned to meet the needs and interests of all people in the neighborhood or community. They should provide a safe, healthful, and attractive atmosphere in which each user may enjoy his or her leisure by participating in activities of a social, inspirational, cultural, or physical nature.

Recreation centers vary in design from the rustic to the contemporary. Present day buildings provide for adaptability and multiple uses. This change from the simple to the complex has stimulated the development of a variety of recreation centers. These are classified by function and size. The size of a recreation center is usually based on the population to be served and the programs and activities to be conducted.

Recreation and Community Center Types

There are different types of recreation centers based on community needs. Traditionally, the two main types have been neighborhood recreation centers and community recreation centers.

Neighborhood centers. The facility that is, perhaps, closest to the grassroots service level is the neighborhood center. A neighborhood center is designed to service a specific area of the city. Such a building encloses 15,000 sq ft to 30,000 sq ft. The size will depend on whether the building is a separate entity or part of a school–park complex where activity spaces are available in the school.

The neighborhood center usually includes
- multipurpose room or rooms,
- gymnasium (if not available in neighborhood school),
- shower and locker rooms when a gymnasium is provided,
- arts and crafts room,
- multimedia/computer/technology room and library,
- fitness and aerobics room,
- dance and aerobics room,
- child care area,
- kitchen,
- restrooms,

- lounge and lobby,
- office, and
- large storage areas.

Community center. The community recreation center functions beyond the primary purpose of serving a neighborhood. It is designed to meet the complete recreation needs of all the people in the community. The size of the building depends on the number of people to be served, the projected programs and activities plan, and whether the building is a separate entity or part of a school–park complex. This building contains 20,000 sq ft to 75,000 sq ft of space and is usually located in a designated recreation area such as a school–park site or community park.

The community center usually includes

- multipurpose rooms that can be organized into one large room and multiple smaller rooms;
- gymnasium;
- climbing apparatus and tower;
- shower and locker rooms;
- stage and auditorium (sometimes combined with gymnasium);
- artistic expression spaces for art, dance, music, and drama;
- game room;
- kitchen;
- restrooms;
- lounge and lobby;
- office and security station;
- large storage areas;
- clubs or classrooms;
- seniors area;
- fitness and exergaming areas;
- dance, yoga, and aerobics room;
- child care area;
- multimedia, computer, or technology room;
- teen or preteen area;
- program specialized areas such as racquet courts, gymnastics, weight and exercise room, photography workshop, or culinary room; and
- picnic and barbeque areas.

Supercenters. There is a new type of recreation center, frequently referred to as a supercenter, which ranges from 80,000 sq ft to well over 100,000 sq ft. Supercenters reflect the commercial trend of creating large, one-stop shopping superstores. The supercenter meets consumer expectations by providing for diverse recreational needs and wants in a single location.

The supercenter typically serves a large metropolitan area or may serve several adjacent communities. The facility is usually not linked to a school–park complex. The size of the facility allows for both indoor and outdoor activity spaces.

The supercenter might, for example, include a water park rather than a traditional swimming pool and have water play equipment, slides and sprayers, lazy river and wave riders, and the like. It usually has large fitness, aerobics, and gymnasium areas and an indoor track. It is likely to have multiple specialized rooms such as preschools, arts and crafts rooms, teen and preteen areas, or a photography room. Most rooms are designed to be multiple use. Adjustable walls allow rooms to be configured in different sizes so groups of 10 or 15 people can be accommodated as well as groups of several hundred people. The child care area allows parents or guardians to leave preschool-aged children in a licensed day care setting while school-aged children and adults participate in activities.

There is no single common design for a supercenter; however, using computers to track facility use, manage the facility and programs, and track maintenance and security operations is mandatory. Patrons expect wireless capacity in the diverse spaces. Open space that is inviting and comfortable is essential. There is usually a single entry that has a front desk monitored by knowledgeable staff members who help patrons find where they need to go, check for membership, take registration for classes, and monitor building use.

Specialized Rooms

Multipurpose Room

The multipurpose room should be designed to accommodate activities such as general meetings, social recreation, active table games, dancing, dramatics, music, concerts, banquets, and the like. The area of this room should be approximately 2,000 sq ft to 3,000 sq ft. It should be rectangular in shape, with a minimum width of 40 ft. The minimum ceiling height should be 16 ft.

Many types of flooring surfaces are available. Wood flooring, usually maple, is always a favorite, but it requires considerable upkeep and does not respond well to some uses. Composite flooring such as a poured or a rollout type of floor is as costly as a wood floor but is highly versatile. The floor should have a nonskid surface to prevent many common accidents.

Gymnasium

If a single court is constructed then the structure should be at least 90 ft x 100 ft with a minimum height of 24 ft. This size will permit a basketball court of 50 ft x 84 ft with additional room for telescopic bleachers seating approximately 325 spectators on one side of the gymnasium. Community centers and supercenters will have multiple courts side by side, typically with 12 ft between the courts. Vinyl walls with netting that descends from the ceiling when desired may be used to separate courts.

Multiple-court gymnasiums will usually have seating for just one court, and it is retractable. Provision should be made for a mechanical ventilating system with air-conditioning considered where climate dictates. It is preferable to have no windows in the gymnasium. However, if desired, windows should be placed at right angles to the sun at a height of 12 ft or more, and the windows should be equipped with protective guards. The wainscoting, or tile, in the gymnasium should provide clear, unobstructed wall space from the floor to a height of 12 ft. Many recreation centers are moving to portable standards or retractable goals, thus removing the basketball-dedicated areas from multiple-use structures.

Floors with synthetic surfaces have become predominant in recreation gymnasiums. Maple flooring continues to be selected as a preferred alternative to a synthetic surface, usually when the floor will have limited conflicting use. If maple flooring is used, the cork spring clip or other type of expansion joint should be installed on all four sides. If suspended apparatus requiring wall attachments is used in the gymnasium, these attachments should be at least 7 ft above floor level.

Recessed drinking fountains should be located where they will cause minimal interference. Fountains should be hand or hand-and-foot operated with up-front spouts and controls. Protective floor covering or drainage at the base of the fountain should be considered to avoid floor damage and slipping hazards.

Locker and Shower Rooms

Locker and shower rooms should be provided for physical activities, athletics, staff, and so forth. When designing or remodeling a locker and shower room, planners should focus on three basic considerations: durability, maintainability, and cleanliness (see Chapter 6). A recent trend is for recreation centers to have multiple locker rooms. Typically, facilities have space for adult women, adult men, and families. An additional option is to design spaces for female and male patrons between ages 8 and 17.

Family-friendly spaces are characterized by their barrier-free entrances, privacy corridors, child-sized sinks and toilets, and a sizable number of hooks and shelves for child-sized gear. The cabana design is often used in the family area and is popular among senior patrons who appreciate the extra space and private changing areas.

Stage and Auditorium

A stage and related facilities were traditionally built in conjunction with the gymnasium or multipurpose room. Contemporary facilities feature separate stages or work with community groups that provide auditorium space. The stage proper should be about 20 ft in depth, and the proscenium opening should be at least two thirds of the width of the crafts area.

The approach to the stage from the floor of the main room should be by inclined ramp with a nonskid surface to promote patron access and to facilitate movement of equipment. The room should be designed to allow for a portable public address system with matched speakers and be equipped with outlets for additional microphones and audiovisual equipment. When possible, a master control from the office of the building should be considered. All stage lighting should be modern and should be controlled from a dimmer control cabinet equipped with a rheostat or professional lighting console.

The base and wall of the room should be equipped with electrical outlets to accommodate floor and table lamps, motion picture equipment, floodlights, and other electrical apparatus. Heavy-voltage electric lines may be necessary. Projection equipment built into the ceiling, wireless systems, and areas where technological equipment can be accessed and used is also desirable.

The entrance should contain double doors. Stage doors should be of sufficient width and height to move scenery. It is desirable to have a door at the rear of the stage area to permit the handling of stage properties and scenery. Door frames and thresholds must be flush with the floor to permit transfer of large objects. Adequate exit doors should be provided and be equipped with panic hardware.

Space should be provided for the storage of chairs, tables, and portable staging. This space can be under the stage or in an adjacent storage room provided with dollies that have swivel ball-bearing fiber or rubber-covered casters.

Acoustics are an important factor in an auditorium and should be kept in mind when selecting materials for walls and ceilings. Rigid acoustical materials for ceilings are more economical and discourage vandalism better than suspended acoustical tile.

The entrance to the auditorium should contain double doors and should be at the end opposite the stage. Each door should have a minimum unobstructed opening of at least 32 in. with a removable mullion.

Game Room

The game room should be approximately 30 ft x 64 ft in size. It is designed for a variety of games including pool or billiards, table tennis, and foosball, as well as console video and computer games or popular board games. The plan for this room should provide sufficient storage space for the various items of game equipment and supplies.

This room should be close to office supervision and should be acoustically treated. The choice of floor material should be carefully considered because of the heavy traffic anticipated in this room. Windows may be placed high in the walls to reduce glass breakage. A chair rail or wainscoting to prevent the marring of walls should be installed to a height of 3 ft above the floor, but wall damage to 6 ft in height should be anticipated. Whenever possible, noncontact (non-marring) furniture should be used.

Kitchen

A kitchen is desirable for most community and neighborhood recreation centers. There is a choice between having a warming kitchen where the food is prepared elsewhere and brought on-site and served or having a full-service kitchen. Warming kitchens have become popular with food preparation done either by a vendor or in a centralized kitchen. All kitchens must meet local and state health board requirements and are subject to regular inspections. The kitchen should be located near the multipurpose rooms and the gymnasium. The kitchen is sometimes placed between two multipurpose rooms and made available to both rooms by the use of aluminum roll-up doors.

Adequate storage space, cabinet space, and electrical outlets for appliances such as the refrigerator, range, microwave oven, dishwasher, and can openers should be provided. Exhaust fans should also be installed.

Arts and Crafts Room

A separate room for arts should conform to local health regulations and have an open floor space at least 15 ft x 15 ft. Ample storage cabinets, closets, or lockers should be included for the safe storage of craft materials, unfinished projects, and exhibit materials. Base and wall outlets should be provided in all club rooms for the operation of electric irons, sewing machines, power tools, movie projectors, and other equipment. If a kiln is used, it should be equipped with a heavy-duty 220-V electrical outlet. Bulletin boards and exhibit cases may be used to display completed projects.

Computer Room

A computer room may have few or many computers and is open to the general public. The room is networked and ideally linked to a T1 line for fast Internet access. It is best to work with information technology (IT) experts to design and manage the network. Issues of security and keeping inappropriate material off the computers are major concerns for most IT managers and recreation staff. Many recreation centers are now organized for wireless access from anywhere in the building.

Information Desk, Lobby, and Community Area

The information desk and lobby is located at the entrance of the recreation center. The information desk is the first contact point for all recreation center users and should be positioned to provide staff a direct line of sight with the entrance area. The counter should be accessible for all patrons. This area has computer terminals and is networked. It provides space for information distribution and registration.

Depending on the size of the center, season, and time of day, it may be staffed by one to five individuals. The adjacent lobby is spacious, so when a number of people are present it does not feel crowded and provides a queue area when needed. It provides access to the remainder of the building. The community area should open off the lobby and, if possible, should be close to the central office and to other recreation center features.

The community area and lobby are often combined into one space. This area should be attractively lighted and should contain a wall-mounted and recessed drinking fountain, comfortable seating, television monitors, wireless access, and other amenities. Adequate space, preferably recessed, and electrical and water connections for automatic vending machines may be included.

Carpet floor covering is desirable; however, terrazzo, quarry tile, and patio tile are preferred when cigarette damage is a possibility in facilities that allow smoking.

Office

Each office area for administrative, supervisory, and building staff has a different function and should be designed with specific tasks and responsibilities in mind. The administrative area may be the primary office for the recreation and park department and should be separate from the entrance to the building. It will be in the same building, but, because of the function, should not be in the main flow of traffic. Supervisory and building staff should be closer to the action. Building staff should be located so they can see the day-to-day operations of the facility. This places them in the flow of activities so that they are available to handle routine challenges and needs. However, provision must be made to ensure privacy when dealing with disciplinary problems, staff meetings, and the like. Secretarial and program offices should be adjacent to the director's office.

Storage Areas

One of the most common errors in planning recreation centers is lack of sufficient storage space for equipment, maintenance, and custodial purposes. An area adjacent to the gymnasium should be provided for such storage. It should have an 8 ft wide roll-up door opening with flush, louvered doors and a flush threshold to permit passage of the most bulky equipment. The minimum size of the storage room should be 800 sq ft to 1,200 sq ft. Provision should be made for storage of inflated balls, bats, softballs, and other supplies, either in separate cabinets or a special closet. Appropriate bins, shelves, and racks are suggested. In addition, a recessed alcove for the storage of a piano is desirable. Storage rooms should be located strategically throughout the building to support specialized needs as well as to reduce the amount of time to move equipment into rooms.

The maintenance storage room varies in size depending on the adjacent outdoor space and the size of the building. The room is ordinarily located on the ground level adjacent to the outdoor areas. An outside entrance should be provided by means of a burglar-resistant door large enough to permit the passage of motorized maintenance equipment. Recessed wall shelving and cabinet storage should be provided for tools, supplies, and equipment. This space should contain hot and cold water, a slop sink, a lavatory, a water closet, and a clothes closet. The floor should be concrete and pitched to a central drain. The junction of the floor and wall should be covered. A supply closet equipped with a utility sink and space for mops, pails, brooms, and cleaning supplies should be centrally located on each floor level.

Meeting and Multipurpose Rooms

Experience indicates the desirability of providing a minimum of 1,000 sq ft of floor space per meeting room. For community recreation centers, at least three to five rooms should be provided for multiple use. At least one large club room should be adjoined to a kitchen or warming room. The rooms may use moveable walls to increase or decrease classroom size.

When windows are placed high in a wall, they are not broken as often as low windows and they also allow more space for furniture, bulletin boards, pegboards, chalkboards, and exhibits. A nonbreakable type of window pane is preferred. Windows may be omitted and sky domes and vent domes may be used, thus eliminating the need for draperies, venetian blinds, and curtains—all items subject to vandalism.

A chair rail or wainscoting to prevent the marring of walls should be installed to a height of 3 ft above the floor. When possible, noncontact (non-marring) furniture should be used. Floor-level radiant heat in rooms where programs for small children will be conducted should be considered.

Photography Room

A special room can be equipped as a darkroom. Ventilation should be provided through lightproof ventilators. Hot and cold running water, special light outlets (both wall and base), and photographic sinks for developing and washing prints should also be provided. A mixer is desirable to control the water temperatures accurately. A filter should also be provided if the water quality is not good. Doors must be lightproof.

Music Room

The size of the music room should be determined by the potential number in the choral or instrumental group using this facility at any given time. A guide commonly used is to allow 20 sq ft for each participant. Provision should be made for the storage of music, instruments, band uniforms, and supplies. Cabinets and shelves that may be locked are commonly used to store music equipment.

Auxiliary Gymnasium

The auxiliary gymnasium (see also Chapter 22) is for activities such as wrestling, weight lifting, tumbling, gymnastics (see Figure 15.1), fencing, and apparatus work. Acoustical treatment for this room is desirable. The size of the room and height of the ceiling will depend on the various activities for which this facility will be used. The floor should be treated with material that will withstand the use of equipment such as heavy weights.

At least one well-ventilated storage room will be needed for equipment and supplies used in the auxiliary gymnasium. If the apparatus is to be cleared from this room, an additional apparatus storage room should be provided.

Specialized Recreation Centers

Many cities and communities provide recreation programs that require specialized facilities. Although the construction of these facilities can be justified in the majority of cases, care must be taken to provide for maximum year-round use. The specialized centers should be centrally located to serve all the public.

Art Center

In recent years, many cities have constructed community art centers to satisfy the public demand for programs in the arts. The size of the facility will be determined by the number of people to be served and type of art programs to be conducted. Generally, art centers will include work areas for ceramics, sculpture, painting, and sketching. Depending on the interests in the community, a center may also include facilities for woodworking, lapidary, stonecutting, and other arts and crafts. Some art centers also include facilities for dance, music, and drama classes and programs.

Preschool Center

Preschool centers for day care, Head Start, and nursery school programs are being built in some communities with the aid of grants or federal funds. These buildings are smaller than neighborhood center buildings, and the design scale is geared to preschool children. Generally, the centers include a large multipurpose room, rooms for small group activities, an office, a kitchen and eating area, and ample storage space. Special care should be taken to ensure good acoustic treatment in the center.

Senior Citizen Centers

Senior citizen centers are similar in design to neighborhood recreation centers. However, more emphasis is placed on spaces for conversation and stationary recre-

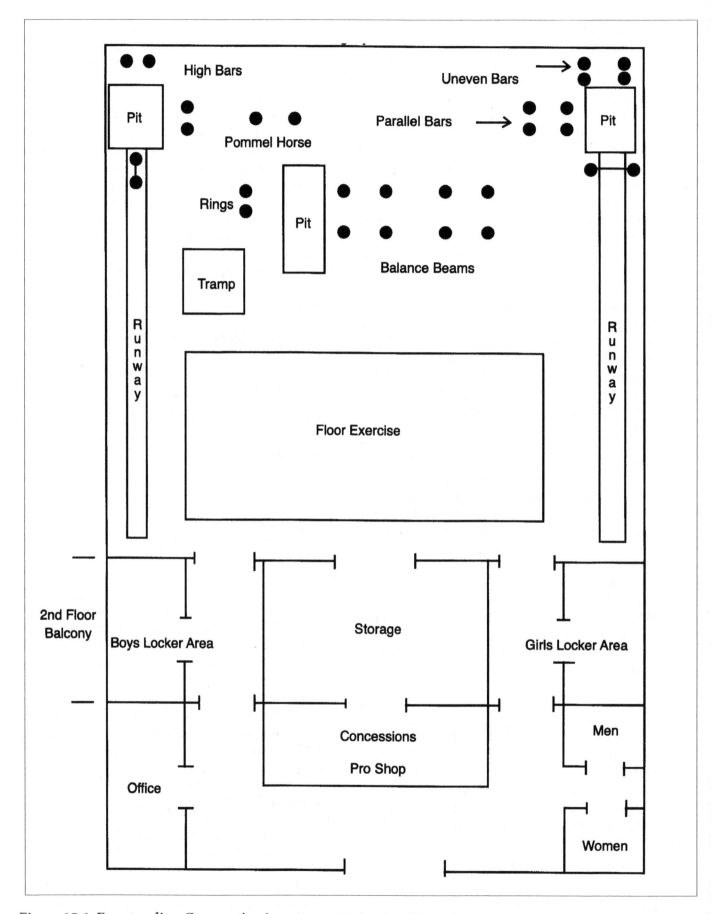

Figure 15.1. **Freestanding Gymnastics Area** (*Source:* Meghan Rosselli)

ation activities (e.g., cards or dominoes) and educational activities (e.g., physician or accountant talks) than for large-scale physical activities. Although a gymnasium is seldom found in a senior citizen area, a large multipurpose room is needed for dancing, games (e.g., shuffleboard), and health and wellness activities (e.g., yoga). A kitchen offers the opportunity of serving low-cost meals. The senior citizen center should be a single-floor building, and special care should be taken to eliminate all hazards such as steps and protrusions on walls.

Aquatic Center (Natatorium)

Many neighborhoods and communities have a considerable interest in water activities and demand that an aquatic center (see also Chapter 13) be included as part of the recreation center. A combination of learn-to-swim and therapy spaces, lap lanes, wave pools, lazy rivers, wave riders, and water playgrounds is becoming more common. As with any good design, several factors such as local competition, demographics, geography, and community expectations and backing must be considered. Mixing the types of aquatic attractions makes more effective use of available space and serves a larger clientele.

A recent trend in new facilities is to have separate systems to control different bodies of water. In a single system design, the entire facility may be shut down for water treatment. In contrast, a separate system design allows for different water temperatures, shutting down low activity spaces, or treating contaminated spaces without closing the entire facility.

Teen Centers

Although teen centers have been popular and continue to be built, the trend today is to construct multiuse centers that will provide opportunities for teen programs along with other activities. For example, a teen office and lounge are provided in many community recreation centers.

When a separate teen center is desired, it could include

- multipurpose meeting rooms;
- gymnasium;
- skatepark;
- shower and locker rooms;
- game room;
- multimedia computer or technology room;
- music, art, and theater areas;
- conversation areas;
- restrooms;
- lounge and lobby; and
- office and security station.

Other Specialized Spaces or Facilities

The planning of any specialized recreation center demands a precise and logical approach. Because a recreation center reflects the unique needs and interests of a neigh-

borhood or community, the specific design will vary, but the preliminary considerations of planning objectives will be the same. Types of spaces include fitness rooms, weight rooms, running tracks, child care, aerobics, and a multimedia center. The successful incorporation of accepted planning objectives will ensure maximum use of the building. The initial functional/spatial specification and the continuous reevaluation of the architectural specifications of the building prior to its construction should be considered in terms of the following checklist for indoor recreation facilities:

- Has the most efficient and effective use of the entire structure been determined?
- Does the preliminary sketch include all the essential activity spaces necessary to fulfill the program objectives?
- Does the layout provide for flexibility in use and for future expansion?
- Does the floor plan permit convenient access to and facilitate circulation within the building?
- Does the floor plan provide for ease of supervision and administration of the building?
- Have individual rooms been located to encourage multiple use within safety limits?
- Has the building been designed to ensure opportunity for its use by all members of the community, including children, older persons, and individuals with disabilities?
- Has the building been designed to minimize the impact on the environment and occupants?
- Does the design encompass accepted aesthetic qualities that relate harmoniously to the surroundings?
- Is the building designed to ensure cooperative use with other public or private agencies?
- Is the building designed to be sustainable when considering daily operations and subsequent maintenance of the facility?

Outdoor Facilities and Open Spaces

Population growth projections suggest that few metropolitan areas in the United States have sufficient open space to meet the demands of the future. Based on these projections, it is imperative that planning boards and commissions on all levels of government review previous planning philosophies with the intent of revision or, when necessary, the development of new master plans.

As open space becomes more expensive and less available, greater consideration must be given to multiple use of available lands and every measure must be taken to use them efficiently and consistently with good environmental management. Municipal and school authorities should acquire, plan, and develop areas for joint use. This process calls for professional guidance in the fields of planning, designing, and engineering and for the advice and counsel of professionals in the fields of education, recreation, community development, and park planning.

The most efficient and successful planning is accomplished when everyone in the organization, particularly those who will be identified with the finished product, have an opportunity to participate in the planning. Those who are to be served also should have a voice in the planning through community meetings.

Standards

Various standards for the size, location, and number of educational and recreation areas and facilities have been proposed over the years by persons with a great deal of operations experience. These standards are formulated to make possible a program to serve the basic needs of people for physical education and recreation. However, they are not valid in prescribing specific activities or facilities for every neighborhood. Although they are a useful guide in the acquisition and construction of a property, standards can seldom, if ever, be applied completely or without modification because a typical or common situation is seldom found. Standards are formulated to provide a basis for the intelligent development of local plans. Therefore, the standards for areas and facilities should be reviewed and appraised for each planning unit and modified whenever changing conditions warrant revision.

Standards for areas and facilities developed by private planning firms, public agencies, and service organizations at the local, state, and national levels have been widely endorsed throughout the United States and have provided the basis for recommendations in scores of long-range plans for school, park, and recreation systems. The proposal that at least 1 acre of recreation and park space be set aside by urban areas for every 100 members of the present and estimated future population has been more widely accepted than any other space standard. However, this standard does not relate to the demographic or physiographic character of particular locales and is becoming obsolete. Professional and governmental authorities, including the National Recreation and Park Association and the National Park Service, have previously suggested the desirability of providing a higher ratio of land-to-population in towns and small cities.

Modification of this general standard has been suggested for all planning entities based upon local requirements for populated cities. Some municipal planning officials believe that developing large outlying properties owned by the municipality will help meet the recognized deficiency in the inner municipality. However, this proposal should be considered as a practicable substitute indicative not only of necessity but also of feasibility.

Previous number standards were related to the number of tennis courts or swimming pools per thousand people. Such numbers do not consider the land or people and the climatic and geographic locale of the planning entity. The specification and allocation of facilities per thousand are arbitrary. They neither reflect the requirements of the community or neighborhood nor are universally applicable. A planning process of interaction and participation by the public should determine the number of facilities from one end of the community to the other.

Recreation acreage should be based on potential usage. Basing acreage and number of facilities on potential usage has serious deficiencies but remains the best possible approach. Marketing demand studies can suggest levels of use but do not account for changing recreation patterns, changes in the economy, unanticipated competition, and the like. Guidelines for acreage allocations for different park types are only illustrative. Every activity has a public demand. The demand for some activities is often met by the commercial, nonprofit, or volunteer sector. Ski lodges, tennis centers, and other corporations all conduct market studies to ascertain the leisure needs of and probable use by their clientele. Public agencies must conduct comparable studies to analyze demand. If the municipality can ascertain the probable use, turnover, capacity, and low/peak load for each activity, it can compute the number of activity stations and facilities for each activity group. The park acreage is then computed for actual facilities, for circulating paths and roads, for landscaping, and for other features.

Park and Recreation Areas

The types of outdoor recreation areas described here represent a variety of service units that may be used in leisure, physical education, and competitive or recreational sport programs. Local conditions will dictate to a large extent which types are to be used in any given locality. Hence, different combinations of areas and facilities will emerge as the solution to the problem of meeting the needs and interests of a particular locality.

There is some controversy over parkland aesthetics as measured by the terms *active recreation* and *passive recreation*. Many individuals with inherent interest in recreation or leisure pursuits associated with nature denounce the intrusion into parklands by activities that alter the natural environment. Battles have been fought over ball diamond location, loss of wetlands, and elimination of native species. Obviously, these two groups have different attitudes about the character and purpose of parklands. Parklands can be designed for active or passive use, or both, without destroying their aesthetic values. The use of parklands should reflect the greatest good for the greatest number and the protection of the health, well-being, and safety of all. Parklands may be of multiple use in many cases, but there are also strong cases for maintaining natural areas. The balance between the two is often difficult to agree upon, but there should be a commitment for both. Community involvement is essential in making these determinations. In some instances, state and federal environmental standards may determine what can and cannot be accomplished.

If a community is split over the use of parklands, a cost–benefit analysis should be made to ascertain the feasibility and costs of various options. There is no sense in preserving a swamp that was created artificially and lacks any ecological value, but a natural swamp might be found elsewhere and preserved to meet specific needs and interests. There are alternatives in every planning process, and they should be considered.

Abandoned industrial sites such as strip mines, waste disposal areas/landfills, and sand and gravel pits offer unique possibilities for park and recreation development. In many cases, recreation use is not only the most beneficial but also the most economic use of such sites. The cost of development of the sites can sometimes be born by the owner, by state or federal reclamation funds, or through previous court settlements. Brownfields, waste disposal sites, and other areas that have been adversely affected by previous use should be carefully assessed and tested before being accepted for recreation and park use. The cost of environmental cleanup can easily run into the millions of dollars. The recreation planner must not overlook the possibility of obtaining these sites for public use. If possible, cooperative planning should be started while the site is still being used by industry so landscape features can be developed to make it more appealing for recreation use.

Playlot/Mini-Parks: Location, Size, and Features

A playlot/mini-park is a small recreational area designed for the safe play of preschool children. As an independent unit, the playlot/mini-park is most frequently developed in large housing projects or in other densely populated urban areas with high concentrations of preschool children. More often, it is incorporated as a feature

Additional examples of play equipment (*Source:* Meghan Rosselli)

of a larger recreation area. If a community is able to operate a neighborhood park within one quarter of a mile of every home, playlots should be located at the playground sites. A location near a playground entrance close to restrooms and away from active game areas is best.

The playlot/mini-park should be enclosed with a low fence or solid planting to assist mothers or guardians in safeguarding their children. Thought should be given to placement of benches with and without shade for ease of supervision and comfort for parents and guardians. A drinking fountain with a step for tots will serve both children and adults. Playground equipment geared to the preschool child should combine attractive traditional play apparatus with creative, imaginative alternatives. Playground equipment should be marked with signs to designate the age group for which it is designed.

Neighborhood Parks

The neighborhood park is land set aside primarily for both active and passive recreation. Ideally, it gives the impression of being rural, sylvan, or national in its character. It emphasizes horticultural features with spacious turf areas bordered by trees, shrubs, and, sometimes, floral arrangements. It is essential in densely populated areas but not required where ample yard space is available at individual home sites.

A neighborhood park should be provided for each neighborhood. In many neighborhoods, it will be incorporated in the school–park site. A separate location is required if this combination is not feasible. A separately located neighborhood park normally requires 3 to 5 acres. As a measure of expediency, however, an isolated area as small as 1 or 2 acres may be used. Sometimes the functions

Celebration Station (*Source:* Meghan Rosselli)

of a neighborhood park can be satisfactorily included in a community or citywide park.

The neighborhood park plays an important role in setting standards for community aesthetics. Therefore, it should include open lawn areas, plantings, and walks. Sculpture forms, pools, and fountains should also be considered for ornamentation. Creative planning will employ contouring, contrasting surfaces, masonry, and other modern techniques to provide both eye appeal and utility.

Community Parks

The community park, like the neighborhood park, is designed primarily to provide facilities for a variety of organized recreation activities, but it should also have the characteristics of a landscaped park. It should include passive recreation areas, provide visibility for security purposes, and have adequate lighting for nighttime security. It usually serves as the playground for the children living in the immediate neighborhood, but its primary service is to a much wider age group. Thus it supplies a greater variety of facilities and more extensive service than can be justified at the neighborhood park. The school child, teenager, young adult, hobbyist, senior citizen, and family group all find attractive facilities at the well-developed community park and play field. Because there is no school building at this area, some type of indoor facility is needed. In many cases, a multipurpose recreation center is provided to meet this need.

Citywide or District Parks

The citywide or district park serves a district of a large city or an entire smaller city. It should serve a population of 50,000 to 100,000 with a wide variety of activities. The ideal location for this area is in combination with a high school as a school–park complex. Where this is not feasible, consideration should be given to placing the park as close as possible to the center of the population to be served.

The land available will be a determining factor in site selection. Although the service zone will vary according to population density, a normal use zone is 2 to 4 miles. The size may range from 50 to 100 acres but is generally recommended to be in excess of 100 acres.

Depending on available acreage, topography, and natural features, the citywide or district park will contain a large number of components. These might include

- fields for baseball, football, soccer, and softball (see Chapter 11);
- tennis center (see Chapter 10);
- winter sports facilities (see Chapter 19);
- recreation or day camp center;
- accessible picnic areas (group and family) with barbeques;
- pavilion with fireplace cycling paths or tracks;
- swimming pool (see Chapter 13);
- water sports lake;
- golf course (which requires considerably more acreage);
- walking trails with intermittent fitness equipment;
- skateparks (see Chapter 19);
- multiple playgrounds for different age groups;
- parking areas; and/or
- outdoor theater.

The above facilities should be separated by large turf and/or landscaped areas to serve as natural buffers between spaces.

Special-Use Areas and Facilities

Trails

Trails used by walkers and joggers have become popular. In many locations in the United States, old, abandoned rail lines have been secured from the railroad companies. In some cases, the companies have salvaged the rails and cross ties. In other cases, they have donated the land, rails, and ties to the government. Once a trail has been established, it should easily blend into the environment. The planners need to consider the climate, flora and fauna, topography, local history, and available materials for the infrastructure.

The width of a walking trail should be between 3 and 6 ft. When developing a walking trail, the following points should be considered: (a) local community preferences, (b) initial cost and long-term maintenance costs, (c) interesting attractions featured along the trail, (d) access to public transportation, (e) appropriate signage (e.g., names of plants and trees, distances, grades or elevations, direction of trail, trail layout and map, warnings of hazards), (f)

A good example of park lighting (*Source:* Meghan Rosselli)

surface preparation (e.g., asphalt, dirt, gravel, wood chips, sawdust), (g) fitness equipment along trail, and (h) loops and networks to provide distance options. Many communities are developing citywide trail systems that link together walking and bicycle paths with the park trails being the anchor for the system.

A walking trail requires basic infrastructure: (a) universal accessibility (e.g., ramps, handrails, appropriate gradients); (b) adequate parking at the beginning of the trail and at select entry points along the trail; (c) rest stops with benches, drinking water, restrooms, shelters, and picnic areas; and (d) a trail design to eliminate water drainage problems and minimize vandalism.

Bicycle Facilities and Pathways

Most of the recommended bicycle programs and facilities will require considerable investments of time and money to bring them to fruition. An alternative program would develop bicycle-touring routes in and across the county using rural and low-volume vehicular routes. The only expenses involved in the creation of this system are for initial system planning, printing bikeway maps, and marking intersections. County and city governments together with educational institutions have implemented touring systems.

The steps to developing bicycling facilities are outlined below:

- Appoint a committee from interested groups of individuals, including representatives of educational institutions and the recreation department.
- Make a survey of county road maps and mark a conceptual bicycle system on a work map. One of the objectives is to create a roughly circular route. "Spoke" routes would radiate from central sites to the peripheral route. Select the safest possible routes. High-volume roads and intersections should be avoided. After the road map is finished, the committee should find that it has the framework for an adequate bicycling touring system.
- Field reconnaissance of the roads marked on the working map is conducted. Alternate routes may be selected if the original roads are not appropriate for bicycling. Actual travel by bicycle is recommended for the reconnaissance.
- The final bikeway map is drafted. Titles and safety information are also indicated on the map. The back of the map may be filled with a variety of safety tips and information about the local community. The bikeway should be marked, especially the abrupt turns. Paint distinctive symbols and arrows on the pavement of the road. Standard highway marking paint may be used, and stencils for the symbols may be cut from heavy gauge linoleum.

Cycle trails require additional planning beyond that needed for a walking or jogging trail. The planners need to include the following additional factors in the design: (a) minimum width of dual path should be 12 ft, (b) the path should have a safety zone on either side extending 5 ft clear of all vegetation, (c) the ideal surface material is asphalt for the path and small gravel or brick chips for the safety buffer, and (d) the cyclists may desire bike racks at rest areas.

Bridle Paths and Rings

Horseback riding is popular with all age groups but is generally restricted to the larger park areas because of space requirements. Riding trails, sometimes called bridle paths, are usually a minimum of 10 ft wide to permit riders going in opposite directions to pass safely. Except on steep terrain, little is required in the way of construction. Clearing, a small amount of leveling, removal of large rocks and boulders, and trimming or removal of low-hanging tree limbs constitute the major items. Most small streams can be forded, but an occasional bridge may be required as well as cross drainage on steep gradients. No special surfacing is required except that a gravel base should be installed in wet or boggy areas that cannot be avoided. Tanbark, cinders, and other materials are frequently positioned on heavily used trails and in areas of concentrated use around hitching racks and in riding rings.

Stables and adjoining facilities such as feed racks, holding corrals, riding rings, and hitching racks should be located at least 500 ft from the nearest public-use area because of the fly and odor problem. The size of these facilities will depend on the number of horses. However, the stable will ordinarily contain a limited number of horse stalls, a feed storage room, a tack room, a small office, and restroom facilities. A fenced enclosure commonly called a holding corral or paddock into which the horses can be turned at the end of the day is required. A surfaced riding ring, sometimes encircled with a rail fence, is frequently provided for training novices in the fundamentals of riding.

Finally, horse riding trails are not compatible with walkers or cyclists. The horse trail cannot be made of hard surface (e.g., asphalt or concrete), but rather should be made of a softer topsoil and clay mixture. The trail needs a good base in order to reduce maintenance costs. The tree limbs need to be cut close to the trunk. It is also necessary to provide good horizontal vegetation clearance (over 6 ft) and vertical vegetation clearance (over 10 ft).

Golf Courses

The design, construction, operation, and maintenance of golf courses is too vast a subject to be covered in detail in this publication. For general information and guidance, write the National Golf Foundation at 1150 South US Highway One, Suite 401, Jupiter, FL 33477 or The American Society of Golf Course Architects, 125 North Executive Drive, Suite 106, Brookfield, WI 53005.

The creation of new golf course facilities throughout the nation continued at a healthy pace during the early years of the new century. As the popularity of the game continues to grow, there is an obvious need to increase the number of golf courses to keep up with demand.

Golf course construction costs vary greatly, but generally planners can count on spending at least $3 million, excluding the cost to purchase the land. It must be emphasized that this figure is intended only as a rough guideline and does not include the cost of entry road, parking lot, other support facilities (e.g., restrooms, chemical storage areas, fuel storage, sand and topsoil storage areas, golf cart storage space, practice putting green, driving range, and tree nursery), golf course architect, and other necessary professional consulting fees. In addition, maintenance costs usually run between $250,000 and $650,000 annually, plus club operations and golf cart fleets.

Assuming the land is suitable for construction of a golf course, the following space requirements must be considered:

- for a standard 18-hole course—145 to 200 acres,
- for shorter executive courses—75 to 120 acres,
- for a standard nine-hole course—70 to 90 acres, and
- for a nine-hole par three course (including a couple of par four holes)—45 to 60 acres.

Some of the most desirable features of the land to be used include rolling hills, interesting landscaping, ravines, creeks and ponds or lake sites, and irrigation resources. The more of these features that can be found on a piece of land, the less the overall construction cost will be. The planners need to also be concerned about environmental issues (e.g., wetlands, invasive plants, and bugs), drainage, and quality of the soil. Other key components for site selection are the ease of utility connections and accessibility to the new project.

Marinas and Boat Ramps

America abounds in waterways. The myriad inland lakes, the rivers and streams, the vast Great Lakes, and the thousands of miles of coastline invite America's citizens to take advantage of this natural resource. Today, boating commands more of the recreation dollar than baseball, fishing, golf, or any other single activity. There is a need for efficient, realistic, and functional planning for facilities to accommodate the present needs and the future growth that this recreation interest will precipitate. The launching, mooring, and storage of yachts and rowboats are the function of a marina that will serve the needs of the recreation boat owner.

It is suggested that knowledgeable and experienced personnel be engaged to study the number, types, and sizes of existing boats in the area, the number and size of existing berthing facilities, and the condition of such existing facilities. The survey should also include the potential population growth in the community and surrounding area to determine the future boat ownership. An accurate and comprehensive evaluation of such a study is the first step in planning a marina.

The study will determine the next important consideration in laying out a marina: selecting the correct number of slips of each size that will be required. Based on the needs of the community to be served, planners will determine the necessary number of slips to accommodate boats of various sizes.

Because marinas vary so greatly in their design, function, location, and capacity, it is virtually impossible to arrive at standard conclusions and judgments concerning a model marina. Each planner will be able to apply the general principles to his or her unique circumstances. From that point, however, he or she must adapt his or her marina to the peculiar needs and characteristics of a community.

A marina, because it is a parking lot for boats, will most likely be surrounded by a repair shop, fuel station, dry dock area, and general marine supply shop. Key planning issues include (a) environmental impact, (b) local politics, (c) waste management, (d) conservation, (e) quality of construction and compatibility with the environment, (f) financing (i.e., initial cost and long-term maintenance costs), (g) management and safety, (h) size of the project, and (i) monitoring of environmental problems.

A boat ramp is necessary for launching boats into a waterway. The initial task is to locate adequate, safe launching and retrieval facilities. Contrary to popular opinion, suitable locations for boat ramps are hard to find. Planners should consider the following when selecting a suitable location for a boat ramp: (a) protection from severe weather; (b) minimal impact on the surrounding environment; (c) large enough space to accommodate the ramp and trail-

Fishing deck (*Source:* Meghan Rosselli)

er and vehicle parking as well as rigging and maneuvering of trailers; (d) accessibility to the proposed site by an all-weather road; (e) ancillary facilities such as restrooms, water supply, night lighting, telephone accessibility, wash down area, and waste disposal facility; (f) legal requirements (e.g., requirement for environmental impact study, zoning requirements); (g) local community input; (h) initial cost and long-term maintenance costs; and (i) water conditions (e.g., wave patterns and currents).

Curling

Curling is an ice sport popular in Canada and the northern United States. The advent of artificial ice has broadened the popularity of curling and has extended its geographical interest zone. Sponsored by clubs and leagues, it is played with hand-propelled 42.5 lb stones, referred to as rocks. The curling sheet is a level ice area 146 ft long and between 14 ft, 2 in. and 16 ft, 5 in. wide. A key aspect of the playing surface is the spraying of water droplets, called pebbles, on the ice. Friction between the stone and pebble cause the stone to "curl," that is, to turn inside or outside. The object is to slide one team's rocks nearest the center of a circle, called the house, at each end of the rink.

The house is a set of three concentric circles. The center of the house is formed by the intersection of two lines, center line and tee line, which divide the house into quarters. This is known as the button. The center line is drawn lengthwise down the center of the sheet. The tee line is drawn parallel to and 16 ft from the backboard. Two additional lines, the hoglines, are drawn parallel to and 37 ft from the backboard. The three rings that make up the button are set with diameters of 4 ft, 8 ft, and 12 ft. Usually distinguished by color, the inner rings are used to determine which stone is closer to the center. The curler pushes off a traction device, called a hack, which is located 12 ft behind each button.

Performing Arts Areas

In the past few years, demand has increased for suitable indoor and outdoor facilities for operas, plays, band and orchestral concerts, pageants, festivals, holiday programs, and civic celebrations. When performed outdoors, such activities usually require a stage or band shell with adjoining amphitheater capable of accommodating large numbers of spectators. Selecting the proper site for an outdoor theater is of primary importance. It should have good acoustical properties and be located in a quiet place away from the noise of traffic or of groups at play. A natural bowl or depression on a hillside with a slope of 10° to 20°, preferably bordered by slopes or densely wooded areas, provides an ideal setting.

At some theaters, people sit on the slope of the amphitheater. At others, permanent seats are installed. Terraces with a turf surface are not recommended because they are too difficult to maintain. Sufficient level space should be provided at the rear of the seating area for the circulation of spectators, and aisles should be wide enough to facilitate the seating of large numbers in a short period of time.

Public comfort stations and refreshment facilities are usually provided near the entrance to the amphitheater. Provision for the nearby parking of automobiles is essential, but parking areas must be located where noises and car lights do not disturb the stage action.

The dimensions of the stage are determined by the proposed uses, but rarely should a stage be less than 50 ft in width or 30 ft in depth. The rear of the stage may be a wall or high hedge, or even a planting of trees, and the wings may be formed by natural plant materials. The band or music shell, however, is more satisfactory for projecting voices and sound free from echoes and interference. A vertical rear wall with an inclined ceiling not only is the simplest and most economical to construct but also affords excellent acoustical qualities.

The band shell usually contains dressing rooms, restrooms, storage space, and control centers for amplifying and lighting equipment, but sometimes these facilities are provided in separate structures near the back of the stage. An orchestra pit is generally located between the amphitheater and the stage.

Mobile storage units with self-contained lighting and acoustical systems are becoming popular because they can be used in many parks instead of restricting programs to one permanent location. Equipped to serve as a band shell, stage, puppet theater, or platform for other performing arts, these mobile units can bring productions to audiences never exposed to such activities. Excellent units can be obtained at a cost less than that required for a permanent band shell.

Archery Range

This sport appeals to a sizable group in most communities. Sufficient space should be dedicated to ensure the safety and enjoyment of the participants. An earth bunker or bales of hay and straw piled up to the top of the target may protect this space. Anticipate errant arrows and plan for proximal use areas.

An archery range (see Chapter 26) should be fairly level. Orientation should be north and south so the archers will not be facing the sun. A fence enclosure is desirable but not essential. The public, however, should be controlled in some manner so they do not walk through the range.

Bocce Ball

A bocce court is 91 ft x 13 ft. Many bocce courts are sunken, with retaining walls constructed out of pressure-treated landscaping timbers. When built aboveground, a bocce court needs side and back walls. These can be constructed of wood, lattice, landscape stones, brick, or cinder block.

The bocce court area should include

- shade trees,
- flowers,
- storage area for equipment,
- lawn chairs and tables, and
- possibly lights for evening play.

Dog Parks

A dog park is a facility for dogs to exercise and play off leash in a controlled environment. A minimum area of 8,000 sq ft of fenced perimeter is needed, but a larger area is preferred. Dog parks vary in design and may contain some or all of the following elements:

- paved or gravel double-gated entry;
- excrement pickup stations and trash cans;
- hills or mounds;
- swim area with pond or pool;
- water spigot with bowl or flushable water bowl system;
- benches, tables, and covered shelters placed in shaded and unshaded areas;
- granite, gravel, sand, or native plants and sturdy grasses;
- gravel or paved warning track around the inside of the fence perimeter;
- coat and leash rack near gate;
- shy/small dog area; and
- time-out area for dogs who need to be contained (e.g., overexcited or aggressive, in heat, bleeding).

Areas for Outdoor Education and Recreation

Outdoor education is a term that refers to learning activities in, and of, the outdoors. Such activities can be provided in the curriculums of schools, colleges, and universities as well as in the programs of recreation; camping; and federal, state, and community agencies. Outdoor education is a means of curriculum extension and enrichment through outdoor experiences.

It is not a separate discipline with prescribed objectives like science and mathematics; it is simply a learning climate that offers opportunities for direct laboratory experiences in identifying and resolving real-life problems, for acquiring skills with which to enjoy a lifetime of creative living, for building concepts and developing concern about humankind and the natural environment, and for getting people back in touch with those aspects of living where our roots were once firm and deep.

Outdoor education and outdoor recreation encompass a variety of activities, many of which can be conducted on a single large tract of land. With careful planning, facilities, some in or near an urban area and others in more rural places, can be used. An outdoor education complex on one piece of land or on several plots in close proxim-

ity has many advantages. Such a site lends itself to wide community use with responsibilities for leadership and finances shared by several agencies. Obviously, the size and physical characteristics of an outdoor education complex, and the resulting equipment and transportation needs, will depend on the geographic location and the topography of the land. Facilities and types of site treatment for a complex that would accommodate a broad program of outdoor education and outdoor recreation, and which would constitute an outdoor laboratory or field campus, are briefly described below. It is assumed that there will be many areas and facilities, public and private, that can also be used in a comprehensive program.

Considerations in Selecting and Developing Park Sites

Size. The type of program planned should determine the size of the site. Size alone does not necessarily mean much except that it affects the numbers of certain species of wildlife that might live in the area. A large area does not necessarily have a diversity of physical features. It may just be level land, harboring only a few species of trees, with no particularly outstanding features. Nevertheless, such an area could be made interesting from an educational point of view, provided good leadership and programming is available.

Many schools, recreation departments, and community agencies already have school sites, parks, and recreation areas that could be developed for outdoor programs. Schools, as well as other agencies, in some sections of the country also have forestlands that could be developed and used in a broad educational and recreation program.

Site characteristics. The type of program planned also determines the characteristics of the site. If plans call for a resident camp, many more requirements must be met than if the site will be used only on a daily basis. If the land and facilities are to contribute to all aspects of the educational curriculum, or if there is to be special emphasis on science, conservation, and outdoor skills, many characteristics will need to be considered, such as

- a location to give privacy and solitude;
- year-round accessibility by road;
- natural and man-made hazards;
- interesting geologic features, such as rock outcroppings, open field, flat terrain, and a variety of soil types;
- a variety of native vegetation including woods;
- wildlife that can be maintained with sound management;
- a pond, stream, seashore, or large body of water;
- demonstration areas for conservation practices;
- woods for practicing outdoor skills and use of native materials;
- sanitary facilities including good drainage and good drinking water;

- simple shelters in the event of inclement weather; and
- proximity to adequate medical and hospital services.

Special features. Many kinds of developments are found in various types of outdoor education areas. Some of these are appropriate for camps, some for outdoor laboratories or nature centers, and some for outdoor recreation and sport centers. An outdoor education and outdoor recreation complex should include many site plans and facilities not possible in more limited areas. The adaptability of the area to the proposed program, the cost of construction, maintenance problems, aesthetic considerations, and available leadership are all factors in determining what facilities might be developed in a particular land area or cluster of acreages.

Listed below are some of the special developments that might be included in appropriate sites. Some of the features listed are discussed elsewhere in this text and are merely mentioned here. Others, not mentioned in other places, are discussed in more detail.

Grass, shrubs, and trees. They provide shade, prevent soil erosion, provide food and cover for wildlife, serve as windbreaks, mark the boundary of the property, act as a buffer zone to ensure privacy against an adjacent (presently or potentially) populated area, demonstrate principles of plant growth, serve as a resource for ecological studies, and give practice in forest management. A school forest offers many popular activities.

Soil erosion demonstration areas. Such an area should be rich in vegetation, feature good conservation practices, be situated on inclined terrain, and be located next to a piece of land denuded of its vegetation and also located on an incline. Comparisons can then be made over a period of time to determine what happens to the quantity and quality of soil in both areas.

Wildlife sanctuary. Wildlife sanctuaries need mixed plantings and birdhouses, feeders, and birdbaths to attract a variety of birds.

Picnic shelter (*Source:* Meghan Rosselli)

Weather station. This is for the study of meteorology and should be located in an area that can be fenced off and locked.

Campfire ring. This facility provides a place for campfires, for conducting orientations before field trips, and for other special programs. The campfire ring should be located in a wooded area to ensure a feeling of isolation. The base of the fire ring should have a barrier to any outside vegetation (i.e., roots). Surface (i.e., plants) and elevated (i.e., tree limbs) vegetation and other flammable substances

Picnic pavilion (*Source:* Meghan Rosselli)

should be restricted from the flame and embers expelled.

Nature trails. If space permits, develop a variety of trails with individual or multiple purposes. Using trail markers, brochures, and naturalist-conducted programs can focus the trail use. One may be a geology trail winding its way through an area rich in geologic features. Another trail may emphasize the study of erosion, and still another may lead to a historic spot.

Pioneer living area. Social studies lessons are vividly illustrated in such an area. The life of the pioneer can be dramatized, including activities such as making dyes from plants, cooking outdoors, constructing shelters, learning to identify edible plants, and learning other survival practices.

Observation platform. This platform can be used for observing birds and for studying astronomy. It should be located on the highest point of the property.

Vegetable, bog, and native plant gardens. Each garden features a particular grouping of native plants found in the typical setting in which they normally grow.

Plant grafting. This demonstration area provides interesting studies in genetics.

Animal-baiting area. Place a salt lick and some meat in a cleared area. Spread loose dirt around the baited spot, press it down with your feet, and smooth it out. Animals attracted to the area will leave their footprints, which can then be observed and studied.

Natural preserve. An area could be set aside in which no developments would be made. It would be given complete protection and would provide a spot for the observation of ecological aspects.

Orienteering courses. Developing several courses for map and compass use would stimulate educational and recreational use of the area.

Greenhouse. A place for the propagation of plants, some of which may be used for area improvement, is important. A greenhouse would make possible an acquaintance with plants and would be a means of providing projects for study during the off-season.

Winter sports area. Places for curling, skating, sledding, skiing, and coasting would be desirable in those parts of the country that have sufficient snow and cold weather to make these sports feasible.

Natural play area. An area set aside for children, containing elements such as climbing logs, ropes for swinging across low areas, sandbanks, and hide-and-seek areas, can provide play opportunities different from those found in the city.

Turtle pond. An attractive pond with water and plantings would make possible the study and observation of turtles and other amphibians.

Rifle and skeet ranges. Such an area will provide opportunities for instruction in gun safety as well as for participation in rifle and skeet shooting. These areas should be located away from high-use areas and should have controls to monitor potential safety issues.

Casting and angling area. Developments for casting and angling would serve both instructional and recreational uses.

Amphitheater. For large group programs, an amphitheater would be important. It could be used for lectures, drama, music, and a variety of demonstrations.

Astronomy area. A special area for astronomy may be developed on a large open area, waterfront, dock, or even a roof. Seating facilities are desirable, and often a telescope is permanently mounted to facilitate observations.

Bird feeding station. A combination of seeds and syrups may attract a variety of bird life.

Historical markers. Sites of old farms, early settlers' homes, Native American trails and village sites, and pioneer roads are illustrations of the kinds of historical sites that might be used for student projects.

Shelters. Adirondack or picnic shelters can serve day camp and day-use groups during inclement weather.

Tree stump. Locate a fairly well-preserved tree stump. Make a sloping cut, smooth the top by sanding, and treat it with clear waterproofing material such as fiberglass resin. Much can be learned about tree growth from carefully studying a tree stump.

Herb garden. This garden features food seasoning and medicinal plants and serves as a useful teaching aid for a home economics class.

Photographic blind. Construct a blind near a bird feeding station for taking pictures of wild birds.

Evergreen tree nursery. Trees can later be transplanted to desired areas.

Field archery. Targets are set up in wooded areas or fields to simulate actual hunting conditions.

Natural areas. Such areas are left relatively undisturbed and man-made modifications should be avoided as much as possible. These places serve as excellent resources for scientific studies of natural phenomena.

Picnic site. It is desirable to locate the picnic site on the periphery of the property.

Seashore areas. Communities adjacent to seashores may have areas set aside for study and observation. Developments might include ramps or walks to facilitate observation. Walkways through tidelands may be developed as nature trails. One of the national parks has an underwater nature trail.

Outdoor Laboratories

The term *outdoor laboratory* is used for a piece of land (including wetlands, lakes, and seashores) set aside by a school for learning experiences directly related to land and its resources. It may be located close to an individual school or it may serve a group of schools. It may be a part of the school grounds or a section of a park–school development. It may consist of only a few acres nearby or of several hundred acres many miles away. It may serve individual elementary schools, high schools, or universities or all of them jointly. Because outdoor laboratories are extremely varied in their site possibilities and their purposes, no rigid format for their development is possible.

The term *land for learning* has been applied to the school laboratory. It implies the opportunity of school groups to study, explore, and experiment with land and its resources. Outdoor study, field trips, and experiments

Horseshoe pit (*Source:* Meghan Rosselli)

with water, soil, plants, and animals constitute its major functions. Developments may range from nothing more than a few trails, with the area left natural, to nature trails, class and museum buildings, horticultural plots, developed ponds, forest plantations, gardens, and small farm operations. The creativity of the teacher or outdoor education specialist, the potential of the available site, and funds available may be the only limiting factors in the development of program facilities.

If a laboratory is heavily used, water and restroom facilities might be essential. A storage building for tools and supplies might also be desirable.

Nature Centers

The term *nature center* is used to designate a particular type of development that will facilitate learning in the outdoors and the growth of recreation interests. The establishment of nature centers is being promoted extensively by several science- and nature-related organizations. Many centers exist across the United States. Children's museums may be considered a part of this development even though some of these museums lack adjacent lands for outdoor education.

Site. Some of the suggestions for the school outdoor education laboratory are applicable here. Nature trails, ponds, bogs, gardens, forest plantings, and the like may provide the variety essential for a rich outdoor education program.

Building. The building should be designed to permit expansion as the program grows and as more funds become available. In its initial stage, the building should contain a minimum space of 2,500 sq ft, which is large enough to adequately contain one program. The building should be designed according to the needs set by the program. The following general spaces are recommended:

- Office.
- Restrooms. Access should be provided to the outside as well as to the interior of the building.
- Large meeting room. The wall space can be used for exhibits. Low cabinets along the walls should be provided for storage of educational equipment and supplies. A long counter providing work and display space should be constructed on top of the cabinets.
- Classrooms. Moveable walls should be provided so that a class may be broken up into smaller groups if necessary.
- Workroom. This room would be used for constructing displays and for arts and crafts.
- Science laboratory. A room should be equipped with microscopes, soil- and mineral-testing equipment, and other materials necessary for scientific studies. Inclusion of GPS and GIS technology has become more common.
- Library. The large meeting room can contain the library, which would occupy one section of the room. The library should contain reference material, field guides, magazines, and novels concerned with the outdoors.
- Storage room. Adequate space should be provided to store the instructional and janitorial equipment that is necessary for operating programs and the facility.

It should be emphasized again that it is not essential for one center to have most of the spaces described here. Creative space management will allow a relatively small center with few amenities to provide a wide variety of programs.

Interpretive Centers

Although the name *interpretive centers* might apply to the outdoor laboratories and the nature centers mentioned earlier, it specifically describes certain facilities of public parks offered as a service to the general public and, in some cases, to school groups. The National Park Service has the most extensive development of such centers. The U.S. Forest Service, Corps of Engineers, and Bureau of Land Management as well as other federal land managing agencies provide interpretive facilities. State parks and larger metropolitan parks have also developed interpretive centers.

The primary purpose of interpretive centers is to help visitors understand and appreciate the natural, historical, cultural, or archeological features of the areas in which the centers are located. Interpretation is tailored for each area. Facility developments are likewise varied and often unique to the site being interpreted.

Interpretive centers frequently contain a trailside museum or interpretive center building. This may vary in size from 10 ft x 20 ft to a large multifocused structure. The size depends on the groups to be accommodated, the interpretive materials available, and the types of programs to be presented. A large building may contain some or all of the following:

- museum-quality display rooms with cultural, historical, wildlife, and other exhibits;
- office space;
- a laboratory for research and the preparation of display materials;
- theater and meeting rooms for lectures, video, or computer presentations;
- restrooms;
- storage space for archived materials;
- a counter for the sale of books and the distribution of pamphlets;
- an outdoor amphitheater or campfire area for lectures and movies;
- trails to points of interest (often self-guiding nature trails);

- parapets or other special observation points, often including mounted telescopes and pointers indicating places of interest; and
- interpretive devices at points of interest.

School and Community Gardens, Farms, and Forests

Gardens, farms, and forests provide direct experiences with growing plants and, in some cases, with domestic animals. Schools, park and recreation agencies, and a few private agencies have been responsible for developing facilities. Even when facilities are developed and operated by park and recreation departments or private agencies, some direct relationship with schools is often provided through an instructional program in which the schoolchildren are enrolled.

Display gardens. Gardens of various kinds should be developed to provide for visual, cultural, and educational equipment. A formal garden may be composed entirely of one type of plant (e.g., roses), of various types of assorted plant materials, or of a series of individual gardens made up of single types of plant units. Features such as a water fountain and statuary can be incorporated into the design. Informal gardens should have long, sweeping lawn areas to serve as a setting for plants and flower beds. Plants may include large specimen trees, flowering trees, shrubs, and vines. The flower borders can be of varied plants. All the plants should be of interest to the average homeowner and should be useful in helping him or her select plants for his or her own yard. Attempts should be made to keep abreast of the latest introductions and to display those types of plants that are hardy to the particular region in which the garden is located. This aspect of planting for the homeowner should be stressed in both formal and informal gardens, and demonstrations of plant cultural practice should be provided.

Naturalistic and native, or wildflower, gardens are established in a wilderness location where the plants native to the region can be assembled in one area so they are easily accessible to the citizens. Developers will probably need an area of varied topography—lowlands, highlands, and prairies—and an area with varied soil conditions—from alkaline to acid—to accommodate the various types of plants.

Tract gardens. In a tract garden, which is the most common type of school or community garden, a piece of property ranging in size from 1 to 10 acres is divided into small tracts for the use of individuals. A typical plot size may be 10 ft x 20 ft, but adults and families can use larger gardens. A garden program with 25 plots can be set up on one quarter of an acre of land; however, more space is desirable. Four acres of land can hold 100 gardeners with plots of varied size and community crops. This size allows space for a service building and activity area. It should be on rich, well-drained soil with water available. Garden

programs may involve instruction, environmental projects, field trips, and science activities. Community projects may include novelty crops such as pumpkins, gourds, Indian corn, and Christmas trees. Gardening appeals to all ages and is an excellent program for families.

Some of the necessary or desirable features of the tract garden include

- garden building—either a small building for the storage of tools and equipment or a building large enough for class meetings and indoor activity during bad weather;
- restroom facilities adequate to care for the maximum number of participants expected on the garden plot at one time;
- greenhouse for plant propagation;
- ready access to water, with spigots and hoses available for limited irrigation;
- fencing for protection of the garden;
- pathways and walkways to provide easy access to all plots;
- a demonstration home yard, with grass, flowers, and shrubs; and
- good landscaping.

Preferably, the tract garden should be located within walking distance of the homes of the participants. In many cases, gardens are developed on or adjacent to school grounds. Tract gardens for adults and families have been established in some communities. They are usually intended for people living in crowded urban centers or apartments who would not otherwise be able to garden. In some communities, these gardens are located some distance from homes with individuals responsible for their own transportation.

Farms. Community or school farms are becoming increasingly important, especially near metropolitan centers, and offer opportunities for a rich and varied program. Farm programs include animal care and training and traditional rural activities such as hayrides, picnics, and nature activities. Families who just want to walk through to see and pet the animals often use model farms. Simple barns and pens contain horses, cows, pigs, chickens, sheep, and other domestic animals, which children can help care for and feed. In an urban setting, it is essential that the facility be attractive and well maintained. An office, restrooms, drinking fountain, indoor and outdoor activity areas, and storage space are needed. There must be water, feed storage, and adequate exercise space for the animals.

In addition to the buildings that are generally found on a diversified farm, there are meeting places and exhibits that make it possible to carry on indoor instruction. Picnic areas, farm ponds, day camp facilities, campfire circles, and hiking trails are often developed.

Working farms are sometimes adapted for recreational purposes. This type of facility actually produces a variety of products, and city residents visit to learn, observe, take part in, and enjoy farming activities. Groups may use the farm on a day basis and overnight accommodations can be provided. In either case, a large room and open outdoor space are needed for activity and instruction.

Farm camps offer opportunities for a farm-oriented camping experience. The farm camp is a farm not worked for production but set up for resident programs in environmental education, farm activities, natural history, science, and other outdoor recreation. There may be a large farmhouse converted to a program building and farm buildings converted to cabins. Facilities needed are a kitchen, dining area, sleeping quarters, restrooms, large activity room, and ample storage space. Additionally, barns, farm equipment, and other facilities may be needed depending on the types of programs offered.

Forests. Numerous school and community forests can be found throughout the United States. Many of these were acquired from tax-delinquent land, through gifts, or through protection programs for community watersheds. Their use has followed diverse patterns. Some schools have carried on field trips, forest improvement projects, and other outdoor education activities. Many of these forests could be developed as outdoor educational laboratories. Some might be suitable sites for nature centers, day camps, or even resident camps. School and community forests may serve valuable purposes even without extensive development. Water, trails, and restrooms may be all the development needs to provide useful educational facilities. Such areas may serve their best function as places to study the ecological changes taking place over a period of years.

Outdoor Skills and Sports Areas

Outdoor skills or sports areas should be included in the outdoor education and recreation complex; however, it may be necessary to acquire special sites depending on the topography of the land. These areas should provide opportunities to learn and practice skills, but they may also be used as outdoor laboratories.

Specialized program facilities that might be included in the outdoor skills and sports areas are

- casting and angling—platforms and open, level spaces;
- outdoor shooting range (see Chapter 26);
- climbing towers (see Chapter 18);
- archery range—target field course, archery, golf, and other games (see Chapter 26);
- camp craft skills area (see Chapter 20);
- overnight camping area (see Chapter 20);
- outpost camping—Adirondack shelters;
- facilities for water sports including swimming, canoeing, boating, sailing, skin diving, and waterskiing;
- area for crafts with native materials—carving, lapidary, weaving, and ceramics—with a simple structure to provide shelter in inclement weather and to house equipment; and
- water sports—ski slopes and tow, ski shelter, tobogganing, and ice-skating rinks.

Natural Areas

Natural areas are generally thought of as representative of native plants and animals of a locale. They may encompass a variety of habitats such as woodlands, deserts, swamps, bogs, wetlands, shorelines, or sand dunes. It is almost impossible today, even in the wilderness, to find undisturbed areas. Most places categorized as natural areas are protected lands that indicate the least disturbance and that, through protection, planting, and development, approximate the original characteristics.

It is characteristic that natural areas are protected from inharmonious developments and activities. Simple access trails, protective fencing, and simple interpretive developments such as entrance bulletin boards are usually acceptable. In designated natural areas, the enjoyment and study of the natural features are encouraged and uses that detract from the natural features are discouraged. Schools, parks, and camps are often the agencies that develop, maintain, and protect natural areas. Such areas are valuable assets in environmental education.

16 Campus Recreational Sports Centers

Thomas H. Sawyer, *Indiana State University*
Tonya L. Gimbert, *Indiana State University*

Over the past 10 years, a number of recreational sports centers have been constructed on campuses to meet the needs of the student bodies and admissions officers seeking to enroll more freshman. These centers have been built for recreational purposes rather than instructional or athletic ones. They have been financed primarily with student fees and state and private funds. Most of the facilities include aquatic centers, entrance/lobby areas, lounge areas, racquetball/wallyball courts, indoor and outdoor tennis courts, basketball courts, dance exercise areas, indoor running/jogging tracks, strength and cardiovascular training areas, climbing walls, locker rooms, indoor and outdoor in-line skating hockey courts, indoor soccer areas, administration areas, pro shops, concessions, and areas for equipment rental.

This chapter provides the planner with an overview of the needs for a campus recreational sports center. The specifics relating to many of the spaces are found in other chapters in this book.

Planning for a New Recreational Sports Center

According to the National Intramural–Recreational Sports Association (NIRSA, 2008, 2009, 2012), there are at least 14 institutional factors to consider when planning a new student recreational sports center, including

- demographic characteristics of the student population (e.g., gender and age);
- enrollment projections by gender and number of students of traditional college age and students of nontraditional age at undergraduate and graduate levels;
- proximity of the proposed facility to residence halls and other housing on campus or close to campus (including future housing plans);

- number of students living on campus or within walking distance to the proposed recreational facilities;
- number of commuter and resident students (current and future);
- demand placed on campus recreational sports facilities by faculty and staff;
- level of participation that is part of the campus culture;
- building program;
- proposed business model;
- climate;
- amount of space for adequate storage;
- peak time for activity usage for each space;
- proposed new offerings and future offerings not yet established; and
- allocated space for regional recreation favorites such as basketball in Indiana, Kentucky, and Illinois; football in Ohio, Oklahoma, Pennsylvania, Texas, and West Virginia and across the South; ice hockey in Minnesota and North Dakota; and squash in New England.

Facility Size

The NIRSA (2008, 2009, 2012) recommended the following minimum sizes for space recommendations:
- total indoor recreation facility space = 20,000 assigned sq footage (ASF);
- total fitness equipment space = 3,000 ASF;
- group exercise space = 1,200 ASF; and
- total outdoor recreation (field space) = 6 acres.

Table 16.1 is based on the NIRSA 2006 College Recreational Sport Facility Inventory (NIRSA, 2009); the numbers represent an average of all the suggested ASF or number of spaces for institutions ranging in student population between fewer than 3,000 and greater than 20,000.

Table 16.1

Average Space Needs for Campus Recreational Sports Facilities

Type of Space	Guideline per 1,000 students
Total indoor recreation space	10,989 ASF
Locker room space for men	217 ASF
Locker room space for women	192 ASF
Basketball courts (indoor)	0.50
Handball and racquetball courts	0.46
Squash	0.12
Table tennis tables	0.34
Tennis courts	0.23
Swimming pools	0.95
Total fitness equipment space	1,288 ASF
Cardio equipment space	439 ASF
Free weight space	337 ASF
Group exercise space	417 ASF
Group indoor cycling space	96 ASF
Multiuse space	377 ASF
Strength equipment space	381 ASF
Stretching & core exercise space	60 ASF
Indoor bouldering walls	39 ASF climbing surface
Indoor climbing walls	0.63 top ropes per 1,000 students
Storage space for trip and rental equipment	163 ASF
Total outdoor fields	0.76
Basketball courts (outdoor)	0.32
Flag football fields	0.39
Soccer fields	0.36
Softball fields	0.33
Tennis courts	0.76
Volleyball	0.28

Note. ASF = Area Square Footage. These guidelines are based on data from NIRSA (2008) and can be used to determine a starting point for planning recreational sport facility space for colleges and universities.

Comparing a Campus With Accepted Standards

To compare a campus with the accepted standards, five steps should be followed. The first step involves the location of existing and potential areas within the boundaries of the campus. This is achieved by physically canvassing the campus and envisioning the potential of all areas. The initial phase of Step 1 should be locating and identifying all areas that are currently used by recreational, intramural, and informal sports.

The second phase is more difficult and requires more effort and imagination on the part of the observer. Potential areas of expansion are spaces (outdoor and indoor) that can be converted from whatever they are currently being used for to usable recreation areas. Costs of converting each area should be kept at a minimum to further enhance the attractiveness of securing new facilities (Mull, Bayless, Ross, & Jamieson, 1997; Sawyer, 2009). For example, the cost of converting a relatively small (50 ft x 100 ft) grassy area to an outdoor volleyball area would only include installing two poles and a net. If further funds were available and the sport popular, this area could be converted to a sand or beach volleyball court at a small additional cost. Providing alternatives or options also enhances the acceptability of the proposal.

Space for conversion should meet the general considerations noted above before being considered for alteration. For example, an indoor area with an 8-ft ceiling should not be considered for conversion to gymnasium space; however, it could be converted to a dance studio or a karate practice room with the addition of mirrors and mats.

After all available and potential areas have been located, the next step requires computations of the area in square feet. For indoor areas, a tape measure is used; however, for large outdoor areas, a cross-country measuring wheel is most effective. When an area is measured, precautions should be taken to allow for a buffer zone of safety around any proposed playing area. An outdoor grassy area measuring 100 yd x 40 yd could theoretically accommodate an intramural football field, but if the boundaries are close to hazards such as chain-link fence poles, trees, or buildings, this area should be considered for another recreational purpose.

The same precautions apply to indoor space. Most areas considered will be fairly easy to measure. Normally, spaces are either rectangular or square in shape. Odd-shaped areas should not be ignored, and their areas should be estimated to the best of the measurer's ability and still allow for the safety buffer zone. Odd-shaped areas are also ignored because they do not fit the shape of a standard playing field. These areas, however, may accommodate a combination of two or more sports in that area. Any particular space should not be viewed as usable only for football or basketball, but rather leftover spaces should be viewed as able to be used for other activities such as a frisbee golf or table tennis.

When standards in terms of square feet per student are used as guides in college or university planning, it is natural to ask where the cutoff begins. Obviously, for a college of 200 students, 9 sq ft per student of indoor area for sports and athletics is inadequate. It would not even provide one basketball court. A university or college meeting the space standards for 1,500 students represents the minimum physical recreation space needs of any college institution.

As a college or university increases in size, these standards are applicable regardless of enrollment. Also, a ceiling effect applies to some subclassifications of space.

In the beginning phases of planning for recreational facilities, area standards must be developed. A variety of standards relative to size, location, and development of school and recreation areas and facilities has been developed.

The standards provide a useful guide; however, standards can seldom, if ever, be applied completely or without modification. Because a typical or ideal situation is seldom found, standards simply indicate a basis for the intelligent development of local plans.

The third step involves a description of current and potential uses of each area. A description of current uses should be done first. It should include uses by physical education, recreation, intramural sports, and "outside" departments. If a particular area is not being used for a specific purpose, it should be so listed.

Potential uses (see Tables 16.1 and 16.2) should be as closely linked to the subclassifications as possible. It is in this phase of the process that the director must make responsible choices about developing a given area. A single area must have the potential to be developed into several different types of space. The director must refer to individual program needs and areas of deficiency to make informed decisions about developing that particular area. Again, it is important to provide campus planners with options. However, the director should limit the flexibility of the proposal to stay within the most urgent needs of his or her particular program.

The next step is determining the cost of converting an area from its current use to its potential use. In some cases, the conversion will cost nothing. This type of space should be accentuated in presenting the proposal before any board involved with campus planning. Often, cooperation between two departments regarding scheduling can vastly increase facilities available for recreational use at no cost to either program.

Table 16.2

Indoor Recreational, Intramural, and Informal Sports Activities

Single Function	Specialized or Multipurpose Function	
Archery range	**Country club**	**Gymnasium**
Badminton court	Golf	Gymnastics
Basketball court	Swimming	Combatives
Billiards	Table sports	Basketball
Bowling alley	Strength training	Volleyball
Combatives room	Tennis	Badminton
Curling rink		Table tennis
Cardiovascular room	**Fieldhouse**	
Dance exercise room	Basketball	**Racquetball club**
Diving pool	Track	Strength training
Electronic games arcade	Soccer	Running
Fencing salle	Lacrosse	
Gymnastics room	Running	**Recreation center**
Handball	Archery	Billiards
Ice rink		Table sports
In-line skating hockey rink	**Fitness center**	Table tennis
Racquetball court	Swimming	Swimming
Rifle/pistol range	Strength training	Gymnasium
Roller skating rink	Cardiovascular training	
Shuffleboard course	Running	
Squash court	Combatives	
Swimming pool	Dance exercise	
Table sports room		
Table tennis room		
Tennis court		
Strength training room		
Wrestling room		
Volleyball court		

(*Source:* NIRSA, 2009, 2012)

Table 16.3

Outdoor Recreational, Intramural, and Informal Sports Activities

Airfield	Hydro-slide
Baseball field	Ice rink
Basketball court	In-line skating hockey rink
Beach volleyball	Lacrosse field
Bike trail	Marina
Bicycle track	Miniature golf course
Boat launching ramp	Motocross course
Bocce ball course	Riding paddock
Bowling green	Rifle/pistol range
Cross-country course	Roller skating rink
Curling rink	Shuffleboard
Deck tennis	Skateboard/rollerblade
Diving pool	course and ramp
Field hockey field	Skeet and trap range
Fishing pond/lake	Skiing course
Fitness trail	Soccer field
Football field	Softball field
Frisbee golf course	Speedball
Go-cart track	Swimming pool
Golf course	Speedball field
Golf driving range	Team handball field
Handball court	Tennis court
Horseshoe pit	Toboggan slope
	Volleyball

(*Source:* NIRSA, 2009, 2012)

Obtaining other costs of conversion generally involves requesting estimates from the physical plant operations staff on campus or from outside contractors. These estimates should be obtained prior to presenting any proposal. Also, the estimates should enhance the flexibility built into the proposal. That is, each option should have its own separate estimate. This allows campus planning boards to examine all suggestions in the proposal independently of other suggestions in the proposal.

Finally, the last step involves defining the availability for use by the major users. If two or more users share facilities, the priority schedule for usage should also be listed. After all, a program may have access to a facility 40% of the total time available, but if those times are at undesirable hours, the facility is not meeting the needs of the program. If the prime-time needs of students for recreational use are not considered, the percentage of availability may be misleading.

After information has been gathered, supporting documents for requesting new facilities must be prepared. The proposal should contain five major parts. The first part should state clearly the objectives of the study. It should also list all areas and departments of the campus involved

in conducting the study. Finally, it should include limitations or qualifications specific to the institution.

The second part should include brief historical developments of the sponsoring program from both national and campus viewpoints.

The third section is a statement of the problem. In this section, all forces generating the study should be explained. All major problems affected by changing facility structures should be included, as well as the majority of the information gathered in the aforementioned steps. Listing the standards with the organizations that use them will lend national support to the proposal. The relationship between the standard and enrollment is explained next. And, finally, the standards are applied to the specific campus in question. The comparison should emphasize those areas in which critical deficiencies exist because the largest deficiencies are not always the most critical ones. Section three should conclude with a summary of the work completed on the study and a restatement of those problem areas.

Section four contains recommendations for immediate action and long-term improvements. Flexibility (options) within the overall goals of the organization should be the guiding principle when preparing this section.

Finally, appendixes should be prepared to support the proposal. Participation figures may be used in this section; however, the major part of this section should contain a map of the campus with all areas clearly marked. The map should be accompanied by a list of all buildings and rooms investigated. The most precise way of presenting existing and potential areas is to list and explain each one according to

- location,
- area (structure footage),
- type of space,
- current uses,
- potential uses,
- cost of conversion, and
- percentage of use.

Indoor Facilities

In planning new facilities, remember that substandard facilities usually result in a substandard program. For this reason, official court and field dimensions should be used when possible. The following list identifies the types of areas that should be considered in planning indoor facilities for a campus recreational sports center:

- Main gymnasium—regulation basketball, badminton, tennis, and volleyball courts with mechanical divider nets. The divider nets should be constructed of solid vinyl for the first 8 ft and the remainder of a mesh material.
- Auxiliary gymnasiums—regulation basketball, badminton, tennis, and volleyball courts; gymnastics

area; in-line skating hockey rink; indoor soccer area; suspended track; fencing; batting cages; and dance exercise. The dance exercise area should have hidden mirrors to protect them when the space is used for other activities (e.g., basketball or volleyball) and a retractable instructor's platform. The planners might consider locating two gymnasiums side by side with a storage area between to store equipment, an audio system, and retractable instructor's platform. The storage area should be at least 8 ft wide.

- Swimming pools—50-m pool, diving pool, and/or instruction pool.
- Combatives room—boxing, martial arts, and judo
- Gymnastics space
- Strength training area—progressive resistance training equipment, free weight equipment, and stretching area.
- Cardiovascular area.
- Handball/racquetball/wallyball courts.
- Golf room—sand trap, putting area, and driving nets.
- Archery/rifle/pistol range.
- Games room—billiards, table tennis, table games, shuffleboard, bowling alleys.
- Administrative area—offices, storage, conference rooms, and audiovisual room.
- Lounge and lobby area—bulletin boards, trophy cases, control center, and artwork.
- Concessions, rental, and merchandise area—concession stand, seating area, rental shop, and pro shop.
- Training room—treatment area only.
- Locker rooms—student and faculty, gender specific, shower rooms, drying areas, locker space, and common spa area (i.e., hydro-tube, sauna, and steam room).
- Equipment and storeroom.
- Climbing wall.

Outdoor Facilities

The following list identifies the areas that should be considered in planning outdoor facilities for a campus recreational sports center:

- lighted fields—touch/flag football, soccer, field hockey, softball, baseball, handball, and rugby (see Chapter 11);
- lighted courts—basketball, badminton, tennis, volleyball, handball/racquetball, and horseshoes (see Chapter 10);
- lighted in-line skating hockey court (see Chapter 19);
- lighted jogging/running/walking trails and/or track;
- golf course and lighted driving range and practice green;
- lighted skating rink;
- swimming and diving pools (see Chapter 13);
- bocce field and horseshoe pits;
- storage building(s);
- concessions;
- scoreboards;
- tennis practice boards and soccer kicking wall; and
- picnic areas with shelters (see Chapter 15).

Security Issues

The campus recreational sports center will quickly become the focus of campus interest. The center will be used heavily throughout the day and evening. The prime times will be 6 a.m. to 8 a.m., 11 a.m. to 1 p.m., 4 p.m. to 6 p.m., and 7 p.m. to midnight. The planners need to consider providing adequate security, including appropriate outside lighting at all sites, security cameras, alarmed doors (silent and audible), pool alarms, spa alarms, lockers for valuables, fire alarms, sprinkler systems, and appropriate signage.

Strength and Cardiovascular Training Facilities

Lawrence W. Judge, *Ball State University*

During the past 35 or so years, the popularity of resistance training has increased enormously. Weight lifting facilities of yesteryear were a novelty, as most athletes were advised that serious resistance training might hurt their flexibility and athleticism. According to the American College of Sports Medicine (ACSM, 2011), strength training should be performed at least twice per week with eight to 12 repetitions of eight to 10 different exercises targeting all major muscle groups. As the benefits of resistance training have been accepted by athletes, coaches, and the mainstream population, the demand for facilities has increased. Many school corporations, colleges, and universities (state-of-the-art recreation centers) and community organizations such as the YMCA have developed multiuse strength and conditioning facilities. As the financial stakes of recreation and sport continue to expand, programs continue to seek opportunities to expand the user base.

Strength and cardiovascular training facilities (SCF) for use in physical education, recreation, athletics, and community wellness programs have become larger and more sophisticated over the years. The increasing use of these facilities, combined with the key administrative issues of equipping and staffing, creates a need to better understand these facilities. Strength and cardiovascular training areas (commonly referred to as the fitness floor) are the lifeblood of any existing or future recreation/sports facility. When facilities motivate their members by captivating their attention and imagination and ensuring healthy activity by promoting safety, the facilities will sustain their existence even with the growing number of competing exercise facilities (Sawyer & Stowe, 2005).

SCF coordinators must embrace the advances in technology and recognize the value of incorporating entertainment mediums (televisions overhead, personal televisions for each piece of cardio equipment, music over speakers throughout the facility that leads someone to a workout site for a tip of the day, etc.) as they develop or refine existing programs, refurbish existing facilities, or plan to expand or construct new facilities. The coordinator's responsibilities are demanding; however, when armed with the correct knowledge base, the coordinator can create a facility through an arduous process with a successful outcome.

Cardiovascular training area at a fitness facility

SCF coordinators must be involved with every phase of the development process and continue to be heavily involved in day-to-day operations. From facility design concepts, to choosing equipment, to facility maintenance, the most successful planners immerse themselves in the process and understand every detail concerning strength and cardiovascular equipment and training. This chapter will take the reader on a journey through the full process of planning and operating SCFs.

Strength and Cardiovascular Training Facility Planning

Defining Objectives: Establishing Facility Goals

Accommodation of membership. Defining programmatic objectives is the first step to successfully planning a facility to meet the patrons' needs. Choices on the amount of free weight equipment, machines, and cardiovascular equipment are principally determined by the philosophy/priorities of the facility's leadership. The organization's goals, type and availability of exercise equipment, and size of the facility ultimately impact the clientele served. The clientele satisfaction can make or break the opening and continuing operation of a SCF. The users of a facility are the financial support. Before even beginning to establish goals for the facility, make a commitment to fully understand the population that will be the primary users (members) of the facility and make their needs the focus of the facility. So it is time to ask questions: Is the facility for sports performance, such as a collegiate football strength facility, is it a facility designed to serve primarily the student body and faculty of a university, or does it have a variety of users/functions?

Team-related facilities. Facilities that focus upon preparation and conditioning of student-athletes for sports teams must devise strategic time schedules for them to use the facilities. The size of the respective team, the instructor-to-student ratio, and the program objectives also impact accommodation. Certified staff-to-athlete ratios are based on the age and experience level of the athlete. Instructor ratios of 1:30 are generally acceptable; however, lower ratios are advisable for team sports that involve free weight and plyometric training. For a facility serving collegiate athletes, it is recommended that the facility does not exceed a 1:20 staff-to-athlete ratio. A high school facility should have a 1:15 staff-to-athlete ratio. A performance-related facility should be equipped with lifting platforms, free weights, dumbbells, medicine balls, plyometric boxes, and a few machines.

General population. Obesity and lack of physical activity have been linked to numerous medical complications and cognitive decline. Regular participation in physical activity is important to sustaining good health. Facilities that accommodate the general public, from teens to senior citizens, also have strategic issues of accommodation to be addressed. Even with a wide variety of benefits and the recent increase in participation of girls and women in sports, research still suggests that women are not lifting weights nearly as often as men. Many women are intimidated by weight training facilities because of the predominant number of men using the facilities. The Centers for Disease Control and Prevention (2011) reported that only 25.7% of women are strength training two or more times per week. Similarly, providing cardiovascular and strength training facilities strictly for women and seniors is highly recommended. It is advisable to design the facility so a variety of clientele can be accommodated. It is highly recommended to separate free weights, machines, and cardiovascular equipment within the facility. Doing so will increase member satisfaction and will reflect positively upon the organization because the unique needs of various populations, including women, can be better met.

Choosing facility goals. Before a facility is evaluated or constructed, have a clear understanding of the programmatic objectives and facility design vision. Outlining programmatic goals is the first step to successfully planning a facility to meet the prerequisites of the clientele. Equipment selection and allocation is an important issue for any strength and conditioning facility. What will be the necessary training philosophy for the target population: Olympic lifts, high-intensity training (HIT), machines, free weights (squat, bench press, incline bench press, military press, dead lift), trunk strength, posterior chain development, dumbbells? Do you need space for dynamic warm-ups, trunk strength, and speed/agility/quickness training?

Decisions on the amount of free weight equipment, machines, and cardiovascular equipment are largely determined by the philosophy/priorities of the facilities. Facilities targeted primarily toward athletic use tend to have more free weights, Olympic lifting areas, and a few machines. Physical education/athletic facilities tend to have a mixture of free weights, dumbbells, and machines. Facilities designed to service athletics, physical education, and community wellness tend to include a mixture of free weights, Olympic lifting areas, lifting machines, and cardiovascular equipment. Advances in technology such as flat-screen television monitors have made the incorporation of sports performance analysis equipment and entertainment mediums a part of the planning process.

After evaluating the membership, the planners should choose goals for the new or reinvented facility. To further analyze the target population, the planners of a SCF should answer a number of questions prior to initiating planning for the facility. The answers to these questions should be written down and should become guidelines for construction, equipment selection, and other planning requirements.

Demographics
- What is the demographic composition of clientele served: children, teens, middle-aged persons, senior citizens?
- What is their gender?
- What is the size of the total membership or the membership registered to use the strength training area?

Activities
- What are the specific training needs (e.g., strength, endurance, circuits, and power)?

- What specific activities or training functions will take place in the space?
- Will the spaces be used for team instruction, group programs, new member equipment orientations, and the like?
- Will the activities cater to individuals or small or large groups?
- What will be the size of classes?
- What equipment is needed to support the respective activities?
- What programs will be offered, for example, circuit training, free weights, cardiovascular training?
- What is the equipment preference (i.e., a mixture of free weights and machines, free weights only, machines only)?
- Is there a high demand for separate or coed areas?
- Has the equipment been chosen? If yes, who is the vendor, what are the specific dimensions of the equipment, and what is the proposed layout?

Limitations

- What are the financial constraints?
- What are the space limitations?
- What are the manpower constraints?
- What other limitations exist?

It is important for the planners to consider the desired outcomes of the completed facility. These outcomes should focus upon, but not be limited to, maximizing the use of existing or future space, ensuring the safety of participants, achieving program objectives successfully, and increasing user satisfaction. As the actual facility building process unfolds, the facility goals as well as the facility design concepts and philosophy should guide the decision-making process.

General Facility Design Concepts and Philosophy

Defining programmatic objectives is the first step to successfully planning a facility to meet the needs of the target population activity. Before any further steps are taken, the facility planner must keep some global ideas in mind as each decision is made. These ideas will be referred to as facility design concepts and philosophies and are fundamentally important because developing even the smallest facilities for the smallest populations can be a complicated process. It is important as selection of equipment and planning of facility layout begin not to lose focus on the global goals of the project. As the planning process unfolds, always consider principles of maximization and minimization.

Maximization

One of the most important concepts to consider is space use. Throughout each step of the facility planning process, the maximization of space must be well thought out. Understanding space utility maximization means having a vision and also entertaining many different ideas for layout. The process of idea trial and error can be arduous, but in many facility planning instances, it may be the only way to ensure the best use of space. It is also crucial to keep an eye on the future; how can the facility grow with populace expansion? Meeting only minimum space standards does not allow for potential membership growth and facility expansion. When designing new facilities, always focus your attention on how the facility can be expanded with structural modifications such as removal of interior walls or exterior walls. Strategic facility design includes preparing for future growth. When considering membership in the facility layout process, use a simple rule of thumb: a minimum space requirement per lifter of 30 ft (2.8 m) and a maximum of 60 ft (5.6 m; Greedwood, 2000).

It is best to always project larger at the beginning of a project. An ideal number is 100 sq ft per person for a room that is spacious and will meet future needs. The floor plan of the room (square, rectangle, L-shaped, round walls, and location of drinking fountains, etc.) must also be considered.

The visual appeal of a facility significantly impacts the ability to attract and engage participants. It is important to design visually pleasing facilities that are easily maintained. The desired outcome is to create energy and to make the visit to the facility an "experience." If facility coordinators do not have extensive experience analyzing the impact of interior design, using a professional interior designer to maximize the visual ambience is highly recommended.

Minimization

Liability will always be an issue for facility managers. Minimizing liability conflicts must begin at the first conceptualization of the facility. All types of exercise equipment for SCFs will be a risk for participants if not set up and placed in activity areas in full accordance with the manufacturer's instructions, tolerances, and recommendations. Accompanying safety signage, instruction placards, notices, and warnings must be posted or placed so users notice them prior to use. Safety in facility design is primarily achieved by providing sufficient walking space to keep members from inadvertently bumping into each other or when too many pieces of equipment are placed in an inadequate space. Also consider including all populations for the facility. The facility manager is responsible for providing facilities, training, programs, services, and related opportunities in accordance with all laws, regulations, and requirements mandating equal opportunity, access, and nondiscrimination. For example, all facilities must be planned in accordance with the Americans With Disabilities Act, which requires public facilities to provide appropriate services for persons with disabilities.

From Scratch: The New Facility

Building Design

The enormous financial rewards for a successful program have fueled a race to build larger, more lavish venues that can attract prospective clients. Designing the new facility from scratch can seem like a daunting process. Because the design process can be complicated, it is important to establish a set of detailed programmatic objectives and be aware of the design concepts and philosophies. These will act as a guide as critical decisions are made. Each facility will have different needs; some may be additions to other facilities and others may be a complete stand-alone facility, but there are general guidelines to follow to generate a successful facility. Table 17.1 represents an all-purpose checklist to help facility creators.

A successful facility begins with the assembling of qualified individuals. The construction of the facility is an exchange between facility planners and contractors. Starting with the facility planners, incorporate all of the management that will be involved with the facility. This may include athletic directors, a college administration, those in charge of the financial backing, and even individuals that will use the facility. It might also be beneficial to involve experienced professionals outside of the concerned administration. This could mean hiring someone well qualified onto the staff, but depending on the project, it may be worth the security to have someone with experience to outsource the project. To ensure that the planner's vision comes to fruition, select a contractor and construction team with a reputable reputation. Ask for and check numerous references from a variety of contractors before reaching a decision. Maintain a solid relationship with the project supervisor, and constantly review architectural drawings and process steps along the way.

Another crucial planning consideration is developing a realistic schedule and checklist for project completion. Making the checklist as detailed as possible will be a great aid during the process, especially as many tasks may be in progress at the same time. A wide variety of project planning software and related tools are now available. For a more complete idea of what to include as part of the facility checklist or project schedule, consult Table 17.1.

Physical Construction

The construction process will be in the hands of the project supervisor and contracted professionals. Before the construction begins, establish and discuss realistic deadlines. It may also be advantageous to establish deadline penalties to prevent the already-long process from becoming not only drawn out but also out of control. A successful facility planner will heavily involve himself or herself in the construction process with constant visits to the site, constant consultations with the project supervisor, and consistent referrals to the programmatic objectives.

Staff Considerations

Hiring staff needs to be a deliberate, thoughtful process. Selecting staff members must comply with federal guidelines for hiring practices. Each position may require a different level of education or certification, so it is imperative to fully understand the position and hire accordingly. A practical viewpoint to effective SCF operation and staffing can only come from years of experience developing and operating SCFs. Experienced planners understand how much square footage is needed, where they should be located, how they should be staffed, and how they should be equipped because of experience working in the profession. At this time, it may also be beneficial to set up in-house employee training. What will be the method for orientation to the facility? Also include, if applicable, continuing education programs.

Designing the Interior of a New or Existing Facility

Location and Access

Two important concepts should be considered when determining the location of the exercise rooms. The equipment involved with strength and conditioning/cardiovascular fitness is heavy and bulky, so for the easiest move, it is best to keep the location on the ground level. If this option is not possible, ensure that the flooring meets a load-bearing capacity of 150 lb/ft to completely compensate structurally for dropped equipment. If possible, allow for the construction of double doors in the facility or choose a room with double-door access. This will make it easier to move wider or awkward equipment configurations into the facility.

Sound is another important issue. For customer comfort, make sure the room chosen for exercise has plenty of sound absorption. Location is also important when considering an office for supervisors or management. The office should be centralized with large windows to oversee the facility from within the office.

Before any equipment enters the facility, carefully measure when developing the exits. All exits and emergency exits should be clearly marked. Entryways should meet a minimum width of 32 in. or 81 cm. The facility must be completely accessible; this includes doorways in and out of the facility, emergency exits, walkways, and ramps if necessary.

Ceilings and Floors

The ceiling height is an important factor when designing a new facility or remodeling an existing facility. The overhead clearance needs to be at least 12 ft to 14 ft high (3.7 m to 4.3 m), especially in platform or powerlifting areas. When creating a new facility, consider plans for ceiling fans, sprinkler systems, and other low-hanging

Table 17.1

Facility Design Checklist

General Features

- A comprehensive master plan has been prepared on the nature and scope of the program, and the special requirements for space, equipment, fixtures, and facilities have been dictated by the activities to be conducted (form follows function)
- The facility has been planned to meet the total requirements of the program, both present and future, as well as the special needs of those who are to be served. Possible future additions or expansions are included in the present plans to permit economy of construction and costs.
- The plans and specifications meet the codes of all governmental agencies (city, county, state) whose approval is required by law.
- The plans of the facility conform to accepted standards and practices.
- The following factors have been considered for the proposed facility and site:
  - feeder streets
  - parking areas
  - electrical supplies
  - water supplies
  - sewage lines
  - gas lines
  - storm drainage
  - soil topography
- The selection of equipment and supplies has been based on a cost-per-use ratio, as well as on ongoing maintenance costs.
- Sufficient attention has been given to fire code, fire and security systems, and emergency escape routes.
- Window heights are appropriate for privacy, safety, maintenance, and natural light.
- Floor and wall surfaces have been selected according to the following criteria: year-round usage, multiple uses, dust and moisture resistance, stainlessness, inflammability, nonabrasiveness, durability, resiliency, safety, maintenance, and cost per use.

Indoor Facilities (General)

- All passageways are free of obstructions so two-way traffic can occur. Every effort has been made to eliminate hazards.
- Buildings, specialty areas, and facilities are clearly defined.
- Administrative offices, exercise rooms, and service facilities are properly interrelated. The same is true for medical, first aid, and emergency rooms.
- Special needs of the people with physical disabilities are met, including a ramp into the building at a major entrance.
- Storage rooms are of adequate size and are accessible to appropriate areas. All dead space is used, such as areas under stairwells.
- Low-cost maintenance features have been considered.
- All areas, courts, facilities, equipment, climate control, security, and the like conform rigidly to detailed standards and specifications.
- Drinking fountains are conveniently placed in the locker rooms and workout areas or immediately adjacent to them.
- Provision is made for repair, maintenance, replacement, and storage of equipment.
- Antipanic hardware is used on doors as required by fire regulations.
- Properly placed hose bibs and drains are sufficient in size and quantity to permit flushing the entire wet area with a water hose.
- Space relationships and equipment are planned in accordance with the type and number of users.
- Warning signals, both visible and audible, are included in the plans.
- Ramps have a slope equal to or greater than a 1-ft rise in 12 ft.
- Minimum landings for ramps are 5 ft x 5 ft, they extend at least 1 ft beyond the swinging arc of a door, and they have at least a 6-ft clearance.

Climate Control

- There is climate control throughout the building (i.e., heating, ventilation, and air-conditioning, or HVAC)
- HVAC systems are on both a zone control and an individual room control system.
- Temperature and humidity are specific to a particular area.

Table 17.1 (cont.)

___

Electrical Control

- Lighting intensity meets approved standards
- An adequate number of electrical outlets are appropriately placed throughout the facility. They should be 3 ft above the floor, unless otherwise specified.
- Service area lights are controlled by dimmer units.
- Natural light, when used, is controlled properly to reduce glare.

Walls

- Electrical wall plates are located within the wall where needed and are firmly attached.
- Materials that clean easily and are impervious to moisture are used where moisture is prevalent.
- Drinking fountains are provided in adequate number and are properly recessed in the wall.
- One wall (at least) of the aerobics room has full-length mirrors.
- Wall coverings are aesthetically pleasing and match the overall decor of the facility.

Ceilings

- The ceiling height is adequate for the activities to be performed in a given area.
- Ceiling support beams are designed and engineered to withstand stress.
- Acoustical materials impervious to moisture are used in moisture-prevalent areas.
- All ceilings except those in storage areas are acoustically treated with sound-absorbent materials.
- Skylights in exercise rooms are impractical and therefore are seldom used because of problems in waterproofing roofs and controlling sunrays.
- Ceiling and crawl spaces are easily accessible for maintenance and repair purposes.

Floors

- Floor plates placed where needed are flush mounted.

Storage and Issuance Rooms

- The storage areas conform to fire laws.
- The storage and issue areas are centrally located and are of sufficient number to handle peak periods effectively.
- The doors to storage areas are wide and do not have a riser. The storage areas have appropriate security.
- Storage areas have adequate ventilation.

Activity Areas

- The floor area and dimensions are determined by the activities to be conducted.
- Adequate space or buffer zones are provided between activity areas.
- Wall surfaces allow use for activities, cleaning, and maintenance.
- The floor surface material allows for a maximum variety of uses.
- Adequate storage rooms are conveniently located near activity areas.
- Acoustical standards are met for all rooms.
- Lighting quality meets all standards.
- There are provisions included for an emergency safety lighting system.
- There is a properly installed, high-quality public address system.
- There are provisions for an intercom system that may be connected with the public address system.
- There are adequate climate control systems.
- Floor plates have been installed.
- There are provisions included for repair, maintenance, and installation of ceiling fixtures.
- There are provisions included for proper and necessary signs, both illuminated and non-illuminated, pertaining to areas, exits, and participants.
- There is a suitable lock-key system for doors, storage rooms, light controls, sound system controls, intercom controls, climate controls, and public address systems.

Table 17.1 (cont.)

Provisions for People With Disabilities

- Necessary provisions are present for parking, loading, and unloading areas, and ramps are provided where necessary. (Elevators should also be considered.)
- All doorways and passageways are of sufficient width to accommodate wheelchairs. The feasibility of electrically operated doors has been considered.
- All thresholds are flush.
- All doorways or entryways to toilets, telephones areas, food and refreshment areas, locker rooms, and special rooms are sufficient to accommodate wheelchairs.
- Restroom facilities are provided for people with disabilities.

items; the lowest hanging item must be at least 12 ft to 14 ft high, requiring the actual ceiling to be higher. Options must be carefully considered before including a drop ceiling in new facility plans. Suspended ceilings may allow for more design options, camouflaged pipes, and better sound absorption. A suspended ceiling may restrict ceiling height and reduce the versatility of the facility. The higher ceiling provides more functionality to the facility for Olympic lifting and medicine ball work and gives the facility a greater sense of openness.

The correct selection of flooring minimizes the potential of slips, falls, and other injuries and is based on a number of factors, including facility usage, facility location, and sound reduction. There are many flooring options, and the option chosen may depend on the concrete base of the facility. A poured floor will not have any seams but is more difficult to repair down the road, and if the floor is damaged, the patchwork is never the same as the original. The concrete base under a poured floor must be smooth and fairly level. Tile and rolled floors have seams, but they also have advantages. They can be moved to new space, can be replaced if damaged, and can be permanent depending on the type of adhesive used.

Square tiles, or a puzzle lock-type system of integration for covering just a part of a room are an option. This is often a nice choice for a dumbbell area. The industry standard for flooring is ⅜ in. thick for a resistance training area. Track surfacing companies such as Mondo® are now installing floors for SCF areas. Track surfacing companies are experienced with installing rubberized surfaces indoors and outdoors and may be competitive in the bid process.

The Deutsches Institut für Normung (DIN) standards (see Chapter 8) are ideally suited for selecting the appropriate flooring for cardiovascular and strength training centers. The following DIN standards should be considered.

Shock absorption. Without appropriate shock absorption, the potential for accruing an injury increases, specifically for ankle and knee joints. This is an essential component for aerobic and other group exercise spaces.

Standard vertical deformation/resilience. Insufficient energy return in a floor causes sore ankles if a surface is too hard. Excessive energy return creates a trampoline effect.

Sliding characteristics/surface friction. Side to side, lateral, rotating, and pivoting movements create strain on joints without the proper friction coefficient to minimize stress. "On a friction scale of 0.1 (ice) to 0.9 (fly paper), 0.5 to 0.7 is the DIN standard" (McPherson, 2004, p. 43).

Rolling load. Rolling load is a floor's ability to withstand heavy weight without breaking or sustaining permanent damage.

Walls and Mirrors

The walls of the SCF can serve as facility dividers, acoustic control, and aesthetic value if done properly. Separate rooms for themed training will be discussed later in the chapter. Different types of exercise produce various loud noises; the facility manager should control for noise when possible. The substance chosen for the walls will determine the amount of acoustical control, so it is important to select a durable material with acoustic value. Aesthetics are an underrated priority for gyms. The right decor can create a productive, happy atmosphere and can affect how a user feels. Options for wall decorations are limitless; you can use posters or painted figures or pictures, but, regardless, be deliberate with decoration. The design should reflect the aura of the organization and the users/membership. Patterned galvanized steel could also be mounted on the walls for protection and aesthetic value in high-traffic areas such as free weight areas where numerous benches, bars, and Olympic plates can come in contact with wall surfaces.

Mirrors should be positioned on walls in various areas throughout the facility, especially in front of powerlifting areas and squat racks. Mirrors will allow for personal trainers or strength and conditioning professionals to check lifting technique from various vantage points and also make the rooms seem more spacious. Be aware, however, that putting in too many mirrors may make certain individuals self-conscious. Mirrors should be placed at least 20 in. off the floor so that rolling equipment cannot hit or break them.

Signs

Keeping the proper signage in the strength training and cardiovascular fitness areas means a safer facility. Signs can be divided into three categories: vendor, weight facility, and cardiovascular area. Vendor signs include the warnings for equipment use. These should be displayed on equipment in the line of vision at all times or posted on televisions in the workout area. Weight facility signs refer to signage in the strength training area, and signs that belong near the cardiovascular equipment are termed *cardiovascular area signage*. Examples are displayed below.

Weight Facility Signage

Replace weights in their designated racks

Do not drop the weights

Children under the age of 14 must be accompanied by an adult

The use of a spotter is advisable

Clean equipment after use

Cardiovascular Area Signage

Cease to use equipment if light-headed or dizzy and notify a staff member immediately

Report any equipment malfunctions to a designated staff member on duty

Clean equipment after use

Electrical Service

A fitness facility has special electrical needs. Because of electrical machines and the necessity for electrical cleaning equipment to operate throughout the facility, a large number of outlets are essential. Grounded 100-V and 220-V outlets will be needed for larger cardiovascular machines. Lighting will also be an important issue for visual appeal and safety. The number of foot-candles designates the level of lighting. Optimal lighting is considered 75 foot-candles to 100 foot-candles, 50 foot-candles at floor level. The facility should be void of dark spots and equipment should be well illuminated. Lighting fixtures should be energy efficient and compliant with Green Seal Environmental Standards. Exit signs and signage for people who are hearing impaired should be illuminated and periodically inspected for burned out bulbs.

Environmental Factors

Air temperature should be kept constant between 72°F and 78°F (22°C and 26°C). If the room is too cold, athletes can become chilled after they finish warming up or between sets; if the room is too hot, participants can become overheated or lose motivation to continue. Keeping constant facility temperature will also prevent condensation, damp floors, and equipment corrosion. Relative humidity should be at 60% or less. Air circulation should be at least eight to 12 air exchanges per hour. The result should be no detectable strong odors in the room and equipment free of slickness or rust due to high humidity. Lack of climate control can significantly reduce the life span of equipment, causing rust and moving pieces to corrode.

Color and Noise

Color. Color is a significant dimension that contributes to the psychological, emotional, and physical response of participants. The coordination of equipment frame colors, upholstery colors, wall colors and textures, and flooring patterns; use of lighting; ceiling heights; and window treatments are all factors that contribute to the overall visual appeal of the exercise experience. Facility enhancements may be as simple as painting accent colors on white walls for the purposes of creating a space that not only is visually appealing but also makes a person feel good.

Noise. A significant amount of noise is generated within an exercise facility. Impact noise and vibrations occur from dropping of weights, participants moving simultaneously during an aerobics class, and members' use of treadmills and other equipment, combined with high-volume music. Strategically placing group exercise activities within the context of the actual center, along with the including built-in acoustical controls, will prevent these venues from negatively impacting other programs such as yoga classes. The strategies for addressing these issues ultimately depend upon whether a group is planning a new construction or trying to remedy an existing acoustical problem. Some weight rooms will provide music from a central system throughout the facility. Music volume should always be low enough so that trainers and members can easily speak. To ensure the music evenly fills the room or rooms, place speakers at the high corners of the wall and ceiling.

Another option for structural modification for new or existing venues is multiple layers of drywall on both sides of studs when activities are going to be placed next to each other. Constructing floating wooden platform floors to support cardiovascular equipment is also another solution. Strength training acoustical issues can be enhanced by using rubber flooring and rubber bumpers between weight plates on selected weight equipment. Addressing acoustical issues with the architect, engineer, and acoustical experts should occur early in the design phase of a new exercise facility. Acoustical problems can be remedied by discussing them before they negatively impact the operation.

Selecting Equipment

Resistance Training Equipment

Just as important as the aesthetic features of the space available for the SCF is the type of equipment used. Defining programmatic objectives is the first step in successfully planning a facility to meet the needs of sports teams. Choices on the amount of free weight equipment, machines, and cardiovascular equipment are principally determined by the philosophy/priorities of the facility's leadership. This makes having an experienced certified strength and conditioning professional involved in the planning of the strength and conditioning facility important. A comprehensive strength training facility will include Olympic benches, bars, and plates; weight trees; power racks that include adjustable spotter's bar for squats or bench press purposes; adjustable benches for dumbbell activities; cable crossover and handle accessories; smith machine; assisted dip; hyperextension; and abdominal boards.

Amount of equipment needed. The number of Olympic benches and power racks is ultimately dependent upon the projected number of participants using the facility during peak hours of operation. Based on philosophy, a room should be laid out based on the "meat and potatoes" of the program, and pieces of equipment fill in that are easily programmable. Pieces that cause bottlenecking (10 to 20 people waiting for one piece of equipment) in workouts should be avoided.

Racks. Racks can range from half racks for a smaller space to a full squat rack. A combination rack can be used for bench press and squatting at the same station. These are usually placed on a platform and have become popular in performance-oriented facilities. The benches and power racks are generally manufactured with 7 gauge to 11 gauge steel. The lower gauge rating (7 gauge) is desirable for heavy loads and tends to be sturdier. Price ranges vary based on the company, quality of equipment, and where it is manufactured. Lifting platforms can have squat racks or be stand-alone stations for Olympic lifting. The selection of the appropriate Olympic bars is determined by the tensile strength. Bars used for squatting, Olympic lifts, and bench press ultimately require the 1,500-lb test. It is generally recommended to have a bar that is used for the squat and bench press movements and a bar that is designed for Olympic lifting movements. The types of Olympic plates available are steel, rubber, or polyurethane coated. The selected style is ultimately influenced by the budget and the desired aesthetic value. Olympic plates and dumbbells can be monogrammed with the organization's logo to re-

inforce the organization's brand identity. It is important to determine whether the plates and dumbbells should be purchased in kilos or pounds. Dumbbell sets generally range from 5 lb to 120 lb. It is common for many strength facilities to have two to three full sets of dumbbells. The dumbbells range from simple plate-loaded bars, to molded cast iron, to the more expensive rubber-coated cast iron.

Selectorized systems. Selectorized or pin select machines have become an important and effective tool for many types of fitness training and bodybuilding. Used in conjunction with free weights and cardiovascular workouts, selectorized machines can help a person achieve goals for strength, weight loss, endurance, and toning. Selectorized weight systems offer a safe workout and an easy way of changing resistance for sets and workout partners. These types of machines work well in a multiuse facility. Upholstery and padding on machines is another consideration. For example, on glute hamstring machines, you can choose full pads or half-moon pads. Commercial strength equipment manufacturers include Body Masters®, Cybex®, Flex, Hoist®, Icarian®, Life Fitness®, Badger®, Nautilus®, and Paramount®. One complete line of selectorized weight equipment should be included in the strength training venue. Typically, a complete line (11 to 18 pieces) will accommodate all major muscle groups. Selectorized equipment is ideal for beginners, women, and seniors because it eliminates the balance component and reduces the technical training associated with using free weights. Many of the selectorized pieces such as the lat pull down will use a pulley system with cables. Pulley machines can be with or without seats. The pulleys can be cables or Kevlar® belts. Cable pulley systems are easier to use but require more maintenance. Kevlar® belts last longer but are sometimes difficult to install and not as smooth or as easy to use as cables. Cables must be constantly checked by the fitness staff for wear and tear.

Plate-loaded equipment. Plate-loaded equipment has gained popularity in recent years. Plate-loaded machines are considered convenient to use because the need for co-

A selectorized weight system

ordination is minimal and the amount of resistance can be narrowly defined. This kind of machine can accommodate a range of users, making it ideal for a multiuse strength and conditioning facility. Hammer Strength® is the dominant manufacturer of plate-loaded equipment in the industry today.

Vendors. The purchasing of exercise equipment is exciting; however, it is a time-consuming and involved process. There are many options to be considered when choosing equipment. With the numerous manufacturers of exercise equipment, selecting a vendor is becoming much more difficult. Purchases should be from reputable manufacturers that meet the fitness and industry standards for commercial equipment. Equipment for the home should never be considered for a public facility. Trade shows such as Club Industry can guide these types of purchasing decisions. Prospective buyers can try out equipment and compare equipment vendors in one location. It is also an opportune time to establish rapport with vendors, particularly when planning to do business with them in the future. Additionally, other fitness facilities can be consulted to determine their level of satisfaction with a brand of equipment being considered for purchase. What do they like or not like about the selected equipment? What common maintenance issues have they had to address? What

was response time for making repairs and the quality of service? Keep in mind that equipping a room all at once might be prohibitive due to the cost. Many schools outfit fitness rooms in 2-year to 3-year phases. Some are completely done by the booster club, a generous donation from someone in the community, PE grant, PE budget, athletic budgets, or a combination of all of these. The projected numbers in Table 17.2 are attainable with a combination of the above-mentioned efforts and funds.

Aerobic Training Equipment

All equipment selected should reflect the needs of the clientele and the limitations of the facility. When making decisions, perform research and probe manufacturers to understand population needs and take inventory of facility electrical supply, budgetary considerations, and equipment warranties (2 years for most). Consider questions such as the number of patrons needed to be accommodated at one time. Consider a mixture of pieces (treadmills, ellipticals, recumbent bikes, spin bikes, upper body ergometer, stairsteppers, rowing machines). How many pieces need to be ADA compliant for individuals with disabilities?

Equipment selection. Are there any power restrictions (110-V vs. 220-V) in the room that would not accommodate certain pieces? After these ideas are properly reflected

Table 17.2

Cost Estimates for Secondary School SCFs

Small Schools
- 500 or fewer students
- 25–30 per class
- Flooring: 2,500 sq ft to 3,000 sq ft; $12,500 to $45,000
- Weight equipment: $60,000 to $150,000
- Cardio equipment (10 pieces): avg. $2,500 per piece, $25,000
- Total to expect to pay = $97,500 to $220,000, depending on bells and whistles

Medium Schools
- 501–999
- 35–45 per class
- Flooring: 3,500 sq ft to 4,500 sq ft; $17,500 to $67,500
- Weight equipment: $90,000 to $180,000
- Cardio equipment (15 pieces): avg. $2,500 per piece, $37,500
- Total to expect to pay = $195,000 to $285,000, depending on bells and whistles

Large Schools
- Over 1,000
- 50–70 per class
- Flooring: 5,000 sq ft to 7,000 sq ft; $25,000 to $105,000
- Weight equipment: $135,000 to $300,000
- Cardio equipment (20 pieces): avg. $2,500 per piece, $50,000
- Total to expect to pay = $210,000 to $455,000, depending on bells and whistles

---

upon, it is possible with some vendors to engage in a trial usage period for equipment. This will allow members to give direct feedback. After receiving feedback from members and inspecting other venues, choose the appropriate pieces of equipment. Again, select a variety of equipment for the cardiovascular area, including treadmills, mechanical stair-climbing machines, bicycle ergometers, computerized cycles, rowing ergometers, upper body ergometers, and total body conditioning machines.

At least one circuit of progressive resistance training equipment, other than free weights, should be included in the cardiovascular fitness area. This could be either a machine or workout station for each of the following muscle groups: gluteus, quadriceps, hamstrings, calves, chest, upper back, lower back, shoulders, triceps, biceps, and abdomen. This area can be used for group exercise classes or circuit training.

Group classes. With the growing popularity and variety of group exercise programs, the number of accessories associated with these activities is also expanding. Each class may have individual needs, and it is important to acquire the equipment with the number of participants for each class in mind. Storage of equipment is a significant priority when evaluating existing and planning future group exercise facilities. Avoiding the appearance of clutter and eliminating potential hazards is possible with the installation of tiered shelving that can be rolled out and put into a storage closet after an activity has been completed. Mirrors serve as functional tools in this area, allowing the instructor to observe participants' form and technique. Along with the equipment for each individual class, storage should be planned for as well.

Cycling classes. The facility requirements of the indoor cycling studio should complement the objective associated with the activity, which is to enhance mental imagery of an outdoor riding experience. To a certain extent, this activity should be perceived as a theater production where the instructor can control the lighting and sound with dimmer controls that contribute to the ambience and visual effect. DVD projection is also desirable. The group facilitator's bike should be placed on a platform for participants to observe the cadence, form, and technique of the instructor, as well as for the instructor to observe the participants. Self-contained heating, ventilating, and air-conditioning (HVAC) systems separate from the main facility are desirable considering the intensity of the activity and the perspiration and heat that accrue. Ceiling fans should also be installed to circulate the air and keep participants comfortable. The total space requirements are ultimately dependent upon the number of bikes to be included in the indoor cycling studio.

Recommendations. The International Health, Racquet, and Sportsclub Association (IHRSA), National Strength and Conditioning Association (NSCA), and the ACSM have recommended that strength and cardiovascular training area planners should consider providing

- a variety of equipment for the cardiovascular area including treadmills, mechanical stair-climbing machines, bicycle ergometers, computerized cycles, rowing ergometers, upper body ergometers, and total body conditioning machines;
- at least one circuit of progressive resistance training equipment (other than free weights) that includes either a machine or a workout station for each of the following muscle groups: gluteus, quadriceps, hamstrings, calves, chest, upper back, lower back, shoulders, triceps, biceps, and abdomen; and
- a circuit for resistance training in a fashion that allows users to train the largest muscle groups first and then proceed to the smaller muscle groups. All compound movement machines should be placed in the circuit before isolated movement machines involving the same muscle(s).

Considerations to be taken under advisement when selecting cardiovascular equipment include

- age and condition of clientele served,
- available space in cardiovascular area,
- sufficient electrical supply to support equipment,
- budgetary considerations,
- maintenance requirements of selected equipment,
- proximity of equipment repair technicians to fitness facility, and
- length of warranty (e.g., 2 years for most common equipment).

Stretching and Bodyweight Exercise Equipment

The designated space for stretching and core body training is ultimately dependent upon the scope and extent to which the following accessories are available: stability balls, speed and agility training accessories, medicine balls, bands/tubing, plyometric training boxes, power wheels, functional training grids, balance and stabilization boards, and pads. Establishing systems to support the use and storage of accessories is essential. It is important to decide in advance whether the area will be used for individual use only or on a formal group instructional basis. A minimum of 175 sq ft to 300 sq ft is suggested for this space.

Delivery and Arrival

The installation of equipment must be handled with caution and the utmost care. A firm delivery date and time needs to be established with the shipping company. An assessment must be made to determine what entrance modifications, if any, need to be made to the facility when equipment arrives.

Questions to consider include

- Should the facility be temporarily closed?
- Is the removal of door jambs required?
- Are pallet jacks or a four-wheel cart required?
- Will additional staff be needed to assist with setup and installation, or is this service included in the delivery and setup process?

Photos should be taken and notes should be made pertaining to the condition of equipment upon arrival, specifically if it is damaged. Upholstery colors and the models of equipment must be checked. The equipment should be inventoried immediately by securing the serial numbers from the delivery sheets or manually recording the numbers off of each piece of equipment. This is important because when you request future repairs, respective vendors will ask for serial numbers before processing equipment repair tickets. Deliveries should be signed off on only after items are received as acceptable. If equipment is not correct, an immediate call to the manufacturer or sales representative will determine the course of action to take, which may include the reloading of equipment onto the truck.

Organizing Equipment

After equipment has been ordered, the next step is to organize the equipment within the facility. This process can seem complicated due to many different types of equipment being placed in sometimes limited spaces. One suggestion to streamline this action is to decide first upon a unifying theme for the weight room. This requires a careful look at the programmatic objectives and specific needs of the membership. One idea is to organize resistance training machines according to the targeted body part and then designate specific areas for other themed activities, such as cardiovascular exercise, stretching, and bodyweight exercise. Some weight rooms begin by separating spaces for the different types of exercise and then organize equipment within those designated areas. Regardless of the strategy, deciding on a theme first will guide the decision-making process.

Placing Equipment

Aside from designating specific areas for the three types of activities, equipment placement should be used to positively affect the visual field and safety policy. An exercise facility's visual appeal depends on equipment placement. To increase the visual field within the facility, the tallest machinery, such as squat racks and lat pull machines, should be placed against the walls and, for safety, may need to be bolted to the floor. Smaller equipment should be placed toward the middle to not only increase vision but also promote easy movement across the room or

rooms. On the same note, taller, more upright cardiovascular machines should be placed near the walls of the facility or toward the back of the cardiovascular fitness area with lower, seated cardiovascular machines toward the middle and front. To maintain safety, equipment should be at least 6 in. from mirrors, with powerlifting exercises placed significantly away from mirrors to avoid glass breakage and collisions. More specific measures to place equipment will be discussed in the next section.

Spacing Equipment

Following are guidelines for equipment spacing suggested by the NSCA in Chapter 24 of the second edition of the *Strength and Conditioning Professional Standards and Guidelines* (Greenwood, 2000). The NSCA established many of the recommended standards for professionals in the field of strength and conditioning. This organization is a great resource when establishing policies and procedures for a SCF.

Facility traffic flow

- Traffic flow should be around the perimeter of resistance training and aerobic exercise machine areas. Different colors of flooring or carpet can be used to identify walkways through the facility.
- There should be at least one walkway that bisects the room to provide quick and easy access in and out of the facility in an emergency.
- An unobstructed pathway 3 ft (91 cm) wide should be maintained in the facility at all times as stipulated by federal, state, and local laws. Resistance training machines and equipment and aerobic machines must not block or hinder traffic flow.
- Although ceiling height does not affect traffic flow on the floor, the ceiling should be free of low-hanging apparatus (beams, pipes, lighting, signs, etc.) and high enough to allow clients to perform overhead and jumping exercises. A minimum of 12 ft (3.7 m) is recommended.

Body weight exercise, flexibility, and medicine ball area

- A 49 sq ft (4.6 sq m) area (7 ft x 7 ft, or 2.1 m x 2.1 m) for each client should be allotted for stretching and warm-up activities.
- A larger area may be needed for medicine ball work and partner stretching.

Resistance training machine area

- All resistance training machines and equipment must be spaced at least 2 ft (61 cm), preferably 3 ft (91 cm), apart. To effectively serve clients who use wheelchairs, more than 3 ft (91 cm) may be needed.

- If a free weight exercise is performed in a resistance training machine area, a 3-ft (91cm) safety space cushion is needed between the ends of the barbell and all adjacent stations.
- More than 3 ft (91 cm) of space is recommended between multistation machines and single-station machines. Multistation machines require more space than single-station machines.

Resistance training free weight area

- The ends of all Olympic bars should be spaced 3 ft (91 cm) apart.
- The area designated for a free weight station should be able to accommodate three to four people.
- Racks holding fixed-weight barbells should have a minimum of 3 ft (91 cm) between the ends of the bars.
- Weight trees should be placed in close proximity to plate-loaded equipment and benches, but not closer than 3 ft (91 cm).

Olympic lifting area

- The dimensions of the Olympic lifting area should be at least 8 ft (2.43 m) x 8 ft (2.43 m) and accommodate three to four people.
- The walkway around an Olympic lifting platform should be 3 ft to 4 ft (91 cm to 122 cm) wide.

Aerobic Exercise Area

- Ideally, a space cushion of 3 ft (91 cm) should be provided on all sides of aerobic exercise machines (placement too close to walls should be avoided) for safety and to allow clients and supervising personal trainers easy access.
- It is suggested that each type of aerobic machine needs its own spacing: 24 sq ft (2.2 sq m) for stationary bikes and stair machines, 6 sq ft (0.6 sq m) for rowing machines, and 45 sq ft (4.2 sq m) for treadmills. These recommendations include the needed space between machines.

Health assessment and testing area. An organization truly having a vested interest in the physical well-being of their membership will have a state-of-the-art fitness assessment, consultation, and educational seminar room (Sawyer & Stowe, 2005). This private area is used to obtain baseline measurements for future programming and personal training.

Programmatic Considerations

The members' achievement of their fitness goals requires that they have a baseline to measure their progress prior to beginning their exercise programs. The health assessment process is an integral part in developing exercise plans. The scope of the health assessment process and the

extent that educational and lifestyle programs will be offered must be determined because these dimensions will dictate the amount of facility space required. Most health assessments include body composition analysis, blood pressure screenings, muscular strength and flexibility testing, submaximal cardiovascular testing, cholesterol screenings, health history appraisals, and nutrition consultations.

The following are specific fitness testing space and facility requirements:

- The scope of space required is ultimately dependent upon the scope of the health and fitness protocol completed. The fitness testing space requires a minimum of 100 sq ft to 180 sq ft, a consultation room (90 sq ft to 120 sq ft), and a seminar room (20 sq ft per participant), all with minimum 8-ft ceilings with suspended acoustical panels and wall construction comprised of dry wall and painted with epoxy paint.
- The electrical outlets need to be strategically located in proximity to the exercise testing equipment and should be ground fault interrupters (GFI). Fluorescent lighting within this area should be at least 50 foot-candles of illumination at the floor surface.
- A sink in the facility is required.
- The emergency response system should include emergency lighting and audible alarms. This is necessary for warning other facility personnel of a medical emergency in the area.
- Because of the function of the space, adhering to these standards is essential. The HVAC mechanical systems must have a temperature environment of 68°F to 72°F (22°C to 26°C), humidity control of 55°F, and ventilation (eight to 12 exchanges per hour with a ratio of 40:60, outside air to inside air).
- Size: The testing area includes a fitness testing space (100 sq ft to 180 sq ft), a counseling room (90 sq ft to 120 sq ft), and a seminar room (20 sq ft per participant), all with 8-ft ceilings (Peterson & Tharrett, 1997). There should be adequate space in this area to house two chairs, a desk, a file cabinet, a storage cabinet, a computer station, a bicycle ergometer, a flexibility tester, a treadmill, control console, crash cart, metabolic cart, 12-lead electrocardiogram (ECG), ECG defibrillator, cholesterol analyzer, examination table, double sink, spine board, and a storage cabinet for equipment such as skinfold calipers, stopwatches, and stethoscope(s).
- Walls: The walls should be a simple drywall construction, epoxy painted with a pleasing color(s), appropriate graphics for the area, and a bulletin board.
- Floor: The floors should be carpeted with an antistatic and antifungal commercial-grade carpet, color coordinated with the walls and equipment in the room.

- Ceiling: A suspended acoustical panel ceiling is appropriate.
- Electrical: The electrical needs of the equipment in the room should be considered as well as the eventual location of the equipment. There should be numerous electrical outlets around the perimeter of the room. The outlets near the sink should be GFI. The recommended lighting for this area is fluorescent units that will produce at least 50 foot-candles of illumination at the floor surface.
- Climate control: The mechanical considerations for this space include heating and cooling (68°F to 72°F [22°C to 26°C]), humidity control (55°F), and ventilation (eight to 12 exchanges per hour with a ratio of 40:60, outside air to inside air). Due to the activities in this room, careful consideration to cooling, humidity control, and ventilation are necessary.
- Plumbing: A facility should ensure that every fitness testing space either has a sink or access to a sink.
- Security: There should be emergency lighting and an audible emergency alarm to alert other personnel to a medical emergency in the testing area.

Equipment for the Fitness Testing Area

The NSCA (Greenwood, 2000) and ACSM (Peterson & Tharrett, 1997) suggested that a facility should ensure that its fitness testing area has the following equipment described below.

The fitness testing area should have a bicycle ergometer, a treadmill or a fixed-step device (e.g., a bench) of a desired height, skinfold calipers or other body composition measurement device, sit-and-reach bench on goniometer, tensiometer, or other device for measuring muscular strength and endurance, perceived exertion chart, clock, metronome, sphygmomanometer (blood pressure cuff), stethoscope, tape measure, scale, and first aid kit.

The health promotion and wellness area requires a computer, overhead projector, video system, LCD projector, conference table, and chairs.

The fitness testing, health promotion, and wellness area should have a system that provides for and protects the complete confidentiality of all user records and meetings.

Operations

Scheduling and Staff-to-Member Ratios

Depending on the facility programmatic objectives, scheduling time in the facility can be a small or a large issue. Most SCFs, however, will need to schedule time in a section of the gym in one way or another, for personal training, for aerobic classes, or for athletic teams. Improper scheduling can lead to crowding and dangerous staff-to-member ratios; both of these negative consequences can and should be avoided.

An important concept to understand before scheduling is the use of space and membership flow. Personal training or one-on-one exercise consultation should not be scheduled during peak hours unless the facility houses a special room for personal training. Aerobic or other themed exercise classes should have their own room so they can be scheduled throughout the day according to staff limitations.

Scheduling. Scheduling becomes more complicated when facilities want to incorporate team sports, for example, varsity college weight rooms or facilities that accommodate youth sports or organized group activities. Typically, teams should be scheduled separately with in-season teams receiving time priority. Some small teams, however, can be scheduled together in larger weight rooms if equipment use does not overlap. For example, if a tennis team is working on plyometrics and agility drills, a powerlifting team can use the platforms at the same time. If one season is crowded with two or more teams, a rotating schedule of alternating days may work best to accommodate all athletes; one team can come in Monday, Wednesday, and Friday, and the other team may come in Tuesday, Thursday, and Saturday. Some bigger teams may not be able to be scheduled all at once for effective training, so it is important to consider the alternative and split the team into groups. The team may be split by position, a situation appropriate for football, or can be split by ability, sometimes appropriate for youth team sports, especially those that include a range of ages.

Staff-to-member ratios. One critical variable to think about when scheduling is staff-to-member ratios. Because of the many different uses of the SCFs, it is important that traffic flow be monitored and investigated in relation to the presence of dedicated and/or certified professionals. Ideally, a higher number of dedicated strength and conditioning professionals should be used in those facilities with greater traffic flow and use levels (Armitage-Johnson, 1994). Having supervision from professionals is key to the safety and lifting technique of exercising members, but making sure the proper number of professionals is in the facility for any given activity is just as significant. A general rule to operate by is the younger and more inexperienced the athlete or member is, the more professional supervision is needed. Junior high athletes and members require a 1:10 staff-to-member ratio, high school-aged athletes and members require a 1:15 ratio, and members older than the junior high or high school level require a 1:20 ratio. It is also recommended that facilities do not exceed a 1:50 staff-to-member ratio.

Maintenance

Proper maintenance of the facility and facility equipment means SCF longevity and safety. The type of maintenance necessary for facility upkeep demands an understanding of the types of materials and machines being dealt with. Maintenance is often a chore balanced between custodial, personal training, and gym supervising staff. Devising a maintenance schedule for both the facility and the facility equipment can ensure appropriate, essential, and regular upkeep.

Facility maintenance. First on the facility maintenance list is the flooring. No matter the type of flooring, the floor should be inspected regularly. Tile, resilient rubber, and carpet floors as well as mats must be either treated with an antibacterial and antifungal agent or must contain these attributes. It is also important that mats and carpeting are nonabsorbent. Wood flooring demands extra attention to loose screws, nicks in boards, and other potentially hazardous problems. All types of flooring should be inspected for malfunctions daily, with daily cleaning suggested.

Walls and wall hangings such as mirrors and signs should be cleaned two to three times a week or as needed with special attention to high-traffic areas. Although the cleaning for walls is not as high maintenance as the flooring, wall safety still must be maintained. Ceilings must also be cleaned, and broken areas of the ceiling must be replaced as needed. Dust should not be allowed to accumulate anywhere in the facility. Regular inspection ensures that small problems never become big problems.

Equipment maintenance. Stretching and bodyweight exercise areas are usually comprised of a mat or another kind of skin-contact flooring and a variety of equipment such as medicine balls, individual mats, elastic cords, or physioballs. Because all of these items are in possible contact with membership skin, daily cleaning and disinfecting are necessary. Signs and employees should also emphasize cleaning by the members. Each individual should be encouraged to spray and wipe down equipment after each use; these items for cleaning should be multiple and available in well-seen areas. To ensure the longevity of the flooring in the area, equipment that could pierce or tear the floor or mat should be kept out of the area, and at the end of each day, all equipment should be inspected.

Resistance training areas are comprised of machines, free weights, and sometimes Olympic lifting areas. Each group has its own challenge for maintenance, but in general each group will include upholstery in contact with skin. The upholstery needs to be cleaned and disinfected daily and should be free from tears and cracks. Resistance training machines should not have loose parts, including bolts, screws, cables, chains, or worn parts. Machines with guide rods should be cleaned and lubricated two to three times per week. Chains, cables, and pulleys should be checked and fixed when normal alignment is disrupted. Free weights include racks, benches, weights, and dumbbells. Bench and rack welds should be inspected monthly or as needed. Dumbbells should be checked frequently for loose parts. In the Olympic lifting area, bar maintenance is

critical; these bars require attention to the rotating areas to ensure the proper rotation and should be free from chalk or other buildup (Greenwood & Greenwood, 2000). Because Olympic lifters use various types of accessory equipment to lift, it is important to make sure leftover items are replaced to their original storage. If the area includes wooden platforms, check the platform for cracks and splinters weekly.

The aerobic exercise area can be a challenge for cleaning. These areas typically, after prolonged use, gather sweat from the user. Encourage users to disinfect the equipment after each use. The same types of cleaning materials provided in stretching and bodyweight exercise areas should also be present in the aerobic exercise areas. Machinery should also be maintained, and no loose parts should exist. Check these monthly or as needed. To conclude the maintenance section, if a piece or pieces of a particular machine or weight are found to be broken, place a sign in the line of vision signifying the equipment is out of order.

Strength Training Equipment Maintenance Checklist

The following are the standard inspections that should be included in a comprehensive maintenance program:

- Inspection of weight stacks, cables, and attachments. Are they appropriately secured?
- Inspection of snap hooks. Are the clasps closed appropriately?
- Are there worn or frayed cables on equipment?
- Are chrome endcaps on dumbbells becoming jagged or flaking shrapnel pieces?
- Are dumbbells tightened and secured?
- Are bolts appropriately tightened on all benches?

Keeping Records

Keeping both accurate and up-to-date records is an essential element of a successful weight training and aerobic facility. Two main categories of records must be a part of the venue documentation: clientele records and maintenance records. Clientele records include payments, workouts with hired trainers, complaints, and other reports. It is hoped that a liability case will never happen, but if such a problem should occur, accurate records may be critical evidence. This is why maintenance records are so important. Abiding by the suggested manufacturer's protocol not only ensures safety but also prevents liability (Greenwood & Greenwood, 2000). Other records may include equipment purchase and warranty, schedules, and contractor receipts.

Conclusion

Before evaluating and/or constructing a SCF, have a clear understanding of the programmatic objectives and the vision of the facility design. It is important for the planners to consider the desired outcomes of the completed SCF. These outcomes should focus upon, but not be limited to, maximizing the use of existing or future space, ensuring the safety of participants, achieving program objectives successfully, and increasing user satisfaction. Access to physical activity facilities is the first step to achieving higher exercise rates among all age groups. Sport/recreation administrators must be ready to evaluate their facilities based on the needs of the population and properly follow through with appropriate accommodations.

Creating ADA Accessible Strength and Conditioning Facilities

The Americans with Disabilities Act (ADA) was created in 1990 by the United States Department of Justice as a federal civil rights law to prohibit discrimination against people with disabilities; now nearly 18% of our population (50 million Americans) (McDonnell, 2006). The 1990 ADA standards set minimum requirements for public facilities according to their market segment. The majority of fitness facilities fall under Title III: Public Accommodations and Commercial Facilities. The requirements for this provision encompassed: minimum heights for countertops and light switches, signage, bathroom fixture selection, walkway widths, railings and flooring choices. These requirements were an attempt to make public facilities more accessible to people with disabilities (Department of Justice, 2012). Since 1990, numerous stakeholders lobbied for changes to augment accessibility standards. As a result, the more stringent 2010 standards were created.

On Friday, July 23, 2010, Attorney General Eric Holder signed final regulations revising the Department's ADA regulations, including the ADA Standards for Accessible Design. The official text was published in the Federal Register on September 15, 2010 (corrections to this text were published in the Federal Register on March 11, 2011). March 15, 2012, marked a significant date for fitness facilities as it pertains to updates to the Americans with Disabilities Act (ADA). New requirements from the 2010 update of the ADA went into effect on that date, and those requirements affected fitness facilities with and without pools (Department of Justice, 2012).

For the most part, the 2010 standards do not impact preexisting fitness facilities that have not completed any new construction or alterations. Existing facilities are considered to be in ADA compliance if they meet the 1990 standards, also referred to as safe harbor. The one exception to this rule is items in the 2010 standards that were not included in the 1990 publications. Such is the case with exercise equipment (Department of Justice, 2012). This includes cardiovascular and resistance training apparatus.

The new ADA standards assert that a fitness facility must guarantee at least one type of each piece of exercise equipment is accessible to people with disabilities. This condition necessitates that every piece of equipment,

unless an exact duplicate of the same model exists, must be accessible. For example, if a facility has two lines of 10-piece circuit equipment, even if two machines target the same muscle group, all 20 pieces must be placed in a way that they can be used by someone with a disability. In short, each piece of equipment needs an open space available (minimum 30 inches by 48 inches) for either forward or parallel position for transfer (space required for a wheelchair user room to enter and exit the apparatus) (Department of Justice, 2012).

Typically, facilities are mandated to eradicate any barriers that limit accessibility, assuming it is readily achievable, which means that the business would not endure any serious hardships (financial or otherwise) by removing the obstructions. Since accessibility compliance involves minimal resources other than repositioning equipment, it easily fits into the readily attainable designation, which means it is a requirement for almost all new and preexisting fitness facilities (McDonnell, 2006).

Noncompliance with these requirements can be expensive for strength and conditioning facilities. The Department of Justice can seek monetary damages and civil penalties up to $55,000 for a first offense and up to $110,000 for each subsequent offense. In addition, many states allow individuals to directly sue businesses for discrimination outside of the Department of Justice. This means fitness facilities can be sued by one or more individuals for any violation (Broadhag, 2012). Risk management must be an active part of facility manager duties. Fitness facility managers can identify risks through a variety of modalities: they can survey participants, employees and evaluate the facilities in question for ADA compliance. Questioning experts in the field and maintaining professional guidelines work to minimize risk.

Cardiovascular Equipment for Special Populations

Cardiovascular equipment represents a large part of the commercial exercise equipment portfolio in the modern fitness center. From treadmills and stationary bikes to elliptical machines and upper-body ergometers, cardiovascular equipment was originally created for a progressively sedentary public. Huang, Macera, Blair. Brill, Kohl, and Kronenfeld (1998) reported a strong association between low levels of aerobic fitness and a higher rate of functional limitations. Cardiovascular equipment that was once designed for the typical exerciser's height, weight, and fitness goals has been modified to fit the expanding membership that now includes the disabled population. Many cardio products are endorsed as appropriate for people of all fitness levels. However, some exercisers need some additional modifications to allow specialization (McDonnell, 2006). Section 206.2.13 of the 2010 Standards requires an accessible route to serve cardiovascular machines and related equipment (see Figure 17.1). Section 236 of the 2010

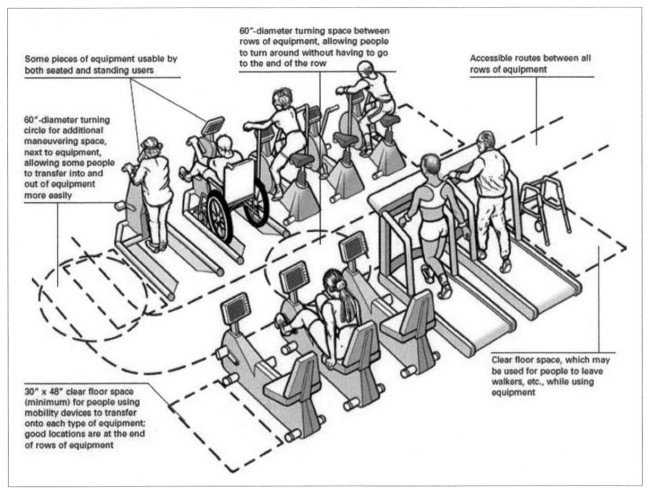

Some pieces of equipment usable by both seated and standing users

60"-diameter turning circle for additional maneuvering space, next to equipment, allowing some people to transfer into and out of equipment more easily

60"-diameter turning space between rows of equipment, allowing people to turn around without having to go to the end of the row

Accessible routes between all rows of equipment

Clear floor space, which may be used for people to leave walkers, etc., while using equipment

30" x 48" clear floor space (minimum) for people using mobility devices to transfer onto each type of equipment; good locations are at the end of rows of equipment

Figure 17.1. Section 206.2.13 of the 2010 Standards requires an accessible route to serve cardiovascular machines and related equipment *Source:* North Carolina Office on Disability and Health. (2008). Removing Barriers to Health Clubs and Fitness Facilities. Retrieved from http://projects.fpg.unc.edu/~ncodh/pdfs/rbfitness.pdf Reprinted with permission.

standards also mandates that exercise facilities must have cardiovascular equipment available for wheelchair users that cannot transfer. The following section describes some of the accessible cardiovascular equipment.

Exer-cycles, especially recumbent bicycles, have been a mainstay for older adults and individuals with disabilities for years. Many bikes offer comfort and ease of use, and many recent improvements have made them even more popular with members. Ease of entry is an important factor that needs to be addressed for the arrangement of all cycles. For ease of use, it is also important to provide alternative mechanisms for fastening feet to pedals on different types of bikes. The upper-body ergometer or UBE has been a useful cardiovascular training modality for those unable to train lower extremities. It is important to provide wheelchair accessible upper-body ergometers for those potential users that cannot transfer (McDonnell, 2006).

Competitive wheelchair racing has become popular in recent years. Advanced aerobic athletes (i.e., Paralympians) sometimes have special equipment needs when it comes to exercising. Many of these athletes are spread out all over the U.S. and workout at the local fitness facility as they prepare in the offseason. Competitive racers need special accommodations to get additional mileage. Wheelchair rollers provide stationary cardio workout capabilities and can provide variable resistance. Design varies between one- or two-roller systems. It is best to consult the competitive Paralympic athlete utilizing your facility for advice on specific equipment needs.

The recumbent stepper is an outstanding piece of equipment for the disabled population. It provides low-impact cardio training and provides both lower- and upper-body exercise. It provides a wide seat (18") for transfer and stability. It also provides back support during exercise and the pivoting chair mechanism can ease transfer.

Once thought of as the piece of cardio equipment for only advanced exercisers and athletes, treadmills now offer many features that make them more user friendly universally accessible. Slower start speeds, smaller speed and incline increments, and shorter step-up heights make exercising on a treadmill easier than ever. A good treadmill can provide both lower- and upper-body exercise. The following features are important for treadmills: wide deck, low speed options (> 1 mph), integrated safety tie-downs, and ramp access to deck (McDonnell, 2006).

The elliptical trainer is one of the most popular pieces of cardio equipment, partly because it can meet the needs of all types of exercisers, from the deconditioned businessman to the elite athlete. Elliptical machines tend to be less intimidating than some other machines because of their simple design. Seniors and disabled clients enjoy the elliptical trainer due to the ease of use and low-impact workout it provides (McDonnell, 2006).

The Vitaglide Pro is a piece of elliptical training equipment designed specifically for wheelchair users that allows a push-pull motion for cardiovascular exercise and for strengthening the upper back and shoulder muscles. The Vitaglide Pro has varying levels of resistance to accommodate users of varying levels of fitness. The Vitaglide Pro can be used by participants with function in one or both arms and has several handle adjustments to accommodate a wide variety of users including those without a functional grasp. The VitaGlide Pro contains electronic features that tracks exercise time, caloric expenditure, and heart rate (McDonnell, 2006).

For the visually impaired, exercise facilities must also provide cardio equipment that has descriptions for controls in alternative formats (i.e., raised lettering, pictograms, Braille, audio, large print). Options such as oversized buttons, easy-to-read screens, and programs designed for beginners are available on many types and brands of cardio equipment. Heart rate monitoring also helps users monitor their intensity when first beginning. For example, many Life Fitness cardio machines come standard with Lifepulse digital heart rate monitoring, wireless telemetry, or both. When used in conjunction with Zone Training workouts, the machine automatically adjusts resistance (on elliptical trainers, cycles and the Summit Trainer) or incline level (treadmills) to help the user maintain a specific target heart rate (McDonnell, 2006).

The Importance of Strength

Individuals with physical disabilities are often confronted with many unique physical challenges as a result of their functional limitations. Maintaining a high level of maximum strength among persons with physical disabilities has even greater importance than in the general population, because a loss in strength could erode a person's functional ability (Krebs, Scarborough, & McGibbon, 2007).

The application of free weights as a means of developing physical capabilities has long been a common practice. The use of other forms of resistance equipment and machines has become popular in recent years (Garhammer, 1982).

Fitness centers today cater to a wide range of members: young and old, novice to elite athlete, able bodied and disabled. The physical challenges that many people with disabilities face on a daily basis are exacerbated by poor strength levels (Krebs et al, 2010). If persons with physical disabilities are unable to transfer from their wheelchair to their car, or get from their home to the bus stop or train station, they will have difficulty partaking in basic daily living. More than ever, strength and conditioning professionals must endeavor to read professional journals, attend conferences and workshops, and join professional organizations to avail themselves of information on how to teach resistance training activities to their clients of varying populations (Craig & Judge, 2009).

Being an informed professional is half the battle in allowing users with disabilities to gain access to lifetime physical activities like weight training (Rhodes, 2007).

Strength Equipment for Special Populations

Equipment selection and allocation is an important issue for any strength and conditioning facility (North Carolina Office on Disability and Health, 2008). Defining programmatic objectives is the first step to successfully planning a facility to meet the needs of the target population activity. Decisions on the amount of free weight equipment, machines, and cardiovascular equipment are largely determined by the philosophy/priorities of the facilities. Many fitness centers provide the majority of members access to the facility, but they lack the equipment and layout necessary to make the facility truly accessible to all individuals. There are two main problems: accessibility and equipment design. Section 236 of the 2010 Standards requires at least one of each type of exercise machine to meet clear floor space requirements of section 1004.1. At least one piece of each type of equipment has an adjacent clear space of 2'-6" x 4'. Section 236 also mandates that exercise facilities provide equipment that does not require transferring out of the wheelchair and provide machines that have back support and have adjustable heights from 18" (Department of Justice, 2012).

Section 206.2.13 of the 2010 Standards requires an accessible route to serve exercise machines and equipment. The new law mandates that health clubs provide a clear floor space of at least 30 inches by 48 inches around each type of weight-training equipment so people in wheelchairs can access them. All pathways around equipment must also free from obstacles and equipment must be arranged in rows with a 5' pathway between each row (Department of Justice, 2012). Common obstacles such as heavy, hard-to-open doors and doorway thresholds must be removed. Floor-to-floor access within the two-story facility is handled by a system of ramps, in addition to stairs and elevators. Accessibility addresses everything from providing adequate passageways into and around the facility and its equipment, plus proper signage on doors and travel routes. Wheelchair accessibility is only one aspect, however. Facility operators also need to consider other disabilities, such as being visually impaired. For instance, it's important to keep equipment out of aisles and to notify visually impaired members if equipment has been rearranged (see Figure 17.2).

Resistance Training Machines

There are several key points for equipping a multiuse facility. Multistation wheelchair accessible weight machines must be provided. Many pieces of fitness equipment should feature wide, adjustable motorized seats and wheelchair tie-downs. All machines should boast storage units attached to frames and designed to hold walking canes, water bottles or other accessories. Multigym pulley systems have remained a fixture in fitness centers for years. Most systems come in two-stack, four-stack, or eight-stack varieties, allowing two, four, or up to eight people to ex-

ercise simultaneously at different stations surrounding the stacked pulley weights. Unlike exercise machines, many of the pulley systems don't include fixed seats or benches, allowing a wheelchair user to pull straight up to the weight stack to perform the desired exercise. Many companies now make single-station pulley systems with adjustable arms, enabling the user to perform almost any exercise at a single piece of equipment. Pulley systems are a way to develop upper-body strength and maintain range of motion. The systems are highly versatile and can be used effectively by anyone, including individuals in wheelchairs. Multiuse cable machines are another piece of equipment that can be excellent for wheelchair users. The key is to select a piece of equipment that has the adjustable lever arm in the middle of the machine so it can be adjusted by a wheelchair user. In addition, handgrips and/or handles on equipment must be provided so that equipment can be moved out of the way to allow for transferring to the machine. Machines must also have the capability change settings without the

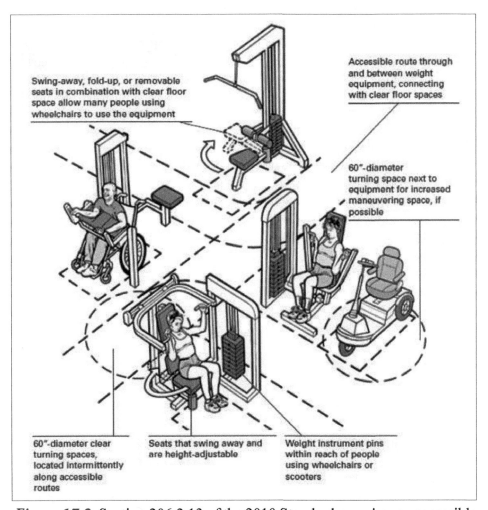

Figure 17.2. Section 206.2.13 of the 2010 Standards requires an accessible route to serve resistance training machines and related equipment. *Source:* North Carolina Office on Disability and Health. (2008). Removing Barriers to Health Clubs and Fitness Facilities. Retrieved from http://projects.fpg.unc.edu/~ncodh/pdfs/rbfitness.pdf Reprinted with permission.

individual transferring off the machine. Exercising with pulley systems is most appropriate for individuals with un-affected grip capabilities, as a solid, firm, grip is required. Gripping the bar and moving the adjustable weight dials are sometimes difficult for individuals with difficulties with their grip. Straps and hooks need to be available for individuals that have difficulty gripping the bar but want to engage in pulling exercises. Equipment must also have the lightest weight setting at less than 5 lb (Bellar, Judge, Patrick & Craig, 2013). Light hand weights, wrist weights, medicine balls, and padded mats must also be available.

Persons with physical disabilities often exhibit asymmetrical weakness. Many individuals with cerebral palsy or persons that have had a stroke have hemiplegia (weakness or paralysis on the right or left side of the body), which results in significant differences in strength between the stronger side and weaker sides of the body (Rimmer, 2005).

It is important to improve the affected side as much as possible without neglecting the non-affected side. Elastic bands are excellent resource to have available, as there are no required grasps or intricate manipulations. The elastic properties of the bands allow them to be tied to arms or legs for those with compromised grasp ability. Elastic bands are typically sold in color-coded levels of resistance based on the progressive thickness of the band.

Iso lateral plate-loaded machines (i.e. Hammer Strength) serve the disabled population quite well. Hammer Strength plate-loaded weight machines were developed by Gary Jones in 1985. While experienced lifters typically use barbells and dumbbells for exercises in order to achieve a natural range of motion, plate-loaded machines can provide a safe alternative to novices, injured lifters, or otherwise disabled gym goers. The Hammer Strength line has several weight machines for every body part, all of which must be used differently. The isolateral design allows users to move both limbs at the same time, one at a time, alternating, or with different weights for each.

Wheelchair users can benefit from utilizing the Smith machine as they can be used without transferring. The Smith machine, an amalgam between free weights and machines, was invented by Jack LaLanne, who developed a sliding apparatus in his gym in the 1950s. A Smith machine consists of a barbell that is fixed within steel rails, allowing vertical movement. A Smith machine requires less balance and coordination to use then traditional free weights and often includes a weight rack in the base to help stabilize it. Unlike a free-weight barbell, the bar on a Smith machine does not move forward, backward, or sideways, requiring less stabilization by the user. It is safe for those who lift without a spotter, as one only needs to twist the wrist in order to lock the barbell in place at the conclusion of a set.

Dumbbells and Free Weights

The use of free weights is an important component of resistance training for all populations. Persons with physical disabilities would especially benefit from participation in resistance training programs that include free weights and would have a greater likelihood of maintaining their physical function and independence with continued participation. Free weights allow for greater freedom of body position and movement, but also require greater balance and stability by the user. Free weight equipment has to be arranged properly so it is readily accessible. A wheelchair user should be able to pull straight up to the dumbbell or barbell rack, select the desired resistance and be able to get to work. Shoulder presses, biceps curls and triceps exten-

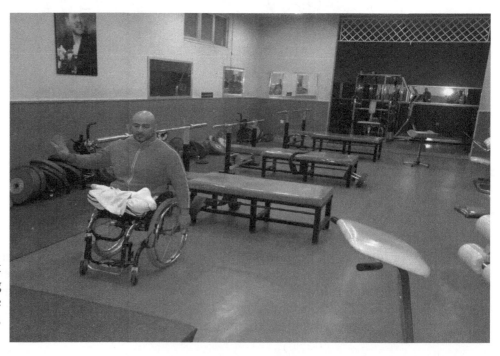

Paralympic athletes that compete in power lifting need special benches that are longer and wider.

sions are just a few of the exercises disabled users can perform easily with dumbbells and free weights. A standard power rack from which the fixed bench has been removed allows wheelchair users to easily pull into the rack and perform shoulder presses. Modified benches for amputees are necessary for competitive athletes (see photo below). Having seat belts readily accessible to help secure disabled users to the bench is helpful.

Competitive wheelchair athletes utilize a full range of dumbbells, using one- and two-pound weights to strengthen rotator cuff muscles. This is a critical joint for a wheelchair user as these muscles are very small and don't need a lot of weight to provide resistance. Meanwhile, heavy weights of up to 100 pounds plus can be used in bench presses. Traditional benches can be adjusted to an inclined and declined position so that lifters can use different sitting positions to mimic movements common to their specific sport (i.e., overhead rebounding in wheel chair basketball or the downward push on wheelchair wheels).

Olympic-style lifts are the core of an ambulatory disabled athlete's resistance training program. Amputees with prosthetic limbs, visually impaired, and hearing impaired athletes are often found in the platform area. Olympic bars, bumper plates, and platforms are traditional pieces of equipment that can serve a variety of clientele. A clear path to the platform area needs to be established and maintained clear for visually impaired users. The types of exercises performed on the platform area are not only marked by high force development but are high velocity movements. This necessitates that this area be located in a low traffic section of the facility. The clean and snatch are two of exercises that require a clear space. The many derivatives of these exercises can be utilized by disabled athletes based on their functional ability. For example, an athlete can choose between doing a snatch from the floor, from the knee, with a close grip, with a wide grip, on one leg, or with a single arm using dumbbells. Disabled athletes with mobility or orthopedic issues, that are unable to perform traditional Olympic-style lifts, can perform modified Olympic lifts on the knees (see photo below). Modified exercises with dumbbells, kettle bells and medicine balls are often prescribed for this population; specialized equipment needs to be available as it can be utilized to build speed strength. Some able bodied and disabled individuals find free weights intimidating, so an experienced staff member can assist with instruction. With the help of a certified strength and conditioning specialist, disabled users will be on the platform pumping iron in no time (Judge et al., 2012).

The power clean on the knees is an excellent adaptation of the power clean for disabled users.

18 Adventure Programming Facilities

Donald Rogers, *Indiana State University*

There are thousands of adventure programs in the United States conducted in schools, colleges, summer camps, recreation programs, commercial adventure enterprises, YMCAs, fitness clubs, and health care settings. These programs offer unique individual and group experiences that are challenging and engaging. Activities in these programs include cooperative games, group problem-solving initiatives, adventure-based recreation, sports challenges, and climbing and challenge course-based experiences.

Adventure activities involve a degree of physical, psychological, emotional, and/or social risks. Programs can be generic in terms of whom they serve, or they can be customized to meet the needs of specific individuals or groups. Typically these experiences foster trust and cooperation, improve problem-solving and conflict resolution skills, enhance self-image and confidence, and improve physical skills, all during a fun and exciting experience. From a facilities standpoint, the least resource-intensive programs involve the games and minimal-prop group initiative activities. These typically require an open space either indoors or outdoors that will allow for safe active movement, such as a gymnasium or open field. As programs seek to provide more complex and demanding adventure activities, the facilities necessary for the activities involved will require more in-depth planning and expertise.

Traditional adventure-based recreation, leisure, and sport activities include mountain biking, kayaking, canoeing, hiking, skiing, and caving. These activities are appropriate experiences to meet adventure program goals; however, because they tend to occur in minimally developed outdoor settings, these adventure activities have few facility requirements associated with them. Therefore, they will not be discussed in this chapter.

Climbing and challenge course (i.e., ropes course) activities introduce risk that is often gauged by how high off the ground the participant is expected or is able to go. In addition to the often unsettling effects of being up high, there are other components of these adventure activities that involve psychological, intellectual, and social challenges. There are also the physical demands on the body that climbing and sustained effort impose. Fatigue is always a factor in climbing that influences how participants think and feel. The heights involved in these activities can range from barely perceptible to 3 ft on low (teams and spotted) courses to a breathtaking 60 ft or 70 ft above the ground on the more extreme climbing towers and high challenge courses. Of course, these extreme heights are not necessary to achieve most climbing-based program goals. Typical heights of towers, walls, and high challenge courses range from 20 ft to 40 ft.

Although there is tremendous variety in climbing wall and challenge course design, each design is guided by standards set by respective professional associations. Indoor climbing facilities may be as simple as holds bolted to an existing wall, as elaborate as premolded replicas of famous rock climbing routes, or low-bouldering faces that mostly involve lateral climbing without belay systems. Outdoors there are freestanding towers framed on telephone poles or steel structures and walls attached to trees. These climbing facilities involve handholds, belay attachments, ropes, climbing hardware, and other safety equipment. Similarly, ropes courses use a variety of indoor and outdoor structural components, including roof trusses, girders, poles, and trees with additional features made of ropes, wires, lumber, pulleys, and extensive safety equipment. This chapter will provide an overview of the common steps in a facility planning process; discuss the structures, equipment, and supporting materials needed for climbing walls and ropes courses; and identify safety and operational considerations for those developing or conducting these types of adventure programs.

The Planning Process

The initial step in planning is to establish clear program goals and determine what type of facility is needed to achieve these goals. The first step will require a needs assessment of the populations to be served. It is a good idea to involve a representative group of stakeholders in the planning process. These stakeholders include other impacted units within the agency, existing customers/clients, potential customers/clients, and agencies that might partner on the project. It is also advisable to employ the services of an established, credible vendor who can provide expertise about types of facilities and to consult with someone in the same industry who is successfully operating a similar facility. Projects such as these require dedicated space for the wall or course, storage space for equipment, extra staffing, ongoing training, maintenance and inspection fees, and equipment replacement and upgrades. The initial costs can be in the tens of thousands of dollars, plus additional recurring costs.

Many agencies establish their programs with what they can afford and over time add components based on need and available resources. Of course, others will be able to afford a sizable state-of-the-art wall or comprehensive challenge course complex. Either way, it is critical to determine in the initial stages of planning that the addition of this adventure component is a good fit for the agency and its partners, that it will serve the needs and interests of customers, and that it is economically feasible. Many agencies have plunged into owning and operating adventure facilities because it seemed like an exciting idea that would appeal to customers, but found that the "build it and they will come" strategy worked better in the movies than in real life.

Once a general facility concept is developed, a detailed construction plan is needed. The facility may be designed and built in-house, designed and built by an outside vendor, or a combination of the two. For example, installing a small bouldering wall (low climbing wall designed for lateral climbing) on an existing wall or as a freestanding unit can be done in-house with the help of maintenance or facilities staff, program staff, volunteers, or climbing club members; however, building a large climbing wall or climbing tower is better left to professional climbing wall designers and builders. If new construction or significant renovation of the climbing facility or challenge course is done by someone other than a credentialed vendor, then it is imperative that an "acceptance inspection" is performed prior to use (Association for Challenge Course Technology [ACCT], 2012).

It is not unusual for a vendor to involve agency volunteers in site preparation, course design, general labor tasks, or even skilled tasks. It is actually helpful for designated agency staff to learn about the inner workings of the wall or challenge course so they can perform periodic maintenance and minor repairs. There are excellent references on the Internet that provide detailed information about building small-scale climbing and bouldering walls. For the more complex projects involving outside professional vendors, considerable planning and coordination will be required.

It is important to select a vendor who is willing to spend time getting to know the needs of the agency and its staff. Many complex decisions need to be made in the planning and construction process that need to happen in collaboration between the vendor and the agency. Ideally, the same vendor should also provide annual inspections, equipment replacement, major repairs, trainings, and consultation. This relationship could exist for many years, so finding a reliable, competent vendor will be a critical early decision. Again, the Internet is a good starting place to locate and research vendors. Some suggestions include the websites for the ACCT and AthleticBusiness.com. The vendor should provide specific information about qualifications and experience with this kind of work. Look for a description of the services offered to customers to be sure it includes the components of planning, design, construction, training, inspections, repairs, and consultation. Consult with the vendor's references to communicate directly with other similar programs about services they received from that vendor. Confirm the vendor is a member in good standing with the professional trade organization and that the vendor designs and builds according to current industry standards. A professional, experienced vendor should guide an agency through the planning, design, and construction process, communicating the steps to be taken and anticipating and preparing to meet the agency's future needs.

Today, adventure programs are widespread and operate in schools, universities, fitness clubs, commercial adventure program facilities, camps, and nonprofit agencies. The growth of the climbing wall industry has been particularly extraordinary. Emerging in the mid-1980s as

Climbing on the Alpine Tower II

a training device for rock climbers, climbing walls have become centerpieces to draw prospective customers and provide recreation, competitive sport, and fitness opportunities for families, youth, and adults alike. Examples of the climbing wall phenomenon include the two large walls on the cruise ship Oasis of the Seas, the world's largest debuting in late 2009, owned by Royal Caribbean International; a wall in the state-of-the-art Center for the Intrepid at Fort Sam Houston, Texas, military rehabilitation facility for wounded American soldiers; a climbing wall as part of an employee fitness center at Goldman Sachs & Co.; and climbing walls or "caverns" within most of the 105 fitness clubs by the chain Lifetime Fitness. Health/fitness centers and university student recreation centers are at the heart of the climbing wall boom. They are no longer simply a secondary option for climbing real rock. The next section will address the design and management of climbing walls.

Climbing Walls

Planning Considerations

Climbing walls can be built indoors or outdoors. They can serve children and older adults. Climbing walls can be part of fitness, recreation, sport, education, and therapeutic programs. Their utility to deliver a range of outcomes is similar to challenge courses as a multifaceted adventure instrument. When deciding to include a climbing wall in a new facility or add one to an existing program, an organization has a number of questions to answer and options to consider.

Initial questions address where to locate the wall, how big it will be, and what kind of wall it will be. More technical questions would explore the safety systems, risk management, staffing, training, equipment, maintenance, and access control. The following are additional questions Sagar (2007) addressed:

- Who are your primary users, and do they represent your desired target markets?
- What are your goals for the users' experience?
- Do those goals reflect the style of outdoor climbing popular in your region, as well as the progression of the sport?
- How do your facility's design and space limitations affect those goals? For example, are the walls too high for beginners? Are the routes not challenging enough to entice more experienced climbers?
- What does your facility offer that others in the area do not?
- Is the overall environment friendly and inviting to climbers of all skill levels?
- Do instructors communicate in a way that climbers understand and appreciate?
- Do business hours and clinic and program schedules fit the needs of the wall's typical users?

- Do you provide related services (e.g., gear rental and sales) and customer service to climbers?
- Does the music played in the facility appeal to the typical climber?
- Does the facility's atmosphere encourage both performance and socialization?
- Is your building conveniently accessible from the street and the parking lot?
- Is it easily identified as a climbing facility? (p. 37)

It is helpful to do initial research in climbing publications and Internet resources, particularly if no one in the organization has experience with climbing walls and adventure programs. At this point, another important factor to determine is the climbing wall vendor. A reputable vendor will be able to answer your questions and present options that stimulate your thinking about the function of a wall in your facility. Unless the plan calls for a small, inexpensive homemade wall, a professional climbing wall designer and builder with plenty of experience will be necessary. There are numerous concerns regarding building codes, engineering, architectural and climbing features, matching program goals with designs, staff training, and long-term strategies that should not be left to chance.

Sagar (2007) encouraged agencies to have a solid mission statement about the climbing wall program. The mission statement should communicate whom the program wants to serve, for example, climbers, families, and/or community. It should also indicate the desired outcomes of the program, such as fitness, skills, and fun. This information provides a guide for the design of the wall and the facilities around it, as well as the development of operating procedures, programming components, and staffing profiles.

Once an agency is clear about whom it is serving and the desired outcomes, it is time to consider what kind of

Climbing wall

climbing wall and climbing experience is needed. The design concept and final products should meet current needs and provide flexibility for future program growth and development.

The climbing wall concept will vary greatly depending on how the climbing wall fits into the overall facility design. For example, the type of wall designed for a commercial indoor climbing gym may be different from a wall designed for an outdoor adventure program in a public school. Determining how the climbing wall will be integrated into other programs and support facilities will also affect the design concept. The location of the climbing wall in relation to entrances and exits, locker rooms, storage areas, offices, pro shops, water fountains, and other program areas, such as the ropes courses, gymnasiums, pools, fitness rooms, racquetball courts, and classrooms, will affect design concept decisions. Designers should consider general design criteria such as visibility, control, and safety. Also, they need to decide whether the climbing wall needs to be near or isolated from other features. Schematic drawings that show general size, location, and adjacencies will refine concept development. More than one design option can be explored at this time.

Design Development

The design development phase is decision-making time. If more than one design concept was developed, whether on your own or with a vendor, a decision needs to be made on which design to carry through to full development. Full development requires decisions on the following questions:

- What is the scope of the project (including budget estimates, funding available, and space allocated for the climbing wall)?
- What heating, ventilation, and air-conditioning (HVAC) systems are needed?
- What features are needed for the walls, floor, and framework? (The wall, floor, and framework designs must meet climbing wall industry standards.)
- Which wall surface is desired (the real rock look, seamless cement, prefabricated panels, wood, or does not matter)?
- How much wall height is desired (a 9 ft to 14 ft high bouldering wall used primarily for horizontal climbing or a high top-roping or lead climbing wall)?
- Will a climbing treadmill meet program needs?
- What wall features are desired, especially the number, type, and location of handholds? Other surface features may be built into the wall, such as cracks, arêtes (corner), depressions, overhangs, caves, ledges, and so on.
- How much wall security is needed? (Will the climbing wall be in a self-contained, lockable area, or will the wall be in an open area and require a way to limit access to the climbing surface?)

- What type of landing surface is most appropriate? Bouldering walls and walls located in multipurpose locations such as gymnasiums often have movable landing mats. Areas used exclusively for climbing may have specially designed impact-absorbing flooring. The standard most followed is the ASTM International standard F 1292-09 regarding impact attenuation on playground surfaces. This standard indicates the need for a minimum of 6 in. of rubber pieces for a 10-ft fall or 9 in. of wood chips at the same height that extends out 6 ft from the wall. Some local practices suggest as much as 12 in. of padding material that extends out 8 ft. There may be state codes or insurance requirements that exceed the ASTM standards, so it is critical to know which will apply in your situation. In any case, the surface must not have gaps, needs to be secured in place, must cover all feasible landing surfaces, and must provide sufficient impact protection given the height of the fall, which can be substantial on bouldering walls that reach as high 14 ft.
- How much storage is required? A lot of equipment is required to operate a climbing program, including ropes, climbing shoes, harnesses, helmets, carabiners, and basic hand tools. The equipment needs to be located near the climbing wall, so the storage areas for some of the newer climbing walls are being built into the back or side of the wall.

Planning and Design Summary

Failure to adequately plan and develop a comprehensive project concept often results in a climbing facility that does not have the desired features or does not meet programming requirements. This can lead to a facility that is unpopular, is unsafe, cannot compete locally, or is prematurely obsolete.

Project planners must develop a comprehensive project concept that will guide specific design and operation decisions. Components of a comprehensive project concept for a climbing wall often address the following questions:

- Who are the target facility users? (Who will be climbing on the wall?) A bouldering facility designed to teach junior high school students will be different from one designed to train lead-climbing mountain guides. Failing to identify the target facility users often results in an inefficient and ineffective climbing facility.
- Will the wall be a stand-alone entity, or will it be used with other facilities? For example, will it be part of a larger adventure or fitness program?
- Will there be festivals or other special events that feature the wall?
- What financial resources are available to fund the project?

- How many climbers will use the wall at one time (peak load)?
- Is this a new build or retrofit of an existing area?
- How much space is available?
- How important are aesthetics? Is a natural rock look more important than having the maximum amount of climbing area? This is an important consideration in situations where the wall will be the centerpiece within a facility or located in a prominent location. Creating a powerful aesthetic impact will likely require more expense with high-end flooring, wall materials, lighting, and access prevention.
- What type of flooring/landing surfaces will be best for the facility?
- Do the design features promote safety, minimize maintenance problems, and meet program needs?

Design Features

As you begin your research locating and identifying what is on the climbing wall market, you may be amazed by the extensive array of designs, features, and options. This is why you need to do the research and why it is important to employ a climbing wall vendor early in the process. You want to get a sense for what is out there without wasting a lot of time trying to answer questions or make decisions that are not relevant. It is like going fishing on a large, unfamiliar lake. There is so much to see and explore, and it is not that you do not enjoy that, but that you have limited time and gas and that you want to catch fish. After many hours of plying those waters and nothing to show for your efforts, you might think, "Maybe hiring a guide wasn't such a bad idea."

Let's explore the types of climbing walls and the features that come with them. Remember, you are working toward an effective means of providing the kind of experiences your customers are anticipating. At the same time, you need to be flexible about the ways this can be achieved and also build in ways to vary and expand your program in the future.

Climbing wall types. Before selecting individual features of a climbing wall, decide what general type of climbing wall is desired. There are essentially two categories of walls: bouldering walls and tall walls (Stiehl & Ramsey, 2004). Bouldering walls will be between 9 ft and 14 ft high, and shorter when used by youth or with overhangs. Consider not allowing preteens to boulder higher than 9 ft. A rule of thumb is to not allow a fall that is greater than twice the height of the climber. Tall walls, which have roped safety systems (belay systems) are generally 20 ft to 36 ft tall. The following is an overview of climbing wall types.

Homemade. These are usually relatively simple walls made of framing lumber, plywood, paint, and handholds. Individual climbers build homemade walls for their personal use, and institutions with limited resources build homemade climbing walls to support their program needs. An outdoor equipment store might build one in the facility to allow customers to try out climbing equipment or have a climbing club.

Prefabricated panel system. Prefabricated panels are usually 4 ft x 8 ft plywood or fiberglass panels with pre-drilled and nutted holes for handholds.

Portable walls. There are three general types of portable walls: disassemble and reassemble, assembled walls on a trailer, and the portable treadmill-type wall.

Steel structure wall systems. These systems are usually professionally designed and constructed walls with a structural steel frame and plywood surfaces. The surfaces may be coated with cementitious material, fiberglass, or blown synthetic material. Some of the cementitious surfaces have natural features such as cracks, ledges, and indentations that are troweled in, and others replicate a real rock-style covering. Surfaces may also be precast or formed and replicate naturally occurring handholds and footholds (cracks, pockets, flakes, and grooves). Some vendors can offer replications of popular real rock climbing routes.

Climbing towers. Towers are usually freestanding wooden towers built outdoors. They can be the only structure or, as is often the case, part of a larger adventure course. These structures use telephone poles and/or steel structure to support the climbing faces. The climbing faces are usually tongue and groove, pressure-treated lumber with straight and angled faces with bolts on climbing holds; however, as the market becomes more competitive, elaborate precast faces are becoming more available. For an extraordinary example, check out the world's tallest climbing tower at http://www.toxel.com/tech/2010/10/25/worlds-tallest-climbing-wall/. It is in the Netherlands and is 121 ft tall with a 36-ft overhang.

Safety features on a climbing wall

Climbing wall features. Most climbing walls have handholds that are attached to the wall using a T-nut or other comparable threaded anchor. These T-nut inserts may be installed by the contractor as part of the construction, purchased as part of predrilled wood or fiberglass panels, or added to climbing panels as part of a homemade project.

Handholds may be simple wood blocks fixed to the wall surface with epoxy glue, wood screws, T-nuts, or a combination of these, although wooden holds are rarely used in this era of custom walls. Although wooden handholds are relatively inexpensive and can be formed into a wide variety of shapes and sizes, they can create splinters and split as they dry or respond to outdoor conditions. They still offer an option, however, for organizations that lack funding and want to construct an affordable program wall on-site.

Most commercial handholds are designed for use with a T-nut system, but some can be attached to the wall with an epoxy process. There are literally thousands of different types, sizes, and shapes of handholds. Handhold packages are available that include handholds that replicate natural features in rocks and require climbers to use specific grip, foot, and protection techniques. Handhold color and texture can effectively duplicate natural rock, match the existing wall surface, or add color and flare to a climbing wall. Color-coded handholds may be used to designate specific climbing routes or difficulty levels. Colored or numbered tags can also be attached to the handholds to mark specific climbing routes. Incorporating movable or removable handholds provides options for changing routes, changing the size of a hold, or rotating the hold. It is common practice to change routes and difficulty levels on a regular basis (monthly) to maintain climber interest and meet the needs of a range of climbers. On an outdoor climbing structure, removable holds are used for the bottom 9 ft to prevent unauthorized access.

Climbing equipment. Climbing wall equipment is matched with the design of the wall and its intended purpose. Although only a narrow range of equipment may be used on the wall on a regular basis, there is a tremendous amount of gear to select at the outset. Numerous factors affect the decisions about climbing gear, such as nature of the program (e.g., competition, sport, or real rock training), ages of the participants, how it will be belayed, and size and adaptability of the wall.

Specific gear choices and quantities of gear should be decided in consultation with your vendor or consultant. Often vendors have gear that they recommend based on their history with the equipment and a relationship that they have with the source of the gear. It is not unusual for vendors to also be a retailer or distributor for specific brands of equipment. This should not be a cause for concern. Actually, it presents benefits for the customer because the vendors can bundle the equipment in the wall package for less than retail and provide discounts later when more or replacement gear is needed.

There are three bodies that determine standards for climbing equipment: Union of International Associations of Alpinists (UIAA), also known as the International Mountaineering and Climbing Federation and World Mountaineering and Climbing; the European Committee for Standardization (CEN); and ASTM International (ASTM). CEN standards are written first with EN (European Norm) followed with a number, such as EN 892, which is the standard for dynamic mountaineering ropes (UIAA 101 equivalent). Climbing equipment standards are concerned with requirements and testing that address personal protective equipment. The CEN standards are legally binding in Europe. The current UIAA standards are based on these CEN standards, but in some cases they are stricter.

The UIAA is recognized around the globe for climbing equipment standards, and therefore purchasing UIAA-certified climbing equipment is a sound practice in terms of safety and legal liability. The specific selection criteria used to purchase equipment will vary with each application; however, the following are general selection criteria for standard pieces of climbing equipment. It is critically important that climbing equipment selection and use is done and supervised by someone competent to make those decisions. Certified climbing equipment is durable and has built-in safety margins, but still requires proper usage and care over time. Improper use or misused equipment can fail, and a climber can be seriously injured or killed.

Ropes. Most climbing programs use 10.5-mm or 11-mm dynamic kernmantle ropes (continuous parallel nylon fibers surrounded by a nylon sheath) as their primary climbing ropes. They provide an excellent combination of strength, stretch, and suppleness as well as a higher falls rating. Kernmantle climbing protection ropes are classified as "dynamic ropes," ropes that stretch so they absorb some of the shock when a person falls. Climbing rope technology is constantly evolving, creating better ropes for specific situations. There are ropes for climbing wall applications designed to meet the rigors of day-to-day use and many falls. An example of this kind of rope would be the Bluewater Gymline.

Harnesses. The harness secures the climber to the climbing rope. Commercial sit/seat harnesses are the standard in the industry. Some programs have used homemade harnesses in the past, but this is an unacceptable practice. Skilled climbers on real rock who need quick protection are able to safely fashion a harness for themselves and others, but this is outside the range of acceptable practice on climbing walls. Harnesses that are manufactured to meet CEN/UIAA standards are the way to go. There are many different types of harnesses on the market with size, adjustability, gear loops, buckles, and other features to consider.

If possible, try different harnesses to determine what will work best for your program and staff needs. Your vendor should be able to offer expert advice about harness selection.

Helmets. Climbing helmets are essential safety equipment for many climbing and ropes course elements. Purchasing quality UIAA-certified adjustable helmets will provide an extra margin of safety, make adjustments easier, and prove to be good investments because they will last longer. Many indoor climbing facilities do not require helmets, or they ask the participant to sign a helmet waiver if they choose to not wear one. On outdoor walls and towers, it is highly recommended they be worn, and on real rock climbs, it is essential.

Belay system. There are numerous types of belay systems, and all are designed to protect the participant from making an uncontrolled fall from a distance of more than 6 ft. Most belay systems are a top-rope design. This design has an approved anchor point at the top of the climb route that provides an attachment for a pulley or shear reduction device. The belay rope is threaded through this hardware and down to the climber's harness at one end and to the belayer/belay system at the other end. In some cases, a 4-in. to 6-in. diameter steel pipe securely welded and bolted in place provides the anchor and radius for the rope to go over. In cases where a pipe is used, be sure participants cannot climb between the pipe and the wall. This would result in them being off belay.

Climbing shoes. Serious climbing programs should have climbing shoes available. Tight-fitting climbing shoes with high-traction rubber soles facilitate good footwork. Climbing shoes make for a better climbing experience, even on outdoor all-wood walls or on bouldering walls for novices. Barefooted climbing should not be allowed.

Carabiners. One of the most recognized pieces of climbing equipment, carabiners come in a variety of shapes, sizes, colors, and materials. Usually these variations have functional implications and are not done to provide options. Generally, a climbing wall program will have a combination of aluminum (12 mm) and steel (11 mm) carabiners on hand. Most will be of the locking-gate variety. These tend to be either screw-to-lock or two-stage self-locking. In some lead-climbing situations, a swing or nonlocking-gate carabiner may be used, but this is a very technical application. Manufacturers will indicate the intended application of their carabiners. Using them in some other manner could result in a malfunction and full assumption of liability by the program organization and/or end user.

Purchasing, inspecting, and maintaining high-quality climbing gear designed for the intended use is important in protecting climbers from injury and owners and operators from costly litigation.

Climbing Wall Standards

The Climbing Wall Industry Group and the Climbing Gym Association, both now disbanded organizations, were subgroups of what was the Outdoor Recreation Coalition of America (ORCA). Replacing ORCA is the Outdoor Industry Association as the trade organization of outdoor industries in the United States.

The Climbing Wall Association (CWA) became an independent 501(c)(6) nonprofit organization in 2003. It is now the only trade association addressing the needs and interests of the climbing wall industry and operators. The CWA sets standards for the industry that guide the design, construction, and operations of climbing walls (Zimmerman, 2008). As a trade organization, CWA can assist in locating qualified vendors, help answer questions about insurance coverage, and provide continuing education and professional affiliation for your staff.

Many states either have or are attempting to regulate climbing walls and challenge courses (currently 24 states) by bringing them under the umbrella of amusement rides or devices using the ASTM F24 standards. The CWA, ACCT, and other organizations have been active in resisting states' efforts to regulate them in this way, but it appears to be the trend. Investigate the laws of your state when planning your facility, policies, and procedures. Local laws and regulations governing zoning, construction, and safe operations must also be reviewed to ensure compliance.

Climbing Facility Operation

Safety in the climbing wall business is always the top priority. It is not simply a matter of having procedures in place, the right equipment, and trained staff at the ready. Maintaining a safe program takes constant vigilance, communication, and systematic evaluation. Climbing is intended to challenge participants as an adventurous experience that is physically, psychologically, and intellectually demanding. It is an adventure because success is not guaranteed. The climber has to make the effort and expose himself or herself to the risks of the activity. Though the climbers may experience some fear, they expect that everything will work properly. The first duty of owners and operators of climbing facilities is to protect the welfare of their customers/participants. To meet this responsibility, owners must fully understand the inherent risks and develop risk and emergency management policies and procedures that are based on professional standards. The staff must be knowledgeable of their responsibilities to manage the risks as specifically detailed in standard operating procedures and have the skills and abilities to implement such a program.

The CWA provides its members with comprehensive standards that address all aspects of owning and operating a climbing wall. These include industry standards that cover areas such as ethics, informed consent, insurance coverage, accident reporting, risk management, record keeping, and a variety of programming concerns. It also provides standards that cover engineering and operations. Using the CWA standards, owners need to work with their vendors to create policies and procedures that work effectively at their facility.

The following is a list of typical risk management and operating policy and procedure areas for climbing and adventure programs. It is not a complete list and should only be used to generate initial discussions and planning.

- Participants should be informed that climbing is a potentially dangerous activity and should know specifically what they are in danger of losing. This is related to the concept of informed consent. If they agree to participate knowing the risks, then they assume part of the liability in case of loss. This is determined greatly by individual state laws.
- Appropriate signage should be posted with safety warnings, rules, policies, and procedures to be followed; emergency contact numbers; and any facility-specific rules, such as "No Horseplay."
- Mature, responsible staff should be hired who are then well trained and stay current with their knowledge and skills.
- Regular formal equipment and facility inspections should be conducted, documented records should be kept of inspections, and corrective actions should be taken.
- All climbing activities should be supervised with a qualified instructor.
- The climbing area should be secured when not in use (access prevention).
- Certified equipment should be purchased that is designed for the specific application and should be well maintained.
- Participant belayers should be trained and certified.
- A written set of standard operating policies and procedures must be maintained.
- Emergency equipment and supplies must be available.
- Documentation of staff qualifications, inspections, maintenance/repairs, equipment retirement and purchases, accident/injury/incident reports, all participant forms/belay training, vendor communications, and meeting minutes should be maintained and organized.
- Participants should be warned about loose clothing and allowing long hair to hang loose because they may become tangled in the ropes or hardware.
- A final equipment check should be made before beginning a climb. (A buddy check with verbal commands and visual checking is recommended.)
- Communications procedures should be reviewed prior to starting a climb.
- Jewelry, including watches, should not be worn while climbing.

Challenge Course Adventures

This section of the chapter will define challenge courses, discuss the philosophy of challenge course programming, provide an overview of the industry, introduce the credentialing system, describe challenge course elements, provide strategies for how to include people with disabilities, and provide guidance on developing and maintaining challenge course elements for an adventure program.

> A challenge course, sometimes called a ropes course, is an experiential adventure program which offers groups and individuals the opportunity to participate in a series of activities involving mental, physical, and emotional risk taking. The ropes course consists of an aesthetically designed series of ropes, cables, and poles combined in such a way as to simulate challenges that might be found in a natural setting. Safety and cooperation, as well as individual achievement, are essential to the program. (Rohnke, Rogers, Wall, & Tait, 2007)

There are two categories of challenge courses that meet the above-mentioned objectives: low courses and high belayed courses. These and other adventure activities, including climbing walls/towers, and ground events are usually used in combination to achieve program, group, and individual goals.

Challenge courses are amazingly versatile. The same activities can be used with variations to meet the needs of a wide range of groups. There are, however, five general programming categories: adventure recreation; personal/group growth; enrichment and education; developmental; and treatment services.

Programs will have a predetermined purpose within one or more of these categories depending on the needs of the customers. In the fields of fitness/wellness, recreation, and sport, most programs will be designed as adventure recreation or personal/group growth, enrichment, education, or some combination of these. Mental and physical health treatment programs such as psychiatric centers, counseling programs, stress care clinics, and physical rehabilitation centers will primarily use developmental and treatment approaches and also blend in techniques as needed from the other categories. Challenge courses are often used to enhance team or group functioning. A team-building program would use design components found in all but the treatment services area.

To provide effective programs, it is necessary to assess client/participant needs. Determining outcome and process goals and individual needs establishes the foundation for program design. In fact, knowing as much as possible about the groups that will use the courses and what they will expect from the experience is critical to course design.

Outward Bound was the first nonmilitary agency to use challenge courses with its participants. Although the courses resembled the military confidence courses, Outward Bound tapped into the educational and personal growth potential of the experience. The first course was built at the Colorado Outward Bound School using hemp rope, wood, and minimal safety systems (belays). Project Adventure was the next significant development in challenge course history. Attempting to reform traditional education methods, Project Adventure built its first course in a Massachusetts high school with a grant from the U.S. Department of Education (Prouty, 1999). This course was used primarily within the physical education program, but it led to applications in a wide range of settings, which today includes schools, camps, community centers, and therapy.

The ACCT is the professional organization dedicated to developing standards for challenge course programs. The ACCT has developed challenge course standards for materials, construction, inspection, operations, and ethical behavior. The ACCT began as an organization for vendors who design and build challenge courses. It has since evolved into a full-service organization that has an associate membership option for programmers, managers, and operators. The challenge courses business has evolved into full-service vendors who build courses, provide customer staff training, recommend equipment purchases, and conduct annual inspections. Though not directly involved in design and building standards, both the Association for Experiential Education and the American Camp Association have accreditation standards that address challenge course staffing, programming, and risk management.

Design and Development of Challenge Courses

The design and development process for challenge courses is the same as described in the previous section on climbing walls. In an ideal situation, the vision of the desired facility and program would be clearly stated and agreed upon by all involved parties. There would be adequate funding to plan and build the challenge course and provide the necessary staff training. To locate a reputable challenge course vendor, contact the ACCT via their website (http://www.acctinfo.org). This website provides a list of vendor members, all of which have gone through a thorough screening process to determine the quality and reliability of their products and services.

Most organizations that want to build a challenge course do not have an ideal situation. They have to find a suitable location, struggle for adequate funding, promote the adventure facility and program, and search to find qualified people to staff the program. These are typical constraints that should not deter organizations from developing a course. Considerable evidence supports the value of using a challenge course. Challenge courses contribute to physical, emotional, and social development of the participants and are high-visibility features that may benefit program marketing and public relations. A well-run program with a quality staff can also be a productive source of revenue.

In the past, agencies have built their own challenge courses. Copying existing courses and coming up with their own designs, they would either rely solely on internal resources or bring in someone with building experience to guide the project.

Although the in-house approach may seem like an affordable option, it is strongly recommended that only experienced and qualified challenge course builders direct the process and build these courses. The designs, materials, and standards have become so sophisticated that the do-it-yourself challenge course builder is all but obsolete. In addition to complex design and construction principles, there are substantial risk management and legal liability issues to consider. It is unlikely that an insurance company will cover a program with a challenge course that is not built, annually inspected, and maintained (major repairs) by a reputable ACCT vendor member. Insurance companies that provide coverage for challenge courses have specific criteria to assess the construction, inspection, maintenance, administration, staff training, clientele, and other risk management concerns. Course builders or the ACCT will be able to identify insurance providers familiar with challenge course programs. In lieu of a build-it-yourself course, some vendors invite user involvement with planning, design, and construction. Organization staff may be able to assist with course design, layout, site preparation, basic carpentry, and physical labor. A collaborative approach effectively fosters staff buy-in and helps them learn about the course, how it works, maintenance needs, and programming potential.

For organizations with limited financing, it may be necessary to develop a multiyear challenge course building and funding strategy that begins with short-term attainable goals and a limited course facility. Additional support and

High ropes course

funding may be forthcoming based on documented program success. With new ideas such as challenge courses, decision makers and funders may be reluctant to commit resources until program benefits can be demonstrated. In this situation, starting with a small project, such as a team course or a scaled-down complex, provides an affordable opportunity to demonstrate the viability of the program. Challenge course vendors can help with course planning and design that may easily be expanded in the future.

One of the first decisions is whether the challenge course will be an indoor course, an outdoor course, or a combination of the two. Many challenge course programs are part of a larger outdoor education program that may or may not have access to a multipurpose indoor facility. Creative designs are available that use indoor spaces, both large and small.

Having an indoor component provides options for rainy days, winter programming, multiple groups, and possibly groups that would have difficulty using an outdoor course. Of course, agencies without outdoor space available will have no choice but to build indoors.

The next two decisions, site location and primary support structures, are often linked. A decision needs to be made whether the challenge course will be tree-based, which uses existing trees to support the challenge course; pole-based, which uses telephone type poles; a combination of trees and poles; or a climbing tower-based course, where a tower is used as part of the support structure of the challenge course. A tower-based course may also use natural trees, poles, or both for additional support points.

Many new designs combine these ideas with steel structures, tree houses, suspended yurts and gazebos, movable platforms, hydraulic systems, and elaborate prefabricated components. Not much can limit the types of designs that may be created.

The nature of the site available greatly influences the support structures used. If there are no healthy, appropriate trees at the proposed site, then poles or towers must be used. Other considerations include substrate composition, ground slope, erosion potential, and environmental sensitivity of the area. Using natural trees is less expensive than using poles or towers, so financial considerations may also be a factor in both site location and support structure. Visiting a challenge course program that is operating in a similar setting, observing the program in action, interviewing the staff, and reading the operating procedures are helpful in the early stage of planning. Be certain that local zoning regulations and building specifications are checked before making the final site and support structure decisions. The ACCT (2007) design, performance, and inspection standards provide direction for site selection.

Selecting challenge course designs. A challenge course is a set of elements and activities that helps programs and participants achieve goals, even if it is to only have a recreation experience. As presented previously, outcome goals fall within the recreation, growth/enrichment/learning, developmental, and therapeutic categories. When participating in adventure recreation, participants are given safe but challenging opportunities to solve group initiative problems and climb on the higher elements. There is little briefing or debriefing of the experience. The emphasis is on participants having fun and being challenged physically and mentally. As program goals become more complex, course designs must provide appropriate options. To meet the programming needs of diverse groups, highly versatile and flexible courses must be designed. A higher degree of design specificity can be employed if the course will only be used with a specified clientele.

Different programming areas may have similar outcomes or benefits, but the methods and goals may differ. The positive outcomes that are possible with challenge course programs include

- improved self-respect and respect for others,
- improved communication skills,
- a sense of physical and emotional exhilaration,
- an expanded personal comfort zone,
- greater leadership skills,
- an ability to manage fear,
- improved teamwork and cooperation,
- learned conflict resolution strategies,
- improved problem-solving skills,
- greater safety awareness,
- improved planning and organization skills,
- developed caring and compassion,
- better physical fitness and coordination, and
- new stress management skills.

Achieving goals with a challenge course requires skillful application of a well-conceived plan. When planning a challenge course, consider

- course layout;
- program goals;
- actions of facilitators (program staff); and
- the needs, desires, and past experience of the participants.

These four primary components are highly interrelated. Given the phenomenal nature of the experience, these factors could be described as having a synergistic relationship. In addition, factors such as environment, weather, and support facilities (restrooms, lodging) will influence the process. The effectiveness of the course depends on the quality of the program and how skillfully it is implemented. The course design is important, but it is just a means to an end within a dynamic cognitive, emotional, behavioral, and social experience.

Some adventure facilities by design include multiple courses; these are called challenge course complexes.

Combining course types into a complex or multiple levels may be done because available space is limited or to provide program flexibility. There are situations in a complex where staff can overlap, allowing economy of staffing. Building the course elements in a central location may reduce building costs by allowing for the sharing of poles or trees among courses/elements. From a programming standpoint, there are important questions to answer before deciding on a complex approach. These questions include the following:

• Will participants on other course elements be distracted?

• When multiple groups are running at the same time, will the visual and audible overlap be a problem?

• Does a complex format create safety concerns with some groups?

• Beyond distractions, will being able to see other groups on the course have a negative effect on accomplishing desired outcome goals?

Complexes tend to offer more logistical, staffing, and economic benefits than programming benefits. Challenge course planners and designers must decide whether the benefits of a challenge course complex outweigh the possible negative impacts on the intended program.

Low Courses (also referred to as Team Courses)

As the name implies, team courses are designed to provide group experiences. The height of a low team course element should not create unsafe situations for user groups. Keeping elements close to the ground (usually 2 ft or less) is the primary factor that allows the entire group to use these elements without employing ropes, harnesses, or extensive spotting when group members or staff members position themselves to provide support if someone falls. On team course elements, spotting is provided as needed while the entire group negotiates the element.

Low ropes course

Team courses are designed to have groups work together to solve problems. These problems or initiatives have physical and mental challenges that the group must overcome. During the process of planning and implementing solutions, the participants interact in ways that generate valuable group dynamics. Team courses are also called group initiative courses because they require the group to use a problem-solving approach to learning and development.

Team courses are relatively inexpensive and lower tech than high courses, which make them a good option for adventure programmers who want a challenge course but have limited funds. They are also a good idea when space is an issue. Each element of a team course is independent of the others, so it is easy to locate specific elements in different configurations. Decentralizing the elements (i.e., placing them away from each other, out of sight and hearing distance) is a good strategy. It limits the "Hey, I wonder how that one over there works?" distraction within the group. Decentralizing also allows for multigroup programming by rotating groups from element to element without them coming into contact with each other. Decentralizing course elements is only one of many strategies that can be considered. Challenge course builders sometimes provide design, operation, training, and maintenance consultation services to program personnel. Many of the well-known team course elements are listed in *The Complete Ropes Course Manual* (Rohnke et al., 2007), which provides details about these and other challenge course elements.

A variation on the low challenge course incorporates elements that are 2 ft to 5 ft above the ground. These elements are generally designed to present individual challenges within a group context. This variation on team building has individual group members negotiate the elements and the others provide spotting, performance feedback, and encouragement. Because the elements are relatively low, participants perform any needed spotting without the aid of ropes and harnesses.

In recent years, the trend has been to make low course elements more team oriented by creating situations where two people are on the element at the same time. These participants work together with the support of the rest of the group. Spotting is still provided by the group, though some incorporation of belay systems (a safety rope attached to the climber's seat harness) is used. Having a belay system benefits programming with a diverse clientele. More information on programming for special populations is provided in the final section of this chapter, Accessible and Universal Designs.

No two low/team challenge courses are exactly alike, though most have variations of common low ropes course elements. *The Complete Ropes Course Manual* (Rohnke et al., 2007) is again a good resource to find additional examples of low course elements.

High Challenge Course

The high challenge course has challenged participants since it was first developed. Innovative design components include steel structures, hydraulic auto belay devices, moveable platforms, suspended yurts/gazebos, shock-absorbing systems, multiple levels, and innovative safety equipment. With these and other cutting-edge designs, high challenge courses have become sophisticated technical facilities. Elements on these courses range in height from 20 ft to 60 ft. Additional safety systems and procedures are required for high challenge courses. Each person negotiating the course must be connected to a belay system. There are variations to how these systems are set up, but generally they consist of a rope connected to a harness that the participant wears. This rope is usually run through a pulley or shear reduction device connected overhead and then down to the ground where another participant or staff member is operating a braking device, prepared to prevent a fall or provide a controlled descent.

Another approach is to employ a pair of short ropes attached to the climber that have carabiner-type clips on each free end that the climber clips onto cables or other approved anchor points. This low-tech fall protection device is affectionately called "lobster claws." The ACCT has developed strict standards for belay system equipment and construction.

Typically, a single participant negotiates his or her way through high challenge course elements. Although this approach is still widely used, more programs are using designs that allow multiple climbers or small groups on individual elements. Benefits are derived from participants collaborating on an element, sometimes called partner or team climbing. Partner climbing seems to more effectively capture and hold the attention of the group members who are on the ground observing. This also provides added value to the process with observers being supporters through encouragement and feedback.

High challenge courses have administrative and financial factors to consider that are not as important for team/low courses. Some of these considerations are listed below.

Increased staffing requirements. One facilitator can manage a group of 12 to 15 on team and low courses. On high courses, a minimum of two or three staff members would be needed depending on the design of the course and the needs of the group.

Additional equipment costs. Typically, all the necessary start-up climbing equipment is part of the course package. This equipment will need to be replaced on a 3-year to 5-year schedule depending on usage and environmental factors.

Possible higher insurance payments. Although the high course is statistically safer than nonbelayed courses, the majority of catastrophic injuries have occurred on high courses.

Access control. Preventing unauthorized access to the high course can lead to an extra expense (fencing, prevention devices, and possibly security technology) and liability concerns.

Staff training. Considerable staff training is needed to safely and effectively facilitate the high course. The safety of everyone on the course, including staff, depends on having knowledgeable and experienced facilitators running the program. An ongoing staff training schedule is recommended to maintain reliable skills and operating procedures.

This list is not intended to discourage agencies from adding a high course to their program. To the contrary, a high course adds features to a challenge program that are not available with a climbing wall or other types of courses. These features include a heightened sense of perceived risk, greater physical challenges, greater awareness of individual effort and concerns, greater sense of individual accomplishment, a visually striking apparatus, and a greatly amplified wow factor. It also complements other courses, if available, by providing powerful individual challenges that take the person's group-based learning to a higher level of commitment.

The structure of high course elements can be similar to those included in low courses. For example, crossing a cable low to the ground with only the other members of the group to help can be replicated on a high course as a small team initiative or using short hanging ropes to assist. This provides a chance to apply newly learned skills under greater stress by adapting skills learned on the lower courses. Again, a more detailed description of many high course elements can be found in *The Complete Ropes Course Manual* (Rohnke et al., 2007).

Universal and Accessible Design Considerations

For the past 15 years, finding ways to make challenge courses accessible to participants with disabilities has been an industry priority. There have consistently been sessions on this topic at Association for Experiential Education and ACCT conferences. The ACCT has a published position statement on its website that supports including individuals with disabilities in challenge course experiences. Standards within both organizations address inclusion, and challenge course vendors have incorporated accessible and universal designs into many of their products and training. The latest ACCT standards (ACCT, 2012), the eighth edition, provide guidance for certifying a person with a disability for any of the available certifications.

The Complete Ropes Course Manual (Rohnke et al., 2007) and the National Center on Accessibility (http://www.ncaonline.org) are excellent resources for additional information on making challenge courses accessible for participants with disabilities. A partial checklist of concerns/considerations is included below:

- **Environment**
  - Are trail systems that lead to and link elements accessible? Planners need to consider slope, cross-slope, surface stability, and trail widths. Trail widths must be a minimum of 32 in.
  - Are areas around individual challenge course elements level and firm with few obstructions?
  - Are drop-offs and steep embankments protected?
  - Are overhead clearances sufficient for participants with vision impairments?
- **Elements**
  - Is independent access available to each element?
  - Are platforms, decks, and elevated walkways large enough and at heights that are usable by all participants?
  - Do transitions from element to element have options that consider the need for intermediate belay clip-ins and movement from one element to the other?
  - Are handholds and footholds of various sizes and shapes used to include enough large holds to improve access?
  - Are options for negotiating (traversing, scooting, crawling, rolling, climbing) individual elements available?
  - Are access ramps accessible to people with disabilities (a slope of 12:1)? Ramps that are part of the element do not have to meet accessibility slope standards.
  - Is edge protection used where participants with bony prominences might hit or have prolonged contact with a hard edge? Rounding edges and using foam to cushion edges and surfaces is recommended.
  - Are belay systems and elements designed so participants with mobility or balance concerns have options?
- **Equipment**
  - Are mechanical advantage systems included to provide access to high courses? (A 3:1 or 4:1 pulley system is commonly used.)
  - Are full-body harnesses available, and are course staff members trained to work with those who may need a harness? Many different harness configurations are available so climbers with disabilities can minimize pain, support critical body parts, and make the best of existing muscle function. Additional padding for harnesses may be needed when prolonged hanging in a harness is a concern. In most cases, no one should hang in a seat harness for more than 15 min. Harness suppliers will provide specific information on safe harness usage.
  - Are body protection systems available for participants with poor balance, diminished sensation, or impaired muscle function? Areas to consider protecting include the head, elbows, hip girdle, knees, and ankles. Padding used in other activities such as skateboarding works well in challenge course activities. Custom-fitting foam and other products to achieve a safe level of protection may be required.
  - Are hauling and counterbalance systems available to assist with access to high elements and climbing structures?
- **Support facilities need to be accessible**
  - Do restroom facilities meet current accessibility standards?
  - Are storage facilities usable by all staff and participants?
  - Are debriefing areas, such as the log circle, accessible to people with disabilities?

Decisions about how to make a challenge course experience accessible to participants with disabilities are important to understand because functioning levels and needs vary greatly. Conducting a needs and abilities assessment on each participant will help with activity selection and determine whether adaptations will be needed. When it is not clear how to include individuals with disabilities, it is best to ask them about their needs to assess their capabilities. Involving the individuals in the inclusion plan becomes valuable to the learning process for everyone involved and begins to develop the staff–participant relationship. It is also advised to consult with a qualified challenge course professional who has worked with people with disabilities. Avoid taking an experimental approach to adapting activities for inclusion. Providing a meaningful experience that maintains personal dignity for participants with disabilities requires unique preparation, but with additional planning and a commitment to inclusion, challenge courses can provide exciting growth experiences for all people.

Challenge Course Operations, Administration and Staffing

The overall safety record of challenge courses is impressive. They are among the safest of all physical activity programs (Project Adventure, 2012). The ACCT has established safety and construction standards to provide guidelines for the safe and efficient operation of challenge courses. Even well-planned and well-operated challenge courses are potentially dangerous; therefore, all participants need to be informed of the potential danger and should sign a waiver of liability (assumption of risk). Other challenge course operation considerations can be divided into administration and staff, equipment, and maintenance issues. An overview of these operations issues is provided below, but is not a complete list of all operational considerations.

Additional operational guidance is available in the *ACCT Technical Operations and Inspection Standards*. There is not a recent comprehensive safety study available similar to the Project Adventure 20-year study. Since that data was published, there have been some tragic accidents in the industry. Most of them have been on zip lines and involve attachment failure, brake system failure, impact with objects too close to the zip path, and human error. More of this data should be available in the near future because states that regulate ropes courses and climbing walls require thorough documentation and investigation of accidents on regulated equipment.

Relatively new to the challenge course industry is the certification of facilitators, managers, and trainers. This certification program was developed by the ACCT, its members, and others across the industry. Vendor members of the ACCT are implementing the program as individual certifying bodies based on their own training and evaluation methods. They will follow the certification guidelines of the latest ACCT (2012) standards, and their certification program and practices are reviewed as part of vendor member accreditation. It is not necessary for all challenge course staff to be certified, though it is recommended that programs have a minimum of one certified practitioner. In large programs with numerous staff and extensive challenge course facilities, it may be necessary to have multiple certified staff and even a certified manager. As the certification program evolves and the industry is able to analyze the many aspects of its implementation and impact, we can expect changes. It is also likely that government regulations and the insurance industry will play a part in the future of challenge course credentialing. For complete information about certification, contact the ACCT or an ACCT Professional Vendor Member through the ACCT website (http://www.acctinfo.org).

Challenge course administration and staffing

- Purchase and maintain liability insurance for the organization and the staff. Provide professional training for all staff members. Administrators must provide sufficient funding to ensure that staff members are up to date on current policies and operating procedures, including rescues, equipment inspection, and emergency response.
- Have a risk management plan that clearly indicates actions and responsibilities. Be certain all staff members are up to date on their responsibilities by providing periodic training. Monitor staff credentials regarding current first aid and CPR certification.
- Keep accurate records of staff training, program operations and procedures, annual and periodic inspections, maintenance and repairs, liability forms, insurance, student training records, and accident/incident reports.
- Maintain a comprehensive equipment inventory and use equipment sign-out sheets to maintain property accountability.

Challenge course maintenance

- Inspect the entire challenge course and the supporting equipment on a regular basis depending on use rates, environment, and nature of the equipment. An ACCT vendor member inspector should conduct, at minimum, a comprehensive annual inspection.
- Use pressure-treated lumber for outdoor challenge courses. Weatherproof (treat) wood parts as needed. (Annually is best if feasible.)
- Use only healthy trees with a solid root system as support trees. Before building in trees, consult a qualified arborist about the condition of the trees (see ACCT DPI standard D-2).
- Use wood chips or bark mulch around the base of trees to protect the soil from compaction. Provide for drainage under the chips or mulch.
- Immediately remove dead or insect-infected trees from the system. Trees are susceptible to weather, insects, disease, rotting, and ground impaction and need to be checked regularly. Trim and clear broken or overgrown limbs. Remove splinters and rough edges on wood parts. Replace and repair rotten or cracked wood. Peen down sharp metal edges and pad protruding bolts or metal ends that are in participant traffic areas. Reset protruding nails as necessary.
- Check for decaying of the poles at ground level and cracks/checks (see ACCT DPI standard D.3.3).
- Use only corrosion-resistant bolts, cable, cable locks, rapid links, and other metal parts.
- Critical cables such as belays, zip wires, and most guy wires should be ⅜ in. diameter galvanized aircraft cable (GAC) that is 7 x 19 (seven strands with 19 wires per strand).
- Tighten nuts and bolts, turnbuckles, and clamps as required. Temporarily cover all frayed cable ends with tape until they can be refitted with a serving sleeve.
- Inspect cables for smoothness and rust. Cables need to be smooth if a participant's hands or feet will touch the cable. Do not wrap or otherwise enclose wire cable/rope. This traps moisture and hinders visual inspection.

Challenge course equipment

- Use UIAA- or EN-certified climbing ropes and locking-gate carabiners (UIAA 101 or EN 892 for dynamic rope).
- Install only stainless steel or galvanized hardware on outdoor challenge courses. For critical attachments, such as belay cable eyebolts, there is a high standard for minimum breaking strength (see ACCT standards or consult with your vendor).

- Have participants wear an adjustable seat harness. A full-body harness is used instead of the seat harness when there are concerns about distribution of forces on jumping or diving elements, such as with the pamper pole activity.
- On static or self-belayed courses, maintain constant vigilance to ensure that participants are using their "lobster claws" correctly when they switch from element to element. (Two auto-locking steel carabiners are attached to the participant by two lanyards.) One carabiner is locked to the next element's belay cable before the other carabiner is unclipped from the previous belay cable. This is a critical procedure.
- Minimize rope wear and damage by using a shear reduction device and edge protection as needed.
- Always have a first aid kit available. Have a communication system in operation, such as two-way radios or cell phones, as part of an emergency response plan.
- Store equipment in a cool dry place, preferably adjacent to the challenge course. Do not put equipment away while it is wet. Lay it out indoors if possible to dry first.
- Include lightning protection on high challenge courses.
- Require helmets to be worn on high elements and whenever anyone is beneath an active high activity.
- Keep a rope log that tracks hours of usage and falls taken on each rope. Also inspect belay ropes regularly for wear, cuts, discoloration, glazing, stiffness, soft spots, and other changes in specifications. If you are not sure about the integrity of a rope or its history, do not use it!

19 Skateparks, Roller Skating Rinks, and Winter Sports Areas

Thomas H. Sawyer, *Indiana State University*
Tonya L. Gimbert, *Indiana State University*

There continues to be a skateboarding renaissance. Facility development, equipment quality, skateboarders' techniques and abilities, and participant attitudes and maturity levels have reached new peaks. High-performance facilities and equipment for every style of skating are available. The abilities of professional skaters visibly advance each month, with athletes literally reaching new heights.

Skaters have become less clique oriented and more open minded. All disciplines of skating are now respected.

These changes have made skating more accessible to people of all ages. Presently, there are over 11 million skaters in the United States, making it the sixth largest sport (AAU Hockey, 2012). Skateboarding has become the third most popular sport among 6- to 18-year-olds (International Association of Skateboard Companies [IASC], 2013). Furthermore, 1 in 10 U.S. teenagers owns a skateboard (IASC, 2013).

The popularity that skateboarding now enjoys is also reflected in the media. Skateboarding is regularly featured on major television networks such as Fox, MTV, TSN, OLN, ESPN (notorious Extreme-Games [X-Games]), and NBC (Gravity Games), thus bringing it into today's spotlight. Finally, this coverage, along with skateboarding appearing in major marketing campaigns for Nike, the National Fluid Milk Processor Promotion Board, Coca-Cola, and Nintendo has provided skateboarding with a much higher media profile. This exposure has greatly expanded public acceptance of skaters and skating.

Skateparks

History of Skateboarding

In the 1950s, surfers created skateboarding to pass the time when the ocean was flat. Roller skate mounts and wheels were innocently nailed to 254s. This was the birth of the "sidewalk surfer." The earlier skateboard parks in the 1950s and 1960s reflected the surfer's passion for fluid, wavelike forms and smooth sensations.

In 1970, the urethane wheel was applied to the skateboard. Skateboard-specific trucks appeared in 1973, which were followed by precision bearings in 1975. Being of higher performance than their predecessors, these new products allowed for an easier, more enjoyable ride. These improvements encouraged advancements in maneuvers and more challenging facilities and spawned a skateboarding boom that supported massive private skateboard parks across the United States and in Europe. The parks perfected the backyard pools, drainage pipes, and ditches that skaters had taken to riding.

However, the demand for parks encouraged the development of poorly designed and constructed parks. This opened the door to insurance and liability problems. As a result, 80% of these parks were bulldozed in 1979, with the rest closing soon afterward. Some public parks remained, but basically skaters were left with nowhere to go, and many simply quit.

Yet during the 1980s, the remaining dedicated and innovative skaters continued to push the value of the sport. Many changes took place in the design of facilities and equipment. The wooden backyard half-pipe ramps began their evolution, which led to today's modern half-pipes.

Presently, there is resurgence in building skateboard parks. This has occurred because of the demand to remove skaters from city streets and public spaces. Skaters took to the streets because most of the skateparks had closed during the 1980s, and they developed the "street style" of skating creatively, adapting moves done in a pool or ramp in the defunct parks of the 1970s to curbs, ledges, steps, handrails, and walls. Communities became concerned about the skaters, and some considered them rebellious and a public nuisance.

Skateparks have come a long way from the early, unsafe private parks to the well-designed, safe public parks of today. The new facilities are larger and safer, and the skaters are using better designed equipment and safety gear. Skateboarding is fast becoming a safe and exciting sport for young (aged 6 to 18) males (74%) to spend their spare time perfecting their skills (IASC, 2013).

Liability

Liability is always a question when dealing with sports in general. Therefore, it is paramount that owners (public or private) carefully plan for a safe facility for participants and spectators. Today most insurance companies do not view skateparks as a high risk for governmental agencies. They are no more dangerous than swings and slides. Yet it is advisable to make sure the facility is covered with the same blanket plan as the city or town.

It is further advisable that the agency seriously considers safety when planning the skatepark. Signs should be posted to indicate hours of operations, pad and helmet requirements, and that the park is used at the participant's risk. The public agency needs to also consider the level of supervision that it should provide. Current common practice with skateparks is to leave the park open to "free play" with no supervision (i.e., similar to playgrounds). This practice will decrease the agency's liability. However, the operator must be certain that the area is safe, free of hazards, inspected regularly, and well maintained (i.e., similar to swimming pools at motels/hotels, where legislation protects those who have proper and adequate signage, a fence around the pool, safety equipment available, and a regular maintenance schedule).

The passage of numerous pieces of state legislation has allowed local public agencies to build unsupervised skateparks and post signs requiring safety equipment to be worn while skating. Unsupervised skateparks are popular with skaters, but they must be built in safe locations. If you do not have an ideal location, you may want to consider supervising the park or partnering with a private skatepark or other youth group, such as a church, Boys and Girls Club, or YMCA.

Immunity for Extreme Sports Parks

The Indiana General Assembly provided in Senate Bill 0141 (2012) that public and private owners and operators of extreme sports parks or recreation areas are immune from civil damages for injuries caused by extreme sports if (a) the extreme sports park or recreation area is designed or maintained for the purpose of extreme sports use, (b) a set of rules governing the use of the facility is clearly posted at each entrance to the extreme sports park or recreation area, and (c) a warning concerning the hazards and dangers associated with the use of the facility is clearly posted at the entrance to the extreme sports park or recreation area. They are immune from civil damages for injuries if the extreme sports park or recreation area is closed and has a warning against entry posted at each entrance. Other states have similar statutes, and it is important for plan-

ners to pay attention to the three provisions outlined above when planning a skatepark.

Safety Statistics

A recent study (U.S. National Electronic Injury Surveillance System [NEISS], 2011) prepared by the U.S. Consumer Product Safety Commission [CPSC] staff indicated that an estimated 108,510 skateboard-related injuries were treated in hospital emergency rooms in 2011 and 4,856 skateboarders were hospitalized. Since 1978, the injuries have dropped 38%. Skateboarders visited hospital emergency rooms with about 18,000 head injuries, and approximately 760, or 4%, were hospitalized. This decrease in injuries may be due to decreased popularity of the activity, the increased use of skateboard parks, and preventive actions by various skateboard safety groups. The parks often require users to wear protective gear such as helmets, knee pads, and elbow pads and require other precautions such as equipment checks before use (CPSC, 2012).

As might be expected, at least half of all roller skating injuries are suffered by teenagers, and over two thirds of the injuries were to girls and women. By contrast, the great majority of skateboard accidents occurred to boys and men. About one third of the injuries were scrapes and bruises, but the rest were more serious—fractures and sprains, mainly to the ankles, wrists, and other joints. Many of these serious injuries might have been avoided if the skaters knew the proper way to fall. Typically, when skaters lose their balance, they try to break their fall in ways that increase the likelihood of fractures and sprains, such as falling forward onto outstretched arms.

Of those injured, 33% had been skating less than 1 week, 20% were people borrowing boards, and 95% received outpatient care (NEISS, 2011). Most noteworthy is that 50% of the accidents occurred in unsafe areas where the skater struck an irregularity in the riding surface (CPSC, 2011). Therefore, the provision and maintenance of a professionally designed skatepark instead of kids skating in the street would likely dramatically decrease the numbers above.

General Planning Criteria

There are many sources of information on skateboard techniques and design of bowls, ramps, and other ancillary facilities. The following information is general in nature and provides the planners a place to begin this type of project.

Location

The planners should evaluate potential sites by considering the following issues: (a) potential usage of area (i.e., demographic analysis and a needs assessment), (b) size of site (i.e., how big is big enough), (c) access to public transportation, (d) drainage for the site, (e) access to public utilities, (f) noise pollution, (g) nuisance avoidance, (h) spectator seating, (i) parking, and (j) emergency access.

Safety

The following design features address safety issues that planners need to consider: (a) safe spectator areas; (b) low-maintenance site; (c) adequate sight lines of the area for supervision as well as viewing activities by spectators; (d) protective netting or barriers to guard against serious falls and to impede flying skateboards; (e) safety lighting; (f) emergency access; (g) exposure to environmental elements such as wind, rain, lightning, or sun; (h) shaded areas; and (i) drinking fountains.

Other Considerations

Planners should also consider the following in the design of the skatepark: (a) adequate lighting for night activities, (b) facilities for skateboarding that are suitable for other disciplines such as in-line skating or roller blading (e.g., recreational speed skating, in-line hockey, and freestyle or aggressive skating) and BMX bikes, (c) noise and light intrusion on neighbors, and (d) a north or south orientation rather than an east or west setting.

Consulting Services

The services that are normally provided by consultants (i.e., architect, landscape architect, skaters, and safety experts) in this area include

- preparing a demographic survey of the local skate community;
- assisting in the site selection;

- determining designs and construction parameters (e.g., wood vs. concrete, size, budget [see Table 19.1 for costs associated with the various types of parks], amenities);
- acting as an intermediary between owners and local skaters;
- organizing and establishing a pro shop (e.g., contacting vendors, preparing initial orders, etc.);
- preparing drawings for public venues; and
- developing design specifications for either wood or concrete skateparks.

Ten Quick Rules for Design

Gembeck (2009) suggested the following 10 quick rules for design:

1. Simplicity
2. Smoothness of surface
3. No kinks
4. Flat bottom
5. No overcrowding
6. Pushing room
7. No ledges over your belly button
8. Edges that grind
9. Pumpable hips
10. Lights

Table 19.1

General Information on Skatepark Costs

Portable parks and wood parks—as little as $10,000 and up to $250,000 with the average park being 10,000 sq ft and costing around $27,000 to $100,000; require regular maintenance; surfaces may be masonite, plywood, birch, Skatelite®, or Skatelite Pro®.
Advantages—portable, movable, affordable.

Steel frame skateparks—steel frame with metal or Skatelite® surfaces; permanent parks; can be bolted to existing concrete pad; some maintenance; more expensive than wood, with a 10,000-sq ft park starting at around $75,000.
Advantages—park can be reconfigured, weatherproof, affordable.

Concrete parks—concrete starting as low as $18 per square foot, averages $28 per square foot, and can be as high as $40 per square foot depending on excavation, grading, drainage, irrigation, water table, and so on; average 10,000-sq ft park costs $280,000, you must work with qualified builders and designers and make sure the concrete crew is experienced with mistakes made in concrete, which are expensive and permanent and are happening too often; two bowls ($132,000) were built and the concrete crew brushed the finish, making them unskateable.
Advantages—no maintenance, permanent park.

Note. A Skatepark designed to meet all skill levels will be between 18,000 sq ft and 25,000 sq ft with the minimum size recommended 10,000 sq ft. From *Skatepark Guide*, by A. Gembeck, 2009, retrieved from http://www.skateparkguide.com.

Design Services

Skateparks are constructed of concrete, steel, or wood. The designs are unique and customized to the specific site, wishes of the local skaters, and the needs of the owners. The park should be designed to provide the skaters with a fun and safe place to skate. Skateparks should include elements for all levels of skating ability, from beginner to advanced with sufficient variety to challenge and keep them coming back for more. Elements are designed with the proper transitions and heights, and the layouts allow flow from one element to the next.

The designer of a skatepark should thoroughly understand skatepark design, site preparation (e.g., surveying, soil testing, etc.), and structural engineering. The designer selected should be able to provide the following services:

- conducting preliminary consulting services appropriate to design considerations;
- preparing custom concept designs for wood, concrete, or combination of the two;
- developing detailed construction drawings for wood skateparks;
- preparing detailed drawings for concrete parks;
- providing budget estimates;

- preparing detailed specifications for wood park construction;
- consulting with concrete and steel contractors on design elements; and
- producing drawings in various formats using the latest version of AutoCad (see Figures 19.1 and 19.2 for samples of skatepark designs from http://www.skatedesign.com).

Specific Design Features

Wood ramp construction. Wood ramps can withstand many years of abuse by both skaters and the weather. The critical factors are that wood ramps are designed properly, built by experienced carpenters, and constructed of the right materials. The advantages of wood parks are that they are relatively inexpensive, are easily built, and can be placed on an existing concrete or asphalt pad. In addition, most wood equipment can be moved to change the configuration of the park to create new challenges for the skaters to enjoy (see Figure 19.2 for types of ramps). Generally, specifications for outdoor wood parks include the following (see also http://www.suburbanrails.com):

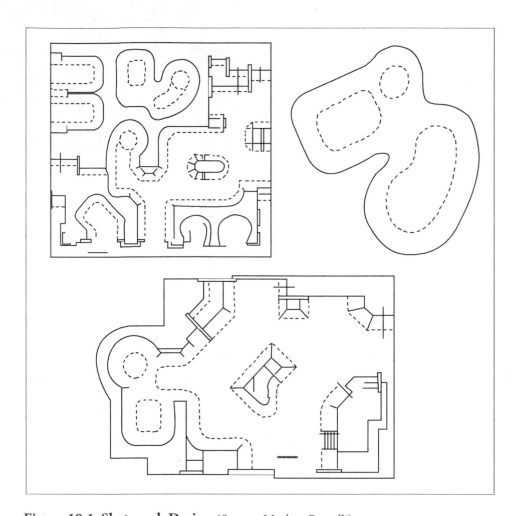

Figure 19.1. **Skatepark Design** (*Source:* Meghan Rosselli)

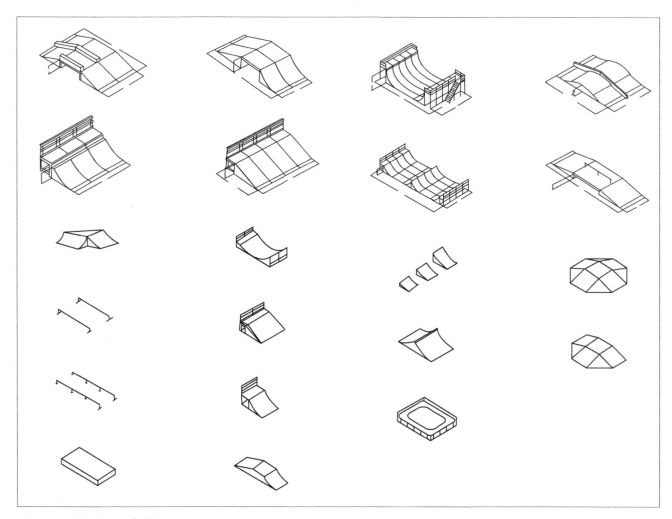

Figure 19.2. **Sample Ramps** (*Source:* Meghan Rosselli)

- pressure-treated wood;
- ¾ plywood transition templates, on ends and every 4 ft or 6 ft;
- 2 in. x 6 in. joists, spaced 8 in. on center, 4-ft spans/double joists every 24 in.;
- two layers of ½-in. plywood subsurface;
- ⅜ polyboard, ¼ Skatelite®, or 12-gauge steel ramp surface;
- 12-gauge x 24-in. steel for all ramp bottoms;
- ¼-in. polyboard on ramp decks;
- coping, 1 ½-in. or 2-in. schedule 40 pipe (2-in. or 2 ½-in. OD);
- ramp joists fastened with #8 x 3-in. galvanized deck screws;
- each layer of plywood fastened by rustproof decking screws on a 12-in. pattern; and
- ramp surfaces and bottoms fastened with #10 x 3-in. sheet metal screws.

Concrete skateparks. Permanent outdoor skateparks are constructed of concrete. The material is fluid and allows unlimited shapes to be integrated into the design. Objects can flow from one to another with no interruptions.

Long, flowing designs that incorporate soft bumps as well as curbs, ledges, rails, and steps can be easily built to make interesting and challenging runs for skaters of all experience levels. If the owner has the budget, this is the way to go.

Ramps at the YMCA state park in Murfreesboro, Tennessee

Concrete skatepark in Greencastle, Indiana

Concrete parks are built from the ground up. This allows for a more aesthetically pleasing park by incorporating varying elevations and by integrating grassy knolls, shade trees, flowers, and observation areas. Critical factors in concrete parks are the design and implementation of the transitions and placement of the coping. If a concrete park is poorly designed or built, the owner could be stuck with an area skaters will not skate.

Perfectly installed coping and forms will act as guides for templates. The templates then guide a blade, called a fresno, which precisely cuts the concrete to shape. The template is then moved to the end of the trimmed section and the process is repeated. The concrete used is called shot-BMX bike on the YMCA skatepark concrete, which is also used for swimming pools.

A gray coat is recommended for bowls, pools, or anything with transition. Working steeply inclined concrete with floats and trowels makes the concrete slump and compresses the transition, forming a kink. Cutting the concrete, then putting a finish coat on later, allows more control to achieve a precise shape and smoother finish.

Lighting. Most outdoor skateparks require lighting. Chapter 5 provides a great deal of detail regarding exterior lighting. Lighting for the park serves two main functions: to provide light for night skateboarding and for security when the park is not in use.

Indoor skateboard park. There are many locations in the United States that have a combined indoor–outdoor park because of climate. The actual design of the park will be the same except it will be indoors rather than outdoors. The other components of an indoor structure include heating, ventilation, air-conditioning, plumbing, electrical, and so on and are found in other chapters of this book.

Indoor skateparks are generally constructed of concrete, and repairs are rarely needed. Those that have steel and wooden structures will require regular inspection and maintenance. The facilities are kept clean by the skateboarders themselves. They do not want to trip on soda cans or other rubbish. A major maintenance concern with

steel is rust and loose bolts and screws. Wooden ramps also have problems with screws loosening and falling out. Weather can take a toll on both steel and wooden ramps.

The major concerns with concrete are cracks and pooling water areas. The cracks need to be properly filled prior to winter. Frost can destroy concrete. Trees and other foliage enhance the visual beauty and provide shade for a park. However, trees require regular maintenance to keep them healthy. Areas around trees require regular cleaning to remove discarded limbs and leaves that could be a safety problem for the park. (See Chapter 9 for additional information regarding foliage, trees, and turf.)

Other maintenance issues focus on cleaning restrooms, concession areas, offices, entrance and lobby areas, and the pro shop within the skate house. Furthermore, exterior trash containers need to be regularly emptied and cleaned. Finally, the grass areas need to be mowed.

Roller Skating Rinks

History of Roller Skating

Roller skating is traveling on smooth surfaces with roller skates. It is a form of recreation, as well as a sport, and can also be a form of transportation. Skates generally come in three basic varieties: quad roller skates, in-line skates or blades, and tri-skates, though some have experimented with a single-wheeled "quintessence skate" or other variations on the basic skate design. In America, this hobby was most popular in the 1970s and 1990s.

The following is a short history of roller skating ("Roller Skating," n.d.):

- 1743: First recorded use of roller skates, in a London stage performance. The inventor of this skate is lost to history.
- 1760: First recorded skate invention, by John Joseph Merlin, who demonstrated a primitive in-line skate with metal wheels.
- 1819: First patented roller skate design, in France by M. Petitbled. These early skates were similar to today's in-line skates, but they were not very maneuverable; it was difficult for the user of these skates to do anything but move in a straight line and perhaps make wide sweeping turns. For the rest of the 19th century, inventors continued to work on improving skate design.
- 1863: The four-wheeled turning roller skate, or quad skate, with four wheels set in two side-by-side pairs was first designed in New York City by James Leonard Plimpton in an attempt to improve upon previous designs. The skate contained a pivoting action using a rubber cushion that allowed the skater to skate a curve by leaning to one side. It was a huge success, so much so that the first public skating rink was opened in 1866 in Newport, Rhode Island, with the support of Plimpton. The design of the quad skate allowed easier turns

and maneuverability, and the quad skate dominated the industry for more than a century.

- 1876: William Brown in Birmingham, England, patented a design for roller skates wheels. Brown's design embodied his effort to keep the two bearing surfaces of an axle, fixed and moving, apart. Brown worked closely with Joseph Henry Hughes, who drew up the patent for a ball or roller bearing race for bicycle and carriage wheels in 1877. Hughes' patent included all the elements of an adjustable system. These two men are thus responsible for modern-day roller skate and skateboard wheels, as well as the ball bearing race inclusion in velocipedes, later to become motorbikes and automobiles. This was arguably the most important advance in the realistic use of roller skates as a pleasurable pastime.
- 1876: The toe stop was first patented. This provided skaters with the ability to stop promptly upon tipping the skate onto the toe. Toe stops are still used today on most quad skates and on some in-line skates.
- 1877: The *Royal Skating* indoor skating ring building was erected in rue Veydt, Brussels.
- 1880s: Roller skates were being mass produced in America from then. This was the sport's first of several boom periods. Micajah C. Henley of Richmond, Indiana, produced thousands of skates every week during peak sales. Henley skates were the first skate with adjustable tension via a screw, the ancestor of the kingbolt mechanism on modern quad skates.
- 1884: Levant M. Richardson received a patent for the use of steel ball bearings in skate wheels to reduce friction, allowing skaters to increase speed with minimum effort.
- 1898: Richardson started the Richardson Ball Bearing and Skate Company, which provided skates to most professional skate racers of the time, including Harley Davidson (no relation to the Harley-Davidson® motorcycle brand). A 24-hr roller skating endurance competition was held in Paris in 1911.

The design of the quad skate has remained essentially unchanged since then and remained the dominant roller skate design until nearly the end of the 20th century. The quad skate has begun to make a comeback recently due to the popularity of roller derby and jam skating.

- 1979: Scott Olson and Brennan Olson of Minneapolis, Minnesota, came across a pair of in-line skates created in the 1960s by the Chicago Roller Skate Company and, seeing the potential for off-ice hockey training, set about redesigning the skates using modern materials and attaching ice hockey boots. A few years later Scott Olson began heavily promoting the skates and launched the company Rollerblade, Inc. (History section)

During the late 1980s and early 1990s, the Rollerblade®-branded skates became so successful that they inspired many other companies to create similar in-line skates, and the in-line design became more popular than the traditional quads. The Rollerblade® skates became synonymous in the minds of many with "in-line skates" and skating, so much so that many people came to call any form of skating "rollerblading," thus becoming a genericized trademark.

For much of the 1980s and into the 1990s, in-line skate models typically sold for general public use employed a hard plastic boot similar to ski boots. In or about 1995, "soft boot" designs were introduced to the market, primarily by the sporting goods firm K2 Inc., and were promoted for use as fitness skates. Other companies quickly followed, and by the early 2000s, the development of hard-shell skates and skeletons became primarily limited to the aggressive in-line skating discipline and other specialized designs.

The single-wheel "quintessence skate" was made in 1988 by Miyshael F. Gailson of Caples Lake Resort, California, for the purpose of cross-country ski skating and telemark skiing training. Other skate designs have been experimented with over the years, including two-wheeled (heel and toe) in-line skate frames, but the vast majority of skates on the market today are either quad or standard in-line design.

Types of Skating

Artistic skating. Artistic roller skating is a sport that consists of a number of events. These are usually accomplished on quad skates, but in-line skates may be used for some events. Various flights of events are organized by age and ability/experience. In the United States, local competitions lead to nine regional competitions that lead to national championships and world championships. The following are the common types of artistic skating:

- figure,
- dance,
- freestyle,
- precision teams,
- singles, and
- pairs.

Speed skating. In-line speed skating is a competitive noncontact sport played on in-line skates. Variants include indoor, track, and road racing, with many different grades of skaters so the whole family can compete.

Group skating. Among skaters not committed to a particular discipline, a popular social activity is the group skate or street skate, in which large groups of skaters regularly meet to skate together, usually on city streets.

Roller hockey (quad). Roller hockey is the overarching name for a roller sport that existed long before in-line skates were invented. Roller hockey has been played on quad skates in many countries worldwide and so has many names.

Roller derby. Roller derby is a team sport played on roller skates on an oval track. Originally a trademarked product developed out of speed skating demonstrations, the sport is currently experiencing a revival as a grass-roots-driven five-a-side sport played mainly by women. Most roller derby leagues adopt the rules and guidelines of the Women's Flat Track Derby Association or its male counterpart, Men's Roller Derby Association.

Designing a Roller Skating Rink

When designing and constructing a roller skating facility, several different aspects should be considered. One of the first steps in designing a facility is determining which components will be included, for example, party rooms, rock climbing wall, skate shop, concession stand, and video games. The actual size of the building should be determined based on need, population size, and budget. Skating rinks come in many different sizes; therefore, dimensions will vary from one rink to another. When considering different-sized buildings, the following issues should be accounted for: the size of the town, the quality of other competition, and whether another skating rink already exists in the same town. Some rinks build small rooms for birthday parties, and others expand the snack bar area. Party rooms allow for more privacy, a place for parents to congregate, and storage space for presents.

Flooring

The skating floor is the main feature of any skating rink. Concrete flooring is cheaper than hardwood flooring. Hardwood flooring is considered the nicest of all flooring. Both of these floors will have a plastic-type coating applied over them, which is what is actually skated on. The protective coating should be recoated at least once a year (high-volume rinks may do this at least twice a year). An average-sized rink is 18,000 sq ft with a skating surface of about 10,000 sq ft (approximately 70 ft x 150 ft). The two most common roller rink shapes are rectangular and oval. A 5-ft wall (or taller) should be constructed around the floor with an opening into the nonskating areas of the rink. This wall should be covered with protective padding to provide safety to patrons, along with a bar for inexperienced skaters to hold on to while skating.

Sound and Lighting Systems

Sound and lighting are important to skating rinks. Most customers are under age 18, and music is important to this population. It is important that equipment will work well across the entire building as well as above the noise of the skaters. It should be heard from all areas/corners of the skating rink (surround sound). Disco balls and colored lighting fixtures may also be used to create dynamic atmospheres. Spotlights and strobe lights may also be used; however, caution signs should be posted at the entrance of the rink warning patrons of their usage on the skating floor (Butler, 2003).

General Design Elements

Entrances to funnel guests to certain areas of the facility should be used appropriately, for example, to areas such as the concessions stand, skate shop or skate counter, locker area, and restrooms or party rooms. An open sitting area where people can put on their skates should be included in the facility design. Lockers or storage cubes, along with a coat rack, allow for storage of personal possessions.

A concessions area should also be considered when designing a skating facility. Typically, there are two sides to the entrance of the rink itself. On one side is the sitting area and on the other is an area with tables and a concessions stand. Restrooms should be part of the facility design process as well. The budget for the facility will depend on other components (i.e., vending machines, skate shop or showroom, video games). Oftentimes, the skating facility is used for various activities, such as yoga, Zumba®, aerobics classes, competitive skating, or even skating lessons. Roller rinks may also host roller hockey practice and/or competitions, skating lessons, and special event nights such as "jam skating" or adult skate night (Butler, 2003; Donahue, 2013).

Winter Sports Areas

Sledding Areas

According to the CPSC (2011), there were 25,131 emergency room visits because of ski accidents but only 1,018 people were hospitalized, and only 2.5% (3,750) were for head injuries. Most sledding accidents occur at a low speed between 10 mph and 20 mph.

Sledding Safety

Sledding is a great activity, but it results in many accidents each year, some of which are serious and even fatal. The following safety recommendations should be considered when developing sledding areas:

- Avoid hills with trees, stumps, holes, fences, and rock walls.
- Never orient a sledding course toward a road, parking lot, pond, lake, river, railroad tracks, or raven.
- Allow for a sled return zone adjacent to the sledding course.
- Have all participants wear a helmet and mouthguard.
- Provide adult supervision.
- Pad all obstructions with hay bales.
- Use sleds that can be steered rather than snow discs.
- Do not allow participants to ride flat. Have the participants sit up and face forward.

- All participants should sled feetfirst, never headfirst.
- Do not allow inflatable tube sleds, they can bounce and throw children.
- Do not allow sitting or sliding on plastic sheets or other materials that can be pierced by objects on the ground.
- Be certain that the sledding area is well lighted during the evening hours.
- Post appropriate signage to warn participants of the dangers of sledding and the dos of good sledding.

Designing a Safe Sledding Area

It is important to consider the points made above when designing a safe sledding area for children. Sledding is a natural winter activity, and communities need to provide for safe sledding areas to protect the children.

A safe sledding area (see Figure 19.3) should include

- an entrance to the area;
- a wide, moderately sloped hill clear of stumps, trees, fences, and holes;
- a length between 50 yd to 150 yd;

- a runoff that is long and flat enough to accommodate deceleration of the sled;
- a clearly marked course;
- return alleys for the sledders that are clearly identified on either side of the sledding course;
- a buffer/safety zone of at least 10 yd between the sledding course and return alleys;
- a course end not comprising roads, ponds, lakes, rivers, or parking lots;
- obstructions padded by hay or straw bales;
- necessary lighting if the area is to be used in the evening hours;
- shelter provided at the top and bottom of the course for sledders to use during resting periods with restrooms nearby; and
- appropriate signage placed at the entrance and shelters outlining the safety recommendations for sledders.

Snow Sports

Ski and snowboard hills. Skiing has become popular. If climatic conditions are suitable and desirable topo-

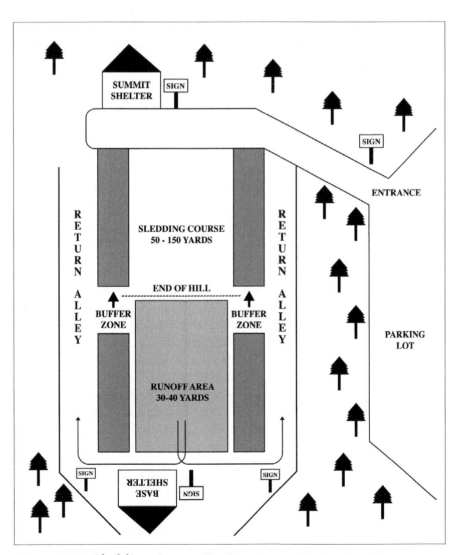

Figure 19.3. **Sledding Course Design** (*Source:* Meghan Rosselli)

graphic features are available, a school or a park and recreation department might look into developing the facilities needed to foster this sport. A variety of artificial surfaces simulating real snow have brought skiing instructional opportunities to all sections of the country independent of climate.

The provision of skiing in a school or public recreation system should be approached from an instructional standpoint, the theory being to give participants some basic instruction so they can enjoy it as a leisure-time activity in the resort areas that have more ideal facilities. If the park system contains ideal skiing hills with plenty of room, regular ski courses may be developed. Basic facility requirements for skiing instruction include proper topographical features; a headquarters building for rental of equipment, a refractory ?, and similar purposes; a ski tow; and various slopes for instructional purposes.

Normally, the series of classes taught is broken into three units: beginner, advanced, and expert. It is the opinion of ski instructors (cite) that the beginners ski class is the most important for recreational skiing. Basic instruction in skiing may be conducted in classes not exceeding 25 to 30 beginners. For this group, a gentle and short slope with a relatively large flat run-out area is desirable because it permits a beginner to have complete control of himself or herself and allows a skier to gain confidence in using skis. In the advanced group, classes are much smaller, and in the expert group, instruction becomes almost individualized. For each successive group, hills become longer and a little steeper.

The following criteria are recommended for selecting facilities for beginners classes:

- flat-top hill area, 50 sq ft per skier, 25 skiers per class;
- slope about 75 ft to 100 ft long, drop in grade of 15 ft, or 4:1 ratio;
- starting line at top of slope that is 100 ft wide;
- run-out at bottom of slope either flat or uphill;
- slope facing east or northeast;
- instructional area free of stones, woods, and other impediments; and
- protective cover, such as trees or brush, around the area.

The following criteria are suggested for advanced classes:

- top of hill about the same as for beginners;
- slope is most important: ratio about 3:1 and length 100 ft to 150 ft; and
- width of hill or slope is a minimum of 150 ft because of speed and space required for turning movements.

The following criteria are recommended for selecting facilities for expert classes:

- either the same hill as advanced classes or preferably a longer and steeper hill;
- enough downhill length to permit a minimum of three turning movements, for example, 250 ft on a 3:1 slope; and
- greater width than that of slope for advanced classes.

Cross-country skiing. Cross-country skiing has a broad popularity across the northern United States. Cross-country skiing, also known as ski touring, has attracted many people who cannot afford to keep up with alpine or downhill skiing price tags or do not want to stand in long lines at the lifts.

One attractive feature of cross-country skiing is that a successful program can be developed with limited facilities. Existing trails can be groomed in the winter using homemade or purchased equipment that is towed by a snowmobile. Trail surfaces are best on a wood chip, grass, or gravel base. Asphalt bases do not work well. Trails can be carved out of almost any park area. If a golf course is used, the greens and tees should have a fence placed around them to keep skiers off of these sensitive areas. Trails should be signed with rules placed at starting points. The signs should indicate direction, distance, and level of difficulty.

Coasting and tobogganing. Often a community has a hill or hills suitable for coasting, which become magnets after every snowfall for children with sleds, toboggans, and other coasting devices. In the absence of a natural coasting hill, some park and public works departments build such a facility. These hills are usually located in a park safely guarded from the hazards of street traffic.

In developing local sledding (coasting) areas, incorporate adequate safety features. Sufficient space should be provided between sled runs, and up traffic should be isolated from the down traffic. The area should be as free as possible from hazards, such as nearby trees, grills, benches, or other park paraphernalia. Municipal risk managers will provide input into the safety of the area.

Communities with an extensive response to sledding or skiing may want to counter adverse weather by using artificial snow equipment or improving the activity with a ski lift. Communities where hills are not available create their own sledding hills. They typically serve as a sledding hill in the winter and as part of a park in the spring and summer where multiple activities can be programmed.

Tobogganing is a thrilling sport that requires designed space. Occasionally, natural slopes are used if they are free from obstructions and have a long bottom run-off. The common practice is to select a hillside with a reasonable steep and even grade. A chute is constructed using a wooden trough. It can be permanent or built in sections. Some communities create artificial toboggan runs with refrigerated chutes. They are expensive to develop and maintain.

Ice-Skating/Ice Hockey Rinks

Ice-skating facilities are feeling the impact of modern technology in more communities each year. With the advent of mechanical freezing, the skating season has been extended from a 20-day to 60-day average season, to a 140-day season, to as much as 240 days depending on climatic conditions.

Although natural ice rinks have not gone out of style, artificial rinks are replacing them as central or regional facilities. Natural ice rinks are continuing to serve as a supplemental neighborhood facility in many communities. A considerable number of skaters still prefer the rugged pleasure of an old-fashioned skating experience.

Ice hockey. Ice hockey rinks have a sports function and provide a recreation service. If ice hockey is to be part of the rink's activity schedule, goals will be needed and a 4 ft high solid fence, called the dasher, will have to be installed to enclose an area as near to 85 ft x 185 ft as possible. Dasher boards are heavily reinforced to stand the shock of players being pushed against them and are lined on the rink side with either wood or plastic. There is normally a chain-link or clear plastic barrier another 4 ft to 6 ft on top of the dashers to enable spectators to view games safely. The dasher board enclosure should have round corners because square corners present a hazard. A kickboard, 6 in. to 8 in. high, is fastened at the base of the dasher boards and is replaced as often as necessary.

Because dasher boards reflect sunlight and cause melting of the ice, they should be painted a dark color. However, it is difficult to follow the puck if the dasher boards are too dark, so a shade of gray is recommended. If the hockey rink is indoors, the dasher boards can be painted a light color without causing a melting problem.

Typical recreational ice floor configuration. The typical recreational ice hockey configurations are as follows:

- full-sized hockey arena floor, normally 200 ft x 85 ft;
- Olympic-sized hockey floor, 200 ft x 100 ft;
- curling sheets, 14 ft x 146 ft, but usually laid out at 15 ft x 150 ft; and
- refrigeration load ranging from 45 tons to 300 tons for an arena.

Cooling the floor. The floor surface is occasionally constructed entirely with sand, but this limits the use of the facility. More commonly, the floor consists of a 5-in. or 6-in. cement pad reinforced with rebar.

The brine is supplied to the floor via 6-in. to 10-in. headers. The headers are constructed of PVC or steel. The headers feed an in-floor-cooling grid consisting of 1-in. polyethylene or steel pipe spaced on 3-in. to 4-in. centers.

The cooling floor brine is usually a calcium chloride solution mixed to a freeze point of -5°F to -10°F. The pH should be maintained at a level of 7.5 to 8.5. The brine should be tested annually by a lab regularly engaged in testing arena brine samples.

Heating the floor. The rejected waste heat from the refrigeration plant typically provides the heat source for the heating floor, but boilers or electric resistance heaters are occasionally used as well.

The heated calcium is usually supplied to the heating floor via 4-in. brine mains. The mains in turn feed a 1-in. polyethylene grid spaced on 12-in. to 24-in. centers. The heating floor is positioned approximately 1 ft under the cooling floor and is separated by insulation and a vapor barrier.

The heating floor brine should be kept at a freeze point of 10°F to 15°F. The pH should be maintained at a level of 7.5 to 8.5. The brine should be tested annually by a lab regularly engaged in testing arena samples.

Solving humidity problems in ice rinks. If you can control the humidity in your facility, you are one large step toward creating the ideal ice-skating environment. Humidity enters an ice rink with incoming ventilation air, with the opening of doors, from the use of showers, and through the normal respiration of the people within the building.

If your facility is in a cold environment, such as Winnipeg, Manitoba, the incoming air can easily be 0°F and 50% relative humidity during a typical winter day. If this entering cold air is warmed up to 400°F , the humidity will now fall to less than 20% because warm air has the ability to hold more moisture. This lower humidity level poses little problem to the proper operation of the facility.

However, if your facility is in Los Angeles, California, the incoming air could easily be 65°F with a relative humidity of 65%. If this entering warm air is reduced to 50°F inside the skating rink, the humidity will skyrocket to 100% relative humidity because the cold air will not hold as much moisture. At this point, there is only one place for the water vapor to go; it condenses into water droplets and the problems begin.

Just as a boiling kettle deposits moisture on a cold window on a winter's day, airborne moisture in an ice rink will also deposit on cold surfaces, and of course, the coldest spot is likely the ice surface itself. When this happens, the ice will cloud over, losing its desired sheen, and will start to become sluggish to skate on. The glass around the ice surface will also fog over, obstructing the view of the audience.

In addition to the aesthetic inconveniences caused by excessive humidity, the condensing moisture releases a tremendous amount of heat into the ice surface that must be removed at the expense of operating the refrigeration equipment longer than would normally be required. Condensation can permeate your building insulation, drastically reducing its effectiveness, and of greater consequence, structural steel will start to rust and wood will start to rot, further reducing the integrity of your facility.

Luckily, with proper design, humidity can be controlled effectively and efficiently. The two commonly used styles of dehumidification systems are the mechanical dehumidifier and the desiccant dehumidifier.

Sand floor versus cement floor. There are good reasons for installing both sand floors and cement floors in an ice-skating facility. Hopefully the following will make your decision easier.

Sand floors reduce the initial cost of an ice surface. A sand floor is generally used in a year-round ice facility but can be installed in a seasonal facility with some precautions to prevent unwanted traffic on the piping system during the off-season.

A sand floor reduces the flexibility of the facility in that no off-season activities can be held directly on top of the sand. An ice covering can be used to facilitate light activities on top of the ice, but there is not enough support for rodeos, tractor pulls, and so forth. If for some reason the building must be sold, a sand floor will reduce the building's usefulness and resale value.

A cement floor for an NHL-sized ice rink will cost between $85,000 and $165,000 more than a sand floor depending on the floor strength, proximity of material, and a good super-flat contractor. A cement floor increases the flexibility of the facility in that dances, bingos, and trade shows can be held in the off-season. With a properly engineered floor, a circus or other heavy event can be held as well. As with a sand floor, the ice surface can be covered for non-ice events while the ice is in place.

To prevent the puncturing of cooling pipes, additional care and attention is required during the initial stages of ice making with a sand floor. Before applying the first water, you must ensure that all of the pipes are in their chairs and the sand has been dressed out to its normal operating level.

To maintain a crisp, clean, efficient ice surface, all arenas should have the ice periodically removed to purge the buildup of solids and old paint that is deposited over time. On a sand floor, the residue tends to cake on the sand surface and can only be removed by replacing the surface sand. This residue is easily washed away on a cement floor.

A cement floor is much easier to make ice on, especially with less experienced personnel. A sand floor requires gently misting the sand surface while avoiding puncturing the pipes until the ice layer is thick enough to walk on and eventually drive a Zamboni on. When installed properly, a cement floor always ensures a precisely level surface to form the ice base. A sand floor can deviate over the years with use.

It is advisable to maintain 1 ¾ in. to 2 ½ in. of ice on a sand floor to reduce the chance of puncturing pipe during ice events. Cement floors only require 2 in. of ice for safe use. Periodically measuring the ice surface thickness by drilling holes (ice taps) is much easier with a cement floor. With a sand floor, added attention must be taken to ensure that no pipes are punctured while edging or resurfacing. This special care is not necessary on a cement floor.

Once the ice is in place, there can be a small amount of difference in energy consumption between a sand floor and a cement floor. The same amount of BTUs (British thermal units) will enter the ice surface regardless of the style of floor. A well-designed cement floor will typically have 1 in. of cement cover and 1 in. of ice cover above the cooling pipes. A sand floor will typically have 2 in. of ice cover above the pipes. Ice has a K value of 1.3 and cement has a K value of 0.54. The K value is the rate a substance conducts heat with a high K value conducting heat faster than a low K value. Theoretically, the cement floor would have to operate a little colder than the sand floor for the same amount of heat to be exchanged. However, in reality, many sand floors usually develop small hills and valleys over the years, which require the ice level to be kept thicker in many areas, which reduces the efficiency.

Whichever way you choose to build your ice-skating facility, rest assured that with proper care and attention, a great ice surface can be maintained on either a sand floor or a cement floor.

Calcium chloride versus glycol. On an indirect refrigeration system, you must select a secondary coolant. Both calcium chloride and glycol have been successfully used over the years, and there are applications where both secondary coolants have an advantage. To a much lesser degree, other heat transfer mediums such as methyl alcohol have also been used in the ice rink industry.

In regard to energy efficiency, calcium chloride is the better choice. Its heat transfer coefficient is much better than glycol. This equates to smaller, less expensive chillers for the same heat transfer. The heat transfer in the floor piping system is also better. Due to the superior heat transfer characteristics in the floor, the brine pump can be smaller, and the required pump horsepower and corresponding energy consumption are reduced with calcium chloride.

Calcium chloride is highly corrosive when not maintained properly. With proper system design and operation, it is still the best choice for most ice rink applications. The system components must be selected specifically for the calcium chloride. Typically chillers are made out of carbon steel or cooper nickle. Brine pump shafts and butterfly valve stems should be made out of stainless steel.

With a system using calcium chloride, it is imperative that the system is kept full at all times and no air is allowed to come in contact with the internal components. A high-grade, environmentally friendly rust inhibitor must be used to ensure equipment longevity. It is good practice to carry out routine in-house brine tests to monitor brine strength and pH on a semiannual basis and to request a lab report once a year.

In systems that are occasionally emptied and filled, such as a portable system, glycol can be a good choice.

Glycol will reduce the effects of corrosion in systems that are occasionally open to the air. It is still important to use good-quality inhibited glycol, such as Dow SR-1, and to ensure that annual lab samples are taken to verify the integrity of the solution.

Should you install a heating floor? If an ice surface is in operation for more than 7 months of the year, a heating floor is generally required. The purpose of the heating floor is to eliminate the buildup of an ice lens below the cooling floor, which can cause the floor to heave and buckle.

High-quality insulation must be installed beneath the cooling floor, which will minimize the amount of heat loss from the soil below. It is considered good practice to install a double layer of 2-in. high-density Styrofoam as well as a vapor barrier beneath the cooling floor (total of 4 in. of insulation). In most installations, the insulation will slow the formation of ice but will not eliminate it unless you have approximately 11 in. of insulation. The cost of 11 in. of insulation is prohibitive, so it is more practical to install a heating floor.

Even if you are not planning on operating your facility more than 7 months of the year, installing a heating floor in the beginning is prudent in case you change your mind later. The cost of a heating floor is typically 7% to 15% of the refrigeration installation.

The result of a heaved floor can have disastrous consequences. An ice rink operating year-round at 150°F without a heating floor will attract moisture from great distances much as a cold window in a humid house will. This steady accumulation of moisture has the potential of forming an ice lens 22 ft thick below the ice surface.

The first obvious result of a heaved floor is an ice surface that is out of level. There have been many ice surfaces over the years that have been more than 10 in. out of level as a result of frost heaves. The only way to level the playing surface is to apply more ice on the low spots. The result is an inconsistent surface temperature over the entire plane and an ice plant that is operating overtime to accommodate the thick spots.

Of greater consequence is the structural damage that takes place. The cement floor can buckle and crack as a result of the heaves. Doors and gates can become impossible to open, and glass can fall out of its supports, causing bodily harm to the players and spectators. In some instances, the whole building can shift and sustain damage.

On many facilities with severe heaving problems, the only recourse is to totally remove the damaged floor and excavate the frozen material. The costs can be tremendous. For this reason, we always recommend a heating floor on new installations.

Selecting a primary refrigerant. The objective of the primary refrigerant is to safely and efficiently remove the heat from the secondary coolant. Several factors must be considered when selecting a refrigerant: budget for con-

struction, the cost of electricity, building design, availability of trained operators and technicians, and local codes and regulations.

Over the years, ammonia and R-22 have been the most common refrigerants employed in the ice rink industry. With the future phaseout of R-22, new alternatives are starting to appear on the market, such as R-410A, 417A, 422A, 422D, and 438A. The following is a brief description of pros and cons of the regularly used refrigerants.

Ammonia. For energy efficiency and equipment first cost, ammonia is still the best choice. Ammonia has a significantly higher heat transfer coefficient than the other refrigerants. This can be exploited in two ways. Selecting a smaller chiller and condenser can reduce first costs. Alternatively, you can select components with the same heat transfer surface area and increase the total system efficiency by operating at lower discharge pressures and higher suction pressures. The higher BTU per pound of mass flow reduces the size of piping and valves. Ammonia's better thermodynamic properties reduce electricity costs. An ammonia system requires less refrigerant than the alternatives, and the cost of ammonia per pound is approximately one fifth of the other refrigerants.

Some facilities cannot use ammonia for various code reasons. Due to its pungent odor and higher toxicity, special precautions must be taken in plant rooms and equipment design. The strong odor makes detection and leak prevention much easier than with the alternatives.

Ammonia systems are built with much higher construction standards than the alternative refrigerants, which results in a higher quality, longer lasting industrial grade system. With the recent improvements in compressor seals, limited charge chillers, leakproof valves, and ammonia detection equipment, we feel that ammonia is still the best choice for an ice rink application.

R-22. Next to ammonia, R-22 is the most efficient alternative. However, due to the .05 ozone depletion factor, R-22 is slated for total phaseout over the next 20 to 30 years. R-22 is reasonably priced in comparison to some of the new alternatives. Compressor sizing is slightly larger than ammonia, and the required horsepower per ton of refrigerant is approximately 8% higher. R-22 is still used in many new installations. Where possible, we suggest using components, piping, and valves so you leave the door open for an ammonia conversion if required.

AZ-50. AZ-50 has been used successfully as an alternative to R-22 since the mid-1990s. It is approximately 12% less efficient than R-22 on a reciprocating compressor application. This efficiency loss can be greatly reduced through creative subcooling techniques. The mass flow of AZ-50 is greater, requiring larger line sizes and valves than R-22. The compressor size must be approximately 10% larger for the same refrigeration effect. AZ-50 requires the use of polyolester oil, which is expensive. Discharge temperatures are significantly lower than R-22 or ammonia, which eliminates the need for oil cooling. The lower operating temperature reduces equipment room exhaust fan run time. The cost of refrigerant is approximately double that of R-22. This price difference will reduce as R-22 phases out.

R-134a. Recently, R-134a has been used in a number of facilities. It is more expensive than R-22 and about 12% less efficient than R-22 on reciprocating compressor applications (20% less efficient than ammonia). The volume flow rate of R-134a is much higher than R-22, AZ-50, and ammonia, which means that the compressors must be approximately 60% larger to do the same job. This translates into higher first costs and maintenance costs.

Comparison of 1-in. pipe in cement versus ½-in. mat-style system. On floors with end headers, the 1-in. pipe permits higher glycol flow rates at lower pressure drops. This results in reduced temperature drops across the grid, faster temperature recovery, and superior temperature control. Better ice surface conditions are maintained during varying conditions. Equivalent flow rates can be achieved with the ½-in. mat-style system if side headers are installed, but this will result in over 400% more mechanical joints and the corresponding potential for leaks.

The lower pressure drops in the large pipe system will result in reduced horsepower requirements per gallon of pumped glycol. When the 1-in. pipes are embedded in the cement floor, this design provides a large thermal mass, which keeps temperature swings to a minimum, further improving ice consistency.

The larger 1-in. pipes are less susceptible to fouling or blockage by foreign objects and have less than half of the mechanical connections reducing the chance of leaks. The 1-in. pipes, when embedded in cement, require no further handling and do not deteriorate as rapidly as the ½-in. pipes that are rolled and unrolled over the years. To provide sufficient pipe protection for the mat-style system, it is normal to operate with a thicker ice surface than is required with a cement floor.

A cement floor is easier to monitor ice thickness by drilling tap holes on a weekly basis. Consistent ice thickness means consistent ice temperature and reduced operating costs. Setup and takedown time is eliminated with the cement floor versus the mat-style system that must be rolled up and put away if the ice is removed.

20 Camps

Thomas H. Sawyer, *Indiana State University*
Tonya L. Gimbert, *Indiana State University*

Historically, the word *camping* signified simple living outdoors and engaging in activities related primarily to the outdoors. Today, the term has broadened tremendously and encompasses a wide spectrum of developments for families and children. Resident centers, day camps, group camps, family camps, and wilderness camps are the common designations used for the various types of camps.

Camps have been developed by public agencies at all levels of government and by many voluntary youth-serving organizations. The rapidly increasing participation of children and adults in camping necessitates careful consideration of desirable areas and facilities.

Although most organized camping takes place on agency-owned or private property, public land is becoming increasingly involved. Public land is one of the major resources for school outdoor educational programs, and many resident centers have been constructed on public property or by public funds.

Schools use the facilities during the school year, and park and recreation agencies use them during the summer. The purposes of outdoor education, whether sponsored by park and recreation departments or by schools, are similar in many respects, and cooperative planning is not only necessary to get the most from the community dollar but also imperative if suitable lands and sites are to be obtained. If adequate facilities are to be provided to meet the needs of both organized camping groups and schools, the facilities must be designed for year-round use.

Program Facilities: What to Expect

The following are facilities used for various camp programs. Specifications and construction details for most are found elsewhere in this book.

Water-related activities are among the most popular in summer camps. During the fall and spring, school groups and other groups may use developments for fishing, canoeing, and boating.

Lakes, ponds, streams, bays, and inlets offer many recreational opportunities. All should be studied in detail with regard to currents, eddies, depth, slope, shoreline, debris, and other factors.

Canoeing, boating, and sailing are activities that may be conducted on a lake, pond, river, reservoir, bay, or other body of water. The water area should have accessory facilities such as floats, docks, markers, or buoys. Various sizes of water bodies are required for different activities and events. For instance, canoe race courses are 100 yd, 200 yd, 440 yd, and 880 yd, as well as 1 mile. Sailing requires a wider body of water because the boats usually finish to windward. The different classes of sailboats, such as Sunfish and Sailfish, require different courses.

Casting is simulated rod-and-reel fishing. Practice casting on a playing field or in a gymnasium is possible year-round. If a pond or lake is nearby, a beach or dock affords an excellent facility for the casting program. To teach all phases of the activity, an area 300 ft x 100 ft is desirable. A football, soccer, hockey, or lacrosse field is ideal for class instruction. Casting targets, which are 30 in. in diameter, are easily constructed and can be an excellent project for any woodshop program. It is recommended that at least 10 targets be made. Others can be added as the program expands. Targets for use on the water also are 30 in. in diameter and are made of hollow metal tubing. They float and can be easily anchored.

Other facilities include campfire circles and council rings for which most camps develop centers for meetings and evening programs and craft centers, which can range from canvas-covered areas with provisions for storing tools to extensive and well-equipped craft shops.

Day Camps

A day camp is an area and facility intended to provide a program similar to that of the resident camp except that campers sleep at home. Many of the considerations of planning for resident camps apply to day camps. However, facility problems are simpler because day campers sleep at home and usually eat two of the day's meals at home. Provisions, however simple, must nonetheless be made for water, restrooms, rainy day shelters, eating and cooking, refrigeration, first aid and health, and program supplies. The focus of this section is selecting an appropriate day camp facility.

Abundant land for programs is extremely desirable, particularly when the emphasis is on outdoor-related activities. Reasonable isolation and a varied topography with outdoor program possibilities are essential. Natural parks, park–school areas, and community forests often lend themselves for use as day camp sites. Some communities have developed special day camp areas; others make appropriate picnic areas available for this special use.

Buses are often used to transport campers to the day camp. If more than a half-hour is consumed in daily travel each way, the effectiveness of the program is reduced.

Day camp groups are divided into units or counselor groups ranging from eight to 20 campers. Most day camps provide simple facilities for each unit, including a fireplace for cooking, storage cabinets, and tables. Some day camps serve a daily meal in a central dining hall to reduce or eliminate the need for unit cooking facilities.

Storage is needed for equipment, food, and program supplies. Some day camps use trailers or trucks for storage, hauling them back and forth each day. Also, a well-equipped first aid station and a rest area facility are necessary.

Group Camps

Many public agencies today provide special campsites for small groups such as scouts, church groups, and school classes. These sites generally accommodate from 10 to 40 persons.

Groups stay from 1 to 5 days. Small units in decentralized resident camps sometimes have facilities that can be used for group camping. Simple fireplaces for cooking, picnic shelters for use in bad weather, restrooms, and safe drinking water are necessities.

The increase in winter camping by small groups often necessitates special developments. Some winter campers live completely outdoors in the cold, even in snow. Usually, however, winterized buildings are used for cooking, sleeping, and evening activities.

Campgrounds

Campgrounds are found in many settings and in many formats. Tent camping is the traditional form of camping, but the increase in motor homes, trailers, and pop-up trailers has changed the camping mix. Public campgrounds such as those found in federal, state, county, and municipal park systems have had to accommodate the changing camper. Traditional amenities have included water somewhere in the campground, restrooms, and maybe showers. In today's marketplace, these are called primitive conditions. Campgrounds desiring to attract motor homes and trailers now provide electrical (usually 110-V and 220-V), sewer, and water. Additional services can include cable television and telephone lines.

Campgrounds should be segregated, or at least partitioned. Motor homes, trailers, and pop-up trailers should be located in one section and tent camping in another. A natural segregation occurs by designating campgrounds as three hookup, two hookup, one hookup, or primitive. The more hookups a section has, the more likely affluent campers will use it.

Roads need to be wide enough to handle a single motor home and most often are one way. Parking areas need to be hardstand, asphalt, or concrete and ideally long enough for a motor home to drive through the site, entering from one side and exiting from the other. This prevents potential problems with motor homes backing up and into other campers. Turns need to be casual enough to allow longer motor homes to make full turns without striking obstructions. The campground should include an entrance station to collect fees or provide information as necessary. Honor systems are available but still require a ranger to manage the site.

Family Camps

Family resident camps offer complete meal and living accommodations for families or for adults only. The facilities are similar to those of resident camps except that some of the sleeping quarters are adapted to families.

Most of the campgrounds in state or federal areas are destination camps. Campers generally stay more than one night and often for several weeks. In recent years, many resort camps have sprung up. These resorts, generally privately developed, are more or less complete vacationlands offering organized programs and facilities, including swimming pools, recreation centers, children's playgrounds, special game courts, marinas, and horseback riding trails.

Waterfronts

Waterfront uses vary with the program offered. The type of program will determine the nature of the waterfront, yet the environmental situation, such as ocean, stream, or lake, may influence the type and design of the facility. The following categories of use identify the specific areas of the aquatic program:

- Familiarization—Familiarization involves programs for acquainting the user with the water.

- Instruction—Instruction involves programs of teaching the user basic activities related to aquatics.
- Recreation—Recreation involves programs that are largely unstructured, for relaxing and refreshing the user, including participating in or watching special events such as synchronized swimming, water shows, and competitive swimming.
- Competition—Competition involves programs of training and competing in swimming and other aquatic activities. The user of a waterfront should be able to participate in a variety of aquatic activities to attain the desired objectives. This is especially true in the camp setting where the camper participates in the constructive fulfillment of inherent attitudes and aptitudes.

Waterfronts for the conduct of aquatic activities are found in children's camps, parks, resorts, marinas, clubs, hotels, residential developments, and other recreational areas. The waterfront, whether it is a beach, floating crib, dock, pond, lakeshore, pool deck, or some other area where aquatic programs take place, must be properly located and constructed to ensure the health and safety of the public using this facility. The post-World War II years saw a tremendous development in children's camps in the United States, particularly day camps. Although many of the aspects of this chapter deal primarily with camps, most of the criteria may be applied to beachfront developments as well. When the location and construction of natural and artificial waterfront facilities are planned, definite criteria should be established. These criteria should reflect not only the camp program but also health and safety requirements.

Criteria for Natural Waterfronts

The natural waterfront site should have certain characteristics to make it desirable for aquatic program use. The recommended criteria for selecting waterfront or beach sites are discussed below, and helpful checklists have been provided for the planners.

Water characteristics. The water content should be of a sanitary quality affording safe usage. The health conditions of a site are primarily judged by a careful examination of both the surrounding environment and the water content.

The first is accomplished by a careful field analysis and the second by a laboratory analysis. Both examinations can indicate the bacterial quality and physical clarity of the water.

A checklist should be used to monitor
- the surrounding water source,
- water quality (bacterial content), and
- water clarity (visibility test).

Water condition characteristics. The circulation of the water through the potential waterfront site should be

examined. Slow-moving water can produce swampy or built-up mud conditions, and fast-moving water can produce undercurrents and erosive conditions.

The ideal water temperature for swimming ranges from 72°F to 78°F depending upon the air temperature. The American Public Health Association (2009) indicated that less than 500 gal of additional water per bather per day is an insufficient diluting volume unless there is sufficient application of disinfection.

A checklist should be used to monitor
- rate of water flow;
- rate of water turnover;
- water level fluctuation;
- water constancy;
- availability of water;
- types of currents and undertow;
- outlet for water;
- eddies, floods, waves, or wash;
- weeds, fungi, mold, or slime;
- parasites, fish, animals;
- debris, broken glass, and so on;
- oil slicks; and
- odor, color, and tastes.

Bottom characteristics. The waterfront bottom should be unobstructed and clear of debris, rock, muck, mulch, peat, and mud. The bottom should be made of gravel, sand, or stable hard ground to afford firm and secure footing. The most desirable bottom is white sand with a gradual pitch sloping from the shallow to the deep end. The bottom should neither be too steep or too shallow nor have holes, pots, channels, bars, or islands.

An investigation, by taking soundings in a boat and by making an actual underwater survey, should be undertaken before a final decision is made on the location of the waterfront. The waterfront should not be in an area where the channel shifts or silt builds up.

A checklist should be used to monitor
- bottom movement,
- amount of holes and debris,
- slope of subsurface,
- amount of area,
- condition of soil,
- porosity of bottom,
- average depth and various depths, and
- bottom color.

Climatic characteristics. Continuous dry spells or numerous rainy seasons may cause the site to have water-retention problems. Dangerous storms including tornadoes, lightning, hurricanes, and northeasters create dangerous waterfront conditions. The severity of the winter can also affect the waterfront. Ice and ice movement can damage waterfront amenities and bottom. A south-southeast orientation is ideal to maximize the benefit from the sun and minimize exposure to the wind.

A checklist should be used to monitor

- number of storms and type,
- prevailing winds,
- amount of ice,
- change of air temperature,
- amount of precipitation,
- fluctuation of temperature, and
- sun exposure.

Environmental characteristics. The locale of the waterfront should be carefully examined for all influences on its construction and use. Zoning regulations, building codes, insurance restrictions, health ordinances, title covenants, and a multitude of other legal restrictions by the Coast Guard, Conservation Department, Water Resources Commission, public works agencies, and fire departments should be studied. The arrangement of land uses and their compatibility to the project, transportation, utilities, community facilities, population, and area economics should also be considered.

A checklist should be used to monitor

- ownership and riparian rights;
- availability of water supply;
- zoning and deed restrictions;
- local, state, and federal regulations;
- adjacent ownerships; and
- water patrol and a control agency.

Program characteristics. The waterfront should be situated so that it can be protected by a fence or other controlled access, particularly in a camp, marina, or other small area. It should be internally segregated (e.g., bathing from boating, boating from fishing, and so on). The site may have storage space for waterfront equipment, adequate spectator seating area during special events, a safety zone near the lifeguard station or post, and ready access to a road.

A checklist should be used to monitor

- distance of waterfront from other areas,
- access road,
- separation of waterfront activities,
- area for unity of controls, and
- space available for adjunct activities.

Access characteristics. The waterfront facility must be accessible by transportation available to the user. There should always be a means of vehicular access for emergency or maintenance use. The site around the waterfront and along its approach should be free of poison ivy, sumac, poison oak, burdock thistle, and other irritating plants.

A checklist should be used to monitor

- location for access road,
- area free of poisonous plants, and
- area accessible yet controllable.

Area characteristics. The waterfront bathing area should allow for at least 50 sq ft for each user. Areas for instruction, recreation, and competition should be available. The depth of the area to be used primarily for the instruction of nonswimmers should not exceed 3 ft. The area to be used for intermediate swimmers should not exceed 5 ½ ft (primarily for competition). Smaller or larger swimming areas may be designed if users are divided differently.

The minimum recommended size for a camp swimming area is 60 ft x 30 ft and the desirable size is 75 ft x 45 ft providing a 25-yd short course.

A checklist should be used to monitor

- space for bathing,
- capacity of waterfront,
- water depths,
- division of bathing area into stations,
- size of boating area, and
- size of fishing area.

Shore characteristics. The shoreline for the waterfront facility should be free of irregular rocks, stumps, debris, or obstruction. It should be a minimum of 100 ft long for bathing in a camp area and can be many miles long in a park beach.

Trees should be adjacent to waterfront areas to provide shade and wind protection. Large, high trees should be eliminated because they attract lightning, and moldy trees have many decayed overhanging branches. Too many trees of a deciduous nature create mucky shores and water bottoms because of their autumn leaves. Coniferous trees cause fewer problems.

A checklist should be used to monitor

- surrounding vegetation,
- slope of the shore,
- existing beach,
- extent of clearing, and
- amount of debris.

Criteria for Artificial Waterfronts

Most of the same characteristics as described for natural areas should be examined for an artificial waterfront. Additional criteria that should be considered are outlined below.

Environmental characteristics. If all available bodies of water are being used, then artificial waterfront facilities must be developed. In some cases, waterfront locations are unsatisfactory or unavailable for new camps or resorts. Thus, undeveloped sites with sufficient watershed (runoff water), water table (underground water), and water bodies (surface water) for lakes, pools, or impoundments must be considered for use.

Water characteristics. Before a site is selected, the percolation rate and, in particular, the permeability of the soil should be carefully checked to be sure that water will be retained. The stability and structure of the soil must also be determined (from test borings and/or test pits) because of the dams, pump houses, dikes, pools, berms, spillways, and other structures that must be built.

Unlike the content of natural bodies of water, the content of artificial bodies can be controlled by chlorination and filtration. Runoff water obtained from storms, and contained in a pond or lake, should be collected by diversion ditches and fed to a reservoir and chlorination plant. This water can then be recirculated until potable water is obtained.

Underground water that is obtained from wells or springs can also be contained in a pond. This type of artificial water body usually has continuous flow and thus needs only a simple filtration system plus chlorination.

Surface water that is obtained from running streams is usually contained in a bypass pond or in a pond in the stream itself. Both methods require the construction of a dam. These artificial water bodies have continuous running water. However, gate valves and floodgates are required, especially during storms when there is a large flow of water to control. Unless there is a constant turnover or supply of clean water, these impoundments will require a filtration and chlorination system.

Climatic characteristics. Climatic considerations are important in developing artificial bodies of water and waterfronts. In most cases, natural bodies of water will fluctuate very little because of weather conditions. On the other hand, artificial bodies are solely dependent upon the climate because the water table, runoff, and stream flow depend on the amount and time of rainfall. All other climatic considerations mentioned for natural waterfronts generally apply to artificial waterfronts as well.

Drainage characteristics. A low-lying area, regardless of its appeal, is not a good location for a pool or pond. Adequate drainage is essential so the surface and deck water will drain away from the water body and so the water body itself can be emptied without pumping. Groundwater and frost action resulting from improper drainage can undermine a foundation by causing it to heave and settle.

Design and Construction of Camp Waterfronts

The camp waterfront is usually composed of either permanent docks or floats to provide safe swimming and boating areas.

Docks and floats. Permanent structures are usually set on concrete, wood, or steel foundations or pier piles. The decks should be made in sections of 10 ft to 20 ft for ease

in removing for repairs or winter storage. The dock should be constructed with at least a 1-ft air space between the deck and water. Underwater braces and other cross beams should be limited to prevent swimmers from becoming entangled in them.

When water levels change, allowances should be made for the piers to be outside the deck limits so the deck can move up and down on sleeves or brackets. Walkways or decks should be a minimum of 6 ft wide, preferably 8 ft to 10 ft. They should be cross-planked so swimmers will avoid splinters. The planking should not be less than 2 in. thick x 4 in. to 6 in. wide. Boards should be spaced a maximum of ¼ in. apart to prevent toe-stubbing. The deck should be treated with a noncreosote-based preservative because creosote will burn feet, plus a plastic, nonlead paint that is not heat absorbing.

The paint should be white with a blue or green tint to reduce the glare and aid in reflection. Flotation structures may be made of drums, balsa wood, cork, rigid polystyrene plastic, steel tanks, or other flotation materials. Many innovations have carried over from war days.

Pontoon decks, for example, are sometimes made from surplus bridge parts and 55-gal plastic containers. All such materials should be treated with red lead after scraping, sanding, and repairing. A frame should be constructed of 2 in. x 8 in. boards to fit over and contain the supporting units. The frame should fit securely yet be removable at the close of the season. Some flotation materials or devices are just placed in the framing under the floats without any anchorage to the frame. Galvanized steel or aluminum straps of ⅛ in. x 1 ½ in. under the floating units will save time and effort to prevent sinking when these units acquire a leak and fill with water. A typical camp waterfront is shown in Figure 20.1. The various designs employed in waterfronts are shown in Figure 20.2.

Construction Criteria for Natural Waterfronts

The natural waterfront facility should have features that make it safe and usable. The following criteria are suggested as a basis for constructing such a facility.

Bottom characteristics. Most swimming facilities around natural bodies of water require the dragging and grading of the bottom subsurfaces to eliminate hazards. In many cases, where improvement of the bottom is required, feed mat, mesh, or plastic sheets have to be laid down on top of muck and staked down. Once these sheets have been laid, sand must be spread over the mat surface. When the bottom is firm, sand can be spread 6 in. thick on top of ice in the crib area during winter. As the ice melts, the sand will fall fairly evenly over the bottom. This can only be accomplished, however, when the ice does not shift or break and float away.

Shore characteristics. When a beach is constructed, a gentle slope of from 6 ft to 12 ft in 100 ft should be main-

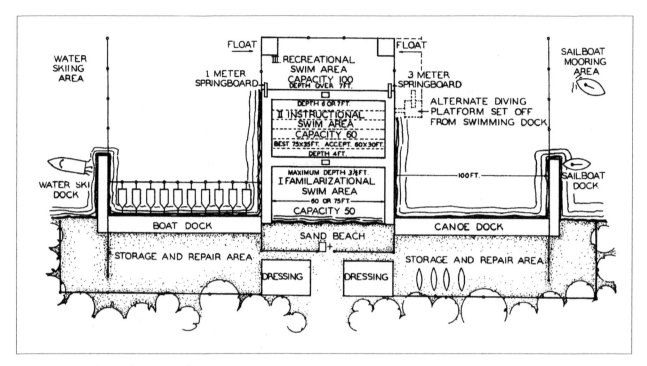

Figure 20.1. **Sample Waterfront** (*Source:* Meghan Rosselli)

tained. Where the waterfront requires a great deal of construction, a dock shoreline is recommended rather than trying to maintain an unstable beach. The ground above the water can then be developed with turf, terraces, decks, and boardwalks depending upon the nature of the project. When the bottom drops off quickly, the shore can be dug out to the grade desired underwater. This forms a crescent-shaped waterfront with an excellent beach.

Access characteristics. The owner should acquire access roads and streets around waterfront areas if possible to keep the area buffered from conflicting uses. These roads should be durable and be attractively maintained. Access roads should have clear horizontal and vertical vision so that pedestrian and vehicular conflict can be prevented.

Program characteristics. The waterfront in small recreational areas such as camps or resorts should be completely enclosed by planting or fencing. There should be a central control for ingress and exit. Many facilities require the use of check in–out boards, tickets, and other similar devices for controlling the use of the area. The waterfront bathing, boating, and fishing facilities should be separated, each with its own control.

Construction Criteria for Artificial Waterfronts

Both artificial and natural waterfronts should have certain features that make them safe and usable. An artificial waterfront can be developed and improved using most of the same considerations as illustrated for the natural waterfront. The following criteria should be carefully considered in providing an artificial waterfront.

Bottom characteristics. For an artificial beach, the grade should be the same as that recommended for natural shores: 6 ft to 12 ft in 100 ft. For reservoirs and ponds, there should be a minimum of 9 in. of large, crushed stone, then 4 in. of well-graded smooth gravel to fill in the voids, and then 9 in. of washed medium sand. Where the sand beach terminates at a depth of approximately 7 ft of water, it is recommended that rip-rapping be established to resist the tendency of the beach sand to move down the slope. The area above the beach should also be ditched where the natural slope of the ground exceeds that of the beach. Thus, the slopes of the beach should be approximately 6% below the water and 10% above. For areas in tidal waters, a maximum slope of 5 ft for 15 ft can be established for the bottom below-water line.

Shore characteristics. In the creation of a shoreline for artificial bodies of water, there should be either a berm or dike if the water is to be confined. A steep slope to eliminate shallow areas is usually required to prevent weeds and other plant materials from growing in the water. If the soil conditions will not allow a steep slope underwater 3 ft deep to retard water plant growth, then bulkheads or docks will be required, or only a limited beach can be provided.

Waterfront Equipment

It is important to plan initially for needed accessory equipment. The amount of equipment required will vary with the size of the waterfront. All necessary safety equipment must be located to afford immediate emergency use.

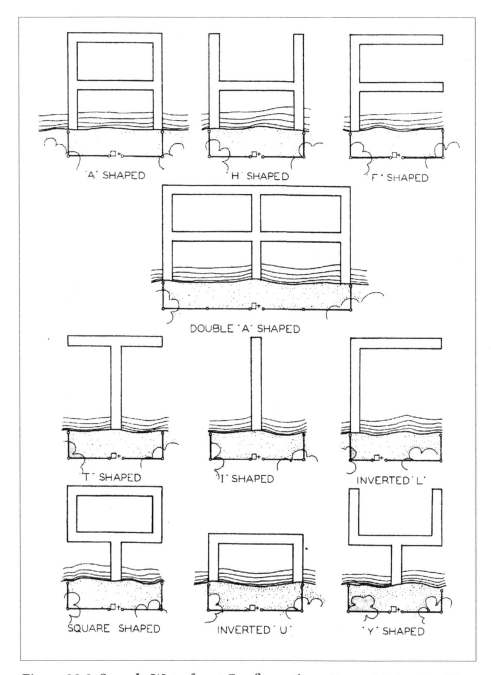

Figure 20.2. **Sample Waterfront Configurations** (*Source:* Meghan Rosselli)

Lifeguard Station

Lifeguard chairs should be placed at a point where the location of beach equipment and sunbathing limit lines does not interfere with the lifeguards' vision of the water areas. Chairs should be a minimum of 6 ft to a maximum of 10 ft above grade. Usually lifeguard chairs are made of galvanized pipe or wood.

Ladders

In all swimming cribs, a ladder at least 2 ft in width should be placed at the sides so as not to interfere with persons swimming the length of the simulated pool.

Log Booms

Logs fastened end to end can form a continuous lifeline around bathing limits in rustic settings and, at the same time, provide the necessary safety to swimmers at a waterfront.

Lemmon Lines

Lemmon lines are small floats attached by a nylon or plastic rope or cable outlining and restricting swimming areas. They can be made of rounded wood, cork, or plastic.

Markers and Buoys

These are floats indicating the limits of areas or channels or for marking underwater obstructions, divers, moorings, and fishing nets. They are usually hollow cans or drums. They can also be flag buoys, a 6-in. square wood block with attached flag, a wooden cross of 2 in. x 4 in. with can on top, or a metal ballast with flag.

Rescue Craft

Boats should be of the round bottom or dory type, between 12 ft and 14 ft long. Lifesaving equipment should be in the boat at all times. The seats should be removable, and oarlocks should be permanent. A catamaran, surfboards, and helicopters (in large beach waterfront facilities) supplement the lifeboat as a means of patrol.

Kick Rails

A rail for practicing and teaching swimming should be placed at water level. This can be made of galvanized pipe, wood rods, or rope.

Towel Racks

Racks for drying towels and bathing suits should be installed at or near the waterfront.

Miscellaneous Equipment

Life ring buoys should be spaced strategically around the waterfront on racks. These racks are usually in the form of a cross, with the ring suspended from the center and the rope wrapped around the ring from pegs protruding from each end of the cross. Torpedo buoys, bamboo poles, grappling irons, lifelines, shepherd's crooks, stretchers, blankets, microphones, and other devices should be available to the lifeguards. Numbers indicating depths and the capacities of the crib and other swimming areas should be clearly visible. Kickboards should be available for practice as well as emergency use.

Section IV

Specialty Areas

Section IV

21 Track and Field and Cross-Country Facilities

Lawrence W. Judge, *Ball State University*
Thomas H. Sawyer, *Indiana State University*

The concept of fairness is an important aspect of sport. Athletes are tested against one another in competition with presumably fair and equal odds. When thinking of competition equality, you probably think of a few primary factors. But it is important to understand that many different factors contribute to fairness. One of these factors is facility construction and design. Sports facilities must be properly designed according to rule books to keep the playing field level for all competitors.

Track and field is one of the oldest sports in the United States, dating from the 1860s. In 1878, the sport of cross-country was introduced and served mainly as training for summer track and field athletes. Nine years later, cross-country running became a formal sport in the United States. Today track and field or athletics and cross-country are governed by the International Athletics Association Federation (IAAF) at the international level, by U.S. Track and Field (USATF) at the domestic professional level, by the National Association of Intercollegiate Athletics (NCAA) at the collegiate level, and by the National Federation of High Schools (NFHS) at the high school level.

Each national governing body level has specific regulations for facility design and construction. Many of these are similar, but some are vastly different. It is important to consult the rule book for each organization before beginning a facility construction project.

Facilities in cross-country and track and field are regulated in great detail to ensure fairness among high schools, colleges, and professional athletes in championships. Facility construction is not often covered in the mainstream media, but it is extremely important to track and field in many ways, not just in keeping competition fair. The safety of participants and the liability of the facility site are completely dependent on meeting the regulations imposed by governing bodies. On the other hand, indoor and outdoor tracks are important to the general aesthetics of the campus facility and are equally important to collegiate recruiting. The aesthetic value of the track facility to the campus and the community is sometime forgotten in the planning stages. A track and field competition complex is complicated at best when compared to other outdoor or indoor sports spaces such as indoor basketball or volleyball courts or baseball, football, or soccer fields. The track and field complex includes areas designed for throwing, jumping, running, relaxation and warm-up, spectators, timing and recording, storage, and officials' dressing room. A cross-country course requires appropriate planning to service girls, women, boys, and men. The distances differ for genders and level of competition (e.g., interscholastic and intercollegiate).

The following chapter is a guide from start to finish in cross-country and track and field facility design. The text in this chapter is based on the NCAA track and field/cross-country men's and women's rules.

Coordinating Site Selection and General Facility Layout

Planning the Outdoor Track

Location considerations. Picking a proper outdoor site is critical to the success of an outdoor track and field facility. A track will require a site of no less than 5 acres, a minimum of 600 ft long x 300 ft wide. Additional area must be allowed for grading, curbs, drainage, and amenities such as grandstands, bleachers, lighting, walkways, and fencing. The site should also be reasonably level. Although the track will be sloped slightly for drainage, for all practical purposes, the track must be level in the running direction. Water should drain away from the track. It is best to locate a track on a relatively level plain, higher than surrounding areas. Additional filling or drainage work required by a low site may add substantial expense to the overall construction costs. Even under the best site conditions, tracks should be constructed with a perimeter drain on the inside of the track to remove stormwater that has drained from the track and playing field. Even the type of soil matters to construction. Poor soil conditions often lead to excessive settling, heaving caused by freeze/thaw action, and drainage problems. The best soil is hard, well drained, and non-heaving. Locations with peat, clay, topsoil, shear sand, or other organic materials at a depth of 8 in. to 12 in. should be avoided. It is also important to consider underground utilities. Although the finished facility will require utility service, it is better to avoid constructing the track over underground utilities. No expense should be spared in developing a good solid base for the running surface.

Wind is also a consideration. Straightaways should be parallel to prevailing winds, which is especially important for dashes and hurdle races. For athlete safety, jumping events should also take place with the wind because crosswinds can be particularly dangerous. Multiple-jump runways should be considered because of the addition of the women's pole vault and time constraints when only one runway is available for men and women for the long jump and triple jump. Throwing events should be located so that participants are throwing into the wind. Likewise, for safety reasons, it is essential that high jump and pole vault runways be located so that the athlete does not have to look into the sun or artificial lighting.

General plan considerations. The first stage in constructing a running track is selecting a site and designing a track to fit the site. The accuracy of a finished 400-m track is essential; no minus tolerance is acceptable, and a plus tolerance must be no more than ½ in. in any lane. These small tolerances and the numerous design and site factors make track design extremely complex and demanding. The construction of track and field areas will follow the International Amateur Athletic Federation rules with respect to grade or slope: "The maximum inclination permitted for tracks, runways, circles, and landing areas for throwing events shall not exceed 1:100 in a lateral direction and 1:1000 in the running and throwing direction" (NCAA, 2010, p. 42). Owners should begin by deciding what size and shape of track is needed. A 400-m, six- or nine-lane track is the standard for high school and college competition, although a few high school tracks and many large college tracks are 10 lanes wide.

Many tracks are built around football or soccer fields, and these instances must be specially considered. In addition to space for the field itself, space must be allowed for player seating, walkways, and other associated facilities. Artificial turf fields require additional space for anchoring detail at the perimeter. Tracks are designed in two basic shapes. An equal-quadrant track has two 100-m straightaways and two 100-m curves, and a non-equal-quadrant track has two straightaways of one length and two curves

of another length totaling 400 m. In the latter case, the result is a track with either a slightly stretched or compressed oval shape. Recently, a third design, nicknamed the broken-back track, has come into use. This design features a squarer track with shorter straightaways and rounded ends made of double curves. This design creates a larger infield that is large enough for an NCAA soccer field (which neither of the two more common designs can accommodate) and is useful for sites where one of the more common track designs will not work. Generally, an equal-quadrant track is desirable, but site factors will determine which design is most feasible.

Will the construction project include field events? Most track projects built today include a high jump pad; long jump runway and pit; pole vault runway and landing area; shot put, discus, and hammer throwing pads and landing areas; and sometimes a javelin runway and a triple jump runway and landing pit. It is more economical to construct field event areas at the same time as the track. It is during the design phase that the design team must consider where the field events will be located. Placing the field events in the infield of the track may facilitate spectator viewing but may cause more traffic over the runways.

Planning the Indoor Track

Location considerations. Designing the new facility from scratch can seem like a daunting process. Because deciding on a location can be overwhelming, it is important to establish detailed programmatic objectives and be well aware of the design concepts and philosophies. These will act as a guide as critical decisions are made. Each facility will have different needs; some may be additions to other facilities, and others may be a complete stand-alone facility, but there are general guidelines to follow to generate a successful facility.

A successful facility begins with assembling qualified individuals. Constructing the facility is an exchange between facility planners and contractors. Starting with the facility planners, it is key to incorporate the management that will be involved with the facility. This may include athletic directors, a college administration, those in charge of the financial backing, and even individuals who will be using the facility. It might also be beneficial to involve experienced professionals outside of the concerned administration. This could mean hiring someone well qualified, but depending on the project, it may be worth the security to have someone with experience to consult the project. To ensure that the planner vision comes to fruition, selecting a contractor and construction team with a reputable reputation is essential. Ask for and check numerous references from numerous contractors before reaching a decision. Maintain a solid relationship with the project supervisor, and constantly review architectural drawings and process steps along the way.

Another crucial planning consideration is developing a comprehensive project plan including timelines and checklists for task completion. Making the plan as detailed as possible will greatly aid the process, especially as many tasks may be in progress at the same time. For more lengthy or critical projects, a variety of software packages and templates are available that offer guidance in developing productive product plans. Available land to support the full building will be the most critical variable facility planners will face.

General Plan Considerations

Many challenges exist for the indoor track and field facility planner. One of the biggest obstacles when planning for track and field events is coordinating the individual events and managing traffic flow to minimize obstruction. This requires an incredible attention to facility layout including plenty of space for equipment storage. This is hard enough because most indoor track facilities are field houses shared with other sports. Planning the space to function for more than one sport adds complexity and requires additional coordination. The design of the facility needs to be analyzed from the meet management perspective to facilitate safe operations, based on the amount of land available and considering—how all track and field events will be run efficiently. This may require tradeoffs, with an understanding that if a greater number of events need to overlap in areas, the scheduling and length of meets will be affected.

Indoor venues pose a number of safety issues, such as low ceilings, any hangings or fixtures, protrusions from walls, proximity of walls to event locations, and placement of throwing nets. Typically, the pole vault venue is laid out in the center of the infield or below the ceiling's highest point to provide enough clearance. Other uses of indoor facilities, such as football or volleyball, may require specific ceiling specifications, which must be considered in the context of field events. To function for track and field, the facility must be able to accommodate a 200-m track complete with safety zones behind the starting line and beyond the finish line. There must be a minimum of 3 m clear distance behind the starting line, and a minimum of 10 m beyond the finish line, although 20 m is recommended. The indoor throwing events present additional challenges because of the space required and safety issues. To that end, many colleges and universities plan dedicated throwing areas outside the infield as part of their field houses. Typically, the throwing area is a double-height space in the range of 3,000 sq ft that opens to the larger volume and may be separated with a fence for spectator safety.

Merging Concepts

Two concepts merge during the planning of the indoor and outdoor track and field facilities: maximization and minimization. When constructing the site, the director of the project must maximize the use of the space with a clean organization of facility components and also must maximize the aesthetics of the facility. The project director must also minimize safety concerns and liability. Through each stage of the facility planning, keeping these concepts in mind will prevent mistakes in the plan and the eventual construction. This will be a difficult task with the constraints of the land available.

Specifics for Outdoor Facility Components

Within the outdoor track and field facility are many components that have different uses but, at the same time, must coordinate and fit together in the specified space. It is important to have a full understanding of each of the components necessary to hold the track meet before constructing the facility. The next step after construction is correctly marking the facility with lines, flags, and circles where necessary. This section of the chapter will discuss these aspects of the outdoor track and field facility.

The Outdoor Running Track

When beginning to determine the precise measurements for the outdoor track facility, first dedicate the project to the metric system. For the facility to be considered official and to comply with NCAA rules, all measurements must be in metric. All measurements included in this section are from the *2011–2012 Men's & Women's Cross Country & Track & Field Rules* (NCAA, 2010). The measurements given are minimums to hold an intercollegiate track meet.

The standard outdoor running track should be 400 m in length and no less than 6.40 m in width in a circular shape with two parallel straights and two semicircular curves of equal design. The track should be bordered on the inside by a rounded curb of suitable material such as concrete, wood, or aluminum approximately 5 cm in height and a minimum of 5 cm in width. The track must hold at least six hurdle lanes of 1.07 m, each marked by white lines 5 cm wide and numbered starting with Lane 1 on the innermost section of the track. Lanes should be the same width, at least 1.067 m wide to accommodate hurdles; this measurement includes the white line to the right. The maximum width is 1.22 m (NCAA, 2010).

It is obviously important for race distances on the track to be exact. Lane 1, and all race distances not run in lanes, should be measured 30 cm outward from the inner edge of the track when a regulation curb is included; when a curb is not in place, Lane 1 should be measured 20 cm from the left-hand lane line. A curb or cones, however, must be in place for race times to be official championship qualifying and also international and national record-setting times. Races run strictly on a straightaway should be measured in a straight line from start to finish. For races run in lanes

Lines on outdoor track

around the track one or multiple times, the distance to be run in each lane should be measured 20 cm from the outer edge of the lane line that is on the runner's left. This does not include Lane 1, which was specified earlier (NCAA, 2010).

The colored markings used on the track are there to standardize tracks internationally. The following is the official color code for both the outdoor and indoor track facilities:

- Starting line (white): 55/60 m, 55/60-m hurdles, 100 m, 100/110-m hurdles, 200 m, 300 m, 400 m, 1500 m, mile, 3000 m, steeplechase, 5000 m, 10,000 m
- Starting line (white with green insert): 800 m, one-turn stagger
- Starting line (white with red insert): 800-m relay, four-turn stagger
- Starting line (white with blue insert): 1600-m relay, three-turn stagger
- Multiple waterfall starting lines (white)
- Finish line (white): all races
- Relay exchange zones: 400-m relay (yellow), 800-m relay (red), 1600-m relay (blue)
- Hurdle locations: 100 m (yellow), 110 m (blue), 400 m (green), steeplechase (black)
- Break line (green)

Visible Starting Line and Finish Line

The visible starting line, 5 cm wide, is marked on the track just within the measured distance so that its near edge is identical with the exactly measured and true starting line. The starting line for all races not run in lanes (except the 800 m) is curved so that all competitors run the same distance going into the curve (Figure 21.1).

The visible finish line, 5 cm wide, is marked on the track just outside the measured distance so that its edge nearer that start is identical with the exactly measured and true finish line. Lane numbers of reasonable size should be placed at least 15 cm beyond the common finish line and positioned to face the timing device. The intersection of each lane line and the finish line is painted black as illustrated in Figure 21.2. Finally, a common finish line is recommended for all races. Lines in the finish area should be kept to a minimum. If additional lines are necessary, they should be of a less conspicuous color than the finish line so as not to cause confusion.

The break line will be the mark designating the point in the 800-m race and second leg of the 1600-m relay when athletes will be able to leave starting lanes and run in the innermost lane for the remainder of the race. This line should also be 5 cm and will arc to ensure that each athlete in each lane will travel the same distance to the innermost lane. The line will be positioned at the entry of the back straightaway.

Relays involve baton exchanges within certain zones. To delegate these zones, the proper track markings are needed. The baton exchange must occur within a 20-m zone; lines must be drawn 10 m on each side of the measured centerline. In some cases, track designers will further designate the limits of the zone with boxes or triangles. These also must exist within the 20-m zone. For races that allow for an international zone, a short mark 10 m

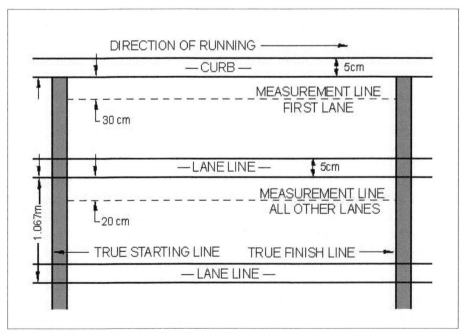

Figure 21.1. **Track Measurements**

Figure 21.2. Finish Line Intersections

before the passing zone will designate the position on the track where runners can begin running before receiving the baton in the 20-m relay zone.

The unique event coined the steeplechase presents a challenge to track and field project managers (Figure 21.3). The standard distance for the steeplechase is 3,000 m with 28 hurdle jumps and seven water jumps. The water jump should be the fourth jump in each lap. If necessary, the finish line should be moved to accommodate this rule. The following measurements are given as a guide, and lengthening or shortening the distance at the starting point of the race shall make adjustments necessary. The chart below assumes that a lap of 400 m or 440 yd has been shortened 10 m by constructing the water jump inside the track. If possible, the approach to and exit from the water jump hurdle should be straight for approximately 7 m.

The hurdles, including the water jump, should be placed on the track so that 30 cm of the top bar measured from the inside edge of the track will be inside the track. It is recommended that the first hurdle be at least 5 m in width and that all hurdles weigh at least 80 k.

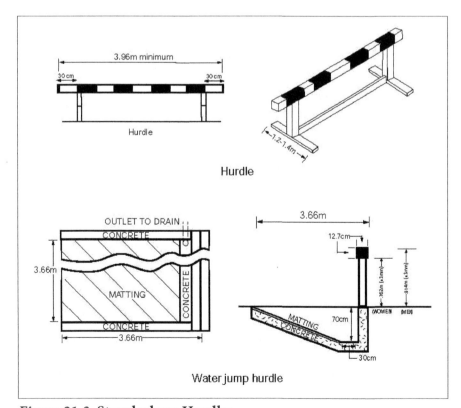

Figure 21.3. Steeplechase Hurdles

Visible start and finish line

The water jump should be 3.66 m in length and width. The water should be a minimum of 70 m in depth immediately after the hurdle, and the pit should have a constant upward slope from a point 30 cm past the water jump hurdle to the level of the track at the far end. It is recommended that the water jump be placed on the inside of the track. The landing surface inside the water jump should be composed of a nonskid, shock-absorbent material. The area between the vertical uprights of the water jump hurdle should be sealed with a solid, rigid material or lattice work to provide safety and to aid the athlete with depth perception. A water source needs to be installed to fill the water jump and a drain installed to drain the water jump after use.

Outdoor Jumping Facilities

High Jump

It is recommended that the high jump approach be an octagon or square with a surface of at least 21 m. The minimum length provided should be 15 m. The length of the approach run is unlimited. The takeoff area is the semicircle enclosed by a 3-m radius whose center point is directly under the center of the crossbar. For a record to be approved officially, no point within this area may be higher than the tolerances.

Pole Vault

The pole vault event requires two components that must be permanent fixtures of the track and field facility: the vaulting box and the runway. The vaulting box is where the pole-vaulter plants the pole to jump. It should be constructed of wood, metal, or other suitable sturdy materials and also should be painted white so that it is noticeable from the runway. The box should also be immovable and all of its upper edges should remain flush with the takeoff area. The angle between the bottom of the box and the stopboard should be 105° (Figure 21.4).

The vaulting runway should have a minimum length of 40 m with a width of 1.22 m (Figure 21.5). The runway also needs to be marked. The full length of the runway may be permanently marked with lines on or touching the edge that are no more than 2 cm wide x 5 cm long to indicate the

distance from the back of the vaulting box. The center of the runway should be marked with seven permanent lines. Each line is 5 cm in width and 30 cm from an adjacent line. Each short line is 30 cm in length. The long line should be 90 cm in length and centered with three short lines on either side. The distance from the edge of the long line farthest from the landing pit to the point where the back of the vaulting box meets the runway is 3.65 m (NCAA, 2010).

Long Jump and Triple Jump

The long jump and triple jump events can be run on the same runway and landing pit, although track facilities usually have two jump runways with pits at either end of both runways to accommodate the wind. The minimum length for the runway for both events should be 40 m from the edge nearest the pit of each event's takeoff board, and the runway material should extend past the takeoff board into the beginning of the pit. Runway width should be 1.22 m. If the runway blends with the general track background, it should be bordered by lines 5 cm in width from the start of the nearer edge of the landing pit. Markers no more than 2 cm wide and 5 cm long may be permanently displayed on the runway to indicate the distance from the foul line. An important piece of the runway is the takeoff board (Figure 21.6). The board should be a rigid material, for example, wood. The board should be 20 cm wide, 1.22 m long at minimum, and no more than 10 cm thick. The board should also be level with the runway surface and distinguishable from the runway, painted white. In the absence of a takeoff board, the takeoff area should be the same dimensions as a board and also distinguishable (NCAA, 2010).

The landing area should be no less than 2.75 m or no more than 3 m in width and filled with damp sand leveled with the takeoff board (Figure 21.7). This next point concerning the distance between the takeoff board and the nearest edge of the landing area or pit is where the two events will differ. For long jump, the distance should be no less than 1 m and no greater than 3 m. For triple jump, the distance should be at least 11 m from the foul line for men and 8.5 m for women. Distances of 12.5 m and 11 m are recommended. Also for the long jump, the distance between the foul line and the farther edge of the landing area should be at least 10 m (NCAA, 2010).

Outdoor Throwing Facilities

The outdoor track and field events include shot put, discus, hammer, and the javelin. The shot put, discus, and hammer are thrown out of circles of various sizes, and the javelin is thrown from a runway. All throwing event areas have general similarities in construction, but there are differences corresponding to each event. This section will discuss similarities such as the circle and the sector and then describe the details unique to each event construction.

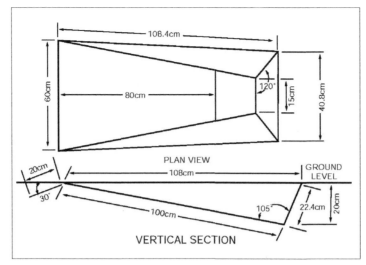

Figure 21.4. Pole Vault Box

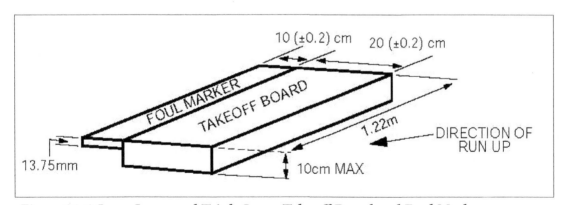

Figure 21.5. Pole Vault Runway Markings

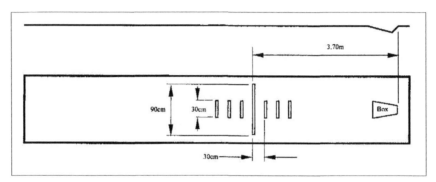

Figure 21.6. Long Jump and Triple Jump Takeoff Board and Foul Marker

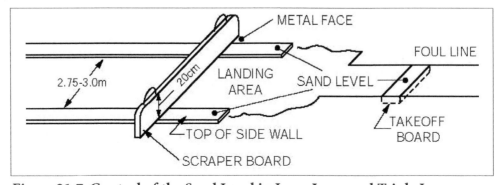

Figure 21.7. Control of the Sand Level in Long Jump and Triple Jump

The Circle

As stated previously, three of the four outdoor throwing events are contested from a circle. The circles are similar in construction, so it is important to begin the throwing facility assembly discussion with the circle. The actual circle or boundary encasing the throwing area should be made of a band of metal or suitable material 6 mm in thickness and 19 mm (± 6 mm) in height; the outside of the circle should be flush with concrete. The interior of the circle should be concrete or a similar material and should be 19 mm (± 6 mm) lower than the surface outside the circle. The inside diameters of the shot put and hammer throw circles should be 2.135 m (± 0.005 m) and the diameter of the discus circle should be 2.500 m (± 0.005 m).

The Sector

Throws made in competition are only valid or legal throws if they land within a specified sector (see Figure 21.8). If the throws land outside the sector, they do not count for the competition. The rules for NCAA throwing events stipulate that the sector will be specified by radial lines 5 cm in width forming a 34.92° angle extended from the center of the circle. The inside edge of the lines will mark the sector. For the discus and the hammer-throwing events, sector flags should be available to mark the ends of the lines and the sector shall be centered within the enclosure. The level of the surface within the landing area should be the same as the level of the surface of the throwing circle.

Shot Put

One particular aspect of shot put that is different from all other throwing events is the stopboard, commonly referred to as the "toeboard." The stopboard is an arc made of wood or other rigid materials. It should be painted white and firmly fixed so that its inner edge coincides with the inner edge of the shot put circle. The measurements are as follows: 1.21 m (± 0.01 m) in length along the chord between the endpoints, 112 mm and increasing to 300 mm in width, and 100 mm (± 2 mm) in height (Figure 21.9).

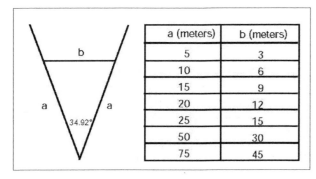

Figure 21.8. **Establishing the Sector**

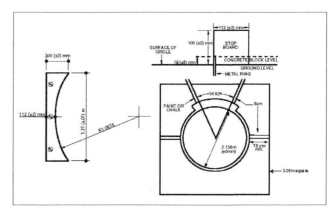

Figure 21.9. **Shot Put Circle**

Hammer and Discus Areas

The circles and sectors for these throwing events have been discussed (Figure 21.10). Because these events involve throwing weighted implements a long distance, safety is a critical issue. As stated previously, sector flags will mark the end of the throwing and landing areas, encouraging spectators and passing athletes, coaches, and officials to remain aware of the sector boundaries. A cage-like structure surrounding the circle is set up to keep hammers and discs that are released in directions outside the sector from hitting anyone standing near the circle area or outside the sector boundaries.

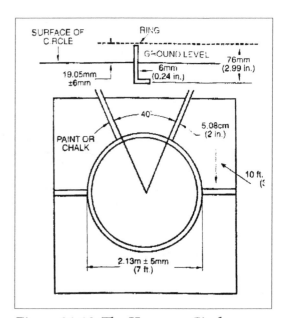

Figure 21.10. **The Hammer Circle**

The cage should be centered around the circle, and the sector should be centered on the nonmovable cage. The specifications for a discus ring and cage are listed in Figures 21.11 and 21.12.

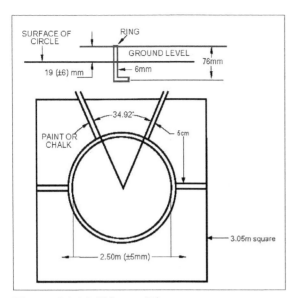

Figure 21.11. **Discus Ring**

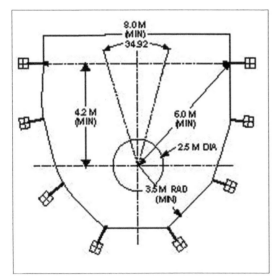

Figure 21.12. **Discus Cage**

The IAAF recently passed new rules for the construction of hammer cages that will dramatically reduce the danger zone for hammer throwing. The IAAF considered the need for new cage designs to be urgent; past specifications did not provide enough safety. The problem with earlier hammer cage specifications and design is that implements could still land on the track front and back straightaway even when the cage gates were operated correctly. In the new design, modifications were made to augment safety by increasing the length (3.2 m) and height (10 m) of the gates as well as decreasing the opening between the front posts (8 m) to accommodate the new throwing sector of 34.92°. But keep in mind the NCAA specifications for hammer cages are different than the IAAF. The NCAA recommendations are far below the IAAF standards for safety.

The following are NCAA (2010) specifications for the hammer or discus cage thrown either outside the

stadium or thrown inside the stadium while other events are in progress:
- The throwing circle shall be surrounded by a cage made with suitable material, hung from and between rigid posts, sufficient to withstand and absorb an impact from the implement so that the implement will not escape over or through and to reduce the possibility of the implement ricocheting or rebounding back toward the competitor. The purpose of the cage is to contain, but not interfere with, the flight path of the implement.
- Rigid posts, approximately six in number, positioned in line with and to the rear of the front edge of the throwing circle, should be approximately 4 m from the center of the circle and allow for panels of suitable material between 2.74 m and 2.90 m in width that are at least 3.50 m from the center of the circle. The height of these panels for the hammer shall be at least 5 m.
- Panels of suitable material between 2.74 m and 2.90 m in width and at least 6.15 m in height should be hung between each of the two rigid posts in line with the front edge of the throwing circle and each of the two additional rigid posts toward the throwing sector that are not less than 2.85 m away from the sector line. The location of these posts will be approximately 6 m from the center of the throwing circle and provide a total fixed cage opening of between 8 m and 9 m.
- When used for throwing the hammer, movable panels of suitable material not less than 4.20 m in length and not less than 6.15 m in height should be affixed to the rigid posts farthest from the circle toward the landing area. For a right-handed thrower (counterclockwise throwing rotation), the right movable panel is to be open so that it is parallel to the sector line on the right side and maintains the minimum 2.85 m distance from the sector line. For a right-handed thrower, the left movable panel is placed in a position so that its non-pivot end is as perpendicular to the sector line as possible and is not greater than 1.5 m into the sector and not less than 6 m away from the center of the circle. For a left-handed thrower (clockwise throwing rotation), the movable panel configuration is reversed.

Even with the cage, spectators, officials, coaches, and athletes should be warned that they are not completely protected. The height of the panels surrounding the cage should be increased when possible. If the discus and hammer are contested inside the track while other events are in action, the movable panel that is normally parallel to the sector line should be positioned closer to the sector line. Changes to the cage positioning that differ from the minimum requirements should be agreed upon by all participating coaches prior to the changes being made (Figure 21.13).

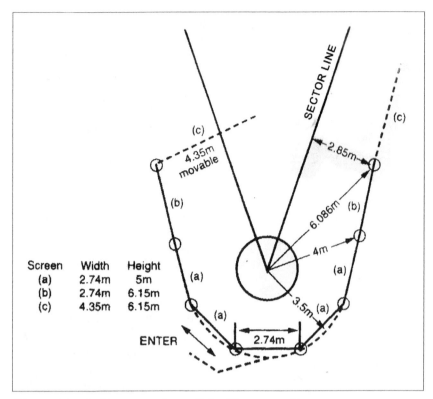

Figure 21.13. **Construction of the Hammer Cage**

Javelin

The javelin event defies the norm of throwing events. It is thrown from a running start on a runway, and the competitor must stay behind the foul line for the completion of the throw instead of remaining in a circle. Throwing into a sector to mark fair throws is a part of the javelin throw, but where the sector begins differs from the other throwing events. The runway should be a minimum of 33.5 m and a maximum of 36.5 m in length, marked by two parallel white lines 5 cm in width (Figure 21.14). The width of the runway should be 4 m from the inside of each white line. If artificial material is used to construct the runway,

it is important for the runway to extend at least 1 m beyond the competition foul line. The foul line should be a 7 cm wide white line in the shape of an arc drawn with a radius of 8 m. The distance between its extremities should be 4 m, measured straight across from end to end. At right angles to the parallel lines marking the runway, lines 75 cm in length and 7 cm wide should be drawn from the extremities. The sector angle, sector line width, and sector color are the same as the other throwing events but will be drawn from the middle of the imaginary circle created by the arc of the foul line. Because the javelin is a long-range event, flags should mark the end of the sector.

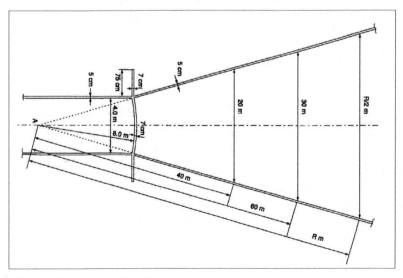

Figure 21.14. **Javelin Runway**

Combining Hammer and Discus Circles in Limited Space

Finding enough field space to hold the sectors for all throwing events may pose a challenge depending on the location of the track facility. The hammer throw and discus events require large landing sectors, and both are thrown from circles; it makes sense to combine the two throwing areas into one. The problem with this idea is that the circles for both events are different sizes. The solution is to use an insert to convert a throwing circle from a 2.5-m diameter to a 2.135-m diameter. This insert should be metal or a suitable rigid material and be flush with the throwing surface. The height of the insert should be 19 mm (± 6 mm). Although rubber inserts are available and easier to manipulate, this material is not rigid enough.

Other Structures/Facilities: Finish Line Towers/Press Box

Towers

The finish line is the control center for running events. The finish line tower should be directly across from the finish line. There should be up to three towers on a track, one at each end of the straightaway and another diagonally across from the main tower at the 200-m start position.

Tower A should be a two-story enclosed structure, 20 ft x 40 ft square with 8-ft ceilings and a roof designed as a deck with railings. The first floor area will contain space for restrooms, a storage area (e.g., for hurdles) with a small roll-up door, and concessions. The second floor will have picture windows facing the finish line. The second floor area will have space for the press, announcer, and the automatic timer, computers, and cameras.

Tower B will be a duplicate of Tower A except the first floor will be dedicated to the storage of hurdles, implements, and pads. The first floor storage area will have a large roll-up door to accommodate the large landing pads. Both towers should have hot and cold water, sewer connection, communications lines (i.e., telephone, computer, and television), electricity, and appropriate ventilation.

Lighting

The track and field area should be lighted for security at a minimum, but lighting the area for evening competition should be seriously considered.

Fencing

The entire facility should be fenced so it can be secured when not in use. The fence should be at least 8 ft high, plastic or vinyl coated, and painted to match the surrounding paint patterns. The fence should have gates in appropriate locations for entrance of athletes, officials, spectators, and maintenance vehicles.

Fences need to be installed to protect athletes and officials from throwing areas (e.g., discus, hammer, and javelin). These fences need to be at least 6 ft high. They should also be constructed with plastic- or vinyl-coated material.

Spectator Seating

Spectator seating is a necessity. The planners should design seating for both sides of the track. The running track will have two finish lines going in opposite directions. Depending on the prevailing wind, a decision will be made as to which direction the races will be run. Therefore, it is necessary to provide seating on both sides of the track for spectators. (See Chapter 12 for standards relative to new bleachers or retrofitting old bleachers.)

The number of seats should be based on historical data regarding spectator involvement over the previous 5 years. The seating can be permanent; be constructed of metal, wood, or other appropriate materials; or be portable aluminum bleachers. The higher the bleachers are, the greater the liability concerns. If money is not a problem, construct concrete seating large enough to incorporate storage areas underneath the seats and a press box on the upper level.

Starting System

Modern timing systems are connected to the starter's gun. Therefore, the hard wiring that is required should be placed underground and junction boxes made available at the various starting lines for the races. These junction boxes should be at least 4 ft off the ground with a storage container for cable to be used by the starter crew.

Landscaping

There should be an irrigation system designed to provide water to grass areas, shrubbery, and flowers. The plan for the irrigation system needs to carefully consider additional water to drinking fountains throughout the complex and water for the water jump. The track and field area should be large enough to provide at least a half-acre of shaded area for athletes between events spread around the facility. The areas at the ends of the straightaways should have trees to provide a windbreak for the athletes.

Track and Field Equipment

Starting Blocks

Starting blocks must be made without devices that could provide artificial aid in starting. They may be adjustable but must be constructed entirely of rigid materials.

Hurdles

Hurdles should be constructed of metal, wood, or other suitable material. The hurdles should consist of two bases and two uprights supporting a rectangular frame reinforced by one or more crossbars. The top crossbar should be wood or other suitable material with beveled edges and a height of 7 mm and a width between 1 cm and 2.5 cm. The center of the crossbar should be directly over the end of the base. The surface facing the starting line should be white in color with two vertical or diagonal stripes. A center chevron should be added to help contestants determine the center of the lane (see Figure 22.15; NCAA, 2010).

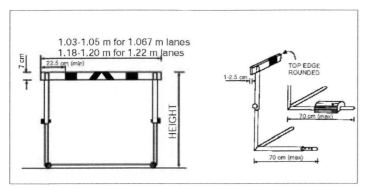

Figure 21.15. The Hurdle

Pullover force refers to the 3.6 k (8 lb) of steady pulling force required to overturn a hurdle when applied to the center of the uppermost edge of the top crossbar and in the direction of the finish line. If the weights cannot be adjusted to the required overturning force, it is recommended that the next greater setting be used because records will not be allowed when the overturning force or the weight of the hurdle is less than the required minimum (NCAA, 2010).

When the manufacturer has not made definite counterweight setting for intermediate hurdles, it is possible to attain the correct adjustment by setting one weight as for the 106.7 cm (42 in.) height and the other weight as for 76.2 cm (30 in.) height. A difference of 3 mm (0.12 in.) above or below the required height will be tolerated (NCAA, 2010).

Steeplechase Hurdles

Hurdles should be constructed of metal, wood, or other suitable material. The hurdles shall consist of a base and two uprights supporting a rectangular frame with a single crossbar. The crossbar shall be made of wood or other suitable material without sharp edges or with a 6.35 mm (0.25 in.) bevel and have a height of 127 mm (5 in.) square. The crossbar shall be white with stripes of one distinctive contrasting color. The ends of the crossbar shall be smooth and not be covered with rubber or another material that has the effect of increasing the friction between the surface of the crossbar and the supports. The diameter of the crossbar must be at least 29 mm but not more than 31 mm (1.14 in. to 1.22 in.). The crossbar should be between 4.48 m and 4.52 m (14.7 ft to 14.83 ft) in length. The maximum weight shall be 2.25 k (4.96 lb). For the purpose of placing the bar

on the supports of the uprights, the ends of the crossbar should be constructed so that a flat surface of 29 mm to 35 mm (1.14 in. to 1.38 in.) x 200 mm (7.87 in.) is provided (NCAA, 2010).

Other Accessory Equipment

The following pieces of equipment will be useful for indoor and outdoor track and field facilities (NCAA, 2010):
- pole vault standards base protection pads;
- countdown timer;
- wind gauge—now required for all collegiate hurdles, long jump, and high jump;
- implement certification unit;
- aluminum water jump;
- foundation tray;
- blanking lid;
- takeoff board with plasticine insert;
- long jump/triple jump aluminum pit covers;
- throwing rings;
- toeboards;
- concentric circles;
- stainless steel or aluminum pole vault box;
- pole vault covers;
- finish post;
- aluminum track curbing;
- rotating track gate;
- hammer cage;
- discus cage;
- indoor throwing event cage;
- lane markers;
- distance marker boxes;
- long jump/triple jump distance indicator;
- performance boards;
- lap counter;
- wind display;
- awards stand;
- judge's stand;
- starter's rostrum;
- hurdle carts;
- platform cart;
- starting block caddy; and
- implement carts—shotput cart, hammer cart, javelin cart, discus cart, combo cart.

Specifics for Indoor Facility Components

The indoor track and field facility will follow similar general guidelines as the outdoor track and field facility. However, differences exist and make understanding the construction a separate project altogether. Not only is the track indoors, but indoor track and field involves a smaller track involving a separate list of track events and a different set of throwing events.

The Indoor Running Track

The standard NCAA indoor track should be 200 m with two horizontal straights and two curves that may be banked. As of January 1, 2004, no track constructed after the date exceeding 300 m will be considered an indoor track. The inside radius of the curves on a 200-m track should be no less than 18 m and no more than 21 m. The curves should be bordered by a curb similar to outdoor tracks, 5 cm high and 5 cm wide. In indoor facilities, the edge of the track may simply be marked with a 5 cm white line. Cones at least 15 cm high should be placed near the white line to designate the boundaries of the track visually. The cones should be placed at distances not exceeding 2 m on the curves and 10 m on the straightaways. Tracks, runways, and takeoff areas should be covered with synthetic material or have a wooden surface with uniform resilience where possible. These surfaces should be able to accept 6 mm (¼ in.) spikes for synthetic surfaces and 3 mm (⅛ in.) spikes for wood.

The track should have a minimum of six lanes. Lanes should be separated on both sides by 5 cm wide white lines and a minimum of 1.067 m and a maximum of 1.22 m in width including the white line to the right. The indoor track lanes are numbered in the same way as the outdoor facility with the innermost lane labeled Lane 1. The intersection of each lane line and the finish line should be painted black. Behind the start line, 3 m of space without obstruction is needed. Beyond the finish line, at least 10 m of space free of obstruction should be the minimum with a recommended space of at least 20 m.

For tracks that are banked on the curves, the angle of banking should not exceed 18° for a 200-m track. The angle may vary for different sized tracks. An inclination toward the inside lane shall not exceed 1:1000, and any facility that exceeds this inclination will be considered a banked track.

Other measuring distances and track markings follow the direction of the outdoor facilities. Consult the previous section for color codes, start and finish lines, break lines, relay zones, and other particulars. One detail, however, that is not a problem for outdoor facilities, but is a concern for indoor facilities, is overhead clearance. From the lowest point of the ceiling including lights and beams, the overhead clearance should be at minimum 9.14 m.

Indoor Jumping Facilities

The high jump, triple jump, long jump, and pole vault can all occur indoors as well as outdoors. These events indoors also need the same dimensional requirements as outdoors. Consult the earlier Outdoor Jumping Facilities section depicting the layout for these events.

Indoor Throwing Facilities

The indoor throwing schedule differs greatly from the outdoor throwing schedule. Outdoor throwing events include the shot put, hammer, discus, and javelin, and indoor events consist shot put and the weight throw. The throwing facility (typically because the facility is enclosed indoors, there is only one circle), however, will remain similar to the outdoor shot put facilities with a few notable differences.

Shot Put

The requirements for the shot put facility are the same as the outdoor shot put facilities mentioned earlier in the chapter. Because the indoor implements roll farther and faster on the indoor surface, stop barriers should be used at the end of the sector. Stop barriers can be of any suitable height and material and should be placed at least 5 m back from the personal best of the farthest thrower in the competition.

Weight Throw

Although the weight throw is specifically an indoor track or winter season event, the event may be contested outside. The event construction should follow the same rules when occurring indoors or outdoors. All weight throws should be made from a circle and sector with the same specifications as the indoor shot put event with the exception of the removal of the toeboard. The cage surrounding the weight throw event should comply with the safety provisions for the outdoor hammer throw. Differences specific to the weight throw include the rigid posts surrounding the circle and two movable panels at the front of the circle. The rigid posts should allow for panels of suitable material approximately 1.91 m in width, at least 3.66 m in height, and at least 2.5 m from the center of the circle. The two movable panels cannot be less than 1.30 m in width and must be at least 3.66 m in height. The sector should be about 90 ft long, and barriers should be placed at the end of the sectors to keep the shot puts and weights from rolling.

Indoor Weight Throw Cage

The weight throw is a throwing event primarily contested in collegiate indoor track and field in the United States. The competitive athlete performs between one and four rotations within a 2.135 meter ring and releases a 40.6 cm long implement with a mass of either 15.87 kg (35 lbs.) for male competitors or 9.07 kg (20 lbs.) for female competitors. The athletes involved in this event must generate as much velocity with the implement as possible, while maintaining balance and coordination through the sequence of turns. There are definitely inherent dangers associated with this event aside from potential managerial neglect of facilities. Athletes, coaches, and spectators participating in the event can be at risk; the event entails hurling a steel implement with weights of 20 pounds for women and 35 pounds for men through the air at great speeds, far distances (70-80 feet), and is often difficult to spot in flight. Due primarily to safety concerns, the throwing circle is sheltered by a C-shaped cage for the protection of officials, athletes, coaches and spectators. At the original inception of the weight throw event, there was no safety cage used; athletes used crude techniques and threw modest distances (30-40 feet). Many facility administrators did not understand the weight throw and underestimated the danger involved with the event. As the event evolved and distances improved, the weight cage was designed to prevent the weight from exiting the throwers' hands in unprotected directions, such as out of the back, sides, and in dangerous angles from the circle.

The NCAA rule book states that the purpose of the weight cage is to contain, but not interfere with, the flight path of the implement (NCAA, 2012). The recommended minimum height for the NCAA weight cage is 3.66 meters in height and at least 2.5 meters from the center of the circle. The gates are required to be not less than 1.30 meters in width and at least 3.66 meters in height. It is also stated in the rules that cage configurations that are more restrictive than the minimums set forth in this rule may only be used with the consent of each participating institution. *Note:* Anchored drop-down nets may be used as a substitute cage in order to satisfy the safety of material provisions of the rule. The weight is the only indoor event that can be contested outdoors in the hammer cage. Universities in the southern part of the United States (i.e. University of Florida) often contest the weight throw outdoors.

Indoor Throwing Cages

There are many different styles of indoor throwing cages: portable to ground sleeve installation, with doors, (meets NCAA rules) or without. Most indoor throwing event cages are manufactured out of the same high-quality materials as the outdoor cages. To meet NCAA guidelines, indoor cages measure a full 13' in height and come complete with a high strength net that withstands the impact of an indoor weight, 4" rounded steel posts and net stabilizer arms. Because of the unique nature of the event with the majority of the weight on the end of a lever arm that is 41 cm long, resulting centripetal forces from the implement during a throw are much greater than the initial weight of the implement. The cage must be anchored to absorb the force of an errant throw. The cage comes complete with crank wheel system for easy adjustments in case the implement becomes caught in the net.

Drop Down Netting

One of the challenges with the indoor throwing cage is portability. The indoor throwing cage would have to be taken down and stored if used in a multiuse facility. Facilities often lack the storage space and manpower to set-up and remove the cage for practices and competitions. It is important that the indoor throwing cage is available for all practices as well as competitions. For multiuse facilities that lack storage space, a drop down netting system is a good alternative. For example, a university in the Mid-American conference shared space in a multiuse facility that lacked storage space for a free standing cage (Figure 21.16) so the university invested in a drop down system (Figure 21.17). With the turn of a key or push of a button, the cage and doors can be raised or lowered to the correct position. The entire cage stores within 3' of ceiling and descends; therefore there is no need for large storage area for the cage (Figure 21.18). Set up and take down times are as easy as 1-2-3. Facility managers will no longer waste time and human capital moving around portable bases, uprights, heavy ballast containers and hoist netting. There is no need for large storage areas that take up valuable floor and activity space. Only the main cage net need be lowered to use as a shot put cage or as an indoor throwing area for the discus. This type of cage meets and exceeds NCAA rules and recommendations for indoor use.

Staging a Competition

Prior to staging a weight competition, a safe zone must be established around the perimeter of the sector lines of the weight venue by flagging off the danger zone of the sector and an area on each side of the sector lines (see Figure 21.19). The danger zones are depicted in red and the throwers and officials should always be instructed to stay in the safe zone in green. Officials, competitors and onlookers need to stand well outside of the flagged off danger zone when someone is throwing in the ring which is usually three to four meters outside the sector lines. Even with a properly installed NCAA cage, onlookers are in potential danger when they are standing in what is considered a safe zone well outside the sector lines. The NCAA rulebook suggests that flagged off areas be set up at 55 degrees prior to a weight throw competition (NCAA, 2012). This would set up a danger zone of 10 degrees along each sector line of the established 34.92 degree sector. The 55 degree danger zone recommended by the NCAA in the rule book would work well for the drop down cage with higher cage doors. The NCAA cage, however, has a potential danger zone, with an elite thrower, of approximately 94 degrees, which puts spectators and bystanders at risk of getting hit with an errant implement even when the cage doors are properly positioned and used. Either the size of the danger zone in the NCAA rulebook needs to be changed to protect athletes, officials, spectators and innocent bystanders when the weight is being thrown or the NCAA needs to adopt the drop down cage as the standard. When the netting drops down from the ceiling, there is no chance of an errant throw going over the cage door and hitting an innocent bystander. Adopting the more stringent drop down cage design will effectively protect more people.

Figure 21.16. Many universities lack the storage space for a free-standing cage.

Figure 21.17. The drop down netting cage is the safest alternative.

Figure 21.18. The drop down netting is stored in 3 feet of ceiling space.

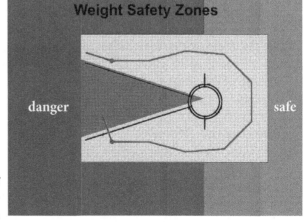

Figure 21.19. It is important for the coach to designate the danger and safe zones .

Indoor and Outdoor Track Facility Certification

All tracks hosting intercollegiate track meets must be officially surveyed. This certification must be maintained throughout the entire use of the track, and the survey record is available from the NCAA upon request. Permanent facilities must be certified after construction and reconstruction, and temporary indoor tracks must be surveyed before the first competition of the season. A certification involves the exact measurements for the following facility components:

- levels of the track, runways, approaches, and landing surfaces;
- permanent track measurements;
- start and finish line;
- track lanes;
- baton-passing zones;
- steeplechase water jump pit;
- hurdle placements; and
- throwing surfaces and all sectors. (NCAA, 2010)

Cross-Country Facility Design

Planning the Course and Course Layout

Properly measuring the cross-country course is paramount; the distance of the course should be measured along the shortest possible route that a runner may take. Men and women cross-country competitors at the collegiate level race at different race lengths. A male cross-country course should be from 8,000 m to 10,000 m and a female course should be 5,000 m. For women and men of high school age, the race should be 3,000 m to 5,000 m and 8,000 m. If race officials, the games committee, or coaches mutually agree to alter the length of the race, it is within the rules to vary from the specified distances. At the high school level, some variations are found between state associations.

The main concern when considering the course layout is participant safety. Confine the course to fields, woods, and grasslands. Dangerous ascents or descents, undergrowth, deep ditches, and, in general, any hindrance detrimental to the contestants must be avoided. Narrow gaps must be no less than 2 m and preferably 5 m in width for nonchampionship courses. Obstacles and other hindrances should be avoided for the first 600 m to 800 m as well as the last 200 m to 300 m of the race. Championship courses must be at least 10 m wide at all points. Continuous traversing of roadways should be avoided. All turns must be gradual.

Marking the Course

The course should also be properly marked so that competitors are easily guided through the course as they compete. The course must be marked clearly by at least two of the following methods presented in order of preference:

- Sign posts not less than 7 ft high with large directional arrows on boards fastened to the tops of the posts so that the arrows will be visible plainly at a distance to competitors approaching the posts. The posts must be placed at every point where the course turns, on the side of the direction of the turn, and wherever there is any doubt as to the direction of travel. The course shall have kilometer and/or mile markings throughout the course.
- A single white or colored line for directional purposes only—not to be assumed as the measured line or two lines that mark the outside borders of the course, one on the measured course marking its shortest perimeter and the second so that runners cannot vary from the proper course. In addition, these two lines serve as restraining lines for spectators. Lines on the turns must vary in color from the color of lines approaching the turn.
- Flags, signposts, or stakes that meet the following conditions:
  - markers at least 7 ft above the ground level;
  - a turn to the left marked by a red flag or arrow of direction on a sign post or stake;
  - a turn to the right marked by a yellow flag or arrow of direction on a sign post or stake;
  - a course continuing straight marked by a blue flag or arrow of direction on a sign post or stake; and
  - all flags, sign posts, or stakes marking the shortest perimeter of the course.

Finally, all of the above course-marking devices must be placed on the edge of the measured line when lines and flags, sign posts, or stakes are used to mark the course.

The Start Area

In cross-country, many competitors and full teams may be competing at the same time. The starting area for a championship course should be wide enough for at least 50 teams. The starting line shall be wide enough to provide at least a 50 cm space for each of the four frontline team starters and a 50 cm space for each individual starter. The area should be flat and well drained. At either side of the starting line, there should be permanent elevated (8 ft to 10 ft high) recall starter stands with steps to the platform and a roof over the platform to protect the recall starter during inclement weather. The lower portion of the platform should be enclosed and used as a storage area. Two more stands should be constructed across from each other at the 100 m mark for the second set of recall starters and one more at the 200 m mark. Finally, the starter should be on a raised platform in the center, 100 m from the start line. The platform should be covered in case of inclement weather. There should be a public address system attached to the platform. The platform should be at least 6 ft tall and padded to protect runners.

There should be a fence (6 ft to 8 ft high) at the end of the starting area to separate the runners from the spectators. Behind the fence should be the official staging area for the athletes and portable toilets. An elevated permanent starter stand should be located in the center of the course. The tower should be equipped with a public address system and communications system to the finish line. The stand platform should be at least 8 ft high with a ladder for the starter to climb to the platform.

The Finish Area

The finish area for a championship course should have an arched entrance with a digital clock embedded into the arch. The finish area should also be 15 ft to 20 ft wide with a face (6 ft) along each side. The fenced area should extend for at least 30 yd. The actual finish line should be a concrete pad (20 ft x 20 ft) on which the timing pads can be placed. Directly adjacent to the concrete pad should be a timing booth to house the timing equipment and personnel. This booth should be covered to protect the equipment from inclement weather conditions. The booth area should have communication linkages to the starter tower and electricity. The final 300 m of the course should have fencing (6 ft) along both sides to keep spectators off the course as the athletes finish. This fencing may stretch from the starting area to the finish area if the course overlaps these two areas.

Control Center Building

The control center building for a championship course is used as a press box and for spectator seating. The building will be a two-story structure near the finish line. The lower portion of the building should be enclosed and used for storage of equipment, mowing equipment, and utility vehicles. The second story will be the press box area. Above the press box will be spectator seating. The press box should be complete with electricity, heating, and communication linkages to the finish and starting lines.

22 Designing Facilities for K–12 Health, Physical Education, and Driver Education

Thomas H. Sawyer, *Indiana State University*

Tonya L. Gimbert, *Indiana State University*

In a public school building, the unit of primary importance is the room or space where teaching occurs. All other parts of the school plant are, in a real sense, secondary. In physical education, therefore, determining the number and character of the teaching stations is basic to the planning process. Furthermore, it is important to locate these facilities in a separate wing for a number of reasons, including noise, evening and weekend use, and nonschool-sponsored uses.

The term *teaching station* identifies any room or space where one teacher can instruct or supervise the learning experience of a class or group of students. For instance, a gymnasium is a teaching station and, if divided, could provide two or more teaching stations. Swimming pools, auxiliary physical education teaching stations, and dance rooms are also examples of teaching stations. The number of students accommodated by a teaching station is controlled by the nature of the specific activity, the size of the facility, whether the facility is indoors or outdoors, and accessibility concerns.

The number of teaching stations required is dictated by enrollment, policies pertaining to instructional physical education, average class size, diversity of program, number of periods in the school day, and other facility uses.

Folding partitions and combinations of vinyl and mesh curtains can be effectively used for flexibility and to increase the number of teaching stations.

Planners should be aware that indoor facilities for physical education, athletics, and recreation are difficult and costly to expand at some future date. School planners should know the peak enrollment potential for each space. The anticipated enrollment 5 to 10 years after completion of construction should serve as a basis for determining the required number of original teaching stations. Long-range planning is imperative to provide for the logical and most economical expansion. The initial design should make provisions for the anticipated construction.

Common Planning Considerations

There are a number of common planning considerations for physical education facilities in public and private schools (see Chapters 1 and 2). These include surface materials (i.e., ceilings, floors, and walls), sound control and acoustics, electrical systems and service, climate control, security, climbing walls, ropes and cargo nets, storage, shower and dressing rooms, folding partitions or curtains, and office space for physical education teachers. These common planning considerations are discussed in detail in the following pages.

Surface Materials

Selecting indoor surface materials for ceilings, floors, and walls is complicated because indoor facilities will be subject to hard usage, excessive moisture, and multiple uses. These surfaces must meet minimum standards in terms of acoustical and light-reflecting properties. Geographic location and the availability of certain surface materials should be considered as well. (See Chapter 8 for greater details on indoor surfaces.)

Floor Surfaces

The best floor surface (see Chapter 8 for further information) to use may depend upon the number of different teaching areas. The main gymnasium area should have either a hardwood or a synthetic surface. Wood, preferably maple, is an excellent all-around surface, although it lacks the durability and flexibility that might be demanded by extensive community use of the facility. Synthetic surfaces have proven excellent for all normal game-type activities and also can better accommodate events that put additional stress on the floor such as setting up chairs, tables, booths, and the like. In an auxiliary teaching station, carpeting is often used but not recommended due to the low coefficient of slippage, which increases the chances of joint injury when quick movements are attempted (e.g., knee and ankle). Tile is also not recommended as a play surface due to the high coefficient of slippage and the lack of adequate resiliency, which increases the chances of joint injury (e.g., knees and hips).

There are at least three distinct types of floor surfacing (e.g., hardwood, resilient synthetic, or common surfaces such as tile, ceramic tile, or rug) required in facilities described in this chapter. Floors in service areas such as locker rooms, shower rooms, toweling rooms, and toilet rooms require a surface impervious to moisture (e.g., concrete or ceramic tile). Classroom, corridor, and office areas may be grouped together for common surfacing (e.g., tile or rug).

Special activity areas require different treatments. For example, a dance gymnasium that is used for instruction in modern dance should have a finished treatment that will allow dancers to slide or glide across the floor. In other areas, such as basketball courts, the finish should be of a non-slip nature. The location of lines for various activities and floor plates for standards or gymnastic equipment should be carefully considered.

Flexibility, durability, and cost are three criteria that have been instrumental in seeing synthetic surfaces challenge hardwood floors for installation in activity areas. The most popular synthetic surfacing materials can be classed into two types: plasticized polyvinyl chlorides (PVCs) and polyurethanes. The PVCs are primarily prefabricated, and the polyurethanes are either poured in place or produced in factory-prefabricated sheets that are adhered down on the site. In general, the polyurethanes possess most of the desirable characteristics sought in a floor surface.

Walls

In addition to segregating specific areas, walls should serve as barriers to sound, light, heat, and moisture. Wall surfaces should be selected based on acoustical properties of the material. In general, moisture-resistant walls with good acoustical properties are recommended. Most modern gymnasiums have smooth surfaces on the lower portion of the walls so they may be used as rebound surfaces. Rough-surfaced walls collect dirt easily and are difficult to clean. Recently, the trend has been to use color, murals, and graphics to add aesthetic appeal. However, in the elementary gymnasium, the need for walls to hold paper, posters, and/or decals should be considered as well.

In locker rooms, shower rooms, and toilet rooms where high humidity is often present, it is important to select wall surfacing that is moisture-resistant and has good acoustical properties. Walls serving as barriers between toilet rooms, handball courts, squash courts, and other areas where noise is a problem should transmit a minimal amount of sound.

Ceilings

Roof design, type of activity, and local building codes should determine the ceiling construction. Ceilings should be insulated to prevent condensation and should be painted to provide pleasing aesthetics and to enhance light reflection. Acoustical ceiling materials are desirable in instructional and activity areas. Dropped ceiling panels susceptible to damage by objects or individuals will require considerable maintenance. False ceilings with catwalks above them have been effectively designed to permit maintenance and repair of lighting and ventilating systems.

Sound Control and Acoustics

The sonic, or audible, environment is the most difficult phase of the total environment to balance and requires the services of an acoustical engineer. In each room, attention must be given to reverberation time. This is influenced by the absorption and reflection qualities of all surfaces within the room. Hard surfaces reflect sound and produce excessive unwanted reflection and reverberations. Thus, the space may be "noisy." Soft or absorbable surfaces turn the sound into another form of energy and can produce areas that are too "dead." Therefore, most areas must have some materials with sound-absorbing qualities to balance the sonic environment for good hearing conditions.

Sound Insulation

Unwanted sound or noise may be transmitted into the room by means of ventilating ducts, pipes, and spaces around pipe sleeves. Sound transmission through ducts can be reduced by using baffles or by lining the ducts with sound-absorbent, fire-resistant materials. The ducts may also be connected with canvas to interrupt the transmission through the metal in the ducts. Pipes can be covered with pipe covering, and spaces in the pipe sleeves can be filled.

Sound can also be transmitted through the walls, floors, and ceilings. This can be reduced to a desirable minimum by the proper structural design and materials. In conventional wall construction, alternate studs can support the sides of the wall so that there is no through connection from one wall surface to another. This is sometimes known as double-wall construction. The space inside the walls can be filled with sound-absorbing material to further decrease the sound transmission.

Sometimes, 3 in. or 4 in. of sand inside the walls at the baseboard will cut down the transmission appreciably. Likewise, sound-absorption blankets laid over the partitions in suspended ceiling construction can frequently reduce the sound from one room to another.

Machinery vibration or impact sounds can be reduced by using the proper floor covering and/or by installing the machinery on floating or resilient mountings. "Sound locks," such as double walls or doors, are needed between noisy areas and adjoining quiet areas. Improper location of doors and windows can create noise problems. It is imperative to pay attention to the acoustical treatment of all areas. Gymnasiums, swimming pools, and dressing locker rooms are frequently neglected.

Materials for Acoustical Treatment

Acoustical materials must be maintained carefully. Oil paint reduces the sound-absorbing qualities of most materials. Surface treatment for different acoustical areas will vary. The most common treatment of acoustical fiber tile is a light brush coat of water-based paint. Most acoustical materials lose their efficiency after several applications of paint.

Electrical Systems and Service

All electrical service, wiring, and connections should be installed according to the requirements of the National Electric Code of the National Board of Fire Underwriters and state and local building codes and fire regulations. (See Chapter 5 for additional information.)

The capacity of each individual electrical system should be determined accurately for safety and economy. Full consideration should be given to present and future program plans when designing the electrical systems. Increased use of electrically operated equipment, higher standards of illumination, and special audiovisual equipment should be anticipated.

Illumination (See Chapter 5 for detailed information)

In addition to the amount of light in any given area, the quality of light is of equal importance. Providing efficient illumination is complicated and challenging, and the services of an illuminating engineer are recommended to obtain maximal lighting efficiency. Gymnasiums, classrooms, corridors, and other specific areas have distinct and different lighting requirements. Planning for electric illumination requires that each area be considered relative to the specific use.

Important lighting considerations. In addition to the quantity and quality of light from the various lighting systems available, factors to consider when selecting an electrical illumination system are maintenance, repair, replacement, and cleaning. The ideal lighting fixture has both an indirect and a direct component, throwing surface light on the ceiling to give it about the same brightness as the lighting unit itself.

There is less need, however, to provide high-ceiling areas with direct–indirect fixtures. In gymnasiums, swimming pools, and similar activity areas, an even distribution of light is required to permit the individual to see quickly

and distinctly in any part of the room. It is advisable to provide supplementary lighting on specialized equipment and areas that may be provided in a main or auxiliary gymnasium. Even with careful planning, it is difficult to make adequate provisions without compromise.

In some activities, such as aquatics, the very nature of the activity necessitates a separate facility. Night lights, sometimes known as safety lights, that burn continually are recommended for gymnasiums, swimming pools, handball courts, squash courts, and other indoor activity areas. Lobbies, corridors, and some classrooms should also be equipped with night lights. These lights are extremely important for safety and security purposes and should have separate controls.

Provisions for outside lighting should be considered. Exit lights must follow the prescribed codes of the local community and the state. Electrically illuminated exit lights clearly indicating the direction to the exterior should be provided over all exit doors from gymnasiums, combined auditorium–gymnasiums, multipurpose rooms, and other areas such as those containing goals or targets. Dimmers should be installed on the lighting in spectator areas. Supplementary light sources should be shielded from the eyes of participants and spectators to provide the proper brightness balance.

Transparent, nonbreakable plastic protective covers will protect lighting units in activity areas where balls may be thrown. Vaporproof lighting units are recommended for damp areas such as toilets, showers, the dressing locker suite, and the swimming pool. Locker room lights should be spaced to the light areas between lockers.

Incandescent, fluorescent, mercury-vapor, sodium-vapor, and metal halide lighting systems are most commonly used in gymnasium buildings. The incandescent light is instantaneous, burns without sound, and is not affected by the number of times the light is turned on or off. Incandescent lights and fixtures are considerably cheaper in initial cost and are easier to change, and the lamp, within limits, may be varied in size within a given fixture.

Incandescent fixtures, however, have excessively high spot brightness and give off considerable heat, which becomes a problem when high levels of illumination are necessary. Fluorescent lamps have the advantage of long life and can be placed over all exit doors from the building and at the head and foot of exit stairways. Emergency (white) lighting systems should be provided for exits (including exterior open spaces to which the exits lead) in gymnasiums, multipurpose rooms, and other places of assembly or large group activity. This lighting should be on a special emergency circuit. All controls should be located so that they are under the supervision of authorized persons, and all other aspects of the installation should meet the specifications prescribed by the Underwriters Exits Code and state and local fire laws and regulations.

Artificial lighting system. Many trends in lighting systems have developed in conventional structures. One system uses primarily skylights and is supplemented with conventional artificial light. In such a system, a light sensor assesses the light level coming through the skylight in the working area just above the floor.

At this point, the sensor signals that information to the artificial light system to shine from 0% to 100% of the wattage capacity depending upon how much light is coming through the skylights. The sensor in this system can raise or lower the intensity of the artificial light to an acceptable and predetermined candle power dependent on the activity. Installing skylights plus a light sensor system will add to construction cost; however, this installation will reward the institution with energy conservation and cost savings. In addition, without the use of a light sensor system, a facility's lights would be required to be on full time whenever the building is occupied. Also, a high percentage of the total kilowatt hours used in a facility are conventionally designed for artificial lighting. A skylight and light sensor system will accrue a significant savings in energy cost. Artificial lights also generate considerable heat, and when the amount of artificial light (heat) is reduced, a skylight and light sensor system significantly impact savings in air-conditioning cost. Such a system has an approximate theoretical savings projected to reduce air-conditioning costs by one half and lighting costs by one third.

Fire Alarm System

Electrical fire alarm systems should be separate and distinct from all program signal or other signal systems and should be designed to permit operation from convenient locations in corridors and from areas of unusual fire hazard. All fire alarm systems should meet the specifications prescribed by the Underwriters Laboratories and by state and local fire laws and regulations.

Program Signal System

Gymnasium buildings can be wired for a signal system operated by a master clock or push buttons from the main administrative offices. Secondary controls may be placed in other administrative units of the facility. Program signals should be independent of the fire alarm system and should not be used as a fire alarm system. Program signals usually include buzzers or chimes in the classrooms; bells in corridors, pool, gymnasiums, fields, and dressing locker suites; and large gongs on the outside of the building. In many instances, signals placed strategically in corridors rather than in individual classrooms are adequate. Electric clocks should be included in all indoor areas in the program signal system.

Services for Appliances and Other Electrical Equipment

There are many needs for electrical wiring and connections, which require careful analysis and planning. The following are examples:

- Basic construction: motors to operate folding partitions, blowers for heaters and ventilating ducts, exhaust fans in gymnasium ceilings or walls.
- Custodial and maintenance services: receptacles for floor-cleaning equipment and power tools.
- Dressing locker rooms: wiring for hair and hand dryers and electric shavers.
- Lounges, kitchenettes, snack bars, and concessions: outlets for refrigerators, water or soft drink coolers, electric stoves, blenders, mixers, coffee urns, and hot plates.
- Office suites: wiring for individual air conditioners, business machines, floor fans, and other mechanical and electrical equipment.
- Laundry rooms: wiring for washers, dryers, and irons.
- Pools: provision for underwater vacuum cleaners, pumps, and special lighting.
- Gymnasiums: provisions for special lighting effects, spotlights, and rheostats or controls to lower the illumination for certain activities.
- Health suites: receptacles and provision for audiometers, vision-testing equipment, floor fans, and air-conditioning units.

Climate Control

The engineering design of heating systems should be based on the technical data and procedures of the American Society of Heating, Refrigerating, and Air-Conditioning Engineers. A heating, ventilating, and air-conditioning (HVAC) system should be selected with special consideration for economy of operation, flexibility of control, quietness of operation, and capacity to provide desirable thermal conditions. The design and location of all climate control equipment should provide for future additions.

Because the number of occupants in any given area of the building will vary, variable controls to supply the proper amount of fresh air and total circulation for maximum occupancy in one area should be considered. Specially designed equipment and controls are necessary to ensure that climate control in major areas can be regulated and operated independently of the rest of the facility.

All three mechanical systems—heating, ventilating, and air-conditioning—are interrelated and should be planned together. The services of a competent mechanical engineer should be obtained not only for design but also for making inspections during construction and for giving operating instructions to the service department. Problems involved in the installation of HVAC systems include

- maintaining a minimal noise level;
- maintaining separate temperature control for laboratory areas;
- insulating all steam, hot water, and cold water pipes and marking them with a color code;
- exhausting dry air through the locker rooms and damp air from the shower room to the outside;
- providing a minimum of four changes of air per hour without drafts;
- installing locking-type thermostats in all areas, with guards wherever they may be subject to damage;
- placing the thermostats for highest efficiency;
- zoning the areas for night and recreational use; and
- eliminating drafts on spectators and participants.

The geographical location of the proposed facility will dictate to some extent the type of climate control equipment to install. Mechanical ventilation is preferred over open windows. Air-conditioning has been strongly recommended for southern climates; however, year-round uses of facilities make air-conditioning a desirable building feature in other areas. Special rooms such as locker rooms, shower rooms, swimming pools, and steam rooms need special consideration for moisture and humidity control.

Security

The athletic and physical education complex presents a unique security problem. The facilities and the programs attract large numbers of individuals who move at all times during the day and week and through many areas in different directions. It is reasonable to believe that all students and visitors who come to the building have a distinct purpose in coming and should be welcome. This is the type of building that people enter through many outside doors and disperse to offices, classrooms, dressing rooms, activity areas, and spectator galleries. There should be a plan for pedestrian control and to handle visitors. Security is accomplished in two ways:
- constructing the facilities according to a plan that allows for maximum security or
- adopting an administrative plan for the direction and control of all persons using the building.

The physical layout will facilitate security but will not guarantee it. A good administrative plan will help. However, a good administrative plan cannot completely accomplish effective security if the physical layout does not lend itself to the attainment of such security.

Security Features of Construction
Entrance doors are the first barriers against illegal intrusion. Open and descending stairways, walled entries, and deep-set entrances should be avoided. The points of entrance to buildings should be well lighted from dusk un-

til dawn. The corners of the buildings should have floodlights that light the face of the structure. So-called vandal lights should be installed and protected to make them vandal-proof.

Corridors, which are continuous and straight, providing unbroken vision, add safety and security to the building, its contents, and its users. Corridors are best lined up with entrance doors to provide a commanding view of the doorway from the corridor and of the corridor from the entrance door. There should be an attempt to avoid angular corridors and to eliminate niches or cubbyholes. Using night lighting within the building and at its entrances will protect against vandalism and other forms of undesirable conduct. Night lighting requires separate wiring and switches to maintain a desirable amount of illumination. Switches for such lighting should be key-controlled to prevent unauthorized individuals from using them. A building chart for day and night "on" and "off" lights should be developed. There should be additional directions for "on" and "off" at every switch, and such directions should be changed according to need. A key-station system for night watch checking is desirable.

Security of the Building
Securing the building and its component rooms against illegal entry is the first and most logical consideration for building protection. Good door framing, substantial doors, and heavy-duty hardware and locks hold up against wear and abuse. In their long life and securing qualities, they are a reasonable investment. Installing good hardware is economical in the long run, reducing replacement costs for materials and labor. To reduce loss through breakage and theft, the additional security factor of quality hardware should never be overlooked at any cost.

A Lock-and-Key System
Enlisting the help of experts in the field of building administration will usually result in a plan that considers the following features:
- A building master plan including a lock-and-key system.
- The use of electronic locks with cards.
- Lock-tumbler adjustments so that an area may have its own control and authorization.
- Area division (vertical division) by responsibility or usage for key assignment; or "level" division (horizontal division) for key assignment; or a combination of both vertical and horizontal divisions.
- A policy of not lending keys is recommended. The person to whom the key is assigned signs a pledge to not lend it out. The keys for the facilities should be identified by a distinguishing mark, and a policy should be established with key duplicators in the areas that the duplicators will refuse to duplicate keys carrying such identifying marks.

- An annunciator system for outside or other doors of importance such as swimming pool doors.

Climbing Walls, Ropes, and Cargo Nets

The trend for the last decade has been to involve the elementary students in activities that allow them to develop upper body strength (e.g., climbing walls [fixed and portable], climbing ropes, and cargo nets). The most recent additions to the elementary school gymnasium are climbing walls and bouldering walls. These walls are either fixed to the gymnasium wall or portable. The fixed versions should have a resilient landing base and a safety rope system to protect the students from falls.

The traditional rope-climbing activities have not changed in great detail over the years. The important facility and safety issues include how (a) the rope is fixed to the ceiling, (b) the rope is stored when not in use, and (c) the landing base is established under the rope. Climbing ropes should be attached to a height of 24 ft and drop to about 3 ft above the floor. If the ceiling is placed below the structural members, the locations of suspended equipment should be planned and eyebolts provided during construction. Ropes should be placed 5 ft apart, allowing one for every five students in class.

Cargo nets are great fun. The greatest concerns focus on how they are secured to the ceiling or wall and the landing base provided. The landing base should include either a landing pad, similar to those used in the jumping events in track and field, or a specially designed pit under the net filled with foam squares.

Storage

Two types of storage rooms are necessary for every physical education facility. The first is the storage of large equipment needed in the gym, items such as volleyball standards and official stands, gymnastic equipment, chairs, mats and score tables, which are safety hazards if left around the gym floor. This room should have easy access to the gym floor through a roll-up door. The room should be planned to provide for current equipment and future expansion and should be equipped with safety lights in case of power failure.

Storage rooms are needed for each instructional area. The room adjoining the gymnasium should be at least 1,000 sq ft to 1,200 sq ft and 10 ft high, be equipped with a roll-up door, and be directly accessible from the gymnasium floor. Consideration must be given to community use of the facility and separately secured storage of related equipment. A separate storage room for each program is ideal. The storage areas should have adjustable bins, shelves, racks, and hangers for the best use of space and the proper care of equipment and supplies. Space to store out-of-season equipment is essential to prevent loss or misplacement be-

tween seasons. An outside entrance assists in the handling of equipment that is used outdoors and/or in connection with a summer playground program.

The second type of room needed is for the storage and repair of small equipment and supplies. Special bins, racks, hooks, and nets, with a workbench for making minor repairs, add greatly to the efficiency of the room. Ideally, this room should be located near faculty offices.

Shower and Dressing Rooms

Although it has been standard practice not to include shower, locker, and dressing room facilities in the elementary school, such facilities are essential if the gymnasium is to be used for intramural or interscholastic competition and community usage. The size, number of lockers, showers, and toilet facilities will depend on the extent of usage. (See Chapter 6 for greater detail on these areas.) If swimming pools are added as part of the school–community complex, such facilities are a must. Outdoor restrooms are desirable if the general public is involved.

Folding Partitions or Curtains

Folding partitions make possible two or more teaching stations in the gymnasium. They should be power-operated, insulated against sound transmission and reverberation, and installed to permit compensation for building settlement. The control should be key-operated. The design and operation must ensure student safety. Partitions should extend from floor to ceiling and may be recessed when folded. Floor tracks should not be used. A pass door should be provided at the end of a partition. When partitions are installed in gymnasiums with open truss construction, the space between the top of the folding doors and the ceiling should be insulated against sound transmission.

Vinyl–mesh combination curtains have become popular. The curtain is rolled to the ceiling when not in use. The curtains generally are vinyl for the first 6 ft to 8 ft with mesh for the remaining distance to the ceiling. The vinyl comes in a variety of colors.

Office Space for Physical Education Teachers

The office space for physical education teachers should be in close proximity to the gymnasium and locker room areas. It should range from 150 sq ft to 250 sq ft and include an attached bathroom and shower facility. The office should have an observation window for the gymnasium and outdoor field spaces. Furthermore, the office should be close to or attached to the storage space for the gymnasium. Finally, the office should be designed to include accessibility to a computer and a telephone.

Other General Considerations

It is important for planners to consider other uses of physical education teaching facilities for extracurricular activities for the students and the community in general at the end of the school day. These considerations are outlined below:

- Additional space will be necessary if all students are to be given an opportunity to participate in an intramural and/or interscholastic program.
- It is desirable to have additional special facilities such as dance studios, gymnastics areas, swimming pools (see Chapter 13), and archery ranges to expand the offerings of the physical education program. Note: It may be possible for the school to obtain some of these facilities through the cooperative use of existing or proposed facilities owned and administered by other agencies.
- As planning for recreation is considered, the entire school plant becomes a potential space resource and all units should be scrutinized and planned with recreational adaptability in mind.

Specific Planning Considerations for Specific School Buildings

Elementary School

The elementary school is defined as follows for this book: kindergarten through fifth grade. These suggestions are based on input from experienced elementary practitioners and the Council on Physical Education for Children.

Indoor activity areas. The elementary school physical education program centers on the teaching of fundamental movement patterns, rhythmic or dance, fitness activities, games and sports, gymnastic activities, combative, self-testing activities, and aquatics. The design and scope of physical education facilities should reflect the activities included in the elementary physical education curriculum. Additionally, the planners should refer to the National Association for Sport and Physical Education's Council on Physical Education for Children (COPEC, 2001) guidelines for facilities, equipment, and instructional materials in elementary physical education. These guidelines will be revised in 2013–2014 and presented to the board in April 2014. Finally, another good resource for planners is Chapter 33, "Facilities, Equipment, and Supplies" in Pangrazi and Beighle's (2012) *Dynamic Physical Education for Elementary School Children.*

Physical education for elementary school children. A major consideration fundamental to the planning of an elementary school indoor activity area is the anticipated use by the community. Future years are expected to see more community use of these facilities.

Several of the standard planning principles apply particularly to the elementary facility. Such planning principles include establishing priority use for the facility by giving basic consideration to the primary age group using the facility, allowing for use by children with disabilities, designing for the participants ahead of the spectators, and remembering considerations for maintenance of the facilities.

Location. Elementary schools are often more compact than other schools, and it is desirable to have the activity area apart from the classrooms to reduce noise disturbance. With the increasing use of such facilities by the community, accessibility from the parking areas must be considered. In addition, it should be adjacent to the outdoor playfields. This allows for easier storage of equipment and increases the efficiency of the area to be used as a neighborhood playground in the summer months.

Teaching stations for physical education. Elementary school physical education classes may be organized by a number of methods. The average class size is usually based on the number of pupils in the classroom unit. Because of differences in pupil maturation, physical education periods generally vary from 20 min for kindergarten and first grade to 45 min for fifth and sixth grades with the school average (for computation purposes) being 30 min per class. The formula for computing the number of teaching stations needed for physical education in an elementary school is as follows:

Minimum number of teaching stations equals the number of classroom students times the number of PE periods per week per class (Total number of PE class periods in a school week).

Example:

- Number of classrooms of students: school contains Grades K to 6, three classrooms for each grade level, or a total of 21 classroom units.
- Number of physical education periods per week per class: one period per class for physical education each school day during the week equals five periods per week.
- Total number of physical education class periods in a school week: There are 5 instructional hours in the school day and the length of physical education period is 30 min. Thus, ten 30-min periods each school day may be scheduled for physical education, or a total of 50 periods for the 5-day school week.

The teaching station needs would be calculated as follows:

Minimum number of teaching stations:
21 classroom units x 5 periods per day,
50 periods per week = 105 ÷ 50 = 2.1

In the above situation, if one classroom section has been dropped each week (bringing the total to 20), then the need would be two teaching stations. Therefore, requiring physical education five periods per week in the school used in the example would necessitate employing two physical education teachers each hour of the day.

In many school systems, the above situation would be too idealistic. More likely, only one physical education instructor would be available (a specialist, the classroom teacher, or a paraprofessional in collaboration with one of the other two). This would then drop the number of sessions per week for each classroom unit from five to an average of 2.5. One teaching station would handle this setup. If only one teaching station can be provided in the elementary school, then a gymnasium would be preferable despite that some other type of auxiliary station might prove superior for instruction in the lower grades. The elementary gymnasium remains the preferred facility because of its heavy use by both the upper grades and the community. If the school system and the community were in need of an indoor swimming pool, this would be the choice for a second teaching station.

The next choice is an auxiliary teaching station, sometimes called a playroom. Particularly when heavy community use is anticipated, another alternative is to build a larger gymnasium and allow for dividing it by a folding partition or vinyl–mesh curtains. Such a setup would provide four possible teaching stations, two on each side of the divider. This area would also allow for two basketball intramural courts, one basketball interscholastic court, three volleyball courts, six badminton courts, and four multipurpose game circles.

Multipurpose, cafeteria–gymnasium combinations, and self-contained classrooms. Multipurpose rooms and cafeteria-gymnasium combinations have been found to be impractical for physical education, especially from the standpoint of scheduling. Self-contained classrooms are restrictive in the types of activities that can be offered and have an additional disadvantages. Furniture must be moved whenever activity takes place, but if there is no way to have a separate facility, make sure adequate storage space is available for the tables, chairs, and benches. This storage space should be separate for physical education equipment and for cafeteria equipment. Both spaces should have roll-up doors for ease of transfer of equipment between uses.

If used, such classrooms must provide an unobstructed area of 450 sq ft, be of a nonskid surface, have no dangerous projections, and ideally have direct access to an adjoining terrace, part of which should be roofed for protection against rain. These self-contained classrooms would only be used in the lower grades.

The gymnasium. In planning the elementary school gymnasium, a minimum of 110 sq ft to 150 sq ft per pupil and a total of at least 4,860 sq ft is recommended. Spectator seating (if provided) and storage rooms (ranging in size from 400 sq ft to 600 sq ft with roll-up doors and a minimum ceiling height of 10 ft) require additional space. Many of the general considerations recommended for secondary school gymnasiums also apply to elementary school facilities.

The specific dimensions of the gymnasium should provide for a basketball court of 42 ft x 74 ft with a minimum safety space of 6 ft around the perimeter. An area of 54 ft x 90 ft (4,860 sq ft) would be adequate. The ceiling should be at least 22 ft high. This space is adequate for activities normally included in the elementary school program and will serve the community recreation program. The gymnasium will be of a larger size if the decision is made to use it as a multiple teaching facility and include a folding partition or vinyl–mesh curtains as part of the design.

Special floor markings. The elementary gymnasium floor may have additional markings beyond the traditional game markings (e.g., basketball). These other markings may include circles of various sizes and shapes. Floor markings facilitate a variety of activities; however, the number of markings should be limited to reduce confusion. The dominant lines should intersect the nondominant lines (e.g., game lines should intersect nongame lines). A nondominant line should be broken (2 in.) prior to intersecting the dominant line, and lines should be in different colors.

Buffer/safety zones. All playing areas must have buffer/safety zones separating them from walls, bleachers, and adjacent playing areas. The distance should be at least 10 ft (although the National Federation of State High Schools Association [NFHS, 2012] rules stipulate a minimum of 3 ft but preferably 10 ft, so the range would be 3 ft to 10 ft) from the sideline to the nearest obstruction (e.g., wall, bleacher, stage, or adjacent playing area). Facilities without buffer/safety zones around playing areas will expose participants and/or spectators to serious injury.

Auxiliary teaching stations. If a second indoor physical education teaching area is built, it should be either a swimming pool or an auxiliary instruction room, sometimes called a playroom. Swimming pools are discussed in this text in Chapter 13. The auxiliary teaching station is most practical when the main gymnasium cannot fulfill all of the school's needs for teaching stations.

At least 80 sq ft per primary pupil, with a minimum of 2,000 sq ft of space, is suggested for this unit. A ceiling height of 18 ft to 22 ft in the clear is preferred, although lower ceilings may be used. One wall should be free of obstruction to be used for target and ball games or throwing practice. A smooth masonry wall will provide an adequate rebounding surface. If included, windows should be of break-proof glass or be protected by a shield or grill and located high enough so as not to restrict activities.

The auxiliary unit should be planned to accommodate limited apparatus and tumbling activities, games of low organization, rhythmic activities, movement exploration, and other activities for the primary grades. Often a 30-ft circle for circle games is located at one end of this room, allowing for permanent or semipermanent equipment at the other end. The equipment could include items such as climbing ropes and poles, ladders, mats, stall bars, rings, large wooden boxes, horizontal bars, and peg boards. These should be located so they do not interfere with other activities or so they may be easily moved out of the way. A storage room for equipment and supplies should be included. A section of wall can be equipped with hangers for mat storage.

Electrical outlets are required for the use of sound equipment. This room will, for the most part, be used by the lower grades and should be accessible to those classrooms. If the area is to serve the after-school recreational program for pupils or community groups, toilet facilities should be accessible.

Use of playroom. The area should be suitable for preschool and for Grades K to 2 or K to 3 for fundamental movement activities including creative games and rhythms, relays, stunts, and climbing and hanging activities.

Size. The area should be a rectangle measuring approximately 50 ft x 40 ft, providing 2,000 sq ft of space.

Ceiling. The ceiling should be acoustically treated, 18 ft to 22 ft high (all beams and supports above the minimum height), with suitable fixtures attached to the beams to support hanging equipment.

Walls. Walls below 10 ft should be free from obstruction. A smooth concrete block sealed with epoxy paint works well. Above 10 ft, walls should also be free of obstruction but made of acoustic or slotted concrete block. A wall free from obstruction will provide practice areas for activities such as kicking, striking, and throwing and a space for the placement of targets and use of visual aids.

Floors. Hardwood maple or synthetic surfaces provide the best floor for general activity use. Both have advantages and disadvantages. The decision should be based on how the floor is to be used. The location of lines and the installation of equipment should be carefully considered.

Lighting. Fluorescent lighting should supply 35 to 50 foot-candles on the floor, and a switch should be installed at each door. Light fixtures should be guarded to prevent breakage.

Windows. If used at all, windows should be placed on only one side of the room to provide natural light. They should be covered with a protective screen. Windowsills should be 8 ft above the floor.

Electrical outlets. Double-service outlets should be installed on each wall.

Equipment storage area. At least 400 sq ft to 600 sq ft should be provided for storage. Cabinets and shelves should be installed. The equipment room should have a double door for wide equipment to be moved in or out easily. A telephone for emergency use should be placed in the equipment room.

Mirrors. Three full-length mirrors should be placed at one end of a wall, side by side, for visual analysis of movement.

Bulletin board. Corkboard should be hung on the wall near the entrance for posting materials and schedules.

Chalkboard. A chalkboard can be wall-mounted to facilitate teaching if this will not interfere with wall-rebounding activities. Otherwise, portable chalkboards can be used.

Drinking fountain. A drinking fountain should be placed on a wall in the corridor just outside the door to the playroom.

Speakers. Two matched speakers should be placed high on the wall or in the ceiling. A cordless headset with a microphone and sound system should be built into a wall.

Paint. Walls should be painted off-white or a pale color with epoxy paint. However, murals, accent colors, and designs can be used for aesthetics.

Other items. If the building is equipped with closed-circuit television, two outlets should be provided for the receiver. There should be a separate entrance for recreational use. The teaching station should be isolated from other parts of the building for evening functions.

Adapted teaching station. Local philosophy and state and federal laws vary as to the inclusion of students with disabilities in regular physical education classes. A separate adaptive teaching station would be an ideal setup; however, special programs for such students often have to be accommodated in the regular facilities. (See Chapter 4 for further details.)

Secondary Schools

A secondary school is defined as the following for this book: middle school (Grades 6 to 8), junior high school (Grades 7 and 8), high school (Grades 9 to 12).

Teaching stations. The type and number of indoor teaching stations for a secondary school depend on the number of students and the specific program of physical education and related activities. In all situations, a gymnasium is required. By determining the number of teaching stations essential for the formal program of instruction, planners will have a basis for calculating other needs. Computation of the minimum numerical requirement is achieved by the following formula:

Minimum number of teaching stations:
700 student x 5 periods per week =
3,500 teaching stations;
30 per class x 30 periods per week = 900;
3,500 ÷ 900 = 3.9 teaching stations

The fraction is rounded to the next highest number, making four teaching stations the minimum requirement. This number would also afford flexibility of class scheduling.

In computing teaching station requirements for the secondary school, do not set the desired class size so low as to require an impossible number of teachers and facilities or so high that effectiveness is impaired. An average class size of 30 with daily instruction is recommended. However, if the physical education classes meet only two periods per week, the total number of class periods per week in the formula must be adjusted accordingly.

The next step for planners is to determine the degree to which the number of teaching stations for the program of instruction will meet the needs for voluntary recreation, extramural and intramural activities, and interscholastic athletics for girls and boys, as well as the possible use of facilities by the community. The needs must be based upon the season of the year representing the greatest demand for facilities.

The following guide can be used to determine the number of teaching stations needed for activities other than the formal program of instruction in physical education:

Minimum number of teaching stations, or fractions thereof, needed for interscholastic team practice at peak load, plus minimum number of teaching stations, or fractions thereof, needed for intramural and extramural activities, plus minimum number of teaching stations, or fractions thereof, needed for student recreation, plus minimum number of teaching stations, or fractions thereof, needed for community recreation, equals the total number of teaching stations needed for any specific after-school period.

To illustrate, assume a school has two interscholastic squads, an intramural program, a voluntary recreation group, and no community recreational use of facilities immediately after school during a specific season. The total needs are as follows:

Required teaching stations equals:
2 interscholastic
+ 1 intramural
+ 1 voluntary recreation
= 4 stations

The need for four teaching stations for the after-school program must then be compared to the number necessary for the formal program of instruction in physical educa-

tion. If the after-school needs are in excess of those for the regular periods of instruction, additional teaching stations should be provided. Careful administrative scheduling can result in maximal use of facilities.

Variety of teaching stations. A wide variety of teaching stations is possible depending on the number of different activities that would appropriately be included in the physical education program. Among the types of indoor teaching stations that might be included are gymnasiums, rhythm rooms, rooms for gymnastics, adapted physical education rooms, wrestling rooms, classrooms, swimming pools, archery ranges, rifle ranges, and racquetball courts.

The problem for some schools is not the lack of an adequate number of teaching stations, but rather the lack of facilities to accommodate the desired variety of activities. For a secondary school with 360 students, a divisible gymnasium will create an adequate number of teaching stations for the program of instruction in physical education but may not meet the peak load requirement for after-school activities.

The facility must be planned and designed to serve all program needs as adequately as possible. Whenever a school's teaching requirements are such that a basic gymnasium is inadequate, planners should consider special purpose stations such as auxiliary physical education teaching stations, a natatorium, or a dance studio.

Secondary school gymnasium. The building or portion of the school that houses the gymnasium should be easily accessible from classrooms, parking areas, and the outdoor activity area. This also makes possible the use of the facility after school hours or during weekends or holidays without having to open other sections of the school.

Size and layout. For general purposes, allow a minimum of 125 sq ft of usable activity space for each individual in a physical education class at peak load. The space requirements and dimensions of a gymnasium floor are significantly influenced by the official rules governing court games, particularly interscholastic basketball and the extent of spectator seating. The minimum dimensions required of a gymnasium for basketball, however, should be expanded, if necessary, to accommodate other activities. In some instances, an entire gymnasium is not required for an activity. Folding, soundproof partitions can be used to divide the area and provide two teaching stations.

Walls and ceilings. The walls of the gymnasium should be of a material that is resistant to hard use, at least to door height. The finish should be nonmarking and have a smooth, nonabrasive surface. All corners below door height should be rounded, and there should be no projections into playing areas. Lower portions (10 ft) of the walls should be finished with materials that can be easily cleaned without destroying the finish. Epoxy paint on cement block makes a durable finish.

Secondary school gymnasium

The ceiling should be 24 ft to the low side of beams or supports with fixtures attached to the beams to support hanging equipment. High ceilings are expensive, and a natural method for cutting construction costs is to minimize ceiling height. If this is in the area for basketball, volleyball, gymnastics, badminton, or tennis, it can be a critical error. However, in an auxiliary gym used for wrestling, dance, combative activities, weight lifting, or table games, a 15-ft to 18-ft ceiling is acceptable.

All ceilings should be light in color, and if support beams are below the ceiling, they normally are painted the same color as the ceiling or background. Contrasting colors have been used effectively; however, such color contrast may make it difficult to follow the flight of an object.

Acoustical treatment of ceilings and walls is important where teaching is to take place. To obtain the best results, at least two adjacent surfaces should be treated. Many types of acoustical treatment are available. However, avoid those that will chip or break when hit with a ball.

Lighting. There are many types of lighting systems that will produce the 35 to 50 foot-candles needed for a good teaching and spectator area. For television, the foot-candles should be closer to 200 foot-candles, and that requires more sophisticated lighting systems. When selecting a lighting system, compare initial costs, annual replacement costs, and operational or electrical expenses. Some are less expensive to install but very expensive to maintain or operate.

Windows. Windows should generally be avoided. When located to take advantage of the sun for solar heat, the glare may cause serious problems. When windows are on the north side, there is less glare, but the loss of heat may be significant. Vandalism is another disadvantage.

Wall padding. Generally, at the end of the basketball competition courts, padding is attached to the wall to protect the students from injury when they run into the wall. This is true even when a recommended 10-ft safety zone (i.e., the standard for a safety zone for a basketball court is 3 ft on the sidelines and end lines according to the NFHS, 2012 basketball rule book) is provided at the end of the court. These pads can be permanently installed or made

to be portable. They are generally 6 ft tall and 16 ft to 24 ft wide and attached approximately 6 in. off the floor. The pads can be designed with almost any graphic desired by the school in a wide variety of colors.

Fixed equipment. If suspended equipment is planned, provision for its attachment should be made before the ceiling is installed. Basketball backstops will need special care in their installation to ensure rigidity and safety. All basketball backstops should be attached to ceilings or walls and swing-up or fold-up models should be used where the backstops might interfere with other activities. In addition to the main court basketball backstops, provision should be made for other backstops on clear sidewalls. Hinged rims that collapse when grabbed are recommended for baskets used for recreational basketball play.

In the interest of safety, suspension apparatus such as bars, rings, and climbing poles and ropes should be placed to allow sufficient clearance from basketball backstops and walls. If wall apparatus is desired in the gymnasium, a strip of metal or hardwood firmly attached to the wall at the proper height is recommended. Wherever necessary, floor plates should be installed for fastening movable equipment such as horizontal bars and volleyball standards. If mats are to be hung in the gymnasium, appropriate hangers placed above head level to avoid any injury must be provided. Rubber-tired mat trucks, which may be wheeled into a storage room, are recommended. For safety reasons, padding should be installed on all walls behind baskets.

Spectator seating. The extent of the demand for spectator seating depends upon each school and the community it serves. Modern design uses power-driven folding or rollaway bleachers (see Chapter 12 for greater detail), which require little permanent space. If possible, the outer surface of folding bleachers should create a flat, wall-like surface so it may be used for ball rebounding.

The width of each seating space should not be less than 18 in. Rollaway bleachers most commonly allow 22-in. depths for seats. The number of rows available in rollaway bleachers varies, with 23 rows being the maximum for standard equipment. In some instances, bleachers with 30 rows can be obtained by special order. Planners should investigate local and state codes.

Balconies can be used to increase the total seating capacity beyond the maximum permitted at floor level. The space at both levels should be considered as activity areas when the bleachers are closed. It may be desirable, in some instances, to provide less than maximum seating at floor level so a balcony will be wide enough to serve as a teaching station for specific activities. Balcony bleachers can be installed to telescope from the back to the front so that they stand erect in the closed position, creating a divider wall at the edge of the balcony. This arrangement affords partial isolation of the teaching station and enhances the safety of participants.

Traffic controls. Good traffic control should permit the efficient movement of students to and from the gymnasium, locker rooms, and other related service areas. All traffic arrangements for spectators should provide direct movement to and from bleachers with minimal foot traffic on gymnasium floors. Spectators should have access to drinking fountains, refreshment counters, and toilets without crossing the gymnasium floor. Steep, high stairways should be avoided. Ramps with nonslip surfaces might be substituted in appropriate places. Local and state building codes and standards of the National Fire Protection Association should be consulted.

Foyers. Where finances and space will allow, foyers should be placed so they will serve as entries to gymnasiums and will guide spectators as directly as possible to seating areas. Toilet facilities for men and women, ticket sales windows, ticket collection arrangements, checkrooms, public telephones, a refreshment-dispensing room with counter, and lockable display case should be provided, opening directly to the foyer.

Spectator restrooms. All athletic events that attract spectators require restroom facilities. Restrooms should be designed for proper light, ventilation, and sanitary care. State health codes will influence the number and location of restrooms.

Concessions. Concessions have come to be considered a necessary service for public gatherings. Appropriate space and distribution as well as adequate fixtures for concessions stands within the field house should be planned. Because plumbing and electrical services are already available in the field house, the concessions stand might be located as a part of or adjacent to the field house. The concessions area will include a double sink, garbage disposal, electric range, microwave, refrigerator, ice maker, popcorn maker, freezer, plenty of counter space, and signage.

Other factors. Provisions should be made for installing electric scoreboards, a central sound and public-address system, picture projectors, radio and television equipment, high-fidelity equipment, and cleaning machines. Floor outlets for scoreboards and public-address systems should be located adjacent to the scoring table. Wall outlets should be installed near cupped eyes to permit special lighting as needed. Controls for gymnasium lighting should be conveniently located, recessed, and keyed.

Drinking fountains and cuspidors should be accessible without causing a traffic or safety problem. It may be desirable to provide a drained catch basin, grilled flush with the floor, to care for splash and overflow.

Cupped eyes can be installed in all walls at approximately 15-ft height and 10-ft intervals for decorating convenience. They may also be used for attaching nets and other equipment to walls at appropriate heights. Bulletin boards and chalkboards should be provided where needed. If wall space is available, such boards may be provided for

Auxiliary gymnasium

each teaching station. Three full-length mirrors should be placed at one end of a wall, side by side, for visual analysis of movement.

The auxiliary gymnasium. Depending on the demands placed on a facility for classes, after-school athletics, intramurals, and student and faculty recreation, more than one gymnasium may be necessary. Careful program scheduling will determine what is best in each situation. However, most schools need at least one auxiliary gym. Room dimensions should be based on the anticipated uses with special attention to the need to accommodate standard-sized wrestling mats.

The other type of auxiliary gymnasium closely resembles the main gym, except there is little or no need for spectator seating and the floor dimensions may be smaller. A 75 ft x 90 ft gym will house two volleyball courts, three badminton courts, three one-wall handball courts, and space for some gymnastic equipment.

The auxiliary gyms can serve a variety of other activities in the instructional, intramural, recreational, or interscholastic program, which cannot all be accommodated after school in the main gymnasium. Some auxiliary gyms are large enough to be divided into two teaching stations. The characteristics of these facilities are similar to those in the gymnasium. A less expensive type may have a ceiling as low as 18 ft. Activities such as wrestling, tumbling, calisthenics, self-defense, and fencing may be conducted in such a room.

Adapted physical education area. Federal legislation requires that special considerations be made for persons with disabilities. Schools must provide programs that meet their special needs. The adaptive area, therefore, becomes essential (see Chapter 4 for additional information).

Gymnastics area for the gymnasium. With a detailed plan, the equipment layout for gymnastics and attachment hardware for the floors, walls, and ceilings can be included in the original design and construction. The manufacturers of gymnastics equipment will supply details for attaching their equipment as well as suggestions for floor plans or layout for the apparatus with proper safety areas. Preplan-

Gymnastics room

ning ensures not only proper installation but also savings on the cost of doing the work at a later date.

Storage of gymnastics equipment requires special attention, for example, a room adjacent to the gym with a roll-up door. Equipment left out or stored around the edge of the gym is a safety hazard and will shorten the life of the equipment. Mat storage requires either a mat truck or a hydraulic lift to ceiling.

The use of light folding mats, however, will alleviate some of the storage problems. Climbing ropes should be attached to a height of 24 ft and drop to about 3 ft above the floor. Apparatus may be attached to the exposed beams. If the ceiling is placed below the structural members, the locations of suspended equipment should be planned and eyebolts provided during construction.

Ropes should be placed 5 ft apart, allowing one for each five students in class. The rings should be at least 5 ft from the walls. End walls at least 35 ft from the point of attachment will afford safety for the participants. Traveling rings are supported from a height of 18 ft to 26 ft and are located 7 ft apart along a continuous line. Lines should be provided for drawing ropes and rings not in use to the overhead so as not to interfere with other activities.

High bars require both floor and wall or ceiling attachments. Adjustable bars for class instruction can be arranged in a linear series. Bars vary from 6 ft to 7 ft in length and require 12 ft of unobstructed space extending perpendicular to their long axis. Bars for interscholastic competition are commonly located as individual units.

Freestanding gymnastics area. Rarely will a freestanding gymnastics area be found in a secondary school. These facilities are either privately owned or part of a nonprofit agency (e.g., YMCA, YWCA, or Boys & Girls Club).

The freestanding facility (Figure 22.1) will include

- an entrance area;
- lobby space;
- a small pro shop;
- concessions;

- public restrooms;
- a day care area;
- a balcony for spectator seating for 300;
- a competition/practice area—boys: runway for vaulting with a landing pit, high bar (2) area with a landing pit, pummel horse area, parallel bars (2) area, rings area, and floor exercise area shared with girls; girls: runway for vaulting with a landing pit, uneven bars (2) area with landing pit, balance beams (3) area with a landing pit, and a shared floor exercise area;
- a trampoline area with trampoline flush with floor;
- office space; and
- a large storage area at least 600 sq ft with a ceiling height of 10 ft and a roll-up door.

Strength and cardiorespiratory area. The current trend in physical education facilities is the addition of a strength and cardiorespiratory area. Student-athletes would use this area for physical education classes before and after school, and community programming after school hours and on the weekends. The details regarding this space can be found in Chapter 17.

Health Instruction

The purpose of health instruction is to provide health information and experiences that will establish attitudes and practices conducive to the conservation, protection, and promotion of individual, community, and world health. This section of the chapter is concerned with the facilities essential to the conduct of health classes, including first aid and safety instruction.

Elementary School

For the elementary school, the general principle of the self-contained classroom is accepted. However, for maximal opportunity for health and safety instruction, it is important to have drinking fountains and hand-washing and grooming facilities and to have accessibility to toilets for the exclusive use of each room in the primary grades. In classrooms for intermediate grades, hand lavatories should be provided. In addition to the central storage space for equipment common to all rooms, each room should have storage space for health teaching aids especially suited to that class. A mobile laboratory table or a resource room equipped with facilities for demonstrations in health and science should be available.

Secondary School

The basic space allotment for the health instruction facilities in the secondary school should be in harmony with generally accepted standards for schoolroom size. However, due to the nature of activities involved in health and safety instructional programs, it is recommended that the

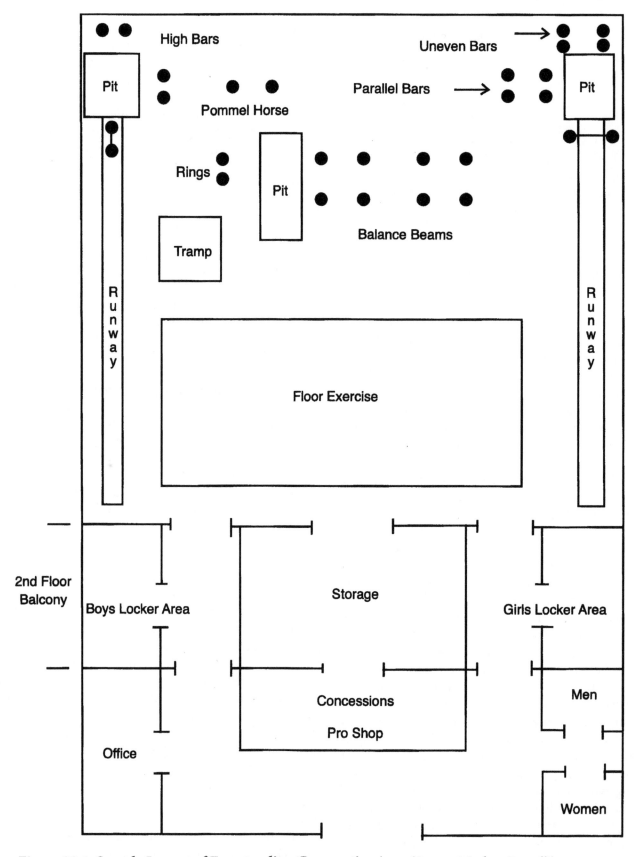

Figure 22.1. **Sample Layout of Freestanding Gymnastics Area** (*Source:* Meghan Rosselli)

space allowed for such instruction be increased approximately 35% above requirements for the regular classroom. This will result in a space allotment of 35 sq ft per student, including storage space.

The space allotment should be sufficient to allow for activities such as vision and hearing screening, first aid and safety instruction, and practical demonstrations and for flexible teacher location. In addition to the conventional teacher's desk, provision should be made for laboratory demonstrations.

This indicates the need for a laboratory demonstration table, which will provide space and facilities for demonstrations. Thus, provisions should be made for water, gas, and electricity as well as storage space for heating devices, test tubes, flasks, beakers, and other essential equipment. The diversity of teaching procedures requires that regular classroom arrangements be used at some times, but at other times floor space must be available for practical instruction such as practice in artificial respiration, splinting, and emergency transportation.

The suggested laboratory method of teaching will require adequate storage space as well as display areas for charts, mannequins, models, and equipment. First aid equipment such as blankets, bandages, splints, and stretchers will also be needed. For instruction in home nursing, equipment such as incubators, rollaway beds, pans, containers, and bedding will be required.

A large amount of display space should be available for the great variety of educational exhibits, literature, and pupil projects inherent in the health education program. This can be provided by allowing liberal space for tables and shelves and by using all available wall space for bulletin boards and tack boards.

The health instruction laboratory should provide for optimal use of additional audiovisual devices such as still pictures, slides, motion pictures, radio, and television. This will necessitate a liberal allowance of appropriately located electrical outlets, shades, or curtains that will reduce the outside light and a screen that may be mounted above the chalkboard behind the laboratory desk.

A convenient access between the health instruction laboratory and the health service suite is desirable so that each may augment the total health program. For example, when home nursing classes are meeting in the health instruction laboratory, there will be times when it is desirable to have free but supervised access to both facilities. Similarly, when there is an occasion to have a large number of people using the health service suite, it may be desirable to have access to the health instruction laboratory for seating or other purposes. In some instances, it may be desirable to consider locating the health instruction laboratory near the science laboratories to facilitate joint use of equipment and supplies. In other instances, location in the area of the physical education facilities may be desirable.

The secondary school health instruction laboratory should be an example of the ideal classroom environment with special concern for color of walls, lighting, ventilation, temperature and humidity control, order, and cleanliness.

Joint planning of school health facilities with public health officials and other community groups who might need access to such facilities is also desirable to strengthening the total community health program. Such arrangements can strengthen the program of all who are concerned with health by providing for dual use of such facilities without duplication and with minimal expense.

The following is a checklist of needs for health instruction facilities:

- space for 35 sq ft per pupil, maximum of 30 pupils;
- flexible teacher location;
- provision for various teaching methods, including laboratory demonstration;
- flexibility of seating;
- hot and cold running water and gas outlet;
- educational exhibit space;
- storage space;
- provision for using audiovisual devices (electrical outlets, window shades, screens);
- access to health service unit exemplary environmental features;
- adequate hand-washing facilities, drinking fountains, and toilets;
- air-conditioning;
- accessibility for persons with disabilities; and
- ability to be used jointly for community use.

Health Services

Health services contribute to the school program by (a) facilitating learning, (b) encouraging pupils to obtain needed medical or dental treatment, (c) adapting school programs to individual pupil needs, (d) maintaining a healthful school environment, and (e) increasing pupils' understanding of health and health problems. Following the principle that program determines facilities, plans would include accommodations for

- appraising the health status of pupils and school personnel;
- counseling pupils, parents, and others concerning appraisal findings;
- encouraging the correction of remediable defects and the proper adjustment of those identified as not remediable;
- assisting in the identification and education of pupils with disabilities;
- helping to prevent and control disease;
- providing emergency service for injury or sudden illness; and

- maintaining a cumulative combined health and accident file for each student.

Health service personnel not only are charged with the responsibility for developing policies and procedures, but also should be consulted in planning programs and facilities. Policies and procedures are essential for attaining program objectives through the proper use of facilities and the protection of school populations under adverse or disaster conditions.

Health suite. Whether in a small rural or a large urban school building, the health service suite will be used for a variety of activities. It may be the center for emergency care of injuries or sickness and health appraisals by nurses, physicians, dentists or dental hygienists, and psychiatrists or psychologists. Various systematized screening tests, such as vision and hearing, may be conducted in this area.

The health suite is the logical place for conferences concerning a pupil's health problems involving the parent, teacher, doctor, nurse, and physical educator. A part of the suite should be used as a dressing room and another section should serve as a waiting room. Some space should be set aside for the isolation of a pupil when the situation warrants, and accommodations should be provided for pupils on a prescribed rest schedule. The suite will also need to provide space for the health service personnel, plus the necessary space for records and equipment.

The common concerns of school health service personnel and guidance personnel suggest the need for a close, cooperative working relationship. This would indicate the desirability of locating the units in close proximity to each other and the possibility of using a common waiting room.

The school health suite may, in some instances, also serve the community. Thus, the health suite and the adjacent health instruction area may be for well-child conferences and other preschool health activities. They may accommodate classes for expectant mothers and other adult education activities. In those situations where the building and grounds are used for recreation purposes, the unit may serve as an emergency care and first aid station for those participating in the recreation program.

Because a health service suite is located within the school does not mean that programs for nonschool groups will be administered or manned by school personnel. Usually, these community health activities will be under the direct supervision of the official health agency. If community usage of the health service suite is expected, then those who will provide the service should be involved in the planning.

Location. In locating a health service suite, consider the variety of activities that will be carried on therein and to conditions that will permit those functions to be carried on conveniently and efficiently. The following are factors to consider in the location of a health service suite:

- It should be located along a corridor near a main entrance to the building so that it may be completely isolated from the remainder of the building yet remain conveniently accessible from all parts of the building.
- It should be located on the first or ground floor.
- The location should be in close proximity to the administrative suite. In situations where full-time health service personnel are not contemplated, direct access should be provided between the area and the administrative office, the teacher's lounge, or an adjacent classroom. In the secondary school, advantages will accrue from locating the health classroom and the service suite so that there is convenient access between the two areas. This is especially true when school health facilities are used for community health services.
- The location and acoustical treatment should be such that corridor and outside noises are kept to a minimum.
- A maximal amount of natural light should be available.

Rooms. All purposes for which the health service suite is designed may be carried out in one large unit, which may be subdivided into (a) waiting room, (b) examining room, (c) resting rooms, (d) toilet rooms, (e) counseling room, (f) dental health room, (f) isolation room, 8) special screening areas (e.g., vision and hearing), and (g) office area for health service personnel and records. Depending upon the size of the school and its health policies, various combinations of the above spaces may be planned without affecting the efficiency of the services. For example, in smaller elementary schools, all services may provided in one room if proper screening is used and the administrative and health service suite are served by a common waiting room.

In larger schools, and especially in high schools, division of the unit into separate rooms is desirable. Thought should be given to the type of wall construction that provides for rearrangement of space allocation because change in policies and school population will affect the nature and extent of health services. The remodel of old buildings requires the same standards that apply to new structures. Guidelines based on accepted standards are recommended in the next section.

Waiting room. Schools with 10 or more classrooms or enrollments of 300 or more pupils should provide a waiting room, possibly in combination with guidance and/or administrative offices. It should be directly accessible to the corridor and the examining room. The waiting room should be separated from adjacent rooms by a full-height partition.

The decorations and furnishings should be designed to create a bright and cheerful atmosphere. The size depends upon enrollment and established health policies of the school (see Table 22.1).

Examining room. Schools consisting of six or more classrooms or an enrollment of 180 or more pupils should include an examining room in the health suite. It should be directly connected with bathrooms and the waiting room and should have access to toilets, the dental space, and any offices that are provided.

The location should provide for natural light and ventilation. The size and arrangement should be such that an uninterrupted distance of 20 ft is available for vision testing. The room should be acoustically treated. If the examining room is to serve as a resting room (in small schools) screened cot areas should be provided. The space should be ample for proper arrangement or storage of the following equipment:

- desk, chair, computer, and possibly a typewriter;
- filing cabinets;
- platform scale with stadiometer;
- vision testing equipment;
- movable spotlight;
- blankets and linens;
- folding screen;
- sterilizer and instrument table;
- cot or couch;
- cabinet for first aid supplies;
- cup and towel dispensers;
- wastebasket and foot-operated disposal can;
- full-length mirror; and
- audiometric testing devices.

The size of the examining room will be determined by enrollment, the types of activities to be conducted, and the extent of use by medical and other health personnel (see Table 22.1).

Resting rooms. Resting rooms are essential in all schools. They should be directly connected with the examining room and toilets or be accessible to them from a restricted hallway. Separate resting rooms should be provided for each sex. A screened cot space may be a necessary arrangement in smaller schools. The location should provide natural light and ventilation and a quiet atmosphere. If no full-time health service personnel are available, the location should allow for supervision of the area to be conveniently provided from the administrative office or an adjacent classroom. Adequate space should be provided for cots (see Figure 22.2), bedside stands, wastebaskets, and blanket and linen storage.

Restrooms. A toilet room with stool and lavatory should be directly connected, or be accessible by a restricted hallway, to the resting rooms in all schools with 10 or more classrooms or with an enrollment of 300 or more pupils. In smaller schools where the resting rooms are a part of the examining room or other space, convenient toilet facilities should be provided. A restroom with a minimum of 48 sq ft should be provided for each sex (see Figure 22.3).

Storage closets. Storage space, opening off each resting room, should be provided for linens, blankets, pillows, and so forth. In the smaller schools without separate resting rooms, such storage should be provided for in the examining room. A ventilated cloak closet should be provided

Table 22.1

Recommended Square Foot Sizes of Health Service Facilities

ENROLLMENT	200-300	301-500	501-700	701-900	901-1100	1101-1300
Waiting Room	80	80	100	100	100	120
*Examining Room	200	200	200	240	240	240
**Rest room (total area for boys and girls)	200	200	200	240	240	240

Toilets.......... 48 square feet total area (provide one for girls and one for boys)

OPTIONAL AREAS

Dental Clinic	100 square feet for all schools
Office Space	80 square feet for each office provided
Eye examination	120 square feet minimum for all schools

* Examining room areas include 6 square feet for clothes closet and 24 square feet for storage closets.

** For determining the number of cots, allow one cot per 100 pupils up to 400 pupils, and one cot per 200 pupils above 400. Round out fractions to nearest whole number. Allow 50 square feet of floor space for each of the first two cots and 40 square feet for each additional cot.

*** In schools enrolling 901 to 1,100, a three-cot rest room is suggested for boys and a four-cot rest room for girls, and in 1,101 to 1,300-pupil schools, a three-cot rest room is suggested for boys and a five-cot rest room for girls.
Note: For larger schools, add multiples of the above areas to obtain total needs.
\# State Department of Education, *School Planning Manual*, school Health Service Section, Vol. 37. November, 1954, Richmond Va.

for school health personnel. If built-in storage facilities are not feasible, space should be allowed for movable storage cabinets.

Isolation room. An isolation room as an integral part of the health service suite is desirable to ensure privacy when required. It should be directly connected with the examining room, but apart from the resting rooms. A space for one cot and the necessary circulation area is sufficient in most instances.

Vision and hearing screening areas. Such areas should be included as a part of the examining room. An uninterrupted distance of 20 ft should be provided for vision

testing. Audiometric testing will require an acoustically treated room.

Offices. The provision of office space for health service personnel will depend upon the time they spend in the school. If office space is provided it should be connected with the waiting room, the examining room, and, if possible, the corridor. The minimum recommended space for two people is 80 sq ft. Health and accident reports should be maintained.

Counseling room. Although such space will not be in constant use, a room where the doctor, nurse, teacher, and parent can discuss a pupil's health is an important unit of the total health facility. Space large enough to accommo-

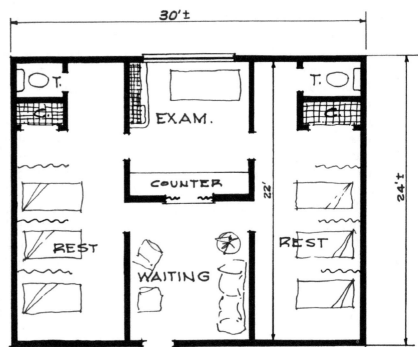

Figure 22.2. Secondary School Health Suite (*Source:* Meghan Rosselli)

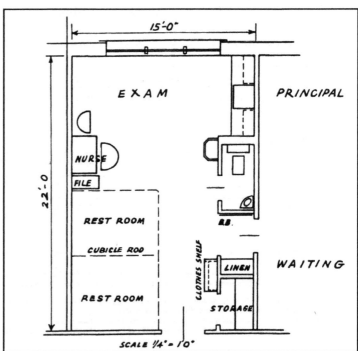

Figure 22.3. Health Suite for Elementary School With Seven Classrooms (*Source:* Meghan Rosselli)

date a small table and four or five chairs is adequate. It may be used as office space for part-time health service personnel.

General suggestions. The entire suite should present an informal and pleasant atmosphere. Flooring material should be nonabsorbent, easily cleaned, and light in color. Lavatories used by personnel functioning within the examining room should be operable by the wrist, knee, or foot.

Driver Education Areas and Facilities

The program of driver education is generally accepted as a responsibility of the school and, more specifically, as a function of health and safety and physical education departments. The guidelines outlined below are based on approved standards and national recommendations.

Indoor Facilities

For the indoor program, there should be a classroom, a psychophysical laboratory with testing devices, a simulator laboratory, and an office.

Location. All indoor facilities should be on the first floor of the building, near the garage or parking space for the dual-control cars, and near the driving range if one is used.

Classroom size. The recommended procedure is to combine the classroom with the laboratory for a combination room of 30 ft x 40 ft. Where separate rooms are used, the classroom should be of standard size.

Furniture and equipment. In addition to the standard classroom facilities and equipment, such as chalkboard, bulletin board, desk, and chairs, the driver education classroom should provide facilities for

- a DVD player and monitor;
- bookcases and storage cabinets for videotapes, flip charts, testing equipment, models, and so on;
- a demonstration table; and
- demonstration equipment, including magnetic traffic board, working models, flannel boards, model signs, and signals.

Driver Education Laboratory

The laboratory contains equipment needed to test the student's physical, mental, and emotional qualifications required for safe and skillful driving.

Size. When the combined room is not used, the laboratory should be at least 24 ft x 30 ft.

Furniture and equipment. The needed furniture and equipment will include a demonstration table, chairs, worktables, and spaces to accommodate equipment for testing visual acuity, depth perception, color vision, field of vision, reaction time, steadiness, night vision, and so forth.

Simulator Laboratory

Driver education simulators are accepted as a means of providing the preliminary steps to behind-the-wheel instruction. Because of the nature of the simulator units, facilities for them should be considered as permanent installations, preferably in a separate classroom.

Size. The size of the simulator laboratory will depend on the number of simulator cars to be installed. A typical eight-car installation will accommodate 450 to 500 students per year and a 16-car installation will accommodate 960 to 1,000. The room size for eight cars should be 24 ft x 33 ft and for 16 cars it should be 30 ft x 40 ft.

Furniture and equipment. The room should be clear of obstructions that might interfere with the projector beam and should be provided with the regular complement of chalkboard, bulletin board, tack board, magnetic board, and so on.

Layout. The cars are arranged in a semicircular fashion with the first row a minimum of 8 ft, preferably 10 ft to 12 ft, from the screen and with the outside cars not exceeding an angle of 30° from the screen. The first row should have the lesser number of cars. A minimum of 24 in. should be allowed between the rows with a 30-in. aisle down each side of the room. Aisle spaces must comply with state safety codes. The projector should be located in the center at the extreme rear of the room, and a 6 ft x 8 ft screen should be placed in the front of the room. Manufacturers' specifications for electrical requirements should be followed. Ordinarily, the standard 120-V, 60-cycle alternating current is required. It should be supplied through a double outlet located in the vicinity of the recording unit.

Lighting. Soft white fluorescent light tubes recessed in the ceiling with semitranslucent shields to provide 100 foot-candles of light at desk height should be installed.

Color. Pastel colors should be used. The woodwork and finishing should be compatible with color used on the walls. A reflection factor of 80% is needed for the ceiling and 60% for the walls. The furniture should have a nonglare finish.

Heating and ventilation. Heating and ventilation should conform to standards required throughout the entire school system.

Driving Area

Behind-the-wheel instruction provides the skills necessary for safe and efficient driving.

Types. An on-street driving area is recommended for schools where traffic congestion is not a problem. First, driving maneuvers should be conducted in locations such as school driveways where there is no traffic. As ability develops, students get experience driving in situations that approximate normal driving conditions and then, finally, in actual normal traffic situations. Blocked-off streets are sometimes used when street traffic is too heavy and school driveways are not available to teach the first driving maneuvers. Arrangements should be made with the residents of the area and with police officials. Because advanced driving skills are taught where other traffic is involved, streets should not be blocked off for an undue length of time. An off-street driving range is recommended where land is available. Ranges should be laid out to simulate most physical situations associated with driving, such as traffic signs, signals, and other control devices; parallel and angle parking; upgrade and downgrade situations; and simulated emergency situations. Space should allow for needed skill-test maneuvers. Different types of road surfaces should be provided. If night classes are conducted, the area should be lighted. The size of the driving range should be no smaller than 350 ft x 450 ft.

The multiple-car driving range (see Figure 22.4) has the advantage of accommodating several cars simultaneously under the supervision of one teacher, thus reducing the per-pupil cost. With this type of range, communication between the instructor and students is accomplished by means of a radio or public-address system.

Recommended equipment and facilities. The following are recommended to simulate actual driving conditions:

- curbs for parking practice;
- intersections for various turning maneuvers;
- gravel area for driving and turning maneuvers;
- streets that are marked properly;
- streets that are both wide and narrow;
- all signs—traffic, control signals, stop, warning, yield the right-of-way, regulatory, guide, and information;
- upgrade and downgrade roadways;
- simulated road surfaces—concrete, asphalt, and gravel;
- muddy surface for emergency situations;
- signboards found on normal roads; and
- stanchions, guide-on, and the like for maneuvers.

Points to remember
- Determine the needs of the student and the objectives of the program.
- Provide as many realistic situations as possible.
- Design the driver-training area equal to the best facilities available.

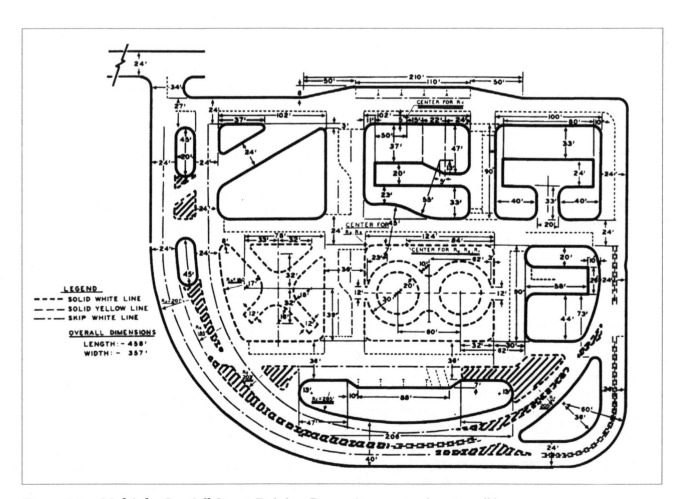

Figure 22.4. **Multiple-Car Off-Street Driving Range** (*Source:* Meghan Rosselli)

23 Designing Combative Areas for Boxing and Martial Arts

Jason Winkle, *Indiana State University*
Thomas H. Sawyer, *Indiana State University*

Boxing

This section provides readers with information that will allow them to use existing space in the physical education area to design a multipurpose boxing facility that meets existing standards for safety and use of proper equipment for boxing.

United States Amateur Boxing Inc.

United States Amateur Boxing Inc. (USA Boxing) is the controlling organization for amateur boxing in the United States. Rules, legislation, and safety regulations are promulgated by USA Boxing and its membership to provide a healthy, safe, and sportsmanlike environment in which young men and women can participate in the sport of boxing throughout the United States.

National Collegiate Boxing Association

The National Collegiate Boxing Association (NCBA) is an umbrella organization under the jurisdiction of USA Boxing that was organized to provide an opportunity for college students to participate in the sport of amateur boxing against other students enrolled in fully accredited institutions of higher learning. Only properly registered students (full time) from institutions registered with the NCBA may participate in this program, and they may only compete against other full-time college students who meet the necessary registration requirements. The NCBA is not a member of the NCAA, but rather is an organization of club teams authorized by their respective institutions and registered with the NCBA and USA Boxing. Numbers of registrations vary from year to year, but there are approximately 30 member clubs (institutions) and over 300 registered participants covering four geographic regions (Northeast, Southeast, Midwest, and Far West). The NCBA conducts educational clinics and annual regional and national championship competitions.

Why a Boxing Facility?

Some may question using physical education space for developing a boxing facility because of boxing's reputation as a violent and potentially dangerous sport. Some of those same people would not question using either outdoor or indoor space for an activity such as football, which is statistically more dangerous than boxing. One might argue that boxing (amateur as opposed to professional) is one of the safest of the contact sports, but that is not the purpose of this discussion. Rather, it is to describe how a facility can be organized for learning and practicing boxing fundamentals and techniques that are ideal for developing physical fitness and self-confidence.

Boxing is now widely accepted and used as a fitness activity. It is universally known that boxers are among the best conditioned athletes and that boxing fitness activities (punching drills, bag punching, plyometrics, associated calisthenics, rope skipping, shadow boxing, distance running, and interval training) are excellent conditioners that reduce stress and are fun at the same time. Add to this the potential for learning the fundamentals of self-defense, and you have an activity that is hard to beat.

Considerable media attention has been recently giv-

Practice boxing ring

en to "white-collar" boxing by young professionals, both male and female. Many of these young men and women have traded their jogging and racquet sport shoes for boxing shoes! It is a relatively inexpensive alternative to many other activities and not only develops aerobic capacity but also can increase strength and muscular endurance. It is also a great opportunity for coed fitness training. Conditioning drills and noncontact offensive and defensive fundamentals can be practiced without regard to gender in an environment that can be designed to push participants to reach beyond their previously self-imposed physical limits. Finally, a properly designed boxing area can be used as a multipurpose facility. If it is set up correctly, a boxing space can easily be turned into an aerobics area, a wrestling or gymnastics room, a practice area for cheerleaders, or a conditioning space for just about any team or activity you can name.

How Much Space Is Needed?

If the space is to be used for boxing only, any space that is 10 ft x 10 ft or larger will suffice. All that is necessary is the proper floor covering, heavy and light striking bags, calisthenic stations, and a small equipment storage area. This area could be categorized as an "all-purpose boxing room" and makes use of almost any available space. The size of a boxing exercise/training area can vary from a large field house, armory, or gymnasium, to a small classroom or similar space suitable for small-group instruction. All that is required for boxing drills/practice is unobstructed space, adequate ventilation, and sufficient lighting.

If a boxing ring is available, or if you desire a multipurpose room, then additional space will be necessary. A space 20 ft x 20 ft is required for the ring setup. A good way to organize such a room would be to divide it into the ring area, a striking bag area (heavy and light), and an exercise section. A 30 ft x 50 ft space would be sufficient for this type of room. If you are converting an old swimming pool space (e.g., 20 yd x 10 yd), you should have all the space you need for an excellent boxing/multipurpose exercise room.

Converting existing space such as a swimming pool into a boxing room is worth considering. Many older instructional pools that no longer meet specifications as competitive venues occupy more than enough space for an excellent boxing facility.

Older pools of this type are usually at least 75 ft x 25 ft (1,875 sq ft) with considerable additional space allotted for the pool deck areas. All that is needed is a way to construct a wooden floor over the surface that will support the weight of 25 to 40 participants (100 lb per square inch). The buildings and grounds staff of a school along with a local architect can plan and construct this project for less than $10,000 (see Figure 23.1).

Materials necessary (other than labor) include

- 2 in. x 4 in. studs,
- 2 in. x 8 in. floor joists,
- wooden bridging pieces,
- ½-in. plywood and ⅝-in. particle board (installed on top of the floor joists), and
- Ensolite® matting to cover the exercise area.

What Equipment Is Necessary?

Floor. If a ring is used, or if contact drills are used, the ring or floor area must be covered with a 1-in. layer of Ensolite® AAC or AL closed-cell foam rubber (or a chemical equivalent). The ring padding must be covered with canvas or a similar material and be tightly stretched and laced securely in place (USA Boxing, 2012). If no contact drills are anticipated, the floor area could be any type of surface, but wood is preferable.

Gloves. Boxing gloves used for sparring or live contact drills must meet the specifications required by USA Boxing. *USA Boxing Official Rules* (USA Boxing, 2012) requires that the padding inside the gloves be "½-inch Latex, ¾-inch PVC (Husitonic), ⅜-inch PVC (Rubitex-313 V) and ⅜-inch Polyfoam or other products that meet the severity (force of blow) index" (p. 115). For instructional purposes, 16 oz thumbless or attached thumb gloves are recommended. Remember that the purpose of the gloves (in contact work) is to diminish the impact of a blow and to protect the hands.

Headgear. The purpose of boxing headgear is to reduce the impact of a blow, reduce/prevent facial cuts, protect the ears, and substantially reduce impact to the head if a fall occurs. Only headgear approved by USA Boxing should be used (USA Boxing, 2007). Several manufacturers produce headgear to the proper standard.

Mouthpiece. During contact drills, use of a mouthpiece is mandatory. The mouthpiece reduces the possibility of jaw injuries, cuts to the inside of the mouth, and injuries to the tongue and teeth. Each participant must wear a custom-made or individually fitted mouthpiece. Examples of the custom-made and individually fitted mouthpieces are the "dentist molded" and the clear plastic types, respectively (USA Boxing, 2007).

Protectors. When contact drills are involved, men and women should wear approved groin or chest protection. For men, this means either a foul-proof protection cup or a jockstrap cup. Women should wear a well-fitted breast protector (USA Boxing, 2007).

Handwraps. Handwraps are recommended for all types of striking drills but are not required for practice (they are mandatory in competition, however). The purpose of the handwrap is primarily to protect the metacarpal bones of the hand. They are not designed or used to add force to a blow. Handwraps can be made of cotton gauze, soft surgical gauze, or Velpeau material. For ease

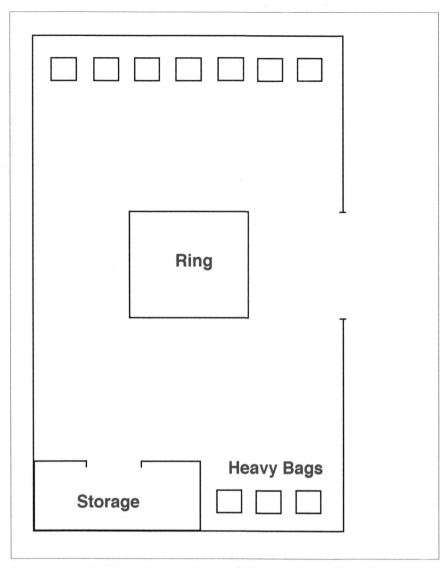

Figure 23.1. **Boxing Instruction and Competition Space** (*Source:* Meghan Rosselli)

of wrapping, the Velpeau type is recommended. Instruction and practice in proper wrapping technique should be given prior to use.

Striking bags. Heavy bags are vital to the organization of a boxing training facility. They are the single best modality to use for noncontact striking/punching drills and are a must in your training area. They are used to simulate an opponent's body and head, and a number of useful drills can be done with these bags. Several types and sizes are available (canvas, leather, nylon, vinyl), and they can be filled with foam, water, or rags (depending on the type). An inexpensive way to make a heavy bag is to fill a duffle or "sea" bag with sawdust, rags, or a combination of the two.

Light striking bags are used for advanced drills and are a "nice-to-have" item in your facility, but the heavy bags are much more practical. Light bags are used for developing speed, timing, and coordination. They are much smaller than heavy bags but require that a bag "platform" be anchored to a wall in order to be used.

Ring. A boxing ring is not necessary for boxing instruction, drills, or conditioning exercises. It is, however, an important piece of equipment if any of your participants are interested in competitive boxing. It is also a good way to control the various boxing contact drills or sparring that is done. Only rings that meet USA Boxing specifications should be used. The ring can be either a platform type, elevated about 3 ft above the floor (not more than 4 ft), or a floor type, built directly upon the floor or on a slightly raised platform that is laid directly on the floor. The platform type is recommended for competition, but for training purposes, many prefer the floor type. According to *USA Boxing Official Rules* (USA Boxing, 2007), "the ring must be not less than 16 nor more than 20 feet square within the ropes, and the apron of the ring floor shall extend beyond the ropes not less than 2 feet" (p. 17). The ring should be equipped with four ropes that are wrapped in a soft material, and all turnbuckles must be covered with protective padding.

Miscellaneous Exercise Stations

The specific purpose of your room and the needs of the participants will determine the number and types of exercise stations you need to develop. At a minimum, there should be exercise stations requiring individuals to use their own body weight as resistance. Among these are pull-up bars (six to eight) and sit-up and push-up stations. If the floor is not already padded, matting will be necessary at the sit-up station. An area set up for rope skipping and shadow boxing (two full-length mirrors) can also be provided.

Cost of Various Equipment Items

The cost of equipment items for your facility will vary slightly depending on the vendor you use, but the following rough estimates will enable you to establish a budget to get your facility started. The amount of equipment, of course, will depend on the number of participants, but the total costs for this example are based on an expected 25 participants (based on 2013 dollars):

- Training gloves (16 oz): 25 pair @ $200/pair = $5,000
- Bag gloves: 25 pair @ $12.50/pair = $312.50
- Training headgear: 25 @ $77.50 each = $1,937.50
- Plastic mouthpiece (upper): 50 @ $2.00 each = $100
- Groin protection (boxing cups): 25 @ $15.00 each = $375.00
- Female chest guards (with support bra): 25 @ $52.00 each = $1,300
- Handwrap: 25 @ $5.00 each = $150
- Heavy bags (canvas; unfilled): 8 @ $75.00 each = $600
- Boxing ring (platform type): $7,200
- Boxing ring (floor type): $3,750
- Total cost (with platform ring) = $16,600
- Total cost (with floor ring) = $13,150

It must be emphasized that these prices may vary from vendor to vendor, and it is important to shop around for the best price. The facility does not have to be completely equipped for 25 persons. Depending upon how exercise/practice sessions are organized, equipment and exercise stations can be shared and rotated so that you may only have to be equipped for 10 participants or fewer. You may also be able to purchase used equipment or construct some of your own.

Organization of the Facility

If you intend to set up a boxing room with a ring, remember that a regulation-sized ring can be from 16 ft to 20 ft, inside dimensions of all four sides. Obviously, this means that you will need more space than if you set up the room without a ring. To use your available space most efficiently, center the ring on one end of the room and place heavy bags and light striking bags on the opposite end, thus leaving the space between for drills, calisthenics, plyometrics, or multipurpose use when the area is not being used for boxing. On either end of the room or along the side walls, you can set up permanent pull-up and sit-up stations using pipe suspended horizontally from the ceiling for the pull-up station and bolted to the floor as an anchor point for feet at the sit-up station. Along one side wall, place full-length mirrors (6 ft x 4 ft) for shadow boxing and technique drills. This arrangement gives you four areas in which to work: a ring area, a bag work area, a calisthenics/conditioning area, and a space in between that can be used as a multipurpose area.

If you decide to set up your facility without a ring, you will save at least 400 sq ft of usable space (not to mention the expense of a ring). This will still enable you to set up three areas for specific fitness training, including aerobics and circuit training. It also allows you to design your facility in a much smaller space than is possible with a ring. The number of exercise stations in your circuit is then left up to your imagination and the available space. The perimeter of this fitness training facility should be set up for specific circuit exercises, with the center area left open for multipurpose use.

A boxing facility that does not have a ring (or the space for one), but is going to be used for self-defense contact drills or sparring, should be set up to ensure that participants are protected from the perimeter walls and objects that may protrude from those walls and that the floor surface being used is properly matted. Floor surface matting has already been discussed (1-in. Ensolite®), and its main purpose is to protect against traumatic injuries to the head resulting from falls or knock-downs. Perimeter walls should also be padded with 1-in. Ensolite® to protect against injuries caused by wall contact. When a ring is not available and the perimeter walls are not matted, you can still conduct contact drills and sparring if you organize the session properly. Participants should form a large circle (16-ft to 20-ft diameter) and be instructed to act as a "human ring." This ring should be centered in the exercise area and at least 6 ft from the perimeter walls. Only two participants should spar at a time, and they should begin in the center. Participants on the perimeter of the ring should be instructed to adjust their positions so as to keep the two sparring individuals inside the ring. Anytime either of the two boxers makes contact with the ring's perimeter, the instructor should immediately stop the activity and have the participants begin again, in the center. This not only prevents traumatic contact with the perimeter walls, but also stops punching activity when one individual becomes momentarily disadvantaged.

Equipment Storage Concerns

Equipment should be of high quality and meet all published safety standards required by USA Boxing. Properly cared for boxing equipment will have a long life and replacement costs will be minimal.

Security of the equipment and, in fact, the entire area, is of paramount importance. The entire facility should be locked when not in use and access should be limited to instructors, coaches, and maintenance personnel.

There should be adequate and assigned storage areas for all equipment that is movable and used on a regular basis. Boxing gloves and headgear, for example, should be stored in an area that is open to circulating air so that the equipment can dry properly. Gloves and headgear should be stowed in open wire racks, on open shelving, or in lockers with steel mesh fronts that allow the circulation of air. Both should be washed with saddle soap and dried thoroughly each week. Both should also be treated weekly with a commercial disinfectant or with a solution of 10% carbolic acid and 90% sweet oil (Deeter, Rubino, & Simmons, 1950). Handwraps should be allowed to dry after each use and should be washed weekly. Obviously, athletic supporters, groin protectors, athletic bras, and chest protectors should be washed thoroughly on a regular basis and stored in a dry, clean area. Usually, this will be the responsibility of individual participants.

Safety Concerns

Headgear. If contact drills or sparring are part of your exercise program, then it is mandatory that the boxing gloves and headgear used meet the safety specifications of USA Boxing. It is also essential that any safety equipment worn be properly fitted to the individual. Protective headgear, especially, should be worn so that it provides maximum protection. All headgear should fit snugly and should not change position on the head if pulled, pushed, or struck. The bottom edge of the padded forehead portion of the headgear should sit just above the top of the eyebrow, approximately ½ in. above the hairline of the brow. The participant's ears should fit snugly inside the ear openings on the headgear, and the ears should lie flat against the inside surface. There should be an additional heavily padded area on the rear of the headgear. This should be centered on the back of the head and should reach down to the top of the neck. If the headgear has cheek guards, they should fit snugly against the cheeks, tight enough so that they cannot slide up into the eye. Finally, the chinstrap should fit under the chin and be as tight as possible, without causing discomfort.

Mouthpiece. If plastic mouthpieces (uppers only or doubles) are used, they should be softened and molded to the individual's mouth. This can be done by placing the mouthpiece in a cup of water and then heating it in a microwave oven. When the mouthpiece appears to be softened (flaccid), remove it from the hot water and rinse it with cool water. While it is still soft, have the individual bite down on it until it is "molded" to his or her mouth.

This may take a few tries, but it is the most inexpensive way to obtain a fitted mouthpiece.

Handwraps. Handwraps should always be worn when striking drills are being performed. Cloth (Velpeau) handwraps are recommended. Furthermore, it is recommended that commercial handwraps be applied as follows:

- Place the looped end of the wrap over the thumb;
- bring the wrap over the back of the hand to the big knuckle of the wrist;
- go underneath the wrist to the base of the thumb diagonally across the back of the hand to the big knuckle of the little finger;
- encircle completely the big knuckles of the hand, wrapping well up toward the middle joints of the fingers;
- go diagonally across the back of the hand to the outside wrist bone;
- completely encircle the wrist once, angling the wrap slightly upward, stopping at the base of the thumb;
- completely encircle the thumb once;
- following the normal contour of the hand, bring the wrap over across the back of the hand to the joint of the little finger;
- completely encircle the large knuckles of the hand a second time, carrying the wrapping down diagonally across the back of the hand and around to the base of the thumb;
- pull it up, completely encircling the thumb for a second time; and
- finally, bring the wrap diagonally over the back of the hand to the wrist, and encircle the wrist once, using a small piece of tape (1 in. x 6 in.) to secure the wrap.

Ensure that participants keep their fingers spread and extended throughout the wrapping process. This will prevent the wrap from being too tight, thus cutting off circulation.

Matching participants. When pairing participants for contact drills, make sure there is as little weight difference between the participants as possible. A reasonable guideline to follow is to allow no more than an 8-lb differential during sparring or contact drills. It is perhaps even more important to also pair individuals according to their respective skill/experience levels. If a new skill is being learned, it is a good idea to pair an experienced individual with a beginner. The experienced person can control the action and can also act as an assistant instructor for the beginner. If the activity involves sparring or any competitive situations, then it is usually best to pair the individuals according to size (weight) and relative ability.

Emergencies. During vigorous activity, injury is possible. There should be a phone located inside the boxing room with clearly posted numbers of the local emergency squad, the school athletic training staff, and the infirmary.

In addition, all instructors should be CPR certified, and a first aid kit should always be on hand. Identifying injuries should be the responsibility of the professional staff, but guidelines for handling suspected head injuries should also be clearly posted inside the room. USA Boxing (2012) published the following guidelines for recognizing a possible head injury. Athletes should be observed for

- dizziness or headache lasting more than 1 hr,
- increasing drowsiness,
- loss of consciousness,
- mental disorientation or confusion,
- unusual or strange behavior,
- restlessness or irritability,
- seizure (convulsion),
- blurred vision or loss of vision,
- repeated vomiting,
- blood or watery fluid from ears or nose,
- inability to control urination or bowel movement, and
- inability to move an arm or leg.

If any of these symptoms occur (or persist), medical personnel should be contacted immediately.

Martial Arts

The term *martial arts* comprises a wide range of fighting systems that are practiced for physical fitness, sport competition, and self-defense. Traditionally martial arts are various Asian fighting systems that teach combat-specific techniques. Most of the modern martial arts have roots that go back to the ancient martial arts of Asia. It is commonly believed that some martial arts started before 2000 BC. Different philosophies, interpretations, and interests of instructors and students have produced the wide range of martial arts practiced today.

Building or renovating a martial arts facility requires extensive planning. This chapter will provide information to assist martial arts facility developers with design and construction decisions. Planners and developers of martial arts facilities must understand at least the general nature

Martial arts competition

of martial arts if they are to make informed decisions. The major classifications of martial arts are summarized in this chapter to provide this knowledge base.

Facility Planning Concepts (see Chapters 1 and 2 for details)

The goal when constructing or renovating a martial arts facility is to produce a facility that is highly functional, cost effective, aesthetically pleasing, safe, and accessible to all. Failure to adequately plan often results in a facility that costs too much and delivers too little. Sawyer (2005) and others suggested participatory planning (seeking information from all interested individuals, especially the representative user group) is the recommended planning strategy. The first step is to conduct a needs assessment. The needs assessment solicits information from the owners and operators, the target facility users, and staff members. The owner and operator may be a person, a group of people, or an established organization. The owners and operators often provide all or some of the finances for the project, so they expect and deserve the opportunity to influence construction or renovation decisions. They often provide a vision for the facility and leadership in organizing and executing both the planning and the construction. Staff members provide an excellent source of information on which features should be included in a new martial arts facility. They have practical expertise and experience and can provide useful recommendations. Gathering information from the target population provides valuable information to determine the demand for martial arts activities and identify which style is most popular. The users or customers are often the best source of information on the desired support facilities, such as parking areas, locker rooms, concessions, and administrative areas.

Armed with data gathered from the needs assessment, you can now take the next step, which is to solicit support from those providing the funding for the construction or renovation project. It is important to present the data collected in a professional and persuasive manner. Oftentimes, important features of a building project are not supported due to a lack of time spent in developing and crafting the justification statements in the proposal. Failing to adequately prepare for this phase of planning could result in a poor presentation and the project being abandoned.

Once a project gets support from a higher authority, establish a planning group or a steering committee. This group will stay actively involved during the entire planning and construction process. It is critical to spend time when making the decision on whom to include on the committee as they will provide guidance and, in some cases, make decisions on issues such as

- renovating an existing facility or building a new facility;

- cost limitations and funding sources;
- promoting the project;
- gathering additional needs assessment data;
- site location;
- selecting an architectural firm;
- approving, rejecting, or modifying architectural firm plans and proposals;
- selecting construction contractors;
- developing construction schedules and phasing;
- specifying material and space requirements;
- ensuring code compliance;
- identifying and solving design and construction problems;
- establishing and implementing maintenance and operation procedures; and
- determining requirements for support and competition areas.

The scope of the project and the complexity of the administrative requirements will determine the magnitude of the planning effort. Whether planning a modest renovation of an existing martial arts room or constructing a new martial arts complex complete with all the support facilities, you will avoid costly mistakes with careful planning.

Overview of the Martial Arts

Martial arts can be defined as numerous systems of self-defense and offensive techniques that may emphasize sports competition, physical development, mental development, or a combination of these aspects. Initially, most martial arts taught in America were taught in wrestling rooms, gymnasiums, multipurpose rooms, or the outdoors. This is still the case in most colleges, recreation centers, YMCAs, and other multipurpose facilities. Martial arts facilities, designed specifically for martial arts, are now being included in the design and construction of many multipurpose facilities. Many commercial martial arts programs are taught in specialized martial arts facilities.

Whether designing a separate commercial facility or a martial arts area in a larger project, planners must decide whether the new martial arts facility will be a general combative facility or a facility designed to accommodate a specific classification of martial arts. In either case, a general knowledge of the major martial arts will help planners make important design decisions. There are almost as many types of martial arts as there are types of ball games. There are too many types and styles of martial arts to discuss the facility requirements for each. A brief summary of the two major martial arts divisions is provided to assist facility planners in making informed design and construction decisions (see Table 23.1)

Grappling arts. The grappling arts have surged in popularity in the past several years due to the television coverage of various mixed martial arts competitions. Although the arts that comprise this classification of martial arts have as rich of a history as their striking counterparts, the grappling arts have resurfaced as a mainstream addition to fitness and recreational facility programming. Their popularity has sparked facility designers to consider devoting specialized areas to this activity. Although multipurpose rooms can accommodate these arts with limited modifications and additional equipment, grappling-specific areas are recommended for safety reasons. Facility planners must consider the characteristics of these grappling arts when making facility decisions. These arts tend to emphasize throwing skills, joint locks, falling, and wrestling-type movements. Participants compete against opponents in close proximity with the goal of physically controlling the other.

Striking arts. The striking arts are systems designed to train participants to make contact with an opponent from a distance (Winkle & Ozmun, 2001). Numerous systems meet this criterion. The most commonly practiced striking arts include karate, tae kwon do, kung fu, and kickboxing. Each of these arts is characterized by its need for mobility and various hand and foot striking techniques. An understanding of the nature of striking arts and grappling arts is required to properly design or accommodate a safe training environment.

Table 23.1

Martial Arts Classification Summary

GRAPPLING ARTS	STRIKING ARTS
Involve throwing skills, joint locks, falling, and wrestling-type activities	Emphasize punching, kicking, and weapon use
COMMON GRAPPLING ARTS:	COMMON STRIKING ARTS:
Judo	Tae Kwon Do
Jui-Jitsu	Karate
Aikido	Kung Fu
Wrestling/Brazilian Jiu-Jitsu	Kickboxing/Boxing

Facility Concerns

Martial arts facilities tend to be simple structures with large open spaces. However, the two classifications of martial arts systems have distinctly different needs from the perspective of facility design. Flooring is the primary difference in each facility. The grappling arts require floor matting, and the striking arts are best suited with a wooden or synthetic floor.

Grappling martial arts facilities. The requirement of floor matting is the distinguishing characteristic of grappling martial arts facilities. Grappling arts often use traditional wrestling rooms with mats and padded walls. These wrestling rooms meet the minimum requirements for grappling martial arts, but a two-layer mat system is recommended for any of the grappling martial arts that require throwing. The standard wrestling mat alone does not provide sufficient protection for high-impact activities such as throws. A two-layer mat system with a lower layer of foam-type matting and an upper layer standard wrestling-type mat is a versatile option. Tatami mats (made of compressed foam) over a spring-loaded base are ideal for the throwing arts.

When designing a dedicated martial arts facility, the planner should include specialized matting specifically selected for the intended activity. Noncompetitive grappling arts only require a firm mat with shock-absorbing properties. The mat should not be slippery or too rough.

For competitive grappling arts, such as judo, the mat must be a minimum of 14 m x 14 m and a maximum of 16 m x 16 m. The top layer of matting is usually a green-colored tatami. Competition mats must have a smooth surface without gaps between sections. Competition mats must also have a competition zone surrounded by a 1-m danger zone marked in red. A 3-m zone on the outside of the danger zone is the safety zone. A resilient wooden platform is the preferred base for judo competitions. Competitive judo venues should also include two scoreboards and three timing clocks. Other competitive grappling arts, such as Brazilian jiu-jitsu, do not require the wooden platform, only competition-quality mats.

Striking martial arts facilities. Karate, kung fu, tae kwon do, and kendo are martial arts that employ mostly striking techniques (Roth, 1974). Karate, kung fu, and tae kwon do all use a variety of kicks with the feet, punches with the hands, and striking skills with other body parts. The majority of these blows are delivered from the feet with full force and strike into a padded surface or stop just short of a human target. Kata, a prearranged series of skills, is also an important aspect for the majority of these styles. Normally, only the advanced students participate in contact competitions where they deliver full-contact blows against an opponent. Additional protective equipment is recommended when practicing striking techniques with an opponent and required for full-contact competition.

The emphasis in each of these martial arts is body control, striking power, and precise technique. The punching, kicking, and striking techniques are delivered from either a linear or a spinning and turning motion. Wrestling-type mats are not recommended when throwing circular techniques because the anchor foot must rotate freely. Flexible hardwood or smooth synthetic floors are preferred for striking martial arts.

The American College of Sports Medicine's (ACSM) health/fitness facility standards and guidelines are commonly used by multipurpose facility designers when determining what type of flooring is best suited for certain activities. Guideline 8 states, "Floor surfaces in physical activity areas should provide the proper level of absorption and slip resistance to minimize the risk of users' incurring impact or fall-related injuries" (ACSM, 2007, p. 37). According to the ACSM, the critical point regarding flooring is that it meets the criteria of the Deutsches Institut für Normung (DIN). DIN standards require floors to meet five criteria: shock absorption, vertical deflection, deflective indentation sliding characteristics, rolling load, and ball reflection.

The goal of these standards is to reduce the number of acute and chronic impact injuries. These floors should have excellent shock absorption, small vertical deformation, and limited sliding characteristics (ACSM, 2007). According to DIN standards, a floor suitable for activities such as the striking arts should serve both a protective and a material-technical function (ACSM, 2007).

General Features for Martial Arts Facilities

Although the primary distinguishing feature of martial arts facilities is the type of flooring and matting required, facility planners must also consider other important features.

Wall coverings. Selecting appropriate wall coverings is critical. All striking martial arts facilities should have at least a portion of the wall covered with mirrors. Mirrors provide a valuable source of feedback for individuals participating in martial arts. Selecting the best location for the mirrors may be challenging because of conflicting priorities. Placing the mirrors too close to the activity area may result in the mirror being broken. Nonglass mirrors are safer and less likely to get broken but scratch more easily and tend to give a distorted image. If glass mirrors are to be used, shatter-resistant glass mirrors are recommended. Placing mirrors too far from the activity area may make it difficult for participants to see themselves. Walls that do not have mirrors are often covered with protective wall mats, to a height of 6 ft.

Water fountains. Martial arts activities are demanding physically, and martial arts participants will need to stay hydrated. A recessed water cooler is recommended for all martial arts facilities. A recessed water spigot is often desired to make facility sanitation easier. The spigot may be located near or as part of the water cooler.

Ceiling. Martial arts facilities tend to be simple functional facilities with few distractions. The simplest and least expensive ceiling is an open ceiling; the roof or floor above and associated piping, conduit, and ductwork is left exposed. An open ceiling area is normally painted white to give the training room an open-area feeling. The open ceiling has advantages for activities that involve weapons and throws. The longer weapons, bows and swords, may damage an acoustic tile ceiling. Acoustic tiles used in drop ceilings can be equipped with spring-loaded clips that will allow the tiles to be contacted without being knocked out of place. The open ceiling is not as aesthetic as an acoustical tile ceiling and does not have as good of acoustic properties. If the facility is to be used primarily as a teaching station, an acoustic tile ceiling may be the ceiling of choice and worth the extra expense. The minimum ceiling height is 12 ft for martial arts facilities, and a higher ceiling is recommended for a martial arts facility used primarily for weapons-oriented activities.

Lighting. The recommended lighting level for martial arts facilities is 50 foot-candles. Recessed lights that have a protective covering are recommended. If the facility will be used for martial arts demonstrations or shows, equip the lights with a dimmer switch.

Storage. Providing adequate storage space for the martial arts facility is an important planning decision. Like storage space in many other facilities, storage space in martial arts facilities is often overlooked or reduced as soon as finances become an issue. Specific storage needs vary with each martial arts program, but should include at least storage for personal items and mesh-type lockers to allow stored gear to dry. The size and type of storage facility required depend upon

- total space available for construction,
- budget constraints,
- type of facility (grappling or striking),
- class sizes,
- whether the mats will need to be taken up and stored,
- whether the uniforms will be stored,
- the style of martial arts to be practiced, and
- the desire to include a trophy case to store and display trophies.

If specific storage needs are not available during the planning phase, allow 8% to 10% of the total martial arts facility square footage for storage.

Scoreboard. A scoreboard with a clock is a practical feature for many of the martial arts, especially those that involve competition. The specific features of the scoreboard will depend on which style of martial art will use the scoreboard. If a scoreboard is desired, but funds are not available at the time of design, include the required power source in the plans. Including the power source in the original construction will cost very little and will save both time and money if funds become available to purchase a scoreboard in the future.

Custodial closet. Martial arts facilities have a lot of skin contact areas that require regular cleaning and disinfecting. Locating a custodial closet in or close to the martial arts facility will facilitate cleaning and sanitation efforts. Rubberized mats require regular cleaning and disinfecting with a liquid disinfectant. A custodial sink is recommended, and a recessed spigot is the minimum source of water for cleaning the martial arts facility. The closet needs to have storage space for mops, buckets, cleaning and disinfecting supplies, and a vacuum cleaner (especially for carpeted facilities).

24 Equestrian Spaces

Michael G. Hypes, *Morehead State University*
Julia Ann Hypes, *Morehead State University*

Many variables are involved in the planning of equestrian facilities. These variables include purpose, budget, image, climate, available material and labor, personal preferences, and future plans, to name a few. These variables make good planning critical to the overall success of the project.

Equestrian facilities incorporate several different components, including

- barns,
- work areas,
- turnout areas, and
- arenas.

Each component serves a specific function in the overall operation of the equestrian program.

Barns

"The atmosphere and safety of all activities within a barn are determined by three main barn features: the brightness and placement of lights, the amount of fresh air, and the material and condition of the aisle floor" (Hill, 2000, p. 27). Although some people prefer their facility to be plain, no frills, and practical, others prefer their facility to make a statement. The image you want to portray with your facility can be a preliminary goal in the planning process. This image goal will guide many of the choices you have to make including architectural style, building materials, interior fittings, equipment, and costs.

Site Considerations

A horse barn's site selection should receive careful consideration. The barn's orientation to wind, sun, and shade should be considered. The ideal orientation would use summer breezes for cooling effect and avoid the harsh winter wind. Trees can be used to

- provide shade,
- serve as windbreaks, and
- screen private areas.

Good water drainage is necessary to avoid standing water. Standing water or marshy areas could be breeding grounds for insects and disease, thus making it difficult to maintain a healthy stable environment.

General Construction Issues

A variety of construction materials can be used for barn structures. These materials can range from wood to precast concrete. Safety features should be the main consideration when choosing materials. Whatever choice in materials is made, it is essential that the structure be as fire resistant as possible.

Many different types or combinations of lighting can be used in a barn. Natural lighting can be used to enhance the overall lighting of the facility through the use of skylights, windows, translucent wall panels, and open doors. Whether incandescent, halogen, fluorescent, or high-intensity discharge lighting is used, it is important to remember that the fixture should be protected from dust and impact. The needed illumination in a given area will dictate the type and amount of fixtures needed.

Another important aspect of any barn is adequate ventilation. Ventilation in barns can be provided by windows, doors, roof vents, and exhaust fans. Adequate ventilation not only keeps barn odor at a minimum, but also helps keep the barn area dry and cool in the summer and contributes to a healthy stable environment.

The main aisle in a barn receives a large amount of traffic. The surface in the main aisle should be durable and easy to clean. It is important for the safety of the horse and handler that the floor is relatively smooth and level. The decision as to what type of flooring to use should be based on a balance of your personal preference, cost, availability, maintenance, and durability. Table 24.1 provides a list of the more common flooring surfaces used in barn structures. Each type of flooring has distinct advantages, and selection should be based upon your specific needs.

Table 24.1

Types of Barn Flooring

- dirt
- wood shavings, chips, shredded bark
- sand
- road base
- gravel
- wood
- brick
- rubber brick
- rubber tile
- concrete
- asphalt
- rubber mats

The size and number of components making up the barn will vary in relationship not only to the size of the facility but also to the requirements placed upon the facility. The following are basic components for a typical barn facility:

- stalls,
- feed room,
- hay storage,
- straw storage/alternative,
- bedding,
- feed storage,
- wash and cleaning room (drying facilities),
- tack room,
- utility stall,
- manure disposal,
- office,
- lavatory accommodations, and
- equipment storage.

The relationship of the components should first be concentrated on the horse. The components should also be considered with respect to other facilities, to the site, to surrounding buildings, and to each other. Careful planning and placement of these barn components can minimize movement of heavy materials, feed, and tack, thus maximizing efficiency and safety of the facility.

Stalls

The stall is the indoor living space for the horse. It should be large enough to allow the horse to move about freely, lie down, and get up without hindrance from banging into the walls. Each stall should be large enough to accommodate separate areas for a horse's three main activities: eating, lying down, and defecating/urinating. In addition, stalls can be used for

- tending to sick horses,
- birthing (foaling),
- sheltering horses from extreme weather, and
- keeping horses clean.

The more time a horse spends in a stall, the larger and more spacious the area should be. Table 24.2 identifies common stall dimensions based on the characteristics of the horse.

Exterior view of horse stalls

Table 24.2

Common Stall Sizes

Feet	Meters	Suitable for
10 x 10	3 x 3	Pony: under 14.2 hands Usually under 800 lb
12 x 12	3.7 x 3.7	Standard Horse: up to 16 hands, 800-1,100 lb
12 x 14	3.7 x 4.3	Large Horse: 16+ hands, 1,100-1,400 lb
12 x 16	3.7 x 4.9	Draft Horse: more than 16 hands, over 1,400 lb
12 x 18	3.7 x 5.5	Foaling Stall: up to 1,400-lb mare with foal

Note. Modified from *Stablekeeping: A Visual Guide to Safe and Healthy Horsekeeping,* by C. Hill & R. Klimesh, North Adams, MA: Storey Publishing.

Stall doors come in a variety of styles. The door size should be sufficient to allow the horse to be led through the door without rubbing the sides and large enough for a cart to be pushed into the stall for cleaning. Stall doors should be a minimum of 4 ft wide and 8 ft high. The edges of the door opening should be rounded to prevent injury. Horse-proof latches should be used on all stall doors. Horse-proof latches are out of reach of the horse or are made so the horse cannot open it. Some of the more common latches include spring bolt, turning, and sliding bolt latches. A lower latch can be used to prevent the horse from pushing the bottom of the door out and possibly injuring itself.

A good stall floor will help reduce the amount of bedding needed. The stall floor should be comfortable for the horse, safe, and easy to clean. The flooring should be fairly easy to install, affordable, and able to withstand the abuse from hooves and acid from urine. Natural soil is the cheapest and easiest floor to install. However, over time, it can become uneven from the horse's movements, pawing, and urination. The size of your horse, function of the stall, and amount of stall use will also contribute to the stall flooring decision. Table 24.3 provides a comparison of different stall floorings.

Table 24.3

Stall Flooring

Material	Advantages	Disadvantages
Soil (clay, dirt)	Relatively inexpensive Good traction and cushion	High maintenance, difficult to clean
Gravel, sand	Inexpensive Good traction and cushion	High maintenance, difficult to clean, danger of colic*
Asphalt	Easy to clean Low maintenance	Cold, hard, and abrasive Can be slippery Hard on legs and feet
Concrete	Easy to clean Good traction if textured Maintenance-free	Cold, hard, and abrasive Hard on legs and feet Slippery if not textured
Wood	Nice sound Warm	Slippery when wet Difficult to clean and disinfect
Draining flooring	Minimal bedding needed Moisture drains through	Urine accumulates under flooring
Conveyor belting	Easy to clean	Very slippery when wet Difficult to handle and install
Rubber mats	Quiet Good cushion and traction Easy to clean	Can be difficult to handle and properly install Can gap and buckle

Note. Modified from *Stablekeeping: A Visual Guide to Safe and Healthy Horsekeeping,* by C. Hill & R. Klimesh, North Adams, MA: Storey Publishing.

*Sand is not recommended because the horse can ingest the sand and develop colic.

Photo by Michael Hypes

Interior view of stall, feed, and water containers

Photo by Michael Hypes

Space utilization at Saint Mary-of-the-Woods College, IN

Photo by Michael Hypes

Double-door entry

Flooring can be categorized as a draining or a nondraining surface. A draining floor allows urine to pass through holes in the material. A nondraining or solid floor is made of material that keeps moisture on top of the flooring, allowing the moisture to be absorbed by the bedding. Bedding provides a comfortable surface for a horse to lie down. It is also used to absorb urine and as an insulator from the cold. Bedding material should be absorbent, soft, dust free, easy to handle, and nontoxic. Possible types of bedding include

- straw;
- pine sawdust;
- pine shavings;
- shredded newspaper;
- hardwood chips, shavings; and
- sand.

Feed Room

This room houses the feed (corn, grains, oats, etc.) for daily use. It should be located close to the stalls for easy human access but still away from animal access. Each type of food should have a separate storage bin. Feed and grain storage bins should be lined with galvanized steel for

Photo by Michael Hypes

Interior stall door

vermin control. It is essential that the feed room be a dry storage area to avoid fungal and mold growth in the feed. Feed spoilage can be costly in dollars and animal health. Hazardous chemicals, cleaners, and disinfectants should be stored away from feed.

Hay Storage

The hay storage area should be directly accessible from the feed room. The size for this area will depend on the size of the facility and the frequency of feeding. The hay should be stored close to the stalls, usually in the loft, where it can be dropped into cribs in each stall. There should be exterior

Tack room at Saint Mary-of-the-Woods College, IN

access to this area for ease of storing hay, either brought in from the field or purchased. It is essential that hay storage areas be dry with good ventilation. The storage area should be free of mold and molding or wet hay. Molding hay can cause serious equine illness, and wet hay can ignite, leading to deadly fires.

Bedding Storage

A variety of materials may be used for bedding purposes. The type selected may be based on geographical location, personal preference, animal preference, or availability. The area for bedding storage needs to be well ventilated and dry. Bedding such as straw can be stored in a separate facility to minimize the risk of fire.

Tack Rooms

The tack room should be accessible to all stalls. The exact size and arrangement will depend on the number of horses and the purposes for which the horses are being used.

Windows are typically omitted from the tack room because they take up valuable wall space as well as pose a security risk. Sunlight exposure can also dry and damage leather and other fine tack materials. The tack room should be designed to fit your needs. Common elements in the

tack room include bridle racks, saddle racks, tack hooks, blanket rods, and shelving for various grooming and veterinary items. If a separate barn office is not available, the tack room may include a refrigerator for storing medications and fireproof file cabinets for storing records. Space should also be allotted for the repair and cleaning of tack.

Many items are common to all horses and should be at hand in all tack rooms. Grooming tools are among the common items, including

- brushes,
- curry combs (rubber and metal),
- electric clippers,
- extension cords,
- scissors,
- shedding blades,
- soft cloths,
- sponges, and
- sweat scrapers.

In addition, all tack rooms should have first aid kits for both horses and people. Depending upon the type of horse stabled, other assorted items are generally stored in the tack room, including

- bell boots,
- lead ropes,
- leg wraps,
- longe lines,
- ropes,
- saddles,
- tail wraps,
- blankets,
- bridles,
- cavessons,
- chain lead shanks,
- crops,
- feed bags,
- halters, and
- hobbles.

Materials and tools for maintenance and repair of tack should also be kept in the tack room. Materials often needed are

- awls,
- hole punch,
- knife,
- latigo leather,
- neatsfoot oil,
- nylon string,
- rivets,
- saddle leather,
- saddle soap,
- sheepskin, and
- waxed linen string.

Bedding storage

Cleaning

From tack to facilities to horses, cleaning is an important aspect of barn operations. The function will dictate the space and location required. The cleaning area for equipment can be incorporated into a tack room or be a separate area. Large, deep sinks, hot and cold water sources, and washers and dryers aid in the proper cleaning and disinfecting of blankets and other accessories. By placing plumbing for workrooms and horse washrooms adjacent to or near each other, you can help minimize plumbing headaches and costs.

Manure Disposal

The manure disposal area should be positioned well away from the stalls but be easily accessible. It should be located adjacent to a road to facilitate collection and dispersal. Care should be taken to ensure that runoff from manure and bedding disposal areas does not contaminate wells, creeks, or other water resources.

Office

The office space should accommodate a desk, chairs, filing cabinets, and storage space for supplies. A fireproof file cabinet or safe should be considered for record storage. An area for a computer with a dedicated phone line should be considered. The telephone should be fitted with an external bell or extensions so it may be heard throughout the facility. The office area should be located to provide supervision over the stable yard, deliveries, and arrival of people. The office can be used as an additional layer of safety for the facility. It is an appropriate screening area for visitors to the facility. The office should be adjacent to toilet and washroom areas. Some facilities have the office adjacent to or located near sleeping areas.

Turnout Areas

All turnout areas should be safe for the horse. These areas are designed to provide limited exercise space for the horse. Turnout areas include pens, runs, corrals, and paddocks.

The pen is usually the size of a large stall. A pen is typically 16 ft x 20 ft. The run is longer, 16 ft x 60 ft, and allows the horse to get more exercise by trotting. A corral can be a square or round pen. The corral is at least 1,600 sq ft. These three areas are usually devoid of grass due to concentrated horse traffic. The paddock area is usually a grassy area from half an acre to several acres and is used for short periods of exercise and grazing.

The turnout areas should have fencing designed for horses. Sturdy 5-ft to 6-ft perimeter fences, complete with latched gates, should encircle the area. Types of fencing range from vinyl to recycled rubber. The type best suited depends on your specific circumstances and livestock type. One of the most practical and inexpensive fences for a horse farm is a 5 ft high, 12 ½ gauge, galvanized 2 in. x 4 in. V-mesh. Pipe fences are attractive, easily maintained, and safe when properly constructed.

Competitive Areas

Arenas

Arena sizes vary widely between the disciplines. Working cows and reining typically require the most room. An arena for this purpose should be 100 ft wide x 200+ ft long. Jumping events are usually at least 80 ft wide and 120 ft long, and more space is preferable if possible. A large dressage arena is 20 m x 60 m (66 ft x 198 ft), and a small dressage arena is 20 m x 40 m (66 ft x 132 ft).

Roof truss manufacturers use standard dimensions, usually in increments of 10 ft. A standard small covered arena truss is 60 ft wide and spaced 12 ft apart. A good rule of thumb for commercial riding arenas is to construct bigger than what you think you need. This allows multiple disciplines to use the facility or accommodates multiple riding lessons simultaneously.

The proper lighting of an arena is an important part of the planning phase. The sheer size of the arena makes it important to plan regarding fixtures, circuit size, and placement.

Jumps

The types of jumps used in Hunter classes are representative of natural obstacles found in the hunt field. These include

- post-and-rails,
- stone walls,
- Aiken,
- chicken coop,
- brush,
- plank, and
- white gate.

The post-and-rails is a natural rail fence, usually of three cross rails. The chicken coop is a triangular wooden obstacle ranging from 2 ft, 6 in. to 4 ft. The Aiken is a split rail over bushes (Price, 1998).

All jumps should be constructed with the safety of horse and rider in mind. They should collapse easily to prevent injury. This breakaway characteristic is based upon the types of cups that hold the rails. The inside dimensions of a cup for a 4-in. pole must be a minimum of 1 ½ in. deep and 5 in. across. The maximum depth must not exceed one half of the diameter of the pole (Price, 1998).

The poles (rails) used in many shows are 12 ft or 14 ft long. The longer the pole is, the greater the weight is and the lesser the tendency to pop out of the cups when hit is. "Fences designed to test for horizontal distances are called spread fences. They may include the oxer, double oxer, hogback, and triple bar. While these obstacles are of different configurations, they can all be raised and lengthened, as for jump-offs" (Price, 1998, p. 245).

The Puissance walls are typically constructed of light plywood with the upper elements able to slide off. Paint is used to create illusions for the horse. Table 24.4 provides a summary of the types of fences used in jumping. New variations are appearing all the time; however, these five categories represent most of the jumps currently used.

Table 24.4

Types of Fences

- Uprights are fences built vertical to the ground with all parts placed one above the other. These include gates, planks, walls, straight posts, and rails.

- Spread fences require a horse to jump width as well as height. These include parallels, hogbacks, triple bars, double oxers, wall with rails behind, water ditches, and open water jumps.

- Combinations consist of two or more elements placed in front of one another. The combination is usually designed with a single or double non-jumping stride between each part.

- The double consists of two fences, which may be of any design. A straightforward distance for non-jumping stride in a double is 7.3 m to 8 m (24 ft to 26 ft) and for two non-jumping strides is 10 m to 11 m (33 ft to 36 ft).

- Trebles consist of three elements of any type of fence or combination of striding.

Note. Modified from *Competitive Riding,* by J. Holderness-Roddam, 1988, New York, NY: Prentice-Hall.

Athletic Training Facilities

Michael G. Hypes, *Morehead State University*

Author note: Recently Joe Brown passed away. This chapter is dedicated to Joe and his memory. Joe was a legend in the athletic training field for over 40 years. We greatly appreciated his service to the field and his contributions to this textbook.

Athletic training rooms are common features in indoor and outdoor athletic complexes, and their specific purposes depend on the type of activities and facilities they support. For example, in multipurpose recreational facilities, the athletic training room often serves as a first aid station for recreational athletes. Conversely, in athletic facilities, it serves as a comprehensive athletic medicine facility for interscholastic, intercollegiate, Olympic, or professional athletes. When housed in a community, the athletic training room may serve the "weekend warrior." Therefore, proper planning, plus an understanding of the essential components of an athletic training room, will make it more effective when it is complete. Accordingly, athletic training room planners should regularly consult with staff athletic trainers during the planning phase to ensure a sound facility for treating and rehabilitating athletes is constructed (Ingersoll & Sawyer, 1999).

Although the specific activities performed in an athletic training room are subject to institutional preference, along with the availability of financial and facility resources, certain activities are performed in all such facilities. These include team preparation, injury evaluation, injury treatment, injury rehabilitation, and administrative functions. It is important, then, to understand these activities before building, retrofitting, or remodeling an athletic training room. To improve the planning process, general considerations for the athletic training room and/or the requirements of organizations concerned with athletic training facilities should be considered (Ingersoll & Sawyer, 1999).

General Considerations for the Athletic Training Facility

Authors in the 1950s (Bevan, 1956; Morehouse & Rasch, 1958), 1960s (Morehouse & Rasch, 1964; Rawlinson, 1961), 1970s (Brown, 1972; Klafs & Arnheim, 1973), 1980s (Forseth, 1986; Penman & Penman, 1982; Sauers, 1985; Secor, 1984), 1990s (Ingersoll & Sawyer, 1999; LaVoie, 1993; Rankin & Ingersoll, 1995; Ray, 1994), and 2000s (Sabo, 2001) have offered a number of options to be considered when contemplating an athletic training facility. Although each author offered specific suggestions, a common thread is associated with each. Generally, these authors agree that the athletic training room is a place specifically set aside for injury care. It has good lighting and ventilation; a constant temperature range; light-colored walls, ceilings, and floors; easily cleaned surfaces; adequate equipment; and ground fault circuit interrupter (GFCI) electrical outlets located on all walls. It is easily accessible by being near the dressing room, but is not a part of it and is not to be used as a passageway to the dressing room or showers. Moreover, these authors support the importance of a facility set aside specifically for the prevention, treatment, and rehabilitation of individuals who may incur injuries.

The Case for Athletic Training Facilities

It is important, then, for organizations without athletic training facilities to promote the need for an athletic training room. First, these management promotion factors include a well-organized plan of action, which outlines why the athletic training room is essential to injury care. These three factors follow:

- Minor injuries often are not reported immediately because there is no one place or person to whom the athlete with the injury should report. Moreover, the person with the injury is often reluctant to be treated for minor injuries in the presence of others. It also is difficult to give minor injuries proper attention during the confusion of dressing and undressing.

- A sanitary and comparatively private environment is generally helpful for treating injuries. Organizations are giving more attention to injury prevention, treatment, and rehabilitation because of the individual's privacy need from a practical and psychological point of view, because of the increased public attention given to sports injury problems, and because injuries adversely affect efficiency. Thus, the presence of an athletic training facility shows an interest in the welfare of athletes.
- A properly fitted athletic training room's cost is minimal when compared with costs incurred for lost time, uniforms, and other equipment. (Brown, 1972)

Second, space needed for an athletic training facility must be determined. Forseth (1986) listed five general factors of facility development he obtained from Coates for determining the space needed for the athletic training room. These factors include

- program needs such as the number of sports and the type of sports offered at the institution,
- projected institutional enrollment and the stability of the number of participants from one year to the next,
- space needed for athletic training instruction,
- cost per square foot estimates to determine what is feasible under the existing economic status, and
- communication with the architect early in the process to ensure a functional athletic training room.

Third, the development of an athletic training facility requires the services of a certified athletic trainer. Such a person has requisite skills in the prevention, treatment, and rehabilitation of athletic injuries. Additionally, the certified athletic trainer has a working knowledge of the national standards for athletic training facilities (Newell, 2003).

Fourth, in retrofitting or remodeling facilities, the athletic training room size will be dictated by a number of unforeseen factors.

Fifth, make sure the athletic trainers are included during the planning phases.

Sixth, emphasize that the primary purpose of an athletic training room is to provide efficient service to large numbers of athletes at one time. Therefore, when building a new facility with a generous budget, follow the Arnheim and Prentice (2010) recommendation, the Penman and Penman (1982) formula, and/or Sabo's (2001) guidelines for minimal size.

Seventh, when possible, use the standards of the National Athletic Trainers Association (NATA) and/or the American Academy of Orthopaedic Surgeons.

National Athletic Trainers Association

The most important organization to consult is the NATA, especially if the athletic training room is in an institution that has a certification curriculum. According to Ingersoll and Sawyer (1999), the Commission on Accreditation of Allied Health Education Programs (CAAHEP) suggests specific guidelines for developing an athletic training room. In this setting, the athletic training room components include team preparation area, injury evaluation/treatment area, rehabilitation area, wet space, maintenance area, storage space, office area, examination space, computer/study/conference area, and a classroom. The specifications for each of these areas are detailed to assist the planner in developing an appropriate floor plan for the athletic training room.

Team Preparation Area

The team preparation area will have a tile floor with an appropriate number of floor drains, treatment cabinets with Formica® tops, a recessed waste receptacle, drawers, and shelves. The ceiling height should be 11 ft to 12 ft, but not less than 10 ft. Furthermore, fireproof tiles are required for the ceiling. The walls should be constructed of masonry blocks for durability and sound control and painted with an epoxy paint to seal the blocks so they will be easier to clean. A deep double-basin sink is suggested. The direct lighting should be with fluorescent tubes. Electrical outlets should be located every 6 ft on all the walls, and those electrical outlets around the sink should be GFCI rated. Finally, this area should have a biohazard waste container and double doors for entrance and/or exit.

Injury Evaluation/Treatment Area

The injury evaluation/treatment area requires different space and equipment needs for performing injury evaluations and treatments. This space has therapeutic modality applications, manual therapy, and treatment activities going on at the same time. Typically, this space includes numerous treatment tables that are used to examine body parts, do special tests on joints, and treat various injuries. There should be a suspended curtain system that, when necessary, can be used for privacy.

Moveable carts between each table are used for transporting therapeutic equipment (ultrasound machine, muscle stimulator, etc.) and storing supplies. The specific space needs of the injury evaluation/treatment area include

- a ceiling with a minimum height of 10 ft (11 ft to 12 ft is desirable) that is covered with fireproof tiles,
- cabinets for storage,
- a deep double-basin stainless steel sink,
- rubberized roll-out sports surface such as Mondo7®,
- masonry block walls covered with epoxy paint,
- GFCI-rated electrical outlets at each treatment site and above the counter on either side of the sink,

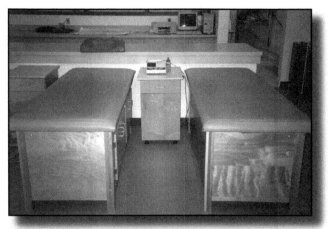

Eastern Kentucky University movable cart

- direct fluorescent lighting,
- biohazard waste containers, and
- double doors for entering and exiting the area.

The rehabilitation area includes space for therapeutic exercise equipment. This area should be separate from other areas in the complex because of the noise level and the movement of the exercising athletes. The needs of this area include

- a rubberized roll-out sports floor surface such as Mondo7®;
- free weights;
- mechanized strength training equipment for exercising shoulders, arms, backs, hips, thighs, knees, and ankles;
- electrical outlets on all walls spaced every 6 ft;
- indirect fluorescent lighting;
- a 10-ft ceiling equipped with fireproof tiles;
- soundproofing in the epoxy-painted masonry block walls;
- double-door entrance and/or exit;
- audio and video system; and
- space for running, jumping, and throwing activities.

Wet Space

The wet space (hydrotherapy) area generally includes whirlpools, ice machines, therapeutic pools, refrigerator, and storage for large drink containers. The area should have

- nonslip tiled floor,
- a minimum ceiling height of 10 ft,
- an appropriate number of floor drains,
- recessed plumbing for whirlpools,
- GFCI electrical supply for whirlpools and ice machines,
- storage area for drinking containers,
- a deep double-basin stainless steel sink equipped with storage,
- extra ventilation and humidity control,

- indirect fluorescent lighting, and
- close to the athletic trainer's office so constant visual contact can be maintained.

Maintenance Area

The maintenance area is where broken equipment is stored and repaired. The area needs are

- shelves,
- worktable,
- concrete floor with a drain,
- epoxy-painted masonry block walls,
- two 8-ft roll-up internal and external door entrances;
- fireproof-tiled 8-ft ceiling,
- enhanced ventilation,
- deep double-basin stainless steel sink with storage,
- GFCI electrical outlets on all walls and an electrical strip above the workbench,
- direct fluorescent lighting in the room and over the workbench, and
- storage space for an electric golf cart and its electrical charger.

Storage Space

The storage space can never be too large. The storage space requirements include

- humidity control to protect the stored tape;
- locking cabinets;
- shelves of various heights and lengths;
- a concrete floor;
- direct fluorescent lighting;
- epoxy-painted masonry block walls;
- a double-door entrance, or at least a 36-in. door, or a roll-up door for easy access; and
- a location close to the athletic trainer's administrative office area and close to loading docks and/or delivery areas.

Office Area

The office area contains all medical records and serves as the administrative hub for the athletic training room. The space needs are

- no smaller than 220 sq ft;
- a location adjacent to the wet and storage areas;
- a sight line to all other areas in the facility;
- electrical, phone, and computer outlets on all walls;
- locking file and storage cabinets;
- a carpeted floor;
- masonry block walls fitted with windows that address each area of the facility; and
- a fireproof-tiled 8-ft ceiling.

Examination Space

The examination space is often the second office area that is used as a physician's examination room. The space includes those items in the athletic trainer's office area, an examination table, and single-sink basin provided with storage above and below it. It should have a locking door, and it could best be used for record storage, as there is less traffic.

Computer/Study/Conference Area

The athletic training students will use the computer/study/conference area. This space should be no smaller than 220 sq ft. The space needs to include

- tables for computers and printers;
- a conference table;
- shelving for a small library;
- appropriate furniture for relaxing and studying; and
- storage lockers for the students' books, coats, and so forth located on the outside wall.

Classroom Design

The classroom must be dedicated for the use of the athletic training curriculum functions. Additionally, this room should have ample storage for instructional equipment and supplies used in athletic training instruction.

The American Academy of Orthopaedic Surgeons

Although NATA is the parent organization for athletic training standards, another good source is the American Academy of Orthopaedic Surgeons (AAOS). Their publication, *Athletic Training and Sports Medicine* (AAOS, 2009), contains suggestions useful for developing a training room when a curriculum is not a factor. The AAOS suggested that each organization should be obligated to provide athletic training room facilities sufficient for enhancing the athlete's health. Furthermore, this athletic training room facility is to be adequately sized; provided with utilities, supplies, and equipment; and staffed by qualified individuals. The services to be provided include preventive measures, assessment of injuries, first aid administration, emergency care, routine evaluation and treatment, and rehabilitation of injuries. The AAOS's specific suggestions are outlined below:

- The size and shape of the athletic training room should accommodate the number of individuals the facility serves.
- The athletic training room should be central to all of the activities the organization provides. Also, the facility must be equally accessible to both men and women.
- The athletic training room should be equipped with electricity, lighting, temperature control, ventilation, and plumbing.
- The walls in the athletic training room should have a minimum of two electrical outlets.

- The whirlpool area should have GFCI electrical outlets.
- Light fixtures should produce a minimum of 30 footcandles at 4 ft above the surface. When illumination varies in intensity, the brightest areas are to be used for evaluation and treatment of injuries or other conditions.
- Because warm water is used in the whirlpools and the hydrocollators, super ventilation must be present.
- The ideal athletic training room temperature is between 68°F and 70°F.
- The basic minimum plumbing requirements include a deep sink with cold and hot water, a whirlpool, and a minimum of one to two floor drains.
- The athletic training room should have a number of locking storage cabinets and closets. Additionally, a telephone, desk, computer, and file cabinet are necessary.
- The athletic training room traffic flow will be determined by the size and shape of the facility, placement of lighting fixtures, location of electrical outlets, site of phone/computer lines, and position of plumbing fixtures.

The athletic training room traffic flow problems can be improved by

- placing a bench outside a small athletic training room to reduce congestion in the treatment area,
- locating those services used less often away from the entrance,
- positioning taping tables nearest to the entrance, and
- stationing the trainer's desk so all ongoing activity can be observed.

Basic Elements for Renovating or Retrofitting an Athletic Training Room

Unfortunately, many organizations do not have the money or facilities to develop an ideal athletic training room or to implement all the recommendations of national organizations. Therefore, renovating or retrofitting present facilities is necessary. Although these two options do not make developing the ideal training room easy, providing a practical and efficient athletic training room is still possible. The elements to be considered when planning this facility include size, location, traffic flow, and structural components.

Size

LaVoie (2009) indicated the athletic training room designer, the administrative requirements of the athletic training staff, number of athletes, type of equipment, storage needs, and expansion possibilities should be considered in determining the initial size of the athletic training room. Furthermore, he stated that a rule of thumb for the size and shape of the athletic training room is unnecessary. Instead, he suggested relying on excellent communication between the designer and the athletic training staff to develop an athletic training facility that will be both productive and efficient. In a way, he agreed with the AAOS (2009) who maintained that the size and shape of the athletic training room help determine an ability to accommodate large numbers of athletes at one time.

Arnheim and Prentice (2010), however, contended that any athletic training room less than 1,000 sq ft is impractical. Instead, they recommended that the facility be between 1,500 sq ft and 2,000 sq ft, with 2,000 sq ft being the preferred size. According to them, an athletic training room of this size accommodates large numbers of individuals, along with the bulky equipment found in athletic training rooms.

Although minimum space requirements have been suggested, Arnheim and Prentice (2010) provided a specific formula for determining a rough estimate of the minimum space needs for an athletic training room. This formula is based on the assertion that each taping or treatment table is sufficient for 20 athletes and occupies approximately 100 sq ft, including the table, work area around the table, and counter and storage space. Thus, the minimum space for the athletic training room can be determined by dividing the number of athletes expected at peak times by 20. This will give the number of treatment and/or taping tables needed. Then, by multiplying by 100, you can obtain the total square footage. The formula follows:

**Number of athletes at peak ÷ 20 x 100 =
Total square footage for treatment/taping table**

Sabo (2001) agreed that the athletic training room space needs can be determined by using this formula. However, he suggested a more accurate means for sizing the athletic training room is by dividing the facility into seven functional areas: taping and first aid, hydrotherapy, treatment, rehabilitation, offices, physician's examination room, and storage. His specific recommendations for each of these areas follow:

- The taping and first aid areas are determined by using Penman's formula. However, Sabo suggested that the minimum space requirements should be large enough for six taping tables to be used at the same time.
- The hydrotherapy area space is calculated by assessing the space needs of equipment in the area. Whirlpool space is based on the assumption that one whirlpool can accommodate three athletes per peak hour. Thus, the number of athletes to be treated during the peak hour is divided by 20 to determine the number of whirlpools needed. This number is multiplied by the

square footage of the appropriate whirlpool to determine area needed. To calculate the square footage for the whirlpools, Sabo used the following guidelines: small whirlpool = 35 sq ft, medium whirlpool = 56 sq ft, and large whirlpool = 64 sq ft.
- The treatment area should be large enough to house six treatment tables with two of these having privacy curtains. According to Sabo, one treatment table will accommodate three athletes per hour. Consequently, to obtain the number of tables needed, divide by 3 the number of athletes to be treated during the peak hour. Then, multiply the required tables by 100 to assess the square footage needed in the treatment area.
- The size of the rehabilitation area depends on the amount and kind of equipment housed in this area. The space required for each piece of equipment, working area around the equipment, further expansion, and storage are added together to give approximate space requirements for the rehabilitation room.
- The head athletic trainer's office should be a minimum of 120 sq ft.
- The physician's office should be a minimum of 120 sq ft.
- The storage area should have at least 100 sq ft; however, a more accurate measure is that the room should be large enough to hold 1 year's worth of supplies.

Location

Working space and traffic flow are important to where the athletic training room is located. When followed, the guidelines listed below will meet these criteria. Ideally, the athletic training room should be
- close to bathrooms;
- close to dressing rooms, but away from the showers;
- close to water and drainage;
- easily accessible for both men and women;
- easily accessible to emergency vehicle loading zones;
- near participation areas;
- located on an outside wall;
- equipped with a street-level double door that can be operated automatically (similar to an accessible entranceway); and
- provided with a janitorial closet that has a large sink, floor drain, and storage area. This janitorial closet should be adjacent to or within the athletic training room.

Traffic Flow

The layout of the athletic training room is designed to maximize the traffic flow of individuals who are using the various services of the athletic training room. Ideally, according to Arnheim and Prentice (2010), individuals should be able to enter and exit the athletic training facilities from an outside doorway and from the men's and women's locker rooms. The design shown in their textbook illustrated an ideal layout. Some of the characteristics of this design are

- it saves unnecessary footsteps;
- it provides completely unhampered and uncomplicated traffic lanes;
- sensitive equipment is placed away from the traffic lanes;
- the athletic trainer's office is positioned in the center of the room so he or she can observe all ongoing activities;
- the physician's office is in a far corner so there will be privacy during the physician's examination; and
- the physician's office is furnished with a desk and chair, treatment table, sink, refrigerator, and storage space.

Structural Components

To a large extent, structural features will dictate the configuration of the athletic training room. Accordingly, the following structural component guidelines will make the athletic training room as functional as possible:

- Ceilings should be a minimum of 10 ft in the treatment area so tall athletes can stand on treatment tables as they are being treated. Additionally, the ceilings should be constructed of material that reflects light and deadens sound. Acoustical tiles are excellent for the athletic training room. For best results, the tiles should be white, ivory, cream, or buff color. These colors tend to reduce glare and provide good light reflection.
- Doors must be large enough to accommodate a wheelchair or a stretcher. Generally, a door 36 in. wide is sufficient for most athletic training rooms. However, if the budget is generous, double doors should be installed in at least one entrance.
- Electrical outlets should be located 3 ft to 4 ft from the floor and spaced at 6-ft to 8-ft intervals. Outlets equipped with GFCI are required in areas where there is moisture. However, it is best if all electrical outlets in the athletic training room are GFCI equipped because moisture could be present in all areas of the athletic training room.
- Equipment in the athletic training room should be a minimum of a desk and chair, bookcase, locking file cabinet, one or two visitor chairs, a computer and printer, and a desk calculator. When possible, the computer should be connected to the Internet.
- Floors should be sloped toward a drainage area, be covered with a nonslip surface, be moisture resistant, and be easily cleaned and disinfected. Good materials for the floor include concrete, vinyl tile, ceramic tile, and poured liquid floors.
- Illumination in the athletic training room should provide even and efficient light on the work surface. Fluo-

rescent fixtures with diffusers for eliminating flickering and that produce a minimum of 30 foot-candles, 4 ft above the work surface, are good choices. For evaluation and treatment areas, 50 to 60 foot-candles, 4 ft above the work surface, are recommended.

- Plumbing should follow all applicable building codes, and the plumbing area must include at least one floor drain equipped with a trap to prevent odors from entering the athletic training room. The plumbing area has a concrete floor covered with a paint that has been modified to prevent slippage, rubber strips, pitted surfaces, or a rubberized liquid coating. The plumbing area should have a backflow device, a deep sink (preferably a double sink) equipped with hot and cold running water, and at least one whirlpool located in an area with a floor drain. Additionally, all electrical outlets must be GFCI rated, and it is recommended that all equipment used in the plumbing area be approved by the Underwriter's Laboratory as safe for use in wet areas.
- Storage facilities are of prime importance, and the storage area should include lockable cabinets, lockers, and closets. For best results, the storage facilities should be near the working space but out of the traffic flow. Another storage consideration is designing the storage area so that it does not require excessive space. An example of efficient use of space is the taping and storage table at Austin Peay State University. This taping table shown on the next page is 42 in. high, 144 in. long, and 48 in. deep. It will accommodate four to five athletes for taping, and it is located near the entrance to the athletic training room and adjacent to the head athletic trainer's office. Beneath the tabletop are lockable cabinets that are used to store tape and other supplies. Directly across from the taping and storage table is a treatment storage cabinet, which is 42 in. high, 84 in. long, and 26 in. deep. This cabinet is approximately 6 ft from the taping table, making it easy for the trainers to obtain the supplies they need for minor treatment and for preventive taping and wrapping activities. Another good feature of this taping and storage area is its close proximity to the athletic trainer's office and that it facilitates preventing waste of materials and supplies and requires very little square footage.
- Temperature control is provided with heating, ventilating, and air-conditioning (HVAC) units capable of maintaining a constant temperature range of 72°F to 78°F and a humidity range of 40% to 50%. Additionally, the temperature control system must be sufficient to change the room air eight to 10 times each hour so vapors from the warm water present in the whirlpools and hydrocollators can be exhausted continuously. Moreover, it is recommended, when possible, that the athletic training room temperature control units be

separate from the rest of the building's temperature control units.

- Windows should be installed in such a manner that all activities in the athletic training room can be observed but, at the same time, the privacy of individuals who may be conversing in the office area is maintained. One-way mirrors are good choices when privacy and adequate supervision are of primary importance.

Equipment Considerations for the Athletic Training Facility

Athletic training rooms contain a variety of equipment with the extent of the equipment being determined by the availability of financial resources and physical facilities. There are three categories of athletic training room equipment: basic, moderate, and ultimate (well equipped).

Basic equipment needs. Basic equipment for the athletic training room consists of a dry and wet heat source, cold source, rehabilitation source, locking supply cabinet, treatment cabinet, training table, and whirlpool. Other features are listed below.

- Heat lamps provide dry heat for treatment of injuries. If a heat lamp is not available, a heating pad is a good substitute. Both of these dry heat devices are inexpensive and safe for use in the athletic training room equipped with GFCI electrical outlets.
- A refrigerator is necessary for maintaining an adequate supply of ice for use in treating injuries. A used refrigerator may be purchased in any locality at a reasonable price; however, it should be remembered that the main feature of this refrigerator is its capacity for making and keeping ice. It is also useful for storing ice bags and cold water.
- A double sink equipped with hot and cold running water, hooked to a trapped drain, and with under the sink storage and counter space of 2 ft to 4 ft is strongly recommended. Sinks are relatively inexpensive and can be purchased at home centers. Sinks may also be obtained from salvage yards or obtained when someone remodels a home or business.
- A supply cabinet is an essential piece of equipment for the athletic training room. The supply cabinet may be either metal or wood and it may be constructed or purchased secondhand. A suitable closet may be used, but it is important that supply storage areas be kept locked to prevent waste and misuse of athletic training materials. The photo on the following page shows a suitable supply cabinet used in the Austin Peay State University athletic training room. The cabinet is 66 in. high (36 in. on the bottom and 30 in. on the top), 18 in. on the bottom section, 8 in. deep on the top section, and 30 in. wide.
- The treatment cabinet must have an adequate working surface and space for holding first aid and other treatment supplies. It should lock to prevent misuse of supplies and to keep the supplies sanitary. A set of regular quart mason jars placed on the cabinet surface is recommended to keep dressing materials clean and available. The size of the treatment cabinet will vary among athletic training rooms; however, a treatment cabinet 78 in. high, 18 in. to 20 in. deep, and 36 in. wide is adequate for most basically equipped athletic training rooms.
- The training table is the most essential piece of athletic training room equipment, as it is used for examining injuries, applying treatment modalities, and applying protective taping and/or wrapping. The training table is usually constructed of heavy wood and measures 78 in. long, 24 in. wide, and 30 in. high. The top is covered with foam rubber or some other form of padding over which an easily cleaned cloth or other covering is applied. Figure 25.1 shows the pattern for a basic athletic training table.

Austin Peay State University taping table

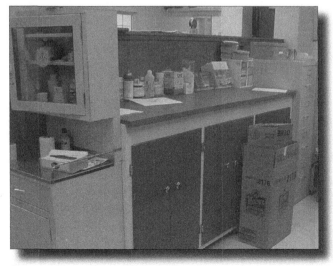

Austin Peay State University taping area storage cabinet

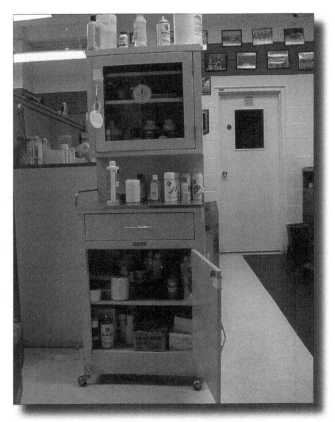

Austin Peay State University supply cabinet

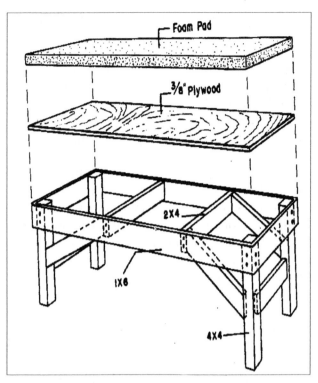

Figure 25.1. **Athletic Training Table Pattern**

- The whirlpool is another essential piece of equipment for the athletic training room for its use in applying wet, moving heat to athletic injuries. It is important that the whirlpool is on a concrete surface and that the area has adequate drains plus GFCI-equipped electrical outlets. The photo to the right shows a whirlpool setup in the Eastern Kentucky University athletic training room. One way of improvising a whirlpool bath is to take an old bathtub and equip it with a portable agitator. Be certain the improvised whirlpool is properly grounded and connected to GFCI electrical outlets.

Examples of Moderately and Well-Equipped Training Rooms

Examples of moderately and a well-equipped athletic training room are those at Austin Peay State University (APSU) and Eastern Kentucky University (EKU). APSU is a retrofitted facility, and EKU is a newly built structure.

Austin Peay State University

APSU in Clarksville, Tennessee, is typical of a moderately equipped athletic training room facility. It was retrofitted from a small athletic training room for football, two locker rooms, three shower rooms, a steam room, a large hallway, a sunken whirlpool and its deck, and an equipment issuing room.

The athletic training room contains 2,138 sq ft, and it is divided into seven components: head athletic trainer's office; assistant athletic trainer's office; team physician's office; treatment room; taping, wrapping, and weighing room; hydrotherapy room; and storage areas.

Head athletic trainer's office. The head athletic trainer's office has 132 sq ft (11 ft x 12 ft). It was retrofitted from an equipment issuing room and has an entrance door from the hallway and a door leading to the taping table. The door leading to the taping table area has glass so it offers a direct sight line to the taping table area and a partial sight line to the treatment room. Yet the office design allows for privacy when it is needed. It contains

Eastern Kentucky University whirlpool setup

- a desk and chair,
- a chair for consultations,
- a computer connected to the Internet,
- a printer for the computer,
- a telephone,
- a recording machine for voicemail,
- a calculator,
- two 2-drawer and one 4-drawer file cabinets,
- a large double-door cabinet that has locking drawers and file cabinets,
- a bookcase with adjustable shelves and a locking cabinet and drawer, and
- a small bookcase with three shelves.

Assistant athletic trainer's office. Two assistant athletic trainers share an office containing 110 sq ft (10 ft x 11 ft). The office was constructed from an area in the rehabilitation area. It has two windows and a glass door with a clear sight line to the rehabilitation activities. This office is equipped with

- two desks and chairs,
- one computer with Internet connection,
- one printer,
- a small worktable,
- two file cabinets, and
- bookshelves along one of the walls.

Team physician's office. The physician's office has 96 sq ft (12 ft x 8 ft) and is located at one end of the treatment area. It has

- a solid door for privacy,
- a telephone,
- a desk and chair,
- an examination table,
- locking storage cabinets along one wall, and
- a sink with hot and cold running water.

Treatment room. The treatment room is located in a separate room that can be partially observed by the head athletic trainer from his office. It was once a locker room, and it has 345 sq ft (23 ft x 15 ft) of space. It has the following treatment modalities:

- Orthotron KT1 exercise table,
- Synatron 500 Electrotherapy CTL CTR,
- Nemectron 2 ultrasound therapy unit,
- Pentium Z station ZSK-8559,
- Electrotherapy ultrasound modality,
- two Mettler electronic stimulators,
- Z station,
- treatment tables,
- examination tables,
- a hydrocollator and hydrocollator tree, and
- a computer with printer.

Rehabilitation room. The rehabilitation room was retrofitted from a dressing room. It has 448 sq ft (28 ft x 16 ft) of space in which the following pieces of rehabilitation equipment are located:

- a Nemectrodyn Model V,
- a Nemectrodyn MDL-2 nerve stimulator device,
- an Orthotron II Fitron cycle-ergometer,
- a Cybex 2450 upper body exerciser,
- a Lifestep 1000, and
- a cable column rehabilitation device.

Taping, wrapping, and weighing room. The taping, wrapping, and weighing room has 228 sq ft (19 ft x 12 ft) of usable space. It, like the rehabilitation room and assistant athletic trainer's office, was retrofitted from a room used for dressing and locker space. It has a taping table that is 144 in. long, 42 in. high, and 48 in. deep; a large weight scale; and a storage cabinet that is 84 in. long, 26 in. deep, and 42 in. high. The taping, wrapping, and weighing area is directly to the right of the entrance into the training room and is situated directly adjacent to the head athletic trainer's office. It is separated from the rehabilitation area by a 5 in. thick wooden partition wall that is 60 in. high and 145 in. long.

Hydrotherapy room. The hydrotherapy room was once a shower room. It contains 60 sq ft (10 ft x 6 ft), and it has a full body whirlpool and two extremity whirlpools. It is located adjacent to the treatment area, but it must be entered through a door from the treatment room, making it impossible to supervise its activities from any of the offices or other areas of the athletic training room. It has GFCI electrical outlets and excellent drainage. Additionally, the area has a curb that prevents overflowing water from entering the treatment or storage areas.

Storage areas. The APSU athletic training room has four retrofitted storage areas other than those already mentioned. One of these is a converted shower room containing 84 sq ft of usable space (14 ft x 6 ft). It houses the ice machine, and it is where all the drinking and ice containers and the crutches are kept.

Another major storage area is located directly across from the hydrotherapy room in what was once a hall leading from the treatment room area to a steam room and a sunken whirlpool. This area contains 240 sq ft (16 ft x 15 ft). It has lockable metal and wooden lockers that are used to store various treatment and rehabilitation supplies and equipment.

The area that was originally a large sunken whirlpool has 255 sq ft (17 ft x 15 ft) including the large whirlpool, the whirlpool deck, and the hallway leading to the steam room. The area is used mostly for large boxes as well as a variety of protective and preventive equipment.

The former steam room is the most secure storage area, as it has a metal door and is away from any traffic flow. It has 180 sq ft (15 ft x 12 ft). It is used to store old records and sensitive supplies and equipment. The room also has temperature and humidity controls not present in the other storage areas.

Eastern Kentucky University

EKU's new athletic training room is an example of a well-equipped facility, and it demonstrates what can be done when building a new athletic training room. It is located on the first floor of the 40,000-sq ft Harry Moberly Classroom, Wellness, and Conditioning Building. The first floor of the building houses the physical education activity/laboratory, the weight room, and the athletic training room. On the second floor, there is a wellness center, three large classrooms, human performance and computer laboratories, offices, locker rooms, showers, and dressing rooms. Primarily, the building houses the College of Health, Physical Education, Recreation, and Athletics and the 16 intercollegiate athletic teams.

The athletic training room is located between the weight room and the physical activity/laboratory. It is entered from the main foyer through glass-enclosed double doors that do not have thresholds. The athletic training facility functional areas include

- a taping/treatment area,
- a rehabilitation area,
- a treatment/therapy area,
- glass-enclosed office,
- therapy storage area,
- hydrotherapy cooler storage area,
- an inground hydrotherapy pool equipped with a treadmill,
- rehabilitation storage area,
- treatment storage area, and
- hydrotherapy room.

In addition to the areas depicted in these photos, the athletic training facility has three aboveground therapeutic pools in the hydrotherapy area, X-ray room with accompanying equipment and exposure control measures, and private examination rooms. All office doors have either full glass or partial full-length glass so activities can be observed from the office. There are artificial and natural light sources in all areas.

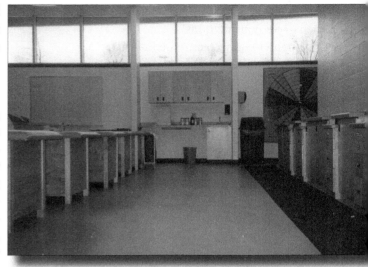

Eastern Kentucky University taping/treatment area

Eastern Kentucky University rehabilitation area

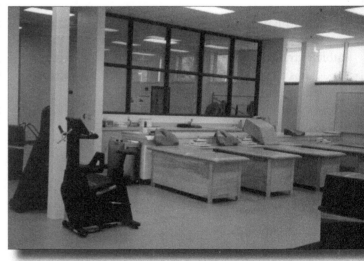

Eastern Kentucky University treatment/therapy area

Eastern Kentucky University office area

Eastern Kentucky University treatment/therapy storage area

**Eastern Kentucky University
hydrotherapy cooler storage area**

Eastern Kentucky University inground therapy pool with treadmill

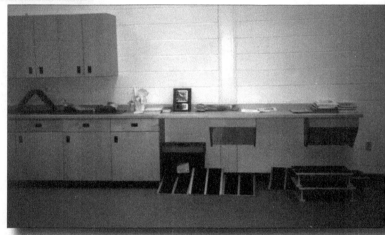

Eastern Kentucky University rehabilitati storage ar

Eastern Kentucky University treatment storage area

Eastern Kentucky University hydrotherapy room

26

Shooting Facilities: Archery, Rifle, and Pistol

Jason Winkle, *Indiana State University*

The evolution of modern shooting sports can be traced back to early man's development of bows, arrows, and spears for protection and to gather food. Around 3500 BC, the Egyptians used archery as a weapon of war (*USA Archery*, 2008). Much of the early development of archery was based on designing archery equipment for a military application. Bows and arrows were used not only as weapons but also for leisure activities and contests. Homer, in the *Iliad*, referenced archery contests in which archers shot at tethered doves. During the 14th century in England, archery practice was mandatory for all able-bodied men (Van Dalen & Bennett, 1971). The advent of gunpowder led to the decline of archery as a tool of war and to the increased development of firearm activities. Organized firearms shooting began in Europe when the first shooting clubs were formed. Public shooting matches were first seen in Europe around the 16th century and in America in the early 1700s.

The rules for shooting sports began to standardize when the National Rifle Association (NRA) was founded in the United States in 1871 and the National Archery Association (NAA) was formed in 1879. Numerous disciplines have developed for rifle, pistol, and archery sports; therefore, the facilities, equipment, and procedures used for shooting activities and competitions vary greatly. This chapter will focus on facilities, equipment, and operational procedures required when developing and operating competitive indoor rifle and pistol facilities and both indoor and outdoor archery facilities. The equipment, facility design, and risk management issues associated with these competitive shooting facilities can be applied or adapted to other shooting activities and facilities.

Planning and Designing a Shooting Facility

Whether a shooting facility is planned and designed from scratch, an existing facility is remodeled to accommodate shooting activities, or an existing shooting facility is renovated, detailed planning will avoid costly design mistakes. The major factors that usually determine facility design are the funding; availability of appropriate space; nature and scope of the program; and quality of the planners, architects, and engineers involved in the project.

Because each planning and design situation is different, the relative importance of each design criteria will vary with each project. Based on guidelines for facility planning and shooting facility-specific design criteria, the following are sound general guidelines for planning a shooting facility:

- **Participatory planning.** Involve the stakeholders in the planning process. This may include establishing a formal planning team.
- **Needs assessment.** Determine past, present, and future needs and desires as early and as accurately as possible in the design process.
- **Site selection.** A large, relatively flat area is ideal because archery ranges are large facilities that usually require a flat shooting area. Consider the type and use of adjacent areas when selecting the shooting facility site. Using natural land features such as hillsides may provide natural backdrops if available.
- **Build to code.** Be certain all construction meets governmental (local, state, and national) building codes and Americans With Disabilities Act (ADA) requirements. If the shooting facility is to be used for competitions, be sure the facility specifications meet or exceed those required by sanctioning agencies. For target archery, the Fédération Internationale de Tir à l'Arc (FITA) and the NAA are the recognized sanctioning

organizations. These organizations publish detailed rules and specifications for sanctioned archery competitions.

- **Support selection.** A careful and judicious process should be used when selecting the architect, engineers, contractors, and other consultants. Select individuals or organizations that have experience in building shooting or similar facilities and have good references. Do not hesitate to contact previous customers.
- **Risk management.** When planning a shooting facility, be certain to address security, access control, and buffer zones around shooting areas.

The specific design features for a shooting facility will depend on the availability of an appropriate site, the availability of funds, the type of shooting, and many other factors. Proper prior planning will help ensure a highly functional and efficient shooting facility.

Archery

Archery is the art, sport, or skill of shooting with a bow and arrow. Although this may sound simple, many archery disciplines and activities have developed over the years. Competitive archery as we know it today originated in England in the 17th century.

Most early competitions fell into one of three general categories of shooting: butt shooting, clout shooting, or roving. Butt shooting consisted of bowmen shooting from set distances at targets mounted vertically on earthen mounds or butts. Most modern competitive archery programs and competitions are based on butt shooting. Clout shooting involved shooting arrows into the air and having them land on a target mounted flat on the ground. The third type of archery was roving, where archers simulated hunting over rough ground and shooting targets representing animals. Roving is the forerunner of today's field archery programs that focus on hunting-oriented shooting. Field archery shots are often made uphill or downhill and may involve shooting around obstacles.

The most popular and numerous archery ranges are basic outdoor designs often referred to as "place-to-shoot ranges." These unmanned place-to-shoot ranges usually have target distances from 25 yd to 100 yd and cater to bow hunters. Some ranges include a field archery course that has targets placed in a natural setting and may even have tree stand stations to simulate bow hunting. Archers bring their own equipment and shoot unsupervised. Few specific design features other than a parking lot, outhouse, and possibly a covered pavilion are normally included. Most archery programs in schools, colleges, recreation settings, and the Olympics are based on early forms of butt shooting. The equipment, facilities, and risk management procedures used for this type of target shooting are well established and clearly defined by FITA and NAA. This section will focus on facilities and equipment to support competitive target archery programs. Most of the facility and equipment issues for competitive target archery are applicable to other less structured types of archery shooting.

Outdoor Target Archery Competitions

Most major outdoor target archery competitions in the United States include a FITA Round followed by an Olympic Round. A FITA Round consists of 36 arrows shot at each of four distances (90 m, 70 m, 50 m, and 30 m for men; 70 m, 60 m, 50 m, and 30 m for women) for a total of 144 arrows. Arrows are generally shot in groups of six (called ends) within a specified time period. Scores are then totaled to determine seeding for the Olympic Round. An Olympic Round is a direct elimination, head-to-head competition shot at 70 m. The winner of each match advances until a champion is determined. All matches are 18 arrows, except the quarterfinals, semifinals, and finals, which are 12-arrow matches.

Indoor Target Archery Competitions

Indoor tournaments are held for the Recurve (Olympic) and Compound Divisions. Recurve Division events are generally held at either 25 m or 18 m. In a 25-Meter Indoor Round, archers shoot 60 arrows at a 60-cm diameter target face. In the 18-Meter Indoor Round, archers shoot 60 arrows at a 40-cm diameter target face. Championship events employ a Grand Indoor Round that starts off with a Combined Indoor Round (both 25-m and 18-m rounds) followed by a direct elimination competition for the top 16 archers. These direct elimination matches are 15-arrow matches shot at a special 20-cm diameter target face. Competitions in the Compound Division usually consist of a Combined Indoor Round of 60 arrows shot from 25 m at a 40-cm diameter target face. A Grand Indoor Round, used in championships, consists of a Double Combined Indoor Round. The top 16 archers advance to direct elimination matches made up of 15 arrows at 25 m.

Target Archery Ranges

Competition target archery ranges must be designed and built to meet or exceed FITA and NAA specifications, the recognized sanctioning organizations for most archery competitions. FITA and NAA have also established standards for field archery and ski-archery, but these standards are outside the scope of this chapter.

Target archery ranges are often set up on multipurpose outdoor fields or in large multipurpose indoor areas. Some schools, clubs, camps, and other agencies have custom designed permanent archery facilities. The Beijing Shooting Range Hall, used in the 2008 Olympics, is an example of a world-class shooting hall. Whether the shooting facility is a permanent facility or a temporary setup in a multipurpose facility, a classroom or meeting room is recommended if the shooting facility is to be used by a club or for educational purposes.

Outdoor archery ranges are most effectively laid out on level turf oriented north to south with shooting aimed to the north. The actual shooting length of the archery range will vary depending on the shooting event being contested, but the range layout is basically the same for all events. The archers shoot from the shooting line at targets placed at the prescribed distance. The minimum spacing of the targets for competitions depends upon the number of shooters per lane. If shooters are shooting singly or in pairs, the minimum spacing between targets is 2.5 m (8 ft, 2 in.); if the archers are shooting in threes, the minimum spacing is 3.66 m (12 ft). All targets should be clearly numbered. Shooting marks, consisting of discs or other flat markers, should be positioned opposite the targets at the shooting line. The shooting marks have the number that corresponds with the target for that lane. A line extending from the shooting line to the target line establishes shooting lanes. A waiting line should be placed at least 5 yd be-

hind the shooting line. An equipment area may be marked off behind the waiting area. Behind the equipment area a space for athletes is recommended. A 50-yd buffer zone must be roped off behind the targets to keep spectators, competitors, and officials safe (see Figure 26.1).

Traditional targets consisted of a boss of tightly coiled roped straw about 4 in. thick and 4 ft in diameter on which was stretched a target face. Targets for both indoor and outdoor target archery competitions are now often made of high-density foam. Targets must be secured to target stands, called butts (buttresses), which are secured to the ground. For indoor archery, targets must be inclined, tilted back, between vertical and 10°. For outdoor archery, targets must be inclined 10° to 15°.

The center of the target for both indoor and outdoor targets must be 130 cm (4 ft, 3 in.; within 5 cm) above the ground for single target faces. All targets must be inclined at the same angle. The target face consists of 10 rings made out of five different colors. The scoring is 10, 9 (gold); 8, 7 (red); 6, 5 (blue); 4, 3 (black); 2, 1 (white) from inner circle to outer ring. The rings all have the same thickness (except for the compound competitions where the 10 is made

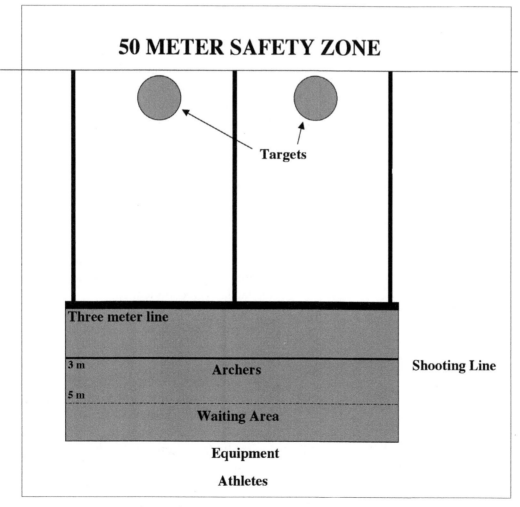

Figure 26.1. **Sample Archery Range Layout** (*Source:* Meghan Rosselli)

smaller). Target sizes vary at different distances and may be displayed as a single face (see Figure 26.2), triple faces triangular, or triple faces vertical.

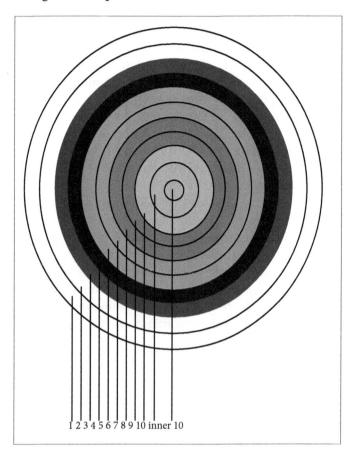

Figure 26.2. **Single-Faced Target** (*Source:* Meghan Rosselli)

·**Targets in front of a protective mound**

Venue Support Equipment

If an archery range will be used for competitions, especially FITA- or NAA-sanctioned competitions, additional venue support equipment will be required. The following are brief descriptions of the additional equipment that may be required to host a sanctioned archery tournament.

Barriers. Some type of physical restraint should be placed on the range to mark safety buffer zones to keep spectators out of the archers' competition areas and facilitate desired circulation patterns. The barriers may be as simple as a rope suspended between two poles or a fenced-in area with directional signage attached. The barriers must clearly designate safety zones and provide a physical obstruction.

Scoreboards. A minimum of one large scoreboard is needed for posting scores. For large sanctioned competitions, smaller scoreboards should be placed near the target butt to display a progressive score for each shooter. For less formal competitions and during match competitions, flip scoreboards may be used.

Flags. Judges and officials are often separated from the archers and other meet officials. Flags or a similar device should be available for judges and officials for signaling or requesting assistance.

Speaker system. Important announcements will need to be made during competitions to archers, coaches, officials, meet organizers, and spectators. A quality speaker system is needed to meet this requirement.

Timing control equipment. Most archery competitions have time limits for the archers to shoot their ends. Enforcing the established time limits is essential in having a fair competition, so both visual and acoustic time signals are required for most sanctioned competitions. Visual time signals can be given with digital clocks, lights, flags, or other simple visual devices. The acoustical signals may be given with a whistle, an air horn, or a similar device.

Archer identification. Tournament officials, organizers, and spectators need to be able to identify archers competing in the competition. In championship tournaments, archers must wear name tags and have a nameplate displayed at the target area. Even at less formal tournaments, archers must wear some type of identification tag, number, or vest.

Field glasses. Some type of visual aid is often necessary for competition administrators and officials to spot arrows. Providing field glasses or a telescope at the shooting facility is recommended.

Shooters Equipment

Bows used for target archery are held in one hand and drawn with the other. They may have an adjustable arrow rest on the riser. The bowstring is permitted to have a center serving to fit the arrow nocks, with one or two nock locators and one attachment to serve as a lip or nose mark. An audible or visual draw checker (clicker) may be used as long as it is not electrical. Stabilizers and torque compensators are allowed as long as they do not touch anything but the bow itself and do not interfere with other competitors on the shooting line.

Recurve bow. A recurve bow is a relatively short bow that was preferred over the longbow by archers who were forced into environments where long weapons could be cumbersome. A recurve bow used for target archery consists of a handle riser and two flexible limbs terminating in nocks supporting a single string.

The distinguishing feature of the recurve bow is that the ends of the limbs curve away from the archer when in the shooting position (see Figure 26.3). This recurve shape reduces loading at full draw (let-off) and will impart more energy to the arrow than a standard longbow of similar top draw weight.

Compound bow. Compound bows have cams and cables, making the holding weight less than half of the draw weight. Bow hunters favor them because of their greater accuracy, flatter arrow trajectory, and ease of use. A compound bow with a peak draw weight of 60 lb or less may be used for target archery competitions. Cables and cable guards are allowed (see Figure 26.4). The bowstring may contain a peep sight or hole for sighting. The bow sight may not have electrical components but may contain lenses and/or multiple aim points. A mechanical string release may be used as long as it does not attach to the bow and has no electrical components.

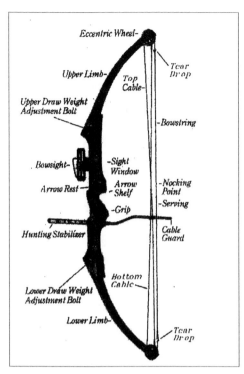

Figure 26.4. The Compound Bow
(*Source:* Meghan Rosselli)

Strings. Strings are usually made by twining several strings of Kevlar®, Dacron®, or polyethylene to make a single cord. Dacron® is relatively inexpensive, but prone to creep, meaning that it may stretch and make for inconsistent shots. Dacron® is recommended for bows with wooden risers and older bows because the other string materials might put too much stress on the bow. Aramid fibers (Kevlar®) have very little stretch, thus giving the arrow a flatter trajectory. The disadvantage of Kevlar® is that these fibers cannot take much shear, so they tend to break more often, usually just below the nocking point. Kevlar® fibers are also susceptible to moisture; therefore, these strings have to be waxed carefully. Polyethylene fibers are the latest addition to string materials. Polyethylene strings last at least as long as those made of Dacron® and are less susceptible to moisture than other string materials.

Sights. The sight can come in many forms, but the most popular sight has a circular sight with a crosshairs or pin at its center. Some compound bows incorporate a "spirit level" that tells the archer if the bow is tilted.

Arrows. Wooden shafted arrows are still used with longbows and for recreational purposes but are rarely used for competitive target archery. For competitive target archery, arrows of any type may be used as long as the diameter is 9.3 mm (.366 in.) or less. Arrows should be marked with the competitor's initials, and all arrows used in an end must be of uniform color, shaft, fletching, and cresting. The most commonly used arrows for target archery are made of aluminum tubes, carbon fibers, or an aluminum–carbon

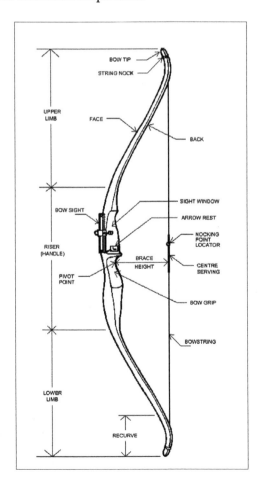

Figure 26.3. The Basic Recurve Bow
(*Source:* Meghan Rosselli)

combination (a thin aluminum tube inside and carbon fibers on the outside).

Aluminum tube arrows are more durable than either of the carbon fiber-type arrows. Carbon fiber arrows and aluminum–carbon arrows are nearly impossible to repair if damaged. Aluminum–carbon arrows are the most commonly used arrows for outdoor shooting. All three arrow types are used for indoor shooting.

Vanes, also called the fletching, are the three feather-like attachments near the rear of the arrow that keep the arrow tracking. There are two options for vanes, either plastic vanes or real feathers. Plastic vanes are less affected by moisture and are recommended for outdoor shooting.

General archery equipment. A bow, arrows, and a target are required for target archery shooting, but experienced archers rarely shoot with only the bare essentials. Archers or those conducting an archery program, whether highly competitive or recreational, should consider purchasing the following general archery equipment:

- *Arm guard.* A piece of leather or other durable material that fits over the bow arm that keeps the string from contacting the arm when the string is released.
- *Chest guard.* Protects the chest and prevents clothing from becoming caught by the string.
- *Finger protectors.* One of a variety of protective finger stalls, gloves, tabs, or tape methods to protect the fingers on the draw hand.
- *Quiver.* An arrow-holding device that can be worn on the body or attached to the bow.
- *Arrow straightener.* A device that measures arrow bend and straightens arrows.
- *Grip/arrow pull.* A rubber grip that helps in removing arrows from the target.
- *Fletching jig.* Allows you to fletch a shaft, put vanes on it.
- *Nocking jig.* Allows you to accurately replace a nock on the arrow shaft.
- *Stringer.* Recurve archers use this device to string their bows. Compound bows are permanently strung and many longbows have built in stringers.
- *Stringing rig.* A device you can make your own strings with.
- *String server.* A device that allows you to create nocking points on the string.

Equipment Care and Maintenance

The Bow
The bow is the most important piece of equipment in archery, so keeping it in good working condition is essential. A sound practice is to never lay the bow on the ground. This can cause dust and other materials to damage or ruin sensitive parts of the bow. If a bow becomes wet for any reason, dry it off as soon as possible even if the finishes are waterproof. Metal bows may rust, reducing bow function. Apply bow wax to preserve the bow's finish.

Bowstrings
This vital part of the bow is perhaps one of the easier areas to damage. To avoid damage, archers should use bowstring wax to keep the string waterproof. This will help keep the string in maximum performance condition and prevent it from becoming tangled.

Arrows
Although numerous and somewhat inexpensive, an arrow which has even the slightest malfunction can cause unexpected and unwanted results. Protect the fletching from getting wet or becoming damaged. Repair or discard damaged arrows. Serious archers should only use arrows deemed to be in perfect condition.

Target Butts
To help prevent fungus growth, mold, and premature deterioration, do not place target butts on damp floors or leave them uncovered in the rain.

Target Faces
Target faces must be in good condition. Remove faces while moistening butts. If the face is torn, use masking tape to bind the tears.

Replacing a Plastic Nock
Nocks may become worn down and will need to be replaced, so inspect the nock regularly.

Replacing a Feather or Vane
Replacing a feather or vane is easy, but restoring an arrow to competition quality is difficult and requires skill, experience, and the use of a feather jig. Feather replacement is only recommended for arrows that will be used for recreation or practice shooting.

Replacing Arrow Points
The condition of the arrow shaft directly behind the point should be checked when replacing points. If the shaft is damaged, the arrow cannot be repaired unless the shaft is shortened. Salvaged arrows may still be used for school, recreation, and practice purposes, but are no longer suitable for competition shooting.

Storage
The amount of storage required for an archery facility will vary based on many factors. If the archery facility is used for instructional and recreational programs where the program sponsors provide the equipment, well-secured storage will be necessary. If the archery facility is simply an outdoor facility that stocks limited personal archery gear,

the storage requirements will be considerably less than a facility that provides equipment. If any bows and arrows are to be stored, they must be stored in a secure area because they could be used as weapons. Archery equipment, especially bows, arrows, and targets, must be stored in a dry environment to avoid damage.

Rifle and Pistol

The first consideration when designing an indoor shooting facility is determining what type of shooting will be conducted. Firearm caliber, muzzle velocity, and the nature of the shooting all play an important role in the construction needs of the facility. Firearms commonly used in indoor ranges include air pistols, air rifles, handguns of various calibers, and rifles with muzzle velocities below 3,500 ft per second. Indoor ranges can also be used for a variety of shooting approaches from basic marksmanship to tactical shooting where participants practice defensive shooting skills. Although each of the above-mentioned shooting variables has unique facility needs, they all share common design characteristics.

This section will examine these common design characteristics and design and construction standards for indoor shooting ranges.

Space Needs

Once the types of shooting that will be conducted in a facility have been determined, the focus can shift to designing a facility to adequately and safely house these shooting activities. The largest expense in range development is usually the real estate that comprises the shooting area. Thorough planning to determine space needs is critical to keep development prices from escalating dramatically. Most competition shooting can be accommodated with a range that provides 50 ft to 100 ft between the target and the firing line. The industry standard length, however, is 84 ft, 4 in. (Navy Environmental Health Center [NEHC], 2002). Be sure to identify all space needs, including support functions such as parking areas, restrooms, storage, office space, lobby area, and circulation space.

Ceiling Height and Construction

An important space consideration is ceiling height in the range. A ceiling that is too low or too high can cause ricochet issues that must be addressed with baffles and other types of ballistic protection. A ceiling height between 10 ft and 12 ft is recommended (NEHC, 2002). This height provides adequate overhead clearance for downrange shooting as well as keeping lighting, ventilation, and target retrieval system costs to a minimum.

A slab ceiling is the industry standard. Slab ceilings require few baffles and guards, thus reducing costs. Guards are required, however, for exposed light fixtures, ducts, conduits, and plumbing. For ceilings other than slab, baffles and guards must be placed at angles that are determined by the length and height of the facility. A 30° angle to the ceiling is suggested for baffle placement.

Shooting Stalls

Shooting stalls function as protective dividers between shooters in the range by preventing interference from expelled casings, misdirected shots, and other distractions. In addition to their protective characteristics, stalls also provide a stable mounting position for range equipment. Stalls are typically equipped with a self-controlled target retrieval system to prevent shooters from stepping downrange from the firing line. A stall width between 42 in. and 48 in. is suggested.

Shooting stalls are typically constructed of double-wall steel liners covered in a molded shell. Although steel has been the industry standard, a new clear acrylic stall is becoming more popular. The acrylic stall is popular in academic shooting ranges due to the unobstructed view the clear dividers provide range personnel.

Shooting stalls for shooters

Wall Construction

Range walls provide a protective shell between the interior of the range and the building exterior or adjacent spaces. In addition to their safety function, walls play an important role in noise attenuation. Most range walls are constructed of poured concrete. Concrete block is also acceptable; however, the block should be filled with grout or cement. Unfilled block is sufficient in ballistic security but has poor sound-dampening qualities. Sound-dampening tiles are recommended for the walls from an area 10 ft forward of the firing line to 20 ft in front of the bullet trap.

Flooring

The flooring in shooting ranges needs to be durable enough to withstand the high volume of stray shots that will strike it and smooth enough to prevent erratic ricochets. Most ranges use a hardened concrete floor. Absorbent material behind padding for construction should include floor drains. It is recommended that floor drains and sloped floors be excluded from the shooting area. Environmental regulations stipulate that all floor drains located between the firing line and the bullet trap must contain filtration systems. These systems tend to be expensive and require substantial maintenance.

The flooring from the firing line backward should be covered with a nonslip surface. Moderate traction in these areas is suggested to prevent shooters from losing their footing. Many ranges have a vinyl floor cover in this area to prevent slippage. Carpeting is not recommended as it tends to collect lead dust and is cumbersome to clean (NEHC, 2002).

Bullet Traps

Bullet traps have evolved substantially over the past 50 years. Environmental standards, particularly during the 1980s, have changed to accommodate environmental and safety concerns, but the object of the bullet trap has remained constant. The goal of a bullet trap is to provide a means of decelerating the bullet into a collection chamber. A brief description of the plate and pit trap, Venetian blind trap, steel escalator trap, and the granular rubber trap is provided below.

Plate and pit trap. The first widely accepted bullet traps used a steel plate that was secured at a 45° angle into a deceleration chamber (NEHC, 2002). The bullet would strike the angled plate and break apart inside the chamber. Although this method accomplished its purpose, it raised environmental concerns due to the generation of lead fragments and lead dust that accompanied a destroyed bullet. Other concerns with this type of trap include high noise levels from bullets striking steel, as well as erratic ricochets.

Venetian blind trap. The first widely accepted improvement to the plate and pit trap was the Venetian blind trap. The trap used a series of impact plates angled at approximately 35° to direct bullets into a deceleration chamber (NEHC, 2002). The bullet's velocity and energy is dissipated via friction. Typically this trap is a small freestanding trap, making it a popular model for shooting ranges.

Steel escalator trap. The next evolution of bullet traps improved on the problem of bullets hitting the front edges of the Venetian trap. This improvement was accomplished by designing a sloping plate that directed bullets into a deceleration chamber. This trap uses sloping surfaces to create multiple striking areas where the bullet loses energy and then drops into a collection tray.

Granular rubber trap. The latest development in high-tech, environmentally sound bullet traps is the granular rubber trap. This trap is constructed with an inclined skeleton of steel that supports a sloped mound of granulated rubber covered with a rubber blanket for containment. This design provides excellent sound attenuation as the bullets strike only rubber. Lead recovery is also simple and safer because the bullets are not destroyed upon impact. Bullets are decelerated and contained in the top 10 in. of the granulated rubber. Erratic ricochets resulting from hitting the trap itself are no longer a problem.

Range Lighting

Shooting range illumination entails general facility brightness and target-specific lighting. Fluorescent fixtures typically generate general illumination. A soft light is preferable for general areas of the range. Target-specific lights need to be much brighter and have the ability to be moved to achieve a direct focus on a target. Recommended downrange lighting should be approximately 100 foot-candles measured 4 ft above the floor at the target face (NEHC, 2002). These lights should be baffled to protect them from misdirected shots. Many shooting experts, however, prefer recessed floor spotlights. Shadows are typically less of a problem with bottom-illuminated targets. It is important to have protective covers for floor lighting because stray shots often strike the floor of a range.

Target Retrieval Systems

The purpose of a target retrieval system is to place the target downrange and retrieve it in a safe and convenient manner. Target retrieval systems allow the shooter to remain behind the firing line. The type of shooting that will be conducted in the range determines the type of retrieval system needed. Most target shooting consists of firing at a stationary bull's-eye target at predetermined distances and then retrieving the target to determine shooting accuracy. Two types of target retrieval systems are commonly used for this purpose: a guide wire system and a steel track sys-

Shooting target system

tem. These retrieval systems have the features described next.

Guide wire system. This system uses a guide wire that is suspended between the bullet trap and the firing line. A target attachment travels along the tight guide wire to place the target downrange or for retrieval. The shooter typically controls the target's movement along the guide wire via a control switch located in the shooting stall. Many models of guide wire systems allow for intermediate target stops for various shooting distances. One limitation of guide wire systems is that they typically do not allow for target oscillation.

Steel track system. A steel track system is the most common target retrieval choice in commercial and law enforcement facilities. In addition to providing shooters with multiple stops, these systems offer 180° turning targets to present tactical situations. A steel track runs along the length of the shooting lane, providing the support structure for an oscillating target system.

Range Control

There are a variety of range control systems on the market, each with unique features. All of these systems, however, serve as the command center for target placement and retrieval. Some systems are controlled from the shooting stall and others use a central control booth. The level of sophistication and the capabilities of a control system depend upon the type of target system being used and the type of shooting desired.

High school and collegiate ranges typically only require a basic system that is controlled at the shooting stall. These systems contain a forward and reverse toggle switch for target placement as well as a Range Master call intercom.

A computer-based control center is often used in military and law enforcement facilities. These systems offer sophisticated options for tactical training. Training scenarios can be created and downloaded into individual shooting stall systems to provide a personalized shooting session.

Range Ventilation

Exposure to lead in a shooting facility is a major concern for all range planners. Lead, when absorbed into the body in certain doses, can be toxic. When a gun is fired, lead dust and fumes are released. The amount of lead dust in the air is greatly increased in a range that uses steel bullet traps.

When a bullet strikes a steel plate, it is destroyed, sending lead fragments and dust into the air. Federal and state health standards regarding permissible exposure to lead (PEL) must be adhered to when developing an indoor range. Ventilation systems should provide airflow from the firing line toward the bullet trap. Exhaust points should be located downrange from the shooter. Heating, ventilat-

ing, and air-conditioning (HVAC) systems are especially important in shooting facilities; therefore, shooting facility planners should enlist the services of an experienced HVAC engineer to ensure the ventilation system meets all safety and government standards.

As industry, state, and federal standards continue to tighten, the need to include a state-of-the-art ventilation system increases. Typically, a ventilation system is a large portion of shooting facility development costs. Professional developers recommend spending the money for a highly efficient and effective system rather than one that only meets minimum requirements. This may prevent the need to do a costly upgrade to meet governmental standards in the future.

The Occupational Safety and Health Administration (OSHA) established a PEL limit of 0.05 mg per cubic meter of air that is based on an 8-hr time weighted average. More information regarding permissible exposure to lead can be found in the National Institute of Occupational Safety and Health's Publication Number 76-130.

Ballistic Security

Range designers must be cognizant of potential ricochet threats and stray shots that may occur in a range. Misdirected shots can be extremely dangerous if protrusions in the range are not covered with protective baffles and guards. The three primary types of ballistic security used in indoor ranges include re-directive guards, air-space baffles, and steel guards. Each of these security devices has a particular function in the range. Steel guards are most often used in facilities that have slab ceilings. These guards are positioned in a manner that directs any impact toward the bullet trap. Steel guards should be used to protect all protruding light fixtures and ductwork.

Re-directive guards serve the purpose of deflecting stray shots in the direction of the bullet trap. These guards are typically located just in front of the bullet trap, as they are the guards that receive the greatest percentage of stray shots. Their composition should match the composition of the bullet trap. Steel bullet traps should use steel re-directive guards, and rubber air-space guards should be earmarked for rubber traps.

Air-space baffles are a critical safety buffer for indoor ranges. These horizontally suspended panels reduce the risk of injury resulting from a vertically discharged shot by trapping the round in the panel.

These baffles are constructed with a thin layer of rubber that is separated from a steel plate. A misfired shot passes through the rubber surface and strikes the steel plate. After striking the steel plate, the bullet bounces back across the air space and re-strikes the rubber face. The baffle decelerates the bullet to where it no longer has the velocity to exit the baffle. The bullet is therefore trapped inside the air space.

The danger zone for vertical shots extends from the firing line to 15 ft downrange. Air-space baffles should be hung at regular intervals for the first 15 ft and then where needed to protect protruding objects. Baffles should be installed with a 30° angle in relation to the floor.

Risk Management

Establishing and maintaining sound risk management policies and procedures is especially important for shooting facilities because weapons are involved. Shooting facility design must consider risk management issues, including

- staffing—training (type, duration, and certification) and ratios (staff to participants);
- insurance—waivers (professionally developed) and liability (specific to activity and venue);
- emergency procedures—first aid and emergency action plans;
- equipment and supplies—safety checks, handling, storage;
- facility inspections, procedures, rules, and signage;
- ensuring that shooters use appropriate eye protection and ear protection;
- properly locating the activity so that it does not pose a hazard to participants or spectators; and
- providing adequate spacing so that the activity may be performed safely.

Dance Spaces

Thomas H. Sawyer, *Indiana State University*

Dance in education is not a new idea. At all educational levels, it has existed by virtue of dedicated individuals. In elementary schools, dance activities under a number of aliases—eurhythmics, rhythms, play party games, singing games, and folk dance—have been offered. Coming into the elementary school curriculum as an offshoot of the playground movement, dance materials presented were usually happenstance (with a few exceptions in experimental schools). A classroom teacher may have been interested in folk dance or faced with the necessity to prepare a May Day, a pageant, or a festival.

Within the past few years, many privately administered elementary schools and some public schools have made provisions for dance in the curriculum. By and large, existing physical education facilities are used.

Since the turn of the century, folk dance (usually European in origin) has been offered in physical education classes for girls in secondary schools. When folk dance lessons were first introduced, they were often limited in content and skill and were, as in the elementary school, an outcome of the playground movement. Toward the end of the 19th century, a few secondary schools in large cities had gymnasiums that were primarily equipped for gymnastics and other sports using limited-sized courts. The use of these areas for dance was spasmodic and usually occurred in preparation for special events.

In the 1920s, dance in education was materially advanced when Margaret H'Doubler initiated the first dance major at the University of Wisconsin. During this period, clog and tap dance assumed a leading role in dance education, and Henry Ford promoted a return to the formal square dances of an earlier day, such as the Lancers.

By the 1930s, the United States was sufficiently removed from its pioneer beginnings to acknowledge the joy and value of square dancing. The teaching of social dance was heavily emphasized as a means of implementing the social values of physical education. Modern dance—stemming from natural dance and from the influences of Martha Graham, Doris Humphrey, Charles Weidman, and others—began a slow but steady growth in curricular offerings. In 1931, great impetus was given to dance in education with the establishment of the National Section on Dance within the American Association for Health, Physical Education, and Recreation (NDA, 2012).

The advancement of physical education programs was not without trauma for teachers and administrators. Until World War I, with its emphasis upon fitness and recognition of the recreational needs of service personnel, it was difficult to finance facilities and staff for physical education. Immediately after the war, mobility and better communications enhanced the athletic program, and as the result of athletic needs, more gymnasiums and stadiums were built. The need for a gymnasium in secondary schools was thereby placed on a firm basis. The depression of the late 1920s and early 1930s, however, curbed these programs and the extensive expansion of facilities. World War II not only emphasized fitness and the recreational needs of service personnel but also added a new dimension: recreational needs of war workers in factories, shipyards, and munition plants. The Cold War and the possibility of increased leisure time have reiterated the needs for enriched curricula and additional facilities.

Until recently, studios for dance at the secondary school level had dropped in priority behind athletic and aquatic facilities. At the beginning of the 20th century, dance was often better off than were sports in the low-ceilinged basement rooms and narrow hallways. As gymnasiums were built primarily for basketball programs, dance was relegated to a low priority in the use of these facilities for both class and after-school clubs. Moreover, the finish or seal on gymnasium floors made certain dance activities uncomfortable and precluded others. Within the past 10 to 15 years, there has been a growing consciousness of the needs of girls in secondary schools. As dance has proved its worth as a physiologically demanding and aesthetically rewarding activity, consideration is being given to the employment of specialized teachers and the provision of specialized areas for teaching dance at the secondary level.

Gradually, clog and tap dance, natural dance, and later ballroom and square dance as well as modern dance have appeared in the secondary school curriculum. Of significance is the increasing interest of boys in the various forms of dance, especially modern jazz. Frequently, dance programs at the secondary school level are the result of grants from the National Endowment for the Arts (NDA, 2012).

As was true in elementary and secondary schools, facilities for dance education at the college level have developed slowly. The gymnasium dominated the scene, with dance scheduled catch-as-catch-can during available hours. As emphasis upon dance in teacher preparation increased and as colleges and universities became more involved in all phases of the arts, auxiliary rooms were planned for dance and related activities.

Basic Dance Facility Assumptions

The essential facilities should be supplied in sufficient quantity and quality to provide for all dance activities in the required and elective curriculums and in extracurricular programs. Particular attention should be given to adequate provision for dance performance, observation, and audience spaces.

Related portions of the activity complex should be provided and meet acceptable standards. These will include
- box office;
- construction rooms for costumes, props and sets, and music (composing and recording);
- costume storage areas;
- custodial space;
- laundry, cleaning, and drying facilities;
- listening areas;
- locker/dressing rooms with makeup areas;
- office space;
- parking area;
- public lavatories;
- rest rooms (remote from toilets and showers);
- shower area;
- storage spaces (props and sets);
- toilets; and
- training room. (NDA, 2012)

The following should be provided and meet established standards:
- electrical installation,
- lighting equipment,
- acoustics,
- ventilation,
- heating,
- floors,
- walls,
- sanitation,
- safety,
- drinking fountains,
- sound systems,
- filming and taping facilities,
- installation of fixed equipment,
- movable equipment, and
- lines of traffic. (NDA, 2012)

Dance facilities should be designed to serve both genders. Furthermore, the dance facility should be readily accessible to outside entrances and be a unit unto itself even if it is attached to, or a part of, another building. Finally, the dance complex should be constructed, decorated, and furnished in an aesthetically pleasing manner and suitable for the pursuit of dance as an art form.

Criteria for Determining Facility Needs

The following criteria can be used to determine the dance facility needs when planning either a stand-alone dance facility or one for inclusion in a larger complex (NDA, 2012).

Total facilities should be determined according to the amount of emphasis placed on various aspects of the dance curriculum, such as classes needed and areas for individual work and for extracurricular and concert practice.

Based on the design of the dance curriculum, facilities should be considered in terms of
- auxiliary space and equipment,
- classroom space,
- dance teaching space,
- office space,
- performance space,
- practice space and choreography,
- rehearsal space, and
- research space.

Preferably three distinct areas should be provided: one area for folk and social dance, one area for modern dance, and one area for ballet.

Construction of Modern Dance and Ballet Areas

The following information is provided to assist in the development of state-of-the-art modern dance and ballet areas (NDA, 2012).

Dimensions

- A minimum of 100 sq ft per person is recommended. An area of 3,000 sq ft will accommodate 30 students.
- If an area is to serve as an informal theater and instructional area, it should be between 4,800 sq ft and 5,000 sq ft to accommodate both the class and the needs of the theater section.
- Ceiling height of 16 ft to 24 ft is recommended for all dance areas. Full height is essential for large dance areas (over 2,400 sq ft), and 16 ft is the minimum height for small dance areas. There is a feeling of height when the ceiling is high. Some dancers prefer a height of 16 ft to 18 ft, but the total construction in the dance areas must be considered. In some instances, any change in the roofline may add prohibitive expense.

Floors

- Dance activities require air space between floor and foundation and "floating" and/or spring floors for resiliency.
- Floors should be made of hardwood (e.g., maple) of random lengths and tongue-and-grooved; they should be laid with the grain going in one direction.
- Portable floors (marley or stage-step) provide flexibility for use when both ballet and modern dance need to be accommodated.
- Floors should be nonslip and constructed for easy cleaning.
- The finish should provide a smooth surface upon which dancers can glide with bare feet or soft sandals. Tung or linseed oil is considered by most to be a satisfactory finish; an alternative might be several coats of wood sealer. Chemical dust mops should not be used to clean such floors, only a slightly damp mop.

Doors

There should be wide double doors to permit traffic flow into and out of the room. The sills of such doors should be level with the floor to allow for moving large equipment such as a piano.

Walls

- Walls should be smooth and easily maintained.
- Consideration should be given to having one unobstructed wall of neutral background for filming purposes.
- Stress factors of the walls should be considered to support ballet barres and mirrors.
- Thin walls are inadequate.
- It is desirable to soundproof walls, especially in listening areas.

Lighting

- Incandescent light is preferable to fluorescent light.
- Rheostat lights that also serve as houselights during performances should be controlled from wall switches as well as from the light control board.
- Natural lighting should be considered. Large windows contribute to an aesthetically and psychologically desirable atmosphere. The best location for windows is the north wall to avoid direct sunlight.
- Windows should be curtained so the studio can be darkened for film showing and studio performances.
- When total construction necessitates no windows, the aesthetics may be improved by using a pastel color on the walls or having draperies serve both aesthetic and acoustical purposes.

Acoustics and Sound Equipment

- When one studio is directly over another or over offices, acoustical treatment is necessary.
- Placement of sound equipment, such as a record player, turntable, microphones, and speakers should be considered in the initial planning in terms of performance and security.
- An adequate number of speakers, installed in or near ceiling height, should be located so participants can hear music and instruction.
- Heavy equipment should be placed on stands of table height equipped with rollers.
- Electrical outlets should be spaced on every wall and located close to where equipment will be used. Four-plex outlets are needed close to the area where most equipment is used (e.g., videotape recorders, tape deck and amplifiers for performance, and stage manager's desk for cueing lights).

Storage Space

- Locked storage space for sound equipment should be adjacent to the dance area. Storage rooms should have double doors and a flush threshold for easy movement of large equipment, such as a piano.
- Built-in storage space for records, sound equipment, tapes, and musical instruments should be provided.
- A soundproof area for use of students and instructors in listening to recordings and tapes and viewing videotapes is highly desirable. This area should have adequate acoustics, ventilation, and electrical outlets.

Wiring

- Heavy-duty wiring is essential for all dance facilities. Wiring should be capable of carrying a portable light board as well as phonographs, additional speakers, tape recorders, and projectors. Wall outlets should be plentiful.

- Television conduits should be installed at the time a building is constructed.

Temperature and Ventilation
- Temperature should be maintained at 65°F to 72°F (22°C to 26°C). The thermostat should be located in studio areas.
- The air should be well circulated, and consideration should be given to the use of natural air. Humidity should be no greater than 95%.
- Mechanisms for heating and circulating of air should be as silent as possible to avoid interfering with the quality of sound and its reception.

Accessories
- Leaf-fold mirrors, which can be folded for protection or curtained during performances, may be installed along two adjoining walls so that movement can be analyzed from two directions. Wall mirrors at least 6 ft high should be installed flush with the wall and raised 1 ft or 1 ½ ft from the floor.
- Ballet barres should be made of wood, preferably oak, or aluminum and be smooth in texture. The minimum length to accommodate one dancer is 5 ft. Barres from 40 in. to 42 in. in height may be installed permanently; they should extend 6 in. to 8 in. from the wall. If feasible, consider double barres—one at 36 in. and one at 42 in. If necessary, barres may be placed in front of mirrors. The barre supports may be screwed into recessed floor sockets just in front of the mirror, thus facilitating the removal of the barre and supports when not needed.
- Custom-made percussion cabinets mounted on rollers are a fine accessory. They may have a carpeted top surface, slide-out drawers lined with felt for small instruments, and larger partitions to accommodate cymbals and drums.
- Heavy sound equipment should be built in or placed on stands of table height equipped with rollers for ease of transportation.
- Because moving affects the tuning of a piano, this instrument should be placed where it will not have to be moved. A piano should be placed on an inside wall where it will not be subject to extreme heat or cold and be protected by a suitable cover and lock. It should be placed on a heavy-duty dolly if it is to be moved frequently.
- Chalkboards and tackboards are useful accessories.
- Telephone.
- A glass-enclosed exhibit case for photographs, costumes, costume plates, manuscripts, and other items may be installed near the dance area. A building foyer may be used.

- The atmosphere for dance should be conducive to artistic endeavors. Soft colors, clear lighting, and spaciousness are pleasing to both dancers and spectators.

Construction of Folk and Social Dance Areas

The following information is provided to assist in the development of state-of-the-art folk and social dance areas (NDA, 2012).

Dimensions
- An area of 5,400 sq ft (54 ft x 100 ft is suggested) will accommodate a class of approximately 60 students.
- Dance areas are generally rectangular with a length–width ratio of approximately 3:2 (e.g., 90 ft x 60 ft).
- Ceiling height should be in proportion to the size of the room but never lower than 12 ft.
- An outside entrance into a main corridor of the building will provide for traffic flow of the relatively large groups using the area.

Floors
Floors, as described in the section on ballet and modern dance, are necessary. However, an epoxy finish, rather than tung oil, will enable the use of street shoes without damage to the floor.

Lighting and Ventilation
- Acoustics and sound equipment (see above).
- Storage space (see above).
- Wiring (see first point under wiring above).
- Temperature and ventilation (see above).

Accessories
- Racks for coats and books should be installed either within the dance area or along the outside corridor wall.
- Tackboards, chalkboards, and display cases are highly desirable.

Dance Production Areas
Although a well-equipped theater is the ideal dance performance area, it is not always possible to have such a facility. The alternative is to provide a large area for both instructional and performance activities. The area may be equipped with a balcony for observation of classes and for audience seating during performances. Other seating arrangements such as portable bleachers may also be desirable. A large area may be equipped to provide for arena, proscenium staging, or both.

Arena Stage Area

The planning for an arena stage area should include performance space, seating, lighting, sound equipment, control booths, and wiring. The following sections describe the specifics needed in each area.

Performance space. The performance area should contain between 875 sq ft and 1,200 sq ft (NDA, 2010).

Seating space. The most desirable seating capacity for performances should accommodate 300 to 500 people. The entire performing area should be visible from all seats. The seating arrangement should be flexible. Seats may be on movable risers so space may be used in a variety of ways. Raked seating is essential. Adequate entrances, exits, and exit lights should be provided for performers and audience in accordance with local fire codes.

Lighting. Lighting should be available from all directions. It should be possible to use gels on all lighting instruments except houselights. All lights should be on separate dimmers. A sufficient number of electrical outlets should be available. When possible, all lights should be operated from a single console within the control booth.

Sound equipment. Equipment should be operated from a control booth. Speakers for amplification should be placed so both performers and audience can hear. Backstage monitors should be used.

Control booths. Provision should be made for control booths with full view of the stage area to operate lights and sound.

Wiring. Wiring should be adequate enough to carry a portable light board, phonograph, tape recorder, speaker system, projector, and follow spots (see local electrical codes).

Proscenium Stage Area

The planning for a proscenium stage area should include performance space, seating, curtains, teasers, battens, lighting, sound equipment, control booths, and live musicians. The following sections describe the specifics needed in each area.

Performance space. The minimum performance area should be 1,200 sq ft (30 ft x 40 ft). The two wing areas combined should be equal to the amount of visible stage space. Space should be provided for musicians, chairs, and lighted music stands. Placement of musicians should not interfere with the visibility of the stage or the sound of the music (NDA, 2012).

Seating space. A balcony with permanently installed raked seating is desirable, with the possibility of portable risers below. The entire performing area should be visible from all seats. The number of seats should be planned for the estimated size of the audience.

Curtains, teasers, battens. Hand control is preferable to a mechanically controlled front curtain. Side curtains (legs) or flats should be provided on both sides of the stage for entrances and exits. Flexible tracks to move the curtain horizontally should be considered. Asbestos teasers and tormentors are needed for safety and masking. Battens to be used for hanging scenery, sky drop, or film screen should be suspended above the visible stage area. Provision should be made for lowering and raising battens for the attachment of scenery. Lines should be attached to a pin rail located at one side of the stage. Metal grids are also usable. The back wall should be free of visible obstructions and painted white for projections. Curtains and flats should be light, absorbent, and neutral or dark colored.

Lighting equipment. Provision should be made for side lighting, front lighting, and overhead border lighting. Three separate circuits should be provided to be used singly or in combination. There should be front ceiling beam lighting, balcony lighting, or both. Crawl space should be provided in the ceiling above the beams to permit focusing and repair work. It should be possible to use gels on all lights except house lights. All instruments should be on separate dimmers. A sufficient number of electrical outlets should be located in floor pockets or wall spaces in the wings. A low wattage light should be installed for cueing performers and crew members at the side of the front stage. When possible, all lights should be operated from a single console within the control booth.

Sound equipment. Equipment should be operated from the control booth. Speakers for amplification should be placed so both performers and audience can hear. An intercom should be used to link the backstage, dressing rooms, and control booth. Telephones to handle outside calls should be located in the box office and backstage. The backstage phone should be equipped with a signal light.

Live musicians. If feasible, space should be allocated for performance appearances.

Control booths. Control booths for lights, sound, and projections should be centered at the audience end of the facility and should include soundproofing, a large window for viewing the stage, built-in counters and shelves for storing equipment, and an intercom for communication with the backstage area.

Auxiliary Areas

The following auxiliary areas need to be included in the planning process for a dance facility.

Costume Room

A costume room for constructing, fitting, cleaning, and storing should be a minimum of 400 sq ft and be equipped with or accessible to

- built-in cabinets with shelves and drawers, as well as racks for hanging and storing costumes;
- cleaning machine;
- control room with toilet facilities;
- cutting table;

- double door with a flush threshold to facilitate moving costume racks;
- dress forms;
- ironing boards and steam irons;
- laundry tubs and drying facilities;
- sewing machines;
- tackboard and chalkboard affixed to one wall;
- three-way mirror; and
- washing machine and dryer.

Dressing Rooms

Dressing rooms should be provided for men and women. They should be equipped with costume racks, chairs, washbasins, lighted mirrors, toilets and showers, and a first aid kit.

Makeup Room

The makeup room should be located between the men's and women's dressing rooms and be furnished with lighted mirrors, built-in shelves, makeup tables, chairs, washbasins, and storage space.

Scene and Prop Room

The scene and prop room should be located as close to the stage area as feasible. It should be a minimum of 400 sq ft to 500 sq ft and have a ceiling height of at least 16 ft, although 24 ft is preferable. The floor should have a paint-resistant surface. Proper ventilation is necessary to avoid fumes from paint and glue. The room should be furnished with built-in bins and shelves for storage of nails, brushes, screws, paints, and glues; a pegboard mounted flush with the wall for hanging tools; a built-in workbench; a wash sink; outlets for electrical tools; and a chalkboard and tackboard. Storage space for props should be a minimum of 500 sq ft with a 16-ft to 24-ft ceiling; it should be easily accessible to the backstage area (NDA, 2010).

Box Office (Ticket Booth)

The box office should have locked racks for tickets, a locked drawer for currency, a telephone with an outside line, and an intercom to the backstage area.

Foyer

It is desirable to provide a social area where the audience and performers may meet following a production. It should be situated adjacent to the performing area and include attractive decorations, a comfortable seating arrangement, display cases, and an adjoining small kitchen for preparing refreshments.

Additional Instructional and Laboratory Facility Needs Based on the Size of the Dance Program and Curriculum

Three areas need to be planned for in the dance facility, including teaching space, office space, and auxiliary space.

Teaching Space

The following are planning considerations for dance teaching areas:

- There should be a minimum of one large teaching and performance area. This area should have a 24-ft ceiling and resilient floors and be equipped with special lighting for performance, sound equipment, a communications media, an observation balcony, and good ventilation and lighting.
- Two additional areas should be provided: an area for ballet and modern dance and an area for jazz, social, and folk dance.
- Provision should be made for well-designed and well-equipped classrooms and seminar and lecture rooms for instructional use.
- In addition to the performance area, there should be rehearsal space that is somewhat larger than the area designed for performance.
- There should be an area for practice and choreography that is equipped with phonographs, tape machines, and videotape equipment.
- A library and reference room with an adjoining study area for books, music, records, tapes, and copying machine should be available.
- Provision should be made for a soundproof recording studio large enough to accommodate a piano and small orchestra, turntables, and tape recorder. It should have built-in shelves for storage and be not less than 300 sq ft.
- Storage space for musical instruments should be provided.

Office Space

The dance facility office space should include

- a centralized office for unified administration,
- a private office and conference space for the director of the dance program,
- office space for faculty members and for technical personnel,
- supporting space for office equipment and storage, and
- laboratory space for faculty.

Auxiliary Space

Additional auxiliary space might include

- a reception/social room (with adjoining kitchen) for use by students, faculty, and community groups on special occasions;

- locker/shower areas for students and faculty of both genders;
- a faculty conference room; and
- a rehabilitation or therapy room.

Adaptation of Dance Facilities and Equipment

Because local conditions may demand modification of ideal dance facilities while a dance program is being developed, this section describes adaptations that may be feasible.

Elementary School

Current practices. Small gymnasiums are used most frequently, with cafeteria–gymnasiums, multipurpose rooms, and auditorium–gymnasiums following in close order. Class sizes range from 25 to 70 pupils, with 30 being the average size.

With regard to floor surfaces used for the instruction of dance, hardwood predominates, with linoleum tile running second. The floors in winter should be heated.

Use of limited facilities and equipment. Practically speaking, securing ideal dance facilities in all situations at the elementary school level is impossible. Community socioeconomic conditions virtually negate such a dream. Lack of ideal facilities and equipment is no reason to omit dance experiences for children. A dance program that includes children's movement experiences can be staged in a multiple purpose space. Further, children can be taught to move lightweight classroom furniture (e.g., desks and chairs) efficiently so that a dance space can be made. By paying constant attention to opportunities for renovations in a school (or a school system), a teacher may ask for use of renovated space, for installation of bulletin boards and electrical outlets, and even for changes in floor surfaces. Teacher initiative is a priority if space for dance is to be acquired.

Recommendations. Dance areas for elementary school children should be large enough to accommodate approximately 30 students. Rooms below ground level are inadvisable because of possible dampness and lack of adequate ventilation. As increasing numbers of elementary schools are being built on a one-floor plan with outdoor exits for individual classrooms, basement facilities will gradually vanish.

Hardwood is advised for dance floors. Tile floors, which frequently are laid directly on cement or concrete, are cold to the touch, often slippery, and conducive to injury. Because tile flooring allows no resiliency for foot action, it can lead to painful shin splints.

There is no answer to the exact type of dance facility that should be provided. Except under unusual circum-

stances, economics rule out the provision for a dance studio. The combination gymnasium–lunch room is not recommended because of loss of time for classes before, after, and during lunch hours, and the health hazards of dust on food and lunch debris in the activity area. A stage–auditorium, stage–gymnasium, small gymnasium, multipurpose room, or large playroom may be used if adequate electrical outlets and wiring for record players, tape recorders, and minimal stage lighting can be provided.

The informal dance programs presented at the elementary school level can often be accommodated by seating the children on the floor and visitors on chairs around three sides of one end of the dance area. Usually storage space for recordings and simple percussion equipment is available in, or adjacent to, such areas. Many physical education items can be used in the dance program. Jump ropes, balls, boxes, benches, mats, and other play apparatus lend themselves to creative uses.

Dance for children has become an established activity in elementary school programs. It can only take place, however, when space and equipment are provided, time is allocated, and leadership is available.

Secondary School

Current practices. It is extremely difficult to secure detailed information on dance programs at the secondary school level. The size of areas used for dance varies from extremely small to extremely large, with a rectangular shape being most common. In height, the areas vary from 8 ft to 40 ft. Record players and tape recorders are usually available. Percussion instruments, drums predominating, are also used. Some secondary schools have closet space set aside for costumes, and some even have a full costume room. Ballet barres and mirrors are used. Wooden floors predominate. One secondary school reported that excellent additional practice space is available, and several schools noted that smaller additional space is available, and several secondary schools noted that smaller additional space is available when not in use by other groups.

Use of limited facilities and equipment. Few secondary schools have specialized facilities for dance. One reason is that dance has not been adequately emphasized in the secondary school curriculum. There is some indication, however, that specialized concentrations (dance, sports, aquatics, gymnastics) in teacher preparation and a cultural emphasis upon the arts are beginning to alter this pattern, particularly in suburban areas and in certain consolidated school districts. As these programs begin to establish their value, obtaining facilities will become easier.

Meanwhile, the standard gymnasium can be used. Teachers who are interested in providing dance experiences for their students can plan curricular units, secure a few portable barres, borrow a record player and/or tape recorder from the audiovisual supply room, find a storage area for a few percussion instruments, and secure space for a costume closet. The floor with the usual gymnasium seal on it is not ideal but can be used. The battle for time allotments and space assignment is perennial. Interest and effort can perform wonders.

Recommendations. A minimum dance facility should provide 100 sq ft per student, one dimension to exceed 60 ft; full-length mirrors at a corner for analysis of skill from two directions; a speaker system designed to distribute sound evenly throughout the room; a control system for record players and microphones; and practice barres on one wall at heights of 34 in. and 42 in. For modern dance, the floor should be hard northern maple that has been sealed and then buffed with a fine abrasive. Additional suggestions are included in the next section (NDA, 2012).

Equipment. As in the case of the elementary school, physical education equipment such as balls, ropes, and gymnastics apparatus may be used. Stall bars, if available, are an excellent substitute for ballet barres and a fine medium for creative activity.

Wise planning can allow basic equipment (recordings, percussion instruments, and portable lighting boards) to be floated from school to school for production use.

Portable percussion racks made in an industrial arts department solve the problems of easy storage and efficient class and program use. Portable mirrors, 6 ft tall and 8 ft wide, can be constructed 1 ½ ft from the floor on rollers and moved into the dance area if wall-mounted mirrors are not feasible. Portable ballet barres of lightweight aluminum are desirable when unobstructed wall space is at a premium.

Floors. Poor floors should be covered by marley dance flooring rather than a ground cloth.

Areas. Investigation of the following areas may reveal available spaces for dance: adaptive rooms, gymnastic rooms, weight control rooms, recreational game rooms. Careful preplanning of new facilities suggests the possibility of combining two or more of these. Two community resources are feasible: churches and local theater groups. Churches are now interested in dance. Either temporary or permanent use of a large classroom or a church auditorium may be possible. Community theater groups are adding dance experiences for all age levels to their gamut of activities. It may be possible to arrange for use of their areas during the school day.

The possibility of pooled resources in the performing arts—dance, drama, music—opens wide potential in the development of excellent facilities, economy in their use by several departments, and rich experiences in multimedia.

Performing arts for modern dance or ballet. The following specific recommendations are made for modern dance and ballet areas:

- The stage should be situated at the end of the room that can best provide entrances for the dancers. The dancers' entrances should be out of the audience's view.
- The stage can be formed by curtains or flats.
- A back curtain should have a center opening and be hung at least 3 ft forward of the back wall to provide crossover space for the performers.
- In the case of a raised stage, the front curtain should be set back about 4 ft from the raised edge to provide an apron (forestage).
- Side curtains or flats should be provided.
- If curtains cannot be used, an open stage is advisable. The folding mats used in physical education can be set on edge to form entrances and exits. Flats and portable screens are alternative possibilities. (NDA, 2012)

Performing area for folk and social dance. The following specific recommendations are made for folk and social dance areas:

- Roll-away bleachers can be installed at one end of the room.
- Provision should be made for storage of folding chairs, which can be placed along the side walls.
- An auxiliary performing space can be a patio or other outdoor area, such as a dance green or a broad, level surface at the entrance to a school building, which can be adapted for occasional use for dance performances. Marley dance flooring may be placed on the cement surface to protect the dancer's feet and legs. (NDA, 2012)

As in the case of elementary schools, specific dance facilities are not feasible in all secondary schools. Dance is possible, however, depending on the teacher's interest, effort, and ability to adapt to the situation.

College/University

As new facilities have been constructed and older facilities remodeled in the larger colleges and universities, there seems to be little excuse for omission of areas specifically planned for dance. The increasing emphasis upon dance as a major field and the increasing interrelationships among the performing arts have placed dance in a position of importance in college planning.

Section V

Trends and History

28 Design Trends in Stadiums and Arenas, 1975–2012

Todd L. Seidler, *University of New Mexico*

John J. Miller, *Troy University*

This chapter will present an overview and analysis of certain recent trends and innovations in stadium and arena design. It is by no means a complete look at these unique sports facilities; many additional trends and innovations are covered in other parts of this book. This chapter will merely try to highlight certain significant trends and concepts that should not be overlooked.

Constructing and Funding Sports Arenas and Stadiums

Stadium and Arena Construction

In the relatively early days of sports in America, many stadiums were designed for teams in different sports. For example, the Polo Grounds in New York City was the home site for the New York Giants of the National Football League and Major League Baseball. Wrigley Field, while being more famous as the home of the Chicago Cubs, also hosted the Chicago Bears. Other stadiums that were used for multiple professional teams included Tiger Stadium (Detroit Lions and Tigers), Comiskey Park (Chicago Cardinals and White Sox) and Candlestick Park (San Francisco Giants and 49ers). Presently, the Oakland-Alameda Coliseum is the only facility that is shared by a baseball team (Oakland A's) and football team (Oakland Raiders). It is important to note that these stadiums should not be confused with the multiuse complexes of today. These stadiums were designed for one team in a particular sport (i.e., baseball) while a team in different sport (i.e., football) used it as well. For the context of this chapter, multiuse stadiums are those designed for a specific sport but shared by one or more teams of another sport. Conversely, multipurpose stadiums (which will be discussed later in this chapter) are designed to accommodate the needs of more than one different sport.

Analysts argue that the rapid changes in design and available amenities over the last decade have rendered any stadium over 10 years old economically obsolete. Since the year 2000, 21 new stadiums were built for the National Football League (NFL), National Basketball Association (NBA), Major League Baseball (MLB), and National Hockey Association (NHL). In fact, the number of functional stadiums and arenas opened to the public before 1990 is dwindling. By the end of 2012, nearly every American sports team was playing in a facility that was 20 years old or newer. Even Yankee Stadium in New York and Lambeau Field in Green Bay, which are arguably the most identifiable venues in their respective sports, have undergone major renovations recently.

Capacity Trends

According to Quirk and Fort (1997) and Sawyer (2009), the median capacity for an MLB field was 36,677, 10,000 for NBA arenas, 13,350 for an NHL arena, and 47,246 for an NFL stadium. Komisarchik and Fenn (2010) reported that MLB stadiums constructed prior to 1995 averaged a total attendance of 45,368, while more current ballparks average 44,419 spectators. Regarding the NBA, Komisarchik and Fenn (2010) indicated that older arenas (pre-1995) held an average of 19,652 fans, while those constructed after 1995 had a average capacity of 19,159. Furthermore, older NFL stadiums had an average capacity of 71,162, while stadiums constructed after 1995 could hold 70,563 fans on average. Interestingly, National Hockey League was the only major North American professional league that exhibited a capacity increase, as the average capacity of an NHL arena constructed prior to 1995 was 18,244, while the more recent arenas seated 18,381 spectators (Komisarchik & Fenn, 2010). Thus, professional football, baseball, and basketball decreased their average spectator capacity for stadiums or arenas constructed after 1995, while professional hockey increased the average capacity of their arenas during the same time period.

Trends in Stadium and Arena Costs

Some of the most impassioned discussions regarding the construction of new sports stadiums or arenas has involved public financing implications of new stadiums and arenas. Komisarchik and Fenn (2010) revealed that an excess of $6.6 billion was allocated to MLB facilities constructed or proposed between 1995 and 2009; nearly $7 billion was distributed to National Football League venues. Furthermore, almost $1.9 billion was designated for arenas that housed NBA and NHL teams, $1.6 billion was allotted for arenas that housed only NBA teams, and slightly more than $1.4 billion for NHL-only sites. Thus, the total cost to construct professional sports stadium or arena North America between 1995 and 2009 was approximately $18 billion dollars (Komisarchik & Fenn, 2010).

A breakdown of the cost of constructing an individual stadium or arena for MLB, NFL, NBA, and NHL use showed significant increases (Komisarchik & Fenn, 2010). For example, the price of an MLB field prior 1995 was $187 million, which was increased by more than double ($389 million) in 2009; NFL stadium construction costs rose from $182 million before 1995 to $365 million. The NBA arena average costs increased by $149 million between 1995 and 2009. The NHL was the only professional North American league in which the average construction costs decreased from $217 million before 1995 to $207 million after 1995

More recently, two new stadiums, New Yankee Stadium and the Dallas Cowboy Stadium, reportedly cost in excess of $1 billion to build. Of major concern to the owners of these facilities is the ability to maximize revenue-generating potential. Some of the most important trends in revenue generation and financing of stadiums and arenas is the selling or leasing of luxury suites, the naming rights to the facility, and personal seating licenses, which will be discussed in the next sections.

Luxury Suites

Luxury suites have long been cited as the most important part of state-of-the-art sports facilities today (Danielson, 1997; Sawyer 2009). As such, one of the most dynamic trends that have developed in the design of spectator sport facilities is the inclusion of luxury suites in professional as well as intercollegiate arenas and stadiums. Additionally, suites are now found at rodeo arenas; PGA, LPGA, and Senior PGA events; the Kentucky Derby; the U.S. Olympic track and field trials; and ATP Tour tournaments; among others. This popularity may be traced to luxury suites becoming a significant tactic to take full advantage of cash flow per seat in most stadium construction projects (Howard & Crompton, 1995, 2004). In 1997, Funk estimated that the 114 teams belonging to the four major leagues (MLB, NFL, NBA, and NHL) realized nearly $1 billion from luxury suite revenues. This incredible increase in revenue can make a big difference in the profitability of an organization and can provide a huge competitive advantage over other organizations that do not have it. It also has become an essential part of the equation for financing a new facility. Thus, not only are luxury suites a design issue, but they are becoming of primary importance for any sport organization aspiring to maximize revenue.

Luxury suites are small, private rooms opening toward the court or field that are usually leased to individuals or companies who desire a semi-private lounge area, typically large enough to accommodate 12 to 20 guests. Suites are normally leased on multiyear contracts and are often furnished and decorated by the tenant. The prevalence of these luxury suites is growing rapidly primarily because they are such good revenue producers. Originally referred to as "skyboxes," luxury suites have become a foremost feature of the majority of new stadiums and arenas constructed since the early 1990s (Heistand, 1999). The Houston Astrodome is generally recognized as being the pioneer facility to include luxury suites in sport venues in the late 1960s (Fischer & Ozanian, 1999). However, while the inclusion of luxury suites is an acceptable, almost mandatory, feature of a spectator sport facility today, its revenue potential did not become fully recognized for 20 years (Heistand, 1999).

The impetus for the luxury suite trend was the tremendous success of The Palace of Auburn Hills in Detroit and Joe Robbie Stadium, now referred to as Dolphin Stadium in Miami (Howard & Crompton, 2004). The Palace of Auburn Hills is a good example of how important suites have become to the economics of this type of facility. The original plans called for 100 luxury suites to be built as part of the arena. About one-third of the way through construction, all 100 suites had already been leased. Some quick design changes by the architect produced an additional upper ring of 80 suites, which were also leased by the time The Palace opened. Total construction cost for The Palace was about $70 million. The income from the lease of the suites alone was almost $12 million per year, which allowed for an unheard of 6-year payoff (Howard & Crompton, 2004).

The Miami Dolphins took in gross revenues of nearly $20 million annually from the 216 luxury suites in their stadium. This amount equaled more than 50% of the entire team's 1990 gross revenues (Howard & Crompton, 2004).

The financial impact of luxury suites may be exemplified by the Dallas Cowboys, who constructed 360 luxury suites that produced more than $23 million annually in potential revenue in the early 1990s (Gorman & Calhoun, 1994). Then, later in the 1990s, they increased the number of luxury suites to 398, which grossed about $29 million per year (Fischer & Ozanian, 1999). The Cleveland Browns' move to Baltimore was based on the assurance of a publicly funded stadium containing 108 luxury boxes that would be leased for between $55,000 and $200,000. As a result, the Baltimore Ravens (formerly the Cleveland Browns) anticipated earning about $11 million annually from suite leases at the brand new Raven Stadium.

Professional sports teams are not alone in reaping the benefits of luxury suite sales. Despite uncertain economic times and criticism from university circles, major colleges around the country are constructing sport facilities at a tremendously fast pace primarily due to luxury suite income potential. It has been estimated that universities invested between $800 million and $1 billion for new athletic facilities in the five-year period between 1999 and 2005 (Garbarino & Johnson, 1999). For example, Auburn University incorporated 71 executive suites into the football stadium renovation. This allowed Auburn University to entirely balance the $1-million-plus yearly debit created by the expansion. Once the facility construction debt is totally repaid, Auburn will realize an annual profit of close to $1.8 million (Simers & Wharton, 1999). Other prominent university facilities that have used proceeds from luxury suites for construction cost repayment include the University of Oregon's Autzen Stadium, the University of Texas' Darrel K. Royal Memorial Stadium, the University of Michigan's "Big House," Virginia Tech's Lane Stadium, and Texas Tech's Jones/SBC Stadium.

Some of the items that are now being included in the design of luxury suites are full-service kitchens, toilets, wet bars, coffee makers, and refrigerators. The Toronto Blue Jays baseball team has been recognized as a leader in designing luxury boxes as upscale hotel rooms. Moreover, previous complaints from those who purchased luxury boxes included being exposed to too much direct sunlight as well as being so far away from the action on the field that they would have to use binoculars. To counteract these complaints, luxury box windows are now offered with the ability to transition from light to dark depending on the amount of sunlight. A second window feature provides binocular-like properties that allow the spectator the ability to see the action on the field from a distance without eye strain. As such, while luxury suites have become a significant design feature, the ability to update them is essential. In summary, luxury suites not only make the construction of future arenas and stadiums more economically feasible, but are becoming a necessity for many sports organizations to remain financially competitive.

Naming Rights

As with luxury suites, selling the naming rights of sports facilities has gained recent importance in sport facility construction. Naming rights deals are agreements made between stadium owners and large corporations that permit the sponsor to connect a brand name or logo to a stadium for a given period of time. It has been alleged that the first naming rights agreement occurred in 1971, when the New England Patriots agreed to have the Schaefer Brewing Company pay $150,000 to rename Patriots Stadium, Schaefer Field. In 1973, the Buffalo Bills signed a 20-year agreement with a frozen food supplier, Rich Products, to rename War Memorial Stadium, Rich Stadium. However, further examination finds that in 1926, William Wrigley, who owned the Chicago Cubs for many years, decided to name the team's park Wrigley Field. This marked the first naming rights agreement in professional sports in the United States.

Between 1995 through 2000, the number and financial magnitude of sport facility naming rights grew dramatically. A primary reason for this escalation was due to the increased number of new sporting venues that were built in the late 1990s. For example, the period 1991–1995 had eight stadium or arena openings compared to a total of eight in the previous 15-year period from 1976-1990. In 1997, one third (41 of 113) of the sport stadiums or arenas used by teams in the NFL, NBA, NHL, or MLB had been named for corporations; however, by 2002, 80 of 121 teams were competing in sports venues that were named for large corporations (Waterman, 2002). According to a businessman who specializes in naming rights agreements there were three naming rights deals in professional sports totaling $25 million in 1988 (Maher, 2003). Presently, there are 69 pro teams with anticipated significant increase of intercollegiate teams, who have naming rights deals that total in excess of $3.5 billion (Maher, 2003). Thus, this new strategy was implemented as a way of helping to ease the financial burden of stadium or arena construction.

Of the current 121 North American major league teams—MLB, NFL, NBA, and NHL—83 (69%) have their home stadiums and arenas named after corporate sponsors. The league with the most naming rights deals is the NHL with 90% of its teams, followed by the NBA with 79%, MLB with 57%, and the NFL with 50%. It is important to note that all eight of MLB's newest ballparks have corporate sponsorships. Conversely, as of January 2013 only the following eight stadiums in the NFL did not have naming rights deals: Arrowhead Stadium (Kansas City Chiefs), Candlestick Park (San Francisco 49ers), Cowboys Stadium (Dallas Cowboys), Georgia Dome (Atlanta Falcons), Lambeau Field (Green Bay Packers), Paul Brown Stadium (Cincinnati Bengals), Ralph Wilson Stadium (Buffalo Bills), and Soldier Field (Chicago Bears) (Crabtree, 2013).

Although there has been a recent history of companies that own stadium- and arena-naming rights deals filing for bankruptcy, such as WorldCom, PSINET, and Enron, corporate names seem to appear everywhere in arenas and stadiums. As listed in Table 28.1, the earliest anticipated expiration of the top ten naming right deals is 2019. However, opportunities for companies to obtain sport stadium or arena naming rights will increase in the near future, as a group of deals is set to expire within the next five years.

For example, the agreement for the United Center in Chicago is scheduled to end in 2014. The HP Pavilion, where the San Jose Sharks play, will complete a $47 million, 15-year pact in 2016. Finally, the naming rights for the New England Patriots home field Gillette Stadium, San Diego Chargers Qualcomm Stadium, and Verizon Center, home of the NBA Washington Capitals and WNBA Washington Mystics are set to expire in 2017. Even in cases where neither a team nor stadium exists, naming rights are perceived as a valuable commodity. For example, in 2011, entertainment colossus AEG put forth a plan to construct a $1 billion football stadium and event center in downtown Los Angeles. At the center of the plan was a naming rights deal worth $700 million, representing the most valuable deal of its kind, with Farmers Insurance for a 64,000-seat, retractable-roof football stadium that has not even begun construction (Garrison, 2011). However, a caveat in the contract states that if construction on the stadium does not begin by January, 2015, Farmers Insurance can entirely back out of the deal (Markazi, 2012). As of January 2013, no NFL team has expressed desire to relocate to Los Angeles (Bachrach, 2013).

Table 1 lists the top 10 most valuable naming rights deals in North American professional sports as of 2013. While this list may change, it is significant to note that the top listed deal is for Farmers Field, which may never exist. Including Farmers Field, the NFL has five of the naming rights deals, the NBA has three, and MLB has the remaining two sports.

While naming rights deals have become commonplace in professional sports, the growing trend has recently been seen in intercollegiate athletics. Stadium naming rights can be sold to variety of organizations that are often not normally associated with sports. The most recent examples include the KFC Yum! Center and Papa John's Stadium at the University of Louisville. For many years, universities named buildings after munificent donors and prominent alumni. As of the time of this writing, more than a dozen have sold naming rights to major corporations. For example, Comcast Corporation has a $25 million contract for a 25-year deal to have its name on the Terrapins' new arena in College Park at the University of Maryland (Weinberg, 2003). At Texas Tech University, SBC Communications is paying $20 million over 20 years to have its name on Jones SBC Stadium, and United Supermarkets has a $10 million, 20-year naming rights deal for the United Spirit Arena, where the Texas Tech basketball teams play (Maher, 2003). The Ohio State University plays its basketball games at the Value City Arena, the result of a $12.5 million naming rights deal with a discount department store chain. While these institutions possess impressive naming rights agreements, the largest intercollegiate deal to date has been a $40 million, 20-year deal for the Save Mart Center at Fresno State University. However, the naming rights trend took an unprecedented course when Florida Atlantic University signed a deal to rename its football building the GEO Group Stadium for $6 million over 12 years (Bishop, 2013). On the face of this transaction nothing seems out of place until a person realizes that that the GEO Group is a private prison corporation (Bishop, 2013). There is significant controversy concerning the naming rights issue as the GEO Group has had numerous allegations by human rights groups for violations and corruption charges (Kunnathon, 2013). As a result, collegiate sports are going to be "the next frontier." The only concerns are which schools are going to be first and how much will they receive. As the price of sports venues increases, new sources of income must be recognized and used to the maximum that the market will bear. Therefore, the importance of naming rights to raise revenue to pay for sport stadiums and arenas will undoubtedly continue, if not increase in the future.

Table 28.1

Top 10 Naming Rights in North American Professional Sports

Stadium	City	League	Sponsor	Price	Number of Years	Avg Annual Value	Date
Farmers Field announced	Los Angeles	NFL*	Farmers Insurance	$600 million	30	$20 million	To be
MetLife Stadium	East Rutherford, NJ	NFL	Metropolitan Life	$425 -$625 million	25	$17-$20 million	2036
Citi Field	Queens, NY	MLB	Citigroup	$400 million	20	$20 million	2028
Reliant Stadium	Houston	NFL	Reliant Energy	$310 million	31	$10 million	2032
Gillette Stadium	Foxboro, Mass.	NFL	Gillette	$240 million	15	$8 million	2031
FedEx Field	Landover, Md	NFL	FedEx	$205 million	27	$7.59 million	2025
Barclays Center	Brooklyn, NY	NBA	Barclays PLC	$200 million	20	$10 million	2032
American Airlines	Dallas	NBA	American Airlines	$195 million	30	$6.5 million	2030
Philips Arena	Atlanta	NBA	Royal Philips Electronic	$185 million	20	$9.25 million	2019
Minute Maid Park	Houston	MLB	Coca-Cola Company	$178 million	28	$6.36 million	2029

Personal Seating Licenses (PSLs)

A third revenue trend that developed significantly in the 1990s was the concept of personal or permanent seating licenses (PSLs). Personal seating licenses are to individuals what luxury suites are to corporations (Yeomans, 2001). Personal or permanent seating licenses have been primarily associated with new facility construction and are used to assist in financing plans (Irwin, Sutton, & McCarthy, 2008). Personal seating licenses have given athletic organizations a tremendous benefit since they provide the opportunity to presell seats in advance of the actual construction or renovation of the sport facility. This ensures that the organization responsible for the financing of the facility will not have to borrow as much (Irwin, Sutton, & McCarthy, 2002).

Typically, PSLs allow the purchaser the right to buy season tickets in special seating areas such as club seats. Club seats are typically larger, are more comfortable, and have more leg room than regular seating. Also, they usually include special considerations such as a wait staff who take orders and deliver food right to the seat and possibly offer access to certain restaurants or lounges.

First identified by the Dallas Cowboys in 1968, the concept of PSLs did not gain widespread recognition until the Carolina Panthers implemented a highly successful campaign in 1993. Using personal seating licenses, the Panthers were able to raise $125 million prior to playing their first game in the National Football League. By 2002, nearly 30 professional, intercollegiate, and racecar speedways had adopted the personal seating license concept (Howard & Crompton, 2004). For example, the Chicago Bears were able to raise approximately $60 million for 27,500 personal seating licenses to help pay for the renovation of Soldier Field. As stated earlier, other examples of the personal seating license trend are not limited to professional sports. The Ohio State University recently raised about $20 million from the sale of licensed seating in its new basketball arena, while Texas Motor Speedway sold 30,000 personal seating licenses, generating $27.5 million of the $110 million construction costs.

It is important to note that the trend of personal seating licenses is not without controversy. Because some critics have accused sport organizations of holding ticket holders "hostage" by forcing them to pay large upfront fees, some sport organizations such as the Pittsburgh Steelers have changed the PSL acronym to SBL (stadium builder licenses). This strongly expresses to the ticket holder that the money raised through personal license sales is going directly to construction of the stadium rather than to owners' pockets. Thus, whereas the corporate support and willingness to pay relatively high prices for luxury suites and naming rights, the trend of personal seating licenses, while an important component for paying for a sport facility, seems to be in an evolutionary, more consumer-friendly stage.

The Need for Multipurpose Design

The newest stadiums today are designed to be multipurpose venues that are capable of hosting a variety of sport and entertainment events. Thus, the fundamental purpose and design of stadiums and arenas has changed radically in the last decade. These changes are so dramatic that many facilities have become obsolete, and even young ones 10 to 20 years old are facing the wrecking ball. The basic idea behind this change is that modern arenas and stadiums are no longer just places to watch an event, but are now designed to provide a total entertainment experience and optimally host as many different events as possible. For example, the Miami Arena was built in 1988 and hosted all of the home games for the Miami Heat, Florida Panthers as well as the University of Miami basketball program until 1999. However, since that time the arena has hosted only an indoor football team, the Miami Moorays, which disbanded in 2005, continued to play in the arena after 1999. Thus, the Miami Arena was shut down before it turned 20 years old.

While many older stadiums were designed for multiuse, the users were primarily professional baseball and football teams. Prior to the modern football stadiums in the United States, multiuse stadiums such as Fenway Park, Wrigley Field, and Milwaukee County Stadium were sites of competition for the Red Sox/Patriots, Cubs/Bears, and Braves/Packers, respectively. Moreover, teams such as the New York football Giant shared the Yankee Stadium with the New York Yankees and the San Francisco 49ers shared Candlestick Park for years. Yet, these two major stadium sports cannot coexist unless a major reconfiguration of the playing field is made for each sport. Such changes often include the leveling of the pitcher's mound, covering the warning track and the infield skin of a baseball field to play football and then reversing the process from football to baseball. Additionally, the spectator seats need to be reconfigured in an attempt to provide the best viewing for both baseball and football in the same facility. However, many individuals did not believe that such a configuration could be satisfactorily accomplished. As a compromise, Kansas City, Missouri voted to have a dual stadium complex that would house 78,000 spectators for the Kansas City Chiefs and 42,000 for the Kansas City Royals.

While few dual-sport facilities exist, such as the Oakland-Alameda Coliseum, the majority of newer arenas and stadiums are being planned and built to avoid becoming "white elephants." This is accomplished by designing so that the multipurpose facility optimally supports many sporting and nonsporting events. For instance, thriving facilities have been used to host a number of diverse events, including a wine tasting contest at Alamodome and a Beatles tribute show at U.S. Cellular Arena in Milwaukee. The Houston Texans of the National Football League possess one of the most lucrative naming rights agreements in all of professional sports in North America. There are three primary reasons that deal with the multipurpose design of the facility that allowed the Texans to command $10 million per year. First, for the next three decades, not only will Reliant Stadium be the home of the Texans, each of three other facilities at the complex will bear the Reliant name. Reliant Park, as the Astrodome complex was renamed, consists of Reliant Stadium, Reliant Astrodome, Reliant Arena (formerly the AstroArena) and Reliant Center, a 1.4 million-square-foot exhibition center. Secondly, the 69,500-seat, retractable-roof stadium also annually holds the Houston Livestock Show and Rodeo, which attracts 2 million visitors during its 2 weeks of operation. Third, the stadium hosted the 2004 Super Bowl and is expected to become a part of the Super Bowl rotation.

These "value-added" multipurpose design aspects played an important part in Reliant's motivation to invest a large amount of money for the naming rights. The $10 million per year that Reliant Energy will pay breaks down in the following fashion: the Houston Texans NFL team will receive $7.5 million (75%), the Houston Livestock Show & Rodeo approximately 1.5 million (15%) and Harris County about 1 million (10%) annually until the agreement expires in 2032. Thus, the naming rights for Reliant Stadium will benefit not only the Texans, but also the Rodeo and the county as well in paying off the arena.

Multipurpose design is playing a role in intercollegiate sports facilities as well. Due to the escalating pressure to be self-sustaining, universities in the United States have begun to investigate traditional and nontraditional options for revenue streams. For example, college stadiums that have been customarily used only for football now are being renovated to accommodate soccer, lacrosse, field hockey, and track and field competitions. With the stress to produce revenue, many of these stadiums may also host motocross events and concerts during nonplaying seasons (Hutchison, 2003).

In order to maximize return on such a large investment as a stadium or arena, every effort must be made to ensure that the facility is able to accommodate as many events and different kinds of activities and generate as much revenue as possible. The information in this table identifies an important facility trend that combines naming rights of the venue with multiuse designs. Such recent trends include design features that allow a facility to change over from one event to another as quickly as possible. Whereas some older facilities would rely on 6 to 10 football games or 30 basketball games per year as their main source of revenue, some facilities now schedule from 250 to 600 events per year, including such varied activities such as basketball, soccer, hockey, arena football, concerts, conventions, trade shows, rodeos, monster truck shows, and professional wrestling. It is not uncommon for a poorly designed facil-

ity to require up to a full day for a crew to change the set-up from one event to another, whereas a well-designed facility can be transformed in a matter of hours. Not only can this provide a significant cost saving in manpower, but it also often means that more than one event can take place in the same day. Several aspects of design that allow a facility to accommodate a wide variety of events and also to quickly alter the set-up for different events include the following:

- Versatile lighting and sound systems that are designed to adequately handle the wide variety of events.
- Heavy-duty lighting grids that can be lowered to the floor in order to enhance the placement of sound and lighting equipment for concerts.
- Loading ramps that allow semi trucks to back all the way onto the floor. Even better, some facilities provide floor access for two or more trucks at a time so that one can be loading after a show while another is unloading for the next.
- Versatile, moveable sections of seats that can quickly change the configuration of a facility.
- Fixed, prewired camera positions that allow for quick and easy set-up for television broadcasts. Many new arenas are constructed with a full television production studio, which permits a television network to broadcast a game without bringing in their semi trucks full of production equipment.
- Computerized curtain systems that can quickly change the layout and size of the facility.

Many sport organizations have made a shift in their fundamental mission and have gone from primarily trying to put a winning team on the court/field to providing a great family entertainment experience. This change in thinking has led to many design changes in the arenas and stadiums being constructed today. In general, this has caused a move toward more upscale facilities with greater service, entertainment and convenience for spectators. Some aspects of this trend include the following:

- Providing more restrooms, especially for women. In the past, many spectator facilities provided only enough restrooms to satisfy the local code requirements. This often resulted in long lines and frustration on the part of spectators. Many facilities are now being designed with more than twice as many restrooms as the minimum required. Since some events may draw a disproportionate number of men or women, consideration should be given to designing some restrooms that can serve either gender simply by changing the sign on the door. Family rest rooms are also becoming common in new stadiums and arenas.
- Taking into consideration the requirements of customers with disabilities. With the advent of the Americans with Disabilities Act, full accommodation of the needs of people with disabilities is now federal law. Recent

lawsuits have established new standards for the placement of handicapped seating. All wheelchair-accessible seats should now be located so that users can see over the heads of the spectators in front of them even when the spectators stand.

- Building larger concourse areas and adding separate concourses to serve different levels. Improved access and less crowding make these areas more attractive. Some concourse areas are being designed to resemble a mini-mall by offering many different choices of food, novelty items and entertainment opportunities. Some concession areas are designed so that customers standing in line still have a direct view of the field while others place closed-circuit televisions so that patrons will not miss the action while spending their money. Opportunities for amusement are becoming more common. These include things such as batting cages, merry-go-rounds, bouncers, museums, and many types of electronic games as well as gift shops. Many facilities strive to provide the atmosphere of an amusement park.

- Improving pedestrian traffic flow into, out of and within the facility. People do not enjoy standing in long lines. This can be accomplished by providing more entrances/exits, as well as wider and more stairways, ramps and escalators.

Innovations in Materials and Methods of Construction

Recent innovations in the methods of enclosing large areas without support pillars and posts that interfere with spectator sight lines are providing many more options for the construction of stadiums and arenas. Stadiums with retractable roofs, tension fabric structures, air-supported fabric structures, wooden domes, and cable domes are examples of building designs that have been successfully used to enclose large sports facilities.

Retractable Roof Stadiums

One of the biggest innovations in stadium design is the concept of having a stadium that is open to the elements when the weather is nice but can be quickly covered when needed. The first attempt at a retractable roof stadium was Olympic Stadium in Montreal, built for the 1976 Olympic Games. The original plan was to build a huge concrete mast next to the stadium that would support a fabric roof supported by steel cables. The roof was supposed to have the ability to be lifted off the stadium and suspended from the mast, thereby becoming an open-air stadium (Holleman, 1996). The roof could then be lowered back on top of the stadium to enclose it again when desired.

The design has never worked correctly, but this ambitious idea eventually led to the successful designs we are seeing today. It is estimated that adding a retractable roof to the design of a new stadium will increase the cost of a stadium between $50 and $150 million.

Examples include the following:

- **Rogers Centre.** Formerly known as SkyDome, the Rogers Centre was the first stadium to have a fully retractable roof. Located in Toronto, Ontario, it was opened in 1989. The Rogers Centre can completely open or close the entire steel-trussed roof in 20 minutes. This is accomplished by three movable roof sections two of which slide and another that rotates. The stadium seats 46,105 (not including luxury suites) for baseball, 45,746 (not including luxury suites) for football, and has different seating arrangements for concerts ranging from 10,000 to 55,000. It also contains 161 luxury suites, a 348-room hotel and health club, a 280 seat restaurant overlooking the field, full broadcast facilities, underground parking, and a 110 by 33 foot video screen. Original estimates of the cost for the Rogers Centre were $184 million (Canadian) but it ended up costing about $585 million.

- **Chase Field.** Opened as Bank One Ballpark for the 1998 season, Chase Field is the home of the Arizona Diamondbacks. Located in downtown Phoenix, it was the first retractable-roof stadium to be built since the Rogers Centre. This air-conditioned, retractable-roof stadium is designed primarily for baseball and seats 48,500. The retractable roof can open or close in just five minutes. It has a natural grass field and was built for a cost of $354 million with 68% coming from public financing. With a total of 69 private suites, six party suites and 5,592 club seats, there is something for everybody, including 350 bleacher seats that originally sold for $1 per game. As with many of the new stadiums, it is more than just a place to watch a ballgame. Chase Field contains three restaurants, two microbreweries and two 10,000-square-foot beer gardens, a mini hall-of-fame fashioned after Cooperstown, a 4,000-square-foot team store, 110 picnic tables, 212 concession stands and a swimming pool and spa just beyond the outfield fence.

- Safeco Field. Opened in 1999, Safeco Field's retractable roof allows Seattle Mariner fans to stay dry during the rainy days of the season. While the retractable roof covers the entire ballpark, it does not enclose it, thus giving the stadium an open-air feel. When opened, the roof sits above and behind the right field seats. The roof consists of three panels that glide on 128 steel wheels powered by almost 100 ten-horsepower electric motors. When fully extended, it encompasses almost 9 acres and weighs 22 million pounds, yet, at the push of a button can close or open in 10-20 minutes depending on wind and other weather conditions. For protection against lightning the roof is self-grounded and is planned to hold up under 6-7 feet of snow as well as winds of up to 70 miles per hour.

- **Minute Maid Park.** Originally named Enron Field, it was completed in time for the 2000 baseball season. In 2001, Enron declared bankruptcy, and the naming rights were sold to the Minute Maid Company for an estimated $170 million for 28 years. Built for a relatively inexpensive $248 million, it seats approximately 42,000 and has a fully retractable steel roof. The roof covers 6.25 acres when closed and is made up of three moveable sections that can be opened in less than 20 minutes. The moving roof panels contain over 5,000 tons of steel as well as an acre of glass to allow for spectacular views even when the roof is closed. Also, the roof has been designed to withstand hurricane force winds. Special amenities within the stadium include a kid's play area, batting cages, more than 60 private suites and 4,850 club seats, a café, retail space and even has a 65,000 lb. full-size locomotive that moves along an 800 ft. section of track after game highlights.

- **Miller Park.** Home of the Milwaukee Brewers, Miller Park opened in 2001. It possesses many unique features, the most obvious one being the retractable roof. The 12,000 ton, 7-panel roof has a unique fan-shape design. The moveable roof panels pivot from a point behind home plate and go along a semicircular track beam powered by 60-horsepower motors. The roof can open or close in 10 minutes, and sits 175 feet above second base. Miller Park has no air conditioning, but an air circulation system keeps the ballpark comfortable when the roof is closed. The roof is designed to withstand snow drifts of up to 12 feet.

- **Reliant Stadium.** This 1.9 million sq. ft. facility opened in August 2002 as the NFL's first retractable roof venue. It is also home to the largest rodeo in the world, the Houston Livestock Show & Rodeo, and was built at a cost of $417 million. The roof is comprised of two translucent Teflon-coated fiberglass fabric panels that separate at the 50-yard line, slide on tracks, and rest over each end zone. It can open or close in just 7 to 10 minutes, depending on wind conditions. The supertrusses used to support the retractable roof transport system are 84 feet tall and 12 feet wide and weigh 3,750 tons. The retractable panels move in opposite directions, similar to the Arizona Diamondbacks' Chase Field's roof but unlike the two moving panels at Houston's Minute Maid and Safeco Field in Seattle, which travel in the same direction. Miller Park in Milwaukee also has two moving panels, but they retract in a fan-shaped pattern. Even though it weighs an estimated 2,000 tons, high winds can create havoc. To counteract this, operable clamps hold the roof in place to stabilize it.

- **University of Phoenix Stadium.** Construction began in July 2003 at the University of Phoenix Stadium, home of the Arizona Cardinals. Opened in August 2006 at a cost of $455 million, it was named by *Business Week* as one of the 10 "most impressive" sports facilities in the world. The facility seats 63,400 and is expandable to 73,719 with 7,000 club seats and 88 luxury suites called luxury lofts. There is space for an additional 16 suites if needed in the future. The roof consists of two large panels that retract to uncover the entire playing field and has been designed to provide a balance of sun on the field and shade in the seats. An additional innovation is their portable grass field, which can be moved outside until needed.

- **Dallas Cowboys Stadium.** Opened in May 2009, Dallas Cowboys Stadium has seats for 80,000 and with standing room will accommodate 110,000. Originally estimated to cost $650 million, it reportedly cost more than $1.5 billion, making it the most expensive sports venue built to that time. The domed stadium is supported by two steel arches nearly 300 ft high and 1,290 ft long, the longest single-span arches in the world. A retractable roof and two huge fully retractable glass walls, 120 ft high and 180 ft wide, on each end of the stadium allow for great flexibility.

- **Marlins Park.** Completed in 2012 just in time for the beginning of the baseball season, Marlins Park is the fifth MLB stadium to be built with a retractable roof. With a seating capacity of 37,442, it is LEED Gold certified and is the greenest park in MLB. The retractable roof is made up of three moving panels that span 560 ft and takes approximately 13 min to fully open or close the roof. Additionally, there are six retractable glass panels in the outfield that offer a view of downtown Miami. When closed, these panels combine to stretch 240 ft long and 60 ft high. The natural grass field has been plagued by brown patches. Because only about 4 hr a day of sunlight come into the stadium, groundskeepers have been experimenting with grow lights to try to keep the grass healthy.

At the time of this writing, several other teams are planning or considering construction of new stadiums, many with retractable roofs. Whereas 10 years ago the price tag for most stadiums was in the $200 million to $400 million range, now it is not uncommon for them to exceed $1 billion. It appears that the retractable-roof stadium has come into its own, and we will probably see many new examples in the coming years.

Trends in Indoor Playing Surfaces

Due to the increase of retractable roofs or domed stadiums, playing surfaces need to require either no or minimal amounts of sunlight. At first, artificial turf fields were categorized as nothing more than carpets, often laid on hard concrete or asphalt bases. These surfaces were hard and presented sports participants with extensive opportunities for injury. Often, players would suffer injuries, sometimes career-ending such as Michael Irvin, as a result of being slammed to the ground. In other situations the footing was too good, thereby creating the potential for ankle, knee, and groin injuries when an athlete's shoe became planted in the carpet. The danger of friction burns when players slid on the carpet with bare limbs posed an additional risk of infection if these abrasions were not treated properly.

In response to these potentially unsafe situations, innovative indoor playing surfaces have evolved to the point that players actually prefer to play on some types of artificial surfaces. Approximately 60 Division I-A schools currently use synthetic turf on their playing fields according to the NCAA (2006). The majority of colleges still play on natural grass, but the percentage of artificial fields is the highest since 1997. In fact, a 2003 NCAA report add ref showed baseball players experienced nearly identical injury rates on synthetic and natural surfaces. The following information will highlight the improvements of playing surfaces for retractable and/or domed stadiums.

New Breed of Synthetic Turf

The last decade has seen a tremendous improvement in the design and manufacture of synthetic turfs. Many of the old concerns about higher injury rates have been alleviated. The new designs are much softer to fall on and do not produce the friction burns of the previous designs. Most participants reported that conditions are more similar to those found on good natural grass fields. The new turfs are typically filled with ground rubber particles and sometimes with sand.

Recently the NFL Player's Association conducted a survey of playing fields. The FieldTurf® surface at Seattle Stadium finished as the third most popular playing surface in the NFL (Waterman, 2003). Additionally, the new FieldTurf® playing surface at the Detroit Lions Ford Field ranked as the 11th most popular playing surface (Waterman, 2003). This is despite that only nine of the 32 NFL teams had the opportunity to play on it. It is important to note that both of these fields were rated ahead of many natural grass fields and that no other artificial turf field rated higher than 20th. An added feature of FieldTurf® is its ability to be installed for football, markings and all, in 8 hr or less; in addition, all the markings can be removed in the equivalent time frame. Therefore, it is also entirely possible that a field conversion from football to another sport may be accomplished in less than 8 hr. This would allow a stadium to stage a soccer game or tennis matches on it one day

and a football game the next without tearing up the playing field as might occur on natural grass (Waterman, 2003).

Examples of professional football teams that have recently installed FieldTurf® at their game or practice facilities are the Atlanta Falcons, St. Louis Rams, Kansas City Chiefs, Houston Texans, New England Patriots, Cleveland Browns, Green Bay Packers, Seattle Seahawks, Detroit Lions, Pittsburgh Steelers, New York Giants, and New York Jets. Additionally, the Florida Marlins and Montreal Expos have, of late, elected to install FieldTurf® for their fields. FieldTurf® recently introduced a system called Revolution Coolplay, which reportedly reduces field surface temperatures approximately 35°. It has become evident that FieldTurf and similar systems are becoming the preferred design choice for the NFL and MLB.

Removable Natural Grass

Another turf-related option that has become a facility design issue in sport stadiums is removable natural grass. This innovative concept was first used in the Silver Dome for the 1994 World Cup Soccer Tournament. A hybrid grass was developed at Michigan State University that was designed to thrive in the low levels of sunlight that could enter through the fabric roof of the Silver Dome. A system of nearly 2,000 interlocking pallets was computer designed and built to provide the regulation soccer field. The pallets were set up in the parking lot where the grass was planted and received plenty of sunlight. Just prior to the first game, they were hauled by trucks and forklifts into the stadium and assembled. The process took 2 days to complete. The field was a success and received good reviews. Unfortunately, it was too large an undertaking to make it feasible to move in and out of the stadium on a regular basis, so the Detroit Lions continued to play on their AstroTurf® field.

The idea of using a removable natural grass field was also hotly debated during the construction of Reliant Stadium because the field would accommodate both professional football and rodeo. A palletized natural turf field was seen as the solution. It integrates portable turf units of 8 ft x 8 ft, including a metal drainage base. The units incorporate a growing medium that is reinforced with Reflex® mesh elements (small pieces of nylon mesh) that increase field stability, aid in water and air management, and provide a forgiving (non-hard) surface for the athletes (Thompson, 2001). The turf was designed so that any unit can be replaced without affecting the unit next to it (Valentine, 2003). They can be easily replaced so as to resist extreme wear as well as the effects of extended time in shade. The field is completely removed to an outside nursery once a year while the stadium hosts the Houston Livestock Show and Rodeo.

The University of Phoenix Stadium addressed the problem in an innovative way. A full-sized natural grass field is contained on a movable, 12 million-lb tray, 234 ft wide x 400 ft long. The tray rests on tracks and rolls on steel wheel sets powered by small electric motors. The entire field can reside outside of the facility where the grass can absorb sunlight and receive nourishment, maintenance, and grooming. Then, when it is needed, the entire field is moved into the stadium, a process that takes about 45 min. This allows for tremendous flexibility and ideal conditions for maintaining strong, healthy grass.

Fabric Structures

One development in the area of physical education, recreation, and sports facilities is the concept of fabric structures. The fabric commonly used is either a Teflon®-coated fiberglass or a polyester material. The fiberglass fabric is, pound for pound, stronger than steel and is also less expensive. It can be designed to allow either a large amount or very little natural light to penetrate. The fabric can withstand temperatures of 1300°F to 1500°F and is not adversely affected by cold or the ultraviolet rays of the sun. Fabric structures offer a number of potential advantages and disadvantages when compared with standard construction.

Advantages. The advantages for fabric structures are as follows:

- **Lower initial cost.** Initial costs are usually lower than the costs of conventional construction. Several factors contribute to this, the primary one being weight. A fabric roof is 1/30 the weight of a conventional steel-truss roof. This reduced weight means that the walls, footings, and foundations are not required to be nearly as strong as in a conventional building.
- **Less construction time.** The amount of construction time is directly related to the initial cost of the structure. The total time necessary to build a fabric structure is usually less than for a conventional roof.
- **Natural lighting.** Because the fiberglass fabric material that is used is translucent, it results in a large amount of interior natural lighting. Without the use of artificial lights during the day, the light intensity inside can vary anywhere from 100 to 1,000 foot-candles depending on weather conditions, design, and choice of fabric. The interior light is considered to be of high quality because it is nonglare and shadow free.
- **Possibly lower energy costs.** In some climates or regions, energy costs may be substantially reduced by the fabric's translucency. The large amount of natural light may reduce or eliminate the need for artificial light during the daytime. This may also reduce the need for air-conditioning required to overcome the heat generated by the artificial lights.
- **Less maintenance.** The nonstick characteristics of Teflon® allow the fabric to be washed clean each time it rains.

- **Full use of space.** Depending on the fabric structure's configuration and support, the area that can be enclosed is almost limitless.

Disadvantages. The disadvantages of fabric structures are as follows:

- **Life span.** The fabric envelope in use today has a life expectancy of up to 25 years, with longer life materials being tested. All other items such as the foundation, flooring, and mechanical equipment have the life span of a conventional building.
- **Poor thermal insulation.** In cold climates, there may be an increase in energy cost when compared with conventional construction due to lower insulating properties of the fabric roof. The insulating value of a typical fabric roof is about R-2 but can be increased substantially (see Lindsay Park Sports Centre). The cost of heating is a significant factor and should be evaluated against that for a conventional building over time. During winter months when the heat is required to melt the snow or to cause it to slide off, a safe level of temperature will have to be maintained at all times, which has an impact on heating costs. If the bubble is not to be heated during inactive hours, it will have to be supervised constantly for the dangers of unexpected snowfall. In the summertime, the heat gain of the air-supported structure may pose a cooling problem.
- **Acoustic problems.** The curved shape of the air-supported structure produces a peculiar acoustic environment. This large reflective surface magnifies crowd noise and can create undesirable noise conditions.
- **Restriction due to wind.** In winds of hurricane velocity, many codes require that the fabric structure be evacuated.

There are three basic types of fabric structures in use: (a) tension structures, (b) air-supported structures, and (c) cable domes. Tension structures are made by stretching the fabric between rigid supports and/or steel cables. Air structures are sealed buildings that, through the use of fans, maintain a positive internal air pressure that supports the roof. These structures are actually inflated like a balloon and must maintain the positive air pressure to remain inflated. Cable domes are the newest type of fabric structure. The cable dome is actually a modified tension structure that uses a complex network of cables and supports to suspend and hold up the fabric roof.

Tension Structures

Some projects lend themselves more naturally to tension structures than to air-supported structures or cable domes. Tension structures may be more favorable

- when free and open access from the sides is desirable or required,
- when a unique design or aesthetics are important,
- when the facility will be largely unattended or not monitored,
- when possible deflation of an air structure would constitute a severe operational or safety problem, and
- when a retrofit to an existing building or structure such as a swimming pool or an outdoor stadium is desired.

Examples include the following:
- **Lindsay Park.** The Lindsay Park Sports Centre in Calgary, Alberta, Canada, houses a 50-m pool, a diving pool, a fully equipped 30,000-sq ft gymnasium, and a 200-m running track. The roof is unique in that it was designed with insulation that is rated at R-16. This compares with a typical fabric roof that has about an R-2 rating. Despite the great improvement in insulating qualities, the fabric roof is still translucent enough to allow for an interior illumination of about 200 foot-candles. This facility was completed in 1983.
- **McClain Athletic Training Facility.** Completed in 1988, this field house is located at the University of Wisconsin at Madison. Due to site restrictions, this $9.5 million facility contains a 90-yard football field instead of a full-sized field. Most of the field is covered by a 42,000-sq ft fabric-tension roof that admits up to 750 foot-candles of natural light into the structure. When the fabric roof is compared to the standard construction, it is estimated that the increased cost for heating and the reduced cost for artificial lighting result in an overall savings of about $21,000 per year. Below the synthetic turf field is a full 64,320-sq ft basement that contains locker rooms for football, track, and coaches; weight room; training facilities; and therapy pool. The therapy pool is 15 ft x 40 ft and goes from 4 ft to 7 ft in depth. Also included in the facility are an auditorium, six meeting rooms, and a film room.

Air-Supported Structures

There are two basic types of air-supported structures: (a) large permanent structures and (b) smaller, more portable structures.

These facilities are actually inflated with positive air pressure that is produced by a group of large fans. In conventional buildings, the foundation, walls, and internal columns must support a roof weight of between 10 lb and 40 lb per square foot. In air-supported structures, a roof weight of about 1 lb per square foot is transmitted directly to the ground by the increased air pressure. This increased pressure of about 4 lb or 5 lb per square foot greater than ambient pressure is usually unnoticed by the building's oc-

cupants. A significant advantage of this type of roofing is the relatively low capital cost, but disadvantages include relatively short design life and vulnerability to damaging the full enclosure (John, Shear, & Vickery, 2007). Some of the instances when an air structure may be preferable to a tension structure or standard construction are
- when column-free spans of greater than 150 ft are desired,
- when large, column-free spans are desired at a cost that is greatly reduced compared to conventional structures—in fact, cost per unit area usually decreases as the size of the span increases, and
- when a low silhouette is desired.

Examples include the following:
- **Dedmon Center.** Located at Radford University in Radford, Virginia, the Dedmon Center was constructed for a cost of $6,750,000 and opened in 1982. Encompassing 110,000 sq ft, it has 5,000 temporary seats for basketball. Used for physical education, athletics, and recreation, the center provides five full basketball courts, weight room, pool, locker rooms, and offices.
- **Carrier Dome.** The Carrier Dome, located in Syracuse, New York, is the home of Syracuse University athletics. The stadium seats 50,000 for football and over 30,000 for basketball. Also a great bargain, total construction cost was $27,715,000, which figures out to $554 per seat. This is inexpensive when compared to conventional covered stadiums. This facility was completed in 1980.

Other examples are below:
- Steve Lacy Field House, Milligan College, Milligan, Tennessee—1974
- Uni-Dome, University of Northern Iowa, Cedar Falls, Iowa—1975
- Metrodome, Minneapolis, Minnesota—1982
- B.C. Place Amphitheater, Vancouver, British Columbia, Canada—1983
- Tokyo Dome, Tokyo, Japan—1988

The primary disadvantage of air-supported structures is the need for the constant positive air pressure. Because this positive pressure is what supports the roof, if pressure is lost even temporarily, the fabric will hang down on the supporting cables. Although this alone should cause no damage to the facility, this is when the structural system is the most vulnerable. Even light winds, snow, or rain may cause extensive damage to a fabric roof in the deflated position. These facilities must be constantly monitored, and precautions must be taken to ensure that all systems are functioning properly. Because cable domes appear to have the same advantages as the large air-pressure structures but without many of the disadvantages, it is entirely possible that we have seen the last large air-supported structure that will ever be built (see Cable Domes).

Combining Air-Supported and Tension

Another development in the construction of fabric structures is the idea of combining both an air-supported roof and a tension roof in the same building. An example of this concept is the Stephen C. O'Connell Center. This physical education, recreation, and athletic complex is located at the University of Florida at Gainesville. This was the first structure to combine both air-supported and tension roofs in one building. The center or main arena is covered by a large air-inflated roof, and the outer areas of the building are the tension-covered spaces. The main arena has an indoor track and can seat 10,400 spectators for basketball. Located under the tension-supported areas are a gymnastic area; dance studio; weight room; locker rooms; offices; and a 3,000-seat, 50-m natatorium. Like most fabric structures, this facility was a bargain. The total construction cost was $11,954,418, which comes out to about $49 per square foot. This facility was completed in 1980.

Temporary Air Structures

This section will outline the merits of the smaller and more portable air structures. Air structures work well as environmental covers placed over existing recreational areas, and for many organizations, the "bubble" is the answer to an increasing need for large covered activity areas at a nominal cost. Cost savings are in proportion to the size of the space to be covered. Spaces over 300 sq ft usually bring a cost savings when compared to conventional roofing. Heat gain seems to present a more severe problem than heat loss and must be considered in warmer climates. Numerous playing fields within communities and around schools and colleges lend themselves easily to enclosure by a fabric air structure

Advantages. The advantages of temporary air structures are as follows:

- **Speed of erection.** Once in place, the actual erection of the structure usually takes only 1 or 2 days. However, additional time is required for the groundwork, site services, foundation, anchorage, flooring, and installation of mechanical and electrical equipment needed in the initial installation. Only minimal field labor is needed.
- **Ease of deflation, inflation, and repair.** Deflation and inflation of the fabric bubble usually does not require skilled labor.
- **Portability.** When deflated and packed, the fabric envelope can be stored in a small space or easily transported elsewhere for storage or use. Depending on the size of the dome, deflation and packing usually require 1 or 2 days.

- **Adaptability for temporary functions.** For temporary use, the air-supported structure has definite physical and financial advantages over a conventional building.
- **Long-span and high-ceiling features.** Clear and unobstructed spaces are an inherent feature of the air-supported domes. Conventional long-span and high-ceiling structures are more expensive.
- **Integrated heating, ventilation, and air-pressure system.** The integrated heating, ventilation, and air-pressure system is simple and less expensive than conventional systems. Lengthy ductwork is not required.

Examples include the following:

- **Memorial Stadium.** A portable inflatable fabric bubble is used to cover the entire football field at the University of Illinois at Urbana-Champaign in the winter. First erected in 1985, Memorial Stadium was purchased for $1.5 million. With an average inside winter temperature of 55°F, the field is used heavily by several departments across the campus. The concept of a portable dome over the game field adds extra use to a facility that would otherwise sit empty much of the year.
- **University of Santa Clara.** The swimming pool at the Thomas E. Leavey Center is covered by a portable air structure. It is removed so the pool is outdoors in the summer months and then reinflated for the winter to transform the pool for indoor use.
- Numerous tennis centers, golf driving ranges, pools, and fitness centers.

Cable Domes

Cable domes are the most recent innovation in fabric structure technology. Through a complex system of cables and girders, large spans can be inexpensively covered by a fabric roof without the need for columns or fans to maintain integrity. Engineers predict that the cable dome concept is feasible for spans of at least 1,000 ft. Cable domes incorporate most of the advantages of fabric structures when compared to standard construction and fewer of the disadvantages. Many experts in fabric roof technology believe that cable domes will replace the air-supported structure as the fabric roof design of choice for the future. Large air structures will probably not be built anymore because of the inherent advantages of the cable dome.

Advantages. Advantages are as follows:
- huge column-free spans can be covered,
- expensive energy-consuming fans are not needed,
- a passive system means someone does not have to constantly monitor the facility, and
- the structure has an extremely low silhouette.

Examples of cable domes include the following:
- **Georgia Dome.** Located in downtown Atlanta, Georgia, the Georgia Dome was completed in August 1992. This $210 million structure was the site of both the

Super Bowl and the Olympics in 1996. The Teflon®-coated fabric roof covers 8.6 acres, weighs 68 tons, and incorporates 11.1 miles of steel support cables. This multipurpose facility seats 70,500 for football and is the home of the Atlanta Falcons. A total of 202 luxury suites are located on different levels around the stadium that range in price from $20,000 to $120,000 per year for a 10-year lease. During the planning process, it was estimated that changing the design from an open-air stadium to a fabric-covered dome increased the cost of the project by only 20% or less. In March 2008, during the SEC Tournament, the dome was actually hit by a tornado that struck downtown Atlanta. It ripped two holes in the roof and delayed a quarterfinal game for about an hour. The remaining games of the tournament were moved to another location, and the dome was inspected for safety.

Wooden Domes

Another recent development in encapsulated spaces is the wooden dome. These spherical wooden structures have several advantages over conventional structures. Column-free spans of up to 800 ft are possible, and they are generally easier to build. There are several wooden dome structures around the country ranging from high school gymnasiums to large stadiums.

Advantages. Advantages of wooden domes when compared with standard construction may include

- efficient construction of huge column-free spans,
- lower initial cost when compared with conventional construction,
- less construction time,
- full use of space, and
- good insulation and acoustical properties.

Examples of wooden domes include the following:
- **Round Valley Ensphere.** Located in Eager, Arizona, this wooden dome is the only high school domed football stadium in the world. Opened in 1991, it was built for a total project cost of only $11.5 million and is unique in many respects. The 113,000 sq ft of unobstructed floor space provides a full-sized synthetic turf football field with seating for 5,000; a six-lane, 200-m, synthetic-surface running track with 100-m straightaway; seven combination basketball, volleyball, or tennis courts; a softball field; and offices, training room, and four full locker rooms. The wooden roof is insulated to a value of R-28 and is energy and acoustically efficient. One of the most interesting features of the dome is that it contains a large skylight in the center of the roof. This skylight is made of clear Lexan® and provides good illumination of the activity areas even on overcast days. At an elevation of over 7,000 ft, the Round Valley area experiences extremes in weather, including snow-packed winters. During the colder months, the skylight also acts as a solar collector, helping to make the Ensphere very energy efficient.
- **Walkup Skydome.** This laminated wood dome is located at Northern Arizona University in Flagstaff. Opened in 1977, the Skydome is 502 ft across and covers 6.2 acres. It contains a full-sized, roll-up, synthetic football/soccer field, a professional-sized ice hockey rink, a 1/5-mile running track, a portable wood basketball court, and seating for more than 15,000 people. The total construction cost was $8.3 million, or about $620 per seat.
- **Superior Dome.** Constructed on the campus of Northern Michigan University (NMU) in Marquette, this state-owned wooden dome was opened in the fall of 1991. With a diameter of 533 ft, the 14-story, $21.8 million structure was envisioned in 1985 as an Olympic training center. It has a 200-m track and a full-sized football field and is home to the NMU football team, with seating for 8,000 spectators. Designed to be constructed in phases as funding becomes available, the facility will eventually include an additional 5,000 seats; an ice rink for hockey, speed skating, and figure skating; locker rooms; sports medicine facilities; and public-use areas.

29 Trends in Equipment and Supplies, 1975-2012

Jeffrey C. Petersen, *Baylor University*

In the process of building a new facility or completing major renovations of an existing facility for physical activity or sport, the planning process typically focuses on the building itself. At times the focus may shift to major building systems such as the electrical; heating, ventilating, and air conditioning (HVAC); plumbing; or structural systems. While these aspects of the building or renovation process are important, the needs of facility users must remain the greatest consideration. Although the facility itself needs to be a high priority in the building process, it is also crucial that the equipment and supplies required within the facility are carefully considered and selected. The equipment and supplies are just as vital as the building itself if the facility is to fully serve its intended purposes for the users.

Consider, for example, a very basic health and fitness center. While a physical space for this center must be created, the space alone will never meet the expectations of the facility users without the procurement of the necessary equipment and supplies.

As the demand for sport and recreation facilities increases, so does the demand for necessary supplies and equipment. When considering the competitive nature of sport organizations (interscholastic, intercollegiate, and professional), as well as the pressure on fitness centers and health clubs to attract and maintain a customer base, it is not surprising that new equipment and supply innovations are regularly entering the sport marketplace. Each athletic program wants to provide the latest equipment innovation that may help their athletes or programs become more successful. Similarly, leaders in the fitness industry search to find the next must-have exercise machine. Identifying trends becomes crucial for success because of both the large capital investments in equipment and the competitive nature of the fitness and sport market. Of course, predicting future trends is just as difficult as predicting a moneymaking stock or predicting what team will win the next Super Bowl. It is more typical to identify equipment or supplies that are experiencing rapid growth in use and popularity. The purpose of this chapter is to examine selected trends impacting the selection and use of equipment and supplies within several venue types. The discussion of various products should in no way be considered a blanket endorsement, because each facility operator or manager must develop her own selection criteria based on the wants and needs of their own consumers.

Supplies and Equipment Defined

A case of athletic tape, a soccer uniform, hockey mouthpieces, football helmets, a case of tennis balls, portable bleachers, a baseball pitching machine, basketballs, a treadmill, wrestling mats, towels, and a pole vault landing pit are all items that might be necessary in a facility used for physical activity and sport. Which of these would be considered a supply and which would be equipment?

According to the Miriam Webster's *Collegiate Dictionary*, equipment is defined as "all the fixed assets other than land and buildings of a business enterprise." A fixed asset is often considered an item with a worth or value above a preestablished dollar value. Equipment could also be defined as durable goods or items used repeatedly over a period of years. Items that have a short duration of use, typically one year or less, are classified as supplies. Many supplies have a one-time-only use, while other supplies may be repeatedly used over a relatively short functional life. Equipment, on the other hand, will have one year of useful service at a minimum.

The cost per item or unit is another method of differentiating between equipment and supplies. Items with higher costs are usually considered equipment; therefore, something as large as a scoreboard and something as small as an external heart monitor may both considered to be equipment. Depending on the established policies of the organization, be it governmental, school, or private enterprise, a price standard may be set to distinguish between supplies and equipment. This may be set at the low end of perhaps $100 per item or at higher levels such as $250, $500 or even $1,000 per item. Items designated as equipment are more closely monitored through item tagging and annual inventory processes. Therefore, the two major considerations in differentiating between supplies and equipment are the cost of the item and the duration of its use.

Another term commonly used that encompasses both equipment and supplies in the planning and building process is FF&E. This is a common acronym for furniture, fixtures, and equipment. The FF&E is a very detail-oriented part of the design process that will often make or break a facility in terms of its overall functionality and appearance.

Cost Considerations

The cost of supplies and equipment is a major consideration in both the initial creation and annual operation of facilities for physical activity and sport. When considering the costs for equipment and supplies, a balance must be maintained between the ultimate wants of the users and the total cost. There is usually a very significant portion of the project cost that should be allocated to properly equip and furnish a facility. Without taking this into consideration, a beautiful facility structure could be constructed, but it would be useless without the necessary equipment and supplies.

Equipment Trends for Stadiums, Arenas, and Gymnasiums

With the 1990s being a decade of unprecedented growth in professional sport venues in the U.S., it is not surprising that many colleges have also seen this prosperous economic climate as a time to build or expand facilities. With such a high rate of growth in spectator sport venues, several equipment trends have emerged. Most of the trends described in this section focus on enhancing the spectator comfort, the spectator sensory experience, or the use of creative management to reduce direct equipment expenses for the owner or operator.

The development of myriad seating options has been one major trend in large spectator facilities, both indoor and outdoor. Gone are the days of standard bleachers with the minimal 18 inches per person seating width allowance. The current trends are expanding not only the seat width, but also the legroom (tread depth) available. Stadium seating now commonly includes various seatback options, different levels of cushioning, custom color schemes, logo or graphic branding incorporations, arm rests, and even cup holders.

Consider the relatively new Sports Authority Field at Mile High (opened in 2001), the home of the NFL's Denver Broncos. This new facility has an official seating capacity of

76,125 with a total facility size of 1,717,000 sq ft. The previous home stadium of the team, Mile High Stadium, had an official capacity of only two fewer spectators at 76,123, but the total size was less than half the total of the new stadium at only 850,000 sq ft. Although this increase of total square footage cannot be completely attributed to seating upgrades, the changes in seating allocation were substantial. The old stadium had an average seat width of 18" and legroom of only 31", while the new facility has a 19" minimum seat width and 32-33 " of standard legroom. The club seating area in the stadium boasts 20"-wide padded seating with 33" of tread depth. The new stadium seating also provides the added amenity of cup holders for every seat regardless of the seating section (Ames, 2001).

From a video board perspective, the Sports Authority Field provides a primary screen of 27 x 96 ft and two secondary screens of 27 x 48 ft (Wolf, 2001). Now in comparison, consider the even newer Met-Life Stadium, home to both the New York Giants and the New York Jets, which opened in 2010. This stadium has been touted as the NFL's most technologically advanced at a total cost of $1.6 billion. Stadium features include a massive size of over 2.1 million sq ft compared to the 900,000 sq ft in the former Giants Stadium. Met-Life also boasts 130,000 sq ft of club lounges and 9,000 club seats and an additional 221 luxury suites (Eisen, John-Baptiste, Phillips, & Berger, 2012). This stadium also includes four high definition video screens each measuring 30 x 118 ft each, as well as energy-efficient color-changing LED lighting that can create either a blue or green coloration of the structure's exterior for each home team (Eisen et al., 2012).

These two examples above demonstrate in a time span of just under 10 years the trends in sport stadium amenities. In addition, massive increases in total space and general seating upgrades, the continued trends of both luxury boxes and club seating areas cater to the expanded desire to provide creature comforts such as: food and beverage catering services, high definition video screens, and full climate control. There has also been increased emphasis in high-quality sound and video systems to enhance the live sport experience in order to better compete with the home theater experience.

While watching a sporting event live at the venue was once considered the best place to view sports, television's use of instant replay (begun in the 1960s) has greatly added to the viewing experience. Replays allow the spectator at home to see plays again that may be either spectacular or controversial. Spectators attending an event at the stadium or arena may miss key parts of the game due to lapses in concentration or their sheer distance from an actual play. However, the installation of big-screen LED (light-emitting diode) panels that serve as large video or television monitors can solve these viewing problems for the live event spectator. The use of this video equipment now allows the spectators at the venue to view both the live action and have access as an entire stadium or arena audience to the replays, game statistics, close-up images, and other video information broadcast on the LED big screens.

The number of LED screen installations in sport venues increased enormously throughout the 1990s and the first decade of the 2000s, and this growth is likely to continue. LED displays are not the only video technology available, but other systems such as projection, liquid crystal display (LCD), and cathode ray tube (CRT) are at a significant disadvantage compared to LEDs. First, the power consumption for LED is lower than the previously mentioned systems. The second major advantage to LED displays is that they will typically operate for 100,000 hours before dropping to 50% of their original brightness (Dahlgren, 2000; Sawyer, 2009). The LED systems are also much lighter than the CRT display options, making them easier to suspend or mount. The major drop in production cost of the blue and green LEDs has also allowed the price for full-color displays to drop and become more affordable for collegiate programs, and minor league professional venue use. The LED displays have even entered into the interscholastic market with installations now in place at fields and gymnasiums across the United States. High schools of all sizes are investing in the latest scoreboard, matrix and video display technologies as they have become more affordable (Steinbach 2008b). The development of integrated sponsorship packages and plans at the interscholastic level has also aided in the expansion of the video board market at the interscholastic level (Popke, 2012). In fact, large-

Outdoor application of LED video technology at Kauffman Stadium, home of the Kansas City Royals. This was the world's largest high definition (HD) LED video display in 2008 with a display size of 105'0" x 85'0". *Photo courtesy of Daktonics*

screen LED displays globally were projected to grow from $639 million in 2004 to $795 million in 2012, and the unit sales should rise from 518,067 square feet in 2004 to over 1,286,200 square feet by the year 2012 (Popke, 2012).

Another reason that LED video boards are expanding in use is that three different types of display manufacturing have been developed, each with its own specific applications. The lamp LED method uses a combination of reflector cups and epoxy lenses to intensify and focus the light. These are typically the brightest systems and can be used outdoors where more light intensity is needed. The surface-mounted lamp method utilizes a metal reflector frame that is mounted directly to the board. This method provides a higher resolution and allows for viewing from a wider range of angles. The drawback to the surface-mounted lamp LED display is that it lacks the brightness necessary to provide an optimal image outdoors. The chip-on-the-board method places the LED directly on the board without any type of reflection or lens system. This method is the least expensive, but it is the least light efficient of the three and it is often harder to maintain. The full-color displays in all three manufacturing options are obtained by the blending of light from the combination of red, blue, and green LEDs, creating up to 4.4 trillion colors. The red LEDs continue to be the least costly to produce; therefore, many scoreboard or marquee sign applications of LED technology continue to use red as the primary color (Dahlgren, 2000).

A major factor in the growing popularity of the LED video display would be the competition between colleges and professional sports organizations. Each venue attempts to keep up with or become the leader with the biggest or best video displays available for their patrons. The inclu-

Indoor LED video display at Thompson-Boling Assembly Center & Arena, home of the University of Tennessee Basketball, in Knoxville, TN with the following LED video features starting from the top, a ringed screen 3'0" x 100'6", four 9'6" x 18'0" main video screens, four scoreboard screens 5'6" x 13'6" and a final ringed screen 3'0" x 58'6". *Photo courtesy of Daktonics*

Figure 28.3. An example of a fascia or ribbon board LED display at Dolphins Stadium in Miami, FL. This display runs between the two suite levels and circles the entire stadium with dimensions of 3'6" x 2,117'6". *Photo courtesy of Daktonics*

sion of large video display screens is considered standard in new large-scale venue constructions. Another advantage of the LED screens is that older venues can easily add these displays to upgrade the facility. This can have a major impact on spectators' impressions of the facility. The wide range of size options allows each stadium to create a more customized fit for its particular needs. Other recent LED video innovations include the use of long, narrow screens,

Figure 28.4. An LED scorer's table application on the John Wooden Court, home of UCLA basketball, provides full-color video display on a 2'0" x 57'0" format. *Photo courtesy of Daktonics*

called fascia displays, such as the two 300' x 5' video displays located along the face of the upper deck of the US Cellular Field, home of the Chicago White Sox. These US Cellular fascia displays, installed in 2003, are used primarily for promotional and advertising purposes but can also display scoring or other data. The universal matrix scoreboard is a growing trend that combines the functions of the LED video board with the traditional scoreboard display partitioned within a single screen, and this LED application is especially popular in smaller scale applications (Vence, 2011).

In addition to the use of LED technology for the traditional scoreboard and the new fascia board displays, the use of LED and other video displays has spread to the scorer's table of basketball arenas. In 2005, the NBA's Portland Trailblazers installed a 58-foot-long rear-projection system at the Rose Garden's center court consisting of 16 digital displays encased in padded modules that provide advertising, statistics and other information (Popke, 2006). This technology trend signals the next step in sports venue signage, one that creates more sponsorship and advertising revenue opportunities for the sport organization while also enhancing the spectator experience.

Another trend impacting equipment in spectator venues is contracting and outsourcing portions of the typical functions associated with the venue. According to Peter Bendor-Samuel, considered a leading outsourcing authority, outsourcing occurs when an organization transfers the ownership of a business process to a supplier. Heywood (2001) more precisely defines the outsourcing process as the "transferring of an internal business function or functions, plus any associated assets, to an external supplier or service provider who offers a defined service for a specified period of time, and at an agreed but probably qualified price" (p. 27). The key aspect is the transfer of control. Outsourcing differs from contracting where the buyer retains control of the process and tells the supplier how to do the work. It is the transfer of ownership that defines outsourcing, and at times, makes it a challenging process. In outsourcing, the buyer does not instruct the supplier how to perform its task. The buyer clearly communicates the desired results and leaves the process decisions for accomplishing those results with the supplier.

Within stadiums and arenas, typical operational aspects that may be outsourced include services such as concessions, laundry, and facility maintenance. One of the advantages of outsourcing can be significant savings in major equipment expenditures. When organizations or teams owning or operating these facilities outsource, the equipment and supplies required can be significantly reduced. For example, at a venue where concessions are outsourced, only a space allocation with water and electrical supply would be provided. The outsourced supplier for concessions would provide all the necessary equipment for the preparation, storage, and sales of all products. Outsourcing of concessions operations has expanded to over 60% of collegiate arenas and stadiums with companies like Sodexho-Marriott and Aramark dominating this sector (SportsBusiness Research, 2012). According to the Outsourcing Research Council, operations and facilities outsourcing had an average growth rate of 21% between 1999 and 2012 in the corporate sector (SportsBuisness Research, 2012). This trend will continue to impact the equipment needs for major venues in the future. The needs for equipment will not decrease, but outsourcing will shift the responsibility of equipment search research/selection, purchase and maintenance on the outsourcing supplier. Additionally, outsourcing of management and leadership functions in the sport realm have been increasing in the area of municipal parks and recreation for sports instruction, league and tournament play (Bynum, 2007). This trend has also impacted management outsourcing of fitness facilities at Jewish Community Centers by Club One Fitness in order to revitalize the viability of many of these locations nationwide (Popke, 2008).

Gymnasiums are facilities in secondary schools throughout the country that serve as both a primary activity space for physical education as well as a primary spectator venue for interscholastic sports. As spectator venues, gymnasiums require safe and ample seating, while as a teaching and practice area, the need is for maximum useable floor space. The most common solution to these two needs has been the telescoping bleachers unit. Most gyms have these seating structures, however current requirements in the Uniform Building Code (UBC) and the Americans with Disabilities Act (ADA) are most likely not met if bleachers were installed before 1990. The replacement of older models of bleachers has become a growing trend in the renovation and improvement of gyms.

The older model bleachers have some serious deficiencies in regard to safety and risk management. Many old bleacher models have open-space area between the seat and the foot rest or tread area. This is a space that small children can often fit through to fall under the structure, or where an adult could slip a foot or a leg into and be injured. Additionally, many old units lack designated aisles, and require that the seating area itself double as an access route up and down the bleachers. The rails on many older units consist of a single or double bar that has a large open area where children could fall through. Older bleacher units often require manual operation to open and close. This process exposes workers to a greater risk of injury. In fact, the rate of injuries associated with bleacher seating, estimated by the U.S. Consumer Product Safety Commission, averages 22,100 injuries each year since 1999, while 1999 saw a record high of 22,308 injuries. There were 4,910 falls involving children under 15 in 2011 (CPSC, 2011).

Because of the significant issues with many older bleacher units, it is not surprising that bleacher replacement is becoming a popular trend. Steel remains the primary structural component of the units, but seats can be made of wood, vinyl-coated metal, or of molded plastic for standard bleacher seating. Tip-up seating with chair backs, either padded or unpadded, is another option for telescoping bleacher units.

The specific UBC regulations impacting bleacher seating begin with row limitations. A maximum of 16 rows is allowed if the bleachers load only from the top or only from the bottom. No row limitations exist if the bleacher section can load from both the top and bottom. Whenever there are more than 11 rows of seating, aisles are required, and no more than 20 seats can separate each aisle. Aisle steps cannot exceed nine inches without providing an intermediate step, and since the typical bleacher rise between rows is more than nine inches these intermediate steps are almost always required. A minimum aisle width of 42 inches is necessary if servicing seating areas on both sides, or 36 inches wide if seating is only to one side. When considering railings, the aisles require discontinuous rails that allow spectators to move laterally as well as up and down the aisle. These rails must also have an intermediate rail 12 inches below the top of the rail for shorter spectators (SPSC, 2011). These P-shaped railings usually attach to the riser face in the center of the aisle and must be attached and removed each time the units are moved. The end railings prevent falls and must have no gaps greater than six inches.

The ADA requirements also specify that the seating areas provided for those with wheelchairs be spread throughout the facility rather than all congregated together for nay facility with a spectator capacity greater than 300. Wheelchair seating is to be an integral part of the seating plan, and a companion seat must be provided adjacent to each wheelchair seating location (U.S. Department of Justice, n.d.). The number of wheelchair spaces for spectator seating should be reviewed carefully to maintain ADA compliance. The required amount of wheelchair seating locations, according to the Uniform Federal Accessibility Standards section 4.12, are detailed in Table 29.1. For example, a gymnasium with a seating capacity of 1300 spectators must provide 20 wheelchair locations plus one additional location for every 100 seats over the initial 1,000. Therefore, this example gymnasium would require a total of 23 wheelchair locations plus 23 companion seating spaces (Access Board, n.d.).

Bleacher replacement (see Chapter 12) can improve a gymnasium facility not just by improving the facilities compliance with ADA and UBC, but also by creating an improved facility appearance. Many models have color options to enhance the aesthetic image of the facility. The

Table 29.1

Accessbility Spaces for Stadium, Arena, or Gymnasium Spectator Seating

Capacity of Seating Area	Number of Required Wheelchair Locations
50 to 75	3
76 to 100	4
101 to 150	5
151 to 200	6
201 to 300	7
301 to 400	8
401 to 500	9
501 to 1000	2% of total
Over 1000	20 plus 1 for each 100 over 1000

use of mechanical opening and closing greatly reduces the injury risk for personnel in facility set-up and teardown. The risk-management benefits and ADA compliance associated with bleacher replacement help make this improvement not only a desired trend but, in many cases, a necessity.

Several suppliers of bleachers and other gymnasium components have taken safety a step further, going beyond the code language to help mitigate injury risk with specialized bleacher accessories and innovations. The bleacher enclosure, as one of these innovations, has gained increasing popularity among athletic directors within the past five years. Bleacher enclosures are available either as heavy-gauge nylon curtains or collapsible wood walls with lockable access doors on the exposed bleacher ends. In either form, they attach to the bleacher system and move in and out with its telescoping motion to deter unwanted access underneath the opened bleachers (Steinbach, 2008a).

Equipment Trends for Fitness Venues

A 2008 report from the National Sporting Goods Association described a rise of 27.5% from 1998 to 2007 in the number of individuals working out in a health or fitness club. In 2012 the International Health, Racquet and Sportsclub Association (IHRSA) noted that health club membership increased by more than 10% in the last three years totaling 51.4 million members in the United States for 2011. Additionally, annual revenues in continue to climb in the American health club industry from the $17.6 billion reported by Archer (2007) for 2006 to the $21.4 billion for 2011 noted by the IHRSA (2012), representing an approximate 22% increase. For exercise equipment, the U.S. Census Bureau (2012) reported an increase in total spending of 98% from 1990 to 2000 with an increase from $1.82 billion to $3.61 billion, and this exercise equipment spending jumped an additional 48% to $5.35 billion in

2010. With this great desire of individuals to use exercise equipment, public and private institutions must continue to focus efforts on meeting these fitness needs with their selection of exercise equipment for both strength and cardio training.

One major consideration in the selection of fitness equipment is the cost. Table 29.2 identifies the average cost of 12 selected weight machines over four time periods. The 1995 pricing from Hasler and Bartlett, is compared to the average prices obtained from price quotes for two lines of selectorized machines in 2004 and from three lines of both selectorized and plate loaded machines in 2008 and 2013. Over this 18-year period, the total price for these 12 selectorized machines has increased by 55.6%. However, when prior year cost were corrected for inflation via the US Department of Labor Consumer Price Index Inflation Calculator (http://www.bls.gov/data/inflation_calculator.htm), the net change in selectorized equipment over the last 18 years has been a more modest 1.9%. For the plate loaded weight machines, there was a 21.6% increase in prices since 2008 while the inflation corrected price for plate loaded machines rose an inflation-corrected 12.4% over the past five years. While the plate loaded weight machines have a lower total price, it should be noted that these prices do not include the weight plates required for use, and three of the included machines are not available in a plate loaded configuration. This data demonstrates the general trends of rising costs for weight-training equipment. The pricing of strength equipment can be influenced by numerous factors including the costs in primary raw materials. The global spike in steel prices peaking in the summer of 2008 impacted the overall cost of the weight machines and plates. For example, hot-rolled sheet steel rose from an average of $400 per metric ton in 2007 to $1,154 per metric ton in June of 2008 representing a 189% increase in market price (Cohen, 2008). While steel prices have moderated back

Table 29.2

Total-Body Weight Workout Sample Equipment Costs

WEIGHT EQUIPMENT	1995 Selectorized Average Cost Per Unit	2004 Selectorized Average Cost Per Unit	2008 Selectorized Average Cost Per Unit	2008 Plate Loaded Average Cost Per Unit	2013 Selectorized Average Cost Per Unit	2013 Plate Loaded Average Cost Per Unit
Lower Body						
Leg Press	$4,783	$4,510	$4,841	$3,148	$5,799	$3,766
Seated Leg Curl	$2,459	$2,975	$3,611	$1,985	$3,799	$2,449
Leg Extension	$2,388	$2,663	$3,645	$1,878	$3,732	$2,399
Multi-Hip	$2,406	$2,550	$4,285	N/A	$4,166	N/A
Mid Section						
Abdominal	$2,394	$2,713	$3,461	N/A	$3,949	N/A
Lower Back	$2,729	$2,763	$3,668	N/A	$3,966	N/A
Upper Body						
Arm Curl	$2,081	$2,563	$3,378	$1,921	$3,766	$2,599
Triceps Extension	$2,256	$2,563	$3,425	$2,038	$3,599	$2,699
Chest Press	$2,546	$2,813	$3,885	$2,081	$3,799	$2,432
Shoulder Press	$2,414	$2,813	$3,885	$2,038	$3,799	$2,332
Rowing	$2,281	$2,813	$3,918	$2,061	$3,732	$2,249
Lat Pulldown	$2,044	$2,663	$3,918	$2,065	$3,799	$2,432
Total Cost	$30,781	$34,398	$45,919	$19,215	$47,905	$23,358

to the $600-700 range per metric ton in 2013, the market forces for this crucial raw material remain important in product pricing (SteelBenchmarker, 2013). In response to rising prices, the purchase of used strength equipment is growing as it has been noted to save 30-70% in equipment costs (McDonnell, 2009). Key issues to consider in purchasing used strength equipment are aesthetics, function, and liability considerations; although risk factors are generally fewer for strength equipment than for cardio equipment (Broadhag, 2006).

Cardio equipment has also continued to see rises in product prices. The National Sporting Goods Association (2008b) reported pricing trends from 2003 to 2007 remaining stable for treadmills, while average prices for exercise bikes rose 16.1% and elliptical machine prices rose 35.3%. While cost is one major factor in equipment selection, the needs and wants of the users cannot be overlooked.

According to the American College of Sports Medicine's 2012 worldwide survey of fitness trends, two of the top 20 trends related directly to equipment include strength training, rated number 2, and spinning, rated number 16 (Thompson, 2012). The use of free weights (including hand weights) is the most prevalent form of strength training with 46.6 million participants in 2012, and another 39.0 million participants reported using weight machines for strength training (Sport and Fitness Industry Association, 2013). While the increasing trend and emphasis on strength training is indeed noteworthy, the use of cardio training equipment still draws more users than strength training. The top cardio activities and equipment used in 2012 included treadmills (50.8 million participants), ellip-

ticals (28.6 million participants), upright stationary cycles (24.3 million participants), and stair climbing machines (13.0 million participants) according to the Sport and Fitness Industry Association (2013). While the total rise in exercise equipment for fitness center or other industrial uses rose 4.7% from 2011 to 2012, the two equipment types with the greatest increase in sales were treadmills and elliptical machines both noting 15% increases in sales (Sport and Fitness Industry Association, 2013b).

There can also be significant variance in the equipment preferences based on the demographic traits such as age and gender. For example, weight training increased 127% from 1987 to 1997 among American women for a total of 16.8 million (Trend Setting, 1999). Exercise equipment preferences by gender were first explored by Patton (1999). His survey of nearly 1,200 collegiate recreation providers found that males top equipment choices were free weights, bikes, treadmills, and steppers, while the females preferred treadmills, steppers, ellipticals, and bikes. The general trends noted above were confirmed in 2011 when it was found that 80% of females preferred cardio equipment and 80% of males preferred strength equipment when designating first choice in exercise equipment.

It is important to note the wide variety of equipment used in the fitness setting, and that the prevalence of the equipment is not always large and costly. The *IDEA Fitness Journal* has tracked the top offered type of equipment within health and fitness clubs for a number of years. Table 29.3 details the 18 pieces of equipment that were all offered at more than half of the facilities surveyed. Over the past two years, the major changes to the top 10 in this list have included the addition of kettle bells and ellipticals and body weight leverage equipment (TRX® Suspension Trainer, GTS® gravity training system, push-up and pull-up devices etc), and computer workout tracking equipment. Dropping out of the top 10 were weighted bars, resistance tubing, steps and platforms, and treadmills (Stone Hearth News, 2011).

Table 29.3

Equipment Offered at Fitness Facilities

Equipment Type	Facility Offering
Stability balls	95%
Resistance tubing or bands	95%
Barbells and/or dumbbells	90%
Balance equipment	87%
Medicine balls	87%
Yoga mats and equipment	85%
Foam rollers and small balls	83%
Weighted bars	82%
Steps and platforms	81%
Treadmills	76%
Elliptical trainers	72%
Pulley equipment	70%
Recumbent cycles	67%
Selectorized weight machines	66%
Upright cycles	63%
Plate-loaded weight machines	60%
Body weight leverage equipment	56%
Stair climbers	51%

Adapted from Schroeder & Dotan (2010)

Weight training has a variety of equipment options from free weights, to plate-loaded machines, to selectorized (weight stack and pin) machines. While novice lifters typically prefer the selectorized machines, there continues to be a significant amount of growth in the use of free weights as well as the plate-loaded systems.

One trend within the strength training modes is a continued focus on safety and risk management. Some selectorized systems have incorporated shrouds that cover much of the weight stack and many moving parts to reduce to risk of injury. On the free weight side, changes in the plate designs, such as the addition of grip slots, has made for easier handling of the weights. The creation of multisided plates and dumbbells that will not roll have also increased the safety in handling free weights (Brown, 2007).

Another major trend in weight-training equipment is the continued integration of computer-chip technology on many selectorized systems. For example, some systems are

able to read users' swipe cards or other input devices and can set resistance levels and record results based on a prescribed workout routine from a personal trainer.

The increasing use of aerobic or cardio machines is another current trend. The "big three" pieces of cardio equipment expected in any fitness center are treadmills, ellipticals, and cycles (Peavey, 2008).

Since walking remains the most popular of all forms of aerobic exercise, with over 112.7 million participants in 2012, it is not surprising that the treadmill is still a very popular piece of exercise equipment (Sporting Goods Manufacturers Association, 2012). Cycling machines have also been a mainstay of cardio exercise machines, but they have continued to diversify. Cycling equipment now includes many options such as the traditional exercise cycle, air resistance cycle, spin cycle, and recumbent cycle. The Sporting Goods Manufacturers Association (2012) reported that group cycling or spinning noted the greatest level of growth in participation from 2011 to 2012 with an 11.3% increase. Other equipment innovations, such as elliptical machines, are also popular cardio options that offer nonimpact aerobic training. While some cardio equipment users may exclusively train on one type of machine, other users tend to enjoy using a variety of machines to avoid stagnation or boredom in their exercise programs. Because of the varied use of aerobic exercise equipment, it is difficult to predict what machine might become the next top-choice machine, but it is almost certain that there will be other creative innovations.

Key trends in cardio equipment revolve around the use of technology for entertainment, tracking workout progress, and personalization (McDonnell & Tucker-Rhodes, 2007). The continued integration of computer technology within cardio machines is related to decrease in price and size for these innovations. The use of direct pulse monitoring while using the cardio machines began in the 1980s, but the development of computer programming that can alter the speed or resistance level of the machine to keep the person exercising within a specified target heart rate is definitely a great step forward in customizing workouts. The computerized workout routines that focus on optimal fat-burning pulse zones (typically 65% of maximal heart rate [MHR]) or optimal cardiovascular benefit zones (typically 80% MHR) are becoming common options on many cardio machines. Additionally, many cardio machines contain other preprogrammed workouts, such as interval or hill sessions. Some manufacturers have installed fitness protocols used in military, law enforcement, or firefighting fitness assessments. Recent additions of touch screen technology to cardio equipment controls as well as accommodating personal devices such as smartphones and iPods have continued to transform the cardio equipment console and the interaction between the user and the equipment (Cohen, 2012). These advances also include equipment directly connected to the network allowing personal workout data to be stored and retrieved using a system key or QR code-based mobile apps (Cohen). A potential drawback to such advances is that the complexity of the controls and interface systems may reduce the ability for consumers to easily transition from one brand to another within the gym setting without significant time to learn the specific control functions and features.

At the same time, there are many users of these machines who simply wish to get on and work out at a steady rate or pace without using these sophisticated controls or programming options. For those types of users, the manual operation or quick-start options are also available to allow a very basic workout. According to King (2003), approximately 80% of exercisers use these manual or quick-start settings; however, several factors contribute to the continued development of high-tech programming on cardio machines. These include the ability to cater to specific customer wants and needs, the ability to respond to more highly educated exercisers, and the creation of unique sales tool for a manufacturer.

The entertainment of individuals using exercise equipment is a current trend that will likely continue to expand in the future. Cardiovascular exercise areas in the past may have provided reading material, a room-wide stereo system, and perhaps a television. More recent trends involve the use of multiple video display screens and FM band audio programming for individual headset listening of either the video programming or music. The addition of wireless broadband technology has also been adapted to fitness applications, allowing institutions to customize audio and video entertainment and to include internal promotions as well. Numerous video monitors, coupled with individual audio broadcasting systems, are now trademarked as comprehensive systems such as Cardio Theater and Broadcast Vision. With the drop in LED screen technology prices, these systems have been moving from large group monitors to small individual screens directly mounted to each cardio machine. These systems meet users' needs by allowing them to select their own programming in news, business, or entertainment. The video portion of these systems can play network or cable programming or they can play specific workout, motivational, or educational programming.

Entertainment while using cardio equipment has also moved into the interactive realm. New options are available such as stationary cycles combined with video gaming devices. The level of cycle performance directly impacts the performance in the video game in this technology termed "exergaming." Some systems have been developed for both individual applications and group competition, where up to 16 riders can compete on the same system. Other technology moved toward virtual reality, where scenery simulation products that create beach scenery, trails, or palm-lined streets that are projected onto video displays. The landscape moves on the monitor according to the rate of performance on the cardio equipment, and the virtual hills are synchronized with the incline on a treadmill or the resistance level on a cycle.

In addition to the expansion of audio and video entertainment options while exercising, personal computers and tablets have been modified for ease of use while exercising. Computers and display monitors have been modified to allow for operation while exercising on a treadmill, stepper, or elliptical trainer. This technology allows the exerciser to access the Internet via a touch screen or modified mouse. Increased use of computer technology has also led to an increase in the use of wireless computer network technology or Wi-Fi. Fitness equipment manufacturers such as Technogym (with Visioweb), Nautilus and FitLinxx have moved to the lead of the wireless-network revolution in fitness. Their systems are typically composed of two parts: a wireless device attached to individual pieces of cardio or resistance equipment, and a wireless fitness tracking kiosk where patrons can obtain personalized data about their workouts (Picozzi-Moran & Brown, 2006). These technology trends allow for an increase in individual choice in the entertainment and feedback options while exercising. It is likely that market forces will continue to drive an expansion of these trends.

Automated External Defibrillators (AEDs)

Automated External Defibrillators (AEDs) are portable emergency medical devices that deliver an electric shock to the heart in order to halt sudden cardiac arrest (SCA). SCA is the onset of a chaotic and unproductive heart rhythm, and the AED works to restore a normal heart rhythm. Published studies have proven that defibrillation within the first few minutes of cardiac arrest can save up to 50% of victims. Sudden cardiac arrest causes the death of more than 250,000 Americans annually; however, an estimated 20,000 could be saved each year with prompt use of AEDs (National Conference of State Legislatures, 2008). The AED uses a two-electrode system. Once the electrodes are in place, the AED itself will analyze the heart rhythm and determine if an electric shock is necessary (see figure 10). If the AED determines the victim is shockable, then the AED instructs the responder to push the shock button. The AED will also instruct the responder to repeat the procedure if necessary.

Much of the growing movement to place AEDs in facilities used for sport, recreation, physical education, and fitness has been in response to the passage of federal legislation, the Cardiac Arrest Survival Act (House Resolution 2498), in 2000. This federal law requires all federal buildings, nationwide, to provide an AED. The law also provides nationwide Good Samaritan protection that exempts from liability anyone who renders emergency treatment with a defibrillator to save someone's life. This legislation has raised the standard for what would be considered customary treatment for a victim of sudden cardiac arrest. Many public facilities, such as airports, professional stadiums ,and arenas, now have AEDs on the premises. They also have personnel trained in the use of AEDs on staff due to the large number of spectators present at sporting events.

In the school setting, AEDs are becoming more prevalent on campuses. The state of New York in 2002 became the first state in the nation to require automated external defibrillators in schools. This state statute requires school districts, boards of cooperative educational services, county vocational education, and extension boards and charter schools to keep at least one functional AED on their premises. It also requires that an AED must be available at school-sponsored athletic events, whether on campus or off site. It is likely that other states may soon follow in requiring schools to provide AEDs in the future, and a total of 23 states have enacted legislation requiring or promoting AEDs in the school setting as of 2013 (National Conference of State Legislatures, 2013). At the college level, there are similar AED needs for both large spectator events in sport as well as for campus fitness and recreation centers. A 2005 study of NCAA Division I universities indicated that 91% of the schools provided AEDs at their spectator sport venues, and that a total of 35 cases of AED use had resulted in 19 successful resuscitations (Drezner, Rogers, Sennet, & Zimmer, 2005).

In the fitness club setting, the state of Illinois became the first state to pass legislation in 2004 that requires all clubs to provide at least one AED and at least one staff member trained in its use. Additional states mandated similar legislation requiring AEDs in health clubs including: New York in 2004, California in 2005, and Massachusetts, Michigan, and New Jersey in 2006 with a current total of 14 states mandating health club or gym AEDs in 2013 (National Conference of State Legislatures, 2013).

AEDs were approximately $3,000 per unit in 2000 when the original federal AED legislation was passed. According to Richard Lazar of the Early Defibrillator Law and Policy Center in Portland, Oregon, the cost for each AED in 2004 was about $2,200 and training might run $100 per person (Kufahl, 2004). A survey of online sources in 2012 noted prices ranging from $1,199 to $2,520 for an institutional-use AED. It would be expected that the increased placement of these devices might create market conditions that would allow for a further reduction in the price of the AEDs in the future, therefore, more facilities can provide them for their users.

Extreme Sports

Adventure-oriented sports continue to grow in popularity and bring unique requirements for facilities and equipment. The media exposure of extreme sports through competitions such as ESPN's X Games and numerous other network spin-offs continues to help fuel interest in and give credibility to these activities. Although some of the events such as street luge may have limited appeal to mass participation, activities such as rock climbing and skating (skateboarding and in-line skating) have large levels of participation. In fact, these activities are attracting so many participants that instead of being viewed as "extreme sports," it might be better to consider them extremely common.

The number of participants in skateboarding, according to the SkatePark Association of the United States of America (SPAUSA), tops more than 12 million regular users. More conservative estimates from the Outdoor Foundation (2012) totaled skateboarders at 5.8 million in 2011 while the Sport and Fitness Industry Association (2013) noted 6.2 million skateboarders in the population of Americans ages six and older. Added to this impressive total is in-line skating that included over 6.6 million participants with an addition 1.4 million playing inline hockey informally (SFIS, 2013). According to USA Roller Sports (2013), the national governing body for the sport, in-line hockey has an official membership list of just over 3,900. When including the number of inline skaters for informal cardiovascular exercise and the additional recreational street and skatepark skaters, there is a significant population with sporting and recreational needs in this area that are very facility dependent.

Skateboarding and inline skating opportunities can be enhanced through the creation of skateparks as designated areas developed for safe, supervised and exciting riding. In addition to accommodating skateboarders, these parks are often very functional for BMX cycling, inline skating, and scooter use. While the annual construction rate of 300-600 public skateparks per year from 2000 (Ahrweiler, 2001) has continued to remain steady, the addition of grant funding has also impacted construction trends. According to the Tony Hawk Foundation (2012), 500 skateparks in all 50 states have been provided grant funding from 2002 to 2012. Skateparks are being constructed in both indoor and outdoor settings, with features primarily in wood or concrete based, and with both publicly and privately funded operational models. Gembeck (n.d.) recommends that a skatepark for all levels of users should include 18,000 to 25,000 square feet along with 5000 to 8000 square feet for a beginners' area.

While some skateparks are elaborate concrete build-in-place systems, there are also modular park components available. These components could be considered the equipment necessary to create a skatepark from an available asphalt or concrete space. The modular components can be made out of concrete, wood, or a combination of steel framing, polyethylene and zinc plating. These components combine elements such as angled and curved ramps, rails, curbs, and bumps to create fairly comprehensive parks suitable for both skateboard and inline skate use. The modular components have even been assembled into portable units such as the "Flip Side" in Caledon, Ontario. This portable system of seven ramp structures and grind rails is transported to various locations throughout the summer in this Toronto suburb.

Inline hockey has allowed the expansion of the traditionally "northland" sport of hockey to be adapted to sunbelt states without the requirement of ice. Inline hockey can be played indoors or outdoors, and the facility space can often be converted for modified soccer use. Equipment needed to create a usable facility includes the dasherboards, goals, and a smooth base surface. The dasherboards are commonly constructed from wood, fiberglass, or plastic. One change is that the Plexiglas upper portion of the boards seen in ice hockey is often replaced with coated fencing or netting for inline hockey. The preferred surface is smoothly finished concrete, but portable vinyl tiling systems such as Sport Court or other similar products can also provide a good playing surface.

While some skateparks are elaborate, concrete build-in-place systems, there are also modular park components available. These components could be considered the equipment necessary to create a skatepark from an available asphalt or concrete space. The modular components can be made out of concrete, wood, or a combination of steel framing, polyethylene, and zinc plating. These components combine elements such as angled and curved ramps, rails, curbs, and bumps to create fairly comprehensive parks suitable for both skateboard and inline skate use. The modular components have even been assembled into portable units such as the "Flip Side" in Caledon, Ontario. This portable system of seven ramp structures and grind rails is transported to various locations throughout the summer in this Toronto suburb.

Inline hockey has allowed the expansion of the traditionally "northland" sport of hockey to be adapted to sunbelt states without the requirement of ice. Inline hockey can be played indoors or outdoors, and the facility space can often be converted for modified soccer use. Equipment needed to create a usable facility includes the dasherboards, goals, and a smooth base surface. The dasherboards are commonly constructed from wood, fiberglass, or plastic. One change is that the Plexiglas upper portion of the boards seen in ice hockey is often replaced with coated fencing or netting for inline hockey. The preferred surface is smoothly finished concrete, but portable vinyl tiling sys-

tems, such as Sport Court or other similar products, can also provide a good playing surface.

The sport of climbing (indoor, sport, and bouldering) continues to attract attention within the fitness facility setting especially at the collegiate setting. According to the Outdoor Foundation (2013), this activity boasted over 4.1 million participants in 2011, and for 2012 the Sport and Fitness Industry Association (2013) has reported just over 4.4 million rock climbers (a 7.3% increase). Rock climbing demonstrated a 9.5% increase in participants from 1999-2009, and it is included among a listing of "challenge activities" projecting a growth of 50-86% through the year 2060 (Cordell, 2012). The clientele of climbing walls continues to expand, especially for young people. A total of 60% of all artificial wall-climbing participants are 17 years old or younger, with 6- to 11-year-olds the most frequent participants (Popke, 2005). Indoor climbing facilities can be traced back as far as the 1960s, and the current 300-plus dedicated climbing gyms and the multitude of fitness clubs and recreation centers with climbing wall components have their own unique equipment requirements (Mac-Donald, n.d.). The equipment required for the use of a climbing structure might consist of a variety of mountable holds (fiberglass or resin fixtures for hands or feet), belay systems (safety harness), ropes and rope hardware, helmets and climbing shoes. Most climbing structures are "custom built" walls or free-standing structures, but in some instances existing wall space of adequate height and structural soundness can be adapted into a functional climbing surface. One recent trend is the conversion of underutilized racquetball courts into climbing facilities (Steinbach, 2008c). Of course the custom climbing areas are much more impressive in appearance and in realistic climbing features. Regardless of the climbing wall type, the ability to alter the holds creates immense flexibility for the climbing wall to be configured for both novice and experienced climbers. This changeability also helps to keep climbers motivated and interested in the climbing experience.

Supply Trends

It is far more difficult to trace supply trends within sport facilities and sport and fitness organizations. Changes in the market for particular supplies, be it towels, athletic tape, or basketballs, would be more likely to be researched by the manufacturers and those practitioners in the field than those in the facility planning process. The specific supply needs also vary greatly based on the nature of the organization. A tennis club has far different supply needs than an arena league football team. Similarly, the maintenance department for a major stadium has far different supply needs than the baseball team that plays at the stadium.

One innovation that can now greatly influence the selection and purchase of supplies regardless of the program or department is the explosive growth of the use of the Internet. The Internet can be used to research products, obtain price quotes, and even place orders for almost any supply needed in the realm of sport and recreation. The use of standard search engines can be used to locate supplies, but the development of sport specific supply websites can also be effective. Athleticsearch.com can be used to research product information from a multitude of suppliers as well as give access to articles from trade magazines and other sources. The bidding and purchasing process can be facilitated through sites like Athleticbid.com that contact multiple vendors and allow them to place bids on your specified needs.

Vendor Websites

The following list of equipment vendor websites may be useful for the case study exercises and for general product research. This listing of vendors is only a small segment of the total market, and any listing or omission from this listing is in no way to be construed as an endorsement or lack thereof of any products or services.

www.americanaed.com—automated external defibrillators
www.body-masters.com—weight equipment
www.broadcastvision.com—exercise entertainment systems
www.bsnsport.com—sport supply
www.cybexintl.com—cardio and weight machines
www.daktronics.com—scoreboards and LED displays
www.diamond-vision.com—LED video display boards
www.edgewalls.com—climbing walls
www.hammerstrength.com—weight machines
www.humanemfg.com—rubber mats and flooring
www.irongrip.com—weight plates
www.keiser.com—performance equipment
www.lifefitness.com—fitness equipment
www.nautilus.com—weight machines
www.netpulse.com—exercise entertainment systems
www.nicros.com—climbing walls
www.nustep.com—performance equipment
www.paramountfitness.com—weight machines
www.power-lift.com—weight machines
www.power-systems.com—performance equipment
www.precor.com—elliptical machines
www.quantumfitness.com—fitness equipment
www.spohnranch.com—skate park components
www.sportime.com—sport and physical education supply
www.sportsystemscorp.com—in-line hockey and hockey
www.stairmaster.com—cardio machines
www.startrac.com—cardio machines
www.truefitness.com—cardio machines
www.yorkbarbell.com—free weights
www.werksanusa.com—barbells
www.wwsport.com—sport supply

30 History of the Council on Facilities

Thomas H. Sawyer, *Indiana State University*
Michael G. Hypes, *Morehead State University*

The Council on Facilities and Equipment (CFE) focuses on concerns regarding facilities and equipment in relationship to physical activity and sport. The CFE develops policies, standards, guidelines, and innovations to ensure the safest and most effective means for quality health, physical education, recreation, dance, sport, and fitness facilities and equipment for the young through the aging populations. This chapter describes the development of the CFE and facility and equipment standards.

Initial Interest in Facilities

Aside from Dr. Edward M. Hartwell's comprehensive report on gymnasium construction in 1885 and occasional articles in *The American Physical Education Review* (the official publication of the American Association for the Advancement of Physical Education), the profession had made no concerted effort to consider facilities (Rice, Hutchinson, & Lee, 1958). In the early 1920s, the Society of Directors of Physical Education in College (College Physical Education Association) appointed a committee, of which Dr. George L. Meylan was chairman, to consider physical education facilities. Its work was published in booklet form in 1923, entitled *Physical Education Buildings for Education Institutions, Part I, Gymnasiums and Lockers* (Hackensmith, 1966). The committee remained active, and following Meylan in the chairmanship was Harry A. Scott until 1927; A.R. Winters was chair from 1927 to 1928, and Albert H. Prettyman was chair from 1928 to 1945 (Van-Dalen, Mitchell, & Bennett, 1953).

The halt in the construction of facilities during the depression was only temporary, and as soon as the federal government entered the picture, building programs were resumed on a grander scale than before. Many obvious and absurd mistakes were made in the early stages of architectural planning (Hackensmith, 1966; Rice et al., 1958; VanDalen et al., 1953). This led the government to provide expert guidance in planning facilities. In addition, the National Recreation Association and the Recreation Division, Work Project Administration, issued many pamphlets as guides in planning recreation facilities. The College Physical Education Association also initiated the practice of collecting and filing architectural plans of college facilities that were made available to the profession on request (Hackensmith, 1966).

By the end of the 1930s, the degree of interest in the planning and construction of facilities was demonstrated by many publications on the subject, including Herbert Blair's *Physical Education for the Modern Junior and Senior High School* (1938), Emil Lamar's *The Athletic Plant* (1938), George Butler's *The New Play Areas: Their Design and Equipment* (1938), Fredrick W. Leuhring's *Swimming Pool Standards* (1939), and Ruth Eliott Houston's *Modern Trends in Physical Education Facilities for College Women* (1939).

Early Physical Education Facilities

Many gymnasiums were erected after the Civil War, starting with the Dartmouth building of 1867, which cost $24,000. Following that, Princeton replaced its earlier red shack with a $38,000 "gym," the finest of its day. Bowdoin's gymnasium had no heat, and the men dressed for class even in freezing weather, changing to cotton shirts and tights and cloth slippers. In 1870, the University of Wisconsin built a $4,000 gymnasium (the first state university to build one). The Yale gymnasium of 1875 had eight long "bathtubes" lined with zinc, which the students used only by paying a special fee. Then 1879 brought the wonder gymnasium of the age—Harvard's $110,000 Hemenway Gymnasium—followed in 1878 by the University of California's modest $12,000 Harmon Gymnasium. During the 1960s and 1970s, many colleges that could not afford gymnasia fitted up vacant rooms as drill halls (Rice et al., 1958).

In the women's colleges, physical education classwork got underway in this period by using the outdoors, corridors, assembly halls, and storerooms. One school used a privately owned gymnasium in the local community—Radcliffe at Sargent's Gymnasium. Vassar was the only college that started its physical education work with a special building constructed for that purpose. In 1860, it built a "Hall of Calisthenics" with footprints painted on the floor to indicate where the students should stand during their exercise periods. Mt. Holyoke built a gymnasium by 1865 that cost $1,900. Other gymnasiums that were constructed included one at Smith in 1875, Bryn Mawr by 1885, Goucher by 1888, and Mills College by the end of the century. Goucher College constructed the first swimming pool for women in 1888, although it did not list swimming as an activity for students until 1904. Vassar built the second pool in 1889, and Smith installed a "swimming bath" in 1892 that could be used by two to five students at a time and was used for over 30 years; Bryn Mawr built its pool in 1894, and by the end of the century, Radcliffe College had built one. There were no pools for women or men in any coeducational college or coeducational university of this era (Rice et al., 1958).

The coeducational colleges/universities lagged far behind the women's colleges in procuring facilities for women students. As a rule, the women were permitted to use the men's facilities on occasion, and in many schools, a large room in the women's dormitory was set aside for a women's gymnasium (Hackensmith, 1966).

American Alliance for Health, Physical Education, Recreation, and Dance

The American Alliance for Health, Physical Education, Recreation, and Dance (AAHPERD) was founded on November 27, 1885, when William Gilbert Anderson, a physical training instructor in Brooklyn, New York, invited a group of people who were working in the gymnastic field to come together to discuss their profession. These 60 people talked informally of methods of teaching, the best system of measurements, normal training classes, and the manufacture of apparatus. After a demonstration of new exercise methods, they embarked on the formation of a permanent organization that was named the Association for the Advancement of Physical Education (AAPE). Forty-nine people, all teaching physical education, enrolled as members of the organization with a pledge to meet the next year at the same place. The first convention ran full-circle with discussions, speeches, a demonstration, enrollment of members, adoption of a plan of organization, and election of officers.

At the second meeting in 1886, a formal constitution was adopted and the name was changed to the American Association for the Advancement of Physical Education (AAAPE). The name was later changed to the American Physical Education Association (APEA). In 1937, the APEA and the Department of School Health and Physical Education of the National Education Association were formally amalgamated to form the American Association for Health and Physical Education (AAHPE). The following year, recreation was added to the title, and the American Association for Health, Physical Education, and Recreation (AAHPER) continued until 1974 when the American Alliance for Health, Physical Education, and Recreation was reorganized. Dance was added to the title in 1979.

The early years of the alliance focused on defining and exploring the field of physical education and encouraging its inclusion in the schools. By the close of the century, the organization had grown in number of members from 49 to 1,076 and was spreading throughout the nation. As the years went by, the alliance grew in structure, size, and scope as it worked toward the acceptance of the study of physical education.

In late 1896, the AAPE approved a plan to begin publishing a quarterly magazine, the *American Physical Education Review*, which became the *Journal of Health and Physical Education* in 1930 and the *Journal of Physical Education, Recreation, and Dance* in the 1970s. The journal is published nine times a year. In 1930, the association began publishing the *Research Quarterly*, now called the *Research Quarterly for Exercise and Sport*.

The years following World War II saw an emphasis on two key issues. One was the need for adequate and well-planned facilities, and the other was the pressing need for improved professional preparation of teachers. The alliance also continued its interest—which had developed during the war—in federal legislation relating to physical education and health services.

The decade of the 1950s was notable for a prodigious expansion of AAHPER activities, evident in three areas: conferences, consultant services, and publications. During this time, AAHPER also provided significant support and service to the cause of fitness. In 1958, the alliance developed the Youth Fitness Test, which was the first program of testing with national norms that applied to the fitness levels of America's school-aged children.

In 1965, a second national study was conducted, and the norms for the test were revised. It was during this year that the President's Council on Fitness joined with AAHPER, using the Youth Fitness Test, to initiate and promote the Presidential Physical Fitness Award.

In 1980, AAHPERD developed the Health-Related Fitness Test, where the items on the test battery related to major health risk factors. From 1980 through spring 1988, the alliance sponsored its Youth Fitness Test and the Health-Related Fitness Test. The Physical Best Program was developed in 1988 and contains both the health-related test and the teaching of fitness concepts.

The alliance went through growing pains in the late 1980s and launched two major initiatives to explore its future. One, the Blue Ribbon Task Force, devoted 3 years of study to the structure and function of the alliance in an attempt to analyze its effectiveness for meeting member needs. Somewhat overlapping this effort was an experimental project focusing on autonomy. This project, called the AAHE Experiment, used a different method of accounting for the cost of doing business and revenue sources. It allowed AAHE to experiment with more autonomous decision making and to take responsibility for those decisions. This experiment, along with the outcome of the Blue Ribbon Task Force, resulted in Model III, a move toward autonomy for all national associations. The AAHPERD is an educational organization designed to support, encourage, and provide assistance to member groups and their personnel nationwide as they initiate, develop, and conduct programs in health, leisure, and movement-related activities.

AAHPERD seeks to

- encourage, guide, and support professional growth and development in health, leisure, and movement-related programs based on individual needs, interests, and capabilities;
- communicate the importance of health, leisure, and movement-related activities as they contribute to human well-being;
- encourage and facilitate research that will enrich health, leisure, and movement-related activities, and disseminate the findings to professionals and the public;
- develop and evaluate standards and guidelines for personnel and programs in health, leisure, and movement-related activities;
- coordinate and administer a planned program of professional, public, and government relations that improves education in areas of health, leisure, and movement-related activities; and
- conduct other activities for the public benefit.

AAHPERD is composed of five national associations and the Research Consortium, including

- the American Association for Physical Activity and Recreation (AAPAR),
- the American Association for Health Education (AAHE),
- the National Association for Girls and Women in Sport (NAGWS),
- the National Association for Sport and Physical Education (NASPE), and
- the National Dance Association (NDA).

American Association for Physical Activity and Recreation History 1949–2013

The AAPAR evolved out of the General Division of the AAHPER. In 1949, the General Division was created as the fourth division of AAHPER, joining the Health Education Division, Physical Education Division, and the Recreation Division. This reorganization plan consolidated the general sections to eliminate duplication of functions and service. At the time of its formation, the General Division included 12 sections, three of which originated in the AAHPER well before 1930.

These 12 sections were

- Aquatics,
- Administration and Supervision,
- Athletics Boys and Men,
- Athletics Girls and Women,
- Camping and Outdoor Education,
- Dance,
- Measurement and Evaluation,
- Professional Education,
- Professional and Public Relations,
- Research,
- Students, and
- Therapeutics.

The General Division's substructures fluctuated in number through the years, beginning with the addition of the Research Council in 1952. General Division councils and sections were differentiated by functions. The sections operated primarily to plan and conduct programs at the annual AAHPER conventions in their specialized interest area.

The General Division 1970 Operating Code stated, "The purpose of the General Division shall be to provide leadership and coordination to those groups developing programs and fostering education activities under its auspices" and to

- provide an organizational structure to serve groups whose professional interest and activities relate to two or more existing AAHPER divisions or whose professional interests do not readily lend themselves to inclusion in other divisions,
- promote flexibility in serving the many and varied professional interests and levels of the AAHPER membership by providing opportunity for growth of new and continuing professional interest groups,
- recognize interdivisional professional interests and activities and to encourage communications and cooperation among the divisions of AAHPER, and
- coordinate and lend intradivisional support to professional interests and programs.

On April 16, 1973, the AAHPER Representative Assembly approved the Reorganization Committee's Model II to change AAHPER from an association to an alliance. This gave the eight AAHPER divisions and their structure self-determination of association status and placement. The premise was that the alliance would "provide unity with diversity," allowing the associations to have full control over their professional programs and to be a united structure of related disciplines. It is within these concepts and at that time that the Association for Research, Administration, and Professional Councils (ARAPC) originated. In October 1974, the Alliance Board of Governors defined the term *society* as an alliance structure and further stated that all societies would be housed in the ARAPC, formerly the General Division of the AAHPER. The name change took place during the early 1960s. The ARAPC was composed of those councils and a professional society that did not clearly fit into the other national associations—National Association for Sport and Physical Education, National Association for Girls and Women in Sport, American Association for Leisure and Recreation, and American Association for Health Education.

In spring 1994, the ARAPC changed its name to the American Association for Active Lifestyles and Fitness (AAALF). This name change was designed to more clearly define the focus and mission of the association. With its 12 councils and one society, AAALF has a broad range of interests and programs. All professional activities are carried on through the special interest areas of its councils. With this format, most of the income received by AAALF is allocated directly to the councils/society for their professional activities, which maximizes allocations for program content.

American Association for Physical Activity and Recreation

The AAPAR, formerly AAALF, is one of five national associations within the AAHPERD. The goal of AAPAR and its 10 councils (Adapted Physical Education Council, Aquatics Council, College and University Administrators Council, Council on Aging and Adult Development, Council on Facilities and Equipment, Council on Outdoor Education, Measurement and Evaluation Council, Physical Fitness Council, Safety and Risk Management, and Professional Recreation Council) is to promote active lifestyles and fitness for all populations through support of research, development of leaders, and dissemination of current information. The membership is provided the latest information in the field, professional development opportunities, career networking and contacts, an annual national convention, regional workshops/ conferences, publication opportunities, advocacy of mission, leadership opportunities, professional recognition, and headquarters support staff.

The Birth of the *Guide for Planning Facilities for Athletics, Recreation, Physical and Health Education*

At the meeting of the Board of Directors of the AAHPER in Washington, D.C., in April 1945, favorable action was taken on a proposal by Caswell M. Miles, AAHPERD vice president for recreation, that a grant be obtained to finance a national conference on facilities. Subsequently, a request for $10,000 to finance the first facilities conference was placed before Theodore R. Bank, president of The Athletic Institute. The project was approved and the money was appropriated to finance the first conference. The conference was held at Jacob's Mill, West Virginia. As a result of this conference, the *Guide for Planning Facilities for Athletics, Recreation, Physical and Health Education* was published that same year.

The second conference was held from May 5–12, 1956, at the Kellogg Center for Continuing Education at Michigan State University in East Lansing. The second conference, like the first, was financed by The Athletic Institute. The second edition (1956) of the *Guide* was the result of this second conference.

The third edition (1965) was prepared at the third conference, which was financed jointly by AAHPER and The Athletic Institute and held at the Biddle Continuing Education Center, Indiana University in Bloomington from January 15–24, 1965. The fourth conference was held 2 years later, from April 29–May 8, 1967, at Indiana University. Among those invited were a number of outstanding college and technical personnel engaged in planning and conducting programs of athletics, recreation, outdoor education, and physical and health education. In addition, invitations were extended to a number of specialists responsible for planning and constructing facilities for these programs. These specialists included city planners, architects, landscape architects, engineers, and schoolhouse construction consultants.

At the 1974 facilities committee meeting, five members were assigned the task of restructuring the *Guide* (fourth edition) so that it would serve as a more practical tool for school administrators, physical education heads, architects, planning consultants, and all others interested in planning new areas and facilities or checking the adequacy of those already in use.

During recent years, there have been many developments in facility planning and construction. These have been due to a number of factors. The need for improving education, recreation, and fitness opportunities for the youth of the nation has been highlighted by many groups. The extensive work of the President's Council on Physical Fitness is one illustration of the growing national interest in health, physical education, and recreation activities. Much of the research and attention devoted to facility planning and construction during the past three decades has been due to the increased leisure time in society and a growing realization that recreation, and especially physical activity, is a fundamental human need essential to the well-being of all people.

The Athletic Institute and AAHPERD Council on Facilities, Equipment, and Supplies initiated the fifth edition (1979) of the *Guide* following a careful review of the fourth edition (1974). A blue-ribbon steering committee was appointed by the council. Edward Coates of Ohio University and Richard B. Flynn of the University of Nebraska at Omaha were appointed as coeditors and contributing authors. Professionals well known for their expertise in facility planning and construction were invited to assist in a complete rewrite.

The sixth edition (1984) of *Planning Facilities for Athletics, Physical Education, and Recreation* represents a continuing effort on the part of The Athletic Institute and AAHPERD to keep the text current and relevant. Richard B. Flynn of the University of Nebraska at Omaha was selected as editor and contributing author. Chapter input was solicited from carefully chosen leaders in the field as well as from outstanding architects. Efforts were made to incorporate the most recent advances in facility planning and construction. Certain program areas, such as planning for people with disabilities, were expanded, and outdated or irrelevant materials were deleted.

Flynn, who edited the seventh edition, was selected to serve as editor and contributing author for the eighth edition (1993). This edition carried the same title as the seventh edition (1988). Many of the same contributors volunteered to revise their sections. The text was revised but not expanded.

For the ninth edition (1999), a new editorial team was put together by the Council on Facilities and Equipment to completely overhaul the book. The editorial team consisted of Thomas H. Sawyer, EdD (Indiana State University), editor-in-chief; Bernie Goldfine, PhD (Kennesaw State University); Michael G. Hypes, DA (Indiana State University); Richard L. LaRue, DPE (University of New England); and Todd Seidler, PhD (University of New Mexico). Twenty-one authors were involved in writing the 29 chapters. The name of the text was changed to *Facility Development for Physical Activity and Sport: Concepts and Applications*, in order to reflect an expanded content aimed at a broader audience.

The 10th edition (2002) used the same editorial team led by Thomas H. Sawyer. This edition was revised and expanded to 37 chapters, including a chapter describing the newest Japanese Olympic Training Center. The book was published by Sagamore Publishing/AAALF publications. The 11th edition was published in 2005 with the same editorial team that was used for the 10th edition. The 12th edition was published in 2009 with the same editorial team that was used for the 11th edition. In 2013, the 13th edition was published again using the same editorial team that has been involved since the 2010 edition.

Evolution of the Council on Facilities and Equipment 1955–2009

In 1955, AAHPER established the Council on Equipment and Supplies, with Thomas E. McDonough (Emory University, Georgia) as chairman and Charles Heilman (Drake University, Iowa) as secretary. The purpose of the council was to assist physical educators, athletic coaches, and recreation leaders in the selection, purchase, and care of equipment and supplies. Since its organization, the council has secured the cooperation of manufacturing companies and stimulated professional interest through exhibits of equipment and supplies at conferences and conventions. In 1959, AAHPER and the Athletic Institute cosponsored a third National Workshop on Equipment and Supplies for Athletics, Physical Education, and Recreation at Michigan State University, whose report was made available in 1960. The name of the council was changed in 1976 to reflect its work in the area of facilities: Council on Facilities, Equipment, and Supplies.

In 1993, the Council on Facilities, Equipment, and Supplies changed its name to the Council on Facilities and Equipment (CFE). The new name better identified the council's focus on concerns relating to facilities and equipment in relation to physical activity. CFE works to develop policies, standards, guidelines, and innovations to ensure the safest and most effective means for quality health, physical education, recreation, dance, sport, and fitness facilities for the young through the aging populations.

The purposes of the CFE are

- to initiate a national cooperative effort to improve the quality of the facilities and equipment for health, physical education, recreation, and dance;
- to improve the quality of undergraduate and graduate instruction in facilities and equipment design and planning;
- to present research findings and to review needed research projects for possible endorsement and development by the council;
- to prepare and disseminate information to aid members to keep abreast of current innovations, promising practices, comparative data, and practical ideas;
- to cooperate with related professions (architecture, engineering, construction, manufacturing), repre-

senting the alliance in all matters within its purview and proposing and implementing joint projects with other councils within AAPAR;

- to initiate and conduct state, district, and national conferences on facilities and equipment issues;
- to plan and develop needed publications through the alliance; and
- to provide consultant services for referral to potential users and developers of facilities.

Who Should Be a Member
- Those teaching courses or a unit within a course in facilities planning.
- Any HPERD professional who has an interest in facility planning.
- Any professional who plans, designs, and manages facilities, as well as manufacturers of equipment involving fitness, physical activity, and sport.

CFE Membership Services
- Consultant service for potential users, planners, and designers of physical activity facilities and equipment.
- Research on current trends in physical activity facilities and equipment.
- Programs and site visits of facilities at the annual AAHPERD national conference.
- *Focus on Facilities* newsletter is published semiannually. It contains news about ongoing projects within the council and important happenings in facility and equipment development.
- Awards are given to members who contribute significantly to the CFE.
- World Wide Web connection is http://www. aahperd. org/aaalf.html.
- Publication of state-of-the-art textbooks used in educating undergraduates and graduates in the field of facilities and equipment; available from AAHPERD Publications.

CFE LEADERSHIP AND AWARDS

Leadership in Facilities and Equipment Since 1920

The following professionals have been on the council since 1920

Leaders in Facilities, Equipment, and Supplies

1920-23	George L. Meylan
1924-27	Harry A. Scott
1927-28	A. R. Winters
1928-45	Prettyman
1928-45	Caswell M. Miles

Chairpersons of the Council on Equipment and Supplies [CES]

1954-56	Thomas E. McDonough
1956-59	Charles Heilman
1959-60	D. K. Stanley
1960-61	Robert Weber
1961-62	James C. Loveless
1962-63	John A. Friedrich
1963-64	William Theunissen
1964-65	John Fox
1965-66	Maurice A. Clay
1966-67	Wayne Brumbach
1967-68	Richard B. Westkaemper
1968-69	Joseph M. Pease
1969-70	John Nettleton
1970-71	James Delamater

1971-72	Alexander Petersen
1972-73	O. N. Hunter
1973-74	Ghary M. Akers
1974-75	Richard B. Flynn

Chairpersons of the Council on Facilities, Equipment, and Supplies (CFES)

1975-76	James E. Sharman
1976-77	Edward Coates
1977-78	James Mason
1978-79	Marty McIntyre
1979-80	Margaret Waters
1980-81	Mike Collins
1981-82	Robert L. Case
1982-83	Edward T Turner
1983-84	Ernest A. White
1984-85	Dan Gruetter
1985-86	Jack Lynn Shannon
1986-87	Larry Horine
1987-88	Armond Seidler
1988-89	Harvey White
1989-90	David Stotlar
1990-91	Maureen Henry
1991-92	Todd Seidler

Chairpersons of the Council on Facilities and Equipment [CFE]

1992-93	Brad Strand
1993-94	Marcia Walker
1994-95	Richard J. LaRue
1995-97	Thomas H. Sawyer
1997-99	Robert Femat
1999-2001	Bernie Goldfine
2001-2003	Michael G. Hypes
2003-2005	Thomas Horne
2005-2007	Jeff Peterson
2007-2008	Julia Ann Hypes
2008-2009	Michael G. Hypes
2009-2011	Michael G. Hypes
2011-2013	Lawrence Judge

The CFES or CFE Award Winners

Honor Award

1979	Richard B. Flynn
1980	Edward Coates
1981	Edward Shea
1982	Martin McIntyre
1983	Margaret H. Aitken
1994	Armond Seidler
1995	James Mason
1996	Harvey White
1997	Todd Seidler & Marcia Walker
1998	Edward Turner
1999	Thomas H. Sawyer
2000	Hervy LaVoie
2001	Donna Thompson
2002	Thomas H. Sawyer
2003	Richard LaRue
2004	No award
2005	Michael Hypes
2006	No Award
2007	Todd Seidler
2008	Michael Hypes
2009	Bernie Goldfine
2010	Julia Ann Hypes
2011	Richard LaRue
2012	Lawrence W. Judge
2013	Thomas H. Sawyer

Professional Recognition Award

1994	Edward Turner
1995	Larry Horine
1996	Alexander Gabrielsen
1997	Arthur Mittelstaedt
1998	Alison Osinski
1999	Dave Stotlar
2000	Richard LaRue
2001	Thomas Sawyer
2002	Todd Seidler
2003	Susan Hudson
2004	Bernie Goldfine
2005	Hal Walker
2006	No Award
2007	Michael G. Hypes
2008	Bernie Goldfine
2009	Gary Rushing
2010	Jeff Peterson
2011	Lawrence W. Judge
2012	Julia Ann Hypes
2013	Hal Walker
	Bernie Goldfine

Chairperson Citations

2007	Thomas Sawyer
2008	Jeff Peterson
2009	Sam Iverson and Chris Neumann
2010	No Award
2011	No Award
2012	No Award
2013	Jeff Peterson
	Julia Ann Hypes
	Peter Bannon

Lifetime Achievement Award

2008	Edward Turner
2009	No Award
2010	No Award
2011	No Award
2012	Thomas H. Sawyer
2013	Richard LaRue
	Mike Hypes

31 Equipment and Facility Design Standards

Thomas H. Sawyer, *Indiana State University*
Tonya L. Gimbert, *Indiana State University*

Standards

Standards are the basis by which fitness, physical activity, recreation, sports products, and facilities can be harmonized between companies, between sports associations, between trade associations, and between countries. Standards that have been developed over the past 50 years have provided a uniform approach to producing devices and parts used in fitness, physical activity, recreation, and sports equipment and in the construction of elements of a facility. Standards have also provided sports organizations with consistency among levels of a sport and variations of the game itself. This perhaps has been the weakest aspect of standardization, as various sports organizations have similarities and differences that become the competitive edge for control of that market.

A standard is something established for use as a rule or basis of comparison in measuring or judging capacity. A standard applies to a measure, principle, model, and so forth, with which items of the same class are compared to determine their quantity, value, or quality. A standard has a set of criteria used to test or measure the excellence, fitness, or correctness of something.

Standards for facilities and equipment are established by associations, societies, trades, or federal and state governments. ASTM International (ASTM) is an example of a society that establishes standards. From the work of 132 technical standards writing committees, ASTM (http://www. astm.org) publishes standard specifications, tests, practices, guides, and definitions for materials, products, systems, and services. ASTM also publishes books containing reports on state-of-the-art testing techniques and their possible applications. These standards and related information are used throughout the world.

Mandatory and Voluntary Standards

Standards may be either mandatory or voluntary. The status of a standard depends on the sponsor's organizational standing (i.e., governmental or voluntary nongovernmental). A mandatory standard is developed by a federal agency such as the Environmental Protection Agency (EPA) and Occupational Safety and Health Administration (OSHA). The voluntary standard is developed by a professional nonprofit agency. A violation of a mandatory standard carries a penalty. In addition to standards, other written documents control the unity and uniformity of equipment and facility development, including legal codes or regulations, technical specifications, guides, and literature and learned treatises.

Legal codes are developed by elected public officials, such as the National Bureau of Standards, EPA, and OSHA. Furthermore, each state or local government has its own building codes. Technical specifications and guidelines are developed by voluntary organizations such as the ASTM or American National Standards Institute (ANSI), which create standards through committee or trade group processes. Many other professional, trade, and organizational associations also promulgate standards, specifications, or guides that are used to measure a standard of care. Literature and learned treatises document common knowledge in a variety of ways, including professional journals, magazines, reference books, textbooks, and reports.

Standard of Practice

A standard of practice is a usual practice accepted by the national or local government regarding some aspect of equipment or facility design or usage. It is a usage or practice of the people, which, by common adoption and acquiescence and by long and unvarying habit, has become compulsory and has acquired the force of law with respect to the place or subject matter to which it relates. It is considered a customary practice that prevails within a geographical area.

Standard of Care

In laws of negligence, the standard of care is that degree of care that a reasonably prudent person should exercise in the same or similar circumstances. If a person's conduct falls below such standard, legal or customary, he or she may be liable in damages for injuries or damages resulting from his or her conduct.

Evolution of Standards

The development of standards began in earnest at the conclusion of World War II. The movement was enhanced by the efforts of the National Bureau of Standards to establish partnerships with ASTM, ANSI, and other groups to standardize materials and methods used by private industry and government. During the 1950s and 1960s, automation of the workplace increased the need for greater standardization of materials and methods. The computer age has again increased the need for greater collaboration between government and the private sector in developing additional standards as well as modifying previous ones.

The development of standards in the fitness, physical activity, recreation, and sport area began in the early 1970s. The F-8 Committee on Sports Equipment and Facilities was organized by ASTM. The initial standards promulgated by the F-8 Committee dealt with footwear and football helmets. Ten years after the F-8 Committee was developed, the Committee on Skiing and Amusements was established. Over the years, a wide range of standards has been developed that influences fitness, physical activity, recreation, and sport. These standards have also made equipment and facilities safer for participants.

Though such standards have been through the gauntlet of objections and reservations, they are here to stay. Some fear standards may inhibit creativity, negatively affect the growth of the sport, and increase its cost. When participants are engaged in a sport, they seem to want to use something to protect themselves. When they do, that something should meet reasonable and meaningful requirements, demonstrating that it provides the protection. The cost of debilitating injuries is reduced by this common denominator.

Organizations Advancing Standards

American National Standards Institute

ANSI is another significant organization that develops standards. It is a nonprofit, privately funded membership organization that coordinates the development of U.S. voluntary national standards and is the U.S. member body to nontreaty international standards bodies, such as the International Organization for Standardization (ISO) and the International Electrotechnical Commission (IEC) through the institute's U.S. National Committee (USNC). ANSI serves the private and public sectors' need for voluntary standardization. The voluntary standards system contributes to the overall health of the economy and the competitiveness of U.S. industry in the changing global marketplace.

ANSI was founded in 1918, prompted by the need for an "umbrella" organization to coordinate the activities of the U.S. voluntary standards system and eliminate conflict and duplication in the development process. The institute serves a diverse membership of over 1,200 companies; 250 professional, technical, trade, labor, and consumer organizations; and some 30 government agencies. The ANSI federation is guided by the national culture and the free enterprise system. For over 70 years, the U.S. voluntary standards system has been administered successfully by the private sector, through ANSI, with the cooperation of federal, state, and local governments. Standards exist in all industries, including telecommunications, safety and health, information processing, petroleum, banking, and household appliances. ANSI's (2012) key functions are to

- coordinate the self-regulating, due-process concensus-based U.S. voluntary standards system;
- administer the development of standards and approve them as American National Standards;
- provide the means for the United States to influence development of international and regional standards;
- disseminate timely and important information on national, international, and regional standards activities to U.S. industry; and
- promote awareness of the growing strategic significance of standards technology and U.S. global competitiveness.

A standards board is a standing organization within ANSI, having planning and coordination responsibilities on a continuing basis for a defined scope of activity under the purview of, and advisory to, ANSI's Executive Standards Council (ExSC). Standards boards serve in a purely advisory capacity. They do not develop standards, and they do not have authority over the activities of accredited standards developers. Membership within ANSI is a prerequisite to service on a standards board. The standards board is responsible for establishing overall planning and coordination for national and international standards activities in the safety and health area. Furthermore, it reviews the standards activity of applicants for accreditation and the initiation of new standards activities by accredited standards developers. It reviews applications for accreditation of International Standards Organization's U.S. Technical Advisory Group (TAG) Administrators and makes recommendations to the ExSC regarding approval of TAG Administrators, TAG membership lists, and accreditation.

The board also reviews lists of candidates for American National Standards and recommends the addition of directly and materially affected interests, and it makes recommendations to the ExSC concerning suggested changes to ANSI procedures.

The scope of the standards board includes protection of the health and safety of employees and the public using buildings, machinery, and other equipment; hazardous materials; workplaces (including construction sites); vehicular traffic; public and recreation areas; homes and schools; and occupational and nonoccupational hazards. Hazards include things such as explosion; fire; radiation (other than ionizing); mechanical, physical, chemical, and environmental hazards; disease; and inadequate or polluted air. Specifically included are personal protective equipment, including personal protection devices for attenuating noise, practices or devices to prevent or minimize fire, explosion or mechanical hazards, safe work practices, and provision for accident reporting and recording. Specifically excluded are building codes and acoustical (other than personal protective devices), electrical, process industry, and nuclear energy standards.

American Society of Testing and Materials

Prior to the 19th century's industrial revolution, craftsmen told their suppliers in similarly basic language what materials they desired. Craft experience was indeed key because artisans had no instruments to measure the tensile strength, chemical composition, and other characteristics of a given material.

The industrial revolution opened a new chapter in the history of material specifications. Locomotive builders, steel rail producers, and steam engine builders who used revolutionary new materials, such as Bessemer steel, could no longer rely on craft experiences of centuries past. Manufacturers encountered numerous quality problems in end products such as steel rails because suppliers furnished inferior materials. American rails were so poorly made, in fact, that many railroad companies preferred British imports, which were more expensive but reliable.

To avoid such problems, some manufacturers issued detailed descriptions of material to ensure that their supplies met certain quality standards. However, suppliers in many industries, such as construction and metallurgy, objected to standard material specifications and testing procedures because they feared that strict quality controls would make customers more inclined to reject items and default on contracts.

The Pennsylvania Railroad, the largest corporation of the 19th century, played a key role in the quest for standard specifications. Its efforts in this field were initiated by Charles Dudley, who received his PhD from Yale University in 1874 and later became the driving force behind ASTM. Dudley organized the railroad's new chemistry department where he investigated the technical properties of oil, paint, steel, and other materials the Pennsylvania Railroad bought in large quantities. Based on his research, Dudley issued standard material specifications for the company's suppliers.

What Is ASTM?

Organized in 1898, ASTM has grown into one of the largest voluntary standards development systems in the world. ASTM is a not-for-profit organization that provides a forum for producers, users, ultimate consumers, and those having a general interest (representatives of government and academia) to meet on common ground and write standards for materials, products, systems, and services. From the work of 132 standards writing committees, ASTM publishes standard test methods, specifications, practices, guides, classifications, and terminology. ASTM's standards development activities encompass metals, paints, plastics, textiles, petroleum, construction, energy, the environment, consumer products, medical services and devices, computerized systems, electronics, and many other areas. ASTM headquarters has no technical research or testing facilities; such work is done voluntarily by 35,000 technically qualified ASTM members located throughout the world. More than 10,000 ASTM standards are published each year in the 72 volumes of the *Annual Book of ASTM Standards*. These standards and related information are sold throughout the world.

What Is an ASTM Standard?

As used in ASTM, a standard is a document that has been developed and established within the consensus principles of the society and that meets the approval requirements of ASTM procedures and regulations. Some of the specific standards developed that relate to fitness, physical activity, recreation, and sport facilities and equipment are E-5 Fire Standards, F-6 Resilient Floor Coverings, F-8 Sports Equipment and Facilities, F-14 Fences, F-21 Filtration, F-24 Amusement Rides and Devices, F-26 Food Service Equipment, F-27 Snow Skiing, and F-30 Emergency Medical Services.

What Types of Standards Does ASTM Produce?

ASTM develops six principal types of full-consensus standards. They are listed in the following section.

- **Standard test method.** A definitive procedure for identifying, measuring, and evaluating one or more qualities, characteristics, or properties of a material, product, system, or service that produces a test result.
- **Standard specification.** A precise statement of a set of requirements to be satisfied by a material, product, system, or service that also indicates the procedures for determining whether each of the requirements is satisfied.

- **Standard practice.** A definitive procedure for performing one or more specific operations or functions that does not produce a test result.
- **Standard terminology.** A document comprising terms; definitions; descriptions of terms; and an explanation of symbols, abbreviations, or acronyms.
- **Standard guide.** A series of options or instructions that do not recommend a specific course of action.
- **Standard classification.** A systematic arrangement or division of materials, products, systems, or services into groups based on similar characteristics such as origin, composition, properties, or use.

Why Are ASTM Standards Credible?

Many factors contribute to the quality and credibility of ASTM standards. Those factors include

- a voluntary, full-consensus approach that brings together people with diverse backgrounds, expertise, and knowledge;
- a balanced representation of interests at the standards writing table;
- intense round-robin testing to ensure precision;
- strict balloting and due-process procedures to guarantee accurate, up-to-date information; and
- an atmosphere that promotes open discussion.

What Is Meant by Full-Consensus Standards?

Full-consensus standards are developed through the cooperation of all parties who have an interest in participating in the development and/or use of the standards. Standards can be developed through varying degrees of consensus. Examples include the following:

- Company standard—consensus among the employees of a given organization (principally within departments such as design, development, production, and purchasing).
- Industry standard—consensus among the employees of a given industry (typically developed by a trade association).
- Professional standard—consensus among the individual members of a given profession (typically developed by a professional society).
- Government standard—consensus often among the employees of a government agency or department.

ASTM develops full-consensus standards with the belief that input from all concerned parties in the development of a standard will ensure technically competent standards having the highest credibility when critically examined and used as the basis for commercial, legal, or regulatory actions.

Is the Use of ASTM Standards Mandatory?

ASTM standards are developed voluntarily and used voluntarily. They become legally binding only when a government body makes them so or when they are cited in a contract.

Who Uses ASTM Standards?

ASTM standards are used by thousands of individuals, companies, and agencies. Purchasers and sellers incorporate standards into contracts; scientists and engineers use them in their laboratories; architects and designers use them in their plans; government agencies reference them in codes, regulations, and laws; and many others refer to them for guidance.

Who Writes ASTM Standards?

ASTM standards are written by volunteer members who serve on technical committees. Through a formal balloting process, all members may have input into the standards before ASTM publishes them.

Anyone who is qualified or knowledgeable in the area of a committee's scope is eligible to become a committee member. ASTM currently has 32,000 members representing virtually every segment of industry, government, and academia.

What Are ASTM Technical Committees?

They are the specific arenas in which ASTM standards are developed. There are 132 ASTM main technical committees, and each is divided into subcommittees. The subcommittee is the primary unit in ASTM's standards development system, as it represents the highest degree of expertise in a given area. Subcommittees are further subdivided into task groups. Task group members do not have to be ASTM members. Many task groups seek non-ASTM members to provide special expertise in a given area.

How Are ASTM Standards Developed?

Standards development work begins when a need is recognized. Task group members prepare a draft standard, which is reviewed by its parent subcommittee through a letter ballot. After the subcommittee approves the document, it is submitted to a main committee letter box. Once approved at the main committee level, the document is submitted for balloting to the society. All negative votes cast during the balloting process, which must include a written explanation of the voter's objections, must be considered fully before the document can be submitted to the next level in the process. Final approval of a standard depends on concurrence by the ASTM Committee on Standards that proper procedures were followed and due process achieved. Only then is the ASTM standard published.

How Long Does It Take to Develop a Standard?

It usually takes about 2 years to develop a standard, although some committees have produced their standards in a year or less. Progress depends entirely on the urgency of the need, the complexity of the job, and the amount of time committees devote to the work.

How Does Someone Initiate a New Standards Activity in ASTM?

A written request, which describes the proposed activity and lists individuals, companies, and organizations that might have an interest in it, should be submitted to ASTM headquarters. The ASTM staff then researches the project to assess whether there is adequate interest, to discover whether parallel activities exist in other organizations, and to determine where the activity would appropriately fit within the ASTM structure.

The process of organizing a new activity includes holding a planning and/or organizational meeting depending on the activity's complexity. These meetings ensure that all affected interests have an opportunity to determine the need for the activity; participate in the development of a title, scope, and structure; and identify areas that need standardization.

Does ASTM Offer Continuing Technical Education?

ASTM provides continuing education and training in the use and application of ASTM standards through technical and professional training courses. ASTM members propose ideas for the courses, work with staff to establish course outlines, and serve as instructors. Attendees learn the practical application of standards and benefit from the instructors' technical expertise and knowledge of standards development.

Occupational Safety and Health Administration (OSHA)

OSHA (a federal agency) has become extensively involved in standards development. The impetus to develop a new standard can come from a variety of sources: OSHA's own initiative, the U.S. Congress, information from the National Institute for Occupational Safety and Health (NIOSH), a referral from EPA's Toxic Substances Control Act (TSCA), public petitions, or requests from OSHA advisory committees.

The standard-setting process can begin in a number of ways: with publication in the *Federal Register* of a request for information (RFI), an advance notice of proposed rule-making (ANPRM), or a notice of proposed rule-making (NPRM). Through an RFI or an ANPRM, OSHA seeks information to determine the extent of a particular hazard, current and potential protective measures, and the costs and benefits of various solutions.

Recently, OSHA has begun to develop new standards through a negotiated rule-making process. Under this process, the agency forms an advisory committee composed of representatives from the various interest groups that the new standard will affect. These labor and industry representatives meet with OSHA to hammer out an agreement (consensus standard) that will serve as the basis for a proposed rule. This process is used to resolve long-standing differences that, until negotiated rule making, could not be resolved. OSHA is using this process to draft proposed rules for steel erection in construction and fire protection in shipyards.

Information from these sources, as well as injury and fatality data, is then used to develop a proposal. Formal proposals are published in the *Federal Register* with notice of a public comment period over the next 60 to 90 days. Occasionally, requests are made to extend the comment period or to hold a public hearing.

Finally, OSHA uses this information to prepare and publish a final standard in the *Federal Register* or, in some cases, to determine that no standard is needed. Standards usually take effect in 90 days or less, although some provisions (e.g., requirements for detailed programs) may be phased in over a longer period.

International Environment, Health, and Safety and International Audit Protocol Consortium

New International Environment, Health, and Safety (IEH&S) requirements are also being developed. These requirements include Great Britain's BS7750; the European Union's (EU) Environmental Management Audit Scheme (EMAS); the ISO's 9000 quality assurance and quality management standards; and the ISO 14000, a global environmental management standard.

Companies are compelled to comply with these environmental management standards for reasons that reach beyond fear of legal reprisal; strong economic and political forces are at work. Consumers are increasingly demanding that companies' products and manufacturing processes be environmentally responsible. One goal of the ISO 14000 standards will be to provide a precise "green" measuring tool for a concerned public. Governments, particularly those in the EU, are also favoring the green company. Companies without an ISO 14000 certification could be shut out of some international markets.

Fitness, Health, Racquet, and Sports Clubs

American College of Sports Medicine

The American College of Sports Medicine (ACSM) has published a fourth edition of the book titled *Health Fitness Facility Standards and Guidelines* (Peterson & Tharrett (2012), which suggests that the "book now sets a clear standard of comparison for use in legal proceedings" (p. vii). These standards are as follows:

"**Standard #1.** A facility must be able to respond in a timely manner to any reasonably foreseeable emergency event that threatens the health and safety of facility users. Toward this end, a facility must have an appropriate emergency plan that can be executed by qualified personnel in a timely manner.

Standard #2. A facility must offer each adult member a preactivity screening that is appropriate to the physical activities to be performed by the member.

Standard #3. Each person who has supervisory responsibility for a physical activity program or area at the facility must have demonstrable professional competence in that activity program or area.

Standard #4. A facility must post appropriate signage, alerting users to the risks involved in their use of those areas of a facility that present potential increased risk(s).

Standard #5. A facility that offers youth services or programs must provide appropriate supervision.

Standard #6. A facility must conform to all relevant laws, regulations, and published standards."

However, IHRSA, the International Health, Racquet, and Sportclubs Association, has rejected the guidelines. The Association for Worksite Health Promotion (formerly the Association for Fitness in Business [AFB]) is developing its own standards and certification process in a reaction to ACSM's failure to recognize the AFB's previous contributions to health and fitness certification standards.

There is a veritable alphabet soup of professional certifications from associations wishing to increase their memberships, improve their images, or turn a profit. The ASCM book defers to the state or local codes when it comes to more technical standards.

The ACSM is a medically based organization with a research focus. In the 14 years since the ASCM issued its initial exercise recommendations, the percentage of people complying has not changed substantially. The medical model works in a hospital or testing lab, but not necessarily in clubs or corporate health promotion or municipal fitness programs.

International Health, Racquet, and Sportsclub Association

IHRSA is a not-for-profit trade association representing 2,500 health and sports clubs worldwide. It is the largest club association in the world. More than 1,800 IHRSA member clubs offer some form of reciprocal access through the association's "Passport" program, which provides members the opportunity to use another club when they travel.

A club must agree to abide by the IHRSA Code of Conduct and comply with the association's membership standards. A member of IHRSA has the mission to enhance the quality of life through physical fitness and sports. It endeavors to provide quality facilities, programs, and instruction and strives to instill in all those served an understanding of the value of physical fitness and sports to their lives.

IHRSA recognizes the following international certifying agencies:
- Aerobics and Fitness Association of America
- Aerobic Pipeline International
- American Aerobics Association/International Sports Medicine Association
- American College of Sports Medicine
- American Council on Exercise
- Cooper Fitness Institute
- IDEA: The Association for Fitness Professionals
- National Academy of Sports Medicine
- National Association for Fitness Certification
- National Dance Exercise Instructors Training Association
- National Federation of Professional Trainers
- National Strength and Conditioning Association
- Ontario Fitness Council
- Sinai Corporate Health

National Fire Protection Association

The National Fire Protection Association (NFPA) publishes the *Life Safety Codes* and jointly developed and published the first edition of the *International Fire Code* in 2010. This agreement came after negotiations between the International Code Council (ICC) and NFPA. The ICC's three model code organizations include the Building Officials and Code Administrators International, the International Conference of Building Officials (ICBO), and the Southern Building Code Congress International.

ICBO is a leading code organization that established a *Uniform Building Code* (UBC) in 1927. That code contained over 200 pages of text, whereas the 1994 version involved three volumes and more than 2,600 pages. The 2010 version involved four volumes and more than 3,400 pages. Modern codes are steadily moving to performance-type codes rather than the specification type because of the proliferation of types of materials, methods, and machinery used today. Such codes also reflect public policy, which has changed in the past 70 or more years. Contemporary society has looked to codes not only to ensure safety of life and limb, but also increasingly to safeguard public welfare or well-being and security. Goals for many public issues, such as air and water quality, energy conservation, recycling, and disabilities, have led to a number of codes that affect recreation, physical activity, and sports facilities.

Codes and standards are sometimes viewed as interchangeable terms. Indeed, a code meets the above definitions of a standard. Codes, or parts thereof, are frequently characterized as being either prescriptive or performance based. Prescriptive code requirements are definitive and easily measurable, such as the minimum width of an exit corridor, maximum slope for a specific type of roof covering, minimum air gap for backflow prevention, minimum size of grounding conductor, and so forth. Performance code requirements, on the other hand, use terms that describe the desired result, such as *watertight enclosure, smoke removal, safe for the intended use*, and so forth. Some of these terms have companion standards as part of the code, such as those for smoke dampers, stairway identification signs, and waterproof paper, and others do not. Adopted standards in this context can be thought of as specification codes.

A review of the 1927 *Uniform Building Codes* (UBC) revealed that 28 standards were incorporated by reference. Today, there over 40 standards. These documents were promulgated by various organizations including ASTM, the American Concrete Institute, the National Board of Fire Underwriters, the NFPA, and others.

Standards are incorporated into the UBC under a code change procedure involving a proposal, a review by a code change committee in a public hearing, and a vote at a final hearing by the assembled membership at the annual meeting. Anyone can propose a code change and argue for or against any code change.

The Building Officials and Code Administrators International (BOCA) and the Southern Building Code Congress International (SBCCI), the respective publishers of the *National Building Code* (NBC) and the *Standard Building Code* (SBC), have similar histories of employing adopted standards in their codes. Together with ICBO, the ICC has been formed as a consortium of these organizations. The ICC published the *International Building Code* (IBC) in 2003 with subsequent editions in 2006, 2009, and 2012, with no further publications of the UBC, NBC, and SBC after 1997.

European Committee for Standardization

The European Committee for Standardization (CEN) is the European standards organization that coordinates all European country standards organizations. It has secretariats in various subject areas that in turn relate to ISO Technical Committees. CEN initiated the EC 1992. This is the array of regulatory and standards initiatives that leads to the common European internal market. EC 1992 also requires testing and certifications requirements. It sets forth alternative approaches to testing, certifying, and proving conformity with the regulatory directives that are set out. It identifies organizations that will perform conformity assessment functions and U.S. testing and certifying organizations. This has implications on many sports products and ultimately facilities used for international events.

International Standards Organization or International Organization for Standardization

The International Standards Organization (ISO) is the worldwide body, and ANSI is the member body of this group representing the United States. ISO sees a world in which global trade between nations continues to grow at a rate 3 to 4 times faster than national economies; a world in which the design, manufacture, marketing, and customer service operations of a growing majority of individual enterprises are distributed across many countries; and a world in which electronic communications have dramatically increased technical collaboration between experts in academia, governments, and industries from all countries.

The increasingly rapid development of technology in many sectors will continue to present major opportunities as well as underlying dangers for the general welfare of society. It will therefore be incumbent on all social and economic partners to collaborate closely in guiding the applications of appropriate technologies toward sustainable economic development and global prosperity.

In this rapidly evolving scenario, globally applicable standards will play a key role. Such standards, whether developed by ISO or others, will become primary technical instruments supporting international commerce. In this context, ISO intends to be recognized globally as an influential and innovative leader in developing globally applicable international standards that meet or exceed the expectations of the community of nations. It will strive at all times to perfect the application of consensus and transparency principles in standardization and, in this way, promote the values of rationality, utility, safety, and environmental protection for the benefit of all peoples.

Standardization is essentially an economic undertaking made possible by the achievement of widespread agreements on the coherent and mutually beneficial use of science, technology, and business know-how. The prime object of ISO and its governance is laid down in the ISO statutes (i.e., to promote the development of standardization and related activities in the world with a view to facilitating international exchange of goods and services and to developing cooperation in the sphere of intellectual, scientific, and economic activity).

National Spa and Pool Institute

The National Spa and Pool Institute (NSPI) has been for nearly 35 years the source of standards for the design, construction, and operation of public and residential pools and spas. The organization has a membership of designer-engineers along with manufacturers, builders, contractors, equipment and chemical manufacturers and suppliers and retailers in every aspect of the pool and spa industry. Many representatives of health departments also belong.

World Waterpark Association

The federal government has had standards for water parks since they became popular over a decade ago. In 1991, the World Waterpark Assocation (WWA) published *Splash Magazine* as a developer's reference. Concurrently, it established a risk management and safety committee. Representatives of this committee were invited by the NSPI to sit on the public pool standards rewrite committee. After a year of deliberations, it was decided that waterslides and flumes should have a standard apart from any public pool standard. As a result, a WWA committee was established in 1997 to write a draft of a standard under the cooperative auspices of NSPI, which is an accredited member of ANSI. This standard is now being circulated.

Sport Indoor and Outdoor Facility Standards

The following organizations establish standards for facilities and equipment for amateur and professional sports in the United States.

Amateur sports organizations, include, but are not limited to,

- National Federation of High School Activities Associations,
- National Collegiate Athletic Association,
- National Junior College Athletic Association,
- Amateur Athletic Union,
- Little League Baseball,
- American Softball Association, and
- the United States Olympic Committee and its various national governing bodies.

Professional sports organizations include, but are not limited to,

- National Football League,
- National Basketball Association,
- National Hockey League,
- Major League Baseball,
- Professional Golf Association,
- Ladies Professional Golf Association,
- United States Tennis Association, and
- American Bowling Congress.

Professional Involvement in Standards

Professionals in the fitness, physical activity, recreation, sport, and related fields are not as involved in standards as they could and should be. Standards organizations involve only a small percentage of the professionals directly involved in the teaching, researching, planning, administering, operating, and maintaining of fitness, physical activity, recreation, and sports facilities and activities, regardless of jurisdiction or the type of entity. Many standards applicable to fitness, physical activity, recreation, and sport are developed by manufacturers, medical specialists, businessmen, lawyers, and others.

Professionals are neither aware of these standards organizations nor familiar with how to become involved. Organizations such as the American Alliance for Health, Physical Education, Recreation, and Dance and the National Recreation and Park Association have not specifically designated professionals to serve as their representatives to these organizations. It is imperative that in the future more professionals be appointed or volunteer to lend their expertise to the standards process.

Governmental Involvement in Standards

Governmental agencies have a long history of involvement in standards. Apparently, many of their efforts now tend to be catalytic in evolving standards. This is a significant change over the past 50 years. In most cases, they have encouraged producers to regulate their own industries. Where such efforts have failed the government, both state and federal agencies have moved to provide regulations and supportive standards to protect the health, safety, and well-being of the public.

The government usually provides standards in the form of legislation that go beyond the base line or minimum level of requirement. As a result, industries and professions are becoming more conscious in recognizing that if they themselves do not develop standards, somebody else will.

Guidelines

A guideline is a standard or principle by which to make a judgment or determine a policy or course of action. A guideline is developed after a standard has been established. The guideline is a series of procedures to ensure the maintenance of the standards.

Appendix A
Planning Checklist
for Indoor and Outdoor Spaces

The following is an abbreviated list of items to be considered during the planning process.

Circulation

- Types: Vehicle (cars, trucks, buses, maintenance, etc.), pedestrians (persons with disabilities, different teams), participants (different teams, players, coaches, officials, etc.), main entry, secondary entries, control and security points, and so forth.
- Roadway: Type of vehicles (trucks, cars, buses, etc.), quantity of traffic (conduct survey), type of roadway system (single or two directional), roadway width (vehicle size and number of lanes), surface systems (materials); protection devices (bollards, guardrails, etc.), and so forth.
- Parking: Type of vehicles (trucks, cars, buses, etc.), quantity of vehicles, sizes (length and width) of vehicles, drainage (surface or subsurface, water collection/detention areas), snow removal (storage areas), protection devices (bollards, guardrails, tire bumpers, etc.)
- Walkways: Type of use (pedestrian and/or vehicle), walkway widths, surface system (materials), elevation changes (walks, ramps, stairs, and lifts), railings.

Activity Areas

- Landscaping: Type of surfaces (e.g., grass), type of plantings (ground cover, shrubs, plantings, etc.), and so forth.
- Game Standards: Applicable association regulations for each sport.
- Activity Configuration: Areas (separate or combined activity), orientation, flexibility, and so forth.
- Surfaces: Type (natural, synthetic, or combination), grading and drainage (surface and subsurface), and so forth.

Sports Areas

- Diamonds: Type of sport(s), type (game and/or practice), size, quantity, and so forth.
- Courts: Type of sport(s), type (game and/or practice), size, quantity, and so forth.
- Fields: Type of sport(s), type (game and/or practice), size, quantity, and so forth.
- Ranges: Type of sport(s), type (game and/or practice), size, quantity, and so forth.

Structures

- Tickets: Type (fixed or portable), surfaces for portable types (pads), utilities, quantity of units (location on site), and so forth.
- Security: Type (fixed or portable), surfaces for portable types (pads), utilities, quantity of units (location on-site).
- Medical Treatment: Type (fixed portable), surfaces for portable types (pads), utilities, quantity of units (location on-site), and so forth.
- Storage: Type (fixed or portable), surfaces for portable types (pads), utilities, quantity of units (location on-site), type of storage (equipment and tools), and so forth.
- Communications: Type (fixed or portable), utilities (supplemental), quantity of units (location on-site), type of systems, and so forth.
- Concessions: Type (fixed or portable, owner or vendor-supplied), surfaces for portable types (tent pads, trailer pads, etc.), utilities, quantity of units (location on-site), and so forth.
- Seating: Type (standing and/or seats), persons (spectators, teams, officials, etc.), natural (beams, sloped areas, etc.), artificial (prefabricated bleachers, type of seat, guardrails, etc.), and so forth.

Signage

- Vehicle: Type (direction, information, safety, etc.).
- Pedestrian: Type (direction, information, safety, etc.).
- Activity: (by sport, area, etc.).
- Scoreboard: activity (single or combined use), type (manual or electronic), size, and so forth.

Barriers

- Vehicle: Type (sound, visual, safety, etc.), natural (plantings, berms, depressed areas, etc.), artificial (walls, fending, railings, etc.),
- Person: Type (sound, visual, safety, etc.), natural (plantings, berms, depressed areas, etc.), artificial (walls, fencing, railings, etc.), and so forth.
- Security: Type (gates, juxtaposition, or open).

Utilities

- Power: Site lighting (pedestrian and vehicle), activity lighting, structures (tickets, security, storage, communications, concessions, etc.), and so forth.
- Water: Irrigation, sanitary, drinking fountains (hot and cold), and so forth.
- Sanitary: Type of units (fixed or portable).
- Storm Drainage: Type (surface and subsurface).
- Communications: Scoreboards, team sidelines to observation booth, public address for game, telephones for public and private use, broadcasting for television and radio, portable communications for security personnel, emergency, and so forth.

Equipment Evaluation Considerations

The following system analyzes the most common exercise equipment used in the fitness industry.

- ❖ Purchase Price ranges will be designated by $ / $$ / $$$; variables that increase the cost of the equipment will also be identified.
- ❖ The maintenance requirements, ease of use and learning curve of operating equipment, popularity of equipment will be designated by: L-Low/M-Medium/H-High
- ❖ The clientele typically using the equipment will be reflected by:
  G- General Population
  SN- Special Needs – Wheel Chair bound (WCB), Rehabilitation (R), or Senior Citizens (SC)

Equipment	Cost	Maintenance (and Variables)	Learning Curve	Popularity	Clientele	Variables that increase cost
Treadmills	$$$	H •Deck replacement •Belt replacement •Motor replacement •Self-lubricating deck	M	H	G	•Number of diagnostic features •Number of programs •Elevation options •Heart rate functions •Entertainment features
Ellipticals	$$	L •Ramp replacement •Elevation assembly replacement	L	H	G	•Heart rate functions •Entertainment features
Stair Steppers	$	L	L	L/M	G	Heart rate function
Recumbent/ Stationary Bikes	$	L	L	L	G/SN-Rehabilitation	Heart rate function
Upper and Lower Body Ergometers	$$$	M •Calibration	L	M	G/SN-WCB	
Rowing Machines	$	L	L	L	G	

Planning Checklist for Indoor and Outdoor Spaces

Lobby/entrance
- peak traffic rate entering and exiting
- energy conservation
- door size
- lobby size
- seating arrangements
- public restrooms
- floor surfaces
- lighting
- ADA requirements
- ticket booth
- concessions

Control area
- number of patrons at peak periods
- number of staff at peak loads
- computers, cash registers, automated check-in
- towel service
- locker registration
- TV surveillance
- light controls
- door monitor system/panel
- fire annunciator panel
- public address system
- emergency alarm system/panel
- equipment issue/return/storage,
  equipment to be stored,
  storage cabinets,
  separate issue and return functions,
  peak load considerations, staffing
- building directory
- phone system

Strength training area
- number of mechanized weight machines
- electrical needs
- flooring considerations
- mirrors
- audio and visual accommodations
- control center
- desk and computer
- storage space and cabinets
- clocks
- peak load considerations
- HVAC considerations
- platforms

Free weight area
- benches
- weight racks

- dumbbells and racks
- weight platforms
- chalk holders and chalk
- floor considerations
- control area
- desk and computer
- mirrors
- HVAC considerations
- audio and visual considerations
- peak load considerations

Fitness testing
- treadmill
- exercise bike
- monitoring equipment
- desk and bed
- storage cabinets
- sink and counter space
- computer
- telephone
- tackboard
- special electrical or HVAC requirements

Cardiorespiratory area
- treadmills
- bicycles
- rowing machines
- stair climbers
- arm ergometers
- wall weight racks
- dumbbells
- floor surface
- audio and visual accommodations
- desk and computer
- storage
- HVAC considerations
- peak load considerations

Aquatics center
- competition pool
- teaching pool
- handicapped pool
- diving well
- diving boards
- diving platform
- underwater windows
- underwater sound
- filtration and sanitation
- vacuum
- lane lines
- bulkheads

- movable floors
- lifeguard stands
- HVAC considerations
- lighting
- accessible pool lift
- whirlpool for divers
- spectator seating
- rescue equipment
- grab rails and ladders
- acoustic treatment
- wall graphics
- starting platforms
- timing devices, scoreboard, diving scoring, public address system
- deck space and drainage
- corrosion-resistant fittings
- emergency telephone or call button
- storage
- control center, desks, computers
- office, desks, computers
- telephones
- automated pool chemical control
- tile or no tile
- pumps and auxiliary pumps
- heater and auxiliary heater
- main drains
- access to pipes

Dependent care
- number of children
- number of aging adults
- state requirements
- number of staff
- adjacent play areas in and out
- adjacent toilet facilities
- audio and visual accommodations
- office, desk, computer
- storage and storage cabinets
- indoor and outdoor play spaces

Pro shop
- display windows
- adjustable wall display system
- adjustable display shelving
- adjustable display lighting
- office
- control area, computer, cash register, visual surveillance
- door alarm system to catch shoplifters

Food service
- juice bar
- vending
- seating area
- small kitchen with microwave,

range, dishwasher, hot water booster, garbage disposal, range hood, refrigeration, sink, and counter space
- health requirements
- tiled floor with drains

Gymnasium/multipurpose space
- activities to be accommodated
- peak number of people
- floor and wall inserts required
- lighting requirements
- folding partitions or dividing curtains—motorized or manual
- baskets and backstops—portable or permanent, motorized or manual
- batting cages
- golf cages
- scoreboards
- seating—portable or permanent
- wall pads
- flooring considerations
- wall graphics
- drinking fountains
- Public address system
- large storage area, roll-up doors
- public restrooms
- concessions
- portable stage
- press box
- press (media) room
- built-in audio and visual hookups
- computer hookups
- ceiling and wall-mounted projection screens
- video monitoring
- loading dock with roll-up door
- adjacent meeting areas
- adjacent locker rooms
- large janitorial space
- adjacent training room
- climbing wall area
- indoor jumping and throwing areas

Running track (indoor)
- laps per turn
- elevated or floor level
- number of lanes
- type of surface
- adjacent strength training, cardiovascular areas
- radius at turns
- banked curves
- automated banking
- lane markers
- pacer lights

Dance areas
- number of participants at peak loads
- audio accommodations
- acoustics
- ballet barres
- mirrors
- dance floor
- storage
- HVAC considerations
- emergency telephone or call button

Handball/racquetball/squash courts
- number of courts
- competition courts
- spectator seating
- instructor observation area
- type of wall and ceiling system
- type of floor system
- glass or solid walls
- remote lighting
- striping
- other activities: wall soccer, walleyball, dancercise, etc.
- lighting
- securing valuables
- accessing lighting
- HVAC considerations
- acoustics

Combative/wrestling room
- number of participants
- padded walls
- padded floor
- no glass areas
- no protruding fixtures
- remote HVAC sensing
- hanging bag
- hanging rope for climbing

Locker rooms
- number of lockers
- type of lockers and locker system
- tile floor with drains
- grooming area: number of sinks, mirrors, hair dryers, soap dispensers, towel dispensers, waste receptacles, nonslip floor, water-resistant electrical receptacles
- accessibility area
- family changing areas
- benches or stools—fixed or movable
- HVAC considerations
- swimming suit drying system
- permanent lockers
- dressing booths

Restrooms
- health code requirements
- accessible area
- family changing areas
- nonslip floor
- floor drains
- mechanical exhaust
- diaper changing areas
- toilet partitions
- disposable seat covers
- sanitary napkin dispensers and disposals
- vandal-proof partitions
- corrosion-resistant fittings
- automatic flush

Showers
- number of people to accommodate at peak loads
- individual showers
- hose bibb
- soap dispensers
- soap dishes
- accessible accommodations
- nonslip floor
- floor drains
- corrosion-resistant fittings
- waterproof membrane as required
- HVAC considerations

Shower drying areas
- number of people
- floor drains
- towel racks or hooks
- nonslip floor surface

Steam room
- number of people
- steam convector units with cover plates—electric or gas
- waterproof membranes
- observation window
- emergency call button
- remote temperature control
- floor drains
- tiled room
- mechanical exhaust
- shower in steam room
- corrosion-resistant fittings
- lighting
- hose bibb
- unisex or separate facilities

Sauna
- number of people
- exterior shower adjacent the sauna

- waterproof membranes
- observation window
- emergency call button
- remote temperature control
- floor drains
- redwood interior, all boards screwed into frame
- mechanical exhaust
- protective covering over rocks
- corrosion-resistant fittings
- lighting
- hose bibb
- unisex or separate facilities

Tanning room
- number of units
- type of units
- adjacent to a changing area
- washup or grooming area

Massage room
- number of massage tables
- heat lamps
- towel, cleaning, and disinfectant storage cabinets

Laundry
- projected volume/required staffing
- number and size of washers
- number and size of extractor units
- number and size of dryer units—gas or electric
- sorting and folding area
- floor drains
- soiled linen area
- carts
- linear feet of linen storage shelving and cabinets required
- HVAC considerations
- office, desk, computer

Administrative areas
- number of offices
- size of offices
- contents

Other miscellaneous areas
- janitorial spaces and break areas
- general storage
- classrooms
- maintenance area
- mechanical areas
- elevators and elevator equipment spaces
- hallways
- stairwells

Outdoor activity areas
- sport fields—practice and game
- basketball courts
- sand volleyball courts
- golf course
- tennis courts
- archery and shooting ranges
- ice hockey/skating
- outdoor aquatic center
- playground
- spectator seating
- concessions
- security lighting
- game lighting
- security fencing
- observation areas
- press boxes
- storage buildings and areas
- scoreboards
- ticket booths
- pump houses
- rope courses
- challenge courses
- fitness courses
- picnic areas
- horseshoes
- croquet area
- bocce area
- shuffleboard area
- parking: zoning requirements, adjacent existing facilities, surface or garage parking, accessible spaces, security lighting, landscaping buffers, asphalt or concrete, entering and exiting, pedestrian areas

Appendix B
Existing Facility Assessment and Future Planning Checklist

Check appropriate facility being assessed:
❑ Cardiovascular Center   ❑ Group Exercise Room   ❑ Indoor Cycling Studio
❑ Strength Weight Area   ❑ Selectorized Weight Equipment area   ❑ Other _____

Rating System:

	Rating MR/YES D/NO	Comments regarding Deficiencies
MR/YES – Meets Requirements (Fitness Facility Industry Standards)		
D/NO – Deficiency (Does not meet Industry Standards)		

❑ Facility Appearance
    Well maintained (No visual signs of structural deterioration)   _____   _____
    Well cleaned   _____   _____
    Ambiance—Inviting and creates a sense of energy   _____   _____
❑ Facility Space Assessment
    Adequate Space to support activity   _____   _____
    Appropriate Traffic Flow throughout space   _____   _____
❑ Compliant with local, state, federal, and ADA requirements:
    Width of Entrances   _____   _____
    Water Fountain levels   _____   _____
    Aisle widths   _____   _____
    Appropriate Signage   _____   _____
❑ Ample Storage for:
    Program related accessories   _____   _____
    Cleaning and Maintenance supplies   _____   _____
❑ Monitor Station appropriately located to activity   _____   _____
❑ Electrical:
    Lighting:
        No dark spots in facility   _____   _____
        Candle illumination appropriate for activity   _____   _____
    Electrical Supply:
        Adequate number of breakers for present needs as well as
    future expansion requirements   _____   _____
        Dedicated breakers for equipment, as required by
    Manufacturer (110 or 220)   _____   _____
        Sufficient # of wall outlets for present and future
    expansion requirements   _____   _____
❑ HVAC System Analysis:
    Air Exchange Ratio is 8-10 per hour   _____   _____
    Humidity is 60% or less   _____   _____
    Appropriate Temperature—68-72 degrees   _____   _____
    Separate HVAC control for designated activity space   _____   _____
❑ Flooring:
    No signs of visible wear of the flooring surface or hazards   _____   _____
    Appropriate flooring for activity (DIN standards)   _____   _____
        Surface is antibacterial, slip resistant, etc.   _____   _____
❑ Ceiling:
    Adequate ceiling height for designated activity   _____   _____
    Condition of ceiling tiles, if applicable.   _____   _____
❑ Walls:
    All apparatus, fixtures, mirrors, shelving, securely
    attached to walls?   _____   _____
❑ Sound (Controllable ambient noise levels)
❑ Entertainment
    Variety of entertainment options offered, when appropriate for
    appropriate venues—TV, stereo?   _____   _____
❑ Equipment   _____   _____
    Storage of items and placement of equipment do not
    block walkways, entrances, emergency exits, etc.?   _____   _____
    State of the art of equipment in place.   _____   _____
    No equipment replacement required.   _____   _____
❑ Appropriate cleaning and maintenance systems in place.   _____   _____

Assessment completed by:_____   Date completed: _____

Appendix C
Indoor Activity Area Planning Checklist

A checklist has been prepared to aid those responsible for planning facilities for athletics, physical education, health, and recreation. The application of this checklist may prevent unfortunate and costly errors.

General

_____ 1. A clear-cut statement has been prepared on the nature and scope of the program, and the special requirements for space, equipment, fixtures, and facilities have been dictated by the activities to be conducted.

_____ 2. The facility has been planned to meet the total requirements of the program, as well as the special needs of those who are to be served.

_____ 3. The plans and specifications have been checked by all governmental agencies (city, county, and state) whose approval is required by law.

_____ 4. Plans for areas and facilities conform to state and local regulations and to accepted standards and practices.

_____ 5. The areas and facilities planned make possible the programs that serve the interests and needs of all the people.

_____ 6. Every available source of property or funds has been explored, evaluated, and used whenever appropriate.

_____ 7. All interested persons and organizations concerned with the facility have had an opportunity to share in its planning (professional educators, users, consultants, administrators, engineers, architects, program specialists, building managers, and builder)—a team approach.

_____ 8. The facility will fulfill the maximum demands of the program. The program has not been curtailed to fit the facility.

_____ 9. The facility has been functionally planned to meet the present and anticipated needs of specific programs, situations, and publics.

_____ 10. Future additions are included in present plans to permit economy of construction.

_____ 11. All classrooms and offices are isolated from background noise.

_____ 12. Ample numbers and ample-sized storage areas are built in flush with walls at all teach stations.

_____ 13. No center mullions or thresholds are on storage room doorways.

_____ 14. All passageways are free of obstructions; fixtures are recessed.

_____ 15. Storage areas are well ventilated, dry, and cool.

_____ 16. Buildings, specific areas, and facilities are clearly identified.

_____ 17. Locker rooms are arranged for ease of supervision.

_____ 18. Offices, teaching stations, and service facilities are properly interrelated.

_____ 19. Special needs of persons with disabilities are met, including a ramp into the building at a major entrance.

_____ 20. All "dead space" is used.

_____ 21. The building is compatible in design and comparable in quality and accommodation to other campus structures.

_____ 22. Storage rooms are accessible to the play area.

_____ 23. Workrooms, conference rooms, and staff and administrative offices are interrelated.

_____ 24. Shower and dressing facilities are provided for professional staff members and are conveniently located.

_____ 25. Thought and attention has been given to making facilities and equipment as durable and vandal-proof as possible.

_____ 26. Low-cost maintenance features have been considered.

_____ 27. This facility is a part of a well-integrated Master Plan.

_____ 28. All areas, courts, facilities, equipment, climate control, security, and so forth conform rigidly to detailed standards and specifications.

_____ 29. Shelves are recessed and mirrors and supplies are in appropriate places in restrooms and dressing rooms.

_____ 30. Dressing space between locker rows is adjusted to the size and age of students.

_____ 31. Drinking fountains are placed conveniently in locker room areas or immediate adjacent areas.

_____ 32. Special attention is given to provision for locking service windows and counter, supply bins, carts, shelves, and racks.

_____ 33. Provision is made for repair, maintenance, replacement, and off-season storage of equipment and uniforms.

_____ 34. A well-defined program for laundering and cleaning towels, uniforms, and equipment is included in the plan.

_____ 35. Noncorrosive metal is used in dressing, drying, and shower areas, except for enameled lockers.

_____ 36. Antipanic hardware is used where required by fire regulations.

_____ 37. Properly placed house bibbs and drains are sufficient in size and quantity to permit flushing the entire area with a water hose.

_____ 38. A water-resistant covered base is used under the locker base and floor mat and where the floor and wall join.

_____ 39. Chalkboards and/or tackboards with map tracks are located in appropriate places in dressing rooms, hallways, and classrooms.

_____ 40. Bookshelves are provided in the toilet area.

_____ 41. Space and equipment are planned in accordance with the types and number of enrollees.

_____ 42. Basement rooms undesirable for dressing, drying, and showering are not planned for those purposes.

_____ 43. Spectator seating (permanent) in areas that are basically instructional is kept at a minimum. Rollaway bleachers are used primarily. Balcony seating is considered as a possibility.

_____ 44. Well-lighted and effectively displayed trophy cases enhance the interest and beauty of the lobby.

_____ 45. The space under the stairs is used for storage.

_____ 46. Department heads' offices are located near the central administrative office, which includes a well-planned conference room.

_____ 47. Workrooms are located near the central office and serve as a repository for departmental materials and records.

_____ 48. Conference area includes a cloakroom, lavatory, and toilet.

_____ 49. In addition to regular secretarial offices established in the central and department chairpersons' offices, a special room to house a secretarial pool for staff members is provided.

_____ 50. Staff dressing facilities are provided. These facilities also may serve game officials.

_____ 51. The community and/or neighborhood has a "round table" for planning.

_____ 52. All those (persons and agencies) who should be a party to planning and development are invited and actively engaged in the planning process.

_____ 53. Space and area relationships are important. They have been considered carefully.

_____ 54. Both long-range and immediate plans have been made.

_____ 55. The body comfort of the child, a major factor in securing maximum learning, has been considered in the plans.

_____ 56. Plans for quiet areas have been made.

_____ 57. In the planning, consideration has been given to the need for adequate recreational areas and facilities, both near and distant from the homes of people.

_____ 58. Consoles for security, information, and checkout have been ideally located.

_____ 59. Every effort has been exercised to eliminate hazards.

_____ 60. The installation of low-hanging door closers, light fixtures, signs, and other objects in traffic areas has been avoided.

_____ 61. Warning signals—both visible and audible—are included in the plans.

_____ 62. Ramps have a slope equal to or greater than a 1-ft rise in 12-ft.

_____ 63. Minimum landings for ramps are 5 ft x 5 ft, extend at least 1 ft beyond the swinging arc of a door, have at least a 6-ft clearance at the bottom, and have level platforms at 30-ft intervals on every turn.

_____ 64. Adequate locker and dressing spaces are provided.

_____ 65. The design of dressing, drying, and shower areas reduces foot traffic to a minimum and establishes clean, dry aisles for bare feet.

_____ 66. Teaching stations are related properly to service facilities.

_____ 67. Toilet facilities are adequate in number. They are located to serve all groups for which provisions are made.

_____ 68. Mail services—outgoing and incoming—are included in the plans.

_____ 69. Hallways, ramps, doorways, and elevators are designed to permit equipment to be moved easily and quickly.

_____ 70. A keying design suited to administrative and instructional needs is planned.

_____ 71. Toilets used by large groups have circulating (in and out) entrances and exits.

_____ 72. All surfaces in racquetball, handball, and squash courts are flush.

_____ 73. At least one racquetball, handball, or squash court has a tempered glass back wall and sidewall.

_____ 74. All vents in racquetball, handball, and squash courts are located in the back one third of the ceiling.

_____ 75. Standard-sized doors are used on racquetball, handball, and squash courts.

_____ 76. All aspects of safety are planned carefully for the weight areas.

_____ 77. Racks are provided for all loose plates, dumbbells, and barbells in weight areas.

_____ 78. Special attention is paid to acoustical treatment in weight areas.

_____ 79. Ample walk areas for traffic flow are planned around lifting areas in weight rooms.

_____ 80. Concessions areas are planned for and built flush with existing walls.

_____ 81. Adequate numbers of concession areas are planned.

_____ 82. Concessions stand cash-handling methods have been planned carefully.

_____ 83. Storage and maintenance have been planned for concessions areas.

_____ 84. Classrooms are planned by instructors, students, and maintenance staff.

_____ 85. Classrooms are planned for the number of users and the styles of teaching to be used in the room.

_____ 86. Careful attention has been paid to storage areas in classrooms.

_____ 87. Faculty offices should be private and secured.

_____ 88. Storage areas and windows are planned in faculty offices.

_____ 89. Laboratories need to be planned for both teaching and research use.

_____ 90. Ample space and subdivisions within laboratories are planned carefully.

Climate Control

_____ 1. Provisions have been made throughout the building for climate control: heating, ventilating, and refrigerated cooling.

_____ 2. Special ventilation is provided for locker, dressing, shower, drying, and toilet rooms.

_____ 3. Heating plans permit both area and individual room control.

_____ 4. Research areas where small animals are kept and where chemicals are used have been provided with special ventilating equipment.

_____ 5. The heating and ventilating of the wrestling gymnasium has been given special attention.

_____ 6. All air diffusers adequately diffuse the air.

_____ 7. Storage area ventilation is planned carefully.

_____ 8. Humidity and ventilation are balanced properly in racquetball, handball, and squash courts.

_____ 9. Thermostats are located out of the general users' reach and/or are secured.

_____ 10. The total energy concept has been investigated.

Electrical

_____ 1. Shielded, vaporproof lights are used in moisture-prevalent areas.

_____ 2. Lights in strategic areas are key controlled.

_____ 3. Lighting intensity conforms to approved standards.

_____ 4. Adequate numbers of electrical outlets are placed strategically.

_____ 5. Gymnasium and auditorium lights are controlled by dimmer units.

_____ 6. Locker room lights are mounted above the space between lockers.

_____ 7. Natural light is controlled properly for purposes of visual aids and to avoid glare.

_____ 8. Electrical outlet plates are installed 3 ft above the floor unless special use dictates other locations.

_____ 9. Controls for light switches and projection equipment are located suitably and are interrelated.

_____ 10. All lights are shielded. Special protection is provided in gymnasium, court areas, and shower rooms.

_____ 11. All lights must be easily accessible for maintenance.

_____ 12. The use of metal halide and high-pressure sodium lighting has been investigated.

_____ 13. All areas have been wired for television cable and computer hookups.

_____ 14. Indirect lighting has been used wherever possible.

_____ 15. All teaching areas are equipped with a mounted camera, 25-ft color monitor, and tape deck securely built in flush with the existing walls.

Walls

_____ 1. Movable and folding partitions are power operated and controlled by keyed switches.

_____ 2. Wall plates are located where needed and are attached firmly.

_____ 3. Hooks and rings for nets are placed (and recessed in walls) according to court locations and net heights.

_____ 4. Materials that clean easily and are impervious to moisture are used where moisture is prevalent.

_____ 5. Showerheads are placed at different heights—4 ft (elementary) to 7 ft (university)—for each school level.

_____ 6. Protective matting is placed permanently on the walls in the wrestling room, at the ends of basketball courts, and in other areas where such protection is needed.

_____ 7. Adequate numbers of drinking fountains are provided. They are properly placed (recessed in wall).

_____ 8. The lower 8 ft of wall surface in activity areas is glazed and planned for ease of maintenance.

_____ 9. All corners in locker rooms are rounded.

_____ 10. At least two adjacent walls in dance and weight areas should have full-length mirrors.

_____ 11. Walls should be treated acoustically 15 ft and above.

_____ 12. Walls are reinforced structurally where equipment is to be mounted.

_____ 13. Flat wall space is planned for rebounding areas.

_____ 14. Walls should be flat with no juts or extruding columns.

_____ 15. Pastel colors are used on the walls.

_____ 16. Windows should be kept to a minimum in activity areas.

Ceilings

_____ 1. Overhead support apparatus is secured to beams that are engineered to withstand stress.

_____ 2. The ceiling height is adequate for the activities to be housed.

_____ 3. Acoustical materials impervious to moisture are used in moisture-prevalent areas.

_____ 4. Skylights in gymnasiums, being impractical, are seldom used because of problems in waterproofing roofs and controlling sunrays.

_____ 5. All ceilings except those in storage areas are acoustically treated with sound-absorbent materials.

_____ 6. Ceilings should be painted an off-white.

Floors

_____ 1. Floor plates are placed where needed and are flush mounted.

_____ 2. Floor design and materials conform to recommended standards and specifications.

_____ 3. Lines and markings are painted in floors before sealing is completed (when synthetic tape is not used).

_____ 4. A cove base (around lockers and where wall and floor meet) of the same water-resistant material that is used on the floor is used in all dressing and shower rooms.

_____ 5. Abrasive, nonskid, slip-resistant flooring that is impervious to moisture is provided on all areas where water is used (laundry room; swimming pools; shower, dressing, and drying rooms).

_____ 6. Floor drains are located properly, and the slope of the floor is adequate for rapid drainage.

_____ 7. Hardwood floors are used in racquetball, handball, and squash courts.

_____ 8. Maintenance storage is located in areas with synthetic floors.

_____ 9. Floors should be treated acoustically when possible.

_____ 10. Hardwood floors should be used in dance areas.

Appendix D
Indoor Activity Dimensions

Ceiling Activity	Play Area in Feet	Safety Space in Feet[a]	Total Area in Feet	Minimum Height
Archery	5 3 60	15e	5 3 75	12
Badminton	20 3 44	6s, 8e	32 3 60	24
Basketball				
Jr. High instructional	42 3 74	6s, 8e		24
Jr. High interscholastic	50 3 84	6s, 8e		
Sr. High interscholastic	50 3 84	6s, 8e	62 3 100	
Sr. High instructional	45 3 74	6s, 8e	57 3 90	
Neighborhood E. Sch.	42 3 74	6s, 8e	54 3 90	
Community Junior H.S.	50 3 84	6s, 8e	62 3 100	
Community Senior H.S.	50 3 84	6s, 8e	62 3 100	
Competitive— College & University	50 3 94	6s, 8e	62 3 110	
Bocce	18 3 62	3s, 9e	24 3 80	
Fencing, competitive	6 3 46	9s, 6e	18 3 52	
instructional	4 3 30	4s, 6e	12 3 42	12
Handball	20 3 40			
Racquetball	20 3 40			20
Rifle (one pt.)	5 3 50	6 to 20 e	5 3 70 min.	20
Shuffleboard	6 3 52	6s, 2e	18 3 56	12
Squash	18.5 3 32			12
Tennis				
Deck (doubles)	18 3 40	4s, 5e	26 3 50	
Hand	16 3 40	41/2s, 10e	25 3 60	
Lawn (singles)	27 3 78	12s, 21e	51 3 120	
(doubles)	36 3 78	12s, 21e	60 3 120	
Paddle (singles)	16 3 44	6s, 8e	28 3 60	
(doubles)	20 3 44	6s, 8e	32 3 60	
Table (playing area)			9 3 31	
Volleyball				24
Competitive and adult	30 3 60	6s, 6e	42 3 72	
Junior High	30 3 50	6s, 6e	42 3 62	
Wrestling (competitive)	24 3 24	5s, 5e	36 3 36	

[a]Safety space at the side of an area is indicated by a number followed by "e" for end and "s" for side.

Appendix E
Park and Recreation Open Space Standards

PART 1: GENERAL

1.01 Introduction

This document is intended as a tool for designers and citizens to use while planning the renovation or development of play areas within the Seattle Parks and Recreation (SPR) System. The standards may appear excessive if the project they are being applied to is small, or they may appear to lack specific details required of large complex projects. The SPR may require some, all, or additional requirements to be met.

1.02 Definitions

Play area. For the purposes of this document, the term *play area* shall refer to any place or space specifically and primarily intended for recreational use by children, generally between ages 2 and 12.

Designer. The design professional is responsible for the assembly of the documents required to implement the intent of the play area design including construction drawings and specifications. The designer must be licensed in the State of Washington to practice design appropriate to the task, including, but not limited to, architects, landscape architects, and civil engineers. The designer may be a volunteer or a paid consultant or be provided by the SPR.

Design team. For the purposes of these guidelines, the design team is a group of interested volunteers and/or paid individuals who have committed to participating in the design process by attending working meetings and public meetings and by performing various research and consensus-building tasks, to achieve a common goal of developing or renovating a play area. The group requires some organization and can consist of any interested parties plus the designer.

1.03 References

The SPR adheres to the standards of several nationally recognized organizations, as well as internal documents where the design, construction, and maintenance of play areas are involved. The following documents are hereby incorporated as part of these guidelines:

A. Published Documents:

1. American Society for Testing and Materials (ASTM) *Standard Consumer Safety Performance Specification for Playground Equipment for Public Use* (F1487; most recent edition).
2. U.S. Consumer Product Safety Commission (CPSC) *Handbook for Public Playground Safety,* Publication No. 235 or most recent edition.
3. U.S. Architectural and Transportation Barriers Compliance Board, Americans With Disabilities Act (ADA), *ADA Accessibility Guidelines for Buildings and Facilities*, Play Areas section; October 2000, amended November 2000 (or most recent edition).
4. City of Seattle *Standard Specifications for Road, Bridge, and Municipal Construction* (most recent edition).
5. City of Seattle *Standard Plans for Municipal Public Works Construction* (most recent edition).

B. Other specifications may be provided by city staff, during the course of design and design review, including storm drainage, concrete, irrigation, and others that may be deemed necessary for the acceptable completion of the design of the project.

1.04 Quality Control

The SPR System has play areas in all types of settings, some nestled among trees and others surrounded by downtown traffic. All of the play areas in the system, however, must be considered within the greater urban context. The extent of use is generally higher than you might find within other municipal settings, and the large number of facilities within the system dictates that with sometimes limited resources and high use, maintenance attention can at times be less than ideal. The quality ideal that the SPR aims for in acceptable play area design balances function and aesthetics with safety, accessibility, durability, and maintainability. With these considerations in mind, the following quality control measures must be upheld during the process of designing play areas:

A. Designer Selection

The SPR requires that the design of play areas be performed with the guidance of a professional licensed by the State of Washington to practice design within an area of specialty appropriate to the task. Generally, this has meant an architect, landscape architect, or civil engineer must be retained to assume the responsibility for performing the essential tasks of producing and assembling the documentation necessary to design and construct the play area (refer to PART 2—PRODUCTS).

Selection of a designer is typically as follows:

1. Paid consultant—When a group of interested citizens or the SPR cannot produce an individual who meets the required qualifications, a Request for Qualifications or Proposals (RFQ or RFP) may be issued soliciting the services of a paid consultant.
2. Park staff—Qualified park staff support may be provided on certain projects.
3. Volunteer—An interested party meeting the above qualifications may voluntarily provide the necessary services to see the process through.

B. Public Involvement

The City of Seattle has a blanket policy of public involvement for all public works performed on public property. Generally, this requires that notification be made within the geographic neighborhood or potentially impacted area, followed by a comment period and most often a public meeting where comment and discussion can take place. Public notifications and meetings may be required on multiple occasions depending on the scale and complexity of the project, on new development, or on projects proposing considerable changes to the use or character of public property.

C. Internal SPR Review

The SPR has a system in place for reviewing capital improvements of all types. For play areas, it is expected that the PROVIEW Project Review Committees (composed of administrative, program, and professionals) and Technical Review Committee (composed of technical staff and shops representatives) each have an opportunity to review and comment on the direction and progress of the design process. The scale and complexity of the project will usually have a direct bearing on the number and frequency of review sessions required by each review body.

D. Review by Other City Departments

Depending upon whether various criteria are met, other city departments may require an opportunity to review the direction and progress of the design process or require permitting. These departments may include Public Utilities, Transportation, Design Commission, Arts Commission, Landmarks Board, Public Works, or others.

E. Review by Other Agencies

Although infrequently required for play area design, it may become necessary to submit for review or permit with state or federal agencies, particularly where shoreline, riparian, or other ecologically sensitive, regulated natural systems are involved.

F. Adherence to Accepted Standards for Safety, Accessibility, Durability, and Maintainability

PART 2: PRODUCTS

2.01 General

This section will focus on the physical products required by the SPR during the design process.

2.02 Predesign

Prior to the production of visual representations of the project, it is important to produce the following preliminary documentation to aid in the actual design.

A. Design Program

Generally a planning tool, this document outlines the basic intent of the project and defines certain specific boundaries—physical, regulatory, fiscal, and conceptual—as well as time constraints. This document may include the results of citizen surveys. Citizen groups or the SPR may produce this document directly depending upon the primary funding source.

B. Site Analysis

Assuming a project location has been selected and approved by the SPR, the consultant or design professional will produce, with the aid of park staff and citizen neighbors of the park, a comprehensive analysis of the site. At a minimum, this document will identify existing conditions including solar orientation and wind conditions, vegetation, pedestrian and vehicular traffic patterns, use patterns both formal and informal, known improvements such as surface materials, site furniture, and underground utilities. A common scale of measurement appropriate to the task should be used.

2.03   Schematic Design

A. Preliminary Schematics

Preliminary schematics are rough sketches showing various options based on requirements and parameters set forth in the design program and site analysis, as well as input at public meetings. Rough estimates of cost to construct should be calculated for each scheme. Review of preliminary sketches by the design team should result in revisions that develop a preferred alternative.

B. Preferred Alternative

This is typically a color rendering illustrating the alternative that has drawn the consensus of the design team for use in presentation to the public and various reviewers. This drawing should be proportional and to scale (except reproductions), showing all key elements to be included in the finished project.

C. Cost Estimate

As the preferred alternative is developed from the preliminary schematics, an accurate estimate of the cost to construct the project must be maintained.

D. Approved Schematic Design

The approved schematic design is a graphic representation and cost estimate of the approved project design intent, as reviewed, revised, and accepted. Often the preferred alternative is an elaborate illustration produced for presentation and cannot easily be revised; however, a photocopy with red-lined revisions reflecting the consensus drawn through the review process and an adjusted cost estimate may be accepted as the approved schematic design. If wholesale revisions have not been required, the preferred alternative may still be used for public presentation of the proposed project.

2.04 Design Development

Design development is the intermediate stage between schematic design and the construction documents where further research and development of the design begins to identify specific details of the project that may result in necessary changes to the physical appearance, functionality, and cost of construction of a project. Design development is performed by the designer (usually a registered landscape architecture firm) and an artist (if there is a known art component integrated into the design) who produce documentation consisting of measured drawings and details of construction, outline specifications for materials and workmanship, and cost estimates. The design team and the SPR review this documentation to ensure that the approved intent of the project as defined by the design program is adhered to and that all required standards for safety, accessibility, durability, and maintainability are upheld. For smaller, less complex projects, this phase may be waived.

2.05 Construction Documents

Project scale and complexity will define the level of detail required in preparing construction documents; however, the following provides a complete example:

A. Construction Documents

Construction documents are measured scale drawings produced on an appropriate title block that provides all of the detail necessary to construct the project as proposed, revised, and approved through design development. The drawings must be clear and concise, with plan views separated by trade as appropriate (i.e., existing conditions and demolition, layout, grading and drainage, irrigation, planting, play equipment, and site furniture). Separate drawing sheets should be used to identify specific details to be used in construction. The details should be organized in a logical manner by trades as indicated above.

B. Specifications

The SPR uses a CSI-based, five-digit specification system consisting of 16 divisions. Division 0 and 1 are the primary and general requirements; Divisions 2 through 16 are technical specifications.

The level of written specification required will depend on the size, complexity, and implementation mechanism being used to construct the work. Below are some examples:

1. **City of Seattle Department of Finance Public Bid**. For projects bid through the Planning and Development Division, the primary City Contract language (Division Zero or "boilerplate" will be provided by the SPR, as will the basic framework of the General Requirements (Division 1). It is the Designer's responsibility to provide all technical specifications.

2. **Department of Neighborhoods (DON) Contract.** These contracts are used by Citizen Groups operating under contract with the Department of Neighborhoods through the Neighborhood Matching Grant Fund, and the SPR requires that approved technical specifications be attached as an addendum to the DON contract.

3. **Volunteer Construction.** Volunteer construction is typically used in the installation of landscaping and play equipment. In the case of landscaping, the SPR will provide technical specifications to be used. In the case of play equipment, the manufacturer's installation instructions and specifications, as well as the reference documents named above in Paragraph 1.03, shall guide the work.

C. Inspection Plan

The inspection plan identifies primary construction systems requiring inspection. Examples are concrete formwork prior to pour, pressure testing irrigation lines prior to backfill, and safety inspection of play equipment.

D. Cost Estimate

A cost estimate is an accurate cost estimate broken down by trades and identifying each separate construction system within each trade, showing quantity, unit price, and total system cost. Trade categories should show a subtotal. Contractor markups can be shown per line item or as a multiplier to the subtotal. Unit price can be expressed as a line unit or broken down by labor, equipment, and materials.

E. Schedule

A reasonable critical path schedule based on the trade and construction system breakdown used in the estimate should be prepared to complete the construction document phase. Identify all major milestones and incorporate the inspection plan. Identify clearly the division of labor anticipated for projects that include multiple implementation mechanisms, for example, physical participation by citizen volunteers, donated contractor work, manufacturer-certified installers, and bid work.

Design Standards for Sport Fields

Regulation football	120 yd (360 ft) in length x 53.3 yd (160 ft) in width includes two 10-yard (30 ft) end zones. Requires 15 ft of clearance from end lines and sidelines to vertical fixed objects. Goal posts are behind end zones, 120 yds (360 ft) apart.
Regulation soccer	110 yd to 120 yd (330 ft to 360 ft) in length x 65 yd to 75 yd (195 ft to 225 ft) in width. Requires 15 ft of clearance from end lines and sidelines to vertical fixed objects. Goal posts are on end lines. For other than regulation-sized fields, length is more critical than width.
Combined football/soccer	Same as regulation football.
Flag football	100 yd (300 ft) in length x 40 yd (120 ft) in width includes two 10-yard (30 ft) end zones. Goal posts not required for kicks.
Rugby	160 yd (480 ft) in length x 75 yd (225 ft) in width includes two 25-yard (75 ft) goal zones. Goal posts are 25 yd (75 ft) in from end lines.
Field hockey	100 yd (300 ft) in length x 60 yd (180 ft) in width. Goal posts are 100 yd (300 ft) apart.
Lacrosse	110 yd (330 ft) in length x 60 yd to 70 yd (180 ft to 210 ft) in width. Goals are 15 yd (45 ft) in from end lines and 80 yd (240 ft) apart.

Design Standards for Athletic Field Lighting

SECTION I: Introduction

Seattle is one of the most densely populated areas on the West Coast; therefore, Seattle Parks and Recreation (SPR) is committed to supporting growth management and comprehensive planning goals by providing an inventory of athletic facilities within Seattle that are safe, high-quality fields. Due to the City of Seattle's geographic location and environmental conditions, the use of synthetic surfaces and field lighting greatly increases the park system's scheduling capacity. The decision to light athletic fields comes with impacts to the immediate residents and area neighbors, even when using the latest technologies. The Joint Athletic Facilities Development Program (JAFDP) and these lighting design standards reflect the commitment to both providing safe, high-quality facilities and the recognition that these facilities impact the communities in which they are located.

Within this context, this document outlines the issues requiring consideration during the design phase of an athletic field lighting project. It also outlines design standards on technical issues such as levels of field lighting, addresses obtrusive light, and establishes design parameters for materials, all while allowing flexibility with regard to emerging technologies.

SECTION II: Definitions

Common lighting systems. The key technical issues to consider when selecting a preferred lighting system include illumination levels, uniformity, obtrusive light levels, daylight appearance (pole number, fixture density), lamp type (affects color rendition), initial capital investment, and operating and maintenance costs.

- *Full cutoff.* These lighting systems incorporate a downward aiming array of fixtures set close to the supporting pole, arrayed around the field side of the pole at various heights. Individual fixtures are composed of a reflector enclosed within an essentially open-bottomed, box-like structure. Full cutoff refers to the fact that the lamp placement inside the box and above the plane of the bottom opening eliminates, or cuts off, all direct light above the plane of the fixture opening. "Full cutoff" system designs may incorporate both metal halide and high-pressure sodium lamps of 1000-W each.
  Pros (compared to shielded aimable). No glare above the plane of the fixture. Minimal sky glow (some glow is produced by reflected light, which varies by field surface). Visually unobtrusive at the mounting point (fewer fixtures, mounted close in), in daylight.

Cons (compared to shielded aimable). Uniformity on larger surfaces is more difficult to achieve. More spill light behind the pole. Difficult to adjust. Does not allow for a reduction in pole quantities. Typically higher initial capital outlay. Poles must be close to the playing surface.

- **Shielded aimable.** Shielded aimable lighting systems incorporate a parabolic (somewhat dome-shaped) metal reflector around the lamp that results in a controlled beam spread. Fixtures are arrayed on supporting crossarms extending outward from the pole. The term *shielded* refers to two typical components: the parabolic reflector, which to some degree shields the lamp as viewed from off-site, and separate visors and shutters that can be bent or hinged to tighten the beam spread and further shield the lamp. The term *aimable* refers to the fact that the individual fixtures are mounted on an armature so that they can be specifically targeted at a predetermined point on the surface to be lighted. Although high-lift equipment is required to do so, each fixture can be re-aimed or have its individual visors and/or shutters adjusted, added to, or removed if necessary. Shielded aimable systems are produced almost exclusively with metal halide lamps with either a 1000-W or 1500-W power output.
  Pros (compared to full cutoff). High degree of uniformity regardless of field size or shape. High degree of control of spill light behind the pole. Adjustability of problem fixtures (on the field or off). Typically lower number of poles required. Typically lower initial capital outlay.
  Cons (compared to full cutoff). Higher glare below the plane of the fixture. Moderate glare above the plane of the fixture. High resultant sky glow from direct and reflected sources. Visually dense at mounting point (numerous fixtures arrayed on crossarms), in daylight.

Illuminance:
The density of the flow of light falling on a surface. This document refers to illuminance as measured in foot-candles, which is defined as one lumen uniformly distributed over an area of 1 sq ft.

- Horizontal illuminance is the normal design criteria used for design calculations and measuring field lighting levels for athletic field lighting projects. It is calculated by measuring the amount of light falling on the horizontal plane 36 in. above the surface.
- Vertical illuminance is critical for sports where the ball spends most of the time in the air (e.g., baseball, foot-

ball, and softball). Vertical levels are typically calculated in four directions and at various heights above the playing field. It is also used to calculate spill light levels.

- Initial illuminance is the measurable output of the fixture with a new arc tube (light source) installed.
- Maintained illuminance is the average output of the fixture following an initial burn-in period. The initial burn-in period is approximately 100 hr.

Illumination—Off-Site:

- **Ambient light** describes the existing light levels in a neighborhood given off from streetlights, building lights, and so forth.
- **Spill light** is the light that falls beyond the athletic field being illuminated. Spill light is expressed in foot-candles and is normally measured in the vertical plane.
- **Glare** is light that hinders or bothers the human eye due to the eye's difficulty in adjusting to different levels of light. Direct glare from a light source is typically an important issue in the design and operation of athletic field lighting installations, in terms of both players and nearby populations. Topography and vegetation can change the impacts of glare. There is no industry standard for measuring glare once a project has been completed. However, there may be design steps that mitigate the effects of glare, such as increased pole height.
- **Sky glow** is the haze or glow of light emitted above the lighting installation and reduces the ability to view the darkened nighttime sky. This is a combination of light emitted directly from the light source and reflected light that casts upward from the surface being illuminated. The level of sky glow is also impacted by atmospheric conditions; clouds and moisture increase the effects of sky glow.

Levels of play classifications. The Illuminating Engineering Society of North America (IESNA) set forth four illumination classifications based on the level of play being accommodated on a lighted athletic field. Recommended levels for social or recreational sports range from 20 to 50 foot-candles; levels for professional play with large spectator attendance and television coverage can reach 300 foot-candles. Field illumination for SPR athletic fields will conform to either Level III or Level IV standards depending on the anticipated use of the field.

- **Level I** illumination is for competition play before a large group of spectators (approximately between 5,000 and 10,000 spectators).
- **Level II** illumination is for competition play with up to 5,000 spectators.
- **Level III** illumination is for competition play with some provision for spectators, such as permanent bleachers for 5 to 100 spectators.

- **Level IV** illumination is for competition or recreational play only with no provision for spectators.

Uniformity:

Uniformity measures the relationship between the brightest area on the field and the darkest area on the field. Allowable variations are set to ensure player safety and are established based on the level of play classification determined for the field.

SECTION III: Design Considerations

Site Considerations

1. **Light levels.** Meeting illumination levels for safe play on the field while minimizing lighting impacts off-site is the priority design consideration for athletic field lighting projects.
   - On-field light levels: Projects will be designed to meet field surface illumination levels necessary for the safe play of the sports that will be played at the project site.
   - Off-site light levels: Project design will include analyses of spill light, glare, and sky glow.

2. **Park amenities.** Replacement and new lighting projects may present an opportunity to consider additional park amenities that might be appropriate for the site, such as comfort stations, drinking fountains, security lighting, seating, and accessible access.

3. **Topography.** The surrounding topography will be considered when selecting a project's lighting system in an effort to minimize impacts of obtrusive light, as well as for aesthetic considerations such as impact to views.

4. **Traffic and parking.** Increased scheduling of an athletic field may cause periodic traffic congestion and constrain available parking. These issues will be considered during a project design through the public involvement process and/or State Environmental Policy Act (SEPA) analysis. Additionally, the department will work with sports organizations, field users, and community organizations to provide site-specific information as to preferred traffic routes and parking areas.

5. **Vegetative screens.** Tall shrubs and trees may be considered as screens to reduce glare and spill light.

6. **Wildlife.** Potential impacts of lights on wildlife vary for each proposed site. Analysis of these potential impacts is performed as part of any required SEPA process.

Programming Considerations

1. **Capacity.** All SPR athletic fields where lights exist or will

be installed should be evaluated and monitored with respect to the type of sports, age group, field dimensions, type of surface, and so forth by the scheduling staff to maximize the opportunities and improve the management of the entire system.

2. **Noise.** In order to practice a "good neighbor" policy in and around parks where lights exist or will be installed, every precaution should be taken to minimize the type and amount of noise to which a surrounding neighbor may be exposed. Therefore, the department will work closely with user groups and encourage them to practice being the best neighbor possible while using park facilities.

3. **Programming.** Recognizing that user needs vary, the department will attempt to balance the needs of users with the impacts to and needs of the neighboring community. Hours of operation for lighted athletic fields are addressed in the department's scheduling and use policy.

Maintenance and Operational Considerations

1. **Energy costs.** The cost of energy will be an ongoing challenge, and therefore the type of lighting systems installed at each athletic field site should be analyzed for short- and long-term energy consumption needs. Current data regarding use patterns, alternative uses, types of lamps used, and the level of lighting to accommodate the users at a given location are all considerations.

2. **Safety of users and neighbors.** On- and off-field safety will be considered in the design and development of athletic fields. Close coordination with user groups and good communication with neighbors to address issues and concerns should be ongoing. Attention should also be given to ensure user safety after field lights are turned out.

3. **Maintenance.** A maintenance plan outlining ongoing services and upkeep will be critical to the lighting program, and therefore project design should consider issues related to future maintenance. In addition, a well-organized inspection program to monitor and evaluate the efficiency and effectiveness of each lighting system should be developed for each site.

SECTION IV: References

- These Lighting Design Standards are based on the 2001 Ballfield Lighting Study, and the various technical references therein, (The Study) prepared by McGowan Bros. Engineers for SPR.

SECTION V: Standards for Illumination Levels

Illumination levels are determined based on the level of play being accommodated at the project site. The lighting consulting engineer shall verify the level of play with SPR prior to initiating design. The athletic field lighting project must conform to the following standards for illuminance levels, uniformities, and light loss factors.

In general, SPR facilities will be built to Level IV illumination standards. Certain baseball/softball athletic fields that can accommodate tournament play with spectator attendance will be built to Level III illumination standards, such as lower woodland.

SECTION VI: Standards for Addressing Obtrusive Light

Spill Light

The environmental zone for city projects shall be E3. Only the precurfew limitations will be considered, in accordance with the lighting study. Therefore, projects at newly lighted sites shall conform to a maximum maintained vertical illuminance level for spill light that does not exceed 0.8 foot-candles (initial 1.1 foot-candles) at the residential property line. The lighting designer shall undertake initial vertical illuminance calculations on a line along the edge of the properties and roadways as defined by the city to establish compliance with the 0.8 foot-candle level. The levels shall be calculated vertically at 5 ft above grade. At sites with existing lighting systems, every effort will be made during the design of a replacement system to meet this standard. However, in order to encourage an expeditious replacement of these out-of-date systems, projects may deviate from this spill light level.

Glare Analysis

Although glare is very subjective and difficult to measure in the field, it can be analyzed during the design phase. Therefore, as part of the luminaire and mounting height selection process, the lighting designer will review candlepower curves and determine the appropriate luminaire mounting height and optical system so that no greater than 12,000 candlepower from any given luminaire is visible from the residential property line. (This analysis is outlined in The Study, pp. 2–40).

Sky Glow Assessment

As it is nearly impossible to measure sky glow in the field, it shall be assessed during the design stage to ensure that the calculated maintained average lighting level on a horizontal plane above the lights shall not exceed 5% of the maintained calculated average lighting level on the field surface. We recognize, however, that this method does not account for the reflected light from the field surface or the atmospheric conditions.

SECTION VII: Standards for Materials

Improvements in technology will be considered when choosing appropriate materials.

- **Lighting system.** Full cutoff, shielded aimable, or a hybrid of these two systems will be used for all SPR athletic field lighting projects.
- **Lamp wattage.** SPR athletic field lighting projects will consider both 1000-W and 1500-W lamp systems, and the optimal system will be chosen based on the design considerations list in SECTION III.
- **Pole material.** SPR athletic field lighting projects will consider galvanized steel and concrete poles, and the optimal material will be chosen based on the design considerations list in SECTION III. Wooden poles are not acceptable due to the susceptibility to twisting and rotting.
- **Safety lighting.** All lighted facilities shall provide pedestrian-scale lighting of sufficient intensity and duration to allow all participants to exit the site safely at the conclusion of any scheduled evening use. Consideration will be made regarding ADA-compliant routes of travel and common points of pedestrian and emergency access and egress from the site. The pedestrian lighting should be designed to incorporate "full cutoff" type fixtures at heights that discourage vandalism but are within the height restriction of land-use development standards for the site. Cost effectiveness shall be maximized by using the existing athletic field lighting poles where possible and by designing fixture heights that minimize the number of additional poles necessary to achieve the intent.
- **Control system.** All SPR athletic field lighting projects will include an on-site control switch that can allow lights to be operated at the site. Projects will also be designed to allow individual fields to be lighted separately so that all facility lights are not required to be on when a limited number of fields are in use.

SECTION VIII: Project Design

Lighting design. Lighting design shall be based on the performance criteria defined by the city. It is the responsibility of the lighting designer to meet the required lighting criteria. The city takes no responsibility for any misinterpretation of these standards. The performance of the installed athletic field lighting system will be field measured as described in SECTION IX.

Project design team. A city-approved electrical engineering firm with thorough knowledge of sports lighting systems, power distribution, and controls systems shall undertake all athletic field lighting projects. The electrical engineer shall be registered in the State of Washington. The electrical engineer shall be responsible for the preparation of the construction design drawing(s), technical specifications, and the review of the supplier's pole and lighting submittals.

The design team shall design foundations to suit the local soil conditions present. An independent geotechnical engineer registered in the State of Washington shall approve the foundation designs. The city may supply a soil report. Where geotechnical information is not provided, the design team shall confirm the soil conditions.

Codes and standards. All electrical design shall be performed in accordance with the latest edition of the National Electrical Code (NEC) and any applicable Washington State or local codes and amendments. All engineering shall follow the latest edition of standards and codes and shall be performed under the direction of engineers competent to practice in those fields. Although the Non-Residential Energy Code (NREC) does not directly apply to athletic fields, energy consumption and energy efficiency shall be given the utmost importance in design.

Design process. A standard design process has been established to minimize confusion and streamline the design.

1. The city selects a qualified electrical engineering firm for the specific sports lighting project.
2. The engineering firm's project team meets with the city to discuss the project specifics and criteria to be followed.
3. A project schedule is developed after the engineer records all discussions and key issues. The engineer submits notes (i.e., memorandum of understanding) to all key persons involved in the project.
4. The engineer determines the specific lighting electrical loads.
5. The engineer meets with the local utility company to establish either a new or an upgraded service including supply voltage and service location.
6. The engineer develops the electrical design drawings, specifications, and cost estimates.
7. The drawings, specifications, and cost estimate are reviewed with the city, revisions are made as required, and a reproducible set of drawings and a digital set of specifications are issued to the city for its bid process. The drawings shall be signed and sealed by the engineer.
8. The engineer provides bidding assistance and shall be available to respond to any questions from bidders. The engineer shall issue addendum as required.
9. After award, the engineer shall review and comment on vendor lighting and technical information submitted.

10. The engineer shall provide construction administration services.

11. Following construction, the engineer shall measure and record all illumination levels in accordance with IESNA LM-5 (refer to the SECTION IX on Performance Verification later in this memorandum). This document shall become a part of the project's permanent record.

Drawings and specifications. Drawings detailing the entire sports lighting installation shall be produced for each installation. At a minimum, the consultant shall supply the following items (supplemental specifications may be produced for each contract to complement these Lighting Design Standards):

- *Site plan.* Showing the fields, pole locations, conduit, wiring, pull boxes, service locations, lighting control cabinet, and other features necessary to properly construct the facility.
- *Details.* One-line diagram, lighting control schematic, panel schedules, pull box details, conduit trench detail, control cabinet details, equipment elevations and other detail needed to properly construct the facility.
- *Drawings.* Drawings shall be prepared in AutoCAD format and shall include the following information:
  - Initial and maintained illuminance designs. The sports field being illuminated shall be presented at a 1:30 scale, or larger, showing all illuminance levels at a grid spacing of 10 ft. Grid points shall be calculated at 3 ft above grade. Grid points shall extend to the edge of the primary play area (PPA) as defined by the city.
  - Summary table. A summary table shall be included on the drawing showing the number of grid points, the design average illuminance levels and uniformities achieved, luminaire model number(s) and types, lamp type(s), wattage and lumen output, light loss factors, tilt factors, and other information as deemed necessary.
  - Pole location. Pole locations and luminaire mounting heights and total number of luminaries on each pole shall be presented on the drawings. Pole locations shall be dimensioned to key control points.
  - Spill light levels. Off-site vertical illumination (light trespass) levels at 20-ft intervals on the boundary lines defined by the city shall be shown on the drawing. Levels shall be shown in vertical foot-candles calculated at 5 ft above grade with the meter oriented in the vertical position facing the lights.
  - Glare levels. The field being illuminated shall be shown to match the appropriate Maintained and Initial Designs and 12,000 candlepower points (as shown in The Study, pp. 2–40). All luminaire aiming points, pole locations, number of fixtures on each pole, fixture types, and NEMA beam patterns shall also be shown.
  - Candlepower cut sheets. The lighting supplier shall provide luminaire candlepower cut sheets showing the vertical and horizontal axial candlepower at 5° increments. These candlepower curves shall be supplied for each luminaire used. An independent testing company shall verify and supply the vendor's candlepower cut sheets.
  - Consultant information. Lighting supplier's name, lighting designer's name, phone number, date of design, project title and location, and bar scale shall be included on each drawing.

SECTION IX: Performance Verification

Lighting

- The engineer shall field measure illuminance levels and document findings in accordance with LM-5. Spill light levels shall also be measured and documented and nighttime digital pictures taken at key points along the residential boundary.
- Where the lighting installation does not meet the required performance levels, the engineer shall coordinate re-aiming by the supplier. Retesting will be required where fixtures are re-aimed. Illumination level measurements shall take place after the lights have been in operation for a period of 50 hr to 100 hr of operations.
- The engineer shall inspect the installation of the sports lighting equipment for general conformance to the performance requirements. Upon completion, the engineer shall submit a drawing showing the final measured illumination levels, uniformities, and spill light levels, along with properly labeled nighttime digital pictures from the residential boundary looking at the lights. A letter of compliance shall accompany the measured levels.

Electrical Systems

- The entire electrical installation shall be inspected by the engineer of record or his or her designated representative for general conformance to the design. Deficiencies shall be listed in writing and submitted to the contractor for correction. Upon correction of deficiencies, the engineer shall submit notification of substantial completion to the city.
- After completion of the installation, the engineer shall prepare a final set of record drawings, commonly referred to as "as-builts," that shall account for all changes through construction. The record drawings shall be incorporated into an Operation and Maintenance (O&M)

manual, which shall include all pertinent information, shop drawing product information, and other salient data deemed necessary to document the installation.

Geotechnical

- All foundation installations shall be inspected and approved by a geotechnical engineer. The geotechnical engineer shall provide a copy of the foundation design and backfill attached to a letter approving the installation.

Environmental Zones

(defined by the Illuminating Engineering Society of North America, IESNA)

Zone	Description	Light trespass (maximum levels at the residential property line)[a] Initial/Maintained
E1	Areas with intrinsically dark landscapes, such as national parks and areas of outstanding beauty.	0.14 fc / 0.1 fc
E2	Areas of low ambient lighting, such as suburban or rural residential areas.	0.42 fc / 0.3 fc
E3	Areas of medium ambient brightness, such as urban residential areas.	1.1 fc / 0.8 fc
E4	Areas of high ambient brightness, such as dense urban areas with mixed residential and commercial uses.	2.1 fc / 1.5 fc

Note. FC = foot-candles.

[a] As a comparison, a 30-ft street lamp located 10 ft from a residential property line would have a vertical illumination level, at 6 ft above grade, of 1.3 fc at the residential property line (IESNA, 2008, pp. 2–17).

Design Standards for Wood Flooring for Gyms and Multipurpose

PART 1—GENERAL

1.01   Intent

To provide a floating maple floor system with a consistent ball bounce, good shock-absorbing qualities, and no dead spots.

1.02   Performance Standards

To be a Deutches Institut für Normung (DIN) certified floor system, the floor must meet the following DIN standards:
1.   Shock absorption—53% minimum to no more than 63% of concrete. Concrete equals 0%.
2.   Ball bounce—98% minimum.
3.   Deflection—vertical deformations at point of impact, minimum 0.091 in.
4.   Deflective Indentation—at 20 in. from point of impact, 15% maximum.
5.   Friction—0.5 to 0.7 range.
6.   Rolling load—337.6 lb.

PART 2—PRODUCTS

2.01   Material

A.   Flooring to be second and better Northern Hard Maple, (MFMA) grade marked, edge grain of 25/32 in. thick x 11/2 in. or 21/4 in. wide, 33/32 in. thick preferred
B.   Playing surface to have painted game lines per STD DTL #09900.51 for layout and color. Provide two coats sealer and minimum two coats finish high solids modified polyurethane gymnasium floor finish system, such as Hilyard® Golden Seal system. Three coats of finish preferred. Sand and clean between each coat. Install game lines after the first coat of sealer, sanded.
C.   Subfloor system: shall meet the performance standards listed in 1.02 above for the total system.
D.   Vapor barrier (not retarder) system—sealed at all penetrations and laps.
E.   Wall base—galvanized steel or clear anodized aluminum, 3 in. x 4 in. x ¼ in. or 3 in. x 6 in. x ¼ in. angle, spaced ⅜ in. away from wall. Shop form all outside and inside corners. Wall base to be easily removable for floor repair and refinishing using metal wall inserts and screws.

Park and Recreation Open Space Standards

Table 1

Acres Required per 1,000 Residents

Facility Category	Total Acres
Sports Fields (i.e., soccer, multiuse, baseball, softball)	4.4
Courts (i.e., tennis, basketball, volleyball)	.3
Outdoor Recreation (i.e., skatepark, BMX, trails, fishing access, etc.)	8.5
Leisure (i.e., playgrounds, picnic, general parkland)	.8
Other Recreational Facilities (i.e., swimming pool, hockey, outdoor events venue)	1.5

Table 2

Design Standards for: Baseball and Softball Field Layouts

	BASEBALL		SOFTBALL	
	Regulation, Colt, and Babe Ruth Leagues	**Pony League**	**Regulation**	**Little League**
Outfield Radius	375 ft	300 ft	300 ft	180 ft
Hood- or Hoop-Style Backstop Distance From Home Plate	14 ft, 6 in.	14 ft, 6 in.	14 ft, 6 in.	14 ft, 6 in.
Distance From Pitcher's Rubber to Home Plate	60 ft, 6 in.	54 ft	46 ft 40'(Women)	46 ft
Radius of Pitcher's Rubber to Skinned Infield	95 ft	80 ft	65 ft or 70 ft**	65 ft
Wing Fences:				
1. Length	96 ft	96 ft	60 ft	60 ft
2. Height	10 ft	10 ft	10 ft	10 ft
Dugouts	All dugouts shall be at least 30 ft long, gated for baseball with entrance at least 40 ft from backstop, and usually open at one end for all types of backstops.			
Distance Between Bases	90 ft	80 ft	60 ft or 65 ft**	60 ft
Outfield Fences:				
1. Distance From Home Plate	375 ft	300 ft*	300 ft*	180 ft
2. Height	8 ft	8 ft	8 ft	8 ft
3. Top Covering	Bright Vinyl	Bright Vinyl	Bright Vinyl	Bright Vinyl
Bleachers (minimum)	2 @ 8 ft x 9 ft sections each side	2 @ 8 ft x 9 ft sections each side	2 @ 8 ft x 9 ft sections each side	2 @ 8 ft x 9 ft sections each side
Warning Tracks	10 ft	10 ft	10 ft	10 ft

Recreation, Park, and Open Space Standards and Guidelines

The National Recreation and Park Association (NRPA) recognizes the importance of establishing and using park and recreation standards as

- a national expression of minimum acceptable facilities for the citizens of urban and rural communities;
- a guideline to determine land requirements for various kinds of park and recreation areas and facilities;
- a basis for relating recreational needs to spatial analysis within a community-wide system of parks and open space areas;
- one of the major structuring elements that can be used to guide and assist regional development; and
- a means to justify the need for parks and open space within the overall land-use pattern of a region or community.

The purpose of these guidelines is to present park and recreation space standards that are applicable nationwide for planning, acquisition, and development of park, recreation, and open space lands, primarily at the community level. These standards should be viewed as a guide. They address minimum, not maximum, goals to be achieved. The standards are interpreted according to the particular situation to which they are applied and specific local needs. A variety of standards have been developed by professional and trade associations that are used throughout the country. The standard derived from early studies of park acreages located within metropolitan areas was the expression of acres of parkland per unit of population. Over time, the figure of 10 acres per 1,000 population came to be the commonly accepted standard used by a majority of communities. Other standards adopted include the "percentage of area" approach, needs determined by user characteristics and participation projections, and area use based on the carrying capacity of the land. The fact that some of the standards have changed substantially is not an indication of their obsolescence. Changes are a measure of the growing awareness and understanding of both participant and resource (land, water, etc.) limitations. Parks are for people. Park, recreation, and planning professionals must integrate the art and science of park management in order to balance park and open space resource values such as water supply and air quality.

Appendix F
Metric Conversion Formulas

Converting from Metric to English:

To Obtain	Multiply	By
Inches	Centimeters	0.3937007874
Feet	Meters	3.280839895
Yards	Meters	1.093613298
Miles	Kilometers	0.6213711922

Converting from English to Metric:

To Obtain	Multiply	By
Centimeters	Inches	2.54
Meters	Feet	0.3048
Meters	Yards	0.9144
Kilometers	Miles	1.6093

Appendix G
Associations Pertinent to Planning

Aerobics & Fitness Association of America
15250 Ventura, Suite 310
Sherman Oaks, CA 91403, (818)905-0040
www.afaa.com

American Alliance for Health, Physical Education, Recreation, and Dance (AAHPERD)
1900 Association Drive
Reston, VA 22091, (703)476-3400
www.aahperd.org

American Amateur Racquetball Association
815 North Weber, Suite 101
Colorado Springs, CO 80903, (719)635-5396
www.usra.org

American Association of Cardiovascular and Pulmonary Rehabilitation
7611 Elmwood Avenue, Suite 201
Middleton, WI 53562, (608)831-6989
www.aacvpr.org

American Athletic Trainers Association and Certification Board, Inc.
660 W. Duarte Road
Arcada, CA 91006, (818)445-1978
www.bocatc.org

American College of Sports Medicine
P.O. Box 1440
Indianapolis, IN 46206-1440, (317)637-9200
www.acsm.org

American Council on Exercise
6190 Cornerstone Court East, Suite 202
San Diego, CA 92121
www.acefitness.org

American Heart Association
7320 Greenville Avenue
Dallas, TX 75231, (214)373-6300
www.heart.org

American Massage Therapy Association
1130 West North Shore Drive
Chicago, IL 60626
www.amtamassage.org

Association for Fitness in Business
310 North Alabama, Suite A100
Indianapolis, IN 46204, (317)636-6621

Athletic Institute
200 Castlewood Drive
North Palm Beach, FL 33408, (408)842-3600
www.athleteinstituteinc.com

Illuminating Engineering Society of North America
345 East 47th Street
New York, NY 10017, (212)705-7926
www.ihs.com/index.aspx

International Council for Health, Physical Education, and Recreation (ICHPER)
1900 Association Drive
Reston, VA 22091, (703)476-3400
http://ichpersd.org/index.php/component/content/front-page

International Dance Exercise Association (IDEA)
6190 Cornerstone Court East, Suite 204
San Diego, CA 92121, (800)999-IDEA
www.ideafit.com

International Racquet Sports Association
253 Summer Street
Boston, MA 02210, (800)228-4772
www.ihrsa.org

Maple Flooring Manufacturers Association
60 Revere Drive, Suite 500
Northbrook, IL 60062, (708)480-9138
www.maplefloor.org

National Archery Association
1750 East Boulder Street
Colorado Springs, CO 80909, (719)578-4576
www.nfaaarchery.org

National Association of Concessionaires
35 East Wacker Drive, #1545
Chicago, IL, 60601, (312)236-3858
www.naconline.org

National Collegiate Athletic Association
700 West Washington Street
P.O. Box 6222
Indianapolis, IN 46206-6222, (317)917-6222
www.ncaa.org

National Employee Services and Recreation Association
2400 South Downing Avenue
Westchester, IL 60154, (708)562-8130

National Institute for Occupational Safety and Health
944 Chestnut Ridge Road
Morgantown, WV 26505
www.cdc.gov/NIOSH

National Intramural–Recreational Sports Association
850 Southwest 15th Street
Corvallis, OR 97333-4145, (503)737-2088
www.nirsa.org

National Recreation and Park Association
3101 Park Center Drive
Alexandria, VA 22302, (703)820-4940
www.nrpa.org

National Rifle Association
1600 Rhode Island Avenue, N.W.
Washington, DC 20036, (202)828-6000
www.nra.org

National Strength and Conditioning Association
P.O. Box 81410
Lincoln, NE 68501, (402)472-3000
www.nsca-lift.org

National Swimming Pool Foundation
10803 Golfdale, Suite 300
San Antonio, TX 78216, (512)525-1227
www.nspf.org

National Wellness Association
University of Wisconsin
Stevens Point, WI 54481
www.nationalwellness.org

President's Council on Physical Fitness and Sports
450 5th Street, N.W., Suite 7103
Washington, DC 20001, (202)272-3421
www.fitness.gov

Sporting Goods Manufacturers Association
200 Castlewood Drive
North Palm Beach, FL 33408, (407)842-4100
www.sfia.org

United States Badminton Association
920 O Street, Fourth Floor
Lincoln, NE 68508, (402)438-2473
www.teamusa.org/USA-Badminton.aspx

United States Fencing Association
1750 East Boulder Street
Colorado Springs, CO 80909, (719)632-5737
www.usfencing.org

U.S. Golf Association
P.O. Box 708
Far Hills, NJ 07931, (201)234-2300
www.usga.org

U.S. Gymnastics Federation
Pan American Plaza, Suite 300
201 South Capitol Avenue
Indianapolis, IN 46225, (317)237-5050

U.S. Handball Association
930 North Benton Avenue
Tucson, AZ 85711, (602)795-0434
www.ushandball.org

U.S. Squash Racquets Association
P.O. Box 1216
Bala-Cynwyd, PA 19004, (215)667-4006
www.ussquash.com

U.S. Tennis Court and Track Builders Association
720 Light Street
Baltimore, MD 21230, (301)752-3500
www.ustctba.com

U.S. Volleyball Association
3595 East Fountain, Suite 1-2
Colorado Springs, CO 80910-1740, (719)637-8300
www.usavolleyball.org

Wellness Council of America
7101 Newport Avenue
Omaha, NE 68152, (402)572-3590
www.welcoa.org

YMCA of the USA
726 Broadway, 5th Floor
New York, NY 10003, (212)614-2827
www.ymca.net

YWCA of the USA
101 North Wacker Drive
Chicago, IL 60606, (312) 977-0031
www.ywca.org/

Appendix H
Associations Pertinent to Planning for Accessibility

American Coalition of Citizens With Disabilities
1346 Connecticut Avenue
NW, Room 814
Washington, DC 20036
(chapters in states)

American Council of the Blind
1211 Connecticut Avenue,
NW, Suite 506
Washington, DC 20036
(chapters in states)

Arthritis Foundation
1212 Avenue of the Americas
New York, NY 10036

Association for the Aid of Crippled Children
345 East 46th Street
New York, NY 10017

Disabled American Veterans
3725 Alexandria Pike
Cold Spring, KY 41076
(state and local units)

International Society for the Rehabilitation of the Disabled
219 East 44th Street
New York, NY 10017

Muscular Dystrophy Association of America
1790 Broadway
New York, NY 10019

National Association of the Deaf
814 Thayer Avenue
Silver Spring, MD 20910
(local chapters)

National Association of the Physically Handicapped
76 Elm Street
London, OH 43140
(local chapters)

National Congress of Organizations of the Physically Handicapped
6106 North 30th Street
Arlington, VA 22207

National Easter Seal Society for Crippled Children and Adults
2023 West Ogden Avenue
Chicago, IL 60612

National Foundation for Neuromuscular Diseases
250 West 57th Street
New York, NY 10019

National Multiple Sclerosis Society
257 Park Avenue South
New York, NY 10010

National Paraplegia Foundation
333 North Michigan Avenue
Chicago, IL 60601
(state and local chapters)

Paralyzed Veterans of America
4330 East West Highway, Suite 300
Washington, DC 20014
(state and local chapters)

United Cerebral Palsy Association, Inc.
66 East 34th Street
New York, NY 10016

Appendix I
Retrofitting or Replacing Facilities

The practice of buying-using-discarding has become unacceptable. This applies not only to paper, aluminum cans, and glass but also to facilities (CEFP, 1985). Due to the high cost of new construction, upper level administration, whether it be in the private sector, at a university, at a municipal agency, or in a public school system, is responsible for making the wisest use of existing buildings. In meeting this obligation, it is necessary for administrators, with input from knowledgeable resource persons, to consider the feasibility of renovating or retrofitting an existing building or of constructing a new facility.

By definition, the renovation of an existing facility is the rehabilitation of the physical features of that building, including the rearrangement of spaces within the structure. Retrofitting, on the other hand, is the addition of new systems, items, features, materials, and/or equipment to a facility that were not installed at the time the building was constructed. These changes may be minor, or they could be significant to the point of changing the primary function of the facility.

To accurately ascertain whether renovation, retrofitting, or new construction is the most prudent alternative, administrators have a myriad of factors to consider. One of the more important is the effect that the construction process has relative to ongoing programs. Consideration must be given to program modifications and adaptions that may occur during the construction process. The advantages and disadvantages of both the present and the possibility of a new building should be closely scrutinized. The following is an adequate representation of the factors to consider.

Cost Considerations
- What is the cost of new construction to provide comparable space?
- What is the cost of construction needed to bring the existing facility up to compliance with safety codes/accessibility?
- Does the cost of renovation or retrofitting exceed 50% of the cost of new construction?
- Will the increased cost of maintaining an older building justify renovation instead of the construction of a new facility?
- Could the existing facility be sold or leased to a private entity to help defray the cost of new construction?

- If the amount of construction time becomes critical, which method—renovation or new construction—could be completed in the least amount of time?

Site Considerations
- Is a site available, and how effectively does the site meet the agency's immediate and long-range goals?
- Is the location of the present structure easily accessible?
- Is the parking adequate at the present site?
- How efficient is the sewer and stormwater control?
- How is the soil-bearing performance of the present site?
- What is the general condition of the grounds?
- Is there sufficient area for all program activities?
- Are vehicular drives well located for safe ingress and egress?
- Are the existing utilities on or near the site adequate to provide the needed services?

Architectural and Structural Considerations
A certified architect and engineer should be sought to determine the following structural factors:
- Is the present facility aesthetically appealing and structurally sound?
- Does the existing facility meet current and long-range program goals, and if not, would renovation or retrofitting realistically elevate the facility to acceptable standards?
- What is the availability of utilities?
- How energy efficient is the present facility? Does it meet all updated energy codes?
- Are there signs of deterioration of footings, foundations, or piers?
- Are structural members adequate and in serviceable conditions?
- Is the exterior masonry sound? Are there structural cracks, water damage, or defective mortar?
- What is the condition of the roof and roofing surfaces, roof drains, and skylights?
- What is the condition of flashing, gutters, and downspouts?
- What are the conditions of doors and windows?
- What are the conditions of door hardware and panic devices?

- What are the locations, numbers, types, and conditions of plumbing fixtures?
- What is the condition and capacity of the present water supply, sewage lines, and drainage systems?
- Is the present HVAC system adequate and energy efficient? Does it meet updated codes?
- What is the condition and adequacy of lighting and power distribution systems?
- Do the existing light fixtures provide adequate illumination in all areas?
- Are stairways, circulation patterns, and exits safe and adequate in number?
- What is the present condition of fire alarms and intercommunication systems?

Educational Considerations
- Is the building now meeting the agency's program?
- What is the current inventory of rooms and their sizes?
- Are laboratories adequately served by all required utilities?
- Is the library adequate to house the required book collection and to provide media and related services?
- Are food service facilities adequate to meet present and projected needs?
- Are physical education, recreation, and athletic areas usable or capable of being retrofitted if required?

Community Considerations
- Will the renovation of the building be consistent with present zoning requirements and policies?
- What are the plans for the area served by the program as projected by city or area planning agencies?
- Is the building on or eligible for placement on the National Register of Historic Places?
- Will a new facility constitute a political problem with businesses in the private sector?

Before a decision is made on the wisdom of renovating, retrofitting, remodeling, or replacing, factors concerning the existing and proposed facilities should be evaluated in detail, both individually and collectively. Administrators would also benefit from projecting a reasonable life expectancy of the facility, accounting for factors such as

- increased or decreased populations served by the programs within the facility;
- growth and development of areas surrounding the facility; and
- the potential reorganization, community rezoning, or consolidation of schools in the district.

Appendix J
Facility Maintenance

by Thomas Rosandich

Most maintenance managers will agree that maintenance requirements are almost never adequately considered when facilities are designed. Even when maintenance is partially considered during the design phase, changes in design during construction often nullify the original plans. The construction contractor is usually most concerned with completing the building in the manner that will generate the most profit and, as such, is not usually concerned with maintenance and repair requirements once the warranties expire. Furthermore, architects have a natural tendency to focus on the visual aesthetics of the design, often at the expense of more utilitarian concerns such as cost efficiency in operations (Beisel, 1998; Sawyer, 2009).

Given that the largest cost of a sports facility is born through the many years of operation following construction and commissioning, maintenance professionals (typically the designated facility maintenance manager) need to participate in the design process. These maintenance professionals should remain involved until the project has been completed. So, although there should be no question at this point that the maintenance manager can have a lot to offer in terms of the planning of the facility, further discussions are in order as to the practical considerations for operations and maintenance (O&M) in the project planning. This chapter looks at some of the design requirements for the sports facility from the perspective of the maintenance manager. The first part relates specifically to maintenance and support areas and the second to general generic maintenance concerns for the facility as a whole.

Design Considerations for Maintenance and Operations

Physical education, athletic, and recreational facilities should be maintained in a sanitary and hygienic condition. The very nature of many of the activities conducted within these facilities and the many uses of water within them magnifies the need for consistent, superior custodial care. Unless custodians are provided with adequate and convenient facilities and equipment, the prospects of achieving the desired level of sanitation are significantly diminished.

Among the facilities required by the maintenance and custodial staff for the care and operation of sports facilities are workshops; storage for tools, spare parts, and supplies; janitorial closets; laundry facilities; office and administrative space; and staff break rooms with locker facilities. The following discussion looks briefly at design considerations for these specific O&M areas within the multipurpose sports facility.

Central Custodial Complex

The size and configuration of the custodial complex in a sports facility is contingent upon a number of factors, the first of which is the size of the building and the nature of the programs being conducted. The needs of a small, privately held health club, for example, will vary markedly in both size and scope from those of a multipurpose municipal facility or a university sports complex.

But even between facilities of comparable size, the nature of the organization that owns them will have a significant impact on the size and composition of the custodial complex and the way that it is managed. For example, the physical education, intercollegiate sports, and recreational facilities of a major university can be similar in size to that of a national sports complex or a municipal stadium. However, in the university situation, there will typically be less space given over to O&M within the sports facility itself because it is likely that elsewhere on campus there will be a centralized buildings and grounds operation that will be responsible for the heavy maintenance activities of the entire university. Thus, within the sports facility, there may, at most, be a small work space with a storage area for tools and spare parts, which would be insufficient for a freestanding, independent operation of comparable size.

Freestanding sport facilities, such as a municipal civic center or a national sports complex, will typically have a self-contained operation for O&M activities. Instead of a small work area for on-site repairs, a freestanding sports facility will need expansive work spaces with a much larger variety of tools and storage for spare parts. Nevertheless, O&M facilities of all types have a number of elements in common.

One approach for the allocation of administrative and support space for O&M operatives is described by Sawyer (2009). In large facilities, a central custodial headquarters should be planned to include a toilet, shower, lavatory, and dressing area with individual lockers. This unit should also have a separate break and meal area equipped with a sink, hot and cold water supply, microwave oven, and a small refrigerator. Additionally, a small, apartment-sized breakfast table and chairs should be provided.

Although there is no question that a properly furnished break area and locker room facilities for the O&M staff are appropriate, there is a definite need for a separate O&M office. The area for the administrative office in a typical collegiate facility should be about 7 sq m. It is important to note, however, that this space allocation for the administrative office is a minimum and that the size of the space allocated will grow as the complexity and size of the O&M operation grows. The administrative area should have enough office space to accommodate a desk, filing cabinets, and communications equipment. With today's communication technology capabilities, the administrative office must have a networked computer (either a networked personal computer or a terminal in the case of a mainframe operation) with a printer. Traditionally, the office of the O&M supervisor has been physically located in the workshop or storeroom area. However, because of advances in the application of communications equipment and powerful management tools, such as networked microcomputers, the physical presence of the supervisor in the workshop area is no longer a necessity (Sawyer, 2009).

A further case can be made that, because of the coordination required between the different administrators who manage the sports facility, the office of the maintenance supervisor should be located in the same area as other administrators. Regardless, however, of where the office of the maintenance manager is physically located, the office (and those of the other facility administrators) should be hardwired for communications and microcomputer networking.

There is little point in having the maintenance manager's office hardwired for data and communications if the work areas of the operatives are not. Thus, each of the main components of the O&M complex, such as the workshop area, storage for spare parts and supplies, and the administrative office, should similarly be hardwired for data and communications and should have a desk area that can accommodate a microcomputer and communications equipment.

With the exception of the manager's office as outlined above, ideally the rest of the maintenance offices and workshops will be grouped together in one of the service areas of the building. General characteristics of the O&M area include direct or easy access to the exterior of the building, preferably with a loading dock to facilitate the handling of deliveries, which will often arrive by truck. The landing area at the loading dock should be spacious enough to allow the easy movement of cargo pallets and bulky containers and to allow sorting and organization of materials being received before they are moved into storage.

The storerooms and workshop areas should be located close to each other. This will reduce work hours wasted in retrieving parts and supplies before they are used. In addition to easy access to the exterior of the building, the custodial complex should be easily accessible via wide and level (i.e., without impediments) corridors. Wherever feasible, the doors between service and storage areas should "line up" so custodial operatives do not have to turn corners with cumbersome loads.

Access to the central custodial complex and its various work and storage areas should be through double doors. If some material other than steel is used for these doors (e.g., for aesthetic reasons), they should be equipped with kick plates and bumper guards. The service or freight elevator, in the case of a multistory building, should also be situated in close proximity to facilitate logistic operations. Such elevators should have a ceiling, if possible, of 10 ft and should be as wide as possible. Quite simply, such elevators are going to have to handle the largest pieces of equipment being moved between floors of a multistory sports facility and should be planned accordingly. Such appropriate logistical considerations will typically yield dividends in the cost-efficient use of personnel and are discussed further below.

However, although easy access to the custodial complex is desirable, the area must still be secured against unauthorized entry. Bear in mind that the typical sports facility will have large numbers of participants and spectators passing through the building, and to have them enter service areas, either intentionally or otherwise, is undesirable.

These are the general guidelines for O&M facilities within the building. Each individual area is discussed below.

Maintenance Workshops

Among the most obvious concerns of the maintenance manager during the design phase of the sports facility are the work and support areas that the maintenance crews will use. The size and location of their work areas will significantly impact how well O&M workers can do their jobs. The argument could be made that perhaps the most important of all of the facilities in the custodial complex is the workshop area.

The workshop itself should be situated against an outside wall of the building in the service area, which will allow an exhaust fan to vent outdoors the hazardous fumes and odors generated by activities conducted within. Preferably it should also be situated immediately adjacent to the loading dock entrance and service reception area and have access to the core of the building.

The floor should be of hardened concrete and have a noncorrosive drain. There should also be sufficient open floor space between permanent fixtures such as the storage bins and shelving, workbench, and slop sink to allow free movement around large pieces of equipment that may be brought to the workshop for servicing. The door into the workshop area itself should be a lockable sheet metal-type without a floor sill or threshold. Because of the level of noise generated in the workshop area with power tools, the walls should be of sufficient thickness to inhibit the transmission of sound to surrounding spaces. The walls should also be finished with a stain-resistant and easy-to-clean surface.

As stated earlier, the actual size of the workshop area will depend on whether it is a self-contained operation and how much activity it will be required to handle. Regardless of the size, however, common characteristics should be considered. The first is a spacious workbench equipped with vises, small mounted power tools such as grinders, and a nonskid surface. The workbench area should be well lighted by fluorescent lighting in the 100-lumen range that is mounted directly overhead. There should be sufficient electrical outlets around the room, particularly in the workbench wall near the vises and bench-mounted power tools. Also, depending on the type of operation, sufficient floor space may be needed to mount freestanding equipment such as pipe threaders and certain types of woodworking tools.

The maintenance workshop area should be both air-conditioned and well ventilated. Because maintenance personnel use highly toxic and volatile substances such as paint, solvents, and cleaners, the workshop areas and central storage areas should have exhaust fans that operate automatically and are vented to the outside.

Another area that needs to be considered is the tool room (also known as a tool crib). Although maintenance workers frequently have a set of commonly used tools assigned to them, such as those contained in a lockable tool box, many specialized or expensive tools and equipment are not assigned to individual craftsmen on a permanent basis. Examples of the specialized tools required for building maintenance may include welding equipment, a variety of metering devices (e.g., volt meters), and certain power tools. Because these types of tools and equipment are typically high-value items, access needs to be controlled and sign-out procedures employed as with any other inventory item. It is therefore cost effective from a labor standpoint to have the tool room physically located near the workshop area and/or combined with other stockroom activities such as the spare parts storeroom.

Storage

Storage falls into a gray area between strictly O&M concerns and sports activity and program concerns. On the one hand, storage space is needed for tools, spare parts, and consumables, such as cleaning supplies and dispenser items (toilet paper, paper towels, and hand soap) to support O&M activities. On the other hand, sufficient storage space is needed to support program activities in the building, such as that required for sports equipment, uniforms, and ancillary activities.

Experienced administrators of the various activity programs and experienced supervisors of storage and distribution rooms agree that the most prevalent fault in the planning of these facilities is the failure to allocate sufficient space. As a result, programs suffer in one way or another, and students do not enjoy all of the benefits they should receive. Operations costs increase disproportionately. Thus, it is useful to consider all the storage requirements for a sports facility for both O&M and sports and activity programs concurrently.

Storage for O&M Operations

A wide variety of spare parts and consumable supplies is required to keep a building functioning properly. Examples of spare parts required for a typical sports complex can range from light bulbs, ballasts, filters, and fan belts for air-handling units to replacement modules for scoreboards. Consumables similarly include a wide variety of materials, ranging from equipment lubricants, chemicals such as chlorine for the pool, cleaning supplies required for custodial work, and dispenser items required for the restrooms and locker rooms. Secure tool storage and space for storing bulky maintenance equipment, such as scaffolding and/or hydraulic lifts, are also needed.

There are a number of considerations in determining the size and location of storage and supply rooms to support O&M operation. Obviously, whether the O&M operation is self-contained is one of them. Another is whether the supply room is run on an open-stock or closed-inventory basis and how much inventory is dispersed to other storage locations around the facility, such as in janitorial closets.

If the nature of the organization is such that the sports facilities are a self-contained operation, then the space required for the storage of O&M-related equipment and supplies will obviously be greater. More space must be set aside for larger quantities of tools and supplies and for bulky equipment such as scaffolding. If the sports facilities are, for example, part of a centralized O&M operation on a university campus, it is likely that the high-value tools and equipment, such as lifts and scaffolding, will be kept elsewhere at a central location.

Whether the supplies are run on an open-stock or closed-inventory basis is another consideration. Low-value, high-usage standard stock items such as nails, nuts and blocks, paints, and lubricants are frequently designated open-stock items. Maintenance personnel can obtain them directly from bins without a requisition form, and there is no control over who takes them or on what job they are used. Such items can be stored in the workshop area, for example, which will further enhance efficiency of the

O&M operation. Although such an arrangement reduces the need for separate storage space and an inventory clerk, it also invites increased pilferage by employees.

Perhaps the best use of an open-stock situation is in operations where maintenance is centralized, such as on a large university campus. As explained earlier, a central O&M complex likely will serve the whole campus with sufficient volume and value of materials to require a closed-inventory system within the central maintenance complex. Thus, the sports facility, which is at best a peripheral operation, will likely have a smaller workshop area and tool crib with an open stock of standard-issue items.

A self-contained sports facility, such as a municipal stadium or national sports complex, on the other hand, will likely have a closed-inventory system or a combined open-stock/closed-inventory system. Because high-value tools and spare parts required for O&M operation must be retained on the premises, access control and accountability, and thus an established inventory system and issue clerk, are necessary. However, in terms of operational efficiency, it still makes sense in this type of an operation to place items such as standard issue nuts and bolts in workshop areas and to disperse restroom cleaning supplies and equipment to the janitorial closets. The point is that the space given over to this storage will be markedly greater.

In terms of the physical characteristics of storage areas and supply rooms, these should be situated close to the areas that they service. For example, tool and spare parts issue should be close to the workshop area, with the space required determined by the criteria discussed above.

The storerooms require temperature and humidity control, as inventory items frequently have specific requirements for storage. The floors should be of hardened concrete with a nonslip surface that is easy to clean. The room should be brightly lighted with luminaries located between rows of shelving to ease identification of inventory, which is frequently described on small punch cards or tags affixed to the shelving.

For limited-access storage, there should be a distribution window that can be easily secured when the inventory clerk steps away from the service area to retrieve an item. Near the distribution window should be space enough for a desk and filing cabinet, which should be hardwired for communications and networked computer equipment (de Booji, 1993). The distribution window should have a counter upon which any transactions can be completed.

Doorway access to the stockroom should be planned to accommodate the largest pieces of equipment or machinery that will enter the area. Unless otherwise indicated, a doorway that is at least 60 in. wide and 84 in. high is recommended, with thresholds that are flush with the floor. The doors will also require good-quality, tamperproof locks and should be made of fire-resistant sheet metal.

Shelving is an obvious requirement for the storage of supplies and inventory. These requirements include adjustable steel shelving with a depth of between 18 in. and 24 in. and a width of 36 in. and 48 in. The first shelf should be at least 6 in. off the floor and the top shelf no less than 12 in. from the ceiling. Shelves should be adjustable and standard sizes used.

Sports Equipment Storage and Repair

In most sports facilities, storage and work areas for sports activity and team equipment are separate from those used for general facility O&M. Regardless, many of the physical descriptions of the space required and fixtures contained in the storage rooms used for spare parts and supplies in the O&M operations are also applicable to storage areas for the sports and activity program. It should be noted that virtually all professional teams and most collegiate programs have professional equipment managers whose responsibility includes inventory control and servicing of team clothing and equipment. Just as a maintenance professional should be included in the design process to review the facilities program from an O&M perspective, so too should the equipment manager be consulted with respect to sports equipment storage and repair areas.

It is recommended that the space given over to the storage of sports equipment include a small area to facilitate the repair of program-related equipment. A well-equipped work area can result in considerable savings over an extended period of time, and sports operations tend to work at a higher level of efficiency with this capability.

Examples of equipment that should be housed in a workshop of this type include a small workbench similarly equipped to that in the main facility workshop area described above. Some of the equipment will vary because the nature of the work to be done is different. Examples of equipment that should be included in this work area are racquet-stringing machines and sewing machines for uniforms. Additionally, the laundry facility will typically be located in or near the equipment manager's facility.

As custodial workers are frequently asked to set up and remove equipment used in various sports activities, of particular interest to the maintenance manager are the location and characteristics of equipment storage rooms situated about the building. Generally, an equipment storage facility should be located adjacent to each major activity area in the building. Each of these auxiliary storage units should be designed to accommodate equipment anticipated to be used in that particular area, such as hydraulic basketball and other game standards in the main gymnasium, racing lanes and recall lines in the swimming pool area, and gymnastics equipment and mats in their specific area. In all cases, design considerations include doors of sufficient size to accommodate bulky equipment (preferably "lined up" to reduce the number of corners to be negotiated when moving equipment), no door sills or thresholds, and appropriate shelving needs.

Janitorial Closets

The janitorial closet is the staging area for all custodial or housekeeping work. If the custodian works out of a room that is disorganized and dirty, it is likely that the cleaning effort will suffer accordingly. Also, much of the damage to custodial equipment occurs in the janitorial closet. Examples of this are how mop buckets are frequently wheeled into the closet and not emptied and how floor scrubbing equipment is not cleaned after use. Thus, janitorial closets should be designed to facilitate custodial work (Sawyer, 2009). A number of variables need to be considered to determine the number of janitorial closets needed:

- the number of floors within the facility,
- the type of floor finishes to be maintained,
- the proposed use of the areas, and
- the number of restrooms in the facility.

There should be at least one 6-sq m custodial room for each 930 sq m of floor space and at least one such room on each floor of the facility. The room should be designed with a large enough open area where equipment can be assembled and checked and janitorial carts properly stocked prior to starting a job (Sawyer, 2009; Walker, 1990). Each janitorial closet should have a service sink with a pop-up drain and a temperature-mixing type of faucet; floor sinks are preferable to large wall sinks for this purpose. Shelves and hanging boards should be constructed in each janitorial closet to facilitate the storage of supplies and tools (Flynn, 1985, 1993; Sawyer, 2009). Hanging boards, however, should be designed so that wet mops do not rest flush against the wall. Last, the janitorial closet should have a good level of illumination (at least 50 lumens) so that equipment can be properly cleaned after the job and before being stowed and the fine print on chemical containers can be read (Sawyer, 2009; Walker, 1990).

Although the foregoing is a general guide to the dimensions required for janitorial closets, the general rule of thumb is that the closet should have sufficient space both relative and particular to the area that is being served. High-volume activity areas with greater traffic flow have greater requirements and will need a larger space to accommodate the supplies and equipment needed to properly service them (Bronzan, 1974; Sawyer, 2009). Additionally, areas serviced on a 7-day cleaning schedule will require 35% to 40% more supplies than those cleaned on a 5-day schedule, which would suggest a larger space allocation.

The size of a janitorial closet should be determined not only by the area being serviced, but also by the open floor space required to store floor maintenance equipment. A closet located in a corridor that features tile flooring would require an area large enough for power scrubbing equipment, whereas one in the vicinity of a carpeted office complex could get by with the smaller area required for a commercial-grade vacuum cleaner. Janitorial closets should also be located in or next to restroom and locker room complexes for a number of reasons. First, this location provides a water and sewage source for the mop sink and thus is cost effective from a design and construction standpoint. The second reason is that locker rooms and restrooms typically must be cleaned more often, and work hours are saved if the supplies and equipment are positioned near these areas. Finally, such a location facilitates storage of restroom cleaners, maintenance supplies, and dispenser stock.

A small room should also be located near each entrance of the building to store maintenance supplies and tools (Flynn, 1985, 1993; Sawyer, 2009). Quite simply, everyone who enters or leaves the building will do so through one or more designated entries, which leads to excessive wear in these areas. The first 12 feet on the inside of an entry doorway is called "the walk-off area" and functions exactly as the name implies: It is within this radius that dust, dirt, oil from the parking lot, and water from rain and melting snow are deposited. Thus, a well-conceived maintenance plan will call for the regular policing of this area to prevent soiling materials from spreading beyond the walk-off area. To facilitate this frequent cleaning, a small custodial storage area should be situated nearby.

The failure to provide janitorial closets in the proper location and of the proper size can be illustrated by the following example. A building was constructed in which the janitorial closets were only 1.5 sq m in size, most of which was taken up by the mop sink. As a result, most of the supplies and power cleaning equipment had to be stored in the basement of the building, and carting supplies and equipment to the place where they were needed each night amounted to 30 hr of labor per 5-night workweek. This amounted to an additional three fourths of a worker-year labor expense, which would have been unnecessary if the facility had been properly planned. Additionally, because of operating conditions that arose from this situation, pilferage of supplies and theft of equipment increased, leading to the additional requirements of building a lock-up room in the basement of the building and the administrative controls (and expense) to run it.

Laundry Room

In most physical education, sports, and recreational facilities, it is now more cost effective to establish in-house laundry facilities than to contract out for cleaning uniforms and towel services. As the operation of the laundry most frequently devolves to the custodial staff, and the laundry facility itself is most likely to be situated within the maintenance support areas of the building, it is appropriate to consider planning guidelines for the laundry operation along with the rest of the O&M facilities.

The laundry facility should be physically located on the ground level of the building against an outside wall to facilitate venting of the dryer. Nonskid concrete floors are recommended because the floors in the laundry should be hardened and impervious to water. Floors should be sloped to a drain trough that leads to noncorrosive drains. The slope should be ⅛ in. per linear foot. The planarity of the floor is important because puddles can be dangerous. Floor materials should extend up the walls at least 12 in., with corners rounded or covered. The thickness of the floor should comply with the equipment manufacturer's recommendations, but in any case, the floor should be able to withstand heavy, vibrating equipment.

As with other maintenance and service areas, the laundry facility should have double-hinged double doors without a threshold or a sill to facilitate the installation of laundry equipment during construction and the subsequent movement of laundry carts and supplies in and out of the premises. As a laundry room is a noisy place, the walls and ceilings should have good sound absorption or nontransmission properties yet be impervious to water. The wall finish should also be easy to clean and stain resistant.

Although the floor space required for the laundry is contingent upon the size of the machines and the projected workload, sufficient space should be included in the plan for the storage of supplies and sorting/folding tables. Sawyer (2009) provided guidelines by noting that the size of the laundry facility is determined by the size of the workload. The capacity of laundry equipment is determined by weight (pound). To calculate the number and the size of the machines that will be required, compare the anticipated daily quantities of articles to be cleaned multiplied by their respective weights with the poundage capacity of the machines under consideration, which will give the number of loads they can handle per day. Most process formulas will handle two loads per hour. Facilities with multiple goods classifications (i.e., nylon game uniforms and cotton-blend towels) should opt for two or more machines. Drying equipment needs to be matched up with the washers/extractors and typically has a larger capacity. For example, a 50-lb dryer is a good match with a 35-lb washer.

Once the number and types of machines have been determined, it is a relatively simple matter to size them, as the dimensions of the units can be easily obtained from prospective vendors. The machines should be mounted a minimum of 2 ft away from the walls and with a minimum of 18 in. between machines. Generally, however, sufficient space should be left around them for circulation and work and for equipment servicing as required. Combine this with the space required for processing the work and storage to determine the net usable footage required for the laundry.

As with all equipment, access to utilities needs to be considered in the plan. Hot and cold water, sewage, and electricity are obvious, and gas dryers are the most cost efficient to use, so an appropriate hookup is in order. The room should also have good ventilation and air circulation in addition to outdoor vents for exhaust generated by the equipment.

In terms of the equipment itself, programmable microprocessor controls on the laundry equipment are highly recommended. Also recommended are liquid detergent supply systems that can provide preset, automatic injections of chemicals; as such, devices may serve to remove judgment calls by operators, especially if the operators are part-time helpers (e.g., students; Lizarraga, 1991; Sawyer, 2009).

Generic Concerns for Building Maintenance

Although the foregoing discussion focused on the design parameters of the facilities specifically required for the O&M effort, aspects of sports facility design as a whole should be considered from the maintenance standpoint. These are nonspecific issues that can nonetheless produce significant operating costs. Many of these considerations are simple, yet because of their very simplicity, they are easily overlooked as more obvious design considerations hold the attention of the architect and design committee.

We have touched on matters such as building logistics in discussing the custodial complex, yet so much staff time is spent moving equipment around the typical sports facility that further, more specific attention is warranted. Simple accessibility to equipment and fixtures requiring maintenance tends to get short shrift in the design process, with potentially disastrous consequences.

Standardizing Building Fixtures and Equipment

By now it should be clear that the variety of building finishes, fixtures, and equipment in a multipurpose sports facility can be staggering. Similarly, the need to inventory and control spare parts and consumable supplies for the maintenance effort can be a large undertaking. However, a conscious effort to standardize building fixtures and equipment during the design phase can significantly reduce the costs of acquiring and carrying building spares.

Such reductions are accomplished in two ways. The first is the direct savings realized through a reduction in stocking spare parts. Standardization of finishes and fixtures allows the maintenance manager to reduce the number of items carried in the spare part inventory, which means a smaller financial burden in carrying costs. As a simple example, consider the effect of standardizing light fixtures. If all the fluorescent light fixtures in the building are the same, the number and variety of ballasts and lighting tubes that must be kept on hand can be considerably smaller than if there were a variety of different fixtures scattered throughout the building. Standardization also prevents the cost of wasted labor that results from bringing the wrong replacement tube to the fixture; the chances of this increase with a wide disparity in fixtures.

The second reduction is more indirect, but significant nonetheless. A smaller inventory requires less room for storage. Additionally, a smaller inventory is easier to administer and control, reducing administrative costs and loss through mishandling and pilferage. Concerted efforts can be made in many areas in standardizing building fixtures, including light fixtures and switches, breaker switches and boxes, bathroom fixtures and dispensers, locker room equipment, door hardware, locks and keys, and movable equipment.

Logistical Concerns

Operating costs can also be realized by accounting for the needs of the maintenance staff in logistical operations. A logistical operation pertains to the handling of furnishings, equipment, and materials within the facility.

One area that tends to distinguish sports facilities from other types of buildings is the nature of the equipment contained within. A multistation weight machine is, by its very nature, a heavy and bulky piece of equipment to move around, particularly without disassembly. Gymnastics apparatus and mats, wrestling mats, and portable basketball goals are other examples of heavy, unusually configured equipment that is frequently moved around the building. An awareness of these characteristics is important during the design phase of the facility. For example (as stated on several occasions already), the doors between spaces should line up to reduce cornering, and the doors from the loading dock (or main access from the exterior of the building) and equipment storage rooms should be double doors with flush sills and sufficient height to facilitate equipment movement.

Other design considerations from a purely operational point of view include using ramps between levels in the sports hall, provided the change in level is not too significant. Another approach is to ensure that freight or building service elevators are of sufficient size (including height) to facilitate the movement of equipment between floors. Similarly, making stairwells and landings large enough to handle bulky items, such as boxes of supplies or furniture, will help with logistical concerns.

Last, the design phase must recognize all the activities that will take place within the facility. For example, food service or concessions within the building will require the movement of groceries into and garbage out of the building, preferably through service passages.

The author is aware of one sports facility in southwest Asia that was built at a cost in excess of $80 million, in which virtually all of these concerns were ignored in the preliminary plan. Fortunately, once construction was underway, a design review was able to rectify the worst of the errors, but only at considerable additional expense. Had not the design errors been caught, the only access to a second-floor food-service facility would have been via the VIP elevator. A worker seeking to get on board with a bag of garbage when the elevator was already occupied by a member of the Royal Family would have been problematic at best. Similarly, the design included three steps between each wing of the building and no way to move equipment between them. It was a situation rectified by the addition of a ramp after the fact.

Access of Building Operating Equipment

As unfortunate as the logistical situation was in this facility, service access to building operating systems was even worse. There was no way to access light and sound fixtures over the pool or the gymnasium floor because of a novel roof design.

The roof in the facility was a translucent, Teflon®-coated fiberglass structure designed as an Arabian tent. But the design did not include access by service passages or catwalks to the fixtures suspended from the ceiling. Lights were changed, for example, by erecting scaffolding or using a personal hydraulic lift, both of which were expensive and time consuming. Unfortunately, the hydraulic lift could not be used in the pool area, which necessitated the erection of scaffolding in the swimming pool. Thus, the only way to change the lights was to drain the pool. This is a classic case of the architect's placing aesthetics before the more pragmatic and mundane concerns of operating the building, with costly consequences.

The point of this discussion is that maintenance requirements of building operating systems must be considered during the design of a facility. By accounting for operational requirements such as easy access to equipment, particularly control panels and lubrication ports, which require frequent attention, accompanying labor costs can be substantially reduced.

Utilities

In addition to access to control panels and operating systems for routine maintenance, the astute placement of electrical outlets for cleaning equipment and water spigots for hoses can effectively reduce labor hours in the maintenance effort.

Most floor care equipment requires electrical outlets, whether they are power scrubbers or vacuum cleaners. Therefore, the placement of electrical outlets needs consideration, particularly in corridors, lobbies, and activity areas. Inappropriately situated outlets can cause considerable additional operating expense, both for labor (the need to continually move power cords) and for supplies (the need to purchase excessive numbers of extension cords). Additionally, the need for exterior outlets on the building should not be overlooked. For example, certain types of window washing equipment require access to power, as do many other types of maintenance and custodial equipment, such as blowers for grass clippings.

Water spigots on the exterior of the building should be treated similarly to electrical outlets on the interior of the building. Water hoses are commonly used for washing down sidewalks and exterior windows, particularly those located near the ground. Thus, careful consideration to the number and placement of spigots similarly warrants close attention in the design phase.

Windows

The whole topic of windows deserves special mention. The arrangement and proportioning of windows is called fenestration. Consideration of the relationships of lighting, color, use of materials, acoustics, and climate control cannot ignore the importance of fenestration. The size and placement of windows cannot be left to chance, personal whims, or merely traditional use.

The generous use of windows has been in vogue in the past few decades, at least in part because of the pleasing visual effects obtained by the architect. But the excessive use of glass in a sports facility may give rise to a host of problems, including high operating costs from heat gain and loss and inordinate cleaning costs.

Glass is a poor insulator. It causes significant heat gain during summer months through the greenhouse effect and a corresponding increase in air-conditioning costs. During the winter, the process is reversed, and large glass areas cause significant heat loss with a similar increase in operating costs. Similarly, large amounts of glass tend to increase maintenance costs as dirt is more visible. Any person who has glass patio doors, for example, can attest to how much attention they require when weather conditions make handprints and streaks more visible. In commercial buildings such as sports facilities, the amount of cleaning required depends on many variables, such as the local environment (rainfall, dust, and pollution) and the extent of the maintenance effort (i.e., how dirty you are willing to let the glass get).

Two basic methods are usually used for window cleaning: "over the roof" or "up from the ground." In both cases, special equipment is required for any structure in excess of one story. The cost for these systems can vary from as little as $15 for a garden hose and squeegee with a 6-ft handle to as much as $50,000 for a scaffold for "over the roof" work. Regardless of the system used, plans for water and electrical power sources for window washing equipment should be included in the design phase.

It should be noted that in sports facilities, if windows are to be incorporated in the design, they should be at least one sixteenth of the floor area. Additionally, it is recommended that windows be placed nearer the ceiling than the floor. For a multipurpose gymnasium designed to accommodate both international-level volleyball and team handball, the minimum total area of glass windows would be approximately 66 sq m (over 700 sq ft) located some 7 m to 12 m (22 ft to 40 ft) off the ground. Under these circumstances, accessibility and labor costs related to maintaining an appropriate appearance must be considered during the design phase.

Returning to the sports facility in southwest Asia cited earlier, the architect achieved a stunning visual effect with a bank of blue-tinted windows 2 m wide and 50 m long extending the length of the sports hall wall some 15 m from the ground and cantilevered at an angle of approximately of 140° to the roof line. However, the design made accessing the windows extremely difficult, and in the 6 years that the author observed the building, the windows were never washed. The result was an originally unique visual effect that was severely degraded because the design did not consider maintenance.

References

410 IAC 6-2-1.

410 IAC 20-1-5.

AAU Hockey. (2012). Hockey rule book. Retrieved from http://aauhockey.org/

Abendroth, T. (2011). Competitive advantage. *PanStadia, 17*(2), 166–170.

Abendroth, T. (2012). Indoor hardwood sport surfacing: More to it than meets the eye. Retrieved from http://www.action-floors.com/pdfs/HardwoodSportSurfacing.pdf

Access Board. (2012). Uniform federal accessibility standards. Retrieved from http://www.access-board.gov/ufas/ufas-html/ufas.htm#4.32

Achampong, F. (1999). *Workplace sexual harassment law.* Westport, CT: Quorum Books.

Action Floor Systems. (2012). Sports flooring safety standards. Retrieved October 16, 2012, from http://www.actionfloors.com

AEDs now required in New York schools. (2010). Retrieved from http://www.padl.org/articles.php3?id=aedsnyschools.htm

Agoglia, J. (2004, January). State of the industry: Taking the industries pulse for 2003–2004. *Club Industry, 14*(1), 17–20.

Agron, J. (2001a, April). Dwindling support. *American School & University: Facilities, Purchasing and Business Administration, 24*(4), 24, 26–28, 30, 32.

Agron, J. (2001b, April). Rising to the challenge. *American School & University: Facilities, Purchasing and Business Administration, 24*(4), 50b, 50d, 50f, 50h.

AHRI Air-Conditioning, Heating, and Refrigeration Institute. (n.d.). HVAC in sport facilities. Retrieved from http://www.ahrinet.org/hvacr+industry+standards.aspx

Ahrweiler, M. (2001, January/February). Extremely mainstream. *Recreation Management, 12*(1), 12–17.

Ahrweiler, M. (2004). Special supplement: Recreation management's complete guide to sports surfaces and flooring. *Recreation Management.* Retrieved from http://recmanagement.com/features.php?fid=200407fe00&ch=2

American Academy of Orthopaedic Surgeons. (2007). *First responder* (4th ed.). Sudbury, MA: Jones and Bartlett.

American Academy of Orthopaedic Surgeons. (2009). *Athletic training and sports medicine.* Sudbury, MA: Jones and Bartlett.

The American Institute of Architects. (2007). *Architectual graphic standards* (11th ed.). Hoboken, NJ: Wiley & Sons.

American Public Health Association. (2009). *ATSDR: Safeguarding community from chemical exposure report.* Atlanta, GA: Department of Health and Human Services.

American Red Cross. (2001). *Emergency response.* Yardley, PA: Staywell.

American Red Cross. (2007). *Lifeguarding.* Yardley, PA: Staywell.

American Safety and Health Institute. (2007). *Complete emergency care.* Champaign, IL: Human Kinetics.

American Society for Testing and Materials. (1995). *Standard consumer safety performance specification for playground equipment for public use* (F1487). West Conshohocken, PA: Author.

American Society for Testing and Materials. (2007). *Standard consumer safety performance specification for playground equipment for public use* (F1487). West Conshohocken, PA: Author.

American Society for Testing and Materials. (2008). *Standard consumer safety performance specification for public use play equipment for children six months to 23 months.* West Conshohocken, PA: Author.

American Society for Testing and Materials. (2009). *Standard test method for shock-absorbing properties of playing surface safety systems and materials.* West Conshohocken, PA: Author.

American Society for Testing and Materials. (2012). *Standard guide for construction and maintenance of warning track areas on athletic fields* (F 2207) . West Conshohocken, PA: Author.

American Society of Landscape Architects. (n.d.-a). Sustainable design. Retrieved from http://www.asla.org/sustainabledesign.aspx

American Society of Landscape Architects. (n.d.-b). What are sustainable landscapes. Retrieved from http://www.asla.org/sustainablelandscapes/about.html

American Society of Landscape Architects. (1998). Landscape architecture. Retrieved from http://www.asla.org/asla

American Sports Engineering and Testing Services. (2006). *Why switching from 'DIN' to 'EN' makes sense in North America* (Educational Document # POS-002). Retrieved from http://www.asetservices.com/Documents/POS-002_DIN_vs_EN.pdf

American Volleyball Coaches Association. (2012, August). GCU adds women's sand volleyball for 2013. Retrieved from http://www.avca.org/articles/index.cfm?action=view&articleID=3763&menuID=1921

American Volleyball Coaches Association. (n.d.). NCAA sand volleyball rules modifications. Retrieved from http://www.avca.org/includes/media/docs/SAND-VOLLEYBALL-NCAA-RULES-MODIFICATIONS3(11).pdf

Americans With Disabilities Act of 1990, Pub. L. No. 101-336, 2, 104 Stat. 328 (1991).

Ames, M. (2001). More elbow, leg room? Invesco has it. *Rocky Mountain News.* Retrieved from http://web.archive.org/web/20060722000347/http://www.denver-rmn.com/invesco/seats.shtml

AMI Graphics. (n.d.). Padded wrappings. Retrieved from http://www.ami-graphics.com/1padwraps.php

Ammon, R., Jr., Southall, R. M., & Blair, D. A. (2004). *Sport facility management: Organizing events and mitigating risks.* Morgantown, WV: Fitness Information Technology.

Andriesen, D. (2007, March 20). Arenas and elephants: How much is too much? Retrieved from http://seattlepi.nwsources.com/basketball/308250_arena20.html

Andrus, S. (1990). Manual labor. *CAM Magazine, 2*(5), 61–64.

Ankeney, J. (2005, April). Large-format LED displays. *Sound & Video Contractor, 23*(4), 54–56.

Anonymous. (1998). Making indoor air quality work for you. *Public Management, 80*(8), A10.

Appenzeller, H. (2000). Risk assessment and reduction. In H. Appenzeller & G. Lewis (Eds.), *Successful sport management* (2nd ed.; pp. 313–321). Durham, NC: Carolina Academic Press.

Archery. (2004). In *American Heritage Dictionary*. Retrieved from http://ahdictionary.com/

Armitage-Johnson, S. L. (1994). Equipment maintenance. In T. R. Baechle (Ed.), *Essentials of strength training and conditioning*. Champaign, IL: Human Kinetics.

Arnheim, D. D., & Prentice, W. E. (2010). *Principles of athletic training* (9th ed.). Boston, MA: WCB/McGraw-Hill.

ASHRAE. (2006). Standards and guidelines. Retrieved from https://www.ashrae.org/standards-research--technology/standards--guidelines

Association for Challenge Course Technology. (2012). *ACCT standards for challenge courses and canopy/zip line tours*. Deerfield, IL: Author.

Association for Challenge Course Technology. (2012). *Technical operations and inspection standards*. Deerfield, IL: Author.

Atchison, J. (2003). Top 10 annuals for landscaping. *Sportsturf, 19*(7), 30.

Author. (1992, November). Blowing hot air. *Energy Ideas, 1*(5), 1–7.

Author. (1993, February). It's a small world after all. *Energy Ideas, 1*(8), 6–8.

Author. (1993, March). Sports vs. efficiency (OT). *Energy Ideas, 1*(9), 8–9.

Author. (2003). ASHRAE studies impact of IAC on classroom performance. *HVAC/R Industry News*. Retrieved from http://www.hvacmall.com/news

Author. (2003). CREON2000 disinfection unit studied under NIH grant. *HVAC/R Industry News*. Retrieved from http://www.hvacmall.com/news

Author. (2003). Sanuvox ultraviolet air purifier reduces school district air contaminants by 66%. *HVAC/R Industry News*. Retrieved from http://www.hvacmall.com/news

Aquatics International. (2012). *The history of aquatics* (3rd ed.). Los Angeles, CA: Hanely-Wood.

Azar, B. (1999). The top ten most common mistakes that retailers make. *Employee Services Management, 42*(3), 37–38.

Bachrach, E. (2013). Football teams seem nervous about moving to downtown LA. *Curbed Los Angeles*. Retrieved from http://la.curbed.com/archives/2013/01/football_teams_seem_nervous_about_moving_to_downtown_la.php

Baechle, T. R. (Ed.). (1994). *Essentials of strength training and conditioning*. Champaign, IL: Human Kinetics.

Bannon, J. J. (1978). *Leisure resources: Its comprehensive planning*. Englewood Cliffs, NJ: Prentice Hall.

Barkley, J. T. (1997). Surfacing. *Cornerstones: A Fitness, Recreational Facility and Parks and Recreation Web Magazine*. Retrieved from http://www.sandfordgroup.com/

Beijing Olympics. (2008). Retrieved from http://en.beijing2008.cn

Bellamy, R. (1998). *Mediasport*. New York, NY: Routledge.

Bellar, D., Judge, L. W. Patrick, T., & Craig, B. (2013). Efficacy of the use of fractional plates during maximum strength testing for the bench press and strict curl lifts. *Applied Research in Coaching and Athletics Annual, 28*, 143-157.

Ben-Joseph, E. (2012). *Rethinking a lot: The design and culture of parking*. Cambridge, MA: MIT Press.

Bennis, W., & Nanus, B. (1997). *Leaders: Strategies for taking charge*. New York, NY: HarperBusiness.

Berry, D. W. (1990). Maryland study shows simple signage works. *Aquatics, 2*(6), 16–20.

Berryhill, T. C. (1985). Service areas. In R. B. Flynn (Ed.), *Planning facilities for athletics, physical education, and recreation* (8th ed.). Reston, VA: The Athletic Institute and American Alliance for Health, Physical Education, Recreation, and Dance.

Bevan, R. (1956). *The athletic trainer's handbook*. Englewood Cliffs, NJ: Prentice Hall.

Bishop, G. (2013). A company that runs prisons will have its name on a stadium. *New York Times*. Retrieved from http://www.nytimes.com/2013/02/20/sports/ncaafootball/a-company-that-runs-prisons-will-have-its-name-on-a-stadium.html?pagewanted=all&_r=0

Bishop, W. (1997). Athletic flooring. *Cornerstones: A Fitness Recreational Facility and Parks and Recreation Web Magazine*. Retrieved from http://www.sandfordgroup.com/

Boeh, T. (1989). A program for selling. *CAM Magazine, 3*(10), 53–55.

Bower, M. (1980). *Foil fencing* (4th ed.). Dubuque, IA: Wm. C. Brown.

Bowers, L. (1988). Playground design: A scientific approach. In L. D. Bruya (Ed.), *Play spaces for children: A new beginning* (pp. 22–48). Reston, VA: American Alliance for Health, Physical Education, Recreation, and Dance.

Branvold, S. E. (1992). The utilization of fence signage in college baseball. *Sport Marketing Quarterly, 1*(2), 29–32.

Breems, M. (2001). Quality above depends on quality below. *Sportsturf, 17*(12), 10.

Brickman, H. (1997, November). Helping hardwood perform. *Athletic Business, 21*(11), 67–70, 72.

Bridges, F. J., & Roquemore, L. L. (1999). *Management for athletic/sport administration* (2nd ed.). Decatur, GA: ESM Books.

Broadhag, K. (2006, June). Purchasing used strength equipment. *Fitness Management*. Retrieved from http://fitnessmanagement.com/articles/article.aspx?articielid=1804&zoneid=13

Broadhag, K (2012, May). New ADA requirements affect fitness facilities. Retrieved from http://clubindustry.com/stepbystep/design/new-ada-requirements-affect-fitness-facilities-20120310

Bronzan, R. T., & Stotlar, D. K. (1992). *Public relations and promotion in sport*. Daphne, AL: United States Sports Academy.

Brown, A. (2006, January). Grain power. *Athletic Business, 30*(1), 32–34, 36, 38–40.

Brown, B. J. (1972). *Complete guide to the prevention and treatment of athletic injuries*. West Nyack, NY: Parker Publishing.

Brown, G. (2003, August). Increased retention with entertainment systems. *Fitness Management, 10*(1), 32–33.

Brown, G. (2007, October). Investing in free weights. *Fitness Management, 23*(10), 48–51.

Brown, M. T. (2003). Risk identification and reduction. In D. J. Cotten & J. Wolohan (Eds.), *Law for recreation and sport managers* (3rd ed.; pp. 308–319). Dubuque, IA: Kendall-Hunt.

Brownell, E. O. (1999). How to keep your service edge. *Employee Services Management, 41*(5), 39–40.

Bruya, L., & Wood, G. (1997). Why provide supervision on the playgrounds. In S. Hudson & D. Thompson (Eds.), *Playground safety handbook* (pp. 38–48). Cedar Falls, IA: National Program for Playground Safety.

Bucher, C. A., & Krotee, M. L. (1993). *Management of physical education and sport* (10th ed.). Boston, MA: Mosby Year Book.

Busiman, K. Thompson, A. F., & Cox, A. T. (1992, July). Risk management. *Athletic Management, 15*(7), 3, 10–16

Butler, E. (2003). Roller skating rinks still feelin' groovy despite changing times. *New Orleans City Business.* Retrieved from EBSCO Publishing. (Accession No. 9372281)

Byl, J. (1990). *Organizing successful tournaments.* Champaign, IL: Leisure Press.

Bynum, M. (2003, November). Clean sweep. *Athletic Business, 27*(11), 86–88, 90, 92.

Bynum, M. (2004a, July). Continental divide. *Athletic Business, 28*(7), 84–86, 88, 90, 92.

Bynum, M. (2004b, November). Analyze these. *Athletic Business, 28*(11), 131–134, 136.

Bynum, M. (2006, November). Sports surfaces: A new, comprehensive guideline tests the DIN standard. *Athletic Business.* Retrieved from http://upload.athleticbusiness.com/articles/article.aspx?articleid=1298&zoneid=41

Bynum, M. (2007, September). Outside help. *Athletic Business.* Retrieved from http://athleticbusiness.com/articles/article.aspx?articleid=1627&zoneid=39

Catalano, J. (2012, February/March). Floor factors. *Athletic Management.* Retrieved from http://www.athleticmanagement.com/2012/02/28/floor_factors/index.php

Centers for Disease Control and Prevention. (2011). Healthy water. Retrieved from http://www.cdc.gov/healthywater/swimming/

Civil Rights Act of 1964, 42 U.S.C. § 2000e-5–2000e-9.

Clayton, R. D., & Thomas, D. G. (1989). *Professional aquatic management* (2nd ed.). Champaign, IL: Human Kinetics.

Clement, A. (1988). *Law in sport and physical activity.* Indianapolis, IN: Benchmark Press.

Codring v. Board of Education of Manhasset Union Free School Dist., 435 N.Y.S. 2nd 52 (App. Div. 1981).

Cohen, A. (1991). Back to the future. *Athletic Business, 15*(7), 31–37.

Cohen, A. (1993). Security check. *Athletic Business, 17*(3), 41–44.

Cohen, A. (1998, September). Beneath the surface. *Athletic Business, 16*(9), 56–58, 60–62, 64, 66.

Cohen, A. (2000, July). Feet first. *Athletic Business, 18*(5), 47–48, 50, 52, 54–55.

Cohen, A. (2002a, May). Reflections. *Athletic Business, 18*(7), 48–50, 52–55.

Cohen, A. (2002b, November). Keeping up appearances. *Athletic Business, 18*(11), 105–108.

Cohen, A. (2003, April). Out of the box. *Athletic Business, 19*(4), 71–76, 78.

Cohen, A. (2008, September). The layered look. *Athletic Business, 32*(9), 52–54.

Cohen, A. (2008, October). Nerves of steel. *Athletic Business.* Retrieved from http://athleticbusiness.com/articles/article.aspx?articleid=1880&zoneid=50

Cohen, A. (2012). Press start: Touch screens and networks are revolutionizing the design of cardio consoles, transforming the user experience. *Athletic Business, 36*(9), 57–62.

Compass Resource Management. (2011). *Towards a green building and infrastructure investment fund.* Retrieved from http://www.compassrm.com/energy&infrastructure/

Conklin, A. R. (1999). Facility follies. *Athletic Business, 23*(9), 28–30.

Cooper, J. (2004, July). The changing face of sports surface selection. Retrieved from http://www.sandfordgroup.com/

Cordell, H. K. (2012). *Outdoor recreation trends and futures: A technical document supporting the Forest Service 2010 RPA Assessment* (Gen. Tech. Rep. SRS-150). Asheville, NC: U.S. Department of Agriculture Forest Service, Southern Research Station. Retrieved from http://www.srs.fs.usda.gov/pubs/gtr/gtr_srs150.pdf

Council on Physical Education for Children. (2001). *Guidelines for facilities, equipment, and instructional materials in elementary physical education.* Reston, VA: National Association for Sport and Physical Education.

Craig, B. W., & Judge, L. W. (2009). The basics of resistance program design: Where do I start? *Strength and Conditioning, 31*(6), 75-77.

Crabtree, C. (2013). Cleveland Browns to sell naming rights to stadium. *NBC Sports: Pro Football Talks.* Retrieved from http://profootballtalk.nbcsports.com/2013/01/15/cleveland-browns-to-sell-naming-rights-to-stadium/

Cuneen, J., & Hannan, M. J. (1993). Intermediate measures and recognition testing of sponsorship advertising at an LPGA tournament. *Sport Marketing Quarterly, 2*(1), 47–56.

Dahlgren, S. (2000a, September). LED technology brings fans closer than ever to the action. *Athletic Business.* Retrieved from http://www.athleticbusiness.com/articles/article.aspx?articleid=24&zoneid=20

Dahlgren, S. (2000b, November). Grade of wood can significantly impact sports-facility aesthetics. *Athletic Business.* Retrieved from http://www.athleticbusiness.com/articles/article.aspx?articleid=36&zoneid=25

Dahnert, R., & Pack, A. (2007) Behind the scenes. *American School and University.* Retrieved July 1, 2007, from http://asumag.com/construction/athetics/University_behind_scenes_3

Danielson, M. N. (1997). Newer, bigger, better. In M. N. Danielson (Ed.), *Home team: Professional sports and the American metropolis* (pp. 37–49). Princeton, NJ: Princeton University Press.

DaSilva, V. (2011). How to develop an HVAC maintenance checklist [Blog post]. Retrieved from http://www.goodway.com/hvac-blog/index.php/2011/06/how-to-develop-an-hvac-maintenance-checklist/

Davidson, P. (2007). It's lights out for traditional bulbs. *USA Today.* Retrieved from http://www.usatoday.com/money/industries/energy/environment/2007-12-16-light-bulbs_N.htm

Dea, F. (2008, August). An outsourcing checklist. *Associations Now, 4*(9), 35–35.

Di Pilla, S. (2001, April). Minimizing 'slip & fall.' *Facilities Design and Management, 14*(4), 48.

Donahue, L. (2013). How to design roller skating rinks. Retrieved from http://www.ehow.com/how_6087703_design-roller-skating-rinks.html

Dougherty, N. J., & Bonanno, D. (1985). *Management principles in sport and leisure services.* Minneapolis, MN: Burgess Publishing.

Drezner, J., Rogers, K., Sennet, B., & Zimmer, R. (2005). Use of automated external defibrillators at NCAA Division I universities. *Medicine & Science in Sports & Exercise, 37*(9), 1487–1492.

Dymecki, D., & Stevens, T. (2007). Facility operators and designers rethink the locker room. *Athletic Business.* Retrieved April 27, 2007, from http://www.athletic business.com/articles/article.aspx?articleid=1495&zoneid=16

Eickoff-Shemek, J. (2002). Minimizing legal liability: Risk management for health fitness facilities (Part 2) [Videotape]. Risk Management for Health/Fitness Programs and Facilities. Standards and Guidelines. Champaign, IL: Human Kinetics.

Eisen, M., John-Baptiste, E. P., Phillips, D., & Berger, J. (2012). 2012 New York Giants information guide. Retrieved from http://prod.static.giants.clubs.nfl.com/assets/docs/pdf/2012-New-York-Giants-Media-Guide.pdf

Ellis and Associates. (2007). *International lifeguard training program* (3rd ed.). Sudbury, MA: Jones & Bartlett.

Energy Independence and Security Act of 2007, Pub. L. No. 110-140, 141 Stat. 1492.

Ensman, R. G., Jr. (1999). Fun and games: Solving problems with playful brainstorming techniques. *Employee Services Management, 42*(2), 9–10.

ESPN Sports Business. (2004). Stadium names. Retrieved from http://espn.go.com/sportsbusiness/s/stadiumnames.html

Evenden, E. S., Strayer, G. D., & Englehardt, N. I. (1938). *Standards for college buildings.* New York, NY: Teachers College, Columbia University.

Ewing, S. (1999). Music influences consumers to buy. *Employee Services Management, 42*(3), 5–6.

FAC 64E-9.018.

Farmer, P. J., Mulrooney, A. L., & Ammon, R., Jr. (1996). *Sport facility planning and management.* Morgantown, WV: Fitness Information Technology.

Farmer, P. J., Mulrooney, A. L., & Ammon, R., Jr. (1999). *Sport facility planning and management.* Morgantown, WV: Fitness Information Technology.

Farrell, P., & Lundegren, H. M. (1978). *The process of recreation programming: Theory and technique.* New York, NY: John Wiley & Sons.

Fawcett, P. (2005). *Aquatic facility management.* Champaign, IL: Human Kinetics.

Fischer, D., & Ozanian, M. (1999, October 20). Cowboy capitalism. *Forbes, 164,* 171–177.

Fitzemeyer, T. (2000, October). Airing it out. *American School & University: Facilities, Purchasing and Business Administration, 16*(10), 20, 22, 25.

Flynn, R. B. (Ed.). (1985). *Planning facilities for athletics, physical education and recreation* (7th ed.). Reston, VA: American Alliance for Health, Physical Education, Recreation, and Dance.

Flynn, R. B. (1993). *Facility planning for physical education, recreation, and athletics.* Reston, VA: The Facilities Council of the Association for Research, Administration, Professional Councils, and Societies.

Ford, R. (2006). *Certified pool operator handbook.* Colorado Springs, CO: National Swimming Pool Foundation.

Forseth, E. A. (1986, Spring). Consideration in planning small college athletic training facilities. *Athletic Training, 4*(2), 23–25.

Francesconi, P. (2012). *Tennis courts: A construction and maintenance manual* (7th ed.). Ellicott City, MD: American Sports Builders Association and the United States Tennis Association.

Fried, G. (2010). *Managing sport facilities.* Champaign, IL: Human Kinetics.

Frost, R. B., Lockhart, B. D., & Marshall, S. J. (1988). *Administration of physical education and athletics: Concepts and practices* (2nd ed.). Dubuque, IA: Wm. C. Brown.

Frost, R. B., & Marshall, S. J. (1977). *Administration of physical education and athletics: Concepts and practices* (2nd ed.). Dubuque, IA: Wm. C. Brown.

Funk, D. (1997). *Economics of professional sports franchises: The role of luxury suites and club seats in the construction of sports stadiums and arenas in North America.* Paper presented at the annual conference of the North American Society for Sport Management, San Antonio, TX.

Future trends in fitness equipment. (1997, November). *Joe Weider's Muscle & Fitness, 7*(11), 26.

Gabrielsen, M. A. (1987). *Swimming pools* (4th ed.). Champaign, IL: Human Kinetics.

Garbarino, E., & Johnson, M. S. (1999). The different roles of satisfaction, trust, and commitment in customer relationships. *Journal of Marketing, 63*(2), 70–87.

Garhammer, J. (1982). Free weight equipment for the development of athletic strength and power. *National Strength and Conditioning Association Journal, 3*(6):24– 26. 1982.

Garrison, J. (2011). AEG unveils $700-million stadium naming rights deal as L.A. sports legends, power brokers celebrate. *Los Angeles Times.* Retrieved from http://latimesblogs.latimes.com/lanow/2011/02/aeg-unveils-700-million-stadium-naming-rights-deal-farmers-football-stadium.html

Gembeck, A. (n.d.). Skatepark design – Listen to the skaters. Retrieved from http://www.skateparkguide.com/design_basics.html

Gembeck, A. (2009). *Skatepark guide.* Retrieved from http://www.skateparkguide.com

Girdano, D. A. (1986). *Occupational health promotion: A practical guide to program development.* New York, NY: Macmillan.

Goatley, J. M., Maddox, V. L., Lang, D. L., Elmore, R. E., & Stewart, B. R. (2005). Temporary covers maintain fall bermudagrass quality, enhance spring greenup, and increase stem carbohydrate levels. *HortScience, 40,* 227–231. Retrieved from http://hortsci.ashspublications.org/cgi/gca?allch=&SEARCHID=1&AUTHOR1=Goatley&FIRSTINDEX=0&hits=10&RESULTFORMAT=&gca=hortsci%3B40%2F1%2F227

Goodbody, J. (1969). *The Japanese fighting arts.* South Brunswick, NY: A. S. Barnes.

Goodman, J. (2000, October). Cushion extends life. *Facilities Design & Management, 18*(10), 54, 56.

Goodstein, L. D., Nolan, T. M., & Pfeiffer, W. J. (1993). *Applied strategic planning: A comprehensive guide.* New York, NY: McGraw-Hill.

Gordon, J. (1990). The suite smell of success. *Skybox, 1*(2), 6–9.

Gorman, J., Calhoun, K., & Rozin, S. (1994). *The name of the game: The business of sports.* New York, NY: John Wiley & Sons.

Greenwood, T. A. (2000). Essentials of strength training and conditioning. In *Strength and conditioning professional standards and guidelines* (pp. 549–566). Retrieved from http://www.ncsa-lift.org/Publications/standards. Shtml

Greenwood, M., & Greenwood, L. 2000. Facility maintenance and risk management. In T. R. Baechle & R. Earle (Eds.), Essentials of strength training and conditioning (2nd ed.) (pp. 587-601). Human Kinetics, Champaign, IL.

Griffiths, T. (2003). *The complete swimming pool reference* (2nd ed.). Urbana, IL: Sagamore.

Gunsten, P. H. (1978). *Tournament scheduling: The easy way.* Winston-Salem, NC: Hunter Textbooks.

Hackensmith, C. W. (1966). *History of physical education.* New York, NY: Harper & Row.

Hamar, D. (2000, November). In S. Dahlgren (Ed.), Making the Grade. *Athletic Business, 24*(11), 77–78, 80–82, 84.

Hamel, G., & Prahalad, C. K. (1994). *Competing for the future.* Boston, MA: Harvard Business School Press.

Hanford, D. J. (1998, March). What's going down. *Building Operating Management.* Retrieved from http://www.facilitiesnet.com/

Harassment cases soar in the nineties. (1999, April 1). *USA Today*, p. 1.

Hard questions, critical answers. (1998, March). *Building Operating Management*. Retrieved from http://www.facilitiesnet.com/

Hasenkamp, T., & Lutz, B. (2001, March). The dash for splash. *Athletic Business, 25*(3), 55–56, 58, 60.

Hasler, A. E., & Bartlett, M. (1995, September). Equipped for exercise. *Athletic Business, 13*(9), 47–54.

Heidrich, K. W. (1990). *Working with volunteers.* Champaign, IL: Sagamore.

Heistand, M. (1999, May 26). Skyboxes gain mass appeal. *USA Today*, p. 3C.

Helitzer, M. (1992). *The dream job: Sports publicity, promotion, and public relations.* Athens, OH: University Sports Press.

Helson, C. M. (1997). Keeping control when outsourcing your store. *Employee Services Management, 40*(8), 30–31.

Helson, C. M. (1998). Employee stores keep growing. *Employee Services Management, 41*(3), 11–14.

Hendy, T. (1997). The nuts and bolts of playground maintenance. In S. Hudson & D. Thompson (Eds.), *Playground safety handbook* (pp. 60–70). Cedar Falls, IA: National Program for Playground Safety.

Heywood, J. B. (2001). *The outsourcing dilemma: The search for competitiveness.* London, England: Pearson Education.

Hill, C. & Klimesh, R. (2000). *Stablekeeping: A visual guide to safe and healthy horsekeeping.* North Adams, MA: Storey Publishing.

Hoffman, A. N., & O'Neill, H. M. (1993). *The strategic management casebook and skill builder.* Minneapolis, MN: West.

Holleman, M. A. (1996). Scoring with stadiums. *Athletic Business, 20*(9), 45–49.

Holzrichter, D. (2001, January). Gymnasium makeovers. *Athletic Business, 29*(1), 59–60, 62–65.

Horine, L., & Stotlar, D. (2003). *Administration of physical education and sport* (5th ed.). Dubuque, IA: Wm. C. Brown.

Howard, D. R., & Crompton, J. L. (1995). *Financing sport.* Morgantown, WV: Fitness Information Technology.

Howard, D. R., & Crompton, J. L. (2004). *Financing sport* (2nd ed.). Morgantown, WV: Fitness Information Technology.

Howe, D. K. (2000, March/April). Nine trends of the 1990s. *American Fitness, 24*(3), 12–13.

Huang, Y., Macera, C. A., Blair, S. N., Brill, P. A., Kohl, H. W., & Kronenfeld, J. J. (1998). Physical fitness, physical activity, and functional limitation in adults aged 40 and older. *Medicine Science Sports and Exercise, 30*:1430–5.

Huddleston, E. (2001, November). The sweet smell of success. *Athletic Business, 29*(11), 63–64, 66, 68, 70.

Hudson, S., Olsen, H., & Thompson, D. (2004). *Playground safety.* Cedar Falls: University of Northern Iowa.

Hudson, S., Thompson, D., & Olsen, H. (2008). *Planning playgrounds.* Cedar Falls, IA: National Program for Playground Safety.

Hussey, D. E. (1991). *Introducing corporate planning: Guide to strategic management.* New York, NY: Pergamon.

Hutchison, C. (2003). More than sports. *PanStadia International Quarterly Report, 10*(2), 64–67.

Hypes, M. G. (2009). Signage. In T. H. Sawyer (Ed.), *Facilities planning and management for health, fitness, physical activity, recreation, and sports: Concepts and applications* (12th ed.). Champaign, IL: Sagamore.

Illinois Park & Recreation Association. (1995). *A guide to playground planning.* Winfield, IL: Author.

Illuminating Engineering Society of North America. (2012). Lighting standards. Retrieved from http://www.ihs.com/products/industry-standards/organizations/iesna/index.aspx

Ingersoll, C., & Sawyer, T. (1999). Sports medicine and rehabilitation. In T. H. Sawyer (Ed.), *Facilities planning for physical activity and sport: Guidelines for development* (9th ed.). Dubuque, IA: Kendall-Hunt.

Inter, F. (2007, Fall). Mounting concerns. *Waterpark Resorts Today.* Retrieved from http://www.waterparkresortstoday.com/2007/fall/07concerns.html

International Association of Skateboard Companies. (2013). Retrieved from http://theiasc.org

International Health, Racquet, and Sportsclub Association. (2012a). 51.4 million Americans are health club members up 2.4%. Retrieved from http://www.ihrsa.org/media-center/2012/4/2/514-million-americans-are-health-club-members-up-24-club-usa.html

International Health, Racquet, and Sportsclub Association. (2012b). Top health club trends for 2012. Retrieved from http://www.ihrsa.org/media-center/2012/1/11/top-health-club-trends-for-2012.html

International Tennis Federation. (2010). Court classification scheme. Retrieved November 17, 2010, from http://www.itftennis.com

Jarvis, R. M., & Colemann, P. (2003). Fireworks, fan cams, and lawsuits: A guide to stadium scoreboards. *Seton Hall Journal of Sport Law, 13*, 177.

Jensen, C. R., & Overman, J. O. (2003). *Administration and management of physical education and athletic programs.* Prospect Heights, IL: Waveland Press.

Jewell, D. (1992). *Public assembly facilities* (2nd ed.). Malabar, FL: Krieger.

John, G., Shear, R., & Vickery, B. (2007). *Stadia: A design and development guide* (4th ed.). Boston, MA: Architectural Press.

Johnson, D. K., & Patterson, D. S. (1997, December). Window and curtain walls: Out with the old? *Building Operating Management.* Retrieved from http://www.facilitiesnet.com/

Johnson, G. (2011). PROP approves rule changes. *NCAA News.* Retrieved from http://www.ncaa.com/news/ncaa/2011-05-26/prop-approves-rule-changes

Jones, T. E. (1990, April). Choosing court colors. *Athletic Business*, 70–71.

Judge, L. W., Petersen, J. A., Bellar, D., Craig, B., & Gilreath, E. (2012). CSCS certification and school enrollment influence upon high school strength facilities, equipment, and safety. *Journal of Strength & Conditioning Research.* [Epub ahead of print] doi: 10.1519/JSC.0b013e3182576fd2

Kaiser, R., & Robinson, K. (1999). Risk management. In B. van der Smissen, M. Moiseichik, V. Hartenburg, & L. Twardzik (Eds.), *Management of park and recreation agencies* (pp. 713–741). Ashburn, VA: National Recreation and Park Association.

Kaplan, D. (1998). ABS: A new way to pay. *Sport Business Journal, 1*(1), 3.

Keller, I. A., & Forsyth, C. E. (1984). *Administration of high school athletics.* Englewood Cliffs, NJ: Prentice Hall.

Kennedy, M. (2000, October). A well-grounded plan. *American School and University: Facilities, Purchasing and Business Administration, 18*(10), 30, 32, 34.

King, J. M. (2003, November). Cardio machine programming. *Fitness Management, 20*(11), 34–37.

Klafs, C. E., & Arnheim, D. D. (1973). *Modern principles of athletic training* (3rd ed.; pp. 33–42). St. Louis, MO: Mosby.

Kocher, E. (1996, April). Gymnasium facelifts. *Athletic Business, 14*(4), 39–42.

Kollie, E. (2004). Sports flooring solutions for your athletic facility. *School Planning & Management, 43*(6), 55–61.

Komisarchik, M., & Fenn, A. J. (2010). Trends in stadium and arena construction, 1995–2015. Retrieved from http://ssrn.com/abstract=1584733

Krebs D. E., Scarborough, D. M., & McGibbon, C. A. (2007). Functional vs. strength training in disabled elderly outpatients. *American Journal of Physical Medical Rehabilitation, 86*(2), 93-103.

Kroll, K. (2002, December). Steps to selecting the best floor. *Building Operating Management.* Retrieved from http://www.facilitiesnet.com/

Kroll, K. (2003, December). Ceilings—Blocking the talk: Acoustics in the workplace. *Building Operating Management.* Retrieved from http//www.facilitiesnet.com/

Kufahl, P. (2004, January). Political push. *Club Industry, 11*(1), 21–23.

Kunnathon, A. (2013). College football naming rights: Where FAU's ranks in dollars. *SBNATION: College Football.* Retrieved from http://www.sbnation.com/college-football/2013/2/22/4015320/college-football-stadiums-company-names-sponsors

LaVoie, H. (1993). Ancillary areas. In R. B. Flynn (Ed.), *Facility planning for physical education, recreation, and athletics* (pp. 147–148). Reston, VA: The Facilities Council of the Association for Research, Administration, Professional Councils and Societies.

LaVoie, H. (2005). Ancillary areas. In T. H. Sawyer (Ed.), *Facilities planning and management for health, fitness, physical activity, recreation, and sports: Concepts and applications* (11th ed.). Champaign, IL: Sagamore.

LaVoie, H. (2009). Ancillary areas. In T. H. Sawyer (Ed.), *Facilities planning and management for health, fitness, physical activity, recreation, and sports: Concepts and applications* (11th ed.). Champaign, IL: Sagamore.

Law-Heitzman, B. (1998). A new tool saves lives. *Aquatics International*, January/February, 12–16.

Lewis, G., & Appenzeller, H. (1985). *Successful sport management.* Charlottesville, VA: The Michie Company.

Lewis, W. (1994). Weeding out unwanted growth: Weed problems on athletic fields can be nipped in the bud by implementing a total weed management program. *Athletic Management, 6*(3), 28.

List of sports venues with sole naming rights. (2008). In *Wikipedia: The free encyclopedia.* Retrieved from http://en.wikipedia.org/wiki/List_of_sports_venues_with_sole_naming_rights#United_States

Logan, W., & Petras, H. (1975). *Handbook of the martial arts and self-defense.* New York, NY: Funk and Wagnalls.

Lorenz, B. (2005). Changing views on fire safety point to an increased role for elevators in evacuation. Retrieved from http://www.facilitiesnet.com/elevators/article/Fire-Escape--3175

MacDonald, D. (n.d.). *The CWA's guide to climbing.* Boulder, CO: The Climbing Wall Association. Retrieved from http://www.climbingwallindustry.org/images/uploads/CWA_Guide_to_Climbing_Web.pdf

Mack, M. G., Hudson, S., & Thompson, D. (1997, June). A descriptive analysis of children's playground injuries in the United States 1990–1994. *Journal of the International Society for Child and Adolescent Injury Prevention, 3*, 100–103.

Maher, J. (2003, June 28). What's in a name? *American Statesman.* Retrieved from http://www.utwatch.org/oldnews/aas_erwin_6_28_03.html

Maple Flooring Manufacturers Association. (2013). *Study to determine life cycle for sports flooring.* Retrieved from http://www.maplefloor.org/literature/lifecyclestudy.htm

Markazi, A. (2012). Construction could start by March '13. *ESPN LA.* Retrieved from http://espn.go.com/los-angeles/nfl/story/_/id/7772949/construction-proposed-football-stadium-los-angeles-begin-march-2013

McArthur, S. (1992). Don't throw in the towel. *Athletic Business, 16*(7), 49–50.

McDonnell, A. (2006, November). Cardio equipment for special populations. *Fitness Management.* Retrieved from http://www.athleticbusiness.com/articles/article.aspx?articleid=3094&zoneid=42

McDonnell, A., & Tucker-Rhodes, R. (2007, December). 2007 end-of-year review: Equipment. *Fitness Management.* Retrieved from http://fitnessmanagement.com/articles/article.aspx?articleid=2275&zoneid=13

McDonnell, A. B. (2009). A primer on buying, selling used fitness equipment. *Fitness Management.* Retrieved from http://www.athleticbusiness.com/articles/article.aspx?articleid=3503&zoneid=42

McKenna, N., & Goatley, M. (2009). *Winter management and recovery tips to optimize athletic field safety and performance for spring sports* (Virginia Cooperative Extension Publication 430-408). Blacksburg, VA: Virginia Polytechnic Institute and State University.

McPherson, D. (2004). Flooring your members. *Fitness Management, 18*(5), 43.

Minnée, P. (2012). *European committee for standardization* (EN 14904). Retrieved from http://www.sportsbuilders.org/events/presentations/1D.pdf

Minnesota Building Codes and Standards Division. (2001). Printouts: Bleacher seating. Retrieved from http://www.admin.state.mn.us/buildingcodes/printouts/bleachers.html

Molnar, D., & Rutledge, A. (1986). *Anatomy of a park* (2nd ed.). New York, NY: McGraw-Hill.

Moore, J. N., Pickett, G. M., & Grove, S. J. (1999). The impact of a video screen and rotational-signage systems on satisfaction and advertising recognition. *Journal of Services Marketing, 13*(6), 453–468.

Moran, B. (1999, June). Mission essential: NIRSA conference highlights recreation's power to recruit and retain. *Recreational Sports & Fitness, 10*(6), 14–18.

Morehouse, L. E., & Rasch, P. J. (1958). *Scientific basis of athletic training* (pp. 216–224). Philadelphia, PA: W. B. Saunders.

Morehouse, L. E., & Rasch, P. J. (1964). *Sports medicine for trainers* (2nd ed.; pp. 214–223). Philadelphia, PA: W. B. Saunders.

Moussatche, H., Languell-Urquhart, J., & Woodson, C. (2000, September). Life cycle costs in education: Operations & maintenance considered. *Facilities Design & Management, 17*(9), 20, 22.

Mula, R. M. (1998). Employee vendor fairs. *Employee Services Management, 41*(10), 31–32.

Mull, R. F., Bayless, K. G., Ross, C. M., & Jamieson, L. M. (1997). *Recreational sport management* (3rd ed.). Champaign, IL: Human Kinetics.

National Collegiate Athletic Association. (2000). *NCAA rule books for baseball, football, soccer, and lacrosse.* Indianapolis, IN: Author.

National Collegiate Athletic Association. (2004). *NCAA guides.* Indianapolis, IN: Author.

National Collegiate Athletic Association. (2006). *NCAA facility fact sheet.* Indianapolis, IN: Author.

National Collegiate Athletic Association. (2010). *Men's and women's cross-country & track & field rules.* Indianapolis, IN: Author.

National Facilities Conference. (1962). *Planning facilities for health, physical education, and recreation.* Chicago, IL: The Athletic Institute.

National Facilities Conference. (1966a). *College and university facility guide.* Washington, DC: The Athletic Institute and the American Association of Health, Physical Education, and Recreation.

National Facilities Conference. (1966b). *Planning facilities for health, physical education, and recreation.* Chicago, IL: The Athletic Institute and the American Association of Health, Physical Education, and Recreation.

National Wood Flooring Association. (2007). Ranking of hardwood floors. Retrieved from http://www.woodfloors.org/

National Conference of State Legislatures. (2008, February). State laws on heart attacks, cardiac arrest and defibrillators. Retrieved from http://www.ncsl.org/programs/health/aed.htm

National Dance Association. (2010). *Dance facility design.* Reston, VA: American Alliance of Health, Physical Education, Recreation, and Dance.

National Federation of State High Schools Assocation. (2012). *Basketball rule book.* Indianapolis, IN: Author.

National Intramural–Recreational Sports Association. (2001). *NIRSA aquatic directors handbook.* Corvallis, OR: NIRSA National Center.

National Intramural–Recreational Sports Association. (2008). *Space planning guidelines for campus recreational sport facilities.* Champaign, IL: Human Kinetics.

National Intramural–Recreational Sports Association. (2009). *Campus recreational sport facilities: Planning, design, and construction guidelines.* Champaign, IL: Human Kinetics.

National Intramural–Recreational Sports Association. (2012). *Campus recreational sports: Managing employees, programs, facilities, and services.* Champaign, IL: Human Kinetics.

National Program for Playground Safety. (2004). *Play elements for playgrounds.* Cedar Falls: University of Northern Iowa

National Safety Council. (2008). *First responder: Skills in action.* New York, NY: McGraw-Hill.

National Sporting Goods Association. (2008a). 2007–1998 sports with over 15% change in participation. Retrieved from http://www.nsga.org/files/public/2007-1998.pdf

National Sporting Goods Association. (2008b). 2007–2003 sports equipment by average price. Retrieved from http://www.nsga.org/files/public/averagepricechangein5yearts.pdf

National Swimming Pool Foundation. (1997). *Official swimming pool design compendium* (5th ed.). San Antonio, TX: Author.

National Swimming Pool Foundation. (2012). *Pool and spa operator handbook.* San Antonio, TX: Author.

Navy Environmental Health Center. (2002). *Indoor firing ranges industrial hygiene technical guide* (Technical Manual NEHC-TM6290.99-10 Rev. 1). Portsmouth, VA: Author.

Neuman, D. J. (2003). *Building type basics for college and university facilities.* Hoboken, NJ: Wiley and Sons.

Neville, W. (1994). *Serve it up: Volleyball for life.* Mountain View, CA: Mayfield.

North Carolina Office on Disability and Health. (2008). Removing barriers to health clubs and fitness facilities. Retrieved from http://projects.fpg.unc.edu/~ncodh/pdfs/rbfitness.pdf

Noyes, B., & Skolnicki, J. (2001). A modest proposal. *Athletic Business, 24*(8), 51–58.

Olguin, M. A. (1991). Vital marketing. *Fitness Management, 7*(3), 45–47.

Olson, J., Hirsch, E., Breitenbach, O., & Saunders, K. (1987). *Administration of high school and collegiate athletic programs.* Philadelphia, PA: Saunders College Publishing.

Otto, C. (2006, May). Recreational water-illness-prevention = healthy swimming. *Journal of Environmental Health, 68*(9), 23–31.

The Outdoor Foundation (2013). *Outdoor recreation participation report 2012.* Retrieved from http://www.outdoorfoundation.org/pdf/ResearchParticipation2012.pdf

Paley, N. (1991). *The strategic marketing planner.* New York, NY: AMACOM Books.

Pangrazi, R. P., & Beighle, A. (2012). *Dynmaic physical education for elementary school children* (17th ed.). San Francisco, CA: Benjamin Cummings.

Parkhouse, B. L. (1991). *The management of sport: Its foundation and application.* St. Louis, MO: C. V. Mosby Year Book.

Parkhouse, B. L. (2001). *The management of sport: Its foundation and application* (3rd ed.). Dubuque, IA: McGraw-Hill.

Patton, J. D. (1999, April). Fitness in flux. *Athletic Business, 23*(4), 51–54.

Patton, R. W., Corry, J. M., Gettman, L. R., & Schovee, G. J. (1986). *Implementing health/fitness programs.* Champaign, IL: Human Kinetics.

Patton, R. W., Grantham, W. C., Gerson, R. F., & Gettman, L. R. (1989). *Developing and managing health/fitness facilities.* Champaign, IL: Human Kinetics.

Patton, R. W., McGuire, A., Greenleaf, C., & Jackson, A. (2011). Sex differences in fitness equipment use. *ACSM'S Health & Fitness Journal, 15*(3), 15–18

Peavey, H. (2008, February). Beyond the big three. *Fitness Magazine, 24*(2), 58–59.

Penman, K. A., & Penman, T. M. (1982, September). Training rooms aren't just for colleges. *Athletic Purchasing and Facilities, 6*(9), 34–37.

Petersen, J. C. (1997). *Indoor activity space and ancillary space analysis for New Mexico high schools* (Unpublished doctoral dissertation). The University of New Mexico, Albuquerque.

Peterson, J. A. (1991a). Ten steps to effective publicity. *Fitness Management, 7*(12), 41.

Peterson, J. A. (1991b). The power and nature of publicity. *Fitness Management, 7*(12), 39.

Peterson, J. A., & Tharrett, S. J. (2012). *ACSM's health/fitness facility standards and guidelines* (4th ed.). Champaign, IL: Human Kinetics.

Picozzi-Moran, A., & Brown, C. (2006, October). Wireless dedication. *Athletic Business.* Retrieved from http://athleticbusiness.com/articles/article.aspx?articleid=1275&zoneid=47

Piper, J. (1997). Restroom planning and design: Form meets function. *Building Operation Management.* Retrieved from http://www.facilitiesnet.com/

Piper, J. (1998, March). Complete performances. *Building Operation Management.* Retrieved from http://www.facilitiesnet.com/

Piper, J. (2000, August). Flooring: The real bottom line. *Building Operation Management.* Retrieved from http://www.facilitiesnet.com/

Piper, J. (2003, December). Flooring for today, tomorrow. *Building Operation Management*. Retrieved from http://www.facilitiesnet.com/

Pollar, O. (1997). Effective delegation. *Employee Services Management, 40*(9), 13–16.

Pope, N., & Voges, K. (1997). An exploration of sponsorship awareness by product category and message location in televised sporting events. *Cyber Journal of Sport Marketing*. Retrieved from http://fulltext.ausport.gov.au/fulltext/1997/cjsm/v1n1/pope&voges11.htm

Popke, M. (2000, October). Skate nation. *Athletic Business, 24*(10), 67–74.

Popke, M. (2001, May). Mixing it up. *Athletic Business, 25*(5), 46–50, 52.

Popke, M. (2002, August). Sound barriers. *Athletic Business, 26*(8), 67–68, 70, 72, 74.

Popke, M. (2003, August). Concrete evidence. *Athletic Business, 29*(8), 79–80, 82, 84, 86.

Popke, M. (2005, September). High times. *Athletic Business*. Retrieved from http://athleticbusiness.com/articles/article.aspx?articleid=1065&zoneid=50

Popke, M. (2006a, September). Tread carefully. *Athletic Business, 30*(9), 76–80, 82–83.

Popke, M. (2006b, May). Scoring opportunities. *Athletic Business*. Retrieved from http://athleticbusiness.com/articles/article.aspx?articleid=1198&zoneid=53

Popke, M. (2007, November). The fix is in. *Athletic Business, 31*(11), 56–57.

Popke, M. (2008, March). Competitive spirit. *Athletic Business, 32*(3), 34–44.

Popke, M. (2012a). Visual aids: High schools are counting on sponsor-supported video boards to generate new revenues. *Athletic Business, 36*(8), 28–32.

Popke, M. (2012b). High school scoreboards just got bigger. *Athletic Business*. Retrieved from http://www.athleticbusiness.com/editors/blog/ default. aspx?id=954

President Clinton signs cardiac arrest survival act. (2005). Retrieved from http://www.padl.org/articles.php3?id=newlegis005

Prins, B. (2004, July). Giving kids something to fall back on. Retrieved from http://www.sandforgroup.com/

Project Adventure. (2012). Testimonials. Retrieved October 16, 2012, from http://www.pa.org

Prouty, D. (1999). Project Adventure: A brief history. In J. C. Miles & S. Priest (Eds.), *Adventure programming* (pp. 93–101). State College, PA: Venture.

Puhalla, J., Krans, J., & Goatley, M. (2002). *Sports fields: A manual for design, construction, and maintenance.* Hoboken, NJ: John Wiley and Sons.

Puhalla, J., Krans, J., & Goatley, M. (2003). *Baseball and softball fields.* Hoboken, NJ: J. W. Wiley.

Puhalla, J., Krans, J. V., & Goatley, M. (2010). *Sport fields design, construction, and maintenance* (2nd ed.). Hoboken, NJ: John Wiley & Sons.

Quirk, J., & Fort, R. D. (1997). *The business of professional team sports.* Princeton, NJ: Princeton University Press.

Raiford, R. (1999, June). Into uncharted territory: Outsourcing redirects the future of business for facilities professionals. *Buildings, 1999*(June), 40–42.

Railey, J. H., & Railey, P. A. (1988). *Managing physical education, fitness and sports programs.* Mountain View, CA: Mayfield.

Railey, J. H., & Tschauner, P. R. (1993). *Managing physical education, fitness, and sports programs* (2nd ed.). Mountainview, CA: Mayfield.

Ramirez, C. (2012). Pickleball's popularity grows locally and across the nation. *Detroit Metro News*. Retrieved from http://www.detriotnews.com/article/20120908/METRO/209080349/1409/Metro/Pickleball

Ramsey, C. G., & Sleeper, H. R. (2011). *Interior graphic standards* (2nd ed.). Hoboken, NJ: John Wiley & Sons.

Rankin, J., & Ingersoll, C. (1995). *Athletic training management: Concepts and applications.* St. Louis, MO: Mosby.

Rawlinson, K. (1961). *Modern athletic training.* Englewood Cliffs, NJ: Prentice Hall.

Ray, R. (1994). *Management strategies in athletic training.* Champaign, IL: Human Kinetics.

Read, D. (2013). Indoor innovations. *Athletic Management, 25*(2), 55–61.

Rehabilitation Act of 1973, 29 U.S.C. § 791.

Rehabilitation Act of 1973, 29 U.S.C. § 792.

Rhodes, R. (2007, October). Equipping for diversity. *Fitness Management*. Retrieved from http://www.athleticbusiness.com/articles/article.aspx?articleid=3277&zoneid=19

Rice. E. A., Hutchinson, J. L., & Lee, M. (1958). *A brief history of physical education.* Hoboken, NJ: Ronald Press.

Rimmer, J. (2005). Exercise and physical activity in persons aging with a physical disability. *Physical Medicine and Rehabilitation Clinics of North America, 16*, 41–56.

Roberts, C. (2000, September). Ceilings: Form, function, and ROI. *Building Operating Management*. Retrieved from http://www.facilitiesnet.com/.

Robledo, R., & Kozen, K. (2008, February). President signs pool-safety law. *Aquatics International*. Retrieved from http://www.aquaticsintl.com/safety/president-signs-pool-safety-law.aspx

Rogers, D. (2000). To the top: Challenge courses for persons with disabilities. *Parks & Recreation, 35*, 3.

Rohnke, K., Rogers, D., Wall, J., & Tait, C. (2007). *The complete ropes course manual.* Dubuque, IA: Kendall-Hunt.

Roller skating. (n.d.) In *Wikipedia: The Free Encyclopedia*. Retrieved October 24, 2012, from http://en.wikipedia.org/wiki/Roller_skating

Roth, J. (1974). *Black belt karate.* Rutland, VT: Charles E. Tuttle.

Russell, R. V. (1982). *Planning programs in recreation.* St. Louis, MO: C. V. Mosby.

Russo, F. (2000). Marketing events and services for spectators. In H. Appenzeller & G. Lewis (Eds.), *Successful sport management* (2nd ed.; pp. 151–162). Durham, NC: Carolina Academic Press.

Sabo, J. (2001, May). Design and construction of an athletic training facility. *NATA NEWS, 13*(5), 10–22.

Sagar, H. R. (2007, September). Tall orders. *Athletic Business*. Retrieved from http://athlethicbusiness.com/articles/

Sander, M., & Altobelli, C. (2011, April). Virtual advertising in sport: Does it really work? *International Journal of Sports Marketing & Sponsorship, 6*(4), 16–21.

Sandorti, C. C. (1995). Court cents. *Volleyball Magazine, 6*(8), 114–115, 140.

Sapora, A., & Kenney, H. (1961). *A study of the present status, future needs, and recommended standards regarding space used for health, physical education, physical recreation, and athletics.* Champaign, IL: Stipes.

Sauers, R. J. (1985, September). Safety built into a flexible design. *Athletic Business, 9*(9), 62–63.

Saunders, K. (2001). Rotational field worth taking a look. *Sportsturf, 17*(11), 24.

Sawyer, T. H. (1999). *Facilities planning for physical activity and sport: Guidelines for development* (9th ed.). Dubuque, IA: Kendall-Hunt.

Sawyer, T. H. (2002). *Facilities planning for health, fitness, physical activity, recreation and sport* (10th ed.). Dubuque, IA: Kendall-Hunt.

Sawyer, T. H. (2005). *Facilities planning and management for health, fitness, physical activity, recreation, and sports: Concepts and applications* (11th ed.). Urbana, IL: Sagamore.

Sawyer, T. H. (2009). *Facility planning and design for fitness, physical activity, recreation, and sport* (12th ed.). Urbana, IL: Sagamore.

Schackter, D. (1983). Using advertising to help boost ticket sales. *Athletic Purchasing and Facilities, 7*(8), 38, 40, 42.

Schaeffler, J. (2008). *Digital signage; software, networks, advertising and displays.* Burlington, MA: Elsevier.

Schmid, S. (1993). Premium coverage. *Athletic Business, 16*(4), 39–42.

Schroeder, C. L. (1999). Staffing your store. *Employee Services Management, 42*(8), 37–39.

Schroeder, J., & Dotan, S. (2010). 2010 IDEA fitness programs and equipment trends. *IDEA Fitness Journal, 7*(7), 22–31.

Secor, M. R. (1984). Designing athletic training facilities or where do you want the outlets? *Journal of Athletic Training, 19*(5), 19–21.

Shaffer, A. L. (1999). Taking stock. *Club Industry, 15*(7), 49–51.

Shank, M. D. (2002). *Sports marketing: A strategic perspective.* Upper Saddle River, NJ: Prentice Hall.

Shaw, L. G. (1976). *The playground: The child's center learning space* (MH 20743034A1). Gainsville, FL: The Bureau of Research, College of Architecture, University of Florida.

Simers, T. J., & Wharton, D. (1999, October 10). How the game was played. *Los Angeles Times Magazine*, 28–31, 128–131.

Skate Park Association USA. (2013). Growth and trends in skate parks. Retrieved from http://www.spausa.org/first-steps.html

Sol, N., & Foster, C. (1992). *ACSM's health/fitness facility standards and guidelines.* Champaign, IL: Human Kinetics.

Solomon, J. (2002). *An insider's guide to managing sporting events.* Champaign, IL: Human Kinetics.

Solomon, J. D. (2004, April 1). Public wises up, balks at paying for new stadiums. *USA Today*, p. 13A.

Sport and Fitness Industry Association. (2013a). *2013 sports, fitness and leisure activities topline participation report.* Jupiter, FL: Sport Marketing Surveys USA.

Sport and Fitness Industry Association. (2013b). *2013 manufacturers' sales by category report.* Jupiter, FL: Sport Marketing Surveys USA.

Sport Surfaces. (1994, November). *Athletic Business, 18*(11), 63–67, 70–75, 80, 82.

Sporting Goods Manufacturers Association. (2012). *2012 tracking the fitness movement report.* Jupiter, FL: Sport Marketing Surveys USA.

Stadiums and arenas: Club seat breakdown. (2003, July). *Street & Smith's Sport Business Journal, 6*(26), 10–11.

Starfish Aquatics Institute. (2006). *StarGuard, best practices for lifeguards* (3rd ed.). Champaign, IL: Human Kinetics.

SteelBenchmarker. (2013). Price history tables and charts. Retrieved from www.steelbenchmarker.com/files/history.pdf

Steinbach, P. (2000, April). Stands that deliver. *Athletic Business, 24*(4), 93–98.

Steinbach, P. (2002a, January). Beauty & brawn. *Athletic Business, 26*(1), 58–65.

Steinbach, P. (2002b, July). Great plane. *Athletic Business, 26*(7), 79–80, 82, 84, 86.

Steinbach, P. (2003a). Gym and arena: Bright ideas. *Athletic Business.* Retrieved from http://athleticbusiness.com/articles/article.aspx?articleid=467&zoneid=44)

Steinbach, P. (2003b, May). Bright ideas. *Athletic Business, 27*(5), 79–80, 82–84.

Steinbach, P. (2004, March). Sudden impact. *Athletic Business,* 51–52, 54, 56, 58.

Steinbach, P. (2008a). High-tech scoreboards and video displays finding favor in high schools. *Athletic Business, 32*(1), 13–16.

Steinbach, P. (2008b, January). Matrix revolution. *Athletic Business.* Retrieved from http://athleticbusiness.com/articles/article.aspx?articleid=1707&zoneid=20

Steinbach, P. (2008c, April). A step further. *Athletic Business.* Retrieved from http://athleticbusiness.com/articles/article.aspx?articleid=1743&zoneid=21

Steinbach, P. (2008d, December). Peak interest. *Athletic Business.* Retrieved from http://athleticbusiness.com/articles/article.aspx?articleid=1929&zoneid=10

Sternloff, R. E., & Warren, R. (1984). *Park and recreation maintenance management* (2nd ed.). New York, NY: John Wiley & Sons.

Stiehl, J., & Ramsey, T. (2004). *Climbing walls: A complete guide.* Champaign, IL: Human Kinetics.

Stoll, S., & Beller, J. (1989). *The professional's guide to teaching aerobics.* Englewood Cliffs, NJ: Prentice Hall.

Stone Hearth News. (2011). Top 10 trends in exercise and equipment for 2012: New IDEA survey. Retrieved from http://www.stonehearthnewsletters.com/top-10-trends-in-exercise-and-equipment-new-idea-survey/exercise/

Stotlar, D. K., & Bennett, C. A. (2000). An analysis of in-game advertising for NCAA basketball. *Cyber Journal of Sport Marketing.* Retrieved from http://fulltext.ausport.gov.au/fulltext/2000/cjsm/v4n1/stotlar41.htm

Stotlar, D. K., & Johnson, D. A. (1989). Assessing the impact and effectiveness of stadium advertising on sport spectators at division I institutions. *Journal of Sport Management, 3,* 90–102.

Strand, B. N. (1988). *A space analysis of physical education activity areas and ancillary areas in big ten universities* (Unpublished doctoral dissertation). University of New Mexico, Albuquerque.

Straus, D. C., & Kirihara, J. (1996). Indoor microbiological garden: A microscopic line separates good and bad IAQ. Retrieved from http://www.facilitiesnet.com/

Subcommittee F08.64 on Natural Playing Surfaces. (2008). *ASTM F2270-12: Standard guide for construction and maintenance of warning track areas on athletic fields.* West Conshohocken, PA: ASTM International.

Surface America. (2008). Picking the right gymnasium floor. Retrieved from www.surfaceamerica.com

Tarkett Sports North America. (2012). New sports flooring safety standards. Retrieved from http://www.tarkettsportsindoor.com/news

Tarlow, P. E. (2002). *Event risk management and safety.* New York, NY: John Wiley & Sons.

Thompson, C. (2001, October 6). First-class Reliant Stadium nears completion. Retrieved from http://www.chron.com/cs/CDA/story.hts/sports/fb/nfl/1077737

Thompson, D., & Hudson, S. (1996). *National action plan for the prevention of playground injuries.* Cedar Falls, IA: National Program for Playground Safety.

Thompson, D., Hudson, S., & Olsen, H. (2007). *S.A.F.E. play areas: Creation, renovation, and maintenance.* Champaign, IL: Human Kinetics.

Thompson, G., & Riley, K. (2002, April). A sound arena. *Athletic Business,* 97–98, 100, 102, 104, 106.

Thompson, W. R. (2012). Worldwide survey of fitness trends for 2012. *ASCM's Health & Fitness Journal, 15*(6), 9–18.

Tiger Athletics. (year). Tiger naming rights campaign picks up momentum. Retrieved from http://gotigersgo.collegesports.com/genrel/042604aaa.html

Tony Hawk Foundation. (2012). 500 skateparks in 50 states. Retrieved from http://www.tonyhawkfoundation.org/news/2012/03/20/500-skateparks-in-50-states/

Trais, R. A. (1973). *The hand is my sword.* Rutland, VT: Charles E. Tuttle.

Trend setting. (1999, February). *Joe Weider's Muscle & Fitness, 19*(2), 27–36.

Turley, L. W., & Shannon, J. R. (1997). The influence of in-arena promotions on purchase behavior and purchase intentions. *Sport Marketing Quarterly, 6*(4), 53–59.

Turley, L. W., & Shannon, J. R. (2000). The impact and effectiveness of advertisements in a sports arena. *Journal of Services Marketing, 14*(4), 323–336.

Turner, E. (1994). Vital signs. *Athletic Business, 18*, 65–67.

Turner, P., & Cusumano, S. (2000). Virtual advertising: Legal implications for sport. *Sport Management Review, 3*, 47–70.

Uniform Accessibility Standards. (2012). Accessibility. Retrieved from http://www.access-board.gov/ufas/ufas-html/ufas.htm#4.1.1

U.S. Army Corps of Engineers. (1990). *USACE design manual for indoor firing ranges* (CEHND 110-1-18). Huntsville, AL: U.S. Army Corps of Engineers Huntsville Division.

US Census Bureau. (2012). Sporting good sales by product category. In U.S. Census Bureau (Ed.), *Statistical Abstract of the United States: 2012.* Retrieved from www.census.gov/compendia/statab/2012/tables/12s1250.pdf

U.S. Consumer Product Safety Commission. (2000). *Guidelines for retrofitting bleachers* (Pub. No. 330). Bethesda, MD: Author.

U.S. Consumer Product Safety Commission. (2008). *Synthetic turf fields evaluation.* Washington, DC: Author.

U.S. Consumer Product Safety Commission. (2010). *Handbook for public playground safety.* Washington, DC: Author.

U.S. Consumer Product Safety Commission. (2012). *Skateboarding safety.* Washington, DC: Author.

U.S. Croquet Association. (2012). Retrieved from http://www.croquetamerica.com

U.S. Department of Energy. (2012). *SSL standards and guidelines: Building technologies program: Solid-state lighting technology fact sheet.* Retrieved from http://www1.eere.energy.gov/buildings/ssl/sslbasics_standards.html

Department of Justice. (2012, May) Revised ADA regulations: Implementing Title II and Title III. Retrieved from www.ada.gov/regs2010/ADAregs2010.htm

U.S. Department of Justice. (n.d.). Accessible stadiums. Retrieved from http://www.ada.gov/stadium.pdf

U.S. Equal Employment Opportunity Commission. (n.d.). Notice concerning the Americans With Disabilities Act (ADA) Amendments Act of 2008. Retrieved from http://www.eeoc.gov/laws/statutes/adaaa_notice.cfm

U.S. Equal Employment Opportunity Commission. (2008). *Performance results.* Retrieved from http://www.eeoc.gov/eeoc/plan/archives/annualreports/par/2008/performance_results.html

U.S. Forest Service. (2008). Accessibility for recreation programs. Retrieved from http://www.fs.fed.us/recreation/programs/accessibility

U.S. Green Building Council. (2012). Retrieved from http://www.usgbc.org

U.S. Indoor Soccer Association. (2009). *The official rules of indoor soccer: Amateur and youth edition.* Retrieved from http://www.indoorgoals.com/PDF/US%20Indoor%20Soccer%Rules.pdf

U.S. Lifesaving Association. (2005). *Guidelines for open water lifeguard agency certification.* Retrieved from http://www.usla.org/

U.S. National Electronic Injury Surveillance System. (2011). Injury data research statistics. Retrieved from http://www.cpsc.gov/en/Research-Statistics/NEISS-injury-data/

US Paddle Tennis Association. (2012). Paddle tennis rules. Retrieved from http://www.the uspta.org

U.S. Professional Tennis Association, Rules Committee. (1996). *Tennis rules.* New York, NY: Author.

US Racquetball Association. (2012). Racquetball rules. Retrieved from http://www.usra.org

U.S. Squash Association. (2012). Squash rules. Retrieved from http://www.ussquash.com

US Tennis. (2011). Tennis rules. Retrieved from http://www.usta.org

U.S. Tennis Association. (2012). Tennis facility design. Retrieved from http://www.usta.com

U.S. Volleyball Association, Rules Committee. (1997). *Volleyball rules.* New York, NY: Author.

USA Archery. (2008). Archery rules. Retrieved from http://usarchery.org

USA Badminton Association. (2012). Badminton rules. Retrieved from http://www.teamusa.org/badminton.aspx

USA Boxing (n.d.). Retrieved April 17, 2012, from http://www.TeamUSA.org/usa-boxing/.aspx

USA Fencing. (2012). Fencing rules. Retrieved from http://www.usfencing.org

USA National Shuffleboard Association. (2012). Shuffleboard rules. Retrieved from http://www.national-shuffleboard-association.us/

USA Roller Sports. (2013). Member lists. Retrieved from http://www2.teamusa.org/USA-Roller-Sports/Resources/Member-Lists.aspx

Urban, P. (1981). *The karate dojo* (12th ed.). Rutland, VT: Charles E. Tuttle.

Valentine, P. (2003, May). Out in front. *PanStadia International Quarterly, 9*(4), 23–38.

Van Dalen, D. B., & Bennett, B. L. (1953). *A world history of physical education.* Englewood Cliffs, NJ: Prentice Hall.

van der Smissen, B. (1990). *Legal liability and risk management for public and private entities: Sport and physical education, leisure services, recreation and parks, camping and adventure activities.* Cincinnati, OH: Anderson.

Vence, D. L. (2011). Center stage: The latest in scoreboards and sports lighting. *Recreation Management.* Retrieved from http://recmanagement.com/feature_print.php?fid=201110fe03

Veterans Readjustment Assistance Act of 1974, 38 U.S.C. § 4212.

Viklund, R. (1995, July). High-performance floors. *Athletic Business, 19*(7), 41–47.

Virginia Graeme Baker Pool and Spa Safety Act, H.R. 6-303 to 309, Title XIV – Pool and Spa Safety (2008).

Vocational Rehabilitation Act of 1973, Pub. L. 93–112, 87 Stat. 355 (amended 1974).

Walker, M. L. (1989). *A space analysis of physical education activity and ancillary areas in selected small colleges and universities* (Unpublished doctoral dissertation). University of New Mexico, Albuquerque.

Walker, M. L., & Seidler, T. L. (1993). *Sports equipment management*. Boston, MA: Jones & Bartlett.

Walker, M. L., & Stotlar, D. K. (1997). *Sport facility management*. Sudbury, MA: Jones & Bartlett.

Walls/ceilings-acoustic tile. (1994, December). Retrieved from http://www.ces.ncsu.edu/

Waterman, S. (2003a, February). Magic carpet. *PanStadia International Quarterly Report, 9*(3), 16–23.

Waterman, S. (2003b, November). The naming game. *PanStadia International Quarterly Report, 10*(2), 52–57.

Weinberg, A. (2003, March 23). Biggest college sports arena naming deals. Retrieved http://www.forbes.com/2003/03/24/cx_aw_0320ncaa.html

Whalin, G. (1997a). Fourteen questions to ask before you buy a point-of-sale system. *Employee Services Management, 40*(9), 30–31.

Whalin, G. (1997b). Using cutting-edge retail trends in employee stores. *Employee Services Management, 40*(1), 26–27.

Which dance floor? (2001). Retrieved from http://www.stagestep.com/

White, H., & Karabetsos, J. (1999). Planning and design. In T. Sawyer (Ed.), *Facilities planning for physical activity and sport: Guidelines for development*. Dubuque, IA: Kendall-Hunt.

Wilbur, R. A. (1999). Teams. . . friend or foe? *Employee Services Management, 42*(5), 9–11.

Wilkinson, H. T. (2002). Topdressing a baseball field. *Sportsturf, 18*(2), 27.

Williams, J. (2005). *Engineering tribology*. New York, NY: Cambridge University Press.

Winderbaum, L. (1977). *The martial arts encyclopedia*. Washington, DC: INSCAPE Publishers.

Wolf, M. (2001). Field's TVs: All that's missing is the recliner. *Rocky Mountain News*. Retrieved from http://web.archive.org/web/20060722000953/http://www.denver-rmn.com/invesco/scoreboards.shtml

Wolkoff, M. J. (1985). Chasing a dream: The use of tax abatements to spur urban economic development. *Urban Studies, 22*, 305–315.

Wong, G. M. (2001). *Essentials of amateur sports law* (2nd ed.). Dover, MA: Auburn House.

World Paddle Association. (2012). Paddleball rules. Retrieved from http://www.wpa.org

Yeomans, M. (2001, June 16). Heinz' naming rights deal. *Pittsburgh Tribune Review*, p. 1C.

York, R. O. (1982). *Human service planning*. Chapel Hill: The University of North Carolina Press.

YMCA of the USA. (2001). *On the guard II* (4th ed.). Champaign, IL: Human Kinetics.

YMCA of the USA. (2003). *YMCA aquatic management*. Champaign, IL: Human Kinetics.

YMCA of the USA. (2008). *YMCA pool operations manual* (3rd ed.). Champaign, IL: Human Kinetics.

Zimmerman, B. (2008, March). Indoor climbing gets serious. *Fitness Management*. Retrieved from www.fitnessmanagement.com

Glossary

Access. A way or means of approaching, entering, getting, using, and so on.

Acoustical engineer. Individual responsible for the design of large and small spaces that are appropriate for good sound (e.g., being able to hear in any seat in a large arena or aquatic complex, or not damaging to one's ears while playing racquetball).

Acoustical treatments. Applications designed to control/absorb sound.

Addendum. A written or graphic instrument issued by the architect prior to the execution of the contract that modifies or interprets the bidding documents by additions, deletions, clarifications, or corrections. An addendum becomes part of the contract documents when the contract is executed.

Advertising rights. Rights sold to various entities who wish to advertise to the spectators within the sports facility.

Aesthetics. A branch of philosophy dealing with the nature, creation, and appreciation of beauty.

Aggregate. Any hard material (usually sand and rock) for mixing in graduated fragments with a cementing material to form concrete, plaster, and the like.

Alternate bid. The amount stated in the bid to be added to or deducted from the amount of the base bid if the corresponding change in the work, as described in the bidding documents, is accepted.

Ancillary areas. Areas that provide support functions for the primary building attractions.

Angle of reflection. The angle between the reflected ray and the normal or perpendicular line to the point of reflection.

Angle of refraction. The angle between the refracted ray and the normal or perpendicular line drawn to the point of refraction.

Annunciator. An electronically controlled signal board that indicates to the building control center which courts/areas are occupied at any time.

Application for payment. A contractor-certified request for payment of amount due for completed portions of the work and, if the contract so provides, for materials or equipment delivered and suitably stored pending their incorporation into the work.

Appraisal survey. A method of evaluating the existing community resources, programs, and services in accordance with some established standards or criteria.

Architect. Designation reserved, usually by law, for a person or organization professionally qualified and duly licensed to perform architectural services, including, but not necessarily limited to, analysis of project requirements; creation and development of the project design; preparation of drawings, specifications, and bidding requirements; and general administration of the construction contract.

Architectural barriers. Obstacles that prevent parties from entering a facility or any architectural restraint that hampers moving throughout a building.

Area-elastic surfaces. Allow for dispersion of impact, where a bouncing object, or an individual jumping, is felt approximately 20 in. around the point of impact.

Area of deflection. The amount of impact that is felt in the vicinity of the points of contact.

Asphalt. A brown or black solid bituminous substance obtained largely as a residue from certain petroleum and which is insoluble in water. It is used in paving, roofing, and paints and varnishes and in combination with other materials for floor tiles.

Asset-backed securities. Investments secured by expected revenue.

Attractive nuisance. It is a doctrine that holds if a person creates a condition on his or her premises that reasonably may be construed to be the source of danger to children, he or she must take precautions as a reasonably prudent person would take to prevent injury to children of tender ages who he or she knows to be accustomed to frequent the area.

Baffles. A mounting or partition used to check the transmission of sound waves.

Base bid specifications. The specifications listing or description of those materials, equipment, and methods of construction upon which the bid must be predicated, exclusive of any alternate bids.

Base bid sum. The amount of money stated in the bid as the sum for which the bidder offers to perform the work described in the bidding documents, prior to adjustments for alternate bids that are also submitted.

Bearing (azimuth). A direction stated on compass degrees.

Bequests and trusts. Agreements made with specific individuals that upon their deaths a certain amount of their estates will be given to the organization.

Berm (or dike). A narrow shelf, path, or ledge, as along the top of a scarp or along a road.

Bid. A complete and properly signed proposal to do work or designated portion thereof for the amount or amounts stipulated in the proposal and submitted in accordance with the bidding documents

Bid bond. A form of bid security executed by the bidder and by a surety to guarantee that the bidder will enter into a contract within a specified time and furnish any required performance bond and labor and material payment bond.

Bidder. A person or entity who submits a bid, generally one who submits a bid for a prime contract with the owner, as distinct from a sub-bidder, who submits a bid to a prime bidder. Technically, a bidder is not a contractor on a specified project until a contract exists between the bidder and the owner.

Bidding documents. The bidding documents include an invitation to bid, instructions to bidders, the bid form, other bidding and contracting forms, and contract documents, including any addenda issued prior to receipt of bids.

Bid form. A form furnished to a bidder to be completed, signed, and submitted as the bidder's bid.

Bid opening. The opening and tabulation of bids submitted within the prescribed bid time and in conformity with the prescribed procedures.

Bid price. The amount stated in the bid for which the bidder offers to perform the work.

Bond. An interest-bearing certificate issued by a government or corporation promising to pay interest and to repay a sum of money (the principle) at a specified date in the future.

Bond period. Most government projects and some larger projects require the contractor to post not only a performance bond but also a 1-year (or some other specified time) warranty on the quality of the work.

Brightness. The luminous intensity created by direct emission of light from a source by transmission through a translucent medium or by reflection from a surface. The unit of brightness is the foot-lambert.

Brightness balance. Specified limitations of brightness differences and brightness ratios within the visual fields that, if observed, will contribute toward visual comfort and good visual performance.

Brightness contrast. The relationship between the brightness of an object and its immediate background.

Brightness difference. The difference in brightness among the various reflecting surfaces and light sources within the total visual field as measured in foot-lamberts.

Brightness ratio. The ratio of two brightnesses in the field of view.

British thermal unit. The quantity of heat (252 calories) required to raise the temperature of 1 lb of water 1°F at or near its point of maximum density (62% to 63%).

Broken-back track. Track configuration that features a more square track with short straightaways and rounded ends made of double curves.

Builder's risk insurance. A specialized form of property insurance that provides for loss or damage to the work during the course of construction.

Building permit. A permit issued by appropriate governmental authority allowing construction of a project in accordance with approved drawings and specifications.

Bulletin. A document issued by the architect after the contract is awarded. It may include drawings and other information used to solicit a proposal for change in the work. A bulletin becomes part of the contract documents only after being incorporated in a change order. A bulletin may also be referred to as a request for a change.

Bulkhead. An upright partition separating two parts in protection against fire or leakage; as a wall or embankment holding back earth, fire, or water.

Candlepower. The luminous intensity or illuminating capacity of a standard candle, as of a lamp measured in candles.

Cash allowance. An amount established in the contract documents for inclusion in the contract sum to cover cost of prescribed items not specified in detail, with provision that variations between the established amount and the final amount of the prescribed items will be reflected in change orders.

Cash discount. The amount that can be deducted from a seller invoice for payment within a stipulated period of time.

Cash donation. Donation of cash to an organization for a general or specific use in return for a personal tax deduction.

Casing. The act or process of encasing a frame, as of a window or a door.

Caulking. To fill in the seams or cracks with a filler.

Certificate of insurance. A document issued by an authorized representative of an insurance company stating the types, amounts, and effective dates of insurance in force for a designated insured.

Certificate of substantial completion. A certificate prepared by the architect on the basis of an inspection stating that the work or a designated portion of the work is substantially complete as of a particular date. This establishes the date of substantial completion with respect to the responsibilities of the owner and the contractor for security maintenance, heat, utilities, damage to the work, and insurance.

Certificates of participation. Involves a governmental entity buying a facility. The government entity then leases portions of the facility to the general public.

Certification of occupancy. A document issued by a governmental authority certifying that all or a designated portion of a building complies with the provisions of applicable statutes and regulations and permitting occupancy for its designated use.

Chair rail. An encircling band on the walls around the room at chair height to protect walls from damage by chairs contacting them.

Chamfer. The surface formed by cutting away the angle formed by two faces of timber, stone, or metal; to furrow; to channel; to flute; to bevel.

Change order. A written order to the contractor signed by the owner and the architect, issued after the execution of the contract, authorizing a change in the work or an adjustment in the contract sum or the contract time. The contract sum and contract time may only be changed by a change order. A change order signed by the contractor indicates the contractor agreement therewith, including the adjustment in the contract sum or the contract time.

Changes in the work. The changes ordered by the owner within the general scope of the contract, consisting of additions, deletions, or other revisions, which result in the contract sum and the contract time being adjusted accordingly. All such changes in the work shall be authorized by a change order and shall be performed under the applicable conditions of the contract documents.

Checkpoint. An obvious feature shown on the map that helps orienteers determine their progress along the course.

Chlorinate. To combine chlorine with water for purification.

Circuit breaker. A device that automatically interrupts the flow of an electric current.

Civil engineer. Individual who is responsible for the following tasks: grading and land movement plans, geometric layout of new improvements, plans for new roads and street pavements, utility plans, and plans for water collection system and sanitary sewers.

Code. Legal requirements legislated by federal, state, and/or local government describing legally how a building must be built, including electrical, mechanical, and structural. In many jurisdictions, they are generically titled building codes.

Comprehensive general liability insurance. A broad form of liability insurance covering claims for bodily injury and property damage, which combines under one policy coverage for all liability exposures (except those specifically excluded) on a blanket basis and automatically covers new and unknown hazards that may develop. Comprehensive general liability insurance automatically includes contractual liability coverage for certain types of contracts.

Concession. Authority, granted under contract with mutually acceptable provisions by all parties concerned, given by recreation departments to operators permitting them to provide services and/or to sell commodities to patrons of recreation areas and facilities.

Concessionaire exclusivity. The sale of the exclusive rights for all concessions within a spectator facility for a specified number of dollars over a specified period of time.

Condemnation. To pass an adverse judgment on; to disapprove of strongly; to censure; to prove guilty of wrongdoing; to declare unfit for service or use; to condemn private property for public use; the processes by which government exercises its rights of eminent domain.

Condenser. That which makes dense, concentrates, or compresses.

Convector. A medium of convection; the transmission of heat or electricity by the mass movement of the heated or electrified particles, such as air, gas, or liquid currents.

Construction document phase. This phase is based on the design development phase. The architect prepares final drawings and construction specifications.

Construction phase. The final phase is the construction phase. The architect shall (1) visit the site at least twice monthly at appropriate intervals at various stages of construction, (2) certify payments for work completed, (3) have the authority to reject work that does not conform to the contract documents, and (4) review.

Contingency allowance. A sum included in the project budget that is designated to cover unpredictable or unforeseen items of work, or changes in the work subsequently required by the owner.

Contract. A legally enforceable promise or agreement between two or among several persons.

Contract award. A communication from an owner accepting a bid or negotiated proposal. An award creates legal obligation between the parties.

Contractor's liability insurance. Insurance purchased and maintained by the contractor to protect the contractor from specified claims that may arise out of or result from the contractor operations under the contract, whether such operations are by the contractor or by any subcontractor or by anyone directly or indirectly employed by any of them, or by anyone for whose acts any of them may be liable.

Contract sum. The sum stated in the owner–contractor agreement, which is the total amount payable by the owner to the contractor for the performance of the work under the contract documents. The contract sum may be adjusted only by a change order.

Control. One of several events to be visited by the orienteer.

Control card. A card carried by orienteers used to verify that the competitor visited the control.

Control description (clue card). A sheet or card with a brief description of the control location, control number, and other clues for locating controls. The International Orienteering Federation control symbols are the internationally recognized symbols for orienteering.

Control marker. A distinct marker that identifies the control, usually a three-dimensional orange and white nylon marker.

Control punch. A small clipper used to make a distinctive mark on the control card to verify visiting the control.

Cost plus fee agreement. An agreement under which the contractor (in an owner–contractor agreement) is reimbursed for the direct and indirect costs or performance of the agreement and, in addition, is paid a fee for services. The fee is usually stated as a stipulated sum or as a percentage of cost.

Critical path method (CPM). A charting of all events and operations to be encountered in completing a given process, rendered in a form permitting determination of the relative significance of each event, and establishing the optimal sequence and duration of operations.

Crowned field. A curved field with the summit or highest point (crown) at the middle, running lengthwise. (A football field is crowned for the purpose of drainage.)

Dado. A term applied to the lower portion of walls when decorated separately.

Date of agreement. The date stated in the agreement. If no date is stated, it could be the date on which the agreement is actually signed, if this is recorded, or it may be the date established by the award.

Date of substantial completion. The date certified by the architect when the work or a designated portion thereof is sufficiently complete, in accordance with the contract documents, so the owner can occupy the work or designated portion thereof for the use for which it is intended.

Decibel. The unit for measuring the relative loudness of sounds (as compared with the loudness of a sound that can just be heard by the ear).

Deck. A platform or floor, such as a ship's deck or a swimming pool deck.

Deduction. The amount deducted from the contract sum by a change order.

Deductive alternate. An alternate bid resulting in a deduction from the base bid of the same bidder.

Desiccant. A substance that absorbs humidity.

Design. The architectural form, pattern, or scheme of construction of health, physical education, or recreation areas, facilities, and their units.

Design–build process. A process in which a person or entity assumes responsibility under a single contract for both the design and construction of the project.

Design development phase. This phase is based on the results of the schematic design phase. The architect prepares, during this phase, drawings including floor plans, mechanical and electrical systems, and structural design; outline of materials to be used; landscape designs; parking lot designs; and other such documents as appropriate.

Dewpoint. The temperature at which moisture will condense out of the air.

Diatomaceous. Containing or consisting of diatoms or their fossils (a number of related microscopic algae, one-celled or in colonies, whose walls consist of two parts or valves and contain silica).

Discomfort glare. Glare that produces discomfort; it does not necessarily interfere with visual performance or visibility.

District. The district is a large geographical planning unit of a large city, comprising a number of communities.

Drainage. Surface and subsurface removal of water and groundwater. When properly designed, surface and subsurface irrigation eliminates standing water and relieves saturated turf. Furthermore, it will maintain the proper amount of subsurface moisture.

Drawings. Graphic and pictorial documents showing the design, location, and dimensions of the elements of a project. Drawings generally include plans, elevations, sections, details, schedules, and diagrams. When capitalized, the term refers to the graphic and pictorial portions of the contract documents.

Easement. A right or privilege that a person may have on another's land, as the right-of-way.

Eaves. The lower part of a roof projecting beyond the face of the wall.

Economy. Costs are kept at a minimum compatible with program needs, durability of materials, low maintenance, and attractiveness.

Egress. A way out to grade level around a building.

Electrical contractor. The individual who will provide all electrical wiring, boxes, switches, receptacles, equipment hookups, conduit for all telephone wires, computer cable, television cable, security wiring, and public address system.

Elevation. A geometrical projection on a plane perpendicular to the horizon; an elevated place; the distance above or below the zero level or ground level.

Eligible individuals. Those individuals who have a physical or mental impairment that substantially limits a major life activity.

Eminent domain. The legal right of federal, state, and local governments to take any property required for public purpose. The right implies that the land must be taken by due process of law and that the owner from whom the land is taken receives reasonable compensation.

Environment. The aggregate of all the external conditions, surroundings, and influences affecting the place or individual.

Equal quadrant track. This type of track configuration features two 100-m straightaways and two 100-m curves.

Equipment. Movable furnishings as opposed to stationary property; relatively permanent articles, furnishings, machinery, and devices used in administering, operating, and maintaining recreation programs and services.

Escutcheon. A shield or plate as around a keyhole.

Estimate. A forecast of construction cost, as opposed to a firm bid, prepared by a contractor for a project or a portion thereof. A term sometimes used to denote a contractor application or request for a progress payment.

Estimate of construction cost, detailed. A forecast of construction cost prepared on the basis of a detailed analysis of material and labor for all items of work, as contrasted with an estimate based on current area, volume, or similar unit costs.

Extra. A term sometimes used to denote an item of work involving additional cost.

Facade. The face or elevation of a building.

Facilities. Areas, structures, and fixtures essential to accommodate the program.

Fee. A term used to denote compensation for professional ability, capability, and availability or organization, excluding compensation for direct, indirect, and/or reimbursable expenses, as an agreement based on a professional fee plus expenses. Sometimes denotes compensation of any kind for services rendered.

Field house. A facility providing enclosed and unobstructed space adaptable to various physical education and recreation activities, services, demonstrations, and meetings. It is often located on or near a playfield or athletic field. The term also refers to a service building used by people using the athletic field.

Fixed limit of construction cost. The maximum construction cost established in the agreement between the owner and the architect.

Fixed turning radius, wheel to wheel. The tracking of the caster wheels and large wheels of a wheelchair when pivoting on a spot.

Fixture. Something firmly attached, as a part or an appendage, such as a light fixture; equipment affixed to the surface of a building in such a manner that its removal would deface or mar the surface. (Legally, it is the property of the building.)

Flashing. Sheets of metal or other material used to waterproof joints and cages, especially of a roof.

Fluid mechanics. The study of the flow properties of liquids and gases.

Flush. Unbroken or even in surface; on a level with the adjacent surfaces; having no indentation.

Fluting. The vertical channeling on the shaft of a column.

Foot-candle. The illumination at a point on a surface that is 1 ft from and perpendicular to a uniform point source of 1 candela (candle); a lighting term used to denote quantity.

Foot-lambert. A unit of brightness of a surface or of a light source. One foot-lambert equals 1 lumen per square foot. Candelas (candles) per square inch is an optional term for a unit of brightness of a light source. One candela (candle) per square inch equals 452 foot-lamberts.

Foot-pound. A unit of energy equal to the amount of energy required to raise a weight of 1 lb a distance of 1 ft.

Force account. A term used when work is ordered, often under urgent circumstances, to be performed without prior agreement as to lump sum or unit price cost thereof and is to be billed at the cost of labor, materials and equipment, insurance, taxes, and so forth, plus an agreed percentage for overhead and profit.

Foreseeability. The reasonable anticipation that harm or injury is a likely result from certain acts or omissions.

Fulcrum. The support or point of support on which a lever rotates.

Fullers earth. A clay-like, earthy substance used as a filter medium.

Function. Measuring satisfaction of purpose, where function is the particular purpose for which a person or thing is specifically fitted or used or for which a thing exists.

Furring. The leveling of a floor, wall, or ceiling, or the creating of air spaces with thin strips of wood or metal before adding boards or plaster; the act of trimming or lining.

Gable. The triangular portion of a wall, between the enclosing lines of a sloping roof.

Gallery. A communicating passage or wide corridor for pictures and statues; upper story for seats.

General conditions. That part of the contract documents that sets forth many of the rights, responsibilities, and relationships of the parties involved, particularly those provisions that are common to many construction projects.

General contractor. Individual responsible for constructing and finishing floors, walls, ceilings, steel structure, built-in cabinets, sidewalks, driveways, doorways, windows, and other things not completed by the electrical and mechanical contractors.

General obligation bonds. A full-faith and credit obligation bond. Refers to bonds that are repaid with a portion of the general property tax.

Glare. The sensation produced by brightnesses within the visual field that are sufficiently greater than the brightness to which the eyes are adapted that cause annoyance, discomfort, or loss in visual performance and visibility.

Glaze. Any impervious material produced by fire used to cover the body of a tile to prevent absorption of liquids and gases, to resist abrasion and impact, or to give a more pleasing appearance.

Glazed tile. A hard, dense tile that has been glazed to prevent absorption, to increase its beauty, or to improve ease of cleaning.

Gradient. The grade or rate of ascent or descent; a rate of increase or decrease of a variable magnitude, or the curve that represents it.

Grid. A framework of parallel bars; a grating.

Groundskeeping. The management and maintenance of the outdoor spaces, including landscaped grounds and play spaces.

Guaranteed maximum cost. The sum established in an agreement between owner and contractor as the maximum cost of performing specified work on the basis of cost of labor and materials plus overhead expenses and profit.

Guidelines. An indication or outline of policy or conduct.

Gutter. A trough or channel along or under the eaves of a roof to carry off rainwater; also around the upper edge of a swimming pool.

Gymnasium. A building or part of a building devoted primarily to group activities, such as basketball, gymnastics, volleyball, and dancing. It is equipped with gymnastic apparatus, a court area for playing athletic and game activities, dressing room facilities, and seating arrangements for spectators.

Gymtorium. A combination facility designed to be used as a gymnasium or auditorium. Other combination facilities are cafetoriums (cafeteria and auditorium) and gymnateria (gymnasium and cafeteria).

Header. A wooden beam placed between two long beams with the ends of the short beams resting against it.

Hose bibb. A faucet with the nozzle bent downward and threaded for hose connections.

Humidity. Moisture content of the air expressed in percentage of maximum.

Hydrology. Refers to the study of the patterns of water flow above and below the surface.

Inclusion (designing for). A concept that supports full facility and full program access to all people.

Indirect expense. Overhead expenses (e.g., general office expense) indirectly incurred and not directly related to a specific project.

Indirect lighting. The act of reflecting light off the ceiling to create a clean and pleasant form of light arrangement in an indoor space.

Indoor air quality. A product of the quality of the fresh air introduced into the ventilation system and the quality of the existing indoor air that is recycled.

In-kind contribution. An organization, business, or craftsman donates equipment or time to the project in return for a tax deduction.

Instructions to bidders. Instructions contained in the bidding documents for preparing and submitting bids for a construction project or designated portion thereof.

Integral. The result of integrating parts into a whole; necessary for completeness; essential; whole or complete.

Integration. Functional interrelationship, the process of making whole.

Interior designer. This individual will assist in selecting paint colors, wallpaper, rugs (color, texture/thickness), furniture, accessories, artwork, and other items to make spaces comfortable, functional, and aesthetically pleasing.

Invitation to bid. A portion of the bidding documents soliciting bids for a construction project.

Invited bidders. The bidders selected by the owner, after consultation with the architect, as the only ones from whom bids will be received.

IP telephony. The use of an IP network to transmit voice, video, and data.

Irrigation. Surface and subsurface supplemental watering. When properly designed, surface and subsurface irrigation provides an even distribution of water for plants and turfgrass.

Jamb. A side post of a doorway, window frame, fireplace, and the like.

Join. A place or part where two things or parts are joined together.

Joint ventures. A joint venture is a project with multiple parties involved in its planning and operation.

Labor and material payment bond. A bond of the contractor in which a surety guarantees to the owner that the contractor will pay for labor and material used in the performance of the contract. The claimants under the bond are defined as those having direct contracts with the contractor or any subcontractor.

Landmark. An easily recognized, obvious feature in the landscape.

Landscape architect. Individual who provides information such as specifications and designs for landscaping a building or green area, types of trees to be planted, types of flowers to be planted, number of walkways, specifications and designs for the irrigation system, and types of grass to be planted or sod to be installed.

Landscape architecture. The art or science of arranging land, together with spaces and objects upon it, for safe, efficient, healthful, pleasant human use.

Latent heat. The heat liberated or absorbed by a substance as it changes phase at a constant temperature and pressure.

Lease agreements. A program to lease facilities to other organizations during the off-season or additional spaces within the facility not used for the sporting activity, such as office space or retail space.

Legend. A section of a map that provides an interpretation of map symbols.

Letter of agreement. A letter stating the terms of an agreement between addressor and addressee, usually prepared to be signed by the addressee to indicate acceptance of those terms as legally binding.

Letter of intent. A letter signifying an intention to enter into a formal agreement, usually setting forth the general terms of such agreement.

Liability. The responsibility of one who is bound in law and justice to do something that may be forced by action; a condition that gives rise to an obligation to do a particular thing to be enforced by court action; a responsibility between parties that the courts recognize and enforce; an unintentional breach of legal duty causing reasonably foreseeable damage.

Liability insurance. Insurance that protects the insured against liability on account of injury to the person or property of another.

Life insurance packages. A program to solicit the proceeds from a life insurance policy purchased by a supporter to specifically benefit the organization upon the death of the supporter.

License. A formal permission to do something; a document indicating certain permission; freedom to deviate from strict conduct, rule, or practice; generally may be permitted by common consent.

Light. Visible radiation, generally considered to be the electromagnetic radiations of wave lengths between 380 and 780 millimicrons, which are the violet and red ends of the visible spectrum, respectively.

Lintel. The horizontal timber or stone that spans an opening, as over doors or windows.

Louver. An aperture or frame with louver boards fitted in a slatted panel for ventilation.

Low bid. A bid stating the lowest bid price for performance of the work, including selected alternates, conforming with bidding documents.

Lowest responsible bidder. A bidder who submits the lowest bona fide bid and is considered by the owner and the architect to be fully responsible and qualified to perform the work for which the bid is submitted.

Lumen. A unit of measure for the flow of light.

Luminaries. Floodlight fixtures with a lamp, reflector, and so on.

Luxury suites. These areas have been designed for VIP use and leased by large corporations to wine and dine their clients as well as to provide them entertainment.

Magnetic lines. Lines on an orienteering map pointing toward magnetic north.

Master map. Large orienteering map near the start line that shows the course and controls.

Mechanical contractor. Individual who is responsible for all plumbing (hot and cold water, sewage), humidity control, heating and cooling systems, ventilation systems, and pumps.

Mechanical/electrical engineer. The individual who provides information such as specifications for heating and air-conditioning equipment, drawings and specification for power and lighting, determinations of plumbing requirements, and the design of any communication system (security, public address, music, closed-circuit television, etc.).

Mechanic lien. A lien on real property created by statute in all states in favor of persons supplying labor or material for a building or structure for the value of labor or material supplied by them. In some jurisdictions, a mechanic lien also exists for the value of professional services. Clear title to the property cannot be obtained until the claim for the labor, materials, or professional services is settled.

Modification. This is a written amendment to the contract signed by both parties. It is a change order. It is a written interpretation issued by the architect. Finally, it could be a written order for a minor change in the work issued by the architect.

Mullion. A slender, vertical dividing bar between the lights and windows, screens, and so forth.

Municipal bonds. Bonds issued by a government or a subdivision of a state.

Named insured. Any person, firm or corporation, or any of its members specifically designated by name as insured(s) in a policy, as distinguished from others who, although unnamed, are protected under some circumstances.

Naming rights. Corporations vie for the right to place their name on the facility for a specific sum of money for a specific number of years.

Negligence. The omission of that care which a person of common prudence usually takes of his or her own concerns.

Negotiating phase. Phase in which the architect assists the owner in obtaining bids or negotiating proposals and assists in awarding and preparing contracts for construction.

Nonconforming work. Work that does not fulfill the requirements of the contract documents.

Non-equal quadrant track. This track configuration resembles a stretched or compressed oval shape with two straightaways of one length and two curves of another length.

Non-guaranteed bonds. These bonds are sold on the basis of repayment from other designated revenue sources.

Nonslip. Having the tread so constructed as to reduce skidding or slipping.

Nonslip tile. Incorporates certain admixtures such as abrasive granules in the body or in the surface of the tile.

Norcompass (thumb compass). An orienteering compass that attaches to the left thumb of the orienteer.

Opaque. Does not transmit light; substances that will not allow light through.

Open space. A relatively underdeveloped area provided within or near urban development to minimize feelings of congested living.

Optimal thermal environment. Provides conditions that make it possible to dissipate body heat in the most effortless manner. Combines radiant temperature where surface and air temperature are balanced; air temperature between 64°F and 72°F, humidity between 40% and 60%; and a constant air movement of 20 to 40 linear feet per minute at a sitting height.

Outrigger. Any temporary support extending out from the main structure.

Owner–architect agreement. Contract between owner and architect for professional services.

Owner–contractor agreement. Contract between owner and contractor for performance of the work for construction of the project or portion thereof.

Owner's representative. The person designated as the official representative of the owner in connection with a project.

Park. An area permanently dedicated to recreation use and generally characterized by its natural, historic, and landscape features. It is used for both passive and active forms of recreation and may be designed to serve the residents of a neighborhood, community, state, region, or nation.

Park district. A subdivision of state government exercising within its jurisdiction the authority of a municipality. It may operate and maintain parks, recreation programs, police forces, airports, and other such facilities and programs as may be designated in the act establishing the district.

Parking fees. Fees generated from parking lots that surround the spectator facility.

Park–school. An area cooperatively planned by school and municipal authorities to provide programs of education and recreation for day-by-day use by the people of a neighborhood or community.

Parkway. Essentially an elongated park with a road running through it, the use of which is restricted to pleasure traffic. The parkway often serves to connect large units in a park system and is rarely found except in large cities.

Performance bond. A bond of the contractor in which a surety guarantees to the owner that the work will be performed in accordance with the contract documents. Except where prohibited by statute, the performance bond is frequently combined with the labor and material payment bond.

Permeable. That which can be permeated; open to passage or penetration, especially by fluids.

PERT schedule. An acronym for project evaluation review technique. The PERT schedules the activities and events anticipated in a work process.

Pilaster. A rectangular feature in the shape of a pillar, but projecting only one sixth of its breadth from a wall.

Plan. A two-dimensional graphic representation of the design, location, and dimensions of the project, or parts thereof, seen in a horizontal plan viewed from above.

Playfield. A recreation area designed to serve the needs of a community or neighborhood having a population of 10,000 to 15,000 persons. Its essential features are a community recreation building, areas for sports and games, a playground for children, picnic areas, public parking, and, occasionally, a swimming area.

Point elastic surfaces. Maintain impact effects at the immediate point of contact on the floor, with the ball, object, or individual.

Post sleeves. Metal pipe installed at ground level or slightly below, which receives posts to facilitate various activities.

Preconstruction conference. A meeting between the contracting agency and the contractor(s) prior to the commencement of construction to review the contract items and make sure there is an understanding of how the job is to be undertaken.

Preferred/premium seating. VIP seating located within the luxury suites or in the club areas of the stadium that are the most expensive seats in the facility.

Prequalification of bidders. The process of investigating the qualification of prospective bidders on the basis of their experience, availability, and capability for the contemplated project and approving qualified bidders.

Prime contract. Contract between owner and contractor for construction of the project or portion thereof.

Progress payment. Partial payment made during progress of the work on account of work completed and/or material suitably stored.

Project. The total construction of which the work performed under the contract documents may be the whole or a part, or it could also include the total furniture, furnishings, and equipment.

Project cost. Total cost of the project including construction, professional compensation, real estate, furnishings, equipment, and financing.

Property damage insurance. Insurance coverage for the insured's legal liability for claims for injury to or destruction of tangible property, including loss of use resulting therefrom, but usually not including coverage for injury to or destruction of property which is in the care, custody, and control of the insured.

Property insurance. Coverage for loss or damage to the work at the site caused by perils of fire, lightning, extended coverage perils, vandalism, and malicious mischief and additional perils. Property insurance may be written on (1) the completed value form in which the policy is written at the start of a project in a predetermined amount representing the insurable value of the work and adjusted to the final insurable cost on completion of the work or (2) the reporting form in which the property values fluctuate during the policy term, requiring monthly statements showing the increase in value of work in place over the previous month.

Public accommodations. A facility operated by a private entity whose operations affect commerce. The private entity that owns, leases or leases to, or operates a place of public accommodation.

Public liability insurance. Insurance covering liability of the insured for negligent acts resulting in bodily injury, disease, or death of persons other than employees of the insured and/or property damage.

Rabbet. A groove or cut made in the edge of a board in such a way that another piece may be fitted in to form a point.

Ramps, ramps with gradients. Because the term *ramp* has a multitude of meanings and uses, its use in this text is clearly defined as ramps with gradients (or ramps with slopes) that deviate from what would otherwise be considered the normal level. An exterior ramp, as distinguished from a "walk," would be considered an appendage to a building leading to a level above or below existing ground level. As such, a ramp shall meet certain requirements similar to those imposed upon stairs.

Ray. A single line of light coming from a luminous point.

Readily achievable. Easily accomplishable and able to be carried out without much difficulty or expense. It constitutes a lower standard than undue burden.

Reasonable accommodations. Requires that employers and facilities make an accommodation if doing so will not impose an undue hardship on the operation of the business or facility.

Record drawings. Construction drawings revised to show significant changes made during the construction process, usually based on marked-up prints, drawings, and other data furnished by the contractor to the architect.

Reflectance (reflection factor). The percentage of light falling on a surface that is reflected by that surface.

Reflected glare. Glare resulting from specular reflections of high brightness in polished or glossy surfaces in the field of view. It usually is associated with reflections from within a visual task or areas in close proximity to the region being viewed.

Reflection factor. The percentage of light reflected by a given surface.

Refrigerants. Any of the various liquids that vaporize at a low temperature used in mechanical refrigeration.

Regulations. An order issued by an executive authority of a government and having the force of law.

Reimbursable expenses. The amounts expended for or on account of the project which, in accordance with the terms of the appropriate agreement, are to be reimbursed by the owner.

Release of lien. An instrument executed by a person or entity supplying labor, material, or professional services on a project that releases that person or entity for a mechanic lien against the project property.

Resident engineer. An engineer employed by the owner to represent the owner's interests at the project site during the construction phase.

Resilience. The ability to bounce or spring back into shape, position, and so forth.

Restaurant rights. The sale of the exclusive rights for all the restaurants within a spectator facility.

Retainage. A sum withheld from progress payments to the contractor in accordance with the terms of the owner–contractor agreement.

Revenue bonds. A bond that can be backed exclusively by the revenue occurring from the project or from a designated revenue source, such as a hotel/motel tax, restaurant tax, auto rental tax, or a combination of these taxes and others.

Reverberation. Reflection of light or sound waves.

Riser. The vertical distance (and pieces) between the steps in a stairway.

Rolling load. The capacity of a floor to withstand damage from external forces, such as bleacher movement, equipment transport, or similar activities.

Safety direction (panic azimuth; safety bearing). A compass bearing or direction to guide the orienteer directly to a road, major trail, or settlement if lost or injured.

Schedule of values. A statement furnished by the contractor to the architect reflecting the portions of the contract sum allocated to the various portions of the work and used as the basis for reviewing the contractor applications for payment.

Schematic design phase. This phase is based on the program developed by the project committee and submitted to the architect. The architect will prepare, for approval by the owner, schematic design documents, including drawings (floor plans and mechanicals), scale model, project development schedule, and estimated costs.

Score orienteering. A type of orienteering where controls blanket the course, and each is assigned a point value based on the distance to the controls and how difficult they will be to find. The individual or team with the most points in the prescribed time is the winner.

Service building. A structure affording the facilities necessary to accommodate the people using recreation facilities such as a golf course, swimming pool, or ice-skating rink. It may contain dressing rooms, lockers, toilets, shower rooms, check rooms and storage rooms, a lobby or lounge, and a repair shop. Also, the term is used in reference to buildings that facilitate the operation and maintenance of the recreation system, such as greenhouses, storage buildings, and garages.

Shadow. The space from which light from a given source is excluded by an opaque object; the area of comparative darkness resulting from the interception of light by an opaque object.

Sheathing. The inner covering of boards or waterproof material on the roof or outside wall of a frame house.

Shelter house. A building, usually located on a playground or playfield, equipped with features such as an office for the director, space for storage, toilets, and a craft room or play-room.

Shop drawings. Drawings, diagrams, schedules, and other specific data specially prepared for the work by the contractor or any subcontractor, manufacturer, supplier, or distributor to illustrate some portion of the work.

Sill. A heavy horizontal timber or line of masonry supporting a wall; a horizontal piece forming the bottom frame of a door or window.

Site analysis. The gathering of information and data about a site and adjacent properties. Its purpose is to find a place for a particular use or find a use for a particular place.

Ski orienteering. Orienteering conducted on cross-country skis.

Sleeper. A piece of timber, stone, or steel, on or near the ground to support some superstructure.

Soft space. Space in a facility that requires little or no special provisions (such as plumbing or expensive finishes) and therefore is space that is easily vacated and converted.

Special authority bonds. These bonds have been used to finance stadiums or arenas by special public authorities, which are entities with public powers that are able to operate outside normal constraints placed on governments.

Specifications. A part of the contract documents contained in the project manual consisting of written requirements for material, equipment, construction systems, standards, and workmanship.

Sponsorship packages. Corporate support programs pursued whereby large local and international firms are solicited to supply goods and services to a sporting organization at no cost or at a substantial reduction in the wholesale prices in return for visibility for the corporation.

Staggered. Arranged so that alternate intervals are used, as to space or time.

Stanchion. An upright bar, beam, or post used as a support; one of a pair of linked, upright bars.

Standards. Norms established by authority, research, custom, or general consent to be used as criteria and guides in establishing and evaluating programs, leadership, areas, facilities, and plans; as measures of quantity, quality, weight, extent, or value.

Stile. A vertical piece in a panel or frame, as a door or window; a set of steps used in climbing over a fence or wall.

Stipulated sum agreement. A contract in which a specific amount is set forth as the total payment for performance of the contract.

Structural engineer. Individual concerned with determining possible structural systems and materials, providing cost of preferred systems and materials, and designing final structure to meet architectural requirements.

Sub-bidder. A person or entity who submits a bid to a bidder for material or labor for a portion of the work at the site.

Subcontract. An agreement between a prime contractor and a subcontractor for a portion of the work at the site.

Subcontractor. A person or entity who has a direct contract with the contractor to perform any of the work at the site.

Successful bidder. The bidder chosen by the owner for the award of a construction contract.

Superintendent. The contractor representative at the site who is responsible for continuous field supervision, coordination, completion of the work and, unless another person is designated in writing by the contractor to the owner and the architect, for prevention of accidents.

Supplementary conditions. A part of the contract documents that supplements and may also modify, change, add to, or delete from provisions of the general conditions.

Supplementary lighting. Providing additional lighting on areas such as those containing goals and targets.

Supplier. A person or entity who supplies material or equipment for the work, including that fabricated to a special design, but who does not perform labor at the site.

Survey. A cooperative undertaking that applies scientific methods to the study and treatment of current recreation data, problems, and conditions. The limits of a survey are prescribed before execution, and its facts, findings, conclusions, and recommendations are made common knowledge and provide a base for intelligent, coordinated action.

Synthetic. Artificial; not real or genuine; a substance produced by chemical synthesis.

Tanbark. Any bark containing tannin (used to tan hides), and after the tannin has been extracted, it is used to cover tracks, circus rings, and dirt floors in field houses.

Template. A short piece placed in a wall under a beam to distribute the pressure; also a beam spanning a doorway, or the like, and supporting joists.

Terra cotta. Clayware having the surface coated with fine slip or glaze; used in the facing of large buildings for relief ornament or statues.

Terrazzo. A type of flooring made of small chips of marble set irregularly in cement and polished.

Thermodynamics. The branch of physics dealing with the transformation of heat to and from other forms of energy, and with the laws governing such conversions of energy.

Thermostat. An apparatus for regulating temperature, especially one that automatically controls a heating unit.

Threshold. A piece of wood, stone, metal, or the like placed beneath a door; doorsill; the entrance or beginning point of something; the point at which a stimulus is just strong enough to be perceived or to produce a response, as the threshold of pain.

Topographical map. A precise map that designates altitude of the land with contour lines.

Topography. Refers to the surface features of a site including variations in elevation.

Trade (craft). An occupation requiring manual skill or members of a trade organized into a collective body.

Trade shows. Expositions that generate sales for a particular industry.

Trail orienteering (control choice). A modified type of orienteering designed for orienteers with disabilities.

Translucent. Transmitting light, but scattering it so that details cannot be distinguished through the translucent medium.

Transparent. Allowing light to pass through so that objects behind can be seen distinctly.

Underpinning. A supporting structure of the foundation, especially one placed beneath a wall.

Undue hardship. Requiring significant difficulty or expense, considering the employer size, financial resources, and the nature and structure of the operation.

Unglazed tile. A hard, dense tile of homogenous composition deriving color and texture from the materials of which it is made.

Unit price. The amount stated in the bid as a price per unit of measurement for materials or services as described in the bidding documents or in the proposed contract documents.

Utility. The degree to which an area, facility, or instrument is designed to serve its purpose, and the degree to which it is used; percentage of usage during the workday adapted or available for general use or utility.

Vendor/contractor equity. Vendor or contractor returns to the owner a specific percentage of the profit generated by the firms during the construction process.

Vestibule. A passage hall or chamber between the outer door and the interior of a building.

Vetting. Checking the orienteering course before competition.

Vinyl tile. Asphalt tile impregnated with vinyl.

Visual task. Conventionally, designates those details and objects that must be seen for the performance of a given activity and includes the immediate background of the details or objects.

Vitreous. Of, pertaining to, or derived from glass; like glass, as in color, brittleness, and luster.

Wainscot. A wood lining or paneling on the lower part of the walls of a room.

Waiver of lien. An instrument by which a person or organization who has or may have a right of mechanic lien against the property of another relinquishes such right.

Walk-off area. The first 12 ft on the inside of an entry doorway that functions exactly as the name implies; it is within this radius that dust, dirt, oil from the parking area, and water from rain and melting snow are deposited.

Walkway. Because the terms *walk* and *walks* have a multitude of meanings and uses, their use in this text is clearly defined as a predetermined, prepared surface; exterior pathway leading to or from a building or facility, or from one exterior area to another, placed on the existing ground level and not deviating from the level of the existing ground immediately adjacent.

Warranty. Legally enforceable assurance of quality or performance of a product or work of the duration of satisfactory performance.

Weephole. To permit or let drops of water or other liquid exude from inner containers, from sources such as condensation or overflow.

Wilderness. A rather large, generally inaccessible area left in its natural state available for recreation experiences. It is void of development, except for those trails, sites, and similar conditions made by previous wilderness users. (No mechanical transportation permitted.)

Workers' compensation insurance. Insurance covering the liability of an employer for compensation and other benefits required by workers' compensation laws with respect to injury, sickness, diseases, or death arising from their employment.

Zone heating. To mark off or divide building areas for the purposes of area climate control.

Architectural Drawings

Axonometric projection. A drawing where the angles can vary depending on the needs of the person drawing it. Axonometric projections tend to offer a view from higher up and thus are especially helpful in showcasing building interiors with the ceiling pulled away, allowing rooms to be shown within the context of the entire building plan.

CAD drawings. Computer-aided design has quickly become a staple of building design, as it allows the creation and manipulation of two- and three-dimensional representations of a building. A plan drawn from an eye-level view can be "entered" by the viewer, with perspective automatically maintained by the computer as the client performs the "walk-through." Additionally, the point of view can be changed, allowing architects and clients to immediately see how their designs translate into actual future use.

Cutaway. Similar to an axonometric projection and shows the building from an oblique angle. Where it differs is in its representation of both interior and exterior building elements.

Elevation. A two-dimensional view of a building's external face drawn on a vertical plane; typically, four elevations will be used to show the building from each of four compass points.

Floor plan. A drawn-to-scale overhead view of each floor looking down from an imaginary plan cut 3 ft to 4 ft above the floor. The plans show circulation paths and recreational and support paths as well as doorways, window openings, furniture, and counters. Elements located above the plane of the cut are usually shown using dashed lines (e.g., suspended running tracks, balconies, overhead cabinets).

Isometric projection. Drawings drawn with a 30-60-90 triangle, so the subject is always in proportion.

Reflected ceiling plan. Ceilings are detailed on a specific drawing type called the reflected ceiling plan, which is a drawing using a similar cut as the floor plan but higher up the wall looking up and down.

Rendering. A perspective or elevation drawing, showing building materials, colors, shadows, textures, and natural features of the site.

Section. Similar to a floor plan, except that its imaginary cut is vertical, not horizontal. It is therefore most frequently used to detail arena bowls and stadium grandstands.

Site plan. An aerial view of the entire project site including the facility, parking lots, pedestrian ways, conceptual landscaping ideas, and other site amenities.

Structural Elements

Building walls. Often used to bear loads. However, building walls do not always serve to bear the weight of higher elements. For example, in post-and-beam construction, vertical elements (columns or posts) support horizontal beams or lintels, which are beams that bridge an opening such as a door or window.

Cantilevers. A beam that is supported only at one end by means of downward force behind a fulcrum to eliminate obstructed-view seats but forces stadium decks to be stacked farther from the field, in order to provide support for the extended portion of the beam. Cantilevered beams are also used extensively in the construction of staircases and balconies.

Ceiling. The underside of a roof.

Ceiling plenum. The space between a false ceiling and a structured ceiling.

Clerestories. Clerestories (clearstories) are traditionally walls containing windows that are vertically above a low roofline and topped with the uppermost rooftop.

Coffered ceiling. This type of ceiling utilizes sunken square or polygonal ornamental panels.

Colonnade. A colonnade is a series of regularly spaced columns.

Columns, stanchions (upright structural members), load-bearing walls. Typically building floors and roofs are supported by columns, stanchions, and load-bearing walls.

Coping. Similar to an eave with a similar purpose, although the term is used liberally to represent a variety of treatments that cover the top of a wall.

Curtain wall. Exterior cladding used as a non-load-bearing wall.

Demi-columns. Half-columns that are half sunk into walls.

Eave. An overhanging portion of a roof to keep rain from running down exterior walls. An eave is sometimes called a soffit.

Engaged columns. A wall that encases a column or part of a column.

Fascia. The horizontal band that joins the roof to the eave.

Fenestration. It refers to the arrangement, proportioning, and design of all openings, including windows, doors, and skylights.

Frame construction. In frame construction, the weight is born by the framework encased within a facing or cladding of light material.

Inflatable structures. A class of tensile structure supported by difference in pressure between the air inside and the air outside. Air is pumped in using fans, with air escape prevented by the use of airlocks at entrances. Inflatable structures enjoy applications from big-league stadiums to practice football fields to tennis courts, both temporary and permanent.

Long-span spaces. Long-span spaces or large-volume spaces are column-free spaces used for arenas, field houses, and ice rinks because of the open height required to accommodate sport-specific activities, as well as vertical height for spectator seating.

Parapets. A low wall projection located at the edge of a building's roofline.

Pilasters. A pilaster projects only slightly from walls.

Skylights. Glass structures set into the ceilings to let in light.

Soffit. The underside of any architectural element, including balcony overhangs and staircases. It also refers to the inner curve of an arch, which is a curved means of spanning an opening, used in place of a lintel.

Span. The horizontal distance between the supports of an upper floor or roof.

Spine. A building spine is the backbone of a building's floor plan. Most often the main circulation pathway in an arena or recreation center.

Suspended ceilings. A false ceiling suspended below a structured ceiling.

Tensile and membrane structures. Flexible systems made of thin, coated fabrics supported by a series of masts and stabilized by cables. These structure are often used as roofs over stadium spectator areas and as domes over stadiums and arenas.

Truss. A rigid frame composed of a series of triangular metal or wooden members that is often used to support flat roofs over long-span spaces. Trusses also support horizontal members in pitched-roof construction, such as purlins, which in turn support rafters, the sloping members that support the roof covering. Rafters are joined together at the apex of a pitched roof.

Vault. An arched ceiling.

Material Elements

Bricks. Bricks are made of fired or sun-baked clay, allowing architects to make aesthetic statements by selecting a certain color or by specifying more than one color and setting them in various patterns, sometimes interspersed with concrete blocks and stones.

Brick veneer. Sliced brick pieces affixed with mortar to a concrete load-bearing wall. It is also known as face brick or finish brick.

Concrete. A combination of cement, sand, water, and various sizes of stone. It is used for foundations, structural beams, floors, walls, sidewalks, parking areas, and many other applications. *Note.* Structurally, concrete is notable for its high compression capability and for its poor tension characteristics.

Concrete blocks. Concrete masonry units can be worked to different textures similar to rustication. Most common textures are split-faced and ground-faced.

Gunite. A popular swimming pool shell material consisting of cement, sand, and water that is sprayed onto a mold.

Masonry. This refers to work with brick and stone, offers many aesthetic options, both in the variety of colors and textures of natural materials and in the different ways these materials are cut.

   Ashlar masonry. Hewn blocks of stone, wrought to even faces and square edges, and laid in horizontal courses (tiers) with vertical joints.

   Quarry-faced masonry. Stones left in their quarry state and not made even and square.

   Polygonal masonry. Masonry utilizing blocks having irregular-shaped faces.

Mortar. Similar to concrete, except it does not have stones. It is used to bind bricks and concrete blocks together, to fill interior spaces of concrete block walls, and in some forms, as a ceiling coating.

Reinforced concrete. This type of concrete has rebar (steel reinforcing bars) added to give the concrete slab or beam the ability to withstand tensile stresses. The rebar in reinforced concrete can be put into tension in the factory (e.g., prestressed or pretensioned concrete precast) or on-site (posttensioned concrete or cast-in-place or tilt-up panels).

Rustication. This is a technique used to lend more texture to exterior surfaces, involves the use of large blocks separated by deep mortar joints.

> *Banded rustication.* Only the horizontal joints are emphasized.
>
> ***Smooth or chamfered rustication.*** Smooth faces separated by beveled joints.

Shotcrete. This material is similar to gunite, except it contains stones.

Stucco. This is a plaster made of gypsum (hydrous calcium sulfate), sand, water, and slaked lime.

Terrazzo. This is a floor surface made of cement mortar and marble chips, which after hardening is ground and polished.

Tile. There are three types of tile: ceramic tile (glazed fired clay), quarry tile (unglazed semivitreous tile extruded from shale or natural clay), and composite tile (vinyl).

Who Does What?

Aquatic design engineers (pool consultants). Persons who design swimming pools and natatorium spaces.

Architectural designer. This person works with architects and engineers during the initial concept/schematic design phases to integrate building systems (mechanical, electrical, plumbing, and structural) into the building concept.

Building systems. Building systems include electrical, mechanical, plumbing, and structural aspects of a building.

Construction manager. He or she supervises all contractors and works with the entire design team to ensure that the project can realistically be built within the allocated budget. Furthermore, this person is charged with keeping costs down and ensuring the project stays on schedule.

Consultants. Specialists in a specific field employed to assist the architectural team in developing a facility, such as acoustic (sound and sound barriers), audiovisual, ice rink, and lighting.

Interior architect. This is a licensed architect specializing in interior space design.

Interior decorator. This is a specialist in accessories and color schemes for upholstery.

Interior designer. This is a specialist in space planning, interior casework, furniture, interior finishes, and furnishings.

Landscape architect. This is an architect specializing in vehicular and pedestrian circulation as well as foliage and site grading.

Land use planner. This person recommends the best spot for a facility and develops site design documents for master plans and analyzes a site's location and related physical constraints.

Project architect. This person converts concept, schematic designs into construction documents and coordinates the site, architectural, specialty, and engineering disciplines.

Project engineer. Working with the project architect, the project engineer integrates the building systems with the design.

Project executive (principal-in-charge). This person provides professionals to complete work in a timely manner and should be contacted regarding legal or staffing questions. He or she may be a licensed architect, engineer, or planner.

Project manager. This person directs all of the personnel assigned to the project, including designers, architects, engineers, and consultants. He or she is heavily involved during the feasibility study phase and manages ongoing financial tasks such as budgets and schedules. The project manager hosts regular project meetings, reviews design details from a cost and buildability perspective, seeks participation of the design team, provides ongoing feedback to the design team, works with the design team to resolve design issues, and ensures that the contract documents become an integral part of the comprehensive design and construction process. Finally, the project manager is a facilitator and mediator.

Design and Construction Overview

Change orders. Change orders are formal documents ordering changes in the construction plans. These changes originate from any of the following requested by owner, site conditions, fire marshall, building inspector, contractor, document omission, or document error.

Construction/project management contracts. Advantages—provides for effective communication; elimination of the general contractor; efficient use of joint expertise in all phases of work; construction may begin early in process; work can be bid sequentially, thus allowing for company expenditures; and high cost of extras potentially reduced. Disadvantages—success of project depends to a great extent on skill of project manager, conflict in control of design and building process, total financial commitment unknown until end of project, procedures result in extra fees to design team, and process necessitates mutual respect of all involved.

Design/build (turnkey) contracts. Advantages—total cost commitment known in advance, very competitive process, builder responsible for all errors, little administration work required by client, the proposal is a single package, and time frames can be dramatically compressed. Disadvantages—builder is in control of all project actions, unless client produces detailed list of requirements, little control over product and process, power of design team reduced as working for builder, liability issues become cloudy as design team, and quality of end product can be compromised.

Engineering systems. Structural—clear span demands, wall projections/pilasters, and internal environmental effects. Mechanical—verification of environmental conditions, air conditioning requirements, detect impact on structural, electrical systems, noise generation, and review of operating costs. Electrical—lighting levels, direct, indirect, verification of ceiling heights, and determination of specialized electrical systems.

Master plan. General site master planning—primary objectives, site characteristics (sun, wind, topographic), massing of facilities, functional characteristics, access and transportation characteristics, connection to services and utilities, and zoning. Building specific master planning—primary objective, priorities of development, phasing requirements, and interface with feasibility study.

Needs analysis. The needs analysis consists of technical audit, physical inspection, history and tradition of organization and community, building systems, quality of building finishes, access for persons with disabilities, user requirements, program requirements, safety issues, security issues, and health issues.

Project cost. The project cost is equal to construction cost plus soft costs. Typical construction costs include enclosed building, landscape/sitework, demolition, utility service, fixed equipment, furniture, fixtures, equipment, and art/graphics. Typical soft costs include architect/engineer fees, building permits, testing and inspection fees, special consultants, sewer connection fees, maintenance endowment, parking replacement fund, construction financing, legal fees, in-house administration, other finance fees, and contingency.

Project team–Design phase. A project team consists of the following professionals: owner, fund-raiser, zoning consultant, legal counsel, surveyor, soils engineer, environmental consultant, special consultants (e.g., programmer, master planner, interior designer, aquatic consultant, acoustic consultant, theater consultant, graphic designer), architect, structural engineer, mechanical engineer, plumbing engineer, civil engineer, estimator, landscape engineer, interior designer, interior decorator, construction manager, and contractors.

Punch list. A list of items that needs to be completed before the project is complete, including aesthetics, quality of construction/finish, code requirements, levels and plumbness, structural deflections, engineering systems, building systems, and maintenance requirements.

Schedule/budget/contingency. This includes identifying total project schedule-design period, bidding phase, contract award, and construction; identifying total project budget-planning and design costs, administration costs, furniture and equipment costs, building costs, and site and utilities costs; and contingencies.

Site influences. The following are the most common site influences during the planning phase: adjacent properties, boundaries of sites, relationships to adjoining streets and roadways, existing trees and vegetation, orientation, wind, sun, shadow and microclimatic control, adjacent building heights, pedestrian and vehicular flow on-site and off-site, utilities and services (water, gas, electricity, sewer, telephone), soils, subsoils, water table, contours, and topography.

Stipulated sum contracts. Advantages—architect in close contact with client, time-tested traditional contract, sequential phasing of design, bidding and construction, best price at time of tender, capital commitment known at time of bid. Disadvantages—sequential process, thus time frame longer; creation of powerful adversary with the general contractor; and changes are expensive and time consuming.

About the Authors

Thomas H. Sawyer, EdD
Editor-in-Chief

Department of Kinesiology,
Recreation, and Sport
Indiana State University

Fellow, North American Society for Health, Physical Education, Recreation, Dance, and Sport Professionals (2000); professor of physical education (1984–2011); professor of recreation and sport management (1992–2011); professor of kinesiology, recreation, and sport (2011–present)

Dr. Sawyer is a 42-year veteran of higher education. He began as an instructor of health and physical education; has been a director of recreational sports, department head, department chair, associate athletic director, director of articulation and transfer, director of a college prison education program, executive director of regional education centers, and interim dean of continuing education; and is ending his career, by choice, as a full professor teaching sport management theory to undergraduate and graduate students.

He has written over 193 peer-reviewed articles for notable professional journals; made over 250 state, regional, national, and international presentations; and written 10 professional books and over 32 chapters in other publications.

Furthermore, he has served as a state AHPERD president (Indiana), district vice president (Midwest), association president (AAALF); chaired numerous district and national committees; is editor of the Indiana AHPERD journal and newsletter; chaired the JOPERD Editorial and Policy Boards; and is a member of the AAHPERD BOG. He has been an AAHPERD member since 1964.

Dr. Sawyer has also been active in the community, serving as a volunteer for the American Red Cross in four communities in four different states since 1964. He has been a first aid and CPR and water safety instructor (over 30 years), a chapter board member (off and on for 30 years), chapter chairperson (off and on for 8 years), chair of a state consortium (3 years), and chair of numerous regional committees and currently serves as chair of the Great Lakes Region, Service Area 5, Resource Council.

Finally, Dr. Sawyer has received numerous awards for his leadership and service to the American Red Cross; YMCA; a regional alcohol and drug consortium; Council on Facilities and Equipment; Indiana AHPERD; American Association for Active Lifestyles and Fitness; American Alliance for Health, Physical Education, Recreation, and Dance; and Indiana State University. Furthermore, he has received Caleb Mills Outstanding Teaching Award, Faculty Distinguished Service Award, Distinguished Research and Service Award from Indiana State University, and the Howard Richardson's Outstanding Teacher/Scholar Award from the School of Health and Human Performance at Indiana State University.

Contributors

Kimberly J. Bodey
Indiana State University

Kimberly J. Bodey is an associate professor of sport management in the Department of Kinesiology, Recreation, and Sport at Indiana State University.

Dr. Bodey is a member of the American Alliance of Health, Physical Education, Recreation, and Dance; National Recreation and Park Association; and Indiana Association for Health, Physical Education, Recreation, and Dance. She has more than 50 publications in scholarly journals and academic textbooks related to policy and procedure development; ethical decision making; organizational ethics; organizational justice; advocacy; legal authority, jurisdiction, and politics; coaching education; and designing park and recreation facilities.

Dr. Bodey earned a doctorate in recreation with an emphasis in sport management and public policy from the University of Arkansas. She holds a master's degree in sport management from the University of Arkansas and a bachelor's degree in kinesiology from the University of Illinois.

Mark Cryan
Elon University

Mark Cryan teaches in the Sport and Event Management Department at Elon University. He has previously served as the athletic director for the Burlington Recreation and Parks Department and as general manager of the Burlington (NC) Indians, a minor league affiliate of the Cleveland Indians. He was also one of the founders of the Coastal Plain League. Other industry experience includes working for the NHL's New Jersey Devils, the Fayetteville (NC) Generals, and heavyweight boxing champion Riddick Bowe.

His first book, *Cradle of the Game: Baseball and Ballparks in North Carolina,* was published in 2008. At Hamilton (NY) College, Cryan earned a bachelor's degree in public policy and played football. He also holds a master's in business administration from North Carolina Central University. He lives with his wife, Dale, and their two sons, Sam and Ty, in Burlington, North Carolina.

Steven Dalcher
Water LLC

Steven Dalcher is the cofounder of World Aquatic Training, Education, and Research, and he performs consulting for a wide range of clients, including local schools and Boy Scouts of America, and legal consultation concerning aquatic operations. He is currently completing an EdD in education at Ball State University and is a adjunct faculty member at Ball State University in physical education specializing in aquatics. He has performed a wide range of aquatic and facilities operations over the last 20 years, ranging from pool and waterfront, to small craft and health and safety operations.

Tonya L. Gimbert
Indiana State University

Tonya Gimbert received her bachelor's degree (2003) in elementary education from Saint Mary-of-the-Woods College and a master's degree in recreation and sport management (2009) with a concentration in sport management from Indiana State University. She is currently working on a PhD in curriculum, instruction, and media technology, with a concentration in teaching of sport management. She currently works in the Department of Intercollegiate Athletics as the NCAA Compliance Coordinator. Ms. Gimbert has served as an adjunct faculty member in the Department of Kinesiology, Recreation, and Sport, as well as Athletic Academics. She currently serves as president of the Graduate Student Association and as student representative to the President's Council. Ms. Gimbert has given presentations at professional conferences and authored articles published in professional journals concentrating on sport management.

Bernie Goldfine
Kennesaw State University

Bernie Goldfine is a professor at Kennesaw State University. He has taught a variety of undergraduate and graduate courses throughout his 23 years in higher education, including sport facility design and management. Additionally, Dr. Goldfine oversaw the operations and management of a wide variety of facilities and events in his 13 years as a high school athletic director. He has written numerous articles and made a wide array of presentations at state, national, and international levels, as well as contributed to textbooks on facility and event management. Dr. Goldfine received his bachelor's degree from the University of California–Santa Barbara and his master's degree and PhD from the University of Southern California.

Ricardo Mario Gonzales
University of Wisconsin–Eau Claire

Rick Gonzales is the director of Facilities Planning and Project Development for the University of Wisconsin–Eau Claire. He has received two national planning awards for his work on campus master planning. He sits on the University of Wisconsin System President's Advisory Committee on Disability Issues (PACDI). He has also received multiple state and local awards for planning and building design. Gonzales has taught as an adjunct professor in sport administration, architecture, urban planning, and civil engineering programs at the University of New Mexico and the University of Colorado. He is a member of the American Alliance for Health, Physical Education, Recreation, and Dance (AAHPERD); Society of College and University Planning (SCUP); and other key professional organizations. Gonzales received his undergraduate degree in architecture from the University of New Mexico. He also holds a master's degree in urban and regional planning and a master's in business administration from the University of Colorado at Denver. Gonzales is currently a PhD candidate in education from the University of New Mexico.

Julie Ann Hypes
Morehead State University

Julie Hypes is an associate professor in the School of Business Administration in the College of Business and Public Affairs at Morehead State University in Morehead, Kentucky, where she teaches undergraduate and graduate courses in sport management. Dr. Hypes has held positions as a sports information director and an administrative assistant for athletic facilities, game operations, and budgeting. She serves as the coordinator for the undergraduate internships and as the sport management assessment coordinator. She has presented at state, regional, national, and international levels. She earned a bachelor's degree in mass communications from Middle Tennessee State University, a master's degree in sport science from the U.S. Sports Academy, and a PhD in curriculum and instruction from Indiana State University. Dr. Hypes also served as president of the American Association for Physical Activity and Recreation (AAPAR) from 2010–2012.

Michael G. Hypes
Morehead State University

Michael Hypes is an associate professor of sport management in the School of Business Administration in the College of Business and Public Affairs at Morehead State University in Morehead, Kentucky, where he teaches graduate and undergraduate courses. He has served as chair for the Council for Facilities and Equipment; vice president for the Indiana Center for Sport Education, Inc.; assistant editor of the Indiana *AHPERD Journal*; assistant editor of the *Journal of Legal Aspects of Sport*; director of Higher Education for Indiana AHPERD; chair of the JOPERD editorial board; chair of the AAPAR Publications Committee; management division representative for AAPAR; cabinet member for AAPAR; and various other leadership positions in professional organizations. He has completed numerous presentations and articles for publication at state, national, and international levels. Dr. Hypes received his bachelor's and master's degrees in physical education from Appalachian State University and a doctor of arts from Middle Tennessee State University.

Susan Hudson
University of Northern Iowa

Susan Hudson is a nationally acknowledged expert in the area of playground safety and is the National Program for Playground Safety educational director. She has made numerous presentations nationally and internationally on playground design and safety and is the author and coauthor of over 150 articles concerning playgrounds. Dr. Hudson has held numerous leadership and committee assignments in national professional organizations, including the American Association for Health, Physical Education, Recreation, and Dance and the National Recreation and Park Association. She holds an endowed professorship at the University of Northern Iowa.

Lawrence Judge
Ball State University

Associate Professor Lawrence Judge is in his sixth year at Ball State University. He serves as the coordinator of the athletic coaching education program and has also served as the undergraduate advisor for the sport administration program. As both an associate head coach and a head coach, Dr. Judge has a total of 18 years work experience coaching Division I track and field/cross-country. In addition to field experience (training eight Olympians, 10 NCAA Champions and coaching over 100 All-Americans), Dr. Judge has firsthand knowledge of NCAA rules and current issues in amateur, intercollegiate, and professional athletics.

In just 5 years at University of Florida, Dr. Judge has tutored eight All-Americans, five Southeastern Conference Champions, two NCAA champions, and three Olympians adding to an already impressive résumé. He has guided eight athletes in the last three Olympic Games. In 2000, five of his former athletes competed in the 2000 Olympic Games in Sydney, Australia. As a scholar, Dr. Judge has coauthored 41 peer-reviewed publications, including 21 first-author publications in prestigious journals such as the *International Review for the Sociology of Sport, Journal of Strength and Conditioning Research*, and the *International Journal of Sports Science and Coaching*. Dr. Judge has also been active in the area of textbook publishing, contributing 12 textbook chapters. Dr. Judge coauthored the textbook, *Sport Governance and Policy Development: An Ethical Approach to Managing Sport in the 21st Century* and authored the books *The Complete Track and Field Coaches' Guide to Conditioning for the Throwing Events* and *The Shot Put Handbook*. He has given 84 peer-reviewed academic presentations at a wide variety of state, national, and international conferences. Dr. Judge is also currently the vice president of the Indiana Association for Health, Physical Education, Recreation, and Dance Sport Council; the past president for the National Council for the Accreditation of Coaching Education; the chair for the American Alliance for Health, Physical Education, Recreation, and Dance Council on Facilities and Equipment; and national chairman of the United States Track and Field Coaches Education for the Throwing Events. Dr. Judge serves as a Level II and Level III instructor in the IAAF coach's education program and also lectures in the Professional Figure Skaters Association nationwide coach's education program. Dr. Judge serves on the editorial board of *The Physical Educator* and *Techniques Magazine*.

David A. LaRue
Landscape Designer

David A. LaRue worked as a landscape architect and landscape designer from 1975 to 2007. He has bachelor's degrees in landscape architecture and community planning from Iowa State University. He has worked in his own landscape design firm as well as within design/build landscape companies, developing plans and supervising installations of residential, commercial, and governmental contracts. Most notable in his work are the initial designing of the Dubuque Arboretum and Botanical Gardens

in Dubuque, Iowa, and the McAleece Park and Recreation Complex, which contains three lighted softball diamonds and two regulation adult soccer fields also located in Dubuque. David finished his professional design career as the landscape manager of Vineyard Gardens located on Martha's Vineyard in Massachusetts, where he designed numerous high-end residential estates. Although officially retired, he is currently the owner of Weather Wood Gardens also located on Martha's Vineyard, where he provides landscape consulting services and does the bookkeeping for two landscape companies. He is actively involved in his local church and serves on the board of directors of SOSEN, a national nonprofit organization that advocates for maintaining our citizens' civil rights as provided for in the Constitution.

Richard J. LaRue
University of New England

Richard J. LaRue, DPE, is a NAS fellow and professor in the Department of Business at the University of New England (UNE). Dr. LaRue served 5 years as a YMCA professional director in aquatics, youth and teen programming, health and physical education, and camping. He is now completing his 33rd year as a college/university professor. For 20 of these years, Dr. LaRue was a department chair at Bradford College (MA), Colby-Sawyer College (NH), and UNE. In 1993, he was appointed visiting scholar in the School of Public Health, Harvard University (postdoctorate, 3 years). In 1997, Dr. LaRue was appointed to the graduate faculty at Indiana State University and to the national faculty of the United States Sports Academy (Alabama). As a member of the USSA National Faculty, he was an invitee of the Amateur Sports Federation and Olympic Committee of Hong Kong and the Singapore Sports Councils to teach in Hong Kong (1997, 2000), and Singapore (1997); and in Aruba (1998) as a guest of their Olympic Committee **unclear**. Dr. LaRue taught in Israel (2001) in UNE' s Health Services Management program. Again, as a member of the USSA National Faculty, he was invited by the General Organization for Youth and Sports to teach in the Kingdom of Bahrain, by the Sports Authority of Thailand, and by the National Sports Organizations in both Dubai and Abu Dhabi, UAE. As a member of AAHPERD, Dr. LaRue was active with AAALF, serving as chair, chair-elect, and past chair of the Council on Facilities and Equipment for 4 years and as AAPAR board of governors representative for 6 years. He was then elected to serve 2 years as president-elect and president of AAPAR. In 2012, Dr. LaRue received AAPAR's Pathfinder Award. He was one of the first 100 individuals to thru-hike the Appalachian Trail (April 2–August 31, 1972).

John J. Miller
Troy University

John Miller received his doctorate at the University of New Mexico in sport administration. He is currently the associate dean and professor in the College of Health and Human Services at Troy University in Troy, Alabama. He has written more than 40 publications in sport management in peer-reviewed academic journals, edited a book on sport management internships, conducted more than 100 presentations at national and international conferences, and serves on six editorial review boards of nationally recognized academic sport management journals.

Miller is a research fellow in research consortium; has served as the chair of the Sport Management Council in the National Association for Sport and Physical Education (NASPE), chair for NASPE Sport Management national convention program selection committee, and chair of the Safety and Risk Management Council in the American Association for Physical Activity and Recreation (AAPAR); and is a member of the Facilities and Equipment Council. He has also been a member of the NASPE national public relations committee. He currently is a member of the NASPE Sport Steering Committee representing sport management. He has served as president of the Sport and Recreation Law Association (SRLA) and was selected as a research fellow in SRLA. He presently serves as the editor of the *Journal of Legal Aspects of Sport*.

Jeffrey C. Petersen
Baylor University

Jeffrey Petersen is an associate professor of sport management within the Department of Health, Human Performance, and Recreation at Baylor University in Waco, Texas. Dr. Petersen received his bachelor's degree from Taylor University, a master's degree from New Mexico Highlands University, and his PhD from the University of New Mexico in sports administration. He serves at Baylor as the sport management graduate program coordinator and also serves as the graduate program director for the department. Dr. Petersen has a prior background in interscholastic teaching, coaching, and athletic administration, plus 14 years in higher education, and he currently teaches undergraduate courses in facilities and equipment and graduate courses in facility and event management, legal issues, and sport finance.

He has been actively involved in professional organizations through both scholarship and service. Dr. Petersen has authored or coauthored 44 peer-reviewed publications in journals including the *Journal of Physical Education, Recreation, and Dance; Sport Marketing Quarterly; Journal of Strength and Conditioning Research; Sport Management Education Journal;* and *Journal of Venue and Event Management.* He has also given 93 peer-reviewed presentations at international, national, and state conferences, with an additional 18 invited conference presentations. From a leadership and service perspective, Dr. Petersen has served a term as the chair of the Council on Facilities and Equipment within the American Association for Physical Activity and Recreation (AAPAR) and has also served within AAPAR as a member of the board of directors and as chair of the publication committee.

John H. Pommier
Indiana State University

Pommier is currently a professor and chairperson for the Department of Kinesiology, Recreation, and Sport at Indiana State University. He graduated with a bachelor's degree from Augustana College (biology/secondary education), a master's degree from Illinois State University (adapted physical education), and a PhD from Texas A&M University (recreation re-

sources development with an emphasis in experiential adventure therapy).

He has previously served as an instructor or professor for Hurricane Island Outward Bound School, Texas A&M University, Henderson State University, and Eastern Illinois University. He currently serves as the coeditor for *Schole: A Journal of Leisure Studies and Recreation Education.*

Donald Rogers
Indiana State University

Don Rogers has a PhD in leisure behavior with a counseling minor, plus a master's degree in recreation therapy with an outdoor emphasis, both from Indiana University. His undergraduate is in recreation therapy from University of North Texas, and he has an AAS in engineering design and drawing from San Jacinto J.C., Texas.

For 16 years, Rogers participated in wheelchair sports, including road racing, track, basketball, tennis, racquetball, and touch football. At one point, he held the world record in the 100-meter dash at 16.49 seconds. His professional focus in the outdoors has been with inclusive adventure-based programming and organized camping. Rogers has been designing challenge courses since 1982 after seeing his first course on an Outward Bound program. He has been professionally active at state and national levels in the Association for Experiential Education, the Association for Challenge Course Technology, and the American Therapeutic Recreation Association. He worked for six summers in organized camping for youth with disabilities at Bradford Woods. Working with Roland and Associates in the mid-1980s, he designed a fully accessible, comprehensive low and high challenge course that was the first to be built in physical rehabilitation facilities. Variations of those designs have been built in numerous other settings around the world.

Rogers started his own design, training, and consulting company, Pro Access, in 1992 and shortly afterward began consulting with Alpine Towers International, Inc. He redesigned the Tower and its training program, establishing it as an industry leader for universal and inclusive designs. Rogers is currently on faculty at Indiana State University. He coordinates the Recreation Therapy program in the Department of Kinesiology, Recreation, and Sport and directs the Sycamore Outdoor Center, which also houses the Keystone Adventure Program. His research and writing interests include universal challenge course design and training, families with children with disabilities, and recreation therapy interventions with people with physical disabilities. He is an author of the *Complete Ropes Course Manual.* He has been married to Dr. Nancy Brattain Rogers since 1994, and they have two children, Laura and Jonathan. His recreation passion is bass fishing and being on and around the water.

Todd L. Seidler
University of New Mexico

Todd Seidler is currently professor and chair of the department of Health, Exercise, and Sports Sciences at the University of New Mexico. He is also a member of the faculty of the sport administration program, one of only a few programs that offers both a master's and doctorate degree in sport administration. Dr. Seidler received his bachelor's degree in physical education from San Diego State University and then taught and coached in high school. He then went on to graduate school and earned his master's and PhD degrees in sports administration from the University of New Mexico (UNM).

Prior to returning to UNM, Dr. Seidler spent 6 years as the coordinator of the graduate sports administration program at Wayne State University and then was the coordinator of the undergraduate sport management program at Guilford College in North Carolina.

Dr. Seidler is currently executive director and a former president of the Sport and Recreation Law Association, a professional organization for those interested in teaching sport law and risk management. He has also served on the executive board and as chair of both the Sport Management Council and the Council on Facilities and Equipment within the American Alliance for Health, Physical Education, Recreation, and Dance (AAHPERD) and is an active member of the North American Society for Sport Management (NASSM). Dr. Seidler is also a certified strength and conditioning specialist through the National Strength and Conditioning Association.

Dr. Seidler's primary areas of interest include risk management and legal issues in sport and in planning and managing sports facilities. He is active as a consultant on facility planning and risk management for sport and recreation and frequently presents, publishes, and teaches classes such as risk management in sport, sport facility planning and design, facility and event management, and legal aspects of sport.

Donna Thompson
University of Northern Iowa

Donna Thompson is an acknowledged national and international expert in the field of playground development and safety and is the executive director of the National Program for Playground Safety. She has more than 20 years experience teaching, writing, and researching about playgrounds. She has done numerous presentations on playground development, including television interviews on ABC's *Good Morning America*, CBS's *Early Edition*, and NBC's *Today* show. She has served as consultant for numerous groups planning playgrounds and has been an expert witness in trials concerning playground safety.

Hal Walker
Elon University

Hal Walker is an associate professor and chair of the Department of Sport and Event Management at Elon University. He earned his doctorate from The Ohio State University and has worked in a variety of higher education capacities for the past 28 years. He has experiences as a director of athletics, coach, consultant, and administrator. He presents frequently at regional, national, and international conferences, along with active engagement in applied research and writing on topics such as student career interests, technology, facility and venue management, internships, and experiential education. He currently serves on several editorial, review, and advisory boards including the *International Journal of Sport Management*, the *Journal for Facility Planning and Design*, and the *Journal of Sport Administration and Supervision*.

Anthony G. Weaver
Elon University

Tony Weaver is an associate professor of sport and event management at Elon University. He earned his doctorate in higher education administration from the University of North Carolina at Greensboro. Prior to his appointment at Elon, he served 10 years in Division I college athletic administration at the University of North Carolina at Greensboro, Siena College, Iona College, and the University of Connecticut. He coached college and high school basketball and gained practical experience in financial organizations before moving into administration. He currently serves on numerous advisory boards for local, regional, and national organizations within the sport industry. He is an active member of the National Association of Collegiate Marketing Administrators (NACMA), the North American Society for Sport Management (NASSM), and the College Sports Research Institute.

Jason Winkle
Indiana State University

Jason Winkle is the associate dean for the College of Nursing, Health, and Human Services at Indiana State University (ISU). He has served ISU in many capacities as a faculty member, faculty fellow to the provost, vice president of academic affairs, interim director for the Corrections Education Program, founder and director for the Center for Leadership Development, director and coordinator of the martial arts program, and academic advisor.

Prior to coming to Indiana State University, Dr. Winkle, as a civilian, was the Director of Combatives for the United States Military Academy at West Point, New York. He also taught in the Values Education Program at West Point. He is the former president of the International Tactical Officers Training Association and the Senior Leadership Writer for *SWAT Digest*.

Leland Yarger
Ball State University

Leland (Lee) Yarger is the coordinator of aquatics/instructor of physical education and first aid and safety officer for SPESES at Ball State University located in Muncie, Indiana. He earned a master's degree in workforce education and development (1997–1998) from Southern Illinois University at Carbondale and a bachelor's degree in administration of justice with a minor in aquatics (1991–1995). His work history includes the operation and management of aquatic facilities ranging from indoor and outdoor pools to water park attractions, non-surf waterfronts, and ocean rescue beachfronts. Yarger conducts certification courses from the AAOS, Aquatic Partners, ARC, ASPSA, NSC, NSPF, and SAI.

Index